ANTONIO ROSMINI

THE PHILOSOPHY OF RIGHT

Volume 2
Rights of the Individual

Translated by
DENIS CLEARY
and
TERENCE WATSON

ROSMINI HOUSE
DURHAM

Translated from
Filosofia del Diritto
Vol. I, Intra, 1865

Typeset by Rosmini House, Durham
Printed by Bell & Bain Limited, Glasgow

ISBN 0 9513211 8 8

Note

Square brackets [ ] indicate other notes or additions by the translators.

[...] indicates an omission from the text.

References to this and other works of Rosmini are given by paragraph number unless otherwise stated.

Abbreviations used for Rosmini's quoted works are:
    AMS: *Anthropology as an Aid to Moral Science*
    CE: *Certainty*
    CS: *Conscience*
    ER: *The Essence of Right*
    PE: *Principles of Ethics*
    RI: *Rights of the Individual*
    SC: *The Summary Cause for the Stability or Downfall of Human Societies*
    SP: *Society and its Purpose*

Foreword

In *The Essence of Right*, the first volume of *The Philosophy of Right*, Rosmini describes the nature of right by positing its essence in person ('person is subsistent right') and in the relationship between persons. He also indicates a principle -- 'ownership' in the broadest sense of the word -- governing the derivation and determination of all human rights. In the present volume, he considers derived right itself from the point of view of the rights of the individual. Social right (domestic, ecclesial and civil) is the subject of later works.

Rights of individuals, Rosmini maintains, are either connatural, that is, come into being together with individual existence, or acquired, that is, dependent upon development in the individual of the faculty of ownership, an inalienable element proper to every person. In both cases rights, whether innate or acquired, are inviolable. Every attack made upon individual rights is an immoral attempt to harm the person who holds them.

The immorality of such a lesion of rights is rooted in the injury done to the person whose rights are invaded. Because rights are essentially concerned with what is 'mine', they cannot be endangered without actual damage to the person I am, whom all are obliged to respect. The composition and generation of rights is dependent upon the power of ownership to promote in others the moral duty to respect the right of ownership, a spiritual faculty by which I extend my personship to all that belongs to me.

This duty of respect for rights is always absolute. Where rights are present, they must be respected. This does not mean, however, that all rights are unchangeable. Innate rights alone are immutable; acquired rights, which are totally dependent upon the person's growing appreciation of his own capacity for moral freedom of action, will correspond with the exercise of moral freedom over the matter of rights. In other words, what can be and is taken over by persons as 'their own' or simply 'theirs' can also be relinquished and abandoned to others.

Acquired rights are therefore limited by their generation (they can be acquired only when persons are morally free to extend their personship to some real fact), and by the elimination, willed or unwilled, of the fact to which personship is extended.

But even when the fact continues to exist, it may be expressed in different ways, or 'modes' as Rosmini calls them. What is essential is that the value of the fact be preserved, although it is not always reasonable that the material aspect of the fact be maintained. The 'modality' of rights is not co-terminous with the existence of rights itself.

The deliberately willed elimination of the fact constituting the matter of ownership takes place when rights are transmitted from one person to another. What was mine now becomes yours. How this comes about through abandonment, contract or succession is examined at length by Rosmini. He also deals extensively with the alteration in rights arising from their attempted violation, and with the exercise of sanctions destined to protect rights or to effect satisfaction for injured rights.

Entwined within this broad framework of derived right, Rosmini's applications of his principles serve to focus attention on the relationship between the rights of individuals and the rights of society, between employers and employees, between masters and servants, between parents and children. His enlightened historical perspective also provides considerable food for thought about the development of rights and their different appreciation at various stages of social existence. In addition, he makes clear the path he will follow in his later treatment of social right in the family, Church and State.

Despite Rosmini's highly philosophical approach, it is possible to see throughout the work immediate, present-day applications of apparently abstract principles. It also becomes very clear that human development is impossible without an ever-deepening understanding of the way in which rights are rooted in human nature and *a fortiori* in the light of being on which human nature depends for its dignity, worth and inviolability.

In our foreword to *The Essence of Right*, we indicated the reasons behind our use of certain terms in the translation. Here we add that *servo* has been translated 'bond-servant'. Rosmini's use of the word in this book always indicates not simply a person who works for a wage ('servant' in the modern English sense), but a person who is in some way bonded to the employer for whom he labours. Such bonding may include slavery of one kind or another. Likewise, *servitù* has been translated as 'servitude', which includes the notion of obligatory service, whatever the source of the obligation. Where Rosmini uses *schiavo* and *schiavitù*, we translate *slave* and *slavery*.

DENIS CLEARY
TERENCE WATSON

Durham,
February, 1993.

Contents

Book 2

ACQUIRED RIGHTS

Book 3

THE TRANSMISSION OF RIGHTS, AND THEIR CONSEQUENT MODIFICATIONS

INTRODUCTION
THE SUBJECT OF THIS BOOK AND ITS CONNECTION WITH THE PRECEDING AND FOLLOWING BOOKS

Book 4

ALTERATIONS TO
THE RIGHTS OF OTHERS;
CONSEQUENT OBLIGATIONS AND
MODIFICATIONS OF MUTUAL RIGHTS

INTRODUCTION
SUBJECT-MATTER OF THIS BOOK

DERIVED RATIONAL RIGHT

1. We have dealt with the nature of *right* in a previous volume,[1] where we also considered the principle of the derivation of rights (*principium cognoscendi* [principle of knowledge]),[2] a principle we founded in *ownership*, that is, in everything proper to a person or unified with him. Because *personal resentment* is a clear sign of injured rights, but is not present where the person is undisturbed, we can only conclude that right is to be found wherever person and ownership, which is always personal, are present.

2. The way to our study of *derived Right* has therefore been prepared. We now have to set in motion the principle governing the derivation of rights. This principle shows us how to note rights wherever they are, and to apply them to the varied states of human existence. We have to acknowledge the rights connected to each state and note the form taken in the midst of

---

[1] *The Essence of Right*, 223-317.

[2] In *The Principle of the Derivation of Rights* [*ER*, 318 ss.]. We have already seen that the ultimate investigations possible in any subject are three: 1. the origin or cause of the thing under discussion; 2. the essence of the thing (these two questions were fused into a single question by ancient philosophers when they dealt with the *principium essendi* [the principle of being]); 3. the *sign* which enables us to recognise where the thing is found (*principium cognoscendi* [principle of knowledge]). Cf. *Storia comparative de' sistemi morali*, c. 8, art. 1. — Properly speaking, investigating the origin or cause of right is part of *ontology* or *rational theology*, not of the science of Right. However, this question has been answered whenever we have indicated that moral law and jural law ultimately lead us back to God, their first origin and essential seat.

diverse facts by the unique, extremely simple essence of right which, as essence, is the same in all rights.

Our next step is to bring together the different forms of the essence of right which constitute special rights, to classify them and finally to expound them in the order best suited to showing their unity of origin and the degrees of relationship binding them together. This is precisely the task of *derived Right*.

3. We prefer to call this Right *rational* rather than *natural* because of the ambiguity springing from the multiple meaning of the word *nature*, which I have noted elsewhere.[3] Moreover, I think that *rational*, in contrast to *natural*, befits the dignity of the Right we are going to study. It will be helpful to explain why this is so.

4. Learned authors have employed two ways to arrive at the knowledge of human rights. Some begin from and follow *nature*; others have been prompted and guided by *reason*. However, although *nature* and *reason* are the two founts of Right and are both capable of constituting two distinct methods of discovering Right, nature will never lead us to all rights nor unveil their formal element.

5. When we affirm that we begin from *nature* and follow its traces in order to discover specific human rights, we take 'nature' as the intrinsic, operative, human principle, in other words, as the human *subject*. Setting out from *nature* to uncover human rights means moving from the *subject*, that is, starting from the propensities and inclinations natural to human beings. According to this way of thinking, which is found at the outset of philosophy and followed by Roman jurisprudence, St. Thomas himself maintains that 'those things to which human beings are naturally inclined pertain to the law of nature'.[4] He goes on to divide into three classes the things to which human nature is inclined:

> First, we incline to what is good, in so far as human nature possesses something in common with all substances, that is, in so far as every substance desires (or tends) to the preservation of its being according to its nature; relative to

[3] Cf.*ER*, 252–255.

[4] *Ad legem naturae pertinent ea ad quae homo naturaliter inclinatur* (*S.T.*, I-II, q. 94, art. 4).

this inclination, those things pertain to *natural law* which are required for the conservation of human life or which impede death. Second, human beings possess an inclination to more spiritual things, that is, we have something in common with other animals. Relative to this inclination, things which animals learn naturally pertain to natural law; for example, how male and female unite, how they bring up their offspring, and so on. Third, human beings have an inclination to what is good according to the nature of their reason, which is proper to them. For example, we have a natural inclination to know the truth about God and to live in society. Relative to this inclination, those things pertain to natural law which are concerned with such types of inclination, for example, avoiding ignorance, not offending others with whom we have to live, and matters which have this as their aim.[5]

6. St. Thomas' argument shows that the phrase 'law of nature' has two meanings. 1. It refers to the physical, *real* order, intrinsic to natures. This is *fact*, and the effect and trace of creative wisdom. 2. It refers to moral, *ideal* nature in so far as it induces moral obligation. In its first meaning, 'law of nature' is indeed common both to animals and to non-feeling things,[6] but does not provide a subject for either *ethics* or *Right*. Both duty and right presuppose moral obligation, not physical inclination alone.

Consequently, calling *right* 'natural' is not as exact as calling it *rational*. Because rationality constitutes the nature proper to human beings, the term 'rational right' inevitably refers to the right proper to human nature.

7. Moreover, it is true that reason, by indicating what is *good* and *bad*, also produces in us a kind of feeling and inclination directing us to good and away from evil.

However, the *natural inclination* of the subject, although

---

[5] *Ibid.* art. 2.

[6] He explains how *natural law* is common to all creatures: 'Because all things are subject to divine Providence which rules and measures them with an eternal law, it is clear that all share in some way in that eternal law in so far as they receive their INCLINATIONS to their acts and ends from the impression left in them by the eternal law. But amongst all other creatures, the rational creature is subject in a more excellent way to divine Providence in so far as it is made to share in Providence by acting with foresight on its own and others' behalf' (*S.T.*, I-II, q. 91, art. 2).

good, does not give rise to moral obligation. Rather, the opposite is true: *natural inclination* to moral good arises from the preceding *obligation* directly revealed to us by reason. We are inclined to moral good because we know it; knowing moral good and evil means knowing something in such a way that we are obliged to follow good and avoid evil. The *inclination* in the subject is never *obligation* but a consequence effected in us by the *obligation* we have already apprehended.

As soon as *obligation* has made itself felt in us (not before and not after), the moral law has been manifested in us. The subject's *inclination* cannot be the *moral law*[7] in any way. On the contrary, this inclination is always a *physical effect* produced 1. in inanimate natures by their innate forces, 2. in animals by the feelings they experience, and 3. finally in human beings by their rational apprehension of moral *obligation*. Even in this last case, inclination to moral good is always a physical effect because it originates according to a type of physical law as a necessary consequence of our apprehension of obligation. However, we can rightly call this *physical* inclination, *moral* because it is produced by moral *obligation*, which it tends to *fulfil*.

8. Maintaining the contrary gives rise to other absurdities. Let us imagine that the *inclination* to moral good, instead of being considered as a type of natural beginning to the execution of the law, that is, as a help or stimulus provided by nature for the fulfilment of the law, is erroneously taken for the *moral law* itself. In this case, moralists would have to show that the *inclination* to moral good is always stronger and more vigorous in us than any other inclination of human nature. In fact, inclination as such depends for its worth on its power. If some inclination were itself the law, its validity would be ensured by its power over other inclinations. Unless it were stronger than all other inclinations, it would cease *to obligate* whenever another inclination were powerful enough to overcome it.

It might be said that such an *inclination* to moral good would have to be followed even when it showed itself weaker than other animal or vital inclinations. But this objection falls if we

---

[7] Cf. *Storia comparativa de' sistemi morali*, c. 4.

consider that inclination, taken as law, produces duty only in so far as it is *inclination*. But as inclination, it inclines, and does so in so far as it has the power to incline. Only to this extent does it obligate. If, therefore, it has no greater power to incline than other inclinations, it does not oblige in the face of superior inclinations. Moreover, because the degree of *inclination* to good varies in intensity, moral *obligation* could be strong, weak or even non-existent relative to the same thing. Variation in inclination would depend on the original disposition provided by nature as well as on acquired habits.

But perhaps we ought to consider this inclination in all the force it *should* have rather than in its weakness? If this were the case, moral *duties* prior and extraneous to the inclination as well as superior and regulatory of it, would be admitted. Inclination would no longer be *law*, as our objectors sustain, but subject to law; it would not form moral obligation, which would have to be sought elsewhere.

However we view the matter, an *inclination* in a subject — even a rational and morally good inclination — can never constitute *moral law*, but only some indication (*principium cognoscendi*) of moral law. And even as an indication of law, it is often highly imperfect.

9. *Rational inclination* is highly imperfect because it does not appear to possess by nature the power to rule and regulate all other inclinations nor, in very many cases, does it manifest itself in such a way that we are rendered conscious of its presence. In other words, we cannot turn to it in order to discover easily what we should do or avoid.

10. This explains why St. Thomas himself, instead of leaving *inclination* as the sole constitutive element of morally obliging natural law, subjects it to *reason*, and considers it only as approved by reason. He shows finally that law is posited not in inclination, which is consequent to knowledge, but in the obligation indicated by reason. He says: 'All the inclinations of any parts whatsoever of human nature (for example, the elements by which we can desire or be roused to anger) pertain to natural law IN SO FAR AS THEY ARE REGULATED BY REASON.'[8] Reason, therefore,

---

[8] *S.T.*, I-II, q. 94, art. 2, ad 2.

lays down the law; inclinations receive the law. A most noble, but naturally weak inclination then issues from the law and prompts us to observe it.

11. It is clear that we can with greater propriety and truth call the law *rational* rather than *natural* because it comes from the *objects* of intelligence, not from subjective nature (the complex of our inclinations). And because *right* receives its form from the moral law, it is as *rational* rather than *natural* right that it will be distinguished from *positive* right

12. The argument gains force if we consider that *rational Right* also takes its matter from facts related to the *will* or free, human decision. *Contracts*, which are certainly not formed by *nature*, are a case in point. Believing, therefore, that the most fitting name for non-positive Right is that which expresses the dictate of reason as its *form*, we also believe that it is best called *rational.*[9]

But having established its *formal* name, we still have to divide Right according to its *matter*. While the *form* of things is one, their *matter* is multiple; and although we must always draw a *definition* from the form of things, we have to find *division* in them according to their matter. If we wish to divide *rational Right* into its parts, therefore, we have to take into consideration its varied matter which on the one hand is given by *nature* and on the other by *facts willed* by human beings. From this point of view, we can fittingly divide *rational Right* into two parts, *natural* and *agreed*. The use of *natural* is better reserved for this division.[10]

13. Nevertheless, we will not order our present study according to this division of Right. It would give rise to many problems. For example, in *agreed Right* we find two quite disproportionate divisions, one of which is too large and important to be united with the other. It is better to deal with

---

[9] I do sometimes call it *natural*, but this is intended to show only that I am not averse to using the normal expressions of many writers. I do not want to abandon their way of communicating with me, which helps our mutual understanding. Moreover, it is impossible to correct improprieties of speech overnight and single-handed. As St. Augustine says: 'Few things are expressed accurately' (he is not speaking of himself, but of ordinary language), 'many inaccurately; but we know what we mean' (*Confessions*, bk. 11, c. 20).

[10] Cf. the *Schema of the Philosophy of Right, ER*, pp. 56-57

this part separately without allowing our attention to be distracted. As I have indicated in the *Schema of the Philosophy of Right*, contracts are divided into those which concern only the *objects* of right, and those which concern the *subjects*. Contracts concerning subjects of right form what we call the state of 'society', human society, which is very different from anything preceding it, although even then agreed bonds were not totally absent.

14. As we said,[11] the aim of *derived Right* is to apply the *principle of derivation* to the various states in which human beings find themselves. With this in mind, the principle is used as a kind of type enabling us to find and recognise these states, and to note and gather together all the special rights which belong to us in each state. The greater part of our present work is to be found here, and we shall deal with it as follows.

15. Careful consideration shows that our human condition is subject to constant variation from the moment of birth to death at extreme old age. Everything around us — non-intelligent things pertaining to material nature (which we use as we wish), and things pertaining to association with our intelligent fellow-beings (to whom we owe respect and love as they owe it to us) — are equally subject to change.

16. Practically all the changes that affect us or take place around us in nature or society greatly influence changes in our *ownership*. By re-drawing the limits in which rights are contained, change extends or reduces their *matter*. In other words, our jural state varies.

17. It is clear that human rights or rights between human beings cannot be explained unless we mentally posit rights in all the states and conditions through which human beings can pass. First, these differing human circumstances have to be classified and reduced to certain general forms; finally, the rights corresponding to these forms have to be seen in their relationship to the forms themselves.

18. Undertaking a complete study of human rights is certainly an extensive and difficult task. Our aim, however, is more modest. Nevertheless, even a restricted project such as this

[11] 2.

essay on the *Philosophy of Right* has to begin from a reasoned consideration of the principal states in which we find ourselves. We have to investigate the different development, conditions and forms taken by human rights no less than by human duties.

19. There are two principal, more general states: that of *dissociation*, in which each person considers all his fellows as strangers with their own individual interests; and that of *society*, in which each makes his very own the interests common to all his associates.

20. This division, the most general of all, gives rise to the two principal parts of our study of derived Right: *individual Right* and *social Right*, as we call them.

RIGHTS
OF THE INDIVIDUAL

INTRODUCTION

21. *Individual Right* considers human beings as co-existing, but co-existing in an isolated state relative both to their interests and to the means of furthering their interests. Each one acts of himself, although even in such a state mutual rights and duties exist.

22. Individual Right can be present, we must note, without our necessarily supposing that all human beings are, or can be, found in such a situation. It would be sufficient if only one were found. The rights of a single human being are sacred, and a book could justifiably be written for the sole purpose of instructing one human being about his rights, and other human beings about respect for those rights.

However, the necessity and importance of individual Right is in fact extraneous to and independent of every reality present in the isolated condition in which human beings are considered relative to individual Right. Even if it were true that no one had ever been shipwrecked, people could still be found co-existing on a desert island without social contact, as has happened many times. Even if we never found a single human being sadly deprived of family, homeland and all human contact, an investigation and lucid exposition of individual rights would always be necessary and important. The rights of the individual may indeed be modified in society but they never cease; they always remain as the basis and body of social rights. Social rights therefore cannot be understood nor their foundation uncovered, if individual rights, which precede them, are not first presented on their own and totally separate from them. Consequently, it is entirely reasonable for the philosopher to proceed rather like the mathematician, that is, he must first expound human rights by abstracting from the fact of society. He must do this not because he aims to destroy such a fact, but because he wishes to consider both that which precedes society in the order of nature and reason, and that which is presupposed and required by society — just as the skeleton is presupposed and required for a beautifully formed body.

23. Hence, a discussion of the mutual rights which exist independently of social bonds involves two principal investigations. The first concerns derived rights themselves; the second, the changes they undergo. I will dedicate two books to each of these investigations. Thus, our *individual Right* is divided into four books dealing with the following arguments:

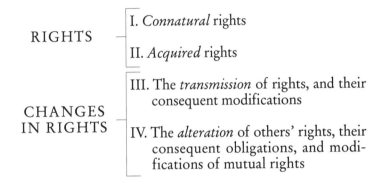

RIGHTS
- I. *Connatural* rights
- II. *Acquired* rights

CHANGES IN RIGHTS
- III. The *transmission* of rights, and their consequent modifications
- IV. The *alteration* of others' rights, their consequent obligations, and modifications of mutual rights

[23]

Book 1

CONNATURAL RIGHTS

[INTRODUCTION]

24. We have said that dissociation and society are the two most general states in which human beings can be considered. In 'general state' we include many other states, because even the individual human beings whom we imagine and suppose in a state of dissociation can be found in a great variety of particular situations and circumstances.

25. Relative to the derivation of individual rights, it is necessary to distinguish carefully two situations. The first is that in which human beings have rights arising solely from their human nature — we call these rights *connatural*, although they are normally said to be innate. The second situation is that in which new rights are added to individuals as a result of their acts; these rights are called *acquired*. We must first discuss connatural rights.

26. The question immediately arises: 'Does a new-born baby have rights? Are there rights which come directly from human nature?' If we consider new-born babies, we find them in a condition so far removed from ours that they seem to have a different life. Consequently we have difficulty in seeing in them the traces of intelligence found in ourselves as adults. And because we find no intellectual acts equivalent to our own, we are inclined to deny them all use of intelligence. This error has continued for centuries. Nevertheless, even though we tend to deny the baby any use of intelligence, we have to grant it fundamental, innate rights in order to avoid the absurdity of an existent, intelligent being without rights, in the way that inanimate and unreasoning things are. It is certainly not the first time that we human beings have been made aware of our errors by the repugnance we would experience in admitting the consequences of those errors; our darkened reason is helped by a more honest feeling. We must therefore investigate the following questions: 'Do innate rights exist? What are they? Can they be modified?' But first of all, what do we understand by innate or connatural rights?

CHAPTER 1

What we understand by *connatural rights*

27. By *connatural rights* we understand only those whose subject (the physical faculty) is contained in human nature in such a way that it exists as soon as human nature exists. Hence, life, the various parts of the human body and natural human powers form the subject or matter of the many rights which are called connatural.

28. On the other hand *acquired rights* are those whose matter is not contained in the nature of each human being who is born, but acquired later through the activity or acts of acquisition of the human being.

CHAPTER 2

Do connatural rights exist in human beings?

29. If 'connatural rights' means rights whose subject is a faculty innate in human nature, we need to ask whether the word 'connatural', attributed to these rights, is to be taken in a proper or metaphorical sense.

30. It cannot be denied that there are innate powers in human nature. But these would constitute only the first element of right, which I have placed in a faculty or activity of the subject considered physically.[12] How then can we show that in the new-born there is also *moral* power or activity, which is the second element of right?

---

[12] Cf. *ER*, 238-273.

31. The following argument against the existence of such rights could obviously be made with some semblance of truth: 'The moral nature of right has the same origin in us as moral duty.'

It is our reason which indicates in different beings what belongs to them. By means of this information our reason becomes aware on the one hand of the duty to avoid anything that harms the dignity of these known beings, and on the other is left free to do all those actions which do not infringe on what is due to those beings.

If the moral nature of right therefore depends on this judgment, there will indeed be a physical power without the judgment, but never a moral faculty of action. There will be action, but not action that we can call 'just'; a fact exists, not a right. Human beings who lack the knowledge to do what is lawful cannot exercise a right. This explains why we said previously that purely animal instincts and actions are not exercises of right, and that animals could never be the subject of right.

32. Moreover, the faculty of knowledge does not operate unless the spirit is acted on by some activity different from the spirit. Hence, if we are to feel obligation and acquire rights and duties, the object of rights and duties must first be presented to us. It does not seem possible therefore for rights to be innate; they must be posterior to the acts of the powers of knowing and willing.[13]

33. If, in order to exercise my right, I need to reflect on what I do, and judge it free of every injustice, not only are innate rights lacking (for lack of innate reasonings), but we must also affirm that rights are suspended every time the use of reason is suspended, as in the case of babies, the insane, drunkards, etc.

---

[13] According to civil law, a donation unknown and unaccepted by the donee does not have the force of transferring the right. If however the assent of the donee is presumed, both he and the will of the donor would be harmed if the donation were kept hidden from him. The same can be said about someone who is not in a position actually to accept a gift. The harm done in this case (denying him what he would fully own as a result of his assent) is always relative to the presumed or future act or at least to the act which would be possible if the material obstruction were removed. This is a consequence of human dignity, a consequence dependent upon the nature of mankind, as I will explain more clearly later.

34. This is what we must say in effect if we accept sensist systems. According to all these systems the reason and will are a sort of later acquisition, an importation, so to speak, from sensation.

35. But the ideological system I have proposed argues quite differently. I have shown that in human nature there is always a light of reason which from the first moments of existence is used by human nature.[14] I have also shown in the moral-anthropological system that the will is moved to its acts even before it has knowledge of itself, and does this as soon as the human being exists.[15] I have shown that *morality* consists solely in a relationship of the will with the law (direct knowledge), even though the will does not yet exercise bilateral freedom.[16] A full reply to the objection will be found in these teachings.

36. My reply therefore is that the human being is unceasingly a moral, rational being, to whom rights can always be due.

37. Rights appertain to human dignity, a dignity residing in the essential act of human intelligence,[17] which constitutes human nature.

38. This universal act of intelligence is spontaneous and essential in human beings.

39. To it, as to its principle, belongs the *intellective spontaneity* that inclines us to good in general, to being, which ceaselessly

[14] Cf. *OT*, 1008, where it is shown that in the power of reason itself there is a first universal act of knowledge from which are generated all posterior acts.

[15] Cf. *AMS*, 605-611.

[16] Cf. *PE*, 193-227; *CS*, bk. 1.

[17] I have already noted that this act of intelligence, essential to human nature, is recognised by common sense. Languages, which are the deposit of common sense, also recognise it. The ancient use of the word 'intelligence' meant an act, a first act of the understanding. Aristotle and the Scholastics understood it in this way. Cicero gave it the same meaning when he defined it as that by which the mind sees BEINGS, a definition taken from the Greeks: *Intelligentia est, per quam animus ea perspicit,* QUAE SUNT (*De invent.*, 2, 53). The very inflection of the word 'intelligence' expresses an act. But this act also names the faculty of understanding. We see here how language expresses what we want to say and how the same word is used to signify both the *faculty* of understanding and its *act*. We are obviously persuaded therefore that the faculty is simply the first, universal act which contains in potency all subsequent acts.

[34–39]

shines before us, spontaneously informing and inclining us to itself. The insane, the drunkard, the baby, all possess this act, and also some use of reason. People as unfortunate as these do not cease to be human. Their defect consists solely in a weak, disordered and false conjunction of ideas and in the reception of defective perceptions and feelings. This fact itself shows that they have ideas, perceptions, and feelings which they unite in some way. Thus, they are already using their reason and their will uprightly.[18] Human beings therefore always have a general and appropriate right to the conservation and use of their faculties, just as they have a right to good in general which they will essentially, with an upright, essential, necessary and fundamental volition.

40. The above reasoning is valid only for duty and cannot be correctly applied to *right*. There is certainly no *duty* where there is no knowledge of having a duty. But this is not true for *right*. Right must be respected in itself; the possessor does not have to know the respect due to it. It is sufficient that the duty of respect is known by those who must practise it, that is, other human beings, not the subjects themselves of right.[19]

[18] To maintain that babies and the insane do not have some kind of *rights* would be contrary to common sense. We can deduce from this fact that common sense is implicitly drawn to see in the human being a moral, reasoning being, even when the external signs of reasoning are not so obvious. — One of the improvements which do great honour to modern times and clearly indicate progress is the way in which the insane are now treated and cared for. The maxim which has emerged is to see at last human beings in the insane, and to treat them as human beings like ourselves. The same progress, worthy of the highest accolade, is taking place in the education of children. The age of reason is being recognised at an earlier and earlier age. I have no doubts that we will eventually discern a flash of intelligence in the first smile a baby gives its mother. In this way we will greatly perfect the valuable art by which the child's and the adult's reason can communicate with each other. A common language will be attained for mutual understanding between adult and baby. All this progress means the death of sensism.

[19] Thomas (*Dottrina della scienza del diritto*, Frankfurt am Main, 1803) denies innate rights. He thinks there cannot be rights where there cannot be duties, as in new-born babies. We grant the dependence of *right* on *duty*, but observe that the duty corresponding to a right exists in some other person, not in the person with the right; right is simply 'an activity protected by the moral law'. On the other hand, although there are no duties in the new-born arising from a formulated law, the baby's activity, both in itself and in its

41. For a human being therefore to have the general right to be respected as an end, only the powers of reason and will, considered simply as powers capable of suffering and enjoyment, are required. As we have said, the activity necessary to constitute a right is simply the activity present in the passivity of feelings.[20] The case would be different if we were talking about the right to certain determined acts. Relative to these, we cannot say human beings have an essential, fundamental right, because such acts are accidental and ephemeral; they are not innate.

42. Hence, anyone who recognises a rational and volitive principle in human beings but denies them innate rights, errs by supposing the following two things as essential to the constitution of right: 1. that the one who has a right, is conscious he has it; and 2. that he knows the moral nature of the right.

43. We say, however, that a right exists 'whenever a person exists capable of at least experiencing pain. If so, other persons have the moral duty not to cause him any suffering.'

All this exists in human beings from the moment of their birth, because the person exists in them together with the faculty of reasoning and will, which lies deep in the essence of their soul; moral dignity exists, springing, as it does, from the intuition of *being* and their inclination towards it. The faculty of will is, by its nature, always moral, even before it acquires the habit of deliberating, because whatever human beings will is always in harmony or disharmony with reason which shines before them. The moral nature of this activity may be unknown to the human being, but ignorance does not affect it.

The rights connatural to human beings cannot therefore be denied.

tendency, is moral and has a moral value. — Cf. what I have said about the existence of some morality prior to conscience in *CS*, bk. 1.

[20] Cf. *ER*, 239.

[41–43]

CHAPTER 3

The connatural rights of human beings

44. We can easily note which rights are connatural if we make use of *ownership*, our principle for determining rights.

45. The new-born baby holds in *ownership* only himself (his spirit and his body), and the faculties of his spirit and body. His *personal activity* has not yet extended outside the limits of his body: his person (that is, the supreme principle of his rational activity) has not attached to itself anything outside the restricted limits of his tiny body, except perhaps the air he breathes. The subjects of his rights, therefore, can only be as yet his connatural and innate capacities, faculties or powers over which his personship rules, even in this imperfect state, .

46. When we speak of faculties as the subject of right, we include passive as well as active faculties. In fact, if the faculties could not be conceived as subject to some kind of passivity they could not be subjects of various rights. As we know, the moral law protects persons against the attacks of others. These attacks, however, presuppose (sometimes mistakenly) that the person is subject to some evil, that is, capable of suffering.

47. If we wish to specify these connatural rights, we have to distinguish in the baby everything that can merit the appellation *personal, one's own*. We shall do this briefly, by distinguishing amongst the connatural rights that which is right of its essence, or *formal right*, and that which is right through participation, or *material right*.

Article 1.
Person, *essential right*

48. Under this heading, some authors speak of 'the right to our own personship', but such language is misplaced. We do not have a right to our own personship. If this were the case, two persons would have to be distinguished, one of whom has the right, the other who constitutes the subject of the right. But the

one possessing right is the identical person who is the subject of right.

49. Precision requires that we say 'the human person is subsistent human right'. It follows that the person is the essence of right.

50. The *essence* of anything is always the principle and origin of everything else in the same species. Things belong to the same species because they share the same essence.

51. It follows from our definition of right ('right is a moral-physical activity which cannot be harmed by other persons') that personship is of the essence of right. Of its essence, *person* has all the elements that form the definition of right. As we said, 'The person is an intellective subject in so far it contains a supreme active principle.'[21] This definition clearly coincides with that of right itself.

52. The supreme, active principle, the foundation of person, which is informed by the *light* of reason, receives the rule of justice. Properly speaking, the principle is the faculty of what is lawful. But because the dignity of the light of reason (ideal being) is infinite, nothing can be superior to the personal principle[22] which of its nature acts on the promptings of a teacher and lord of infinite dignity. Such a principle is naturally *supreme*; no one has the right to command that which depends upon the commands of the infinite.

If the person is of its nature supreme activity, it is clear that each person has a duty of not harming others, either in thought or by an attempt to offend or subject them through despoiliation of the supremacy bestowed by nature. This is clear if we apply the moral principle already established: 'Acknowledge things *practically* for what they are.'[23] The *person*, therefore, has

[21] Cf. *AMS*, bk. 4.

[22] St. Augustine turns to God with the following words: 'And I stood, and was founded in you, IN MY FORM WHICH IS YOUR TRUTH' (Confessions, bk. 11, c. 30).

[23] It is of the utmost importance to note this analysis of the human person, which shows that our share in personal dignity arises from *essential being itself*. This essential, and hence infinite being communicates itself to us in so far as it is essentially manifestative. It is called *ideal*, that is, *light* for this very reason. It follows, therefore, that human dignity is received by us. It comes from outside. Consequently all our rights, strictly speaking, arise not from

in its nature all the constitutive elements of right; consequently, it is subsistent right, the essence of right.

Article 2.
Human nature, *rights through a share in personship*

53. Everything included in the human being, but not constituting the supreme principle of its operations, forms part of human nature, but is not properly speaking the human person.

54. Nevertheless, whatever is found within the sphere of human nature is intimately bound to the human person and subordinate to it.

55. I have shown that the different active principles contained in human nature are bound to the human person by means of an intimate connection subordinating them physically and morally to the person. In the *Anthropology*, I explained the nature of this twofold *moral-dynamic* connection by which the active principles of human nature are united to the person, and I refer the reader to the appropriate passage.[24]

56. This intimate, dynamic and moral union of the inferior principles with the human person gives rise to the dominion that the person has over these active principles. It has the *physical power* to command them and also the *moral duty* because it

our own activity but from an extraneous cause, that is, from God. — It may be objected that in receiving both nature and dignity from outside ourselves we cannot be said to possess the quality of 'end', but only to tend to a supremely noble end. — From one point of view this is correct (cf. *PE*, 66-68); from another point of view the human person can be called 'end' in so far as it shares in the infinite dignity of *being*, to which it is essentially joined. In this sense, offending the person means offending being. It is true that the good which the person finds in adhering to being is subjective, that is, proper to person, but it is nevertheless as noble as being itself. Any attempt to deprive the person of such a good would be an offence against infinite being. From this point of view, the human person itself can be called 'end' because the infinite good, in which all human beings participate and in which they are destined to participate ever more fully, can be called 'end'.

[24] *AMS*, 838-850.

[53–56]

'must acknowledge *in practice* the subordination of these principles to itself.'[25]

57. It follows that these principles are *proper* to the human person, and are rightly called personal because they are grafted as parts into the person itself.

58. Hence seigniory of the human person over human nature delineates the sphere of innate *materiated* rights.

CHAPTER 4

The first seat of freedom, and of ownership

59. The distinction between *formal* innate right and *material* innate rights clearly indicates the seat of *freedom* and of *ownership*. These two words play a large part in any discussion on rights, but their concept has not perhaps been sufficiently clarified.

60. We can safely say that the human person is the first, proper seat of *jural freedom*, and human nature the first, proper seat of *ownership*, if we consider human nature as pertaining to and subordinate to person, that is, as something *proper* to person.

61. *Jural freedom* is something simple, and consists in a supreme faculty of action.

62. Every supreme faculty is necessarily *free*, and no active principle can physically and morally violate and subjugate it. Conversely, if a faculty is completely free, it is supreme.

63. *Ownership* on the other hand is not a simple concept because it includes two things: something that has ownership and something proper to that which has ownership.

64. Person alone, therefore, if considered without any addition and in relation to its simplicity, cannot strictly speaking supply us with the concept of *ownership*; it can only supply the

25 The reader is already aware that for us the phrase 'in practice' means 'efficaciously', that is, not in thought alone, but in fact and as a result of real force.

concept of *freedom*. Indeed, to say that 'the human person is master of itself', or 'has ownership of itself' is, when closely examined, to say nothing. If the person is master, it is not mastered, and if it is owner, it cannot be what is owned; the two concepts are the opposite of each other. They cannot therefore concur in the same subject, nor compose a valid proposition. They can only be the matter for a proposition whose terms contradict and cancel each other.

65. This explains why we placed the supreme principle of rights in person, in personal *freedom*.[26] When we investigated the principle of derivation and determination of rights, however, we turned to the concept of ownership.[27]

66. Right is a faculty of free activity. Personal freedom therefore must be the formal principle of all rights.

67. But because this formal, universal principle is the element common to all rights, it does not determine special rights. Rights are specified by their different matter, which cannot be considered in itself but only as united to the form of right, to person, to personal freedom and governance. We called this union of the matter of right with the form of right (that is, the connection which brings the matter into the sphere of right) *ownership*. Hence ownership taken generally was understood by us as 'the principle of the determination of rights'.

CHAPTER 5

The limitation of connatural rights

68. The nature of connatural rights will be seen more clearly if we consider them relative to their limitation.

69. A very important question immediately arises: 'Are

[26] Cf. *ER*, 224-237.
[27] Cf. *ER*, 318 ss.

our connatural rights (that is, the personship and personal ownership of the faculties innate to human nature) injured when the exercise of these faculties is impeded by other persons?'

70. We must first distinguish between the *power* to act and the *action* itself of the power.

71. As we have said, it does not necessarily follow that because some *power* is ours of right, all possible *actions* of that power are ours of right. Even though some particular *power* to act were shown to be ours of right, we would still have to show that each *action* done with this power was ours of right — each *action* is the matter of a new, simple right, and simple rights have to be demonstrated individually, not as a whole.[28]

72. Furthermore, we have distinguished between simply *lawful* actions and actions constituting a true right.[29] An action may have been found to be lawful, but this does not entitle us to conclude straightaway that the action is the matter of a full right in such a way that we would be harmed if anyone impeded it in any way.

73. In our innate powers therefore we must distinguish activities which actually exist from those which do not yet exist but can be produced.

Every power contains the actuality called 'first act';[30] this is immanent and constitutes the power itself. The acts which come from the power, however, are transient, although they leave some effects in the power (which is always modified and, as it were, enveloped by certain of its *habits*). Relative to first act, they are called 'second acts' or simply and more commonly 'acts' or 'actions'. It is clear that first acts form one thing and constitute one right with the powers themselves.

74. Second acts can be considered from three points of view: 1. as not yet existing but only possible; 2. as actually existing at the moment the power posits them; 3. as having already taken place.

---

[28] Cf. *ER*, 322-323, *The principle of derivation*. — Hence, in the definition of right we give 'activity' a more general meaning than 'faculty' or 'power', etc. Activity is present both in potency or in act, present not only in every action but in every experience.

[29] *Ibid.*, 324-345.

[30] Cf. *OT*, 1005-1019.

75. If they have already taken place, they no longer exist and cannot as such be the matter or subject of a right. They can however leave behind certain consequences which produce the matter of right, as we will see in the next book when we speak about the acquisition of dominion over external things. But because they no longer exist, they are not themselves rights.

76. These transient acts, when posited and thus subsisting, can be subjects of real rights. But because none of these second acts is inborn in the human being, they can be classed only as acquired, not as connatural rights.

77. Finally, if we consider second acts as merely possible and not subsistent, they cannot be the subjects of rights, precisely because they do not exist in themselves and are therefore nothing.

78. As we have seen, right must be a subsistent activity, that is either the personal principle, or something joined to the personal principle by the moral-physical bond of *ownership*. But an action that does not *really* exist cannot have any of these characteristics. A non-existent action is not an activity, nor is it joined to the human person by any moral-physical bond; the person has not taken possession of the action because it has not been posited. Consequently, this kind of action does not pertain to real things.

79. Actions which I can do, but have not yet done, are not mine by right. Nevertheless I am certainly able to do them, just as the new-born baby will be able to use the faculties given it by nature. When the new-born posits second acts with all its powers, it does something *lawful*. Moreover, as soon as it does whatever is useful to itself, it exercises its *right* in a true sense, provided it does not harm another's ownership. But the actions, up to the moment when the baby actually does them, can only be considered as simply *lawful* rather than *jural* or rightful.[31]

80. If a right were always exercised simply by positing lawful actions, no one could obstruct or impede it, because to impede the exercise of a right is to violate the right. But each human being can limit another's sphere of action and diminish the quantity of another's lawful actions by first positing some

---

[31] Cf. *ER*, 322-323.

lawful actions which exclude another's. The principle we propose for the *limitation* of the natural activity of every human being is: 'Do not harm another' or 'Do not harm another's activity in so far as it is personal' or 'Do not diminish another's ownership'. To harm others means in fact to harm their personal freedom or their ownership. We can therefore perform, and do truly perform lawful things as long as we do not diminish or injure another's ownership. Every human being different from us is able to do the same and, as long as another law does not forbid him, always does what is harmless and lawful. Human beings, therefore, when they posit lawful actions, reciprocally limit the sphere of their mutual activity. They do this by changing the state of things so that the action of a neighbour, which was previously harmless and lawful (doing no harm to any ownership), now becomes harmful, and injures another's *ownership* established by previous, lawful actions. Thus, if someone takes a seat previously unoccupied, others cannot take it without removing and therefore harming the occupant. But prior to its being taken, the seat was free and could lawfully have been taken by anybody.

81. Everyone, therefore, by his *lawful* action can impede another's actions because such actions, while remaining unposited, do not constitute a real right. If they are not obstructed by another's ownership, they are simply lawful, but unlawful if impeded by another's ownership.

82. It is true that *possible* actions can also be considered as existing virtually in the powers. But in this case their virtual existence constitutes a right only relative to lawful actions which another has no reason to impede.

Hence, we can easily recognise a double right in every innate power: 1. a right whose subject is the power alone; 2. a right whose subject is the *virtuality* (present in the power) of lawful actions, which no one has reason to impede.

83. This second right (reducible to the right of *jural freedom*) would be violated by anyone who diminished the sphere of my possible actions without a just and lawful motive, that is, not in order to take possession of a good which has no owner (a lawful action), but for mere caprice or malevolence, or solely to exert dominion over me, all of which is unlawful and injurious.

Chapter 6
Injury to innate rights

84. Lawful actions therefore which do not harm another's *ownership* do not injure the *innate rights* of others; they simply limit the sphere of their lawful actions, which, as we have said, are not of right, precisely because they are only lawful.[32]

85. We now wish to see when and to what extent connatural rights are injured. For this we must turn to the general principle we have posited regarding the determination of injury[33] and apply it to this kind of rights.

86. The principle states that 'innate rights are injured whenever an attempt is made which disturbs or harms our innate faculties, person or human nature.'

Article 1.
Injury to pure-formal right
which consists in personal *freedom*

87. Formal right is determined by the exclusion of *ownership*,[34] and consists in pure *jural freedom*.

88. Hence, in order to determine if formal right has been injured, we simply have to recognise injury in any *attack* on pure jural freedom.[35]

[32] Many writers have not made this important distinction between simply *lawful actions* and *actions of right*. They have supposed that innate rights include not only the innate faculties but the possible actions of these faculties. And because *possible, lawful actions* can vary and be limited in different ways, one of which is by positive law, they have supposed that innate rights could be modified by positive laws. This supposition is clearly evident in the Austrian code where it reads: 'Everything conformable to natural, innate rights will be held to be subsistent, as long as a legal restriction of these rights is not proven' (§17).

[33] Cf. *ER*, 360 ss.

[34] Cf. *ER*, 59-67.

[35] Formal right is the form of all rights. Every injury to right therefore is an

89. When does an attack on pure jural or personal freedom take place? If this freedom consists, as we have seen, in the *supremacy* the human person has over all the other principles of human nature, 'an attack on this freedom, which constitutes innate formal right, will take place whenever the attack tries to rob the personal principle of its supremacy and subjugate it to some lower principle.'

90. But when exactly do we attempt to rob the human formal principle of its supremacy and subjugate it to some lower principle of human nature? To answer the question, we must investigate what constitutes, properly speaking, the supremacy of the personal principle over the other subsistent principles in human nature.

91. Our investigation shows us that such supremacy consists in the subject's participation in an *infinite entity*, and in the subject's ability to obtain from this infinite entity, in which it shares, an *activity superior* to all its other activities. As we have said, the subject does this in a way similar to that by which obedience given by a human being to a higher authority is of its nature immune from every subjection to a lower authority. The infinite entity is *being* itself in all its purity, without adjunct or limitation.

92. Whenever the attempt is directed to disturbing or altering the natural union and order of the subject to pure *being*, there is an attack on the supremacy of the personal principle and consequent injury to person.

93. In order to apply this principle and see when and how it is verified, we must carefully consider that the human subject can adhere to being in three modes: 1. through the intellect, by sharing in *truth*; 2. through the faculty of will, by the practice of *virtue*; 3. through feeling, by the enjoyment of *happiness* or *bliss*.[36]

94. When we examine *truth*, *virtue*, and *bliss* attentively, we discover that they are simply an adhesion or adherence of the human spirit to pure being, that is, a communication of this *pure*

injury to formal right. But we are speaking about injuries which concern merely formal right and pure jural freedom in itself, unmixed with any matter of right.

[36] Cf. the difference between *happiness* and *bliss* in *SP*, bk. 4, c. 1.

being, essential to the human spirit; it is a triple communication because effected in a threefold way.

95. In *Certainty* I showed that *truth* is *being* as the light of minds, where it produces knowledge.[37] I showed that all knowledge terminates in an entity, because the opposite of entity is nothingness, which cannot in itself be the object of knowledge. Knowing a truth is the same as knowing an entity. By means of knowledge or its faculty (the intellect), the human being adheres to being.

96. In my works on *Ethics* I showed that virtue consists in adhering *willingly* to being, that is, in acknowledging and loving the whole of *being* without excluding any part of it.[38]

97. Finally I have observed elsewhere[39] that, because we are not sufficient for ourselves, we tend to complete and fully satisfy ourselves by uniting ourselves to beings different from ourselves. Only by uniting ourselves to and enjoying the whole of being do we understand how it is possible to be in a state of such complete satisfaction that we cannot think of a higher state. This state is called *happiness* or *bliss*.

98. The three modes by which the human subject unites himself or is united to being are perfectly distinct. This distinction does not originate from the difference of the powers to which being is communicated. It originates from the threefold nature of being itself which, by communicating itself in its triple mode, produces three distinct powers to receive it.[40]

99. *Being*, in fact, when considered in its purity and fullness, is seen to be endowed with a triple act. The act in which it appears as *object*, and in so far as it is this act, we call *ideal being*. The act in which it appears as active *subject* which *feels* its passions and actions, and in so far as it is this act of feeling, we call *real being*. Finally, the act with which this real being, this *subject*, determines itself to feel and act in conformity with the

[37] Cf. *CE*, 1055-1064, 1112-1135.

[38] Cf. *PE*, etc.

[39] Cf. *SP*, bk. 4, especially c. 6.

[40] As long as this communication has not begun, we cannot have the concept of the relevant powers; at most we can conceive a truly indeterminate receptivity which simply proffers the mind a concept similar to the *prime matter* of the ancient thinkers.

rule of ideal being (*object*), and in so far as it is this act of adherence, we call *moral being*. When any *real being* whatsoever, a human being for example, intuits *ideal being*, the real being is said to share in *truth*. When the real being takes *ideal being* as the rule of its feelings and actions in so far as they depend on the real being, it is said to be endowed with *virtue*. In so far as it comes to love and enjoy the fullness of being, guided by the rule of ideal being taken in its universality, it is called *blessed*. Truth, virtue and bliss are therefore the three terms of the human person, or rather of person in general; they are the purest founts from which flows to person its own excellence, its dignity and its supremacy.[41]

100. We can now clearly see that every attempt to rob a human being of truth or virtue or happiness is an injury to the formal right that person is.[42]

But these three kinds of injury must be considered separately and a few words said about each.

§1. *Injury to personship arising from an attempt to deprive the human being of truth*

101. What we have said so far indicates that injury to person by an attempt to deprive the human being of truth is perpetrated in three ways:

1. By positively harming the *understanding*, which is the power of truth. For example, the Hottentots' practice of placing boards on the temples of their babies in order to stupefy them

---

[41] In *SP* I have shown that *happiness*, the full satisfaction of the spirit, is a *personal* act (bk. 4, c. 2).

[42] Truth is an absolute good and not relative to the subject, even though it endows the subject with a good beyond price. The subject is ordered to absolute, objective good. By means of this order alone, or more properly speaking, by means of the dignity of objective, absolute good, the subject has the right to tend to it. This order and tendency are not properly speaking the title of these rights but solely their condition. We can therefore say that some rights have as their object *absolute good*; others, good relative to the subject. This observation allows us to explain and fully understand the third element of right (cf. *ER*, 294-308).

is clearly a violation of a human right. The same right is injured by making someone drunk, intemperant, or by performing acts against a human being which result in weakening or disordering the power of knowledge.[43]

2. By limiting without just reason the exercise of the power of knowledge through caprice, evil will or display of superiority, etc. This violates innate *jural freedom*.

3. Finally, by attempting to introduce harmful errors into the mind of another. These diminish the possession of truth.

102. Here the general question arises: 'Is lying an injury to the human right to truth?'

103. The opinion of jurists is divided on the matter. Some emphasise the evil consequences of lying, considering it an injury to right only when the consequences are really harmful.[44] But this is to depart from our question; we wish to talk about lying itself and the evil intrinsically contained in it.

104. In the first place, it is certain that a human being *per se* has no right to claim that the knowledge possessed by another be communicated to him. Such a communication pertains to beneficence, not to jural duty. If someone says to another, 'I will tell you nothing about what you wish to know,' the speaker acts justly, from a jural point of view, and remains within the sphere proper to him without invading the other's sphere.

105. If the other, therefore, without a just motive, wants to apply pressure by using force or menacing the speaker in order to be told what the speaker does not wish to reveal, the aggressor injures the speaker's right. Having been violated or threatened, the speaker can now defend his right against the aggression even with force, provided he observes *moderamen inculpatae tutelae* [moderation in justified self-defence], about which we will have more to say later.

106. But an important question now presents itself: 'Does a

[43] Cf. C. A. Titman, *Dissertatio de delictis in vires humanas commissis*, Leipzig, 1795.

[44] 'In a jural sense,' says Zeiller, 'only that subjective, moral lie must be considered a transgression of a jural duty which, because of its natural and easily foreseeable consequences, harms another's right.' — He notes that 'as a result, no one in the State thinks of accusing someone before the courts as a liar except in the case of harm to the victim of a fraudulent, proven deceit' (§54 of his *Diritto privato naturale*).

person who unjustly attacks another to make him say what he does not wish to say lose the right we all have to hear words used with the meaning given them by common use?'

107. Note carefully, I am not asking whether speaking contrary to the truth is always an evil relative to God, a question which concerns moralists. I am not discussing the *duty* of a speaker but the *right* of someone who unjustly claims that he be given information. To repeat, I am asking whether one who unjustly attacks another to make the latter say what he is not obliged to say loses the right to have the words spoken in reply used with their common meaning. For a long time I was persuaded that this right could in no way be lost, but now my persuasion inclines more to the opposite opinion.

I fully grant that we have the reciprocal duty and right to use words according to their accepted meaning, and never to use them in another sense when we speak spontaneously without pressure from injustice. It is equally clear that the fear of some harm, when such harm is just and not caused by another's injustice, does not in any way release me from the jural duty of telling the truth or of remaining silent.[45]

---

[45] A special case is that of a judge in the external forum, who certainly has the right to interrogate. It is also clear that in civil cases the parties questioned must reply, and reply exactly in accordance with truth, because they themselves are equally bound to seek only truth and justice. Finally, in criminal cases, witnesses must on interrogation speak the truth fully and precisely. But the matter is not so clear when we are dealing with a criminal judgment concerning oneself. If the guilty person wishes to speak, he certainly may do so, and in this case must always speak the truth, because the judge has the right not to be deceived. But is a guilty person always obliged to confess his crime, even when he foresees the punishment that will be applied as a result of his confession? — Jurists are inclined to answer affirmatively; they think that the contrary would destroy the force of laws restraining crime. Some laws however (for example, English laws) do not require a confession from the accused, and do not in fact admit it as evidence. Nevertheless some moralists make a distinction worthy of serious consideration. In their opinion, if the punishment inflicted by criminal laws were absolutely just, that is, if retribution for the crime could not be made in another way, the accused would certainly be obliged to confess the truth and undergo the punishment. But external punishment inflicted by the State does not have this characteristic. An accused can make retribution for his crime before God and before human beings without ascending the scaffold. In this way he can restore the justice he has violated to its prior integrity. Without any doubt, an accused

Finally, whenever a person has the right to know something from me, I have the corresponding jural obligation to speak, and to speak the truth, whatever the consequences of my honesty.

Our question therefore does not concern these cases, which are beyond discussion, but only the case where a person who has no right to know the truth and to whom I am not obliged by law to tell the truth wishes me to tell the truth contrary to my will and, by inflicting on me or menacing me with physical evils, violates my right of jural freedom .

108. In this case, it seems, the person loses the right he might have to require the common use of words. Furthermore, if I replied giving my words a false meaning, I would not be doing him any harm, because what I said would be neither true nor false, but simply a means of defending my right, a measure available to me for avoiding his violence.

109. An unjust person such as this could not claim to have been deceived. He has lost his right to the legitimate use of words, and therefore is obliged to know that my words have lost all value for him as a punishment for the injustice he has committed and continues to commit. If he takes the words according to their normal meaning, I am not deceiving him — he is deceiving himself with his own ignorance.

110. I repeat however that this argument can be applied only in the case where there is no duty to reveal the truth independently of the right of a person violently demanding knowledge. If the duty to say or confess the truth comes from elsewhere, it must always be fulfilled, even in the face of certain death. There are situations in fact where the truth must be stated and proclaimed in the face of torture, because truth certainly has

can fully repent of his misdeed, resolve to compensate as far as possible the harm done, and by his life to give as good an example to the world as he gave scandal in the past. Finally he can resolve to satisfy divine justice in the way divine justice prescribes. What further debt need he pay? The laws are not rendered useless in any way by his action, because they obtain their purpose superabundantly. However, this decision, as we see, is valid only for criminals fully converted from their evil ways. Those who remain obstinate are jurally obliged to confess their crimes in the external forum and to undergo the punishment imposed on them by the State judge.

[108–110]

its own rights which are more sacred than those of any human being.[46]

111. We shall leave this case aside, however, and deal with the case discussed previously. The speaker has no intention of deceiving the unjust oppressor, as he does when telling a real lie. His sole intention is to hide from the oppressor the truth which he does not wish to reveal; he has no duty to do reveal the truth, and the oppressor has no right to know it, particularly when its revelation would greatly harm the innocent person responsible for its disclosure.

112. But this explanation would, of course, have no force if words naturally signified things. In this case I could not pronounce a word without signifying something; my intention cannot change the nature of things. However, words in themselves are sounds without any meaning whatsoever. Their meaning depends entirely on an expressed or tacit agreement among human beings, who by that fact show they intend to use them to express their concepts. We note therefore that the obligation to use words to mean something, and particularly one thing rather than another, does not come from the nature of words, as if they were born servants of truth and falsehood, but solely from the tacitly approved agreement or intention to use words for the purpose of expressing concepts. But in my opinion nobody intends to bind themselves by such a rigid and

---

[46] The above opinion cannot therefore be applied in any way to the obligation of every Christian to confess the Gospel even before tyrants. As an obligation, confession of the Gospel originates not from a tyrant's right but from the sublimity of gospel truth and from Christ's precept given to all Christians as his followers. It arises from the intrinsic right of God to be known, honoured and glorified in every way and before all creatures, from the duty of everyone to desire the establishment and spread of his kingdom on earth, from the merits of Christ, to follow whom must be considered infinitely glorious, from the Christian's perfect friendship with Christ, which spurs him on to glorify his friend, and finally, from supernatural charity to one's neighbour, by which the Christian must ardently desire that the Gospel be promulgated in all possible ways and that everybody will embrace it. Witness to all this is greatly aided by confession and the shedding of one's blood. — The teaching which we have given above concerning our duty to use words in their normal sense pertains to natural law and is therefore altogether different from the obligation of confessing Christ before violent men of the world who seek to snuff out his law and followers on the earth.

unjust agreement to use words necessarily in this way. This is especially true when one party abuses the entirely arbitrary agreement in order to force the other party unjustly to do something to which they are not bound, that is, to reveal truths which they wish to conceal because they would do themselves great harm by revealing them. Can anyone who acts so unjustly claim any right, or have the right to abuse his own right in this way? Can there be a right whose object is injustice and injury to some other person?

113. I gladly leave the solution of this delicate case to the judgment of wise people, but maintain nevertheless that every time a real, fraudulent lie is told, another person's right is injured, that is, the right each has 'not to be deceived' by other people.

114. This injury is present even when no deception actually results from the lie because, as we have said, the *attack* itself without its effect is sufficient to constitute a jural injury.

115. Despite all this, we cannot in my opinion conclude that every lie injures pure formal right. We can only conclude that every lie injures every human being's acquired right, and this kind of right, we said, enters society by means of tacit agreement about the use of words. But rights acquired through *agreement* are not innate.

116. Does the case exist, and when, of a falsehood or lie that violates our connatural right not to be cut off from the truth or disturbed in our union with it?

Truth ennobles human beings, and any attempt to deprive them of it is an attempt to rob them of their inborn dignity. *Truth*, however, does not mean *all that is true*[47] nor all true knowledge. There are certain kinds of knowledge which do not increase personal human dignity, and certain kinds of false knowledge or material errors which do not diminish it. For example, surely no one will tell me that I would be improved by the knowledge that a hundred chickens were fed in Pip's courtyard? or that I would have lost something if I falsely believed a hundred and one were fed, instead of a hundred?

---

[47] I have indicated the difference between *things that are true* and *truth itself* in *Saggio sull'Iddio e sulla nuova letteratura italiana* in *Opuscoli filosofici*, Milan, 1828, vol. 2.

Such an error would obviously not affect my personal dignity in any way.

117. It is equally true, however, that there is no knowledge, no matter how frivolous, which in certain circumstances cannot be useful to me. Ignorance itself can be useful, and even error in certain determined cases (legists and the writers of weighty tomes on the privileges of ignorance know this). However, we must note that here we do not calculate the value of truth from its consequences or from the advantages it can bring us. We calculate it from its own intrinsic value. Its simple adherence to our spirit ennobles and enhances us, without regard to all the other advantages we might be able to obtain from it.

118. If we now investigate which truths are useless to the personal dignity of our spirit, we will find that they all concern merely contingent things. Knowledge of such things is useful for what it produces, but its whole nobility is due to that element of universal knowledge which is united to it and makes it knowledge. This element is present in our mind even without other kinds of information. Our mind can in fact know the essence of a contingent thing and have its idea without knowing whether the thing really subsists or is a mere possibility.

119. Conversely, because our mental lights depend upon essences, our spirit is always ennobled and enhanced by the intuition of possibilities, that is, of essences of things. Other kinds of knowledge are obtained from the application of the lights. What is added to the lights in these applications is neither light nor truth, and therefore not the infinite element which renders us persons.

120. There is however a being, knowledge of which ennobles us. It is a real, subsistent being, which, although real, is not contingent. This necessary Being, as infinite reality and complete, subsistent truth, ennobles us by communicating itself to us.

121. This teaching means that not every lie offends pure-formal right, but only those lies in which there is an evil attempt to infuse erroneous principles, whether *logical, moral,* or *religious,* into our minds. These are the errors which truly disturb and diminish the adherence of our spirit to the light of truth.

[117–121]

§2. *The injury to personship arising from an attempt to deprive a human being of virtue*

122. This injury also can be perpetrated in three ways:

1. By attempting to destroy someone's good dispositions towards virtue. We do this when we introduce obscure errors into their mind, or affections contrary to virtue into their spirit. This injury is very often an effect of the preceding injury which seeks to deprive human beings of the light of truth and to diffuse in them the darkness of error.

2. By attempting without just cause to limit the sphere of free actions which can help the acquisition of virtue. This is done either through caprice or evil will, such as the mere pleasure of exerting superiority, etc. It is an abuse which violates every person's *jural freedom*, that is, the right to acts contained virtually in our powers.

3. By attempting to seduce someone to commit a crime or carry out any action whatsoever opposed to duty, or simply by attempting to maliciously prevent someone from performing an act of virtue.

All these attacks are injuries to the right to the moral *virtue* we each have in our personship, even if the attacks have no real effect.

123. The second way of offending the right to virtue (by limiting the sphere of lawful actions helpful to the acquisition of virtues) includes in a general way the removal of means useful for their acquisition, when the deprivation is carried out for no reason at all or for a frivolous or culpable reason, and therefore unjustly.

124. Everybody therefore has the right 'to choose the mode of life they judge to be more conducive to obtaining moral good, provided they do not harm the rights of others'.[48] This in turn means that the right to virtue is injured whenever an individual or government places obstacles to free choice.

[48] I refer the reader to *SP*, bk. 2, cc. 12 and 13, where I have discussed this right at length.

§3. *The injury to personship arising from the attempt*
to deprive a human being of fulfilment and happiness

125. Personship is also injured directly whenever there is an attempt to deprive human beings of their present or future fulfilment and happiness. This kind of injury sometimes results from the preceding kinds, because the state of fulfilment and happiness depends on the possession of truth and virtue.

126. Moreover we can hinder another's state of fulfilment by impeding or disturbing his *jural freedom* of action, or by harassing another in any way at all, when the degree of harassment exceeds the strength of the person being maliciously harassed.

127. We sometimes see wickedness and hatred so engrained in the human heart that it endeavours to deny the hated person happiness in the life to come. This is the greatest violation imaginable of natural and supernatural personal right,[49] a monstrous fact frequently encountered in the history of the factions and bitter hatreds that raged between the leading families of Italy during the 12th century and afterwards.

Article 2.
Injury to the connatural right of *ownership*

128. *Connatural ownership* extends to everything contained in human nature. Hence this right is injured whenever anyone with a positive act harms any part or faculty whatsoever of the human nature which envelops every individual, whether babe or adult.

129. *Slavery* is a multiple and total violation of this innate right.

130. If by slavery we understand the use which one human being claims he can constantly make of another simply as a means for his own ends, the state of slavery contains many actions which are as injurious to innate *ownership* (nature) as to

---

[49] Rights and *duties* also exist in the *supernatural order*. A study dealing with rights of such a sublime nature would be something new, and would throw great light on how the social system should be conceived among Christian peoples relative to the well-being of Christianity.

innate *jural freedom* (person). Indeed, we can say that slavery virtually includes within itself every possible violation of every single human right.[50]

131. Understood in this sense *slavery* cannot be maintained for a single instant, nor abolished only gradually by governments — it must be annihilated at one stroke.

132. The concept of slavery in Roman laws was not explicitly of this kind. Roman law conceived a human being as having no *civil state* or rights recognised by positive laws. The slave was a human being who was not a member of *society*.

133. The concept of a human being who is not a member of civil society would not in itself, properly speaking, be the

---

[50] A principle exists in human beings which is not only *morally* but *physically* inalienable. It is the principle of *personal freedom considered in itself* independently of the good or evil objects to which its action is directed. To talk about a true alienation of the principle would be an absurd, contradictory discourse, a simultaneous affirmation and denial. Whenever we are talking about *personal freedom*, we are speaking about the *essence of freedom*. 'Essence of freedom' contains a concept contrary to that of *alienation*, or belonging to another. Although the good sense of humankind has not succeeded in formulating this truth, it has always intuitively seen it, and our most ordinary reasonings take it for granted. For example, Plautus clearly expresses it in 'Glorious Soldier':

Palaestrius: Sceledrus, I want to know now
               whether we belong to ourselves or to someone else.
               Perhaps someone has changed us into
               examples of our improvident neighbours.
Sceledrus: Certainly I am part of us, Palaestrius
Palaestrius: And I am too.
                              (Act 2, Sc. 5, vv. 20-23)

In 'Amphitruo' the slave Sosia tells Mercurius unhesitatingly:
     I swear YOU WILL NEVER PREVENT ME FROM BEING PART OF US.
                              (Act 1, Sc. 1, v. 243)

He does not see how he can cease to be proper to himself, which would indeed be an absurdity. For the same reason human laws do not recognise ownership in a person subject to the dominion of another. The principle of all external ownership is ownership of oneself, which terminates in personal freedom as its ultimate root and apex. We have said that 'immorality is simply an attempt to perform the absurd, to contradict the truth, to oppose being'. This truth which stems from the *essence* of morality is once again clearly evident here. Slavery, after all, is simply an attempt to prevent that principle from being free in the human being which cannot but be free, because it is freedom itself.

[131–133]

concept of a slave in the sense first mentioned. But it was implicitly the concept of slavery among pagan nations, because they claimed that *civil society* was *everything*; they did not recognise or tolerate anything outside that society. To be excluded from this kind of civil society (whose concept belongs to paganism and is thoroughly unjust) was the same as being excluded from the state of nature. Anyone who was not a member of the society was in fact no longer considered a human being, and consequently could be used like an animal. The natural principle itself, *neminem non laedere* [harm no one], was recognised by the laws as relative to members of the association, but not considered applicable to those who were not part of the association. Hence the pretensions of pagan civil laws which vaunted themselves as the absolute authority, superior to all other authority, even the natural law, and possessing the power to limit and alter this law at pleasure; their laws were a true *tyranny of law*. To be just, State laws must always recognise an authority superior to them: the authority of the rational law and of God. Christianity has subjected civil laws to this limitation, rendering them just and worthy of respect. But we will have to return to such an important topic when we discuss social Right.

Article 3.
We cannot say there is injury to right if we consent to the attack on our freedom or on our connatural ownership

134. Granted the distinction we have made between nature and human person, the attacks on personship discussed above, or at least some of them, can be perpetrated not only by other human beings, but by ourselves against ourselves.

135. In this case, although we sin against the moral law, we cannot say there is injury to right, because, as we have seen, right is always relative to another person.[51]

136. The same can be said when we consent to the attack on ourselves. This is confirmed by the common human feeling

---

[51] Cf. *ER*, 299.

[134–136]

expressed in the dictum, *scienti et consentienti non fit injuria* [no injury is done to the person who knows and consents].

137. But *injury* begins at the moment our consent is retracted, which can and must always be done.

138. This is one of the principal characteristics of the difference between simply moral duties and jural duties. Duties to oneself cannot be other than moral duties.

CHAPTER 7

The use of force in defence of connatural rights

139 Right is an activity rooted in the supreme, active principle of the human being (person). As we have seen, one of the characteristics of right is to act with force either to remove obstacles opposed to it or in general to maintain its activity at a constant level.[52]

140. Because the use of *force* at the moment of exercising an act proper to right is inherent to right itself and manifested concurrently with the act, such use could more suitably be called a *function of right*. However, if we are to proceed with strict logic and provide proof of everything we say about jural force, it will have to be dealt with separately, as though it were a right on its own account. This is particularly necessary because the use of force in the exercise of rights often requires special consideration and reflection.

We shall examine the possible use of force in the exercise of connatural rights by dealing first with personal freedom, and then with force relative to connatural ownership.

[52] Cf. *ER*, 246-251.

Article 1.
The use of force in maintaining the act of *personship*,
and the exercise of its jural freedom

141. As we have seen, the immediate injuries done to person are of three kinds because they are attempts to deprive human beings of *truth*, *virtue* and *happiness*, that is, of the elements which constitute the threefold origin and term of personship.[53]

142. Any attempt to deprive us of one of these three terms of our personal act can itself take three forms: 1. an attempt to despoil us of any one of the three terms of our personal act; 2. an attempt to destroy the power with which we arrive at and adhere to that term; 3. unjust prevention of those acts pertaining to the sphere of our jural freedom which could help us arrive at or better adhere to the threefold term in which our excellence is founded.[54] Thus, altogether, there are nine kinds of injury.

143. We shall now consider these ways, by which our personship can be directly offended. We shall look especially at the way in which the attempted injury threatens not the *power* of which we are speaking (person), nor the *free acts* of this power, but the threefold *personal good* to which this power is ordered of its nature.

§. *The right to use force in defence of the person when others attempt to despoil the person of truth, virtue and happiness*

A.
The general right to do justice

144. First: 'Can the supreme active principle, which is able to carry out its own acts with all the force of which it is capable and

---

[53] Cf. preceding chapter.
[54] Cf. preceding chapter.

which it finds at its disposition, lawfully use this force in favour of justice in cases concerned not with its own justice (there would be no doubt in the case of injury to its own right) but with injury done to the right of another?'

145. If this question relates to human beings in fully constituted civil society, it is certain that an individual cannot undertake to set right the offences committed against himself or others. In such circumstances, this will be done more surely on his behalf and in accordance with what has already been decided by the judiciary.

146. If the question is considered solely in relationship to personship, without reference to constituted civil society, it seems we could resolve it positively provided certain precautions and limitations are observed.

147. With this in mind, we also remember that these rights cannot be exercised in civil society possessing a judiciary except in rare, extraordinary circumstances. Granted this, we have to affirm in general that each of us possesses the following rights, which have to be considered relative to the strength of our personship (the extension of this strength is the extension of connatural right):

1. To speak the truth.

2. To judge actions in the light of truth and justice (if we can do so, and according to our capacity).

3. To reprove anyone who sins.

4. To act with force in order that justice may prevail.

5. To re-establish justice, by means of just punishment, when justice is threatened.

6. To restore things to their pristine state through forced restitution if such restoration is just and possible.

148. If all this were done prudently, carefully and justly, the person performing such an action would be considered a great benefactor. The benefits he bestowed would be a prelude to the establishment of civil society and to his own elevation as head of that society.

149. Such rights are effectively exercised at the origin of civil governments. Many just, courageous people have set out on the path to government by carrying out beneficent acts of this kind.

150. The feeling for such rights is clearly prevalent in the early

days of established nations. And careful consideration shows that these rights are exercised at the beginning of civil history. The constitution of ancient nations is very much inclined towards democracy despite the obedience proffered to an individual. What happens is this: each individual person retains the rights he previously held in the state of nature only a short time before, but now united in assemblies, all exercise these rights collectively. Each individual votes, and all are happy that each has an equal vote, or can even set up before the public a kind of tribunal whose equity is judged by the people itself.

Until the end of the period of the *Judges*, something similar often took place amongst the Hebrews; and the people never entirely abandoned the exercise of this right, which had been received and established by their law.[55]

Moses exercises a natural right of this kind[56] when he revenges

---

[55] The Hebrew law was entirely devoted to impressing ideas of justice deeply into the hearts of that primitive nation. By means of the law, divine wisdom, seconding *the instincts of human nature*, tempered and directed these instincts so that they did not act blindly. For example, in Deuteronomy (c. 17: [4-10]) God permits, or rather commands, all the people to stone those guilty of adultery: 'You' (he speaks to the whole of Israel) 'shall bring forth to your gates that man or woman who has done this evil thing, and you shall stone that man or woman to death with stones.' But he requires 1. that the crime should be carefully ascertained: 'You shall enquire diligently, and if it is true that such an abominable thing has been done in Israel ...' There should be three, or at least two witnesses of the crime: 'A person shall not be put to death on the evidence of one witness.' Moreover, the witnesses are held to the truth by being made the first to throw stones at the condemned, an act by which they protest their willingness to take responsibility for the blood of the innocent: 'The hand of the witnesses shall be first against him to put him to death, and afterwards the hand of all the people.' 2. If the crime is uncertain, and the people are not sure how to judge it, God makes them turn to the priests and to the judge: 'If any case arises requiring decision between one kind of legal right and another, or one kind of assault and another, any case within your towns which is too difficult for you, then you shall rise and go up to the place which the Lord your God will choose, and coming to the levitical priests, and to the judge who is in office in those days, you shall consult them, and they shall declare to you the decision. Then you shall do according to what they declare to you from that place which the Lord will choose, and you shall be careful to do according to all that they direct you.' The Mosaic law limits to this case of doubt the need of recurring to the established priest and judge.

[56] St. Ambrose not only recognises that Moses, although a private individual,

his companions; the young Daniel exercises a similar right in the story of the unjust condemnation of Susanna at Babylon. The people, who permitted and applauded what took place, recognised fully that despite the presence of appointed judges, Daniel did not usurp undue authority, but acted according to natural justice which obliged the people to accept and protect him.

151. These rights, proper to individuals, were then attributed also to the tribes of the Hebrew people, each of which as a collective person was persuaded it possessed the faculty of overseeing, judging and reprimanding the faults of the other tribes.[57]

152. The reason behind this faculty of the human person for exercising justice, even when the case is not concerned with one's own well-being, is found in the objective nature of justice, which is absolutely and essentially good. Whoever does justice therefore, provided he does it *truly*, does something which cannot not be good. He becomes an author of good.

153. In the second place, the human person tends to the objective, personal justice for which he was made in such a natural way that he forgets himself in the act of justice. This altogether special and most noble spontaneity brings about forgetfulness of self for the sake of seeing justice living and

---

was exercising a right in killing the Egyptian whom he struck down, but calls this act a duty. He says: 'Anyone ... who does not defend a companion from injury when he is able to do so, is as guilty as the one who does the injury' (I, *Officior.* 36). St. Thomas and other commentators also acknowledge that Moses exercised a natural right in his action, and some, like Toledo (in Lk 12, ann. 27) note that there was no judge to whom recourse could be made. Cajetan considers the overseers of the Hebrew workers as their public enemies, and affirms quite mercilessly that the Hebrews could kill them as enemies are killed in a just war (I think this is going too far). The fact that Moses exercised a natural right is not contrary to what some say about his being inspired from above in what he did. Rather, it harmonises better with what happened.

[57] Giovanni Jahn in his *Archeologia biblica* speaks about the right presumed by each tribe, §212: 'Each tribe possessed a kind of right of inspection over all the others in order that the law might be observed. If the law had been abandoned, the negligent tribe could be denounced to the others and punished in war, if there were no other remedy.' He cites Scripture, Jos 32: 9, Judges 20: 1 ss., as his authority.

triumphant. It is impossible to fight or repress this spontaneity because it is produced and authenticated by justice itself.

154. Those acts of justice, to which people are moved by pure zeal for justice, are particularly praiseworthy and just. As Scripture says, zeal 'devours' man, that is, makes him forget himself and every other consideration except that of the rights and glory of justice, ardour for which grips him and draws him out of himself.

155. However, these rights cannot be exercised by individuals 1. if individuals are not certain of the truth of the justice they are carrying out; and 2. if there is a more secure, orderly and complete way of maintaining and restoring justice. Consequently, it is not easy for the exercise of these rights to be carried out fully and equally in every human being, especially where there exists well-developed civil society in which the maintenance of justice is in great part suitably provided for. Moreover, it is rare for an individual to be undisturbed by passion; he may also pass judgment lightly, and often rashly therefore, on his brother.

156. In general, the right to carry out justice is not concerned with harm to one's own right alone, but harm to any right whatsoever, even that of another. Moreover, this right to carry out justice, although it can be extended to the defence of one's own and others' materiated rights, remains pure-formal right whenever it is exercised purely, that is, for love of justice alone which pertains solely to the person.

157. It would be different if, in exercising this right, we sought something other than the triumph of justice alone — for example, the protection or maintenance of some other just, eudaimonological good. In this case, the right would belong to the class of materiated rights. But when there is a question of pure, objective, impersonal justice, even in the defence of some materiated right, pure-formal right is exercised.

158. Of itself, the universal right to defend and fight for justice contains pure-formal right; but it can concern the defence either of pure-formal right, or of a materiated right.

159. We need to note this because fighting forcefully for a pure-formal right is very different from fighting for a materiated right. Here defence is mentally conceived as possible because it is clear that circumstances inherent to a case of this kind can

always impede the exercise of a materiated right. But this is not so when we are dealing with the defence of a pure-formal right. The use of force in this case can be sustained only with difficulty: it is neither necessary nor sufficient to achieve the purpose intended.

160. We shall first deal briefly with the question of doing justice in the case of an attack upon pure-formal rights themselves. This may occur either when we are dealing with the removal of some obstacle to our own rights or in the case of the defence of anyone else's pure-formal right.

B.
The right to enforce justice in defence of one's own pure-formal rights

161. Force must not be used unnecessarily to uphold one's own rights, that is, when there are other means of making them prevail.

162. This limitation in the use of force seems to exclude almost entirely any possibility of using it to protect our pure-formal rights. There is, indeed, no doubt that the good (that is, truth, virtue and happiness) which involves these rights, depends upon the *freedom* that a person possesses. In fact, by using our freedom, we can avoid being evilly deceived, led astray or made unhappy. In these cases, therefore, we must not react with force to those who injure us. By offering moral resistance, it is always possible to avoid in some non-violent manner the harm springing from the assault. And this is truly the great foundation of evangelical meekness.

163. In most cases the validity of this argument cannot be denied. Moreover, if the *practical force* of freedom were full, as it could and should be in perfect human nature clothed in grace, the argument would be effective in all circumstances, and thus exclude the possibility of any right to use external force in the defence of pure rights rooted in person. In such cases meekness alone would reign in place of just force. The Gospel was able to proclaim such a law of perfection because only the Gospel was

capable of bringing to the human spirit the moral virtue that stands unconquered before all pleasure and all pain.

164. Writers on natural Right have for the most part considered human beings abstractly. Their abstract view of human nature has in turn presided over the formation of many positive laws in every age and in all States. As a result, positive legislation, which supposes that pure-formal right pertains more to ethics than to Right, normally excludes coercion in cases of violation of such right. It does this because in human nature the internal personal principle, whose dignity alone is in question in the cases indicated, enjoys, abstractly considered, a force of resistance greater than the attacking force. Consequently, it has no need of help from any external force.

165. Nevertheless, peoples in every period have been conscious of something different. History provides examples of nations rising as one man to vindicate or defend such pure-formal rights as religious freedom, one of the greatest and most solemn of such rights.

166. A more complete consideration of human beings, and of the state and events in which these intelligent animal beings are implicated, shows that the consciousness of peoples is correct. We would have to deny all experience in order to disregard the fact that the forces proper to freedom are in reality limited (although freedom considered in itself is also a physically supreme force).[58] We simply do not have available the proximate power to conquer all temptations by opposing them with the power of free will alone. Hence the origin of the *moral duty* to avoid everything that could be a *proximate occasion* of sin for us.

The *right* to use force corresponds with this moral duty whenever 1. the attack springing from another's perversity becomes a *proximate occasion* of sin, that is, a temptation capable of making us waver in virtue, and 2. we cannot avoid it except by use of force. Thus a virgin, already in the power of someone attempting to defile her, may even go so far as to kill her aggressor if she is afraid that her spiritual constancy in virtue will fail.[59]

---

[58] Cf. *SP*, bk. 2, c. 12, for the *rights* arising in human beings from the limitation of the powers proper to their free will.

C.
The individual's right to repel with force
the proximate occasions of sin presented
by the malice of others. — Wars of religion

167. What is said about one's own rights has to be affirmed also about the defence of the rights of others. A parent can kill a person intent on undermining the innocence, virtue and religion of his children if the assault is sufficient to place them in proximate danger of prevaricating and there is no other means of liberating them from the overbearing power of the tempter.

168. Everyone who acts like this on behalf of a fellow human being, granted the conditions we have mentioned, exercises humanity to a splendid degree. It is a case in which courage shines with purest light — a case where bravery and glory form a single truth.

169. We can judge certain wars of religion according to this principle. In fact, we are obliged to say a few words about them because they are often judged badly, or rather very lightly. But I would ask my readers to listen and consider peacefully and calmly what I am going to say peacefully and calmly.

170. People exist, apparently religious, who seek only temporal good from religion. Polytheism of any kind, for example, offered only temporal good to human beings. We must note carefully, however, that by 'temporal' we mean not only good things existing on this earth, but whatever has such a nature even though it is imagined and longed for as part of future life. Muslims, for example, look forward after this life to enjoying the company of beautiful women of an angelic nature. The good proper to such apparent religions, and in general any good of this kind sought in any religion whatsoever, is not the object of the pure-formal right which we are considering. Here, the right to use force in defence and maintenance of personship cannot be upheld.

171. But there are people who conceive religion in a true,

---

[59] The loss of material virginity without interior consent does not entail damage to personship as such. We are not dealing with this, but with the question of effective danger to personal dignity, to morality. If the virgin doubts her constancy she can kill her aggressor.

elevated manner. They think of it as a moral truth, and seek in it the realisation of justice and the happiness that flows from the attainment of justice.

172. This moral justice and perfection, together with its consequent bliss, which human beings seek in a moral religion,[60] can have different subjective grades, that is, grades relative to ignorance and wisdom in the subject.

173. Let us imagine that someone has lived in a wilderness, or even in the midst of ancient paganism, and has adhered with his spirit almost entirely to that complex of truths which religion and natural law present to the mind. This person's religion would be imperfect, but would interiorly possess morality. The heart's desire of such a person could be focussed directly on a moral good, the term of the person.

We could also imagine someone before or after Christ who lives where the Gospel is still unknown, or who at least has not heard it. This person could have added to his religion and to the natural law certain revelations and traditions of divine truth which illustrate and complete the natural law, although the religion itself is still not perfect in the way that Christianity is. The Hebrews, and others scattered amongst the peoples, were in this state before the coming of Christ. Certain peoples are perhaps still in this state and, more generally speaking, some human beings alive today, who are known to God.

Amongst Christians, there are very probably persons of good faith who, because born of heretic parents, are divided from the body of Christ although they believe explicitly in many Christian truths, and adhere to others implicitly. They suffer no harm if through invincible ignorance they mingle errors with truth, provided the errors are held only on the authority of their teachers and in such a way that the errors do not diminish the moral quality contained in their general faith.[61]

---

[60] Morality in religion is that endowment by which religion, through the relationship it establishes between the person professing it and God, effectively betters the worshipper. A religion without power to draw human beings near to God or (and this is more important) of joining God to human beings by making them sharers in the divine nature (*holiness* and consummate justice are found here), is not *entirely* moral.

[61] The teaching of the Catholic Church has always acknowledged the presence of persons of good faith amongst the children of heretics. These

Finally, we have the Catholic Christian Church, 'the pillar and bulwark of the truth', as Paul calls it. Those giving it their adherence in the way they should possess in an altogether complete way both natural and supernatural justice and the means to increase this justice in themselves continually.

174. We still have to see the right that each of these classes of persons has to defend their own religion by using force against others who assail it through seduction or violence or in any other way. It is understood that we consider the use of force only in the case of these persons, their children or others, when there seems no other method of defence against the proximate danger of perversion or abandonment of their religion.

It is also part of our argument, as we have seen, that all those under threat see and seek in their own religion the truly moral good which it offers them. Without this, there would be no question of the personal right of which we are speaking. This right refers solely to a moral good.

We must also keep in mind that the religion upheld by the first class of persons we have considered offers a moral good less perfect than that of the second class; that the religion of the second class of persons offers less moral good to human beings than that of the third class; and that this religion in turn also offers less moral good than the religion of the fourth class of persons. Finally, the last religion we have mentioned contains the fullness of both natural and supernatural truth and moral good. Consequently, it is also taken for granted that the fourth religious state we have indicated contains the moral good of the third, the third all the moral good of the second, and the second all the moral good of the first; at the same time, each contains in a more advantageous manner the lesser moral good of the prior class.

175. Granted these conditions, which are undeniable, at least

people are therefore said to be separated from the *body* of the Church, but not from its *spirit*. They can obtain salvation; Baius' proposition (n. 68), 'Purely negative infidelity in those amongst whom Christ has not been preached, is a sin', was condemned. — St. Augustine denies that those born of heretics and educated by them deserve the title 'heretic' if they love the truth with a sincere heart, seek it and, were they to find it, would be ready to embrace it. Cf. Ep. 43 in the Maurine edition. — Tract. 45, *in Jo.* — *De Util. Cred.*, c. 1. — *De Haeres. ad Quodvultdeus*, c. 1.

[174–175]

for that large portion of the human race who profess Catholicism, and considering the matter simply, the following propositions immediately present themselves to the mind as apparently true.

First proposition. — One or more persons of any of these four classes see that their own religion or the religion of their religious counterparts is in danger through the efforts of one or more persons wishing to despoil them of that religion by putting an immoral false religion, or atheism, in its place. In this case, those attacked could defend themselves with a just religious war if they had no other way of defending themselves.

176. *Second proposition.* — The first class of persons sees some danger to their religion or that of their religious counterparts through the efforts of one or more persons attempting to despoil them of their religion in order to substitute another which not only preserves all the moral good of their own religion, but elevates it to a higher and more perfect plane. This would happen if there were a question of substituting the second, third or fourth of the above mentioned religions for the first. The attack would not endanger moral good; on the contrary, such a good would be preserved, stabilised and enlarged. In this case, it could not be maintained that pure-personal right authorised this class of persons to defend their religion with force. Rather, moral duty would oblige them first to come to know exactly the newly presented religion and then, having found it morally better, to embrace it as a benefit bestowed upon them.

177. *Third proposition.* — For the same reason, if the second class of religious people we have described were to see some danger to their religion, but from an attempt to substitute the third or fourth morally better religion, they would wage an unjust war by defending their own religion.

178. *Fourth proposition.* — In the same way, there would be unjust religious war if the third class were to undertake the defence of their own religion against an attempt to substitute it with the fourth degree of religion.

179. *Fifth proposition.* — On the other hand, the fourth religion could be defended in a just religious war against the three preceding classes of religion, the third against the other two, and the second against the first. In each of these wars an infinite, personal, moral good would be defended.

[176–180]

180. I have said that these propositions are apparently true. But are they true in fact? We cannot decide until we have heard the objections against them which have now to be weighed carefully and impartially.

181. The first objection is very common. Everyone will say that such teaching deprives many people of the right to defend their own religion against attack. If we grant that one human being has this right, we must grant that all have the same right whatever religion they profess. In fact, everyone professing a religion will believe that it is the true religion and better than all the others. Everyone, therefore, has the right to defend his own religion. This right arises from individual persuasions whose sole competent judge is the individual holding these persuasions.

182. 'No one is judge of other people's persuasions'. This proposition, if understood in the sense that no one is judge of the truth and morality contained in a religion professed by others, is true only for those who affect a kind of universal scepticism. They consider themselves unsure of every single opinion they hold, and think that all they know (if this word can be used in their regard) is only probable or likely, but nothing more.

I would be the first to agree that such people are totally without the right to judge the opinions and beliefs of others. They do not possess this right because they lack the physical faculty that forms the first constitutive element of right. And they lack this physical faculty because they themselves are persuaded that they possess nothing that is absolutely certain. Consequently they remain deprived of every certain principle and criterion according to which they may regulate their judgment and come to some decision. I agree completely that 'judgment about the truth and moral worth of a given religion is impossible for all those in this world who profess scepticism in theory or in practice. Such people have no *firm persuasions*, and do not believe that they undoubtedly possess the truth.' It follows that the five propositions explained above cannot be applied to a society composed of such persons. It also follows that the objection would be altogether valid if the world were made up only of people uncertain about what they know. At the very least we would have to say that 'the right to defend one's own persuasion would be possessed by all or by no one.' Everyone would be in the same state of uncertainty as everyone else; no one's persuasion, opinion or belief would have any advantage over that of another; everything would be equally uncertain for everyone; no one would feel himself capable of judging others' opinions without leaving himself open to rash judgment.

183. We have to admit that many persuasions have been disturbed in the human spirit from the time of Luther's pretended reform until today. It is not a question only of doubt about errors and prejudices buried deep in minds; doubt has arisen about the most incontrovertible truths. The second half of the last century is a case in point. If we take into account those whose opinions prevailed through books, speeches or public administration we would find that the majority perhaps were totally bereft of firm persuasions, devoid of unshakeable theoretical opinions, and incapable of following any guide other than that of the utility to be derived from the senses. The great principle marking the passage from the medieval to the modern world is that of *utility founded in feeling*.

The same practical criterion flourished during the decadence of Greece and of the Roman empire amongst sceptics who on the one hand denied any human capacity for knowing the truth, while on the other desired human beings to direct their activity according to the utility derived from experience. Only this kind of utility was to be the practical criterion, as they called it, of true opinions.

Note that laws and the accepted dicta of public opinion are established by the influential majority. As we said, this majority was composed of people, unsure and hesitant in all their beliefs, who had no faculty (and therefore no right) to judge the truth

[183]

and morality of the different religions professed by mankind. It is clear that in such circcumstances *maxims* of a particular kind relative to religious truths would prevail amongst the public. These *maxims* necessarily harmonised with the capacities of their authors who, doubtful about everything, were unsuited to pass judgment on anything. Their maxims had to be reduced, therefore, in our present argument to this: 'People must abstain from judging about religious truths professed by others.' Another maxim followed from the first: 'Indifference in religious matters.' This indifference consisted in treating all religions as more or less equal, that is, as more or less equally uncertain. With religions thus placed on the same level of uncertainty, it is clear that 'anyone preferring his own religious belief absolutely to that of someone else, and in such a way as to condemn the other's religion, must be considered temerarious.'

In these circumstances the choice of one belief rather than another does not depend upon the truth known about the belief, but on mere conjecture and the great principle of utility, that is, on the feeling and taste that each person has for one belief rather than another. Each individual must be free to satisfy his own individual tastes and feelings, and the conjectures made by each must be equally respected. Because no one knows which may be true and which false, an injury could be unconsciously inflicted upon the truth if all religions are not given due consideration. Every effort to take away a person's religious belief, whatever this may be, is an injury inflicted upon that person's right — and an injured right can be defended by force. We have to conclude not only that the truest and most moral religion can be defended against a less true and moral religion, but in general that each person has the right to maintain and defend his own belief however true or false, moral or immoral, it may be.

184. This is the doctrine of religious sceptics and indifferentists. It has been confused with the doctrine of *freedom of conscience*, although the two are totally dissimilar.

185. Here I wish to declare myself a supporter and promoter of *freedom of conscience*, properly understood, but at the same time opposed to the teaching of sceptics and religious indifferentism as I have explained it above. I grant, however, that the teaching I have expounded is the only equable, logical doctrine

available to a society made up of the indifferent and sceptical. But how does the *jural teaching about freedom of conscience* differ from the *jural teaching* of *religious scepticism?*[62]

186. The use of force to constrain another to adhere to a religious belief, even to a true belief, is a logical absurdity and a manifest injury to right.

187. It is a *logical absurdity* because a useless, improportionate means is used to bring about the adherence of an individual to a given belief. The intellect is convinced by reason alone; the spirit bows only to persuasion; physical force has power only over the body.

188. It is an *injury done to right* but not however to the right claimed for each human being by which we can all hold any false opinion, even when it is known as erroneous. I can only protest in the strongest terms against this totally absurd right. There is no right, no moral faculty for consenting to an error known as error, or to immorality known as immorality. The injury done to right, in the sense in which we are considering injury, does not consist in an attack on such an imaginary and absurd right, but in the use of force to inflict harm upon another by imposing some penalty upon him. In inflicting harm and imposing punishment upon another, we enter the sphere of the other's ownership; each of us, as we know, has the right 'not to be harmed in our ownership'.

189. Nor may we say that a deserved punishment can be inflicted upon another in virtue of each one's innate right, indicated above, to do justice. This right cannot be applied without a prior, firm decision about fault. But which of us is capable of passing a sure sentence on the good or bad faith with which others follow religious opinions that are not absolutely and intrinsically immoral? No one is able to discern the hidden depths of the spirit visible only to the eyes of God,[63] invisible to

---

[62] This sceptical teaching about religion has wrongly been called 'theological tolerance'. The word 'tolerance' does not express teaching, but conduct. Moreover, it implicitly contains doctrinal disapproval of the object of tolerance; we tolerate only what is bad. — I think it more important than ever today to avoid imprecise language of this nature which leads to endless questioning, and to discord where harmony should reign. I do not think it useless to remind my readers of this on occasion. My only desire is unity: 'Peace! Peace! Peace! is all my cry.'

human eyes. The right of each to remain unharmed and sure in his ownership is under attack when one person decides to inflict punishment upon another by brute force in order to constrain that person to abandon certain false religious beliefs and to hold certain other religious beliefs which the attacker believes true, and which in this case I suppose to be true.

This is the teaching about freedom of conscience which I fully accept.

190. But it is immensely different from that of religious scepticism.

As we said, this kind of doctrine asserts that each individual has an equal right to hold any belief whatsoever. Because all beliefs are considered uncertain, individuals cannot judge that one is true in preference to others. Each person has to believe that he could be mistaken in his opinion, if indeed he has an opinion. In this system, religious belief is a need independent of truth and dependent upon individual taste. Religious beliefs have to be considered as satisfying religious feeling in various kinds of way, and individuals have a free right to choose whatever satisfies them most. All tastes can be catered for. I cannot in any way give my assent to such teaching, so contrary to human nature's essential need for truth and virtue.

191. We can take comfort, however. Scepticism is a temporary transition now past as we move from one state of the world to another. We have entered a new age in which great strides are being taken towards solid persuasion. We are gaining confidence in our activity and can turn like the man who

> thrown from the sea upon the beach
> looks back upon the threatening waves.

192. We now have to examine possible jural teachings about religious beliefs when society is composed of people who believe fully and are deeply persuaded that the opinions they

[63] The same cannot be said about individual, external and immoral acts damaging to humanity and resulting from false religious opinions: for example, cases of human sacrifice, the burning of Indian widows, sacred prostitution, and so on. Eliminating these injuries to human nature and saving their victims, even when this is done with the use of force, would be a benefit to humanity and a service to justice. — In practice, however, the exercise of this right would be dangerous. It could be used by the devious and powerful to carry out many violations of right.

profess cannot in any way be deceptive. We are not dealing, therefore, with doubtful, indifferent or sceptical society. In explaining these jural teachings we believe that we can open a path to reconciliation between the opposing parties into which the world is divided, that is, between those who have no firm religious beliefs and those who do. We have already seen what the former teach; now we have to examine what is and what should be the teaching of the latter.

193. The reconciliation we are talking about consists in showing that the first group, devoid of religious beliefs, acts coherently and equably in following the teaching it professes (as long as its adherents remain in a state of uncertainty). However, if the second group wished to follow the same teachings as the first and make these its rules of conduct, it would be untrue to itself and act unjustly. The principles of the second group must be different because they spring from a different state of mind and spirit. Moreover, it is not at all reasonable for one side to complain about the other because of this difference. As far as I can see, the mistake made by each side, by each of the two societies, lies in their claiming that the jural teachings proper to each of them are absolutely and universally true and just, and should be followed by everyone without distinction. But this is not how things stand. Such teachings pertain not to absolute but subjective justice, that is, justice relative to the state of the different subjects who make up society.[64]

194. The jural doctrines about religion, in the case of those who hold firm and unshakeable religious beliee the following:

First, we have to note the error present in the all too common belief that individuals can deceive themselves in good faith about everything. This is totally false. Things exist about which we cannot deceive ourselves in good faith. Proof of this assertion will be found in *The Origin of Thought*[65] where we have shown explicitly that good faith is impossible in all intrinsically immoral beliefs.[66] If, therefore, we are dealing not only with a

---

[64] This is an example of the way in which the same species of rights assumes different *modes* in various human accidental states, as we said in the Introduction to this work.

[65] Cf. *OT*, 575-629.

[66] Cf. *CS*.

false, impious belief, but also with one that is intrinsically blameworthy and immoral, persuasion about it, however strong, never gives an individual the right to propagate it in the minds and hearts of others. Every effort in this direction, granted the intention of propagating such immorality, is an injury done to human nature. Everyone can defend himself against this injury provided the rules moderating just defence are observed.

195. The usual objection ('Who can possibly judge the immorality of a religious belief?') has no force here. Every individual has the right and duty to discern that which is intrinsically immoral and that which is not. Without such discernment, it would be impossible to live a good life. Moreover, this discernment is possible because, as I said, no one is forced to assent to what is intrinsically immoral, nor can such an error be made in good faith.

196. Second, it is possible to find beliefs which, although not immoral considered in themselves, are false and senseless. Like the previous kinds of belief, these beliefs are not truly religious, but superstitious. Nevertheless, good faith can be present in so far as these beliefs have been received into the spirit on authority from others rather than reached through one's own reasoning. However, persuasion about these beliefs, whatever its force, does not give rise to a right in those who are thus persuaded to propagate their superstitious errors. There is no right precisely bec are errors and vain superstitions.

197. A person holding these persuasions and communicating them to others is in the same condition as a person who believes in good faith that he exercises a right, or at least makes use of his jural freedom and perhaps confers a benefit upon others, although this is not in fact the case.

198. In such a case, we have to act as though we were dealing with an individual who is following an erroneous, but innocent persuasion. In other words, his endeavours have to be combated with the same arms that he himself uses. If he is content simply to discuss the matter, we can argue peacefully with him and provide him with information and explanations in favour of the truths opposed to his errors. If he uses force, force can be used against him, not because he is a false believer but because he has first used undue violence against us. If he then goes on to use

[195–198]

seduction, fraud and lies, he can be confronted as an already blameworthy individual, convicted of bad faith and immoral assault.

199. We can add that any individual who possesses truly moral beliefs worthy of God is competent to act as judge in deciding which superstitions are devoid of morality. Every human being can and must distinguish moral belief from that which possesses no morality.

200. The contrary is true in the case of an individual whose faith is immoral. He is equally obliged by the natural law itself to listen peaceably to the arguments of others and to acknowledge their moral truth. It is only blameworthy passi blameworthy passion, or a blind, unreasonable attachment to the authority of others that impedes the tranquillity of spirit with which he listens and assents to the truth known through another's reasoning. Anyone refusing to do this is *ipso facto* blameworthy and unjust.

201. There is, however, a more frequent and complicated case of opposition between two religions, both of which contain true and moral elements. In this case, one of them also contains many errors and the other few (or none at all because it is entirely true). Here, good faith is possible on both sides which should therefore treat each other with great sensitivity.

202. In saying that each side should treat the other sensitively, I am speaking of the manner with which each should use its right. I am not speaking of the right considered in itself.

203. A careful distinction has to be made between questions about the existence of a right, and the just manner of exercising it.

204. It is certain that 'moral-religious truth can always be justly defended, and that error can never be justly defended.' This is a conclusion that must be safeguarded relative to the existence of right. We have dealt with this in the five propositions explained above.

205. There is, however, a totally different question to be faced relative to the just, equable manner of putting this defence into effect in particular cases and circumstances. A person upholding error in good faith has the right to be treated without punishment. He is without blame, although without any right to sustain his error despite his belief in it.

206. If, therefore, he upholds his error only through argument, and without the use of force, he should also be dissuaded from it by reasoning. For example, a person who in good faith possesses what belongs to another, must not be immediately dispossessed by force. Another's title to the thing under consideration, and his own unlawful possession of it (which means that he cannot retain it in good faith) should be proved to him.

207. The sole difference between unlawfully holding a material object and upholding an erroneous opinion is this: when a person in good faith possesses a material object, he ceases to be in good faith after sure titles of another's dominion over that object have come to his notice. In this case, the true owner can dispossess him of the object even with force if he does not listen to reason. The same cannot be said about error. It cannot always be said that the one who errs ceases to be in good faith even after others' convincing opinions against the error have been expounded. On the one hand, the person in error may not have understood them sufficiently; on the other, it is impossible for one individual to deprive another of an error by force as though the error were some material object like a coin, clothing or some possession. All that remains to the one possessing the truth is the right to defend it for himself and others with the mildest means possible. These means should also be graded in the sense that they should cause the least disturbance to a person who remains fixed in his error after hearing the contrary reasons, and even wants to propagate it.

208. At this point the usual difficulty arises: who is to be judge in this case? If both sides think they possess the truth, will either be convinced of his error?

209. It is a serious prejudice to suppose that a third party is always necessary to act as judge between two litigants in order to bring about a just settlement, which can sometimes be reached without the presence of any judge.

210. In fact, two parties who have recourse to a judge to end their dispute only do so in order to hear which side is right and which wrong. The judge could not say that one side was right unless it were already in the right even before he said so; nor could he declare a side in the wrong without its being wrong independently of his judgment. The judge does not create justice

and injustice. He simply acknowledges the presence of justice and injustice in the conditions of the case laid before him.

Justice therefore exists independently of the judge, whose only responsibility is to state where justice lies. Our work in writing this essay is designed to establish the rules of justice and right according to which the judge himself can correctly give his decision; the purpose of the essay is not to discover ways of making justice and right prevail, or bring them to be recognised in society. We must remember that we are dealing with the science of 'rational right which continues to exist even after the establishment of civil society, whatever certain absolutist writers maintain. It does not draw its titles from society itself, which it ignores, but from human nature.

It is impossible, therefore, for anyone to maintain that if two people have a dispute in the state of nature where no court exists to resolve the question, one of them cannot be right and the other wrong. It is equally impossible to maintain that one of the two parties, because of the lack of a judge to uphold his right, cannot defend that right against his assailant when he sees the right to be injured. Certainly, the one who believes himself injured must ascertain the fact carefully before proceeding to inflict damage on his assailant. He has a moral-jural duty to examine the case carefully and impartially. But if, in the last analysis, he finds that he has been attacked and injured, he has the right to defend himself fittingly and to demand reparation.

211. — 'But he could be deceiving himself!' He could indeed be deceiving himself because this is the lot of all mankind. But does this matter? If an *infallible* decision about the truth of the right and of the injury were necessary for exercising a right, no one, either in the state of nature or even in civil society, could make his rights prevail. *Infallible* decisions about human things are impossible here on earth. The individual judging his own right, the judge and the tribunal called to intervene and pronounce between the parties, are all fallible, as we can see continually from the differing decisions which tribunals, even within the same State and following the same legislation, make about identical questions. Not only courts of different instances, but different judges in the same instance, and the same judges when they change their minds — as they often do — provide examples of this fallibility.

Totally infallible *certainty* is not necessary, therefore, if human beings are to make their rights prevail. It is sufficient 'that an individual remain *sincerely* certain about his right, and act with good faith while using the means within his power to avoid self-deception.' Once he has acquired this certainty, which in our case could be called *jural*,[67] he can act inculpably to defend those rights of his which he believes have been violated or are under attack.

212. These are general principles. They are valid relative to the defence of any right whatsoever. They can therefore be applied to the personal right to preserve for oneself and for others the truth and morality of one's own religion.

213. I must insist on the certain duty to ensure that only truth and morality are being defended in one's own religion. No extraneous element must be involved. This is especially the case when force has to be used as an element of defence either as a reply to force already exercised against oneself, or because all other means within the person's power have been undertaken fruitlessly. But, granted these precautions and limitations, the defence of such precious beliefs for oneself or others against all sophistry, seduction or violence will always lie within one's right. The absence of a human judge, recognised by both parties to decide which of them is right and which wrong, is irrelevant in cases of this nature. It is always a fact that only the one who defends for himself and others the possession of religious truth and morality is right and acts according to justice; the other is wrong. And that would still be the case even if there were a judge with human authority who decided in favour of the one who was wrong, and against the one in the right.

214. But can there be a competent judge in such a case? — A careful answer is necessary to this question because it will provide greater evidence for what we have said.

215. We must first note, therefore, that no human being what-soever, precisely because each is a rational being, can be judge in such a case without being part of the case itself.

216. This is very clear. No human being exists without his either possessing or not possessing some religious belief. If he

---

[67] We have spoken at length about this kind of certainty in *CS*, 474-528.

has no religious belief, he takes his place with the indifferent —
he has already given his adherence to one of the two sides
previously mentioned, and will necessarily judge according to
the principles of indifferentism which we have explained. He
will judge, therefore, as one of the sides in the question, that is,
he will make his judgment in favour of his own state of spirit
relative to religious beliefs. If he professes a given belief, he will
judge in favour of this belief and consequently as one of the
parties to the case, according to his own principles, and in his
own favour.

217. It is impossible, in the decisions about religion that we are
considering, for an individual to be neutral. There is no one in
all the world who can be put up as third-party judge of the
opposing sides, equally distant from them both. We have to say
that each individual, who is necessarily both judge and party, has
the right and duty to judge uprightly in this matter. We conclude
that there are as many judges as there are human beings; that the
more popular religion has more judges in its favour, the less
popular, less judges; that we are suffering not from a lack of
judges, but from a superabundance of discordant judges. Each
one is responsible for doing his own duty, the only way in which
all can be brought to agree. Those who do not carry out their
responsibility, and consequently make themselves the cause of
discord, stand subject to one single judge, GOD. No human
authority can intervene without entering the case as an individual who is both judge of and party to the dispute. If such a
person takes it upon himself to judge without admitting that he
is a party to the dispute he lies by pretending to be God.[68]

---

[68] An individual opposing the judicial authority of the Church would show
that he has not understood my argument. There is no doubt that the Church
is the supreme judge in matters of faith, but its decision is in fact valid only
for its own children, in other words, for those who have the joyful courage
to believe in her authority. But it is impossible to believe in the Church
without first acknowledging the authority and worth of that in which one
believes. And this is the internal judgment under consideration, which can be
made only by the individual, not by others. — For a proof that this first
judgment is necessarily individual, cf. my first letter to the Abbé Lamennais
in vol 4, *Prose Ecclesiastiche.*

218. 'This teaching provides not only a faculty for self-defence to those who hold true and moral religion, but for attacking other believers in so far as their religions are immoral and false.'

REPLY

219. As we have said, it is not lawful for anyone to attack another's religion by inflicting or threatening to inflict physical punishment. Lies, deception and other immoral ways of opposing the religion of others are even worse.

220. The use of words is different; freedom to speak cannot be denied to truth and morality.

221. The word of truth is essentially free. It does not offend personal right; and its exercise is supremely holy. It is a benefit which renews the personship offended in others by error and immorality. No sophistry or hair-splitting can prevail against this precious freedom; it shines with the clarity of evidence.

222. — But if you admit freedom of speech for an individual because he *believes* that he possesses the truth, you should admit it equally for another who also *believes* that he possesses the truth —

It is not correct to say that I admit freedom of speech for an individual because *he believes* that he possesses the truth; I admit it only because he truly possesses the truth, that is, on condition that he possesses it.

223. — But who judges between two people holding different opinions, both of whom believe they possess the truth and therefore have a right to freedom of speech?

I have already shown that there is no need for any hypothetical judge to act as a third party in the dispute. Moreover, judges are not lacking in this situation because there are as many judges as there are onlookers. And all are fallible.

224. — What can government do then?

Government can certainly prevent external violence and punish the first contestant to introduce intimidatory force, or calumny or other injury into the discussion. But government will only do this because the attacking party has, independently of the argument he is sustaining, offended the other's rights.

225. — In that case, government would also have the right to silence error. —

The case between truth and error, morality and immorality, concerns human persons; it is not a case for government, but for humanity.[69]

226. — Is it impossible for government to do anything in this exigency?

As far as I can see, what I have said shows that I am opposed to considering things in the abstract. I do not want to look at matters in the systematic, exclusive way used so far for political questions, and often jural and moral questions. If I understood as 'government' some kind of mental entity that remained suspended as it were in the clouds beyond contact with human individuals, I would undoubtedly have to grant the consequence which according to you seems to flow from my principles. I would have to say, as someone has affirmed recently, 'the law is atheistic'.

But in my opinion government is only an aggregate of human beings, of real flesh and blood, who govern society. They may do this of their own right, or through delegation by those who are or who wish to be governed by them. As we have seen, all human beings, including those employed in government at any level, are judges in cases of truth and morality. All of them are judges, from the highest to the lowest. And it is lawful and sometimes obligatory for those who govern, as it is lawful and obligatory for all other human beings, to defend their own and others' religious beliefs, if true, when they are threatened. In the same way, they can, like all other human beings, use the means in their power for defensive purposes. Amongst these means is government influence.

Any opinion contrary to this constant, common sense way of considering matters would either be a contradiction or provide

---

[69] I have shown, in *SP* (bk 4, c. 2), that *human good or satisfaction* is personal, and that governmental responsibility consists not only in removing obstacles to the freedom of individuals who have to act of themselves to attain this good, but in helping individuals to do this (bk. 2, c. 10).

rules of conduct not for human beings, but for imaginary entities.

227. We have to add, however, that persons composing government must observe, in their defence of the truth and morality in which they believe, the same moral laws which moderate the defence offered by an individual for his own or others' rights. That is:

1. This defence must be carried out with upright means, not deceptively, etc.

2. It must be the minimum possible defence in which methods of persuasion are employed when the aggressors are not guilty of deception or violence. If they are guilty in these respects, their deception and violence can be punished and repressed for what they are, independently of any religious motive.

228. If it is a question not of defending one's own true religion but of opposing the false religion of someone else, government can act in the same way as all those intimately persuaded of possessing the truth and certain that in propagating it they are performing a benefit to mankind. In other words, government can do this provided it does not enter the sphere of others' absolute or relative rights, and provided it always uses persuasive means, not brute force or punishment, or actual or threatened harm.[70]

229. Within these strict limits, laws and all other means

---

[70] In the Middle Ages, some rulers employed violence to constrain others to embrace the Catholic faith. This brutal method of action seems to have been introduced into religious affairs as a result of the rough and ready customs of the northern peoples who preyed upon the Roman world. Mgr. G. B. Duvoisin, bishop of Nantes, notes this in his *Saggio sulla tolleranza*, an addition to the final Paris edition (1805) of his *Dimostrazione evangelica*. He says: 'Although religious dogmas and morality are always the same, religion in practice takes on the characteristics and customs of the people professing it. The northern peoples who conquered the rest of Europe and knew no other law than that of war preserved their barbarous and bellicose mores even under Christianity. Their zeal for religion was the same as their zeal for honour, and they were under a self-imposed obligation to defend both by force of arms. The spirit of chivalry was not in favour of tolerance, and the unhappy prejudice which caused the introduction of duelling could not fail to make wars of religion an affair of honour.' — And, as we said, wars of religion in defence of true religion are truly holy.

available to governments can and must be ordered to the defence and the propagation of truth, morality and true religion. As we have shown at length elsewhere, this is the final end of civil society.[71]

230. Moreover, while laws and all other means available to government can and must be ordered to propagate what governments have solid reason to believe is truth, morality and true religion, this corresponds to the way in which things have always been done. They could not have been done differently in any rational, coherent system, whatever its denomination: absolutism or liberalism in politics, *atheism* or *Catholicism* in religion.

231. Theorists of any kind in politics or religion should pay careful attention to this last proposition. Provided they grant me two truths, which I think are evident and which I believe I have demonstrated elsewhere with the rigour proper to mathematical theories,[72] I would submit: 1. that civil society is formed and can be formed by human beings alone, for the sake of mutual help in progress towards true human good (moral-eudaimonological good); and 2. that those who govern have the responsibility for promoting this good which is the aim of the existence of civil association, and which they must achieve with civil means.

232. Granted these two principles, common to all who have not abandoned morality and reason, it must be obvious to all rulers of society that in order to reach their aim they have to use the concept they have formed of the aim itself. And this concept of the ultimate aim of society, that is, of true moral-eudaimonological good is formed by them (and by all other individuals) as the result of their own beliefs and interior moral-religious persuasions.

All those who govern, whoever they may be, hold one system or another if indeed they intend to steer the boat entrusted to them to the port for which it is destined. In doing this, they can make use only of the knowledge and persuasion they have about the location of that port, and about the journey needed to reach it. A helmsman can steer the ship only in the light of his

[71] Cf. *SP*, bk. 2.
[72] *Ibid.*

own knowledge of geography, maps and compasses, knowledge which he uses as best he can.

233. — Some may affirm that this is not the case: government, they maintain, must not concern itself with religious or moral matters; its responsibility extends solely to material things. —

But this kind of objection depends either upon people's ignorance of the final and principal end for which civil society is instituted (the end for which human beings operate and which they cannot renounce), or upon people who contradict and oppose themselves, or finally upon *indifferentists* in religious matters, that is, people who recognise nothing as true, or people who believe it impossible to recognise the truth amidst everything else.

The last category (individuals without any firm beliefs) is composed, as I was saying, of the great multitude of those who would have government totally disassociated from everything religious. However, in maintaining this opinion, they do not avoid the necessity we have indicated. In fact, they themselves are acting in conformity with the principle that we hold as a *de facto* universal and necessary rule of conduct for all human beings alike. When they affirm that government, that is, the people who govern, must not pay any attention whatsoever to religion because it provides nothing stable, they simply act according to their own persuasions. If people of this kind were placed in government, they would without doubt act reasonably and coherently in accordance with their own convictions. In other words, they would act in the same way as those who are inwardly sure they possess what is true, just and holy, and use their influence and power to communicate such a good to their fellows. The error of indifferentists is found rooted in their indifferentism.

234. — Nevertheless those who hold firm persuasions and beliefs can always be mistaken. —

The objection is always the same. They can indeed be mistaken, but this does not mean that the teaching they propound is false. Or are we going to say that the helmsman's only possibility of not mistaking his direction is for him to let his rowers and the wind take the boat where they will? Is there to be no navigation because we are over-anxious about the captain's possible mistake?

235. In the second place, we are speaking about rights and, as I have already said, I acknowledge a true right not in the individual who erroneously believes he has a right, but in the one who actually possesses a right. I have also said that it is necessary to treat urbanely those who exercise a right which in good faith they believe is theirs. Finally, I said that the fear of a mistake about one's belief is not a sufficient reason for having to abstain from the exercise of what one believes is one's right. However, each individual is always bound by moral jural duty to proceed calmly with sufficient self-scrutiny.

236. Finally, careful attention should be given to the difficulty and quasi-impossibility of adverting to self-deception in the case under discussion as we have defined it.

I grant that error would be possible and extremely easy in the case of religious beliefs in general, that is, of all beliefs improperly called 'religious'. But I allow a right of defence only to those whose religion is first of all moral. There is no right of defence or of proselytism for those who simply profess 'some religious belief'. In the case of *morality*, nobody is *completely* deceived, strictly speaking, about the universal principles. If through self-deception people believe that something immoral is moral, they would not as a result attain any right, even the right which pertains to error in good faith. A *formally erroneous conscience* is not free from fault even when the person forming such a conscience seems to have no disquiet about his fault.[73]

237. — Your teaching encourages false zeal in rulers, who thus offend and irritate their peoples. —

This kind of statement shows that the question has been misunderstood, and two questions confused. The first question

---

[73] For a demonstration of the voluntariness of informal error, cf. *CE*, 1279-1334 and *CS*, 236-372. Further confirmation may be found in a recent work: 'Every error is in general freely chosen. We are not deceived; we deceive ourselves. There is no falsity in our perceptions. Whatever we feel about the origin of our perceptions, we have to acknowledge that they come from God in a more or less direct way because he is the author of our means of knowledge. That is why perceptions are always true, although incomplete. "The intellect (that is, simple perception) spoken of by St. Thomas is never false as long as it is not mingled with any judgment. It simply does not embrace all its object" (*S.T.*, q. 85, art. 6).' *De la perfectibilité humaine*, by A. M., Paris 1835, c. 4.

is general: can the person possessing moral-religious truth communicate it to others with every upright means available, and in doing so does he offend the rights of those who do not yet possess it? The second asks if the individual possessing moral-religious truth can try to propagate it even if he foresees that his activity would have an effect contrary to his intention and produce more harm than good. In other words, can he communicate it to others with means that, because of the evil they produce, are more likely to damage the good at which they aim?

238. The first question is one *of right*. This we have dealt with. The second is more concerned with *prudence* than with right. The first considers personal right in itself, devoid of the circumstances that are often found in its exercise; the second considers a precise, particular circumstance which sometimes impedes the exercise of that right. The first aims at establishing the existence of the right as faculty; the second limits the acts of this faculty according to the principle we have established (a principle scarcely ever taken into consideration): 'No one has the right to misuse his right'.

Article 2
The just use of force to maintain connatural ownership

239. After the defence of moral-religious truth, rational Right acknowledges as a result of war and violence that there is nothing more just than the attempt to defend oneself against the threat of slavery (taken in the strict sense) or to free oneself from such a state, so degrading to human nature.

240. Nevertheless, we have to note that a slave does not exercise a right if he is so corrupt that he wants freedom simply to abuse it and thus become more immoral than he would have been in the state of slavery. In regaining his freedom for this purpose, he is as unjust as the owner who keeps him in slavery. It is indeed sad for lovers of humanity, but true, that such things occur,[74] and there are facts to prove it. Indeed, there are many

[74] This kind of injustice occurs more easily when the owner acts humanely

reasons drawing us to think that the profound immorality of the human condition disguises a hidden justification for Providence's permitting the slavery of so many thousands of unhappy wretches.

241. Let me point here to two opposite opinions about the natural right of slaves to liberate themselves by force: pagan opinion, which is entirely evil, and Christian opinion, which is highly beneficial.

242. Pagan opinion can be summed up in the words of Florus: 'Who amongst the chief people of the world can possibly tolerate in tranquillity wars waged against slaves?'[75] The people ruling the nations thought it a disgrace that they had to fight against slaves who wanted to cast off their fetters. Such contempt arises from a feeling of habitual supremacy, now changed into a civil right. Subjective pride draws jural reason towards error. It dominates it to such an extent that lengthy oppression and permanent injury become a right of dominion and ownership.

243. Christian opinion originates from a totally opposite principle. Its source is not *subjective* feeling, but moral perfection, which is altogether *objective*. Dominion or the domination by one individual over many, ceases to be good for Christians, whose sole good is justice and beneficence. Christian opinion does not seek to subdue anything to itself, but wants to give to others. Armed with this sublime notion of good, such opinion is no longer interested in what it sees as useless questions about slaves freeing themselves with violence from slavery.[76] As it progresses, Christianity does indeed encounter the question, but bypasses it. The difficulty is resolved of itself, as it were, as Christianity goes forward, casting light in its path and sowing peace in human spirits. Christianity has no doubt that in accord with rational light an affirmative answer must be given to the

towards a brutalised slave. Every time a slave who wishes to lay aside the yoke desires greater moral evil than that to which he is constrained by his master, he commits an injustice. He wishes to leave one immoral state for the sake of something worse.

[75] *De gest. Rom.* 3, c. 19.

[76] Note that we are speaking here of true slavery not about lawful dominion. The principle we are discussing is: 'Can a master use his slave as a thing and even go so far as to destroy him?'

question, and labours simply in order to make the question inapplicable.

As we have seen, the use of violence is justified only on condition that there is no other milder means for arriving at the preservation of one's right which, however, is right simply to the extent that rationally speaking it contains some value.[77] But Christianity provides us with another, peaceful means for freeing slaves from injustice. Enlightening the owner about the injustice of slavery and about his obligation to see a brother in every slave, it shines upon his mind and enhances his spirit — and slavery exists no longer. This simple change produces of itself upright, moral servitude. Moreover, Christianity diminishes and even wipes out in the eyes of the slave the price of his freedom; it shows him that in slavery itself he can exercise heroic virtue, obtaining *moral good* to the highest degree and its consequent divine reward. And the content of this reward is the highest and most perfect freedom, which alone fulfils the concept of true good.

Christian wisdom saw that material freedom from slavery did not necessarily result in the betterment of the slave. On the contrary, the badly-disposed slave could be harmed in his moral good in passing from abasement to arrogance, as indeed occurred.

This sublime teaching of Christ, preached by his immediate disciples, is witnessed to by the great St. Ignatius of Antioch who, according to tradition, was the child put in the midst of the disciples as a symbol of humility and innocence.[78] In his letter to Polycarp he writes: 'Do not despise bond-servants, male or female. On their part, they should not puff themselves up. Rather, let them serve more eagerly for the glory of God to obtain an infinitely better freedom from him. They should not desire to be granted their common freedom if afterwards they become only the bond-servants of desire.'[79] How great the

---

[77] The third constitutive element of right. Cf. *ER*, 252-254.

[78] Matt 18: [2]. — St. Ignatius had listened to Peter, John and Paul.

[79] *Letter to Polycarp*, 4. — We find the same wisdom in the extant letter of St. Barnabas, the apostle: 'Do not give orders with a bitter spirit to your bond-servants, women or men, who hope in the same God. Be careful not to fall away like this from the fear of God who is over you all. He did not come

wisdom, concept and new light for the times contained in these words!⁸⁰

244. But is it then impossible, according to Christian principles, for the slave to throw off undue servitude?

I can only reply that the exercise of this rational right remains in force amongst those who have not reached the apex of gospel virtue. Freedom is indeed a natural good which is not compensated or sublimated in those who either do not fully possess supernatural good or who possess it in an insufficiently sensitive and operative manner. Even amongst Christians a distinction has to be made: some, the majority, remain at the normal level; others, but few, reach final perfection.

CHAPTER 8

A more detailed determination of connatural rights: their relationship with acquired rights

245. I must now continue the determination of connatural rights and detail them more specifically. I will also consider them in relationship with the whole complex of human rights. Investigating them in this way from new points of view will help, I hope, to further clarify our ideas on this important subject, which still contains many difficulties. I will begin with a summary classification of all human rights, making use of

to call us according to rank; he came to call those whom the spirit had prepared.' I omit the well-known passages of the Apostle of the Gentiles.

⁸⁰ Every jural consideration is contained in this evangelical teaching. Amongst others we find the principle we have previously indicated: 'If an individual abuses his right, it does not follow that others can deprive him of it; they can only impede its use.' This principle is fully respected. The Gospel eliminates all that is abusive and unjust in slavery, leaving intact those aspects of seigniory and subjection which do not overstep the bounds of justice. Strictly speaking, what was unjust about seigniory over slaves was its excess. If excesses are removed, justice is re-established without need to break the bonds of seigniory and upright servitude, which can well remain.

[244–245]

what has so far been discussed about their nature. We shall then see the role played by those rights which are fittingly called 'connatural'.

Article 1.
A summary classification of all connatural and acquired rights

246. All human rights can be divided into four summary classes as a result of the principles established above.

247. I. The first class contains those rights which consist in *ownership* or jural possession of some good.

248. They subdivide into the same divisions as the different kinds of good of which we can have ownership or jural possession.

249. For the present we will restrict ourselves to classifying every good as either *connatural* or *acquired*. I have already spoken about the former; the latter I will discuss in later books.

250. In passing, I note however that every lawful spontaneous act (transient act) must be classified as an acquired good, because every spontaneous act, once posited in being, is a good of which we have actual jural possession.

251. II. The second class embraces those rights which consist in *absolute jural freedom*, that is, in acts which, although not yet posited, are ours by right and cannot be obstructed without the violation of justice and our right.

252. These acts are contained and implicitly rooted in rights of the first class, rights which result from a good whose jural ownership we enjoy.

Actions not yet posited cannot be truly said to be ours by right, unless they exist implicitly in our actual rights, that is, in whatever good we jurally possess. A jural *title* necessarily exists in these kinds of good and gives us a right to the actions of which we are speaking.

253. For example, we have seen that the jural title to acts which unite us directly to truth, virtue and fulfilment, is founded in the *person* (the basic, essential good). The jural *title* to acts with which a father exercises his paternal authority over his son, is rooted in *paternity* (an acquired right). The *title* of an

employer's right to acts with which he exercises his authority over others, lies in *seigniory* (also an acquired right). The *title* of the acts with which a proprietor disposes of his possessions, is founded in *ownership* relative to external things (another acquired right).

254. III. The third class includes those rights which consist in *relative jural freedom*.

I must explain this way of speaking.

255. We have said that non-existent actions cannot be the object of our rights. If all the possible actions of our different powers were truly ours by right, we could carry them out fully without their being obstructed or reduced in number by others. But if this were the case, human co-existence would no longer be possible. All things would be within our ownership, and no one could touch them without impeding what we could do with them. If this argument is true for us individually, it must for the same reason be true for everybody else. But this would be absurd because the things involved in actions can belong in their totality only to a single individual. We have to say therefore that some actions, although lawful in themselves and possible for me, are not exclusively mine by right as long as I have not in reality posited them; they can in fact be impeded by fellow human beings who actually carry them out or posit them ahead of me. And if others have taken possession of them, I can no longer perform them without encroaching on their rights.

It is clear therefore that nature has granted freedom to us all to take possession of any unclaimed good. This freedom, understood generally in all its extension, cannot merit the name of right, precisely because no corresponding jural duty to leave it intact (which is the fifth constitutive element we have given of right) exists in others, who may however limit it provided they do not invade *ownership*.[81]

---

[81] We should note that Kant drew his principle of 'co-existence' from his limited view of *free actions*. He failed to realise that not all rights can be reduced to these *actions*; there are prior rights consisting in *ownership* which are the primitive sources of the rights human beings have and can have to actions. But having seen that unlimited freedom of actions could not be reconciled with the existence of the human race, he thought he had found the principle of right by 'positing it in that limited sphere of actions which do not prevent co-existence'. Careful examination would reveal that this highly

Actions which do not invade another's ownership would, however, cease to be lawful if, as I have said, they irresponsibly limited the other's freedom, that is, their author did not do them to procure some good and a natural, legitimate pleasure for himself. In this case we would be moved to action by waywardness or obvious stupidity, but not by natural-reasonable spontaneity. This manner of acting, whether wayward or stupid, cannot limit another's freedom to do lawful things. Consequently, freedom for lawful actions becomes a right relative to the element corresponding to the jural duty not to restrict such freedom for wayward or stupid motives.

256. A right exists therefore 'preventing the limitation of the sphere of my lawful actions through waywardness or mere stupidity on the part of others'. I call this 'the relative right of jural freedom'.[82]

257. IV. Finally the fourth class embraces rights for applying force and sanctions. These rights have their roots in the three previous classes.

We have said that every right is a faculty (for acting or experiencing) considered either in potency or in act. And wherever there is a faculty and an act, there is also force. All the force of person can be utilised by the person in exercising his rights, and therefore for the removal of obstacles and difficulties encountered in such action. Sanction is an activity proper to the faculty in which right consists.

258. To this last class belong:

1. The right to forestall, that is, the right to forestall an unjustly threatened assault.

2. The right of defence, or of not being subjected to non-moral, brute force. Here we have the right to repel force with force in order to *a*) remove the unjust obstacle blocking the

---

limited principle does not in fact include all human rights nor, as I have observed, determine 'the limit' to be placed on those actions which would prevent co-existence. On the other hand, I have posited the limit in *ownership*, that is, in 'the jural possession of any good and any action'.

[82] It is clearly very difficult to decide in particular cases whether some action of my neighbour is due to waywardness or stupidity. We need to be very strict in this judgment; when in doubt, we must presume in favour of the lawfulness of my neighbour's action.

exercise of our right, *b*) defend our right which has been attacked and invaded.

3. The right to use force to obtain retribution for harm to ourselves and to others (the right to retribution, or to forced or tacit compensation).

259. These four classes of rights could be reduced to the first class. If we did this, the meaning of the word *right* would be reserved to rights of the first class, and rights of the other three classes would be called *functions of right*. The latter are rooted in the first, just as the functions of a faculty or power are rooted in the faculties or powers from which they come.

260. What has been said harmonises very well with the definition that makes right consist in a faculty, that is, in something usually understood as still in potency and not in act. According to this way of speaking, right would remain wholly in the faculty (power) which would have a sphere of jural functions whose limits would be marked by distinguishing the last three classes of rights described above.

261. The sphere of *jural functions* and of their acts cannot in fact be extended to match the sphere of the acts of a faculty or power physically considered. It extends only to the jural *title* to the acts virtually contained in the faculty.[83] The notion of this kind of title is founded in what I have said when discussing the three classes mentioned above.

262. However, it is sometimes quite acceptable to call these groups of jural acts, *rights*; at other times the argument is helped more by calling them *functions* of right. I will use both names as the occasion demands.

Article 2.
A more detailed determination of connatural rights relative to the complex of all human rights

263. We can now easily distinguish the connatural rights within the complex of human rights. We see at once that there are connatural rights in all four classes.

---

[83] Cf. the difference between *title* and *law* in *Storia comparativa e critica de' sistemi morali*, c. 7, art. 7, where I have developed the two concepts at length.

264. *First Class.* When we are born we have ownership, or jural possession, of our total self. All the natural activities, faculties, powers, forces, together with every natural good, are connatural rights; they cannot be weakened or taken from us. Supreme among these powers is the person, the apex and centre, from which, like radii from a centre, spring all the other powers and all rights. These other powers constitute human nature.

265. A human being therefore has:

I. The right not to be invited to evil in his personship whose good is truth, virtue and happiness.

This right can be specified into many others, among which are the following:

1. The right not to be misled either by word or action in the case of ideal or necessary truths.

2. The right not to be tempted or provoked to vice by false praise or violence.

3. The right not to be made unhappy by another's testing his moral strength.

4. The right to reputation, praise, glory and earned reward as consequences and appendages of virtue.

266. II. The right not to suffer attacks on his nature.[84]

This right contains a large number of lesser rights, which can be determined in proportion to our activities, to every innate good and to the ways each good can be assailed.

267. *Second Class.* An innate *absolute jural freedom* exists which includes all acts of right having a *jural title* to the rights mentioned in the previous class.

I. The title to all acts tending directly to truth, virtue and happiness lies in personship, the supreme right. Thus the following rights, amongst others, come into being:

1. The right to meditate on, communicate, preach and write the truth.

2. The right to search for the truth through calm discussion, etc.

---

[84] This right ceases to be in act only through our own fault. If we maliciously and violently invade another's right, or obstruct the jural exercise of the right, the person we have offended may use force to overcome the obstacle, injuring our nature and justly punishing it. The same must be said about defending our neighbour against unjust aggression.

[264–267]

3. The right to judge uprightly what is just and decent.

4. The right to do justice orderly and truthfully, using words to praise or blame, and deeds to suppress injustice, etc.

5. The right to perform acts of all the virtues.

6. The right to choose the means and state of life believed to be best for oneself or conducive to one's own moral perfection.

268. All these rights, considered in themselves, are absolute, because truth, virtue and happiness are each a universal and common good which can be sought by us without in any way diminishing their possession by others.

269. We must note however that, under the pretext of exercising these rights, we may not perform external, material acts which injure another's rights to external, material things.

270. II. Human nature also contains the jural title to all acts done with our innate powers without exceeding the bounds of human nature. Nothing exterior to human nature is required to do these acts. All internal acts therefore, except those concerning personship, belong to this category.

271. To all these, we must add rights to certain kinds of good which, although exterior to us, are continuously necessary for our existence; for example, the right to a portion of the air for breathing, the right to a place to live, etc. These kinds of good can be said to be part of ourselves because conditions of our basic existence.

272. Nevertheless, our *jural title* to these kinds of good stems not from their being necessary for our preservation, but from our taking *jural possession* of them through our existence, as if they were constitutive elements of our own individual self. People, therefore, cannot apply pressure to our *occupancy* of these kinds of good to the point of completely depriving us of them. Such action would be a direct, positive injury against us, a removal of something naturally proper to us, and hence an injury to our right. We can say therefore that we have a connatural right to these things. Consequently their use pertains to our *absolute freedom* just as the use of the internal powers of our individual self pertains to the same freedom.[85]

---

[85] The rights to a part of the air for breathing, to a place to live, etc., are *innate* because we take possession of these things at birth. Nevertheless we have to admit that the word 'innate' is understood here in a wider sense, since

273. *Third Class.* We have a connatural *relative freedom*, that is, a right to do all that we can with the upright use of our powers unhindered by another's caprice or wickedness. However, these acts can be prevented and limited by another's jural freedom and ownership.[86]

274. To list these rights one by one would be the same as listing individually all those things which for us can have the concept of good, and which we can enjoy with the acts of our powers. Each of these kinds of good, each of these acts, pertains to our *innate relative freedom* in which our connatural right to them is located.

the act of birth itself has played a part in bringing these rights into existence. It may be better to say 'rights born with the human being' (connatural), but not acquired, because we suppose them and cannot exist without them. However, I do not think we need pay too much attention to this subtle distinction; it is enough to have mentioned it in passing.

What is more important, I repeat, is that these rights are not deduced from our right to self-preservation. In my view this right concerns only *relative*, never *absolute freedom*. Our right to preservation exists solely because we have the right to perform all those acts which are joined to us and do not positively harm others. Self-preservation is not a right, but a good obtained for the most part (though not always) with the *exercise of our rights*. For example, we may not kill an innocent being to save our life, although we could so, if we had an absolute right to our preservation.

We could also ask: 'Can another's ownership of external things impede my use of the means for my preservation?' But I will deal with this when I discuss the limits of this kind of right of *ownership*.

[86] Here I make no mention of just punishment, which is another means of impeding the exercise of these rights. Properly speaking, punishment cannot be an impediment imposed by another on the exercise of our activity. It is rather an abdication that we ourselves make of our own right. But we cannot abdicate or deprive ourselves of a right we do not possess. Hence, guilt and punishment, which do deprive us of our rights, is rather a proof of their existence: it does not remove them, it suspends them. This suspension, to which human rights are subject, also extends to the innate rights of the first and second classes — as we have seen, rights of the first class concern our *nature* (in contrast to *person*), and those of the second class result from a title innate to *nature* (in contrast to *person*). Moreover, the suspension does not change our jural freedom from absolute to relative. The title to the right remains, although it is restricted and superseded by the greater title of punitive justice. In rights of the third class, however, the limit placed by another's activity immediately terminates their title.

[273–274]

275. The most important of these innate rights belonging to this third class are as follows:

1. The right to speech and to seek help.

2. The right to corporal freedom — our body must not be bound or restrained, but allowed the use of its free movements.

276. These two rights are so obvious that we could be led to think they belonged to absolute, rather than relative freedom.

277. In fact it is very difficult for us to conceive that simply by a *request* we can encroach on another's sphere of rights. But requests can sometimes be troublesome precisely by their unreasonableness and their tiresome repetition, importunity, etc.

278. Similarly it is very difficult to conceive that even movement might injure another's rights. But this also is not absolutely impossible. For example, it could be required for a fixed length of time by contract, as in the case of a someone who, having agreed and been paid not to move while his picture is being produced by daguerreotype, may not move during the session.

279. Both rights, taken in all their extension, concern *relative freedom*, but an element is present in both which applies to *absolute freedom*. Everybody therefore has the possibility of using them, at least sometimes and within fixed limits.

280. We can now clearly see how so-called workhouses and detention centres can be justified by rational right only if they accept 1. the poor who willingly go there, and 2. those held because guilty of habitual deceptions, lies, frauds, burglaries, dissoluteness, drunkenness and sloth.[87] All these faults must first be *proved* by exact procedures and not gratuitously supposed or gathered from public hearsay, the judgment of politicians, or the hardness of heart of the rich who would prefer not to see human misery and, thus wallowing in selfishness, become ever harder on their fellow human beings.

281. 3. The right, generally speaking, to all useful or pleasurable, lawful actions, and the right through them to acquire other rights.

---

[87] Furthermore, the limits and conditions necessary for a just application of the penalties must be present. One such condition would evidently be that the penalty has previously been threatened by law.

282. *Fourth Class.* Relative to the preservation of innate rights, the right of *sanction* is also innate, because, as we said, it is simply the 'energy present in the physical faculty which is the first constitutive element of right.'

CHAPTER 9

Conclusion

283. This book has dealt with connatural rights. The titles to these rights are placed in us by nature. We see therefore that their study could strictly be called *natural Right* or *Right of nature.*[88]

---

[88] This is the strictest meaning of the expression *Right of nature. Natural Right* is close to this meaning but has a wider sense. *Natural Right* is the opposite of *agreed Right*, and we have taken it in this sense in the *Schema of Right.* Cf. *ER*, pp. 56-57.

Book 2

ACQUIRED RIGHTS

284. Among the connatural rights of the third class, which make up *innate relative freedom*, I stated the general right 'to posit all the lawful actions that are useful to us and cannot reasonably be impeded by others, and to acquire other rights by means of our connatural rights' (cf. 273).

When exercised by us, the connatural right to posit these actions becomes the universal source of all our acquired rights.

285. Because all *rights acquired* in this way are founded in a *connatural right*, the present work, dealing with acquired rights, continues and flows from the previous book on connatural rights. I have therefore already expounded in the previous book the effective principle of the whole study of acquired rights.

286. We will begin by seeing how acquired rights come into being, and by investigating their act of acquisition and the nature of their efficient cause.

CHAPTER 1

A summary of the cause of all rights in general

287. To be coherent with these teachings, the cause of all human rights in general, including connatural rights, must be found in a *fact*. This is the primary result of all that has been said so far.

288. This first fact, which brings rights into being, is more commonly called the *title* to rights.[89]

289. For a fact to be the cause of a *right*, it must first be free from all injustice in so far as it constitutes a title of a right. Second, it must impart to us the *moral activity* or governance in which the essence of right consists, as we have seen from the definition of right.

---

[89] Two things are required to constitute a right: a *fact* and a *law*. The law is the *form* of the right and gives it its *possibility*; the fact is the *matter* and root of the right. The fact, considered in its relationship to the law, is called a *title* to the right.

290. We saw however that this *moral activity*, based upon a fact, can be considered either as a simple activity acting by itself, in which case we called it *jural freedom* or freedom by right, or else as acting through some instrument. We called the instrument *ownership* — it could also be called an instrumental power in so far as it adheres to the activity using it. Thus all possible rights were reduced to two ultimate kinds: *freedom* and *ownership*.

291. We also saw that *pure freedom* of right was located only in the *supreme active principle* constituting the person. Because the person uses all the lower powers as its instruments, they can be called natural *ownership*.

292. In the rights classed as *ownership* we can always note the characteristic of a *moral-physical connection* with the personal principle. By virtue of this connection the supreme personal principle develops the aptitude for, and intention of using the faculties or powers as instruments for its ends without violating morality. This is equally true for every right of ownership.

Let us now see the different ways in which connatural rights and acquired rights come into being.

CHAPTER 2

The cause of acquired rights

293. In connatural rights, the *fact* containing the title to the right is given by nature without any human intervention. In acquired rights the fact is posited by the human being and called an *act of acquisition*.

294. The fact given by nature as the first of all connatural rights (*pure* jural *freedom*) is the existence of the person. We have seen that person is the very essence of right.

295. The fact given by nature for the second of innate rights (*connatural ownership*) is the *connection* between the supreme

power (person) and the different powers and parts of the human being. This connection is given by nature itself.[90]

296. What facts then do we posit to procure rights for ourselves, that is, rights which in their origin receive nothing from nature? To answer this question accurately we must consider both what is experienced and what is done by a human being in so far as all such actions influence the complex of his rights relative to jural freedom and ownership, the two great categories to which we have reduced rights. We begin with the rights of freedom.

Article 1.
Acquired freedom

297. The human being undergoes experiences and posits actions from the moment of birth. He finds around him beings devoid of intelligence, and intelligent beings like himself. They are all in a given state or position, which is not determined by his nature or will, but by causes foreign and antecedent to him. Furthermore, those devoid of intelligence continually change, while the beings similar to him change their position, state and experience, and act just as he himself does. All this notably alters the complex of his rights. Other rights, which we call *acquired rights*, also accrue to him.

298. But is every change and modification to which the human jural state is subject, an acquisition? Is it a case of other rights always being added to connatural rights without a diminution in the number of connatural rights? This question must be examined; let us consider it relative to freedom.

299. If we are talking about pure, simply personal freedom, this freedom cannot by its very nature be increased or diminished. It does not have *quantity*; it is a *quality*, an essence; it is jural, essential freedom itself.[91]

[90] There are some rights whose bond is effected by nature although they arise from a human act, for example, marital rights. But I will speak about this special class of acquired rights later.

[91] Nevertheless human freedom can be raised to a higher degree of

300. But if we are talking about the sphere in which *personal* freedom can act, this sphere can certainly be extended and diminished. Indeed, its extension and diminution can take place simultaneously.

301. The position of inanimate things does not depend on the nature of human beings. At the moment of our birth this position is fixed. Sometimes it can help our development; at other times it retards development. At different times it offers us wider or more limited scope for exercising our freedom; many accidental things succeed one another, independently of us, helping or hindering our actions in varying degrees.

302. But leaving aside the question about greater or lesser development, we can affirm that there is at the same time, as I said, an increase or restriction in the *sphere* of human freedom. The increase comes from the actions with which we exercise our freedom; these actions increase our sphere of freedom. The restriction originates from the actions with which those around us exercise their own freedom — their actions limit and restrict our freedom.

It is clear that by exercising our freedom we both develop our powers and create external ownership for ourselves. This ownership is then pervaded by freedom, because, as we said, ownership is only a kind of extra instrument acquired by persons, in order to operate according to their ends.

Conversely, another's ownership, like all rights in general acquired by others, restricts more and more our sphere of freedom, which was already limited by the mere fact of our co-existence on the earth with our fellow human beings.

303. The increase of the sphere in which freedom operates, an increase resulting from the acquisition of external ownership, is inherent to this ownership and does not form something different from it. I will speak about this in the following article, where I will deal with ownership.

---

excellence by a supernatural, divine action. This is one of the sublime truths contained in the Christian system, the religion of civilised peoples. I will deal with it in *Supernatural Anthropology*. We should not be surprised therefore that a new kind of freedom given to human beings can modify the teaching on right, elevate it and constitute a new right immensely different from, and superior to right in nature.

[300–303]

304. The only acquired rights to be classified amongst rights of freedom are those which come into being through the abilities and skills we learn with the use of our powers.

Our activity, extended by means of these habits added to our native powers, is rendered capable of greater activity. All other human beings must respect activity which has increased in this way. Its exercise therefore, when it does not harm the rights of others, itself acquires the characteristic of a right.

305. We must also consider the contemporary limitation of our liberty consequent on the activity of others. It has two causes.

We have already spoken about the first: acquired rights and the connatural rights of others diminish the sphere of our freedom because our freedom can no longer take possession of the things they possess, nor can we perform actions which disturb or obstruct the rights they have taken possession of.

306. The second cause arises from the right of defence and security. This right reveals itself in all human beings as soon as it is clear that either through malice, ignorance or incompetence others are going to act without regard for their rights, which they put at risk.

307. As I have said, this can happen from *malice*, when a person will not respect the sanctity of another's rights; or from *ignorance*, when someone makes no effort to know another's rights or, if an effort has been made, either does not know them well or how far he may go without offending them. Finally, I said it sometimes happens from *incompetence* in the use of our faculties. If we exercised our faculties competently, the quantity of our exercise could be the same, but if the exercise is incompetent, inexpert or imprudent, it conflicts with others' rights especially when it could easily avoid them.

308. Under these circumstances, not knowing how to use our freedom competently, we cannot use it to the full extent to which we would otherwise have a right.

309. If because of malice some will not make good use of their freedom, or, because of ignorance and incompetence, cannot make use of it, people will naturally be more on their guard, taking further precautions and requiring more guarantees.

310. This *feeling of the need of defence* explains the varying rigour and strictness of State laws. It also explains different

forms of government or political constitutions of varying be-
nignity, which allow their citizens various degrees of exercise
of freedom.

311. If therefore freedom at the level of nature is 'the faculty
to do all that is lawful', freedom in civil society can be defined
with greater precision as 'the faculty to do all that is lawful in
itself except what is forbidden by law.'[92]

Article 2.
Acquired ownership

We come now to acquired rights consisting in ownership. We
will first speak about the act of acquisition itself.

§1. *The act of acquisition as the cause of ownership*

312. We have said that the common characteristic of all ownership, whether connatural or acquired, consists in the *connection*
of a thing with the personal principle, so that the thing can be
used as an instrument by the person for his own ends.

313. The *act of acquisition* therefore is the act by which a
person joins to himself things different from himself in order to
use them for his own ends.

But how is this union possible and really brought about?

314. The act of acquisition of external ownership can be found
only in morally free or lawful actions.

315. Morally free actions are of two kinds: some leave no
observable result, others leave a result in which the action itself
seems to continue habitually, as it were, in us. For example, I
want to rest under an oak. If someone else has taken the place I
want, the action is morally forbidden me. I cannot do it without
harming another, because I cannot take the place without send-
ing the other away. If the place is empty, I can occupy it; my

---

[92] Justinian's *Institutes* define civil freedom as 'the faculty for everyone to
do as they please unless prohibited by law' (*De jure personarum*).

action is morally free. However my action leaves no result if, after resting under the tree, I go on my way without further ado.

On the other hand, if I build a house on unoccupied land as my family home, I am still doing something morally free. Without harming anyone else I am making use of an unoccupied area, intending my family to live there . But the action of building the house, together with my intention of living there permanently, leaves a result, because it extends into the future. An action of this kind, we can say, will never completely cease; it will continue habitually and virtually in me, even when my positive act of will ceases.

316. The result of the final act of building is a moral-physical connection acquired with me by the house, or better by me with the house. The house I have built with the aim in view belongs to me, is connected with my being and becomes part of my feeling, part of myself.

317. This is so true that if the house were burnt down, I would find it more painful than if one of my fingers had been cut off or I had been physically assaulted. I would consider that a good had been taken from me, from my very person; a good, whose loss would be extremely upsetting. All this clearly indicates that the house was joined to me in my feeling, forming a single thing with me, as my finger is joined to my person, although it is not my person.

318. It would be just as painful, and perhaps worse, to have another man force me out of the house so that he could live there. Clearly, his action harms what is proper to me, cutting me off from a part of myself. He cannot morally perpetrate such an action that causes me pain. Here precisely is jural duty, the fifth of the characteristics of right mentioned above,[93] and the certain sign of its existence.

319. My occupation of the vacant spot, the construction of the house and my intention to reside there have all morally prohibited everybody else from an action which earlier had been free for them. And the prohibition endures until I abandon both the house and the place. At the same time I have acquired a right to both.

[93] Cf. *ER*, 301-303.

320. My rest under the oak, therefore, followed by my abandoning the place without any decision to reserve it for my use in the future, was a lawful action which left no effective consequence morally prohibiting the actions of another person. But my decision to live in the house I had built brought with it a consequence morally preventing the use of the place by others, so that I would be hurt if another used it. On the other hand, before my decision, anyone could have used it without upsetting me in any way.

321. We have then two kinds of actions: the simple use of something and a decision about its continual use. These are two natural human acts, and the primitive sources of external *ownership*. The first, as the simple use of something, is short-lived,[94] while the second endures. The second requires a greater act of reflection than the first; to carry it out, we need to have reflected on the future use of the thing. To do the first act, however, we need to know only its present use. It is probable therefore that people performed the first act before passing to the second.[95]

322. Analysis of the *act of acquisition* by which we became owners of the land and of the house built upon it reveals four successive levels, each of which is a right. These four successive rights are present every time we acquire something external:

---

[94] Here again we have an example of jural duty in another, although it lasts only as long as the action lasts. If, while resting, I am forced out of an otherwise unoccupied place, the aggressor causes me harm and acts immorally. He injures my right, which is posited in being by my action. The action is momentary, of course, but is mine, however short its duration.

[95] Very probably, when people were few on the earth and everything was available in abundance, no one would have thought of reserving the use of things exclusively for himself. Instead each would have been satisfied to use for a short while what first came to hand. Virgil speaks of this in the following verses:

Before Jove settlers did not assign arable land to anyone
Nor was it necessary that the fields be indicated or divided
    by boundaries.
People were modest in their claims;
the earth yielded everything more liberally
and no one needed to ask for anything
                    (Georg. 1, 125-128).

This is the way we must understand the poets of the golden age, when there was no fixed possession of land. — Cf. Hesiodus, *Opere e Giorni.*

323. 1. The first level and right, origin of the other three, is innate. This right, which pertains to *relative freedom*, is the right to lawful actions not encroaching on another's ownership.

324. 2. When we exercise the first right, we produce the second level, the action itself. Every time the action is posited in the actuality of its being, something real is done which adheres to, and is part of us. The thing we do is also our right as long as it endures in act. This right pertains to *ownership*.

325. The first of these rights can be called the *right of relative freedom of action*; the second, the *right of ownership over action*.

326. 3. If the action is such that it can join an external object to us, we also have, granted our right to the action, a right to join the object to ourselves and make it our own.

327. 4. Finally, when the action has been posited in reality, we have joined the thing to ourselves and at the same time increased our power to act. The union gives us the faculty or right to do all the acts contained in the complete, continuous use of the thing, a faculty we did not previously possess.

328. The first of the last two rights can be called the *right of relative freedom to the thing*; the second, the *right of ownership over the thing*.

§2. *Opinions on external ownership*

329. It seems to me that this deduction of the right of ownership over external things is very simple, and I am surprised that it escaped the minds of many writers on *rational Right*.

However it will receive greater light if we compare it with the principal opinions put forward so far concerning the origin of the right under discussion.

A.
Systems which deny external ownership in the state of nature and attribute its institution to civil laws

330. The deduction of the right of ownership over external things, when considered in the state of nature, seemed to certain

authors to present insuperable difficulties. They joined those who completely denied its possibility until the institution of civil society.

331. Such a system is not only gratuitous, but contradictory.

332. If ownership of external things could not exist before the institution of civil society, how would a society's laws have attained sufficient authority to establish as a right that which nature had not made a right?

333. If ownership did not exist and could not exist before civil society, the founders themselves, before establishing civil society, did not own anything. How therefore could they have made laws without an arbitrary decision about something to which they themselves had no right?

334. It may be objected that the law of ownership was established by the consent of all in the civil society. —

335. First, it is impossible to explain how present consent could bind future consent, especially if the consent appears merely arbitrary and without any necessity in nature.

336. Second, we are talking about either an explicit or a tacit, universal consent.

Explicit consent given by all at the beginning of civil societies is an empty hypothesis and a vain pipe-dream.[96]

337. Tacit and arbitrary consent, capable of creating agreed rights, is also entirely imaginary and false. In order to consent tacitly and validly to a particular law or custom which needs the support of our consent, we must first have substantial knowledge of the whole extent of the law or custom. Second, we must be able to withhold consent, even if we do not wish to do so.

A large section of the human race has never reflected on the extent of the law of ownership, and has not made any internal judgment on its utility. People have simply adapted to the fact and submitted to circumstances as they found them.

338. Moreover, let us suppose that ownership of external things has no justice of its own and that the justice we believe it has originates solely in the arbitrary consent given it by all individuals from one generation to the next. It is clear that they

---

[96] In saying this, I do not deny that human beings have often divided land among themselves, either by private agreements or by some kind of agrarian laws. But these procedures regulate ownership, they do not create it.

would give their consent only on condition that ownership was divided equally among them all. It would be absurd to think that the poor would consent to the rich retaining their riches if the latter's ownership depended on the arbitrary consent of the poor.[97]

339. Again, in this system where the justice of ownership depends not on ownership itself, but on the common consent of those who judge it useful for themselves, theft would be a protest against this so-called unanimous consent. And theft of this kind would be more than sufficient to destroy a system of ownership founded on the unanimous consent of all in pursuit of their own utility.

340. Finally, we must not confuse the question, 'Does the establishment of ownership require a tacit consent?' with 'Does the establishment of ownership derive its authority from civil laws?'

341. These are entirely different questions although very often intermingled. This becomes clear when we consider that human beings could give their tacit consent in the absence of established civil regimes; they could consent tacitly or expressly among themselves in the state of nature. Consequently, it could reasonably be maintained that for the establishment of ownership tacit consent, but not necessarily the authority of civil government, is needed.

342. I answer this as follows.

If we are talking about arbitrary consent, the supposed universal unanimity of consent is absurd, as I have shown.

If we are talking about consent originating in a feeling of justice and reason, ownership is indeed admitted and certainly consented to by all, because it is just — but its justice does not come from unanimous admission and consent.

I acknowledge that there is tacit consent by all human beings to the fact of ownership. But this consent is guided by a feeling

[97] Even if we supposed *per absurdum* that children could be bound by the arbitrary agreements of their fathers, it would be quite unlikely that the fathers would readily consent to an agreement exposing some members of their family to the danger of extreme poverty, while other members were able to enjoy great riches. Great human inequalities like these are indeed the work of nature, but cannot be the work of a valid but arbitrary human agreement.

of justice, not simply by a consideration of utility. Hence we are obliged to give this kind of consent in the way we are obliged to consent to all just natural laws. If we failed to do so, we would be reproved by synderesis.

This kind of consent presupposes, but does not explain the right of ownership. The consent itself needs explanation: why, for example, does the common sense of humanity see in ownership a just law; what is this justice?

343. I have tried to derive the justice of ownership from the principle of 'not doing harm to anyone'. We harm others every time we touch, damage or remove what is joined to them and to their *feeling of themselves* by nature and by their own natural acts. We have seen that human nature is so made that it can in *fact* join to itself things which are different from person and from human nature itself. This fact becomes a right immediately the duty of *not doing harm* is established, because by destroying the fact we harm our fellow human beings, causing them trouble and distress.[98]

344. Thinkers who attribute the origin of the right of external ownership to civil laws are themselves divided in opinion when giving their reasons.

345. I. Some authors attribute the establishment of external ownership to civil laws because, they say, in the state of nature everybody has a right to everything and consequently no one can peacefully retain anything

346. This is Hobbes' system. — The so-called right of everybody to everything results from an illusion dominating the mind of its author. According to Hobbes, everything in the state of nature is considered unoccupied and free. But it is clear that everybody can lawfully take possession of things that are free and unoccupied. Therefore, in that state, everybody has the right to everything. —

347. We reply: the right to take possession of things causes no difficulty whatsoever, provided possession has not already been taken.[99] Something already occupied and appropriated cannot

---

[98] Cicero wisely said that natural love for our fellow human beings is the foundation of right: 'These things arise because we are inclined by nature to love human beings, WHICH IS THE FOUNDATION OF RIGHT' (*De leg.*, 1, 15).

[99] Cf. Martini, *De Leg. Nat. Positiones*, etc., c. 13.

be occupied or appropriated by another. To do so would be *to harm the other*, and therefore to act immorally.

In order to avoid this ambiguity, I said that the right to occupancy is relative, not absolute. It is conditioned and endures only as long as things lack an owner. Before their appropriation, things must not be thought of as belonging to everybody; in fact they belong to no one. After appropriation they belong to the one who has first appropriated them. Thus there is never a time when they belong to all.[100]

348. II. Others attribute the establishment of external owner- ship to civil laws because, they argue, the sanction of ownership is found solely in a civilly constituted society.

349. Bentham holds this opinion. He claims that there cannot be a right without physical force to protect it, that is, coercion sufficient to make it enforceable. But we have seen that right is a moral, not a physical power; it is a freedom to act without injury to our fellow human beings.[101]

---

[100] Cicero's statement, 'Nothing is by nature private' (*De Off.*, 1, 7) seems to contain an ambiguity. It could lead us to believe that natural public ownership existed. But such an ownership is a pipe-dream. We can conceive the public as a proprietor only on condition that they are constituted a collective person, and that things are appropriated under the same conditions as the acts and methods of acquisition of private persons. Thus the ownership of a public body is also private.

[101] On this point, the confusion and contradiction in ideas is at its worst in Romagnosi. In some places he does admit the common sense distinction between *fact* and *right*; he says, for example, '*To have a reason* for doing something is not the same as *being able* to do it in practice' (*Assunto I*, etc, §7). In other places he abolishes the distinction by confusing right and fact. For example, he maintains that 'rights and duties are not *really* different from effective human power; in themselves they are simply external or internal human force acting in a given way' (*ibid.*, §3 and 6). He then explains the *given way* as a mode of operation of human force, regulated by reason in such a way that reason directs the operator to obtain *maximum satisfaction*. But if rights consisted in force, only the strong, not the weak, would have them; only the strong would have the force on the one hand, and reason on the other to guide the force to *maximum satisfaction* for themselves. I too have said that right is an activity, or if preferable, a force, but it is activity protected by the moral law. Physical activity, even when directed by reason towards maximum satisfaction, can certainly constitute the material part of right, but never the formal. This distinction easily frees us from the sophistry by which Romagnosi required the existence of civil society not only as a *guarantee*

350. He says, 'Even the most uncivilised human can possess something, but this is simply direct, uncertain possession which lasts only as long as it goes undisputed by any other person, or for as long as the holder can defend it. But a right supposes both present and future guarantee and enjoyment.'[102] These words contain a further error: they presuppose as essential to the constitution of right that right extends to the future, but they do not distinguish the two categories of rights we spoke about earlier: rights *to actions*, which do not extend to the future, and rights *to things* (cf. 325, 328), that are acquired by actions in which we had a right, and extend to the future.

351. An apparently more acceptable explanation for those who do not recognise rights of ownership outside civil society, is the condition of *reciprocity*. This condition seems to be necessary for constituting jural duty, and can be described as follows.

352. Outside the civil state no sufficient guarantee for the rights of individuals can be found. When this guarantee is lacking, infringements of rights become very frequent. But our duty to respect others' rights binds us only when others generally respect ours, that is, our duty is conditioned by reciprocity. Therefore, outside the state of civil society, jural duty, the fifth constitutive element of rights, disappears;[103] rights are not fully constituted in these conditions.

353. The argument seems conclusive. But if we examine it carefully, we will find it lacks solidity.

354. The proposition: 'It is impossible to find a sufficient guarantee of rights outside the civil state', is too universal and cannot be accepted. — Early human beings lived for a long time in a state of domestic society. In this state, and granted the favourable circumstance in which they lived, they easily found sufficient defence of their rights in a common, reciprocal feeling of uprightness, in the reciprocal interests which often impelled them to form alliances,[104] and in the adequate strength of the

of right but also for its *existence*.

[102] *Traité des sophismes politiques. — Examen critique de la déclaration des droits de l'homme, etc.*

[103] *ER*, 301-303.

[104] For example, the treaty between Isaac, Abimelech, Ochozath [Ahuzzath]

family for maintaining itself in the midst of other families. This was the state of the patriarchs, and is still the state of many nomadic tribes on the earth.

355. *Reciprocity*, as necessary to give binding force to the duty of respecting others' ownership, is another case in which the principle is extended too far and causes interminable sophistry. It must be kept within just limits and be deduced from the principle of justice which in the state of nature authorises human beings 'to redress offences against them, to be indemnified for damage and, if necessary, to protect themselves by strong measures against those whose will to do evil has shown itself, and been proved habitual'.

356. When the principle of reciprocity is limited in this way, we can truthfully say that, provided we ourselves were at peace, we would not be obliged to respect others' rights of ownership if those amongst whom we lived lacked all feeling of justice and were always intent on doing us harm. We would be at war relative to such people, and therefore could defend ourselves, seek redress and indemnity, and claim guarantees.

357. Nevertheless, if we were strong enough to require and obtain all this, we could not afterwards harm those people in the least way, because we would still have duties to them. All this shows that rights or jural duties exist even in these conditions.

358. But the conditions are hypothetical; they never were universal, and never will be. Human beings, no matter how evil, cannot lose entirely all feeling of what is upright and just; in fact they act justly on a great number of occasions. And we must act justly towards them, particularly in the case of actions which give us no cause for encroaching on the sphere of their ownership. Furthermore, no matter how foolish we think these people are, they are not so foolish as to be unaware of what is advantageous to themselves in reciprocal respect for ownership and rights.

Hence, throughout the whole human race, and even amongst human beings not bound into civil associations, a common exchange of respect, regard and feelings must always be present. This is particularly so when we consider that we are not born

and Phicol (Gen 26), and the treaty that Abraham had previously made with these leaders (Gen. 21).

into isolation but into the warmth of a domestic society, where so many affections arise and increase with us. All this affection, esteem and natural, reciprocal respect, which never ceases in the mass of human beings, is foundation enough for the duty (exercised at least to a corresponding level) to honour another's ownership.

359. The principle of reciprocity, therefore, as an absolute condition of jural duty, does not exclude in any way the existence of rights and duties in any period prior to civil societies.[105]

B.
Systems which recognise external ownership in the state of nature but lack sufficient reasons to support it

360. Nearly all writers who accept ownership as a right pertaining to the state of nature, agree that its origin is *occupancy*. They differ however in their explanation of the moral force necessary for occupancy, in order that occupancy may be the mode of acquiring the right.

361. A). Grotius,[106] Pufendorf and De Felice had recourse to the tacit and implicit assent of all human beings, which we have already discussed.[107]

---

[105] Blackstone attributes the establishment of the right of ownership to civil laws without giving a satisfactory reason for his opinion (cf. *Commentaires sur les lois anglaises*, bk. 2, c. 1). He is not the only writer to adhere gratuitously to a system because of the difficulties encountered in all other systems.

[106] 'We must have due regard for the intention of those who first introduced individual dominion. We must accept that they intended to depart as little as possible from fairness' (*De Jure B et P.*, bk. 2, c. 2, §6). — Here we see what effect the habit of living under positive law has on the human mind: the natural law is easily forgotten, and authority substituted for reason. And when there is no authority, it is invented. Grotius argues that, although we have no trace at all of the will of our ancestors who instituted ownership, we can guess at it by mentally conceiving what is *fairer* or what harmonises more closely with *natural fairness*. He has to have recourse to *fairness* in order to interpret the will of our ancestors who established ownership. But would it not be easier to have recourse to fairness in order to know what we ourselves must maintain about ownership? Even if the first proprietors had been unjust, is it any less true that we must pursue fairness? What role then does their will play if we of ourselves know what is just and fair?

[107] Gribner explains the right of ownership as an special agreement between

362. But what is the origin of this assent? How do all the people of a nation, in the absence of any assembly or discussion or even knowledge of each other, always agree fully in judging that ownership must be respected? Cicero's excellent opinion is relevant here: 'The consent of the people must in every thing be considered a law of nature'[108] If all peoples agree that the first occupier has the right to the thing occupied, they recognise in occupancy a just title to that right. But, to repeat, their consent is purely an act of recognition, not of creation.

363. B). Barbeyrac, Titius and Locke deny this implicit consent.

364. To deny it however is to reject a very obvious fact.

365. These authors give occupancy moral force by positing a principle of corporal labour and substituting this principle for the common consent of the people. Because a person's labour on a thing makes the thing the work of that person's hands, the thing therefore is the person's property.

366. This is a contrived solution. First of all, not all labour on a thing makes the thing the property of the labourer. But why do other labours on the thing not render that thing a person's own, while the labour of occupancy does? This is the heart of the problem, and still remains unanswered despite the opinion above.

367. Second, even if we grant that labour renders a thing a labourer's own, we are justified in requesting an explanation of the supposition, with all due respect to these authors. Does labour in fact have the power to appropriate to an individual the things he is working on? What is this appropriation, and what is its moral nature? How do others come to have the duty of respecting the appropriation? — All these questions are concerned precisely with the origin of ownership. Our authors ignore this question and content themselves with only a superficial answer, which simply veils the problem by diverting attention from it. It certainly offers no solution.

368. Accepting labour as the universal source of the right of ownership means failing to see that the essence of right is moral, and that its moral essence is found solely in a corresponding

neighbouring families.

[108] *Tuscul.*, 1.

jural duty. The determination of the jural duty is therefore the explanation of right. We began from the very obvious fact that 'the human being clearly has a moral duty not to harm, injure or molest another.' Having established this very simple principle, we investigated the human person and found the extraordinary but general and abiding fact that 'while some things are naturally joined to the human person, others are joined by his own act (a moral-physcial act) and cannot be taken from him against his will without causing pain.' If we now apply the ethical principle to this psychological fact, the direct consequence is: 'No one must separate from the human person that which he has lawfully attached to himself.' In other words, 'Everybody must respect others' *ownership*', which we have defined as 'that which is united by a moral-physical bond to the human person'.[109]

369. We can easily discern the weakness of these teachings about the origin and foundation of the right of external ownership. Nothing is more familiar to us than our needs, nothing

---

[109] It may be objected that, if human beings possess stable and movable good things which they restrict to their own private use, they harm all other human beings by preventing them from using things they previously had power to use. But if an action done in accordance with the principles you lay down harms another person, it is already forbidden and unlawful. Possession therefore cannot give a right to the exclusive use of anything, because possession causes harm to another. — The objection has already been fully answered, but I will say a few words more about it here. I do not deny that possession of external things could *indirectly* cause harm (if you wish to call it that) to human beings by reducing the amount of good things they could use and by forbidding previously free actions. However, the harm does not consist in taking from them what they have, but in preventing their having what they could acquire. We are talking about *potential*, not *actual* harm. In the second place, potential harm cannot always be avoided, because the very use we make of a thing prevents another from using it. If we intended to avoid all *potential* harm, we would have to forbid the use of anything at all and thus cause real, universal harm. Furthermore, the objector confuses *harm* done to a person with *injury to right*, and sees a lesion of right wherever there is harm. I answer: not all harm is an injury and lesion of right. Lesion of right is an injury to person, but person is not injured by disposing of something that has as yet no real connection with it. This is demonstrated by the fact that a person shows no natural resentment if another takes possession of something which the person has not joined to himself. No *natural* pain is caused, and the harm forbidden by law is not experienced.

[369]

more familiar than what we frequently discuss and common sense least doubts.

Let us now see whether the German philosophers succeeded better in unravelling this important problem of rational Right.

370. C). A number of these authors accepted Kant's principle that 'everyone has the right to do anything which does not prevent others from living in the same way.' In this principle (which I have discussed above)[110] they thought they could find the intrinsic reason for the right of external ownership.

371. However I must acknowledge that some of these writers had expressly indicated that the ownership of a thing consists in some kind of connection with personship. The Italian, Baroli, makes the following astute and important observation: 'Consequently the acquisition of a right necessarily requires a fact, by means of which an object is so joined to the personship of a particular subject that it can be considered (partly or entirely) within his sphere of freedom.'[111]

372. Much earlier, some theologians had said that ownership was rooted in a kind of *connection*.[112] However no one had explicitly stated that the connection must be with *personship*. Kant has the merit of focusing his thoughts on the dignity of person, and of finding appropriate expressions for focusing the thoughts of others on the matter. Nevertheless, he was unable to give a truly satisfying definition of person; in fact he did not try.

373. So far everything would be quite acceptable, although the right of external ownership has not yet been explained. In order to establish the foundation of this right, its moral necessity must

[110] *ER*, 342.

[111] *Diritto naturale privato*, §95. — I think it would have been more accurate to say 'within his sphere of ownership'.

[112] For example, Giovanni de Lugo had excellently stated: 'Right, relative to commutative justice is defined as a certain moral choice, by which a particular human being is morally preferred to others in the use of some thing because of a special CONNECTION between the thing and him. For example, a wild animal has a special connection with its captor. But if the owner gives it to someone else, its special connection is now with this second person in so far as the donor has morally transferred to another the connection which he had through his capture of it' (*De Just, et Jure*, bk. 1, Disput. 1, Sect. 2, 5. Cf. the same author, *De Incarnat.*, Disp. 3, Sect. 3, n. 42.

be shown. How then do these authors we are discussing explain and demonstrate the moral necessity of the connection between things and person which constitutes ownership?

374. To begin with, they do not examine and analyse the connection as an anthropological fact — an omission which itself is of great importance in theorists dealing with the science of Right. They are satisfied with having summarily indicated the connection as known and incontrovertible, and so pass on to their jural law. Zeiller says:

> Anyone who for his own pleasure uses things that have no owner, and allows every other human being to use for his own private purposes things that are free, acts in conformity with a rule according to which the activity of all can be compatible with his own activity.[113]

375. This affirmation is gratuitous. How can everybody else's activity be compatible with the activity of the person who has already taken possession of all the things the others could have taken? The first possessor's activity has in fact nullified the activity of all the others. Hence the real limitation of freedom is not equal for everyone; they cannot co-exist in the same way.

376. Let us suppose that the first person or his family, or a society he has formed (for example, a nation that takes possession of a whole country), had not occupied everything but only a major part of what is available. This alone is sufficient to make the limitation of the activity unequal. Everything that the first party has occupied limits the real activity of the others, while the others, who have not yet taken possession of anything, do not in any way limit his activity; they are not therefore truly on a par with him. They could invoke the Kantian principle and say to those who had preceded them in taking possession of the things: 'According to the law of rational Right we must also limit our freedom in such a way that an equal portion remains for all. But this principle cannot be applied unless all external things are divided equally among us. If anyone has an advantage over another, we will not be able to co-exist in an equal way. The freedom of some will have to be sacrificed for the freedom of

---

[113] Il *Diritto privato naturale*, §59.

others more fortunate who alone would fully maintain their freedom.' Clearly, the argument would be unanswerable if this sole principle were to be the law by which the disagreement is settled.

377. Zeiller says that 'such a procedure would almost entirely remove the use of things from human will and right, which is contrary to the law of Right.'[114]

378. First of all, it is not true that the partition we are talking about would almost entirely remove the use of things from human will and right. The partition would in fact make the use equal for all.

379. In the second place, this kind of partition would in no way conflict with the Kantian law of Right which Zeiller has accepted. It would only be a rigorous and legitimate application of it. The law simply states that 'another's freedom must not be limited for one's own advantage. Others must be left a part equal to that which is kept for oneself,' which would indeed happen in the case of the equal division of external goods.

380. But have I misunderstood the jural law I cited? Kant, its author, is precisely the man who applies it to deny a stable, permanent ownership in the state of nature. It is Kant who finds that the only way to deduce the right of external ownership is recourse to a reciprocal agreement. At the same time he states that the agreement is obligatory for all, not arbitrary. But if there is a moral obligation to determine private ownership by agreement, it is clear that such an agreement could only be the recognition of a right in nature, that is, of something morally necessary, not indifferent. There can be no duty to agree about things which do not have within themselves an intrinsic moral necessity. It is also clear that any agreement which determines the ownership of each individual, would need to begin from a principle of justice, for example, from the principle *unicuique suum* [to each his own]. The law of ownership would be presupposed by means of this principle, and the agreement under discussion would deal solely with the way in which the ownership indicated by the right is put into practice.

381. The jural principle of the German philosophers, therefore,

114 *Ibid.*, §62.

is in itself powerless to produce the right of external ownership.

CHAPTER 3
Nature of the right of acquired ownership

382. We shall continue, therefore, to investigate the nature of
the juncture between things and persons that constitutes the
right of ownership.

Article 1.
The juncture of things to persons constituting ownership
is threefold: physical, intellectual and moral

383. This juncture must be threefold: physical, intellectual and
moral.

384. If we possessed only one or two of the three manners of
the juncture of anything to person, ownership over the thing
would not be present. We would at least lack that first ownership which is acquired by occupancy of things which are free.
However, once the thing has been acquired, that is, as soon as
ownership has been formed through occupancy, the physical
juncture is no longer necessary in the way it was when the origin
of ownership was in question. But we shall explain this more
clearly later in the book.

385. The *physical juncture* arises from two things:

1. From a real *relationship* of utility between something and
a person (this is the third of the constitutive elements of right
that we have indicated).[115]

2. From *taking possession* of the thing. This occurs when the
thing is taken and retained with one's own *real* forces.

386. The *intellectual juncture* also arises from two things:

[115] *ER*, 252-255.

[382–386]

1. From an *act of intelligence* with which the thing is mentally conceived and conceived as good for oneself. This gives rise to the thought of taking possession and making use of the thing.

2. From another *intellective act* with which we judge that the thing, when known as free, may lawfully be taken possession of without our injuring the ownership of anybody else.

387. Finally, the *moral* juncture arises from two things:

1. From the *act of will* with which the person intends to take stable possession of the thing, and retain it exclusively for his own use.

2. And from the *jural quality* inherent to this act in which the formal appropriation of the thing consists. This jural quality is established through the thing's becoming part of the feeling of myself in such a way that touching it means touching me,[116] as we can see from the pain we feel and the injury we think we receive when it is touched. Thus jural duty arises in everyone else of not causing me pain by placing an obstacle to the full use of anything joined to me in this way.

388. The chronological order of these elements of the *jural juncture* which constitute external ownership is as follows:

1. the *utility* of the thing in providing some benefit;

2. an *intellectual act* conceiving the thing and conceiving it as advantageous;

3. an *intellectual act* judging the thing as free and jurally capable of occupancy;

4. an *act of will* which desires to take possession of the thing with jural occupancy (hence the jural quality of the act);

5. another act of will which moves real forces for the purpose of taking possession for the sake of occupancy.

I will comment briefly on each of these elements.

389. 1. *The suitability of the thing in providing some benefit.* — If the thing were altogether useless to us, we could not acquire a right to it as a result of what has been said, nor prevent others from taking it if it were useful to them.

390. It follows that if the thing remains suitable for use by others outside the use we make of it, we cannot prevent such use; blocking its use by others does not increase in any way the

---

[116] I have shown, mainly in *AMS* (764 ss.), that *subject* is a *feeling-substance.*

advantage that we can draw from it. Hence, several authors have observed that an object has to be *exhaustible* by the use a person makes of it if it is to become the exclusive property of that person. As Zeiller explains: 'It is of such a nature that an individual cannot use it perfectly for his own ends unless he also excludes all others from making use of it.'[117]

391. This explains why intellectual and moral good, such as *truth* and God, never become the exclusive property of any individual possessing them.

392. This is also a new reason (to be added to that given in 271, 272) demonstrating that all atmospheric air, all light and all spaces cannot become the exclusive property of a single person or of a particular society.[118]

393. The same principle also provides that when a person uses something, or takes possession of it, he must do so in such a way (as far as he is able) that without diminishing the advantage he can obtain from it for himself he does not prevent the least possible good to others or place a narrower limit to their freedom to gain possession.

394. 2 and 3. *Acts of understanding by which we perceive the thing and judge it suitable to be possessed jurally.* — These acts, considered in relationship with those of the will, render right something moral and jural. They show that right does not depend on a simple appropriation or physical juncture, such as that between beasts and their own body, their food, their nests, etc.

395. 4. *The act of will which uprightly desires the thing, and uses physical forces to take possession of it.* — This act, which presupposes those we have already mentioned is, as we said, the *formal* part of occupancy. In other words, it makes occupancy a *way of acquiring a right.*

396. 5. *The real or physical act* with which an individual appropriates or takes the thing for himself so that right is

---

[117] §65.

[118] 'Anyone making a fire with his own wood can indeed exclude all others from use of the wood and the ash because these are exhaustible objects, but he cannot prevent another from looking at any object in the light coming from the fire' (Zeiller, §65). The light of the fire, we may add, and the eye seeing it, have a *juncture* established by nature.

posited in its own real being. — Considered by itself, this physical act is only the *material* part of right and does not of itself alone constitute right, which needs the *moral* element.

We shall analyse later the act of physical juncture in so far as it concerns *occupancy*, and indicate the modifications to which it is subject during the time that an individual is owner of an object.

397. Here it is sufficient to note that for the sake of simplifying language and using it more expeditiously we can reduce the three manners of juncture to two, that is, to a *physical* and a *moral juncture*. The intellectual juncture is included in the moral juncture where in fact it is implicitly contained.[119]

398. These two kinds of juncture gradually come to acquire the following mutual relationship. The *moral juncture* is founded upon the *physical juncture*, which it presupposes; this is its matter. It is clear that I cannot set aside something for my own use without believing that it can be useful to me, nor can I take possession of it with an act of will unless I somehow unite the thing to myself physically.

399. The physical juncture comes from the nature of the *subject* which seeks in the juncture the subject's own good. This juncture arises, therefore, from the *eudaimonological* faculty.

400. The moral juncture comes from the nature of the *object* in so far as the object, clothed with all its circumstances, shows itself as susceptible of occupancy without injury to anyone. In this case, moral reason acknowledges the object's appropriation as lawful, and declares that no one else may lawfully disturb possession which has already taken place. This juncture springs, therefore, from the *moral* faculty.

401. As we said, the physical juncture is only the *matter* of right. The *form* consists in the moral juncture, without which there is no right.

402. Authors on natural Right have not always distinguished clearly between these two kinds of bond, which are contained

---

[119] Roman laws indicate very clearly this twofold connection which gives rise to external ownership. For example,: 'As no possession can be acquired without SPIRIT AND BODY, so no possession is lost except that in which BOTH act in a contrary fashion' (L. 8 ss. *de acquir. et amitt. poss.*) — *Spirit* and *body* indicate the two connections which we have called 'physical' and 'moral'.

in the ownership of external things, and it will be helpful if we offer a brief comment on the principal cause of their errors in such an important matter.

Article 2.
A brief comment on some of the principal errors, present in various writings, about the nature of the jural juncture constituting ownership, and their disastrous consequences

403. The cause of such errors is, as usual, the limited, imperfect observation of these authors.

404. Some writers gave all their attention to the physical juncture while disregarding the moral juncture; the right they sought was crude, material and fictitious — in other words a non-right.

405. Others, on the contrary, gave all their attention to the moral juncture, overlooked by the first writers. The result was an abstract, ephemeral, systematic right, different altogether from that universally acknowledged by human common sense as right.

406. The common defect of both classes of authors consists in their not having stated clearly the *juncture between the thing and the person* which establishes ownership. They had, of course, taken it for granted but paid attention only to its consequences; their lack of clarity shows that their minds had not reached the *order of reflections* necessary for observing and pronouncing directly on the jural juncture.

§1. *Comment on writers who concentrated only on the physical juncture; the consequences they drew from it*

407. The writers we are speaking of did not reflect directly upon the *jural juncture* constituting ownership. We cannot, therefore, describe in their own words any systematic treatment

of the matter. However, the spirit with which they approached it may be gathered from the way in which they reasoned and from their teaching which shows the consequences they unconsciously deduced from their implicit system.

408. A necessary consequence for those giving partial and exclusive attention to the physical juncture was their affirmation that right is founded in the *real nature* of things.[120]

409. Starting from this observation about the physical juncture, they elevated self-preservation, paternal governance, natural instinct (even in those cases or modes in which it was condemned by reason) into absolute, unlimited rights, and granted such rights to beasts.[121] Cicero says: 'First, nature granted to all kinds of animals the right to defend themselves, their lives and their bodies, to abandon things that appear harmful, and to acquire and attain everything needed for existence, such as food, lodging and the like.'[122]

410. As we said, there is a truth here but contained within a very imperfect mental conception. The truth is that ownership requires a physical juncture, but the defective conception is that physical juncture alone constitutes right. The authors we are investigating had forgotten about moral juncture.

411. Nevertheless, Cicero realises that the law, and therefore right, had to spring from certain eternal norms, and be founded in the rational nature of human beings.[123] We can say that his

[120] 'That which can be called and entitled 'right' is so by nature' (Cic., *De Finib.*, bk. 3, c. 21).

[121] Blackstone, speaking of animals, wrote: 'They, too, have a claim to a kind of permanent ownership relative to the area around their lairs, especially for the defence and protection their young. Birds have their nests, wild beasts their caves and woods, and it would *seem an evident injustice to them*, which they would oppose even by risking their lives, if their territory were invaded' (bk. 2, 1). If we want to give a reasonable meaning to the word 'injustice' as it is used in this passage, we have to take it as a figurative expression and, therefore, something which should have been avoided by an author on Right who wishes to prevent doubt and ambiguity in the minds of his readers. If this were not figurative language, the author would be predicating right, and therefore knowledge of what is just and unjust, of animals. He would also be contradicting his other opinion which states that no right to external ownership existed before the institution of civil society.

[122] *De Off.*, 1, 4.

[123] Cf. *De Leg.*, 1, 5. He says: 'The nature of right has to be explained, and

mind saw all the ideas necessary for a complete notion of right, but that he lacked the power to unite those ideas and derive from them the complete concept they should provide. He saw all the elements individually, but not together.

412. The error of those fixing their attention entirely on the physical juncture has its origin in their deriving rights from the *subject* rather than the *object*. — How did this come about?

413. The cause, I think, lies in the fact that the subject provides the *matter* of rights, which is a subjective good. We know the matter of rights only through and in the subject, who experiences in himself (in his own feeling) good and evil. We know that something is good for us or not, we know that it is useful or harmful, solely in the feeling experiences of our nature which always tends to enjoyment. The subject, that is, the primitive feeling of which all other feelings are modifications, is always inclined to move towards good and away from evil, and finds in his various feeling experiences the reason why one thing is good for him and another bad. The subject finds the worth of things and the measure with which to evaluate this worth within himself. He goes on to reserve them for himself, making them the matter of his right.

From this point of view, the subject can indeed be called the source of rights to the extent that his experience of good and evil enables him to understand what it is that other human beings love or detest. The subject comes to know how he does good or evil to others through his actions, and consequently realises when these actions are faultless and when they are morally impeded. In other words, when they can form part of his right, and when they cannot.

Properly speaking, therefore, rights and duties do not arise from the subject; only experience and hence knowledge of them springs from the subject.

414. Spedalieri, a very upright person, was caught in this trap. First, he defined right as 'a power in harmony with reason',[124] but without realising that reason's very own activity is to receive

this explanation is to be found in human nature.' Shortly afterwards, he adds: 'For it is a power of nature; it is mind and the understanding of prudence; it is the rule of right and of injury,' etc.

124 *Dei diritti dell'Uomo*, bk. 1, c. 2.

the law from known objects. He then proceeds almost immediately to forget his definition, and makes right arise from some 'attribute essential to the human being', which he discovers to be 'the instinct for happiness'![125] Having established this new source of rights, he shows he has already forgotten what he has seen immediately beforehand, that is, that the instinct for happiness is a kind of physical impulse insufficient to form a right. Reason has to establish the manner and quantity according to which instinct is permitted to operate. But leaving this aside, he states absolutely:

> We notice in all human beings an impetus drawing them necessarily towards the attainment of happiness. Granted this as a principle, it follows immediately and generally that nature gives us the right over all that reason finds to be an opportune means for reaching this end. This is the extent of our dominion.[126]

In this passage, he introduces reason only as that which teaches the means for satisfying rights which have already been produced by the instinct for happiness without the use of reason. It is now easy for Spedalieri to derive from this instinct all the rights that he assigns to human beings: the rights to preserve one's own individuality, to perfect it, etc.

415. But it must surely be obvious that a theory of this kind can only result in perpetual strife amongst mankind. If people have a right to all that their reason shows them to be a useful means to their desired happiness, all have the right to everything that pleases them without regard for other people. Taking notice of others would mean losing one's right to those things, which is against the supposition.

The author vainly tries to ward off this consequence by affirming that from rights on one side corresponding obligations flow on the other to preserve and respect such rights.[127] It is entirely reasonable that I respect the rights which others can have over something, but only when I have no right over it myself. It is impossible to defend the peace of mankind, therefore, by making obligations arise in human beings after and as a

[125] *Ibid.*, bk 1, c. 3.
[126] *Ibid.*, bk 1, c. 3, §2.
[127] *Ibid.*, bk 1, c. 4.

[415]

consequence of their rights.[128] Agreement and peace amongst human beings is guaranteed only by means of the opposite procedure, that is, by making rights spring from moral obligations, as we have done, not vice versa. We must remember that the nature of right is such that its execution can never be morally prevented. If it could, it would no longer be right, and no longer be moral freedom to act on our part. It is absurd and contradictory to admit first rights in all human beings equally, and then make these rights the source of obligations that impede the exercise of the rights.

416. The world stood back horrified when Spinoza unambiguously maintained the same teaching.[129] However, although all were agreed in rejecting the final fruit of the principle that draws rights from the subject, not everyone abandoned the root

[128] It is certainly true that there are obligations in others corresponding to the rights present in a human being. These obligations arise, however, from the law as their first source. Rights are such only in relationship to the moral law. The error in Spedalieri's system consists in making rights themselves the cause of the obligating force, in making rights the law itself. 'When rights and obligations correspond, no one can lord it over others, and no one can complain; but this is a state of peace, not of war' (bk 1, c. 5, §5). I grant that rights and obligations can exist together if rights and obligations *in the same person* have different objects, but it is absurd to suppose that this is the case when they have the same object. For example, how can I impose an obligation on myself not to use an object which I know I have a right to use?

[129] The following passage from Spinoza's *Tractatus theologico-politicus* (c. 15) is a summary of his system. 'I understand as natural right and institution only this: the rules of nature for each individual according to which we mentally conceive each one as determined to exist and act in a certain way. For example, fish are naturally determined to swim, and larger fish to devour smaller fish. Fish therefore use water, and bigger fish eat smaller fish, with full natural right. It is undoubtedly the case that nature, absolutely considered, has full right to whatever lies within its powers. In other words, the right of nature has the same extent as nature's power. Nor do we accept the existence of any difference between human beings and other individuals in nature. The natural right of each human being, therefore, is not determined by sound reason, but by desire and capacity. Consequently, the individual, considered under the rule of nature alone, lawfully desires whatever he judges useful for himself, either on the basis of sound reasoning or as a result of stimulus from his desires; he does this because full natural right enables him to take what he desires for whatever reason by force, fraud, request or in any way he thinks easiest. And it follows that he can lawfully consider as an enemy anyone who wants to prevent him from fulfilling his desire.

[416]

whence it sprang. Unrecognised in its true colours, it continued to be propounded in books and lectures which nourished and fertilised it. Its development slowed down, but it was encouraged to grow a little at a time. Hobbes' social contract, and the poison of consequent theories, find their origin here.

417. Spedalieri also turned his attention to a false social contract. We should note carefully how he proves the necessity of making sure that civil society is justly formed:

> It is helpful to recall that there are necessary, immutable, natural rights even relative to divine omnipotence. It follows inevitably, therefore, that human beings, whatever state they are in, must be in that state in accordance with their own will and consent if the state is to accord with nature. Otherwise, violence would be done to their imperishable and valid right of freedom.[130]

418. First, if natural rights are necessary and unchangeable even relative to divine omnipotence, what power has the human will to restrict or enlarge them?[131] It is also strange to see how Spedalieri's great argument for showing the truth of his imagined contract is the same argument as that used to show that it is morally impossible.

The absurdity contained in this so-called proof stood out clearly for another writer who saw very well that a society resting upon such a poor foundation can easily be undermined and brought down. 'We have to see,' affirms an author of the last century, 'if mankind has the right to take upon itself lawfully the

---

[130] *Dei diritti, etc.*, bk. 1, c. 12, §6.

[131] Spedalieri teaches that rights are equal in all human beings, and goes on to explain social inequalities by means of a subtle distinction between *right*, and the *matter of right* (bk. 1, c. 7, §9-14). But surely it is clear to everyone that, if the matter of a right differs, the right is different. His recourse to the inequality of human faculties is also unfortunate. He begins by affirming that each individual has the right to use all the means which he judges useful to acquire his own perfection. But if this is the case, it is not the inequality of their faculties but the difference in their judgment, opinions and desires that makes them unequal in their ownership. No one can prevent an individual endowed by nature with extremely limited faculties from desiring the whole world if he believes its possession to be useful for his own perfection. In Spedalieri's system, therefore, inequality of intellective faculties cannot be the source of inequality of ownership amongst human beings.

formulation of such an agreement (the social contract), that is, has mankind the right to undertake such a responsibility?'[132]

In fact, if rights spring from the nature of things, and if God himself cannot change nature or the rights springing from it, how can the human will change or alter them? Let us grant that all rights come from the instinct for happiness in such a way that human beings have the right to all the means they judge useful for this end. If this were so, no one could alter it. Nor could we take upon ourselves any task today that we could be sure of tomorrow because we cannot in fact judge that what is useful today may not be harmful tomorrow, and vice-versa. Is there any possibility, therefore, of any valid contract between human beings?

What I mean is this: granted the cause, the effect must follow. At whatever moment I judge that something is useful for my perfection or my happiness, both the cause of my right and the right itself exists, according to these sages. But this right is unchangeable because its cause is unchangeable. What I know as useful, I know as useful, and not even God himself can bring it about that what I actually know as useful I do not know as useful. My right, therefore, is unchangeable, and any pact that I make to restrict and alter it is invalid and null. The right is as necessary as the nature of things, and as unchangeable as the instinct for happiness which is in my nature. God himself could not make any change here without destroying human beings.

If it is true, therefore, as these authors claim, that all natural right originates from the nature of things as from their source, everything is determined; the human will is despoiled of any power of free choice. We have to begin by eliminating all pacts from the list of the sources of rights because such agreements are simply a momentary declaration of the judgment we make upon the relationship between things and our own utility and happiness, and cannot be brought to bear at other times. We make a judgment, but this could change an instant later.

There is no doubt that if we posit the foundation of right within ourselves we shall indeed be setting our sights on the

[132] *Des Erreurs et de la verité etc.*, Edinburgh, 1782. — Part 2, pp. 7-9.

stars, only to find ourselves travelling into the abyss by the road of arrogant pride.

419. These difficulties were sensed by people whose common feeling, although still confused, affirmed that 'the doctrine demanding that rights precede duties is a source of violence'[133] and reasserted 'the doctrine that duties precede rights.'

420. Was it impossible then for people to see that in deducing rights from the subject, a system was formed which carried within itself a nucleus destined to destroy rights themselves and the whole of humanity? — Yes, this was seen, or at least suspected, but people hoped to remedy the disorder by patching it over. Two principal methods were devised, and these corresponded to the two natural limits whose task it was to contain and limit human actions.

The first of these limits was located in right judgment.

Human beings have a right to a thing only if they judge it useful to their perfection (so the argument runs). Consequently each individual must abandon many things to the power of others, that is, all those things from which he derives no utility.

421. This train of thought was perfected and a system devised which prescribed that human beings should be instructed and persuaded from the beginning of their education that everything helpful to the common good constitutes also their own particular good. This persuasion would depend upon how civil society was regulated so that the common good had the greatest possible bond with the good of private individuals.[134]

422. This would be an excellent argument, provided that the means for carrying it out did not involve any infraction of rights. They are, however, insufficient for their purpose.

In the first place, it is impossible to persuade anyone that all men and women would everywhere think in the same way.

---

[133] This is the argument used by Giuseppe Droz in his *La Morale applicata alla Politica etc.*

[134] Spedalieri proposed this in bk. 2. But he found it insufficient even when it received the support of all possible natural means. To save society this author is forced in the end to turn to the Christian religion, that is, to abandon the system he had embraced. Christianity, in fact, instructs us about our rights only after having found us faithful to our duties. The last five books of Spedalieri's work, which are devoted to showing the necessity of religion, can be considered as a refutation of the first book.

[419–422]

Whatever method and form were taken by education and society, no one could ever be sure that an individual's judgment about things would not change in a flash. — It would be impossible to persuade an individual who had arrogantly escaped from great danger that private utility coincided with public utility. The same is true about a thief in the process of getting away scot-free with his loot, or about some ambitious usurper who thinks the circumstances favourable for a coup d'état, even if thousands of lives have to be sacrificed for his aggrandisement and that of his family: neither thief nor usurper would be persuaded that their private utility was the same as public utility. — Nor would they be held back by remorse: they would simply be exercising their right to use means towards their own perfection and happiness, means to which they have an immutable right!! — Finally, before deciding that children in general should be persuaded of a given opinion, it is necessary to be sure that the opinion is true. Unfortunately, the opinion we are considering is false.

423. It was thought that a second limit could be found in the degree of physical force possessed by each individual. This was the source of the system of force. Some authors claimed that human society could be constrained by force in such a way that the individual's exercise of his rights would be unable to inflict harm upon his fellows, even if he wished to injure them. This is how the problem was set out in the last century. Even a little knowledge of human nature is sufficient to show its absurdity.

For instance, overpowering force is certainly not necessary in order to do harm. As we know, a malicious child can inflict harm. Moreover, anger and other passions find an outlet even when they are clearly going to bring grief to their perpetrator. — There is also the difficulty of preventing association in the world at large. — Imagine for instance, that the whole of mankind had been imprisoned under the illusion that forestalling its propensity to harm was a benefit conferred upon it. Nothing could now prevent the jailers from inflicting every kind of injury upon the beneficiaries of such a system. — And generally speaking, if we grant that force can always be checked by greater force (although this is not true), the superior force must be exercised by someone. In this case, there is no one to prevent injury by this force or check its exercise; no right is available to

[423]

check another's right. — It is incredible that Kant's sophistry disregarded this. But his mind, twisted by the infection present in his century and by Protestantism, brought him to clothe the absurdities of his time in the most perfect philosophical forms. He was a great mind and could have raised up an immortal, scientific monument to truth if he had availed himself of the assistance of Catholic principles.

424. These two systems indicate a total lack of knowledge about the reality of the human condition.

After all, who are the people expected to instruct the human race sufficiently to enable such a prudent, although unlawful, rule of force to be enacted? — Do these people form part of the human race, or do they descend upon us as blessings from outer space? If mankind had to act as a brake upon itself, either with persuasion or force, it would be a double-headed monstrosity, simultaneously restraining and being restrained. —

Again, is the responsibility of restraining oneself and others by persuasion or force a moral duty, or not? — It cannot be if we wish to be coherent. The whole system is in fact a surrogate for non-existent moral duties in the face of existent rights.

Will utility be the stimulus to action? — First, we have to see if people think it useful to follow without any obligation whatsoever the systems imposed upon them by a horde of philosophers, no two of whom agree. — After that, there is no doubt that individuals who consent to the system will accept the common utility as their own utility and endeavour to persuade everyone else of their worthy opinion. But who is then going to prevent them from awaiting a secret opportunity to profit by this belief of others and thus, according to our philosophers, act with perfect justice by seeking their own good in such a cunning way. In the end, the individuals we have in mind are going to turn the argument on its head by maintaining that if the common utility is their own utility, their own is the common utility.

425. It follows that morality is finished, and society with it, if rights and consequent moral obligations are deduced in any way from the subject rather than the object. Authors who teach these principles may deny their consequences, but they cannot forestall their pitiless, inexorable progress.

426. If we look more closely at the logical formation of these errors, we shall see that their authors did not distinguish

[424–426]

sufficiently between *obligation* and the force necessary to mankind to *execute it*. They saw that human beings could not carry out obligation without following the impulse to good provided by nature — an impulse against which the individual cannot act. They went on to conclude from this that obligation consists in satisfying this impulse to good. But here they confused one thing with another.

427. It is not true that obligation consists in satisfying the impulse to good. Obligation exits independently of this impulse just as the notion of what is true and false exists independently of the love bestowed upon what is true and false. We receive obligation, but we can only carry it out by means of the *forces* with which we act. Human operative forces are summed up, however, in the tendency to eudaimonological good which is as it were their principle. It follows that if we want to carry out our moral obligation, we have to believe that we are obliged to consider its fulfilment as containing our superior eudaimonological good. And this is always possible for human nature (which does not lack help from on high) because it is endowed with free will. The power of this wonderful potency of free will consists precisely in making prevail for itself the good it wants. To say that obligation arises in us from the principle of happiness is the opposite of the truth. What happens is that with our free power we authoritatively direct this principle to the object we want; and it is morality which constrains us to turn it to morality itself. In fact, the *supreme genus* of human *duties* could be expressed in the following proposition: 'We must direct the instinct for happiness to the execution of the moral law' or: 'With our free will we must make our greater eudaimonological good consist in the acquisition of moral good and in its consequences.'[135]

428. The subject's good, therefore, is always that which makes us act. But we have to note that although this is totally true, the good is itself subject to the free will with which we determine it.

---

[135] When we say 'principle or tendency to happiness or eudaimonological good', we do not always mean a calculated good, but in addition the good to which we incline spontaneously. As we noted in *Storia comparativa dei Sistemi morali* (c. 4, art. 4), we cannot call this good either *selfish* or *unselfish*.

And free will is always obligated by the law to determine the good in favour of moral goodness.

In the second place, the subject's own good reveals to the individual the good of his fellows. In doing so, it provides us with the opportunity of carrying out the moral law in their regard by doing them good, not evil.

The desire for good and for the felt experience of good provides two kinds of service to morality: it is the *instrument* which the will makes use of in order to carry out moral obligations, and it gives us knowledge of what is good for our fellow human beings and of what we should do to help and protect them.

Because the subjective good enters into the *execution* of moral obligation in this twofold way, it is easy to confuse the *principle of morality*, the source of obligation, with the *principle of happiness*, the source of the execution of the principle of obligation.[136]

§2. Authors whose attention was confined to the moral juncture alone, and its consequences

429. We may rightly say that philosophers who gave exclusive attention to the *physical juncture*, and posited ownership within it, are characteristic of the ancient world. The opposite error pertains to modern times in which many authors have devoted

---

[136] This enables us to see the place occupied in morality by Hutcheson's *benevolence* and Adam Smith's *sympathy*. They cannot form the principle of morality, but have to be considered as modifications of the system of *happiness*, presented by their authors in a noble or ignoble way. By establishing the system of happiness upon the natural propensities of human beings, it was possible to fix one's gaze upon one propensity rather than another. If a noble inclination was kept in view, the moral system deriving from it had the appearance of nobility; if an ignoble inclination was the object of vision, an ignoble, despicable moral system resulted. It is clear, therefore, that we must all feel pleasure in acknowledging the pure feeling to which the two authors we have mentioned endeavoured to recall mankind, just as on the contrary we all find cynicism hateful. Nevertheless, sympathy and the inclination to love of our fellow human beings can only constitute aids to our *execution* of virtue; they do not have any power to impose on us obligation, which they presuppose.

[429]

their entire attention to the *moral juncture* while totally forgetting the physical juncture on which alone the moral connection can be founded. Among these writers must be numbered the ultra-radicals of every country, whatever their name: Sans-Simonists, Chartists, Communists and so on.

430. These authors are divided into four classes.

The first class maintains that 'each individual has the right to an equal portion of external ownership'; the second, 'to each should be given according to his merit'; the third, 'according to need'; the fourth, 'that ownership of things belongs to no one in particular but to humanity as a whole, although the use of things belongs to individuals.' The fourth group are split about whether to understand 'use' on the basis of arithmetic equality or merit or need.

431. As we can see, all these principles equally ignore the physical juncture. They err in presupposing that for a thing to be mine, it is sufficient that I judge on the basis of certain speculative reasons that it belongs to me. I do not need to take possession of it, nor is it relevant that others have already done so.

432. Our first answer to this error, common to ultra-radicals, is that the human race has never understood the word 'ownership' in this manner. Common sense has always understood *mine* and *yours* to refer to something that either has of itself or by means of some act has acquired a certain physical connection with the person expressed in *me* or *you*. This connection is unique and of such a nature that it does not break any other previous connection between the thing and another person who may be injured by the collision.

433. A second answer, sufficient to illustrate the fundamental deficiency of this system, is its gratuitous, false supposition that an individual has a right to the use of all things.

434. Affirming that human beings have the forces needed to use things proves nothing relative to right. Moreover, it is not true that we have the physical forces to use all things.

435. Saying that human beings need to use things (and these needs are limited if we abstract from fictitious, imaginary requirements) proves nothing. Having a need for things does not form a right.

436. Appealing to intentions of the Creator in order to prove

[430–436]

the point means taking the matter beyond its proper limits. It is impossible to know the mind of the Creator without turning to revelation. But if we depend upon revelation, the argument is ended by reference to the seventh commandment, which acknowledges ownership in the sense always recognised by mankind, not in that accepted by the ultra-radicals.

437. Nevertheless, a system would be *useful* (this is truly the Achilles' heel of these people) which, dependent upon the principles expounded earlier, wanted to have things or their use distributed independently of any existing possession.

438. My first answer is that the ultra-radicals, who do not recognise ownership in the sense in which it is recognised by the human race and safeguarded by civil laws,[137] are still in disagreement on this matter. The three or four principles they profess, and which we have indicated, are utterly irreconcilable.

439. Second, the calculation which claims to resolve the problem about 'the most useful system for humanity' is so complicated and difficult that it is beyond the power of human understanding. And if some god-like genius existed capable of making the calculation, he would never succeed in persuading others who did not grasp it. And what obligation would there be for everyone to solve the problem in the same way? If each individual were free to resolve the calculation according to his degree of intelligence, which of the many solutions would become the universal law? Finally, individuals will necessarily find varying solutions because each will be in a different position and governed according to a rule of action modified as a result of his circumstances

440. Third, if all could and should agree about a solution to the problem and decide harmoniously about the greater common utility, it does not follow that utility, common to all mankind, forms right, and that each individual is obliged to renounce what

---

[137] I do not want to justify those laws which either safeguard ownership insufficiently (because they do not safeguard it completely nor always in the same way) or which may go so far as to damage some part of ownership. I acknowledge the presence of such laws which have always existed and which still exist even in the best known codes. But this proves nothing. Positive legislation requires centuries for its perfection. I am speaking of civil laws as a whole, according to their spirit, and relative to what has been perfected in them.

he has until now possessed. I agree that this would be a wonderfully generous and beneficial thing to do, but it cannot be shown that it is an obligation in justice. In order to prove this, we would first have to remove the distinction between just actions and beneficial actions, or establish as a principle 'that each is obliged, by a title of strict justice, to do the greatest possible good to all human beings.' But this unheard-of tyranny is utterly cruel although cloaked, as we have seen, under the apparently kind appearance of changing all beneficent actions into equivalent jural obligations.[138] This is not the freedom and equality we are looking for.

441. Fourth, and finally, before seeing whether the system proposed by the ultra-radicals is *useful* for mankind, we have to decide whether it is *possible*. What is impossible can never be useful. Its impossibility will be seen, however, as soon as we consider it closely.

442. Some of those urging the adoption of this system require the distribution of property to be made in arithmetically equal parts although it is clear that if substances are divided in this way some people will have plenty and others insufficient.

443. Moreover, the proposed division will be carried out either by the whole of mankind or by a few individuals.

It would be absurd to imagine that the whole of mankind should divide all available substances.

But if responsibility is given to a few, will they be judged by the multitude in cases of injustice? In this case, the whole of mankind would again have to intervene either as distributors or as judges of the distribution. But it would be impossible for all mankind to reach agreement even if all could take part in the operation and had the time and all the necessary conditions available for engaging in such work. It is rare enough to find a few reaching agreement about matters touching upon their own interests. Children, when they arrived at the age of discretion, would have reason to complain that their rights had been damaged by their absence from the division to which all have an equal right. — But let us imagine that against all the odds the sharing out has been completed satisfactorily: if a single person

[138] Cf. *SP*, bk. 2, c. 13.

is now born or dies, the immense work is rendered useless and has to be restarted.

444. Similar comments may be made about the other system which would share out substances according to merit. An additional difficulty arises, however, as we search for a human tribunal capable of infallibly judging true merit, the only foundation on which we could hope to sustain ownership. The desire to found ownership on apparent merit only (which is not merit) would not result in discussion about principle, but in worthless talk about fantasy. Granted even that we could measure each individual's true merit with some kind of moral yardstick, we would still have accomplished nothing useful because different people exist at different times, and the merit of each person ebbs and flows from moment to moment. Moreover, if merit can claim what is available, demerit (which is something over and above merit) requires deprivation of what is available. A good number of people are going to die of hunger, I suspect, granted the kind of legislation these ultra-liberals would produce.

445. Need is also an insufficient explanation as a rule for the division of what is available as long as we are discussing a division of right, not of beneficence. There would be no one to judge the needs of individuals. Each person would claim, with apparent reason, that he should measure his own needs. After all, he is the one who feels his needs, especially in the case of his right. Again, therefore, agreement in these cases would be impossible.

We would also have to consider that needs are of many kinds. Some, such as intellectual and moral needs, cannot be calculated, although they are at times more pressing and acute than physical needs. Needs are also subject to continual, rapid change in various periods, circumstances and moments of life. They increase and decrease in an extraordinary fashion.

446. Claiming that everything available should be administered in common, and that only income from what is available should be distributed, has all the disadvantages of the preceding systems as well as the dubious privilege of being a totally arbitrary disposition. The impossibility of administering in common all that is available cannot be overlooked. Because we are dealing always with rigorous right, all should take part in the administration, or act as judges of what is being done in the vast

business. And no individual or group could impose upon even a single person the obligation of renouncing his right and his opinion. In a word, there would be as many administrators and judges in this system as there are human beings. No one could stand outside the inevitable conflicts to intervene as supreme judge when necessary. Strife and war would be necessary because every possibility of discussion would be impossible.

447. We must conclude that all these systems are *gratuitous* relative to their first fundamental propositions and *impossible* relative to their execution.

448. But let us reflect now on the system that I am proposing. There is no need to prove that it is possible because we can see it put into practice throughout the whole world, and followed everywhere, from the earliest times or at least from the time of Peleg.

449. It is not gratuitous, as we can see if we consider that it revolves around a totally clear, moral precept and a fact of nature. The precept states: 'It is forbidden for one human being to cause pain to another.' The fact is: 'Pain is caused whenever a part of anything united to an individual through feeling and upright will is detached from him.'

But taking possession of something real is a juncture which is felt and willed. Consequently, once such juncture has taken place, the moral law forbids our separating occupancy from the person because it is forbidden to cause the person pain. I cannot, therefore, unite that thing to myself or use it for my own advantage without at least the consent of the person who already possesses it; I must respect this jural possession called *ownership*.

450. It will perhaps assist us if we come to understand better the series of reasonings which led the writers we have been discussing to abandon the physical connection, the foundation of ownership, and go on to believe that ownership arose simply from speculative principles, whether eudaimonological or moral.

As we said, this is a modern error. In fact, it could only have arisen long after people had taken possession of unoccupied territory and divided it amongst themselves. After that, occupancy, the original title of ownership, became less important; fewer occasions of using it were available. Other agreed titles

(titles of *transmission* of ownership such as *succession, donation* and *bilateral contract*, etc.) took its place. These titles were *indirect modes* of acquisition; the *direct mode*, occupancy, had almost vanished, *absorbed*, as it were, by the acts of those who had first taken possession of ownerless things. We have to consider now that only the *moral bond* changes when already constituted ownership is transmitted in various ways from one owner to another. The owner changes, but the physical bond of occupancy and possession remains substantially what it was before. Our attention however is drawn more to what changes, and we easily forget that which remains the same. As a result, occupancy, the felt, physical juncture, was totally overlooked by our publicists who concluded that ownership arose solely from intellectual and moral principles.

451. They were led to confirm this error with some force by their having observed that loss of physical possession on the part of an owner who suffered unjust depredation by others did not in any way affect his right of ownership. He could in fact make it prevail by using force against the unjust aggressor. This fact permitted the publicists to believe that the entire substance of ownership consisted solely in a rational or moral law. The error could only be detected by noting that a factual invasion or usurpation cannot take place unless the owner has already taken possession. It is this occupancy that he is vindicating. All acts of ownership, therefore, which are carried out by successive owners of any thing are referred in the last analysis to the first taking of possession, that is, to the first corporal bond of a thing with a person. This is both the origin of ownership and the aim of all acts of ownership.

[451]

CHAPTER 4
The first way of acquiring ownership: occupancy, and its limits

Article 1.
Conditions of occupancy

452. The nature of jural occupancy resides, therefore, in an intimate and natural connection between things and persons. Because persons are simultaneously physical and moral beings, we have to distinguish the physical and moral parts of this personal connection. The conditions of jural occupancy are reduced, therefore, to ascertaining the reality of this twofold connection. In other words, occupancy is present when the physical and moral bonds of things with persons are in place.

453. Consequently, the conditions of occupancy are also the conditions determining the limits of occupancy. It is in the establishment of these two conditions that we have to look for the limits of occupancy.

Article 2.
Limits of occupancy

§1. *Limits arising from the physical bond*

454. By beginning with the physical bond, we see the limits placed upon occupancy as a result of the difficulties of effecting the physical bond. When an individual takes possession of something from which he is unable to draw any benefit whatsoever, he does not occupy it jurally, nor does he acquire any ownership over it. The third constitutive element of right is lacking.

455. No true, real connection can arise if the benefit intended and hoped for by the occupier from the thing is false and totally untrue, that is, if it is the result of an erroneous calculation dependent upon some vain hope created by the imagination. In

this case, the connection is not founded in the *nature* of the human being and the thing; it is rather an aberration of nature. It cannot, therefore, constitute the matter of a natural right.

456. All that remains to do now is to distinguish between an involuntary, innocent error, and one generated by harmful passion. An example of the latter is the activity of possession or envious malice seeking to prevent possession on the part of others.

457. In the case of innocent error (we always take it for granted here that the error is fully certain — the least doubt would be sufficient to make us presume in favour of the occupier), the moral law obliges us to take all possible care to avoid disturbing an individual labouring under error or illusion. If we are dealing with malicious error, the moral law does not provide for such careful treatment. But in neither case does the moral law extend to taking from the owner the moral-jural freedom to repossess something held by others without right.

458. This teaching has to be put into practice with the greatest caution. Otherwise it could be used maliciously as a basis for disturbing the first occupiers of things under the pretext that these things are of no use to them.

459. But the need to take great care in applying some teaching in order to avoid difficulties in practice does not make the teaching untrue. While fully acknowledging that certain teachings are dangerous when applied by unskilled practitioners, I feel obliged to confess their truth. It would be false prudence to declare true teaching false, as some do, because it seems difficult to put it into practice without danger.

As far as I can see, the difficulty never arises from the quality of truth in a teaching, but solely, as I said, from the difficulty present in its application and from the lack of skill on the part of the person attempting the application.

If a proposition is difficult to apply, there is certainly danger of its being applied wrongly and a consequent need for awareness, caution and care in its use, but nothing more. If we were to go further and say that it is false, we would be lying and committing a genuine misdemeanour. In fact, there is nothing more dangerous and imprudent than affirming that something true is false. Although a true teaching is *dangerous*, a false teaching substituted in its place is always *harmful*. Danger, therefore, is exchanged for actual harm. There can be no greater imprudence than this, to my way of thinking. We find it, unfortunately, in certain writers and sometimes in certain civil rulers who set themselves up as judges of what is being taught without having first asked themselves if such a sacred office is proportionate to their capacities.

My attitude is not to substitute false for true teaching because the truth is difficult to apply, but to affirm as true everything that appears to me to be true (after having consulted the best authorities) without paying heed to the consequences. These I abandon to the Providence of him who is subsistent truth; this Providence orders everything, and from my point of view it alone is prudent.

I shall, therefore, continue to follow my normal custom here. I shall indicate the difficulty, that is, the difficulty in the application, and I shall go on to suggest the precautions that may be adopted in order to avoid the suspected danger (if the nature of my argument and its connection with the difficulty allow, or I think it can be done). I will also put forward rules to be followed in the application of the truth which, in so far as we can easily abuse its title in the service of our passions, we think dangerous, or which is actually dangerous. My past and present hope is thus to have fulfilled the duty incumbent upon every writer, and especially upon a Catholic writer.

460. It is true therefore (and we return now to our argument) that someone could disturb a possessor in his occupancy with the pretext that what is possessed is of no benefit to the occupier: this is the danger. But it is also true that anyone who judges *erroneously* that what is occupied is useless for the owner does not adhere to the principle we have established. This principle justifies neither pretext nor false judgments, but only true and certain judgments.

461. But is the judgment about the benefit that a thing can bring to its occupier to be made by the occupier or by the one who wants to occupy it because he thinks it helpful to himself and useless for the occupier? Both have an equal right to judge provided they judge truly. If they judge according to truth, they will agree; if they judge falsely, the false judge will be wrong; he injures the other's right and can be brought back to his duty by force on the part of the other.

462. Both, however, think that they are right; one of them judges wrongly; who is to decide between them? This is the inevitable question in all cases of discordant judgments, and has to be resolved by means of the general principles capable of putting an end to controversies amongst human beings. In civil and ecclesiastical society, tribunals are available, but if we consider human beings as still in the state of nature the principles are as follows:

463. 1. Whoever sincerely believes in the soundness of his conclusion can use force to maintain his right; but in using force when his conclusion is incorrect he leaves himself open, in the moral-jural order, to wrong-doing and to harming the other's right. — If both use force, therefore, one of them is certainly wrong and blameworthy. In this case, it is impossible for each of them to be fully convinced of the truth of his own case with total security and as a result of logical proof; this truly logical and impartial conviction, however, is always a necessary, prior condition in the individual who considers using force in defence of his own right.

464. 2. The use of force, therefore, is justified only by the party who is totally and evidently *correct*, and moreover correct in such a way that the opposite party (to whom the argument has been fully submitted) must acknowledge and admit the argument as *correct*.

465. 3. If there is the least doubt or obscurity about the correct decision, the parties would be obliged by moral jural law to come to some peaceful agreement amongst themselves by way of treaty. They may either consider the matter themselves according to the principles of equity, or leave it to their lawyers, experts or procurators, or finally entrust it to an arbitrator in whom both have confidence.

466. 4. If one of the parties were unwilling to use these means for ending the dispute peacefully and, as we said, did not have any evident argument in his favour, he would oblige the other to defend himself with force. In this case, the use of force would no longer offend justice.

467. By keeping to these rules, individuals facilitate the application of the principle which is thus totally bereft of the danger it presented at first sight.

468. The same principle of limitation also enables us to determine

how far a person in the state of nature may lawfully go in occupying things which afford him some utility. It is clear that:

469. 'Each one can take possession of unoccupied things useful for him to the extent that he has the power to administer or turn them to some advantage.'

470. For example, a single individual who wished to take possession of thousands of acres of fertile land which he then had to leave uncultivated would not lawfully have made that land his own.

471. This would not be so, however, if he were able to cultivate it through his children, or servants or settlers. In this case, he would have the capacity to obtain the fruit of that land.

472. But would the simple hope of acquiring the necessary capacity for administering and developing what is occupied be sufficient? — This is difficult to answer within the ambit of natural Right.

473. Our reply has to begin from the principle that 'occupancy is possible where the physical connection, founded in nature, is possible between things and persons.'

474. It is clear, however, that if the forces necessary to administer and draw fruit from the thing do not yet exist in any way (even in *proximate potency*), the required connection, which is formed through relationship with these forces, cannot exist. The thing in question is, therefore, not yet open to occupancy.

But if these forces exist, at least in proximate potency (for example, if there are offspring who are only infants, or agricultural tools which, although not yet produced, are about to be made with suitable raw materials by skilled labour), the physical connection is already possible because a real relationship exists between the thing to be taken possession of and the incipient, growing forces; and moreover it is reasonable for the prospective owner to count on forces that are *undoubtedly* at hand.

475. But the uncertain development of these forces and a mere hope or probability of their arrival is not, I think, sufficient to produce the physical connection through which a thing is assigned with absolute certainty to its holder or occupier. In this case, even the jural occupancy should be regarded only as a hope for the future, not as an actual fact. Consequently, the things under consideration should be seen as free and unoccupied. The possessor's *certainty* of obtaining the desired benefit from the

things in question — that is, a certainty founded on the forces which have already made an appearance and which will undoubtedly appear in the future — is the necessary condition for being able to effect the natural bond of which we are speaking.

476. Before proceeding, I shall comment briefly on the principal opinions of some authors about the standard needed for occupancy of things in the state of nature, and compare it with the standard we have laid down.

Some, like Tieftrunk,[139] claim that human beings in the state of nature cannot take possession of anything except what is necessary for the preservation of their lives. It is clear, however, that this is an arbitrary rather than a natural law. Human nature certainly aspires to good beyond the mere preservation of life.

477. Others, Schlettwein[140] amongst them, maintain that people in the state of nature can make their own more than what is necessary for subsistence, but only on condition that it is not required for the preservation of their fellow human beings. In such a system, an individual would have to calculate the needs of all his fellows before becoming the owner of anything. This would be altogether impossible in the state of nature in which each person is certainly not obliged by the natural law to come to know everybody else. This obligation would be arbitrarily and (I would maintain) tyrannically imposed under a cloak of humanity.

478. Kant[141] says that the right of occupancy extends to everything an individual is capable of defending. This assertion, however, is as gratuitous as the preceding affirmations. It is also vitiated by the error deriving ownership from *force* rather than from the *moral law*. I do not cease to be the lawful owner of what is mine if I am unable to defend it against a thief or an assassin. On the other hand, while I could perhaps defend less than I am capable of administering and enjoying (and perhaps less than is necessary to preserve my life), I could in other circumstances defend more than I can enjoy and administer. In this case, I would remove from my fellow human beings a great

---

[139] *Ricerche filosofiche*, part 1, p. 272 ss.
[140] *Diritti dell'uomo*, §96.
[141] *Giurisprudenza, etc.*, §15.

quantity of good which is totally useless to me. This is obviously against the law of nature.

479. In confuting these opinions, Zeiller, a very sagacious person, substituted as a legal standard for occupancy the possibility of taking possession of a thing and marking it as one's own. But this standard is no better than those we have already examined.

If I were able to take material possession of some land that was totally useless to me but very necessary for my fellow human beings, and were able to mark it as my own, I would still have injured my fellows in exactly the same way, and damaged their natural right. Rational nature 'forbids us from doing that which injures others while providing no good for ourselves.' Reason never gives a right to such a stupid action, but grants the right of exclusive occupancy of things only on the basis of the utility that we can naturally draw from them, that is, in accordance with the laws of our upright nature.

480. It is precisely in the utility which we can derive from things that we have to find the first determination of the quantity of things that we can occupy.

481. The *limitation* of occupancy arises, therefore, from the quality we call jurally *occupiable*, a quality necessary in the thing we wish to make our own. However, it is not sufficient for the thing in itself to be jurally occupiable if it is to enter into our ownership. Actual occupancy is also needed, that is, we have to take possession of it. Here we have another condition effecting ownership, and hence another limitation to it.

482. What is required, therefore, in order to take possession of something?

This phrase 'to take possession' is ambiguous in the treatises on Right. Sometimes it is used as synonymous with *occupancy* which produces a right; sometimes it is considered as a simple preliminary step which does not of itself produce a right, which is formed later by *occupancy*.[142]

---

[142] Zeiller distinguishes as follows between *detention, possession, taking possession and occupancy*. 'If we employ something for our own ends, we *use* it in the broadest sense. If this thing is within our physical power in such a way that we have the physical faculty for using it to the exclusion of others, it is related to our person with what we call (physical) *detention*. If it has been

483. We hold that possession or detention of something with the intention of making it one's own does not as such form the right of ownership, but what we have called the 'physical bond'. However, irrespective of semantics, let us continue with our attempt to describe the formation of this physical bond between thing and person, a bond which comes about by 'taking possession' of something. We shall then be able to deduce from 'taking possession' the limitations of ownership that we are seeking.

484. Persons naturally form a bond with what is useful to themselves (provided they can make use of it) as soon as a thing on which they have set their sights is reserved for them, and they have put their mark upon it by immediately starting to work it for their own benefit.

485. Granted the existence of something useful, and of forces within a person for making use of it, the elements of this bond are:

1. The act by which the person knows the thing, and knows that it is useful for him.

2. The act with which the person, as a consequence of this knowledge, wants and proposes to reserve that thing for his own use and advantage.

3. The act with which he begins to work with the intention of drawing from the thing the advantage that it can give him.

486. Properly speaking, only the final element is a physical act; the two preceding elements are acts of the understanding and will presupposed by the physical act which, although physical, has to be moved causally by an intellective-volitive principle.

conjoined to us with the intention of being used exclusively by us, we have (physical) *possession*. The act by which possession is effectuated is called *taking possession* and this in its turn is called *occupancy* when it is united with the intention of disposing of the thing perpetually to the exclusion of others (in other words, we exercise dominion over it)' (§46).

Here it would seem that *possession* does not involve the intention of having the thing as one's own (ownership in the strict sense implies the concept of *exclusive* and *perpetual* use); it would seem to refer only to *occupancy*. Zeiller, however, is not altogether in harmony with the Austrian code which defines the possessor as one 'who holds the thing with the intention of having it as his own' (§309). This seems to me to contain the true, legal notion of possession.

For the moment, we shall deal solely with this physical act, and return later to the preceding spiritual acts. These will lead us to consideration of the moral bond and of the limits it sets to occupancy.

487. We have said that possession can be taken of something useful when forces are available for enjoying it. They must exist in such a way that although not completely ready for what is intended, they can nevertheless certainly be made ready by the person who has them, and are in fact actually being prepared (cf. 472-474). As we said, it is necessary that a thing seen and intended as one's own begin to be worked upon immediately with the intention of obtaining from it the advantage it can offer. The *work* intended must consist at least in bringing into play *existing* forces for the purpose intended. For example, an individual may have already begun to make the tools necessary to cultivate a piece of land on which he has set his sights and his mark. This is sufficient to unite the land to himself by means of his physical force. Anyone taking the land away from him at this stage would be causing injury to him in his nature.

488. This could seem a very low requirement for the formation of the physical bond, and it would indeed be so if we accepted the physical bond as occupancy pure and simple. But this is not how I understand the *physical bond*. It is only one element of occupancy, which is not carried through to completion without the addition of the moral bond and the designation implied in the moral bond (we shall speak of this later).

489. Meanwhile it is certain that having decided to cultivate a piece of land, and having taken the trouble to prepare what is necessary for cultivation, an individual would be distressed if someone else took over the land. This natural, not arbitrary, pain is a *symptom* of the union between the person and the thing. This union has already been brought about by the physical work entailed in the preparations. It would now be interrupted and lost if the land for which it was destined were to be snatched away.

490. We say, therefore, that the start of work destined to prepare forces already substantially *existing*, but not yet fully developed relative to the full activity for which they are certainly available, is the minimum physical act sufficient to put into being the physical bond of which we are speaking. It

follows that work exercised immediately on what has been made one's own will be more than sufficient provided that the work is done in order to use the thing and gain the fruits or advantages it offers when the work has been completed. Starting to use the thing (for example, by deforesting and ploughing land or by other preparatory work, or by actual cultivation) immediately becomes a further tightening of the physical bond joining an individual to what he intends to make his own and has already made his own.

491. Some authors claim that making a thing one's own in the state of nature entails providing it with a new form.[143] It is certain, however, that things can be enjoyed without their form being changed, and that it is not necessary for the owner to change their form if they are truly his. Moreover, the object of ownership is not the *form* conferred upon a thing, but the *advantage* that can be drawn from it.

492. But not even Counsellor Zeiller seems to have grasped the correct idea we want to expound. Although he dismisses the system which requires a new form, he says that if 'new form' means any application whatsoever of forces and labour to something, 'the designation applied to the thing would be sufficient because even this could not be placed on the thing without the external use of forces. Moreover, simply taking possession (for example, of an animal located at a distance) is capable of requiring more expense and labour than the entire transformation of the thing.'[144]

Note, however, that neither *effort* nor *expense* constitutes the matter of the right to occupancy, but 'the effort involved in its use'. Mere effort or heedless expense which is not directed to utility has no power to bind anything to a person in such a way as to make it the person's own.

493. If, then, we add — to the new form with which the thing is furnished — the directive by which we draw some advantage from the thing, the new form will be more than sufficient to constitute the physical bond of which we are speaking. As we said, the bond can be brought about by starting any work

[143] Cf. Teod. Schmalz, *Il mero Diritto naturale* (Köngisberg, 1792), §62, and *Spiegazione dei diritti dell'uomo e del cittadino* (*ibid*, 1798), §12.

[144] §67.

sufficient to utilise the thing in question. The usefulness springing from things cannot always be attained instantly; sometimes
it comes about immediately, sometimes after a certain delay. We
cannot therefore require things to be immediately useful; it is
enough if our work sets their usefulness in motion.

494. According to the principle we have explained, the bond
is formed physically or rather we take possession of something,

a) by means of *work preparatory* to obtaining some benefit
from the thing. For example, we make agricultural implements,
we build walls or plant hedges around arable land to protect it
from animals and humans; we shut up animals with the intention of using them for food or some other use. In other words,
we do whatever is helpful for enjoying the advantages the thing
can provide.

b) by means of *productive work*, that is, work which immediately produces some result. For example, we cultivate a field
which has already been prepared.

c) by means of *work which uses or consumes* the thing in
question, in so far as it can be used or consumed.

d) by means of *formative, inventive or craft work*, that is,
work which renders something useful to its owner and is done
with the intention of reserving the thing for its owner.

495. This last type of work, by which things are bound to
persons, can be subdistinguished in various ways. For example

1st. the work of *generation* by which a father brings a child
into being;

2nd. the work of *formation*, production, development, by
which an artisan constructs a machine with raw materials that
he owns, an artist paints a picture, a technician constructs a new
clock, an author writes a book, and so on.

496. If we compare these two modes of production with that
of *creation*, we see without difficulty that creation constitutes a
title of absolute ownership over all things for the Creator. This
ownership is of a different nature from human ownership.

497. Creation gives being to substance itself and to the matter
of things. It is therefore a title embracing all other titles. These
do not *subsist* except in and by means of the first title proper to
the Creator.

498. A third limitation to *ownership* arises from the same
principle (that utility is always the true object of right).

[494–498]

Occupancy does not completely destroy in other people the faculty for an *innocuous* use of the things taken possession of.

499. This has to be understood carefully, however. In order to be truly *innocuous*, the use made of the thing must be incapable of causing any reasonable trouble to the owner. It must not cause him the least discomfort nor take from him the least amount of present or future advantage, use or pleasure that he can have from what he owns.

500. This freedom to an innocuous use of other peoples' things is admitted by Grotius,[145] Daries,[146] Wolff,[147] Martini[148] and others.

501. Martini adds only that if the appearance of innocuous use proves deceptive, the owner should be asked. This is, in fact, the easiest, and I dare say the *jurally* obligatory way of clarifying the matter. The moral-jural law obliges me to use every possible precaution to avoid danger of harming the rights of others. In doubt, I cannot posit this action, and an owner can prevent me from doing so even with the use of force.

502. Nevertheless, if the thing under consideration were obviously innocuous, enquiring of the owner would be nothing more than a question of protocol. If he should then proffer a clearly irrational refusal, one could make use of what he owned (which at this point is not his) even to the extent of employing force to overcome any violence he may have initiated.

503. Zeiller denies this freedom of innocuous use of others' things[149] because, he says, 'using them in any way always harms the rights of others.' But this is a totally gratuitous affirmation which cannot be derived from his principle of co-existence. Innocuous use of something certainly cannot eliminate co-existence amongst the human race. Nor can this affirmation be derived from our own principle of 'natural displeasure': an owner's displeasure at the innocuous use of his goods is not natural, but rather reproved by his rational, moral nature. Nor is the innocuous use of things forbidden by the quality

[145] *De jure, B. et P.* 2, part 2, 11, 21.
[146] *Observ. jur. nat.*, bk. 2.
[147] *Jur. N.* Tom. 5, §686.
[148] *Post. de leg. nat.*, §383.
[149] §88.

'non-renewable' that Zeiller assigns to ownership (cf. 389). If the use is truly innocuous on the part of others, it cannot be said that use by the owner is capable of exhausting it.

504. To Martini's restriction (that the owner first has to be asked), Zeiller replies that 'the owner cannot be obliged to make his opinion known.' But why not? Such a crude, abrupt right not to speak his mind is a consequence of an error in which nature is taken as a state where individuals are altogether isolated and act without reference to others.[150] This is certainly not the concept that we form of the state of nature: for us it is a state in which people, although not yet members of civil society, have nevertheless a relationship with others. Without such relationships the very notion of right would vanish: in the last analysis this notion is a relationship.

505. That may be so, Zeiller will say, but do you want to impose a jural obligation on an owner to reveal his opinion on the use of all that he has? At the most, this would be a moral obligation only in certain cases. —

According to me, people even in the state of nature have a moral-jural obligation to reveal their opinion whenever this is necessary to clarify mutual rights. Their obligation is similar to the moral-jural obligation of forming a pact or endeavouring to reach some kind of agreement necessary to avoid discord and war in cases of doubt (cf. 462-467). Such obligations are jural to the extent that the other party remains free to use force even to uphold his own dubious rights if he is denied discussion and other steps necessary to arrive at an equable solution.

506. It may be objected that circumstances do not always permit an owner to reveal his motives for refusal. This could happen and, if it does, will provide an exception to the general principle.

---

[150] Even Zeiller himself says (§77) that *ownership* 'is merely a negative right, that is, a right with the purpose of preventing an owner from being impeded in the free disposition of what is his. He can claim this from everyone.' Here Zeiller considers the relationship of the owner with other people. But in this relationship it is the moral law that forbids others from impeding the free disposition of what a person owns. If, however, this respect for ownership is imposed by the moral law, it is clear that the prohibition is totally reasonable. Otherwise the moral law would command what is unreasonable while supporting inhumanity and capriciousness.

[504–506]

507. At most, it would prove that others cannot make use of an owner's property when the owner declares that its apparently innocuous use is not in fact innocuous. Others would be free to use it if the owner, after agreeing that the use does him no harm whatsoever, adds that the sole reason for his refusal is that he is the owner.

§2. *Limits arising from the moral bond*

508. Passing to the moral bond, I note that this pertains to *designation* which is correctly required if all are to know that something has been taken possession of.

509. In fact, we could not say that a right of ownership has been formed if others do not know what has and what has not been possessed. Right, as we have defined it, is a moral faculty. The *morality* of this operative faculty does not, however, consist simply in the lawfulness of its activity, but in its being an activity defended and guaranteed by a moral law obliging others not to impede our action in any way, but leave us totally free to carry it out. Others cannot be constrained by such an obligation if they have no means of deciding which things are possessed and thus inalienable, and which are freely available. Some kind of designation is necessary, therefore, to show that a given thing is possessed, and to inform others that they are obliged to leave it alone.[151]

510. What does this designation consist in?

Almost all authors on Right confuse *designation* with the physical bond between things and persons. But if we examine the notion of designation we see that it presupposes the formation of the physical bond. The sign by which a thing is known presupposes the thing itself.

511. According to us, anything capable of making occupancy

---

[151] If the occupancy were known to some people but not to others, the right would exist relatively to those who know about the occupancy, not relatively to those who are ignorant of it. Right, as we have already seen, is *relative*, and consists in a relationship with other intelligent beings who have an obligation to respect it.

known is sufficient to designate it. We agree, therefore, with Grundling[152] that a verbal or written declaration is sufficient.[153]

512. Those opposing this opinion maintain that words or written declaration are not signs connected with the thing in question, which therefore is not designated sufficiently.

513. A sign, however, only exists to distinguish one thing from another. There is never any requirement for the sign to be connected with the thing rather than separate from it provided that in both cases it does act as a sign, that is, serves to show that the thing has been taken possession of. A sign is always united, spiritually if not physically, with what it signifies whenever it designates the thing in such a way that it cannot be confused with something else.

514. The nature and work of a sign is independent of the sign's being affixed to what it is intended to indicate.[154] That authors

---

[152] C. 31 ss.

[153] The sign placed upon a thing has the advantage of reminding others, whenever it falls under their senses, that occupancy has taken place. The obligation of respecting the occupancy would cease for someone who had only heard of it and then forgotten what he had heard. It would not cease in the case of those who remembered that occupancy had taken place. The right of ownership would not be removed, therefore, because it is relative, as we said. This explains why the ownership of some chattel for which money has been paid, but the chattel not consigned, goes unrecognised if it is sold again but this time actually consigned to the buyer, who is recognised as the owner (cf. Austrian Civil Code, §430), although the seller is still responsible for the damage done to the first buyer. This is correct, because the second buyer could not have known that the chattel was already sold. But if the chattel were clearly marked as belonging to someone else, and were declared as such verbally or through signs to the new buyer, his acquisition in bad faith ought not to be protected by law.

[154] Many facts could be cited to show that the actions of government agents indicated their persuasion that a small sign left, for example, in a deserted land, was sufficient for possession of the land to pass to their government. The captain of an English ship, the Olive, took possession of the island of Barbados, in the Antilles, in 1605 on his return from Guinea. He landed with some of his sailors, put up a cross, wrote on a tree: 'James, King of England and of this island', embarked and set sail. The island was colonised only 19 years later by Sir William Courtney. The thirty people he sent there founded Jamestown, the city of King James. I realise that these claims are not recognised for the most part. Schmalz writes in his *Diritto delle genti*, 'The European powers do not grant the person discovering new lands the right to impede their cultivation by others. Consequently, these powers have never

on Right should require an accident so extraneous to the nature of sign shows that they are seeking something more than a mere sign. They confuse the *sign* with the *physical bond* which, in our opinion also, is certainly necessary to the jural occupancy of any thing.

515. For the rest, if a pure sign is required, there can be nothing more perfect than written or spoken words which indicate things far and near without uncertainty or indetermination. Words can of themselves express clearly the act of will of whomsoever takes possession; they can determine if the occupant intends to reserve the thing *exclusively* or *perpetually* to himself — two conditions for the full right of ownership. Other signs can allow us to conjecture, but not know without doubt, the presence of these two conditions.

Words also allow us to express the extension of the right claimed by the occupant, and in fact acquired with his acts. Finally, words are the appropriate and most perfect signs for

considered simple taking of possession as sufficient to establish ownership, nor have they accepted a flag or inscription raised on a beach by mariners claiming that such a sign gave right of exclusive possession to their nation.' (bk. 4, c. 1). It is clear that the party taking possession is concerned to follow the opinion favouring the minimum requirement for constituting possession; the party having to recognise possession will uphold the maximum requirement. It is also clear that some work must be initiated, as we said (cf. 485) for a true appropriation of deserted land. But the question of work is a question about the *bond*, not about the *sign*. I maintain that after the bond has been posited, anything will serve to indicate it. — It is, however, worthy of note that taking possession of *sovereignty* over a deserted land is one thing; taking possession of its ownership is another. Granted, however, that the government of a nation could take possession of an island discovered by it or its agents simply by erecting a cairn, it does not follow that such a government has acquired ownership of the land and therefore the right to prevent others from cultivating it. In this case, the land remains unoccupied. However, those who come to occupy it should recognise the sovereignty of the government that has taken possession of it, provided this government is prepared to exercise its rights and fulfil its duties. This is the only condition permitting the occupancy of unoccupied sovereignty. In other words, the claim to sovereignty must be made by someone capable of exercising it and, therefore, of defending the occupied land in the first place. Defence is the first duty of governments. Nevertheless, we could still go on to ask if sovereignty can be acquired over an uninhabited land.

[515]

human beings because they are more in conformity with their intelligent nature.

516. It is also true, we may add, that a *sign* alone, without the *physical bond*, is not sufficient to bring about occupancy. Moreover, even the reality of the physical bond has to be known by others in order that they may be obliged to refrain from use of the thing which has been possessed. In this case, the rule: *Non esse et non apparere idem est in jure* [Not being and not being obvious is the same in right], prevails.

517. It is also true that while words are sufficient to demonstrate in the speaker a *will* to take possession of things, they are not sufficient to prove that this individual has already effected the physical bond with them. No one is obliged to accept his word; all can claim to see for themselves those acts with which the occupant starts to make use of the thing or work it or prepare himself to obtain some possible benefit from it. If a person were to affirm that he is doing this, but nothing were seen to be done in fact, he could appear to be making a fool of others or holding them at bay by insisting that he is doing something when in fact he is not.

518. This is another reason for authors' claiming that a sign should be physically joined to a thing. But if they had taken full account of this reason, they would not have been content with requiring a simple sign denoting the thing; they would have said expressly that this sign should be a clear, public undertaking with which the occupant at least begins to prepare himself to make use of the thing. This work, when seen, is also a sign of his intention.

519. Hence, *detention* of a thing is itself a valid, natural sign of such an undertaking. The same can be said about *capturing* birds or other beasts, dead or alive; about means of defence placed around a thing to prevent its being ruined or taken by others, and so on; and about other dispositions which are not merely signs but also a true start to work designed to draw some utility from the thing. Usage of this kind, done so that others see it, also indicates the intention of the person doing it.

520. Occupancy is not fulfilled, therefore, unless all these conditions are verified. Only within the limits that we have described can the originating title of external ownership be achieved.

Article 3.
Changes in rights dependent on occupancy, according to variation in the occupying subject

521. A further limit has to be added to those already described. This has its origin in the diversity of the occupying subjects who can be one or more individuals.

522. If several individuals are occupants, they may either be separate individuals or individuals associated in a collective body. For example, two hunters fire simultaneously at a deer; the deer is hit by both shots. In this case, separate individuals take dominion over the same prey at the same time. On the other hand, a society of persons may be formed to take possession of an uninhabited island. Here the occupant is a collective body.

523. In both cases, multiplicity of individual occupants places a limit to ownership, which must be divided between the co-occupant parties.

524. Such a limitation brings with it a duty to reach some agreement. In each of the individuals, therefore, a *jural obligation* arises to divide equably and peacefully the thing simultaneously taken into possession.

525. If one of the parties refuses to share, or seek an agreement about sharing, the others could use force against him (cf. 466).

526. In cases of this kind the right of ownership would always be acquired through occupancy, but an *agreement* would be made to modify such a right, that is, to share the object amongst several persons.

527. This is not the place to speak about contracts, but it was necessary to offer this brief comment because we are dealing with a *contract contemporaneous with occupancy*, that is, with a contract having a different condition from the usual kind of contracts. These are formed about rights already in being (as we shall see in the following book), not about rights which are being established but need a contract in order to be actuated.

CHAPTER 5

**Continuation — Occupancy considered as
a cause of dominion over persons**

528. We must now discuss another question concerning the
limits of occupancy: can *occupancy* give us rights of seigniory
over persons?

Article 1.
Occupancy of self

529. Occupancy gives us rights over self because person, by its
gradual action, takes possession of those different parts of
nature which form the human individual.

530. This right, by which we become master of ourselves, our
powers and our faculties, will be discussed in later Articles; it is
sufficient to have indicated it here. However, by comparing it
with the seigniory that human beings can exercise over others,
we will better understand the nature of the right of seigniory we
gradually acquire over self.

Article 2.
Occupancy of others: the meaning of our question

531. In my opinion, occupancy cannot in itself produce any
right of seigniory over other adult individuals.

532. There is, however, a species of occupancy which can be a
title to the right of seigniory over adults when they consent to
it. But because this occupancy requires the other's consent, it
cannot form part of our discussion on the formation of new
rights. It is a case in which one free person submits and simply
transmits to another a previously existing right, allowing the
second person to take seigniory over the first. In the next book
we still have to speak about this *transmission* of rights; here we
restrict ourselves to speaking about their *formation*.

[528–532]

Is it possible therefore to form a right of seigniory simply by occupancy?

Article 3.
Occupancy of human beings who have not yet fully attained seigniory over self

533. In the case of those who have not yet acquired full seigniory over self, we can reasonably maintain that some rights are acquired over them by occupancy.

534. Let us suppose that a baby abandoned by its parents and family has been given a home and is cared for at the benefactor's expense. Let us also suppose that the benefactor uses the baby for his own advantage, perhaps to alleviate his wife whose own child has died or as a companion for his children. Does he not acquire new rights by caring for the abandoned baby? No one could reasonably prevent him doing so. The child was not *occupied*; the benefactor acquired it by legitimate occupancy; he has thus obtained the right of possession of the child, the right to do good for it and to make harmless use of it. Anyone attempting to steal the child would certainly do him great harm, which he could resist with force.

535. It may be objected that we cannot occupy a human person as if he or she were a thing. In my book, *Society and its Purpose*, I have explained how we acquire dominion over human beings without harm to their personal dignity.[155] I showed that relative to nature there are many parts united to the human person which can all be matter for dominion by others. This dominion is limited to certain parts of human nature and can be exercised only on condition that the personal element is always respected. For example, I may have a right to the physical labour which others have contracted to do for me. In using their work, however, I must respect them by not applying it to any shameful or unbecoming purpose, and I must apply moderation in such a way that neither life nor health is seriously endangered.

[155] *SP*, bk. 1, c. 3.

[533–535]

The ownership that I can have over the faculties attached to person (but not over person itself) is entirely different therefore from the unlimited ownership I can have of things which lack intelligence. I have indicated this difference by calling the former 'dominion' and reserving the term 'ownership' for the right over things.

536. It is not absurd therefore to grant in general this limited dominion of human beings over their fellows. But another question presents itself: is occupancy the title which causes and effects this dominion? And if occupancy is the title both to ownership of things and to dominion over persons, why is it that adults cannot be occupied? Babies are as fully human as adults, and we grant that connatural rights exist in them, not only before the age of discretion but from the first moment of their being.[156]

I fully agree. But let me now explain precisely why, in my view, the occupancy of babies is possible, while that of mentally sound adults is not.

537. Human will and intelligence are in act as soon as the human being exists; personal dignity subsists and cannot be violated in any way whatsoever, nor obstructed in its natural operations. But the baby can certainly be helped to carry out its actions. An infant needs this kind of help, expects it and receives it gratefully — mothers tell us so. Caring for and educating an abandoned child therefore means simply helping it in its powerless state, and aiding it to preserve, develop and enrich its person.

538. Is this a kindness done by the benefactor, or a right exercised by him? It is both. First of all, the benefactor, in acting this way, is using his jural freedom; secondly, we may doubt whether he has acquired a real dominion over the baby relative to the baby itself, but we cannot deny that he has a real dominion relative to other human beings. We have seen that the notion

---

[156] Zeiller maintains that we cannot acquire the right of seigniory over others without the consent of their will (*Diritto naturale privato*, §93), and many other authors are of the same opinion. But my argument would seem to indicate that some rights over human beings (not *over persons*, strictly speaking) are acquired naturally without their consent, that is, by natural titles similar to those by which we acquire ownership of things.

of right is relative: by taking the baby into his home, the bene-factor has truly acquired a right over it before all others, who have not taken it in as he has done. The love he lavishes on the baby would make it precious to him, a real good. Surely no one could legitimately deprive him of the child? His good action in exercising charity towards it can only obtain moral merit for him. He could indeed defend himself with force if others wished to usurp a tender responsibility which can only be measured by the loving affection of his heart, and from which he derives his greatest treasure, the virtue he exercises in the baby's regard.

539. The fact that he may derive some advantage from the baby is another reason why the baby can be the object of his right. The advantage he wishes to obtain is just and legitimate because he sees that he can make use of it without harming the child. He certainly cannot force bad milk or poison on the baby in order to assist the woman feeding it, but he can provide good milk. If this helps him and his wife, this is clearly within his right.

540. I maintain therefore that, although rights can be acquired by occupancy which have human persons as their object, these rights are vastly different from those over irrational things. Dominion over occupied persons is limited to 'doing all we wish with an occupied individual, provided that we do not harm him in any way whatsoever and do not violate his personal dignity'. It is obviously a great limitation.

541. I must now retrace my steps. I have shown that dominion over a baby, acquired by occupancy relative to other human beings, does exist; I did not say whether this dominion extends to the occupied baby itself.

One of the differences between the right of ownership over irrational things and the right of dominion over rational things is that irrational things (the object of ownership) can neither dissent from nor consent to the right of their owner, nor have they any moral obligation corresponding to the right others have over them. Such an obligation exists solely in people co-existent with the owner. In the case of dominion, however, the corresponding obligation can be twofold: it can be present in those co-existent with the owner (who must respect the domin-ion) and in the individual who, as the object of the dominion, must acknowledge and respect his master. In this case dominion is relative both to others and to the one who is its object.

542. But this dominion, like ownership, clearly has only one of the two relationships, if the person who is the object of the dominion were not in a condition to give his consent or have some moral obligation.

543. In the case of the abandoned baby, it would seem obvious that the baby cannot give its consent to the dominion its benefactor exercises over it. Consent requires the use of reflection.

544. In fact the case is not as obvious as it seems. Although the condition of babies is mysterious and virtually unknown, I am convinced that human beings use their understanding and will from the very first moments of their existence; babies do indeed consent with all their will, utterly grateful for the loving care given them. I am convinced that they acknowledge the superiority and just dominion exercised over then by those who feed, govern and care for them. Finally, because morality begins with the use of will at the first moment the human being exists, I am convinced that babies are moral beings [*App.*, no. 1]. It is certainly a fact that babies act spontaneously. Thus, they must fulfil those duties that are in complete harmony with their natural inclinations. In such cases, however, morality has no accompanying merit.

545. I said earlier that I doubted whether dominion over an occupied baby extended to the baby itself. I did so for two reasons: 1. to avoid an involved discussion on the nature of a human baby which would require a book of its own, but is not necessary here; and 2. because legitimate occupancy would, in my opinion, take place and in turn produce a right of occupancy for the occupier, even if the baby did not consent, or expressly refused consent.

I have spoken only of this kind of dominion because our question was: 'Can occupancy alone, independently of the consent of the occupied individual, give rise to dominion over the individual?'

546. I answered 'Yes', and in the case of babies, whose consent is not required for occupancy, I argue as follows.

We have seen that no one can restrict another's freedom to occupy things except by occupying them himself and preventing further occupancy. He can do this only by designating them for his own use and beginning to use them. A baby however cannot do all this. It cannot exercise to its own advantage the possession it has of its powers, nor can it provide for itself without the care and help of others. Thus, even granted that a baby has the right of ownership over those parts of itself which constitute its nature, not its person, other human beings are free to make harmless use of them, because, as I have shown, we can use others' possessions when we do them no harm (cf. 498, 506). This is all the more true if the use is to the advantage of the owner.

547. Moreover, although there is no doubt that a baby has ownership of all that is in its nature, it is doubtful whether this ownership is a right. The physical bond is certainly present, but it would seem the intellectual and the moral bond are not present, at least not completely, because the baby has not yet learnt to use its powers; it has not, it seems, entered fully into possession of itself. In other words, its person has not completed the occupancy of its nature.[157]

548. If therefore the baby is considered simply as the object of the right that all human beings have to harmless use of others' possessions, this right can be called 'dominion', at least relative to other human beings. In their regard, we are simply exercising a seigniory acquired through the preceding act of occupancy, of which the child is the object.

549. On the other hand, if we consider the child as not yet having the full right of ownership over some part of itself, that is, over a part it cannot use, the right of dominion in the occupier is all the more evident.

550. We must admit however that when this kind of dominion is considered as a species of acquired ownership, the ownership

---

[157] In the Latin expressions, *compos sui, compos animi, compos mentis*, etc., which mean a person is 'sane', we find a witness in the common sense of antiquity to the teaching I am expounding. *Compos* means 'who has power over', and *compos sui, compos animi*, etc., mean 'the one who has power over himself, his spirit, his mind, etc.' This clearly shows that anyone who could not use his mind was considered as having no dominion or seigniory over himself. In the etymological sense of these expressions, therefore, the seigniory is vacant and can be occupied just as unpossessed things can be occupied. However this can be done only with due regard to the person, whose essential and entirely free act never ceases.

takes on a more special limitation than the normal ownership of dominion: it is a *provisional* occupancy, producing a provisional, impermanent ownership.

551. Indeed we have seen that the immediate use of an unoccupied thing is not necessary for possessing it. It is enough that someone, having set his sights on it, organises it for himself and begins to work it for his own use, or else systematises the forces and means necessary to exploit the usefulness it can offer (cf. 472-474). Even if a baby has not asserted seigniory over itself, it continually strives to establish this seigniory, and for this purpose is moved by the spontaneity of its nature to use and increase its already existing forces.

552. It may be that a baby, once it is aware of its powers, lacks the internal act of will for reserving these powers to itself. — For my part, I say that this act is implicit in human nature. The very close juncture between nature and person is such that nature is immediately felt by the person, which, bit by bit and without regard for anyone else, works towards possessing nature.

553. A child for whom others have assumed care and government, therefore, acts in the same way as someone who, having reserved something for himself by an internal act of understanding, is preparing to use it. No harm is done to him if others make use of the thing at the time he cannot use it himself. Indeed they assist rather than disturb his dispositions for taking full possession.[158]

---

[158] What has been said so far about our care for children who have not come to the use of reflection clearly indicates 1. that many enactments of civil law concerning the care and rearing of children are founded on rational Right; and 2. that when we apply in practice what has been said, we see the circumspection and limitation necessary for drawing up such laws so that they can be beneficial and within the limits of rational justice. — The *political reasons* put forward in order to adapt this important part of legislation in a particular way may indeed be valid, but only on condition that they do not contradict rational Right.

[551–553]

Article 4.
The right of seigniory over an abandoned child (continued):
does the right continue to exist
when the child has become adult?

554. We must now consider whether the benefactor's acquired dominion over the child remains, diminishes or ceases entirely when the child becomes an adult in full command of itself.

555. The dominion ceases by its very nature: once someone has acquired full seigniory over what is his, any outsider must withdraw.

556. This is true whether we consider the dominion over the child as the harmless use of what belongs to another, or as the provisional occupancy of an object not yet completely occupied by someone else.[159]

557. Does the caring foster-father of the abandoned child, therefore, the one who conscientiously reared it, have no right?

Article 5.
Duties of the grown child to his foster father

558. To answer this important question ('Has the foster-father any rights over the child and, if so, of what kind?') we must first consider the child's duties to the father. In our system we always move from duty to right, not viceversa.

559. In my opinion the child has, or at least can have, three different duties towards the benefactor:
  1. the duty of gratitude,
  2. the duty of submission
  3. the duty of restitution
We shall examine whether the nature of each is only moral or both moral and jural, and consequently whether true rights correspond to these duties.

---

[159] Hence Gratian's law, although intended to save abandoned babies, seems unjust. He had decreed that an abandoned baby should be a slave of the person who had taken care of it and fed it. Cf. Bodino, bk. 1, c. 5.

§1. *The duty of gratitude*

560. The *duty of gratitude* is simply a moral obligation incumbent upon anyone who has received a benefit or has simply been the object of some benevolent affection.

561. It is therefore a duty of the heart, and consists entirely in loving the one who has loved us, in wanting to help those whom we love because they have loved and helped us. Duties which impose affection are not classed among those to which true rights correspond, because affections, that is, simple affections,[160] are essentially free and hence the exclusive property of the one who nourishes them deep in his soul.[161]

§2. *Moral duty, and the jural duty of submission*

562. The *duty of submission* — does a duty of submission to a benefactor exist in a grown child? Is the duty by its nature simply moral, or both moral and jural? In other words, can it be obtained by force if denied?

563. The duty of submission towards a rescuer certainly

---

[160] By 'simple affections' I mean to indicate that special class of benevolent affections manifested naturally by means of the *real relationships* between natures. These affections are raised to the dignity of *moral duties* because the moral law commands that the relationships between us and other natures be maintained. This precept concerns the 'respect merited by the nature of things generally and by the intrinsic order of nature'; it does not concern 'the respect merited by some particular being'. To see the truth of this, let us suppose that someone returns hatred for his benefactor's love but hides the hatred and feigns love. In addition, he lavishes every care on the hated person for secondary reasons of self-interest. He sins, even though the hatred in his heart does no external harm to his benefactor, who is ignorant of the hatred and believes his own love is reciprocated. Hence, the duty of gratitude does not have its source in the author of a kind act. Rather there is in the nature of things a real relationship between hearts and intelligent wills, a relationship which we cannot violate if we respect nature, that is, being and its order. Reflections such as these should, it seems to me, occupy the minds of writers on ethics so that they can separate into distinct classes duties imposed by the 'intrinsic order of things in general' and duties imposed by the 'exigencies of particular beings'.

[161] On gratitude cf. *PE*, 200-205.

remains in the grown child (and in every human being saved from death). The reason is as follows.

564. In the natural fact and relationship between *person* and *human nature*, person takes possession of and has seigniory over the human nature. Person begins to do this naturally, as soon as the human being exists, because the will immediately begins to act and command the other powers. But in order to do all this, both person and the nature to be dominated by person must exist. Person, in the exercise of its domination, depends on the one from whom both it and the human being (of which person is the noblest part) have existence.

Hence, if we accept that the one who takes in a baby has saved it from certain death (which is the case when abandoned babies are taken into someone's home), there is no doubt that the child must *acknowledge* at the first possible moment that the full exercise of his freedom depends upon the one who saved him from destruction. He must attribute this exercise of freedom to his new father.

565. It may be urged that morality required the benefactor to save the baby. This however is a requirement of charity, not justice; a passer-by who ignored the abandoned baby would not deprive it of anything, nor would the baby consequently be able to demand back anything of its own; it would die through natural deficiencies, not because the passer-by had taken its life. The act therefore, by which the baby was taken in, pertains entirely to the beneficence and jural freedom of the compassionate passer-by.

566. I mention *beneficence*, because this requires *gratitude* from the child, and *jural freedom*, because this is a cause of rights and requires *submission* from the child.

The benefactor could certainly have saved the baby for himself, for his own advantage (provided the moral dignity of the child's person is safeguarded); he was saving something that belonged to no one and would have perished. He took possession of it without harm to anyone, just as we might retrieve from a river a piece of wood which would otherwise be lost in the sea: the wood belongs to the one who retrieves it because it has already perished relative to the owner who does not retrieve it. The benefactor therefore becomes the master of the baby, provided personal dignity is safeguarded.

567. This teaching is confirmed by the unanimous witness of antiquity and the laws of all peoples. If these laws seem to offend in the dispositions they lay down for the case in question, their offence consists in requiring an excessive submission of the fostered child. This submission was viewed as necessary for the public good, but it exceeded the limit prescribed by rational Right.

568. We then asked whether the dominion acquired in this way ceased when the child attained the use of reflection and of the freedom corresponding to reflection. We wanted to know whether at such a time the duty of submission, which clearly still subsisted, was a moral duty lacking a jural quality or also a jural duty with its corresponding right.

569. Our opinion on the matter will be clear if we separate the following two cases: 1. If the adult child spontaneously lives in submission to the will of the father who has chosen him, he does a virtuous, honest act. His father does not injure his rights when he reasonably exercises the authority to which the adult child warmly and unresistingly consents.

570. 2. If the adult child lacks full dominion of himself and consequently is to this extent something of a child, he remains subject in this regard and has a jural duty. The father who chose him retains dominion of that part of freedom which is inactive in him.

571. Let us look more closely at this second case. It is based on the fact that human beings acquire power over themselves gradually and more or less rapidly. This is characteristic not only of individuals but of nations, which as a result modify in various ways Right relative to *patria potestas*. Both natural and fostered children obtain their freedom in accordance with the development of their individual freedom.

572. Hence, among primitive peoples and among the present poorly developed peoples of Asia it was and is very easy to retain *patria potestas* in its full vigour and even make it hereditary, establishing great families which later become tribes. The explanation is that individual, reflective freedom does not come fully into act; a part of it remains dormant, as it were, and is not easily taken possession of by individuals.

573. In the fact we must therefore distinguish the principle from its application.

574. The *general* principle is: 'No human being, by occupancy

alone and without permission, can acquire dominion over another who has taken possession of himself.'

575. The *application* depends on the accurate determination of the factual condition applied to the principle, as follows: 'Has the person taken actual possession of himself or not?'

576. Because the fact varies, the decision varies for each particular case. Consequently, at a definite age in a particular people and family, the hypothetical father can both have and exercise, according to rational Right, a degree of dominion over an adult he has brought up. But another father cannot do this in a different age, people and family without harm to the individual over whom he exercises the dominion.[162]

577. This shows us the futility of those abstract theories of rational Right which apply general principles to all cases without distinction. Such theories pay no heed whatsoever to different factual conditions; their authors are persuaded, for example, that they can decide 'what kind of power the father has or has not in general over his child'. They risk condemning without further investigation any laws which attribute to him either more or less than the exact amount of power they are pleased to assign him. On the contrary, the variety of laws enacted by different peoples on these and similar matters clearly demonstrates that common sense, which is more reliable than the remote speculations of philosophers, easily sees how such disputes have many solutions, all of which are accurate and decided by the application of a unique *principle* to multiple, various *facts*.

578. The adult therefore is naturally free from *patria potestas* to the extent he has acquired dominion over himself. Otherwise he is subject to *patria potestas*.

579. It is however difficult to decide where the division is to be made, and what rule can be applied in order to separate *patria potestas* from seigniory over oneself. Nevertheless a sufficient rule can be deduced from the very principle from which I have drawn the notion of right.

580. We said that right arises from the moral duty imposed on us to do no harm to a person. When this duty is applied to

---

[162] This is another example of the different *modes* which the same *specific right* can take. We spoke about this in *ER*, 83 ss.

natural ownership, the ownership becomes the condition of right. *Natural ownership* is a union between a thing and a person, founded in their nature and real relationship. If we disrupt this union we injure the person concerned. Precisely because *duty* forbids evil being done to him, his *right* is harmed when he is subjected to the evil of disruption. Therefore, whenever we regulate a thing or exercise some authority over a person without causing him any normal harm, we do not injure his right.

Hence, the general rule for knowing which part of authority the father can exercise over the person whom he chose and has cared for is: 'He can exercise that amount of authority over him which does not cause him any natural upset.'

581. The most general symptom for knowing whether an act of authority causes upset or not, is JURAL RESENTMENT, that is, the resentment we show when we are persuaded of some offence to our rights.

582. Not all resentment is of this kind. Sometimes a child is sad because he does not like what he has been commanded. This is not resentment, and certainly not jural resentment, which is present only when 'a person suffers because his freedom has been obstructed'.

583. I say 'the most general symptom' because the symptom is not always visible when right is violated.

584. Sometimes it is invisible because of extraordinary virtue. Some very virtuous people happily submit to the unjust and brutish exercise of authority.

585. Nevertheless, generous people such as these suffer some *natural upset*, which is always caused by violated right. Their virtue consists in their not defending themselves and not seeking reparation. Solely for love of their fellows, for whom those who are truly free often sacrifice their own cause, they even suppress the resentment that demands reparation. .

586. The fact that there are people who resent authority because they lack control of their passions and do not have real dominion of themselves is not a source of objection. If they really need to be directed and governed, and are totally incapable of governing themselves, they cannot have a right to freedom. In this case the symptom of resentment is false.

587. But objections of this kind show that our theory and what we said about the jural possession human beings take of themselves has been misunderstood.

588. *Jural* possession and dominion over self is different from the *moral* possession and dominion over self which is described by moralists as an effect and characteristic of virtue.

589. *Jural* dominion is simply a faculty, a dominion in potency, by which human beings themselves know and desire to be free to do as they please; this is *jural freedom*, which pertains to bilateral freedom. *Moral* dominion is a virtuous habit, a dominion in act, exercised habitually by a good will over the lower faculties; it is what I call 'freedom of intelligence'.[163]

Whenever we wish to be free to do what we like, we do neither good nor evil. This faculty, which we claim for ourselves, cannot be impeded or taken from us unless we have partly alienated it or contracted jural obligations which limit it. To do the opposite would be an offence to our natural right. However, our right would not be offended if we were restrained from doing acts which abuse our power.

590. It may be objected that it is precisely the wicked with their great abuse of freedom who are quick to claim the use of their freedom. As I have said it is certainly true that to persuade a person to give into another for love of peace is an act of the highest virtue. This is equally true when we encourage submission as a result of diffidence towards oneself and the renunciation of one's rights for another's good. It is also certain that the wicked person demands his right at the point of the sword, so to speak, because he is ignorant of such a generous feeling. But this is not a reason for denying him the existence of his right. If we did, we would in this case be unjust towards him, placing him in the right and ourselves in the wrong.

591. But, it may be objected again, he is asking for what he is going to abuse. — Let us wait for the abuse to take place first, and then we shall be justified in taking steps to suppress it with the force our right permits. The freedom he demands, which can be turned to both good and bad, is not something evil in itself.

---

[163] Cf. *AMS*, 603-611.

[587–591]

Our only guard against the abuse of such freedom is to exercise virtue and make people good. This is what enables them to use their rights well and to be more generous with their rights, preferring to give rather than exact what right demands. This is the sole, legitimate means of opposing any feared, but as yet unactivated abuse of freedom on the part of others. We assume that the abuse has either not begun or has not been previously revealed by its perpetrator. As far as I can see, rational Right does not, generally speaking, permit any other preventative means. But once the abuse has begun or been declared, the means used against it acquire by that fact alone the nature of repressive means.

592. There is one extraordinary consequence of all this: 'The jural freedom of a person not bound by any agreement is as great as the person desires (note, we are speaking about *freedom*, not *licence*, about something good in itself, not about its abuse).' Therefore: 'Rational Right prescribes that individuals or peoples who claim greater freedom should gradually be granted it.' Retaining constantly an unaltered portion of power over people is contrary to Right itself. Power is not apportioned like a piece of land whose owner holds it within fixed boundaries that cannot be altered without harm to the owner.

593. Judgment about dominion over human beings has up to this point been made as though it were the same as dominion over a piece of land: once dominion has been obtained, it is, according to this opinion, an ownership with unchangeable limits; anyone trying to restrict these limits would be committing rebellion.

594. This is an illusion, a consequence of not bearing in mind the immense difference between ownership of an irrational object and ownership of a rational object. Ownership of an irrational object always retains the same limit because an irrational object can never possess itself; it is passive to others' right. On the other hand, ownership of a rational object changes because the object in this case possesses itself, is the first occupier of itself and can only be possessed to the extent that it has not taken possession of itself, which it does gradually. This is the extent to which it can be possessed provisionally by another as long as the real master does not use what is his

own. In this case, others can use it without harming or upsetting him.[164]

595. This teaching is the key to understanding political revolutions, and explains all the various forms of government.

596. Power and people follow different systems of Right. The former holds to a system that fixes an unchanging limit to dominion, as it does to material ownership. The latter, guided by a certain intimate sense of human nature, follows in practice the opposite system. The former is the opinion of erudite philosophy and of lawyers; the latter, the manifestation of the consciousness of humanity. The result is a great conflict between theory and practice.

Our teaching, however, brings about the reconciliation of both, and lays down a firm foundation for peace in the world.

597. We can confirm our teaching by another observation. Frequently a person saves another's life by rescuing him from a fire or from drowning. This, however, does not give the rescuer any right over the person he has saved. On the other hand, anyone who saves a baby and rears it as his child believes he has acquired a certain right of authority over it.

The difference between the two cases is obvious. Saving someone from death is not in itself taking possession of the person; it is an act of kindness. But taking in a child to care for it and make it of service to oneself is to take possession of it and make use of the faculties and powers which the child cannot yet use.

598. In the first case there is clearly no possession for the following reasons:

First, the rescuer is totally intent on the rescue and finds great satisfaction in doing it; he is not thinking about his own interest. The intention of making use of the rescued person for his own advantage is absent.

Second, even if this intention were present, it would not be sufficient for taking possession. The individual would not be

---

[164] All civil codes suppose that the natural dominion of one human being over another has a changeable limit. We can see this clearly in the regulations governing *patria potestas*. These increase, decrease and terminate relative to the offspring's degree of need, or varying ability to govern himself. The same must be said about the regulations concerning husbands, teachers, guardians and all those who in fact exercise power over their fellows.

occupiable unless he were an abandoned child or insane, in other words a person lacking jural government of himself. Only in this case could the rescuer take him in and keep him as something of his own.

Human beings, therefore, in their behaviour towards an adult saved from death or a baby given a home, show total agreement with what we have said.

§3. *The moral-jural duty of restitution*

599. The benefactor can require from the emancipated child restitution for the expenses necessarily incurred for the child's advantage.[165]

600. He can require this restitution not only from the adult child but also from anyone whom he may have saved from death at the cost of loss to himself.

601. A person who has been rescued and a foster- child have this sole jural duty, the credit of which can consequently be exacted even with force.

602. Some questions now present themselves, and it will be helpful to pass comment on them.

First Question. An adult may prefer not to receive aid rather than incur the obligation of repaying expenses; either he does not see the gravity of his danger and hopes to extricate himself without any cost, or he may resist for some other reason. This kind of reluctance to receive help is impossible for a baby, but it can show itself when the child has become adult. According to rational Right, therefore, can someone be saved who refuses to be saved? And if he is saved, is he bound to compensate the losses necessarily sustained by the rescuer?

603. The first question is contained in a more general question: 'Can good be done to someone against their will?' The reply is very extensive in its application.

---

[165] This right was recognised in the most distant past. Among the Thebans, children of fathers unable to care for them were consigned by the magistrate to citizens who looked after them on condition that when the child became adult it remained in the service of his guardians for a certain number of years as compensation for the care received.

604. Authors who hold to strict right unhesitatingly say 'No'. But we must note that if the question is resolved by a cold, absolute negative, it follows that a great number of regulations of civil law, enforced without or contrary to the assent of the individuals to whom they refer, violate rational Right. If helping someone against his will were absolutely an infringement of his right, the good obtained would also be unjust, when done both by one individual against another, and by a society against an individual.

605. This alone must give rise to a persuasion in favour of the opinion that doing good to someone against his will is not an injury.

606. This is really a corollary of the third characteristic of right[166] which requires a good as the object of right if a right is to exist. Thus, anyone who refuses a good acts outside the sphere of right because the action does not have good for its object; a right to evil or to refuse good does not exist. Resistance to this kind of unjust will cannot therefore be injurious to anyone.

607. This opinion however can be clarified by dividing it into parts based on some necessary distinctions.

First, we must distinguish the abstract question, 'Can good be done to someone against their will?', from the concrete question, 'Is it true that in any particular case I am really doing good to the person who refuses the help offered?'

608. The solution of the first, abstract question is much easier than that of the second, concrete question; the first is not accompanied by the many different circumstances of the second. Concrete questions must be solved by considering all the factual and frequently accidental circumstances surrounding them.

609. Moreover, the difficulty in solving the last question increases with the need to solve another question first: 'Who is competent to judge what is good or bad for a person?'

610. If we begin with this question and consider rational Right alone, I have to say that 'the person for whom these things are considered good or bad is the competent judge.'

611. We must note however that the *competence* of the

166 Cf. *ER*, 252-255.

judgment does not free the judge from the obligation of pronouncing a just sentence. *Competence* is too often confused with *justice*; too often we suppose that a competent judge can pronounce as he likes, and that everyone must submit fully to his sentence, from which there is no appeal. On the contrary, I maintain an appeal is always possible provided that it is made to truth and justice whose tribunal has an unprescribable right to overrule the contrary sentences of every other tribunal.

612. The only usefulness I attribute to the tribunal of first competence is that whenever there is doubt, its sentence should prevail, that is, whenever there is no clear evidence that the tribunal is mistaken — but with one limitation: the doubt (which remains independently of the decision of the competent tribunal) must not expose me to the danger of doing something intrinsically evil. In this case we have to hold to the safe course which ensures us that we are not sinning.[167]

613. In our case therefore madness, idiocy, sudden rage and unusual, confirmed criminality can be clear and sufficient indications of the falsity and error of another person's judgment. In these circumstances, not even a competent judge can pass an authoritative sentence.

614. Consequently, it is clear that without doing any harm whatsoever I can prevent someone attempting suicide, even if my effort is against his will and seen as harmful. I can hide food and drink from a drunkard, even though it is his property, when he is looking for it in his drunken state. I can do any obviously helpful action to someone who is wrongfully refusing my help. The refusal itself is proof that the person is mentally ill and unable to judge.

615. There are undoubtedly cases where the maxim of doing good to others and preventing evil is verified in practice not only without, but against the other's will. It is in fact a kindness, not harm.

616. To the second question, 'Does the benefactor have the right to restitution of the loss sustained in rendering assistance?', the answer is clearly 'Yes'. This is true at least if the

---

[167] Cf. what I have said regarding this last clause in *CS*, 471-654.

recipient of the kindness has in fact benefited, that is, has received more than is claimed from him by title of restitution.

617. This reply is based on the very nature of personal possession. Anyone who has helped another and lost something essential, for example, life, education, etc., could willingly either donate or lend what is his in order to procure the same good for the other. If it was his intention to lend it, he is still beneficent to the one to whom he lent it, because he had no jural obligation to make the loan. Thus, if he obtained for the other a good equivalent to 100% and lost only 10%, he could take the 10% back leaving the 90% to the advantage of the benefited person.

This is clear, because a person who is not obliged to give anything of what is his, is free if he wishes to give 90% rather than 100% — it is within his jural freedom to determine the quantity of his beneficence.

The benefactor therefore can take from the beneficiary sufficient to repair the loss he has suffered. But it is also clear that the beneficiary has a jural obligation to make this restitution.

618. *Second question.* How must this restitution be made? Can the benefactor retain authority over the beneficiary until the latter through his own efforts has made restitution for the losses necessarily sustained on his behalf?

619. The question can refer to both true and foster fathers. The rights of true fathers over their children will be discussed in the next chapter. Here I will speak only about those previously mentioned who simply foster a child, and about benefactors generally.

620. If we are considering the nature of ownership purely as ownership and not as right,[168] we have a case of *res clamat ad dominum* [a thing calls for its master] interpreted so strictly that neither extension of time nor any respect for the debtor is allowed; the owner is justified in claiming his possessions with all expedition and in the way he wants. But the case is different when natural ownership assumes the noble quality of right. We must always bear in mind that right is moral, in itself and in its exercise. Its exercise is entirely hedged about with moral

---

[168] For the difference cf. 895 ss.

obligations, which certainly require us to safeguard ownership, but in the way least harmful to others.

621. Granted this, the creditor, in virtue of his right, can claim:

1. To be paid *in full,*

2. To be paid *promptly,* although allowing reasonable extension of time for the debtor in difficulty. If the extension causes any harm to the creditor, the harm must be compensated.

3. To be assured that the extension he grants does not make the payment of the debt less certain.

All three rights concern the creditor relative to the debtor.

622. The first right is clear in itself; it needs no discussion.

623. The second presents a very difficult and delicate question: 'What *extension of time* must the creditor grant by natural Right to the debtor so that the latter can pay?'

624. First of all, it is clear that if the debtor is able to pay, the creditor has the right to be paid at once.

625. But if the debtor lacks the means of payment (for example, a child taken in care) what time must be allowed for payment? No Right exists, of course, to require that the debtor pay what he does not have.

626. The answer must be: 'The time is to be at least as long as is needed for the debtor to obtain sufficient with the use of his faculties to pay the debt while allowing for his support.'

627. But there are different ways in which he can work to obtain the amount necessary to pay the debt. Can the creditor require that the debtor choose the work which will allow him to scrape together as quickly as possible what he owes?

628. He must certainly apply himself expeditiously to satisfying the debt, and to the upmost of his ability.

629. Consequently, if he showed obvious, voluntary and serious negligence, the creditor could undoubtedly require him to do more.

630. He could suggest a more expedite way of earning money and require that the debtor use this way. The work however must not be too much of a burden, or harm the debtor's bodily health, or do any other serious harm. In other words, the creditor can only require the debtor to make an effort compatible with human nature and proportionate to his forces, and thus without detriment to self. Insisting to the detriment of the debtor would be an injury and violation of the debtor's right.

[621–630]

631. The *competent judge* for deciding whether some particular task is beyond the natural forces of the debtor, is the individual who must perform the task. The same person is also the competent judge for deciding which among the tasks proportionate to his natural forces is more profitable and better suits him, with due regard for his natural inclination which is an indication of stability and an augur of success.

632. The only appeal open to the creditor against these judgments is that which everyone has against an unjust sentence of a competent judge, which we discussed above (cf. 611-612).

633. Hence, we see why it is unlawful for the creditor to confine the debtor and keep him in his employ against his will. This can be done only when the debtor shows by words and facts that he is unwilling to pay, in which case the creditor has the right to use force to obtain satisfaction.

634. But does he have the right to be firmly assured of his credit? And how can he have sufficient guarantee if he leaves his debtor free? In the natural state, and if we exempt the case where the debtor is guilty of bad will, the right of a guarantee for the creditor extends only to a guarantee that does not harm the debtor.

635. If the debtor cannot provide a guarantee without suffering harm, the creditor must be satisfied with his word.

636. The creditor would therefore be committing an injustice if he claimed to keep the debtor in prison or in his employment until he had worked off what was due. Such employment would be detrimental to the debtor, retarding his free development and harming the plans he might have or make for the future. Thus, although the jural duty to the creditor of a debtor who is unable to pay is to apply himself as best he can to earning what is owed, this duty does not require him to bow to the work imposed by the creditor, except by agreement. The creditor's right extends no further than this. The debtor's clearly expressed will to fulfil this duty must be sufficient pledge for the creditor, who has no cause for thinking his fellow human being lies. But if he does discover that the debtor is lying, he has a new right, the right of guarantee owed by bad debtors, and generally speaking, by offenders. I will speak about this right later.

Article 6
At what stage, according to rational right,
must a child be left in his own power?

637. No definite year or time can be assigned for this stage, because children attain possession of their jural freedom at varying rates.

638. JURAL RESENTMENT, the only natural *symptom* telling us when a child has reached this moment has already been discussed. This is not the resentment a wayward child manifests against good discipline and against the order of life imposed upon him, nor his opposition to what he is commanded; it is the uncomfortable feeling he experiences relative to the command, as if the command were some kind of superfluous intimation. This kind of reaction must have its origin in the internal consciousness of his own ability to act reasonably and properly.[169]

639. Jural resentment, felt by people held in subjection and experienced naturally when subjection is no longer needed, can be overridden or mitigated by solid moral virtue. In this case they willingly honour their benefactors with their spontaneous subjection, and thus by following the benefactors' guidance, better assure the uprightness of their own behaviour. Here the only indication that they have taken or can take possession of self is wisdom in thought and actions.

640. I say 'when they have taken or can take possession of self' because taking possession must be carefully distinguished from simply being able to take possession.

641. Simply to be able to take possession of self, we need know only the beneficial and harmful consequences to ourselves.

642. But to take possession of self in reality we need an act of will: we must will to act of ourselves and apply the foresight we have already acquired to the effects of everything we will do.

643. Hence, those who are mentally sound and fully developed and know as well as others the consequences of their

---

[169] This ability to act reasonably pertains to *prudence*, not to *morals*, as we have observed. Wayward people abuse their jural freedom, but we cannot say they lack it. They do not lack the rational power but the will to do good. They can be restrained from the misuse of their right but not deprived of the right itself.

actions may, because of their goodness, remain subject to father or benefactor. Nevertheless, although they have not yet really taken possession of themselves, they may do so whenever they will.

644. However, we want to know the age at which human beings *can* take possession of self, whether they do so or not, because the choice is entirely theirs.

When can they do this and claim to be allowed to do it?

645. First of all, it is clear that we cannot determine exactly the time when we know the consequences of our actions, as we have said. This knowledge does not occur at a given hour of the day; on the contrary it comes about slowly and gradually.

646. Human beings begin as babies to calculate the consequences of their actions: even in old age they never complete their study, which is so vast that it exceeds all human forces.

647. If the knowledge we require of the consequences of our actions is restricted simply to the knowledge attained by the majority of us after adolescence, we have *ipso facto* determined the degree of knowledge recognised by civil laws when they prohibit or allow the free exercise of our civilian rights; they either provide for the care and protection of those who seem to lack the ordinary degree of foresight or they free from care and subjection those who seem endowed with foresight.

648. But civil legislators recognise a gradation even in this measure of knowledge of the consequences of our actions. Thus the knowledge necessary for us to be civilly declared capable of acting in our own right is acquired only little by little. Legislators command that people be gradually admitted to the exercise of their civil rights.

649. For this reason the best known civil codes distinguish three kinds of human beings, who through lack of age are deprived of the full exercise of their rights: *babies*, who are denied all exercise of their civil rights; *children who have not reached puberty*, who are granted only a part; and *minors*, to whom a greater part is granted but not the whole.[170]

---

[170] In the Austrian code, *babies, children who have not reached puberty* and *minors* are those who have completed their 7th, 14th and 24th year respectively (§21). According to this code, *patria potestas* ceases with minority at the end of the 24th year (§172). Nevertheless the code allows

650. According to many positive laws, majority is reached when the human being is fully emancipated from *patria potestas*, if nothing else intervenes. But what is the age of majority?

651. We cannot establish it for all times, or for all peoples, or for everyone[171] at the same time in the same nation — I repeat, a fixed year or moment in nature does not exist in this matter.

652. Nevertheless civil legislators have to fix an age, and they do so by choosing the moment when a particular year of life ends and another begins. Which year therefore can be determined for everyone alike?

653. Because human beings reach the age of majority at different times, legislators must take an average year which they establish for everybody. This necessarily means that those who

---

that *patria potestas* may need to continue (§173), and also that the child can be emancipated earlier (§174). Other codes fix different stages in addition to the three mentioned above. According to the Albertine code, the child always remains under *patria potestas* except when there is fault on the part of the father or inability to exercise his authority (in which case the court decides emancipation, §239), or when the father himself gives the child his freedom by tacit or express consent. The child's age is fixed at 18 years (when a minor can be enabled to administer his goods, §353-366), for the validity of the father's consent through the child's acceptance of it (§238). The father's tacit consent however has effect only when the child has passed the age of majority by 5 years, that is, has completed his 26th year (§242). According to the Albertine code, *patria potestas*, which never ceases of itself while the father is alive, decreases in its acts and becomes more expansive as the child grows older. The code's authors recognise that the father's right to punish changes with the child's age, and determine two ages for these changes: the 16th (§215) and the 25th year (§116). The 16th year is also laid down as the age for the exercise of the right to make a will (§701): completion of the 25th year for the exercise of the right to leave the paternal home (§213). This right however can be anticipated (§212) or postponed (§213) by a court ruling. The Albertine code also fixes the 30th year for the restriction of *patria potestas*; after this, the father's right of usufruct of the goods coming to the child under his authority (§224) ceases. But if the child should marry, usufruct ceases on completion of the 25th year in the case of males, and of the 21st year for females (§225).

The code of the Canton of Ticino makes *patria potestas* cease: of itself, at the child's 25th year (§104); with the father's express consent, at the 18th (§105), and with the father's tacit consent, on completion of the 20th (§106), which is the age of majority for the child.

[171] This is another example of the different *modes* which can be taken by the same right according to circumstances. Cf. *ER*, 80 ss.

[650–653]

attain the required level before that moment must wait to be emancipated; those who have not attained the required level at that moment are considered to be in possession of self, although this is not actually the case.

654. How do the legislators calculate and determine this average year?

655. They cannot all agree because they have to calculate an average, and this can only be obtained by approximation or estimate.

656. Thus, Roman laws required the completion of the 25th year for legal majority. The Austrian code requires completion of the 24th year. The French code, and those that follow it, are satisfied with the 21st year. The Constitutions of 1770 of the king of Sardinia, and the present code of the Canton of Ticino, reduce the age of majority to the completion of the 20th year. These differences of opinion indicate that in the view of modern legislators people today generally speaking take possession of self somewhat earlier than those considered by the ancient legislators.[172]

657. But let us leave aside positive regulations; we have mentioned them solely for the purpose of knowing the kind of rational Right which secretly guided the minds of legislators. It was indeed this right which dictated positive laws, and the founders of these laws have, in my view, great authority. Instead, we shall see what nature itself has to say about the age when human beings can terminate their subjection to others, and when dominion over those held in possession ceases to be just.

658. We shall return to the example we have already used, continuing the comparison between the possession of an irrational thing and that of a human individual at the infant stage. These can be likened to two vases owned by the same person, one of them full of money, the other filled with a spirituous liquid. When the owner comes to inspect them, he finds the first still full but the second empty, not because its contents have

---

[172] The Albertine code, following the French, makes the completion of the 21st year the age of majority, but the preceding legislation of the royal constitutions fixed it for the 20th year. This seems to be an anomaly of the law of human progress, which evidently requires that the development of the human person (within certain limits) should accelerate.

been stolen but because they have evaporated. It is the same with the two things under discussion: material things are stably possessed, but the human person (a spiritual nature), which does not allow itself to be possessed permanently, escapes all unseen from the possessor. The person is not snatched away. What is possessed removes itself by the use of what nature has given it; like the spirituous liquid it disappears little by little — and the owner cannot complain.

659. Anyone who considers this teaching will see that it has important, useful corollaries.

660. First of all, it takes for granted the great principle that the quantity of right (that is, jural freedom) is equal to the amount of knowledge we have of the *consequences of our actions*.[173]

661. This principle is admitted and supposed by all civil legislations,[174] when it is applied to human beings coherently and courageously (courage is always necessary for one who wishes to be coherent). Our first conclusion therefore is that, absolutely speaking, no one has full and absolute jural freedom. None of us can claim to know all the consequences of our actions — only God sees human actions with their whole infinite series of consequences.

662. Relative to God, therefore, we are by nature minors; jural freedom is not proper to us.

663. This explains the supreme gospel precept which imposes 'not our own, but the divine will' as the necessary rule of our actions. Thus Christ, the archetype of human perfection come down from heaven, declares, 'I have come down from heaven, not to do my own will, but the will of him who sent me.'[175] Will, freedom, right do not exist in us relative to God; God alone is free and lord because he alone is wise.

---

[173] Knowing the consequences of our actions is the same as knowing good and evil. Right exists only when its object is a good (the third constitutive element of right). Thus anyone who is able to judge more accurately what is good has a greater extension of rights and a wider sphere in which to exercise the moral faculty called right which he possesses .

[174] For example, Austrian legislation defines people who are under the special protection of the law as those who 'cannot know the consequences of their actions' (Civil Code, §21).

[175] Jn 6: [38].

664. Consequently all the jural freedom we have in respect of other human beings is a relative freedom.

665. According to natural right, human beings are mutually free only in so far as we have an approximately equal amount of knowledge and of foresight of the consequences of our actions, or at least in so far as we must *presume* this equality of knowledge of consequences in each other (unless the opposite is evident). We cannot judge, without reasonable evidence, that someone has less knowledge of the consequences of his actions than we have; we all have the same human nature and can competently judge what is helpful or harmful to self.

666. We can say with complete certainty that only the supreme Being, who knows all the consequences of every action, can decide who among us comes closest to a correct judgment of the totality and result of the consequences, and who is most mistaken in that judgment.

667. Generally speaking therefore we must judge that we all have equal knowledge of the consequences of our actions. This presumption is a foundation of civil law for all those considered capable of every act of civil life.

668. Laws are not based on the supposition that people have full knowledge of the consequences, but solely on the supposition and presumption that they have an equal amount of knowledge. This *equal amount of knowledge of the consequences of our actions* becomes therefore the basis of the civil-juridical equality of human beings.[176]

669. But the equality of knowledge of the consequences of our

---

[176] The amount of knowledge which civil laws require and suppose to be equal in all human beings is expressed by the phrase 'common sense'. This amount of knowledge and use of intelligence is generally sufficient to enable us to judge the *immediate* or *quasi-immediate effects* of our actions and so either avoid any direct harm caused by them or directly profit from them. All this is necessary in order that we can *sufficiently* maintain our individual self, our freedom, family and external property, and acquire what is necessary for our own and our family's preservation. Many people, however, are incapable of calculating this maintenance and preservation beyond the immediate or quasi-immediate effects of their actions. It often happens therefore that they are subject to misfortunes resulting from remote, unforeseen effects of their own behaviour (which explains the origin of the working class and the poor). Civil laws have not yet cast their sights so far ahead but the time will certainly come when they will do so.

actions cannot always be supposed, because the supposition ceases in the face of the obvious truth, just as the authority of a competent judge ceases in the face of obvious justice.

670. Supposition of this equality ceases therefore as soon as certain proof shows that someone cannot rightly use his reason.

671. Hence civil laws make an exception to the rule for minors, the mentally incapable, the insane and even for wastrels.

672. Furthermore, civil Right cannot take account of all the levels present in reality in natural Right concerning the proofs which indicate different amounts of knowledge of the consequences of one's actions in different individuals.

673. The laws must therefore be restricted to determining the more obvious levels, and neglect innumerable others which, even if determinable, would multiply the positive regulations *ad infinitum* and make their application very difficult.

674. Civil Right is also limited, as we have seen, by the necessity of determining an age when everybody is considered as having attained the full exercise of their rights. This age is non-existent in nature, because human beings do not attain the same level of knowledge simultaneously. We will see later if the civil legislator can fix this age for everyone without offending natural Right.

675. For the present we can conclude as follows: 1. A child takes possession of self little by little as it grows older. Consequently natural Right requires the foster-father to gradually allow the child more freedom in using its powers, especially if the child itself wants its freedom.

676. 2. Full freedom can be due to the child before or after the age of majority; in certain cases it is never due.

677. 3. Respect for old age and a certain dependence of the young on their elders (dutifully acknowledged throughout the centuries and by all peoples) has its foundation in natural Right, and thus acquires a jural characteristic. Natural Right requires that the extent of the exercise of each person's freedom must be relative and proportionate to the level of knowledge each has of the *consequences of his actions*. It is clear therefore that generally speaking the experience acquired by older people in their long life gives them a greater degree of foresight and consequently a greater right to exercise their freedom, because they have a wider sphere for exercising it. This means that in every younger

person a corresponding limitation of the exercise exists and that younger people are to some extent dependent on and subject to their elders.

678. This is one of the reasons for the ancient authority of the first-born over the other members of the family after the death of the father, and for their precedence at home even during the lifetime of the parents.

679. 4. For the same reason the superiority of the more intelligent, perspicacious and prudent over the less intellectually gifted (verified in all nations and recognised as good) must not be considered unjust but in conformity with natural Right which, relative to all the consequences of our own or others' unseen actions, requires us to submit to and allow ourselves to be guided by those who see and weigh the consequences carefully, just as the blind must accept the guidance of the sighted, or a ward accept the care of society. Viceversa, those who can weigh remote consequences have the right to choose the results of their reasonings in preference to the results of persons who can only weigh proximate consequences. A prudent person, *certain* that another is mistaken about the final good or evil, can oblige the other to act in such a way that no harm is done through inexperience or shortsightedness.

680. 5. When the principles themselves are applied to relationships between nations, which are social bodies in the state of nature, one nation can justly exercise authority over and influence another, and up to a certain point can subjugate the other, provided the results are good, or at least not harmful, to the subjugated nation. In the same way, a nation can claim from another what is helpful to the latter or at least not harmful, and is helpful or at least not harmful to the claimant. Consequently the fact, repeated on every page of history and read every day in the media, that nations which are Christian, moral and civil lord it over infidel and barbaric nations must not be ascribed indiscriminately to usurpations by force and gain by cunning. On the contrary the fact, considered globally and not always in its accidents, is a natural effect of a Right not discussed by philosophers but fully and clearly manifested in intelligent creatures whom it guides with a hidden and powerful influence [*App.*, no. 2].

681. Although all these teachings (denied, as to be expected,

only by philosophers) find irrefutable support in human consciousness, their application is clearly very difficult.

682. Because they are defined not as mere moral duties but as jural obligations obtainable by force, an educator or a elder or someone of great insight could forcefully bind a pupil, a junior or someone of limited vision to a certain degree of subjection, relative however only to certain acts dependent on age and particular circumstances. But it is impossible for us to define in practice the degree of this subjection and relative authority; it varies almost each day and hour according to different intellectual states. We have no rule for determining this degree of servitude.

683. On the other hand, even if the degree of servitude and that of seigniory were indefinable in the state of nature, the principles of justice established above would still remain true. Although the application of these principles may be very difficult, they are true and right, and must be accepted with all their difficulties. The difficulties are an indication of human limitation, not an argument against the truth and rightness of the principles. Anything found in nature as a fact or inscribed on our reason as a necessity and a law of the world of ideas cannot be rejected on the pretext that it is too difficult for us to use. With such limited, feeble vision we cannot be so reckless and insane as to persuade ourselves we are able to change external things and alter the principles of reason. Yet we vaunt our irrational recklessness precisely at the moment our consciousness reminds us deep down of our own nothingness. I feel compelled to speak like this because of the very frequent objections we hear against the truth, and against virtue: the truth is difficult and impossible, it cannot be applied, it harms. Prudence, it would seem, requires us to hide the truth and not speak about it because, when taught, it can be misunderstood! No thanks are due to the light of this century as it grows dim under the influence of such hesitant and dismal human prudence.

684. But let us move on and investigate whether, in the cases discussed above, it is really impossible to know when force can be applied without offending another's right. Determining this 'when' must be a very noble and important investigation despite the great effort it demands. To indicate even a few points which

make the way more secure for others will be no mean achievement.

685. I have given two indications which show when a person has taken possession of self.

1. The first consists in proofs of intelligence and wisdom which show us whether the person is as aware of the consequences of the action or actions in question as the person to whom he is subject.

686. If so, we can see that the person, relative to the particular action or actions (we need not speak about all actions, because we want to determine the successive levels, not the totality, of his emancipation), is capable of governing himself and has the right to do so.

2. The other indication is the *jural resentment* manifested against acts of subjection.

687. This shows us that the person has not only the right to govern himself but has in fact taken possession of self, wishes to exercise self-government, and renounces nothing of that which comes to him by right.

688. The following maxims result from these two indications: 1. If a person is content to be subject to another without resentment or displeasure, it means 1st. that he has not yet attained the usual ability to govern himself or 2nd. is not conscious of it. It can also mean 3rd. that he feels his own ability to govern himself is overridden by the wisdom of the one governing him so that he willingly remains subject for his own utility or 4th. that out of a feeling of justice or generosity he cedes the government of self in the things prescribed him by placing acts of gratitude and love before the exercise of his own rights, that is, of those rights which he can forego.[177]

689. 2. In the first case, where the subject has not yet obtained the ordinary ability to foresee the consequences of his actions relative to the actions in question, the superior can certainly maintain his authority.

690. 3. In the second case, where the subject has the ability to govern himself but is not conscious of this or does not think

---

[177] A person might have no interest in governing himself through laziness or cowardice, or timidity of spirit. This is another case in which he foregoes his right.

about it, the superior can maintain his authority without damage. But he must be convinced of his real ability to direct his subject relative to the actions in question or, better, be convinced that his subject would not do them so well or even do them at all. Only in these cases does his guidance do no harm.

691. If the superior did not do this, he would sin against *morality* and, if harm resulted to the subject, against *right*.

692. The obligation of restitution would still remain even if the subject did not require restitution or know that he had a right to restitution. We cannot and must not presume that a subject agrees to losses incurred of which he is ignorant. Nor can one person's waywardness ever be the source of harm to others' rights.

693. 4. The third case, in which the subject submits for his *own utility*, because he is persuaded that his superior will direct him better than he could himself, is solved in the same way as the second case (cf. 690-692).

694. 5. The fourth case, in which the subject really foregoes his own right because of affection and virtue, is also resolved in the same way as the second. If, however, the subject has greater wisdom and intelligence than the superior, the superior sins by retaining guidance of the subject, because he clearly knows he does harm to the subject by doing so. In this case, the sin would be moral not jural because of the subject's tacit renunciation of his right (cf. 134-138).

695. This should be the only comment possible in this final case because guidance here is in itself upright and, of course, in good faith. If, however, the harm resulting from the extension of the guidance beyond the required time were caused by the superior's wrongly wishing to draw profit for himself from his government of his subject, irrespective of harm to the subject, such a heartless deceit would require restitution and could always be resisted and punished.

696. In all these cases we have supposed that the person lives peacefully and quietly subject to the other's guidance. But let us now suppose that in all four cases the subject resists and wishes to rid himself of the yoke. When and how does the superior have the right to use force to keep him in subjection, and when must he grant him his freedom? — We are not speaking about universal freedom but freedom particular to one action, then to a few,

then to many, and gradually to all actions. As we have bserved,[178] every action is the object of a right and can itself be a separate case.

697. In the first case, where the person does not know even the proximate consequences of his actions and would do harm to himself by acting on his own, the superior can use force to make him obey if he resists, provided the obedience concerns an order of things which have the good of the subject for their purpose, or at least concerns something which in no way harms him.

In this case the individual's resistance is not *jural resentment* but displeasure at doing what is commanded because it is contrary to his feeling, instinct, habit and desire, not because he feels it as harming and obstructing his legitimate freedom.

698. The second and third cases concern a subject who has already attained knowledge of the consequences of his actions (which are generally calculated according to the utility or harm they might do) but is unaware of this knowledge or considers it inferior to his superior's. It is clear that if he withdraws himself from subjection, he is acting on what is false, not on a truly jural title. However the superior who is unable to verify the falsity of the title on which the subject bases his request because it lies concealed in his spirit must accede and allow the subject government over self. The superior is obliged to presume that the request is just in itself and justly thought out by the petitioner.

699. We would do well at this point to consider the rights generally arising from the relationship between one who has greater foresight and consequently is naturally superior and one who has less foresight and is therefore naturally inferior. These rights are present at nearly every moment of our lives and yet have not been observed and listed by philosophers. We must therefore ask some important questions about them.

700. First: can a person with greater foresight use this foresight, even with force, to avoid the harm he would experience by leaving his subject free to direct himself with less foresight? Can he do this if the subject, acting without malice or entering his sphere of ownership, has simply not foreseen an indirect, remote but inevitable consequence of his action?

[178] Cf. *ER*, 322-323.

The question supposes that the only harm done to the subject by the superior's use of force is to hinder the freedom claimed by the subject, who believes he has a right to his freedom or wishes to do as he pleases.

In my opinion the case as stated within these limits allows the superior, after counsel and exhortation have failed, to use force to constrain the subject to do or omit what does not harm himself and prevents harm to the superior. *Jural resentment* can certainly show itself here, but only because of the *mistaken* belief that one's rights are infringed.

701. In fact the problem is often settled as follows: older, senior people, and people of great perspicacity who frequently find themselves able to persuade or force others to do their will, use these means without scruple, persuaded that, if no harm results, they are not doing any injustice to anybody whatsoever. The royal Right of nations offers many similar examples.

The great problem of intervention or non-intervention can be fully resolved only by the application of the above principles.

702. Second: 'Under the same circumstances can force be used by someone whose purpose is not to avoid harm but to obtain some good for himself?'

703. We must reply 'No'. It is true that I can constrain others to forego activity whose consequences would be harmful to me, but it is not true that I can expect others to act advantageously in my regard when the consequences of some other activity are harmless to me and advantageous to them. Their only jural obligation is to avoid harming me; they are under no obligation to do me good.

704. Third: 'Can force be used under the same circumstances not to remove something harmful from oneself or obtain something advantageous, but to remove harm from, or obtain a definite advantage for another who would be subject to the harm or lose the advantage solely through ignorance and lack of reflection, not through malice or opposition to what is good?'

705. Common sense, and all legislators who follow common sense, constantly affirm that this can be done in the case of children, the insane and wastrels.

706. We must note however that civil laws do not deal with all the cases where the exercise of superiority is required if the

subject is to benefit and the humanity of the one who is superior in mind and force is to be satisfied.

Nevertheless, such cases do exist in nature, and rational Right acknowledges them at every age of life and in every relationship between wise, discerning persons and persons of little discernment. These cases have definite limits and involve a kind of coercion which causes no harm, not even indirectly, except the privation of freedom.

707. In no case are we concerned with unlimited coercion, or any kind of violence which may do initial harm to others under the pretext of doing them good afterwards. Removing material freedom in the case under discussion does no harm to our subject; this freedom ceases to be his of right. Consequently even his jural resentment proves nothing, because it is certainly founded upon on a false persuasion. Nevertheless, if the resentment were very deep, it would have to be respected because it implies profound pain and therefore the presence of harm and injury.

708. In all these cases, the difficulty consists always in *verifying* in the action itself that one person's foresight is greater than another's. This raises a further question: 'What degree of certainty must the person have whose title to the right of superiority over another is based on his greater foresight?' Note that we are discussing a superiority exercised in a special case, not a general superiority — we are persuaded that the other person has mistakenly calculated the consequences of his actions, and that we have not.

709. The answer varies: are the harmful consequences[179] to be removed from us or from the author of the actions?

[179] Note that we are speaking about harmful consequences, not about the violation of our ownership. In fact, harm can result from another's action without the perpetrator entering into the sphere of our ownership through his action. Let us suppose that someone has informed the bank of disastrous political news which lowers the value of shares. Because I have many shares, I suffer serious harm, but I cannot say that I have been robbed. If the news is true, I cannot really complain and I cannot justly stop the news spreading. If I did so, I would be guilty of unjustly harming those who were still ignorant of the news. But this is not the case we are discussing. To deal with our special case we need to suppose the accidental events which accompany bank business. I know, let us say, that a certain, very credulous gentleman will be going

710. It also differs according to its harmful or advantageous consequences.

711. If I have good reason to fear harm to myself, I have the right to avoid it, even though I am not fully certain about it. This is always the case when harm is more likely than not. My right to avoid it increases, and the amount of probability necessary to take just precautions decreases, in proportion to the extent of the feared harm.

712. If, however, the person who acts without foreseeing the consequences of his actions, is liable to harm, I can in the first place always warn him about the evil. But I cannot use force to stop him doing harm to himself except when I am certain of the damage, and solely on condition that the violence I must use to stop him acting imprudently does him no harm other than oblige him to act differently.

713. The difference between the two cases depends on the principle that 'in natural right each of us is the competent judge of our own evil and good'. An appeal against a competent judge is possible when there is moral certainty to the contrary but not in case of doubt. Thus, in the first case I am the competent judge about harm to myself; in the second the one who acts is the competent judge about harm to himself. Even if I am doubtful, I must respect the other's decision; otherwise I violate his right of competence.

714. For the same reason I cannot restrict another's freedom simply in order to bring about consequences useful to the agent if he does not want anything useful from his actions. We all have the right to renounce any good where privation does not produce natural harm but simply a lack of an unnecessary good.

715. 6. Finally, in the fourth case where the subject overrides the superior in foreseeing the consequences of his actions, the superior may not use force to maintain his superiority against

---

to the bank today and quite innocently will relate false or at least unproven news — he has heard it by chance or some speculator has told him. I am aware that if the news spreads it will cause panic among the buyers with a consequent drop in the value of the shares, of which I need to sell a certain number the same day. I cannot interrogate the gentleman or have no time to do so. Instead I take him home and make sure he is occupied, while I go off and sell my shares without loss. According to rational Right, can I act in this way? This is the question we are dealing with.

the subject's will. The latter can be free because he has sufficient foresight to be free, and is free as soon as he desires. Resistance to his just will is, generally speaking, a violation of his right.

716. I say 'generally speaking' because those who know the consequences of their actions can generally be presumed to use their foresight for avoiding every evil and procuring every good for themselves and others. This happens whenever a person is not only sound and prudent of understanding but sound and upright of will. If, however, people abuse their foresight because of malice and cause moral or eudaimonological harm to others, it is clear that persons with the same foresight, even when threatened indirectly, can defend themselves and others from evil provided the defender is certain about the evil. But in this case we are no longer talking about *right of superiority* but of *defence*.

717. In conclusion therefore we can say: 1. The *right to exercise one's natural freedom* results from three elements:

   a) foresight of the consequences of one's actions;
   b) the will to use this foresight for guiding oneself;
   c) moral soundness of will.

718. 2. The acquired right *to exercise* one's free will must be classed among the rights we have called 'relative',[180] because it is impossible to assign an absolute, general degree of freedom.

719. Hence, the degree of freedom due to human beings by right must be derived solely from their relationship with other persons as a result of the three elements we have mentioned. For example, John, who is free relative to James, can be a subject relative to Paul and a natural superior relative to Michael; these three states of subjection, freedom and superiority can change at any moment. Right is posited by the fact constituting its title. Thus if the fact changes, so does the right. In our case, the fact is 1. the existence of a *relative amount of foresight of the consequences of one's actions* possessed by different people, and 2. the existence in them of a *morally sound will*. The relationship which the different amounts of foresight and will have with each other constitutes, properly speaking, the root of the acquired

---

[180] Cf. *ER*, 322-328.

right of freedom considered in its exercise, and the relationship it assumes in different people.

Article 7.
Does positive law offend natural right by determining stages at which civil acts begin to function *ipso facto* for everyone?

720. As we have said, all rights whose object is the exercise of external freedom are relative and consequently variable; there is no determined moment in nature when a child and, much less, all children enter into the full exercise of their freedom.

What authority therefore enables civil laws to determine precise stages when all citizens enter equally into the free exercise of their rights? It would seem that such laws contradict natural Right by injuring both those to whom nature gives possession of self prior to the legal moment and those whose entry is delayed by an underdeveloped nature. It is an important question, which we propose to solve in this Article.

721. The first response, after a cursory glance at the question, would be to condemn this kind of positive regulation. No human authority can ever oblige an individual to forsake the possession of himself given by nature; it would be an unjust, empty judgment. On the other hand, an individual who has not yet been given possession of self by nature, cannot be made by human law what he is not. Moreover, if someone is allowed an exercise of their freedom greater than they really have by nature, all others are injured. As we have seen, each person's freedom must be measured by the relationship it has with the freedom of others (cf. 719).

722. This teaching might be welcomed by a philosopher devoted to paradox, but it would still be false; positive laws can and must be justified in this case.

723. I do not mean that civil laws have reached their perfection in any particular country. On the contrary, I think and have

often said[181] that much remains to be done to perfect positive legislation. Every line of this book points to this.

724. Nor do I mean that the perfection of civil laws can ever reach a point where they faithfully proceed hand in hand with rational Right. On the contrary, we could probably show that it is impossible, strictly speaking, to allow citizens the exercise of freedom in civil acts at exactly the moment when nature grants it. Amongst other things, we would lack the means for knowing with certainty the infinite degrees by which an individual takes possession of self. But I do not wish to discuss this problem here.

725. What I wish to say is that we must not claim instant perfection for positive laws. Indeed, we can never claim they attain an absolute, invariable perfection, precisely because 1. positive laws are the work of human beings, and 2. in order to be perfect the laws would have to be changed, just as human nature is changed in its accidents, by means of society which is constantly in flux. Both are impossible: the first, because nature is immense and the legislator limited; the second, because nature precedes and the legislator can only follow. Thus, no matter how quick the legislator is, he will never catch up with nature.

726. Nevertheless, although we must not claim perfection for positive laws, rational Right still obliges us to renounce our own right when the imperfection of these laws disowns and removes our right. This is explained as follows.

727. Rational Right requires that we modify, limit and even partly renounce our right when we cannot exercise it in a certain way or to a certain level or in some definite circumstance without harming an innocent person. The obligation is both moral and jural, so that the offended innocent person could defend himself with force.

728. A special obligation springs from this general obligation: we must be ready to settle peacefully quarrels and problems arising between ourselves and others.[182] If in a case of doubt one of the parties refuses a peaceful settlement and is ready to use violence, he would offend the other's right and could be forced to submit to arbitration or any other peaceful and just means more acceptable to him.

181 *SP*, bk. 1, c. 2, 12; bk. 3, Intro.
182 Cf. what I have said in *SP*, bk. 1, c. 9.

729. However, jural obligation is clearly not present if it is obviously a question of intolerable bullying or deception in bad faith. But this obligation is present 1. if the question is doubtful or certainly difficult to solve in itself, and 2. if it is doubtful for only one of the two parties, provided the doubt is in good faith and cannot be settled by reasoned discussion.

730. Laws made for all the members of a civilised society are acknowledged as the best means for settling pacifically the problems and quarrels which can arise among the citizens.

731. By 'best means' I understand those in which the portion of natural rights sacrificed by the members of a civilised society is the least possible. Let us imagine that in certain circumstances individuals have to sacrifice a small part of their natural rights for the sake of peace and mutual respect. The sacrifice I am referring to is the sum total of all the losses and gains that occur during a person's lifetime. As in a game of chance, this sum is with equal probability as advantageous or disadvantageous for one party as for another. If therefore the sum is the least possible, the means used to settle these problems will be the best possible. And this is precisely how people of all ages have considered the means used by universal laws, to which all submit themselves with an equal chance of profit or loss.

732. Positive laws, therefore, as the means for preserving the highest possible sum of natural rights by the sacrifice or rather the transformation of the least portion of these rights, is that means to which, by jural obligation, we are all obliged to submit. It is clear that the general obligation we have explained above gives rise not only to the special obligation we are under to resolve questions peacefully, but also to the other special obligation 'incumbent upon each member of a society to be satisfied when a dispute is settled by the most equitable means available for preserving the greatest portion of rights for everybody.' Because this obligation is by its nature jural, it can be upheld with the sanction of force against those who refuse to fulfil it.

733. Everybody therefore is naturally obliged to accept civil laws in possible controversies (unless the parties come to agreement some other way). This may require the sacrifice of some part of the good which would be our right by nature, if nature itself had not withdrawn in part by imposing on everybody the obligation we have explained.

734. But is this true in the case of imperfect laws? Although generally speaking positive laws may be the best means for settling controversies and as such be obligatory for disputing parties who do not settle matters among themselves, are these imperfect laws necessary? Must we tolerate the injury which their imperfection causes to the natural rights of all?

735. The problem must not be confused. Our question does not concern the person in society responsible for drawing up laws. The legislator may be anyone; it makes no difference to our present problem, provided the positive laws we are discussing originate from a competent legislator. Granted this condition (without which laws are not laws), we see immediately two other self-evident natural, jural obligations which bind all those for whom the laws are made:

1. We can expect a competent legislator to make the best possible, but not necessarily perfect laws.[183]

2. We must all presume that the laws made by a competent legislator are the best he can provide, unless there is evidence that the legislator had his own interest at heart rather than the public's. Without contrary evidence a competent legislator or judge must be favoured before everyone else.

736. All the above obligations give rise to another jural obligation: every member of society must 'submit to positive laws even at the sacrifice of a part of their own natural rights.' A part of these rights must in any case be sacrificed by each. The part sacrificed by submission to the civil laws is the least possible, all things beings considered, for each person and for all. In fact, strictly speaking, it is nothing for each person. Having accepted the laws, each can expect overall as much injury as profit; what is harmful to one is advantageous to another. Hence, because injury is compensated by the expectation of profit, no one is really exposed to injury.

737. In fact an individual's accidental sacrifice of a larger portion of his rights depends not on positive laws, which are the same for all, but solely on chance. Chance brings about accidents which subject a person to greater losses than others. In this case, the individual would have to resign himself in the same

[183] Cf. *SP*, bk. 1, c. 9.

way as a person who has insured himself against fire has to resign himself to similar possibilities; he agrees to pay insurance to avoid greater loss. If the insured house is not burnt down, he has indeed paid for the other members, but he has no reason to complain. Before he knew what would happen, the danger existed equally for him and for the others, and he safeguarded himself by paying the cost of the danger. He cannot complain and withhold due payment if he now sees that membership is by chance harmful to him but profitable to another; he reasonably and duly accepted this possibility. In the same way, it is reasonable and dutiful that each member of civil society should accept the outcome resulting from the equal application of positive laws which form the best guarantee of the rights of all.

738. These principles concerning the necessity of positive laws, and their obligatory force founded in rational Right itself, clearly provide us with an adequate reply to our question: 'Does positive law injure rational Right by determining stages at which everyone or nearly everyone begins of himself to perform civil acts?' We answer: 'These laws do not by their enactment injure rational Right. Competent legislators (that is, legislators of all peoples throughout history) have always considered such laws necessary to safeguard the greatest possible part of the natural rights of seigniory and freedom present amongst human beings, and to ensure that whenever a portion must inevitably be lost or rather changed, it is the smallest possible.'

739. Civil legislators had a complex problem to solve. The following considerations will help us to understand it better.

First, we must not think that the families who united in new civil societies were capable of knowing all the advantages obtainable from association. They were ignorant of many of these advantages and thus unable initially to apply them all to the purpose for which they were uniting.

740. At first civil societies were particular societies, that is, they had a particular purpose, for example, mutual defence of life and possessions.

741. Their limits extended however as time passed. Little by little people saw that their association could obtain previously unnoticed benefits, all of which became part of the purpose of the formed society by which they could gradually obtain every known possible good.

742. This is one of the past and present developments that civil societies undergo. All these developments will need to be taken into account by the noble genius who writes *The Philosophical History of Civil Society*, a highly desirable work, which forms a large part of the *History of Humanity*.

743. As society gained new purposes, its nature changed, and so did the work of its legislators. The problem to be solved changed because its elementary data changed.

744. Here I cannot and do not wish to deal with all the different facets of the problem of seigniory and dependence resulting from the work of different legislators in the varying conditions of what we now call 'civil society', a blanket name which is a great source of illusions and errors because society has never been one and the same. On the contrary there has been a succession of different societies which should really have different names. One day perhaps the author we hope to see will provide these names.

745. To avoid an endless task, therefore, I repeat that I am only discussing civil society in Europe, whose laws have as their primary purpose 'the defence and protection of the safety and property of all its members, considered as heads of an actual family or seeds of a future family' [*App.*, no. 3].

746. In civil society, therefore, whose laws have a particular purpose, the question of the right of superiority and of freedom is only secondary. The possible superiority of one person over another is not considered as a right with its own value but as a means to the end of the laws themselves, that is, to the protection 'of the safety and ownership of families'. *Patria potestas* is viewed in this way: the child is entirely or partly freed from this authority when it is no longer necessary either for the child's safety as initiator of a future family, or for the preservation of his material goods.

747. Hence, the legislation of present civil societies does not claim to include and express in numbered articles the whole of rational law.

748. This law is written on the human heart as it has always been, not on paper. It cannot be abrogated, but it is possible for it not to be sanctioned externally. Civil society takes only a part of this law to which it adds the weight of its sanction without prejudice to the part outside the codes.

[742–748]

749. As long as child and father, or the one who takes the place of the father, are in agreement, positive laws do not intervene: father and child, adult and baby, are all subjects of the natural Right not written in codes. No law prohibits a child from living subject to his father by nature or from love, even for the whole of his life.

750. But does the civil law intervene when disagreement arises between father and child?

751. Not always. The disagreement must be such that it harms each particular good which positive law intends to defend, that is, the *safety* or the *ownership* of one of the two parties considered as *elements of families*. For this reason, many disagreements between fathers and their children begin and end within the home without any intervention of public laws.

But this is not the case if the father and child harm one another or threaten harm. The law would intervene here because safety (the purpose of the law) would be in danger. Nor is it the case when the father threatens to squander the child's substance, that is, the substance of the child's future family. As soon as the civil court became aware of this, it would protect the child by law, declare the father excessive and take both father and child under its protection.[184]

752. For this reason, the Council of State opposed discussion of the first article under the title of *patria potestas* in the Napoleonic code, which said: 'A son must always honour and respect his father and mother.'[185] According to the Council the article seemed to concern a matter outside legislation.[186] No one denied that the article did not belong to legislation; on the contrary, that appeared clear to all. The article was retained however so as to serve as a point of reference for judges in certain cases.[187]

753. Civil legislation, therefore, in its present state has only

---

[184] For the same reason civil laws distinguish the father's goods from the child's. The laws consider the child as the seed of a future family whose possession they protect — the child is not considered solely as part of the paternal family.

[185] Art. 371.

[186] The same difficulty arose for art. 212 concerning the moral duties of spouses.

[187] Cf. Report to the Court, made by the Tribune Vesin on behalf of the Section of Legislation on the law relative to *patria potestas*.

a limited, not a universal purpose. It intervenes only when required by the limited purpose which the law itself has determined.

754. Its regulations must be understood in this light. For example, when the law frees the child from *patria potestas*, we must not think that the child is completely freed from all this authority. We must simply understand that if the child requests freedom, the law grants and upholds the request, but only relative to the acts the law intends, that is, civil life, physical freedom and material ownership. The law is neutral relative to all else.[188]

755. Rational law must therefore rule alongside positive law in all those parts which the latter completely abandons to the former.

756. Even when the civil law helps the father by publicly penalising the child, it is not properly speaking concerned with the paternal right but with the child's good, in which society protects its own hopes.

757. All these considerations significantly limit the questions we have dealt with. They show that we must not require from civil laws a sanction of the whole of rational Right in all its length and breadth, but only of that part which the laws intended to sanction without prejudice to the rest of rational Right.

758. This part is concerned with the conclusion of contentions in the most equitable way and for the greatest good of the new families, of which the children are the precious seed.

759. Legislators had to allow for contentions between children and true fathers or foster-fathers. Here, to prevent its further complication by other elements, I take for granted that the question concerns only a foster-father.

---

[188] In the Napoleonic code, the son attains majority at 21 years of age, and with this is declared to be outside *patria potestas* (§372). However, he may not marry without parental consent until his 25th year (§148). But this is a contradiction: parents still retain a part of their authority even after their child is declared free of that authority. To save the code from this contradiction, we have to say that *patria potestas* means the father's general authority, not a particular authority relative to certain determined points covered by laws. These equivocations, ambiguities and apparent contradictions will continue as long as legislators do not express their intentions clearly.

In this kind of contention the child requests his freedom from his foster-father. Natural Right requires the contention to be settled peacefully and justly, and if this is not possible, the case must be handed to arbitrators trusted by both. When the arbitrators have been chosen, the two parties must accept the judgment handed down. The one whose right is lost must accept the decision, because the case was submitted and had to be submitted by him to arbitration. There are therefore, even in natural Right, cases where a moral-jural obligation to cede part of one's own right is present.

We must conclude therefore that human beings have decided to form laws and submit themselves to them for the sole purpose of restricting and reducing as much as possible the portion of rational right which jural obligation required them to sacrifice or alter in any given case. They asked themselves the following question: 'Will a smaller portion of our natural rights be altered by our use of discussion and constantly new judgments to settle contentions, or by establishing fixed judges, common to all, who are obligated to judge according to fixed laws?' The common sense of all peoples decided in agreement with the fact itself: 'It is very probable that our rights will be changed less if contentions are settled by fixed judges, fixed laws and judgments strengthened by common force, than by acting in any other way.'

760. Common sense was undoubtedly correct, because permanent judges are impartial, and gain more competence and experience as they resolve controversies. And permanent laws are also useful because they provide instruction for judges, and reduce arbitrariness which is so easily found in unrestricted decisions.

761. Relative to the laws therefore, the problem consisted in knowing 'whether that portion of rights whose obligatory change was imposed by rational Right would be more probably reduced to the minimum if permanent judges were allowed to pronounce decisions according to their own understanding or by following fixed laws.'

Here, too, the answer is clear: fixed laws guarantee rights much more than judgments made without them. And even though, despite fixed laws, a portion of rights must be changed (rights can never be lost), it is very probable that the altered portion is far less than it would be otherwise.

762. Consequently we all have a jural obligation to obey fixed laws, because we are each obliged by rational Right to submit in the way most equitable and advantageous for all in solving questions.

763. Let us return to the legislators chosen to make laws for the settlement of contentions about freedom requested by a child from his guardian or foster-father. We shall try to express their problem in clear language.

764. We have said that legislators cannot intend to deal with all possible cases of conflict between a child and his guardian, but only with those concerning both the *safety* of the two parties to the quarrel and the greatest good of the *future family* of which the child is the seed.

Legislators therefore do not intend to defend any abstract right of the guardian's superiority, but only 1. the quantity of his natural right of superiority which can safeguard him and protect his external goods from his child's waywardness; and 2. the quantity which helps rather than harms the child and his future family.

765. The guardian's or foster-father's right of superiority extends even further, that is, to acts which are indifferent to the child's good and his future family and at the same time are not necessary for the guardian's safety and the defence of his property. But even these acts do not come within the scope of the legislators; they are natural and rational Right which is not written into laws nor sanctioned by them.[189]

766. Within the limits restricting the purpose of the intended laws, the legislators' problem is to determine what laws must be established to safeguard the greatest possible portion both of the *superiority* they wish to guarantee for the foster-father, and of the *freedom* they wish to guarantee for the child. They know

[189] Natural acts of superiority not sanctioned by civil law must retain some natural sanction. In my opinion a legislator would definitely be erring whose laws supported the appeal of even an elderly child on whom the father had inflicted some punishment for a just motive. We need to note once again that declaring 'a child free from *patria potestas* at a certain age' seems ambiguous if left unexplained and unqualified.

[762–766]

that in solving the various contingent contentions a portion of the right of superiority on the one hand and of the right of freedom on the other is inevitably lost. Their general problem however is to determine laws which would reduce to a minimum the portion of these rights which may be lost.

767. But this gives rise to another, more definite problem for the legislators: will the superiority they wish to guarantee to foster-fathers and the freedom they wish to guarantee to the children continue to be guaranteed if they allow judges to decide of themselves the time when children have naturally attained the sufficient level of knowledge of the consequences of their actions and can therefore be allowed to act for themselves?

768. As I have said, the problem is answered by the common sense of peoples which preferred the system of fixed ages. Common sense reasonably feared the arbitrariness of judges which, without the establishment of laws, would have had a wider field in which to act. Because common sense had not yet been able to find safe and clear indications of the moment each child attained command of its freedom, and at what level — indications which would have excluded arbitrariness on the part of judges — it considered fixed ages, which would have eliminated this danger, as the lesser evil.

769. It is true, of course, that legislations which depend on this method use it more or less perfectly. It is also true that legislations which gradually introduce the child into its exercise of freedom by dividing the acts of a child's jural freedom into many categories and assigning many ages corresponding to these different categories, are closer to nature which makes the child enter gradually into possession of itself.

770. Finally, it is true that legislations which are able to establish wisely a greater number of exceptions to the law of age, increasingly reduce the imperfection of the law for particular cases.

771. Civil laws are perfected therefore by prudent knowledge of the rate of development of young people, according to the state of the nation receiving the laws (a state which varies with the times) and by care that the advantages accruing from gradual perfection of the laws is not overridden by the disadvantages arising from their great number.

[767–771]

CHAPTER 6
Generation, the second title by which
ownership or dominion over persons is acquired

772. We come now to generation, the second title by which dominion over persons is acquired.

Article 1.
Various rights involved in *patria potestas*,
and their different titles

773. Some authors, like Hobbes, deduce *patria potestas* from *occupancy*. Others, like Pufendorf, deduce it from the fathers' provision of food for their children.[190]

774. But, in my opinion, these titles are different and produce different rights.

775. Provision of food produces no more than the right to repayment or compensation, as we noted when we discussed foster-fathers.

776. Occupancy, whose purpose is excessively limited and entrenched by Hobbes,[191] is common to both natural and fostering fathers. It cannot be a true father's proper title to rights over his children.

---

[190] Pufendorf adds the children's consent (*De jur. nat. et gent.*, 6, 2, §4). If he means explicit, positive consent, it would be absurd to attribute such consent to babies. But, as I have said, if he means negative consent, that is, the child makes no request and is content to receive necessary aid, I would recognise it. Properly speaking, however, such consent concerns the *fosterer* and benefactor, not the *father*, and cannot therefore be the title of rights proper to a father; negative consent, relative to the rights of a fosterer, is a *condition*, not a title. For example, unoccupied land is the condition of my ownership, not the title. Granted this condition, I can occupy and appropriate the land.

[191] Hobbes claims that the purpose for which parents take occupancy of children is to prevent them from being hostile and harmful (*De Cive*, 9, 3). The hearts of mothers and fathers are vilified here, although they are the competent judges in the case.

For this reason, we dealt with the matter in the preceding chapter with a view to discussing the *title of generation* in this chapter. Generation is the sole source of *patria potestas* considered in its proper sense.[192]

777. If fathers do not abandon the children they have begotten, but care for them for the sake of consequent joy and utility, they enter into possession of their rights in the same way as foster-fathers acquire their rights by caring for an abandoned child.

778. In so far as he feeds, rears and generally benefits his baby, he acquires those rights which the foster-father acquires by feeding and rearing an abandoned baby.

779. But in the true father there is also the title of generation, which modifies the above-mentioned rights and produces new ones.

780. We have therefore three titles, *fostering*, *occupancy* and *generation*, involved with *patria potestas*. The last, which is the proper title, gives a new form to the rights stemming from the first two.

Article 2.
Generation as the source of *patria potestas*

781. As we have seen, everybody generally admits that the author of anything is also its master. Indeed no physical connection is more intimate than that between cause and effect.

782. There is in generation something which is absent from all other human production: the parents form their child's physical substance and animal principle from their own substance and animality.[193] The whole of antiquity saw in children a kind of extension of the parents' existence.[194]

---

[192] Grotius and Rottek derive *patria potestas* from this title.

[193] Cf. on the nature of generation, *AMS*, 323-349, 812-831.

[194] In the language of divine Scripture, the child forms one thing with the father and is considered as his accession. For example, God says to Jacob and David: 'You will be this or this, you will become powerful, you will have a kingdom without end, etc,' meaning their children. For the same reason, the children as a whole are given the name of their father; they are all Israel or

783. Antiquity however went to excess, and considered the child as a thing belonging to its father, in such a way that the father could do what he liked with his child, as with his own body or clothing.

784. But modern laws seem to offend in the opposite way. Just as ancient laws made the father the end and the children the means, so viceversa modern laws tend to consider the father solely as a means for the good of the child.

785. But civil laws, as we have said, involve only one part of natural and rational Right, and are judged according to their intended, partial purposes. No matter what we may say about them, therefore, it is certain that philosophical Right cannot be limited to considering the relationship between father and child when one is seen exclusively as means for the other.[195]

786. Both *person* and *nature* are present in children. It is certain that person cannot in any way be used as an end by another human being. A child therefore is an end.

787. But it is also certain that what pertains to *nature* can be used as means by another human being, when no harm threatens personal dignity. Hence, in a child we must recognise a double condition relative to the parents: the condition of *means* relative to all the joy and good they can draw from the child, and the condition of *end* relative to the care they take of him.

788. The parents' rights arise from the child's condition as means. Rights always have for their purpose some subjective good of the one who has the right, although the subjective good sometimes comes directly from objective good.

789. Viceversa, the parents' duties emanate from the child's

David or Juda or Ephraim. The same practice is found among all the ancient eastern nations: the tribes bear the name of their descent. Amongst modern authors, the two Germans, Meister and Egger, use something analogous to *accession* to explain the natural seigniory of parents over their children.

[195] Zeiller, in many other respects a man of great discernment, has in my opinion made this mistake. According to him, parents' authority over their children arises *solely* from their duty and right to educate their children (§164-167 of his *Diritto naturale privato*). Thus, only the children are end; the parents serve this *end*. If I am not mistaken, a similar theory can be seen in the spirit of modern civil laws tending to provide for the good of the younger rather than of the elder. They have the tendency to broaden the bonds of freedom rather than protect the rights of authority.

[783–789]

condition of *end*. Duties always have an objective good as their purpose.

790. The duties of parents limit their rights; duties and rights are in a certain way opposites. When talking about parents' rights, therefore, we must always bear in mind their duties.

Article 3.
Modifications affecting the rights which arise from the simple title of rearing joined to the title of generation

791. The benefit of rearing produces duties in the child who has received the benefit from someone who has not generated him. I have reduced these duties to three: perpetual *gratitude*, *repayment*, and *submission* during rearing (cf. 559).

792. Gratitude and submission during rearing are the child's duties towards all those who have exercised the great benefit of rearing him, whether true father or not. But in as much as paternal love and care are incommunicable and more altruistic than any other love and care, duties towards a father are stricter and more sacred.

793. The duty of repayment does not apply to a child reared by its father, but it does apply to a child reared by others.

794. The reason for this, it seems to me, does not lie in the father's responsibility for rearing his offspring, as Zeiller maintains,[196] but in the nature of paternal love which naturally draws a father to rear his child.

795. I cannot in fact agree with those writers who admit *a jural duty* in a father to rear his offspring. Such paternal duty is, I am sure, very strict and serious, but purely *moral* in nature. Consequently I do not recognise any right in a child to obtain education by force from its father, even if the child had the force to obtain education, or others had it through him. An unnatural

---

[196] Cf. §164. — Karpe expresses the same opinion in his *Institut. Philosoph. Jurisprud. universalis*, §116-117.

father who fails to fulfil his sacred duty to feed his children deprives them of nothing because they have nothing.

796. Similarly, although I recognise a right in all people to shelter and rear a child abandoned by its father (a right to the occupancy and therefore the education of the child), I do not recognise in anyone the right to use force to constrain a father to shelter and educate his own son, except in civil society.[197]

797. Zeiller claims to demonstrate that a *jural* duty exists in parents to rear their offspring because he imputes the childrens' wretched condition to the parents who brought them into the world subject to such great need. He says: 'Anyone who by their own act abandons a moral being to a condition of indigence without the being's consent has by that fact the obligation to carefully protect the being from every evil whatsoever.'[198]

798. But the abandonment of a being does not harm him positively; he is not deprived of what is his, nor is his freedom under attack. The starting principle of the derivation of rights, *ownership*, does not apply here. A sick person, for example, does not acquire a right to be helped for the sole reason that I abandon him against his will after caring for him for a long time. If someone born and reared in my house has such need of me that he must live with me or die without me, he has no *right* to require me not to abandon him. My abandonment violates a grave, ethical, humanitarian duty, not a strictly jural duty.

799. If, however, I have helped him or anyone else in need of me, or lived with him, because I am jurally obligated to him, my abandonment would be an injury to his right.

800. Similarly, a father's abandonment of his children cannot be a reason in justice for blaming the children's woes on him, unless the abandonment were an injury to the childrens' right to be reared and not abandoned. Zeiller's reasoning goes round in a circle, presupposing the definition we are seeking.

801. We should therefore rely on the opinion of those authors who consider that natural right always consists in 'not taking from anyone' (principle of ownership), and understand that abandonment does not deprive a baby of what it possesses, but

[197] We will see elsewhere how this right of society originates.
[198] In the footnote to §164 of his *Diritto naturale privato*.

simply does not provide what the baby does not possess and greatly needs. These authors see in rearing an ethical duty of the same kind as, but much stricter than, the duty we each have to come to the aid of our suffering, indigent fellow human beings.[199]

802. In fact the indigence of human beings born into the world is not properly speaking the work of parents but of nature itself. Human nature is very wretched and needy, but the baby has this nature in its entirety with all its good and evil; nobody has deprived the baby of a part of its nature. The parents are authors of the baby, not of the laws, conditions and accidents to which human nature is subject. Strictly speaking therefore a baby, relative to its parents, has no right; it is in fact the object of their humanity and tenderness, and of their sacred, moral duty.

803. This explains why nature has implanted tenderness and affection in the hearts of parents towards their offspring. Such affection was necessary to make them constantly give their baby what its right could not oblige them to give.

804. From the nature of this affection I deduce that the care and effort given by parents to their children is of a totally different kind to the care and effort of a foster-parent, provider or benefactor, and I do so as follows.

805. Parental affection is a natural feeling, an undefinable mixture of infinite, particular feelings and infinite ideas. The prevalent, characteristic feeling is always that of seeing and continuing an extension and reproduction of themselves in their child, a reproduction which develops and is young, better, rich in hopes, promising them a kind of perpetuity on earth.

806. Every simple feeling of human nature has a certain nobility of being. There is no selfish reckoning in it; it obeys its own laws without any further thought.[200]

807. The feeling of parents towards their offspring, implanted by nature in their hearts, is of this kind but to the highest degree. It moves those who have procreated a human being to love this

---

[199] Cf. Achenwall, *Observ. jur. nat.*, §57; Jacob, *Giurisprudenza filosofica*, §662; Hoffbauer, *Diritto naturale*, §407; Fichte, *Principj del Diritto naturale*, §46.

[200] Cf. the observations I made about this characteristic of feelings devoid of all selfish reckoning in *Storia comparativa de' sistemi morali*, c. 4, a. 4.

being with a very simple, spontaneous abandon, without any return for themselves. We see, for example, how brute animals expose themselves to death to defend and save their offspring. A man and woman have eyes only for the good and evil of their child, the sole object of their cares, worries and fears, of their efforts to protect it from threatened evils and to help it prosper and develop; and in doing so they completely forget themselves. I am thinking in particular of the pride, generosity and even harshness of a mother's heart as it passes from joy to tears, from happiness to desperation. The maternal heart is more inventive, energetic and strong than any human wisdom or power.

808. I do not mean that besides having this feeling of affection parents cannot give any thought to the advantages which will come to them later from their children. Even if they think of this, the nature of the feeling of affection remains unchanged. Paternal and maternal sentiment is fully satisfying in itself. It can be called self-interested only in so far as the child's good is considered the parent's own good, in fact their greatest good.

809. This affection of the parents, as something good and their greatest treasure, offers a new reason for their exclusive right to possess and educate their children. Relative to them, no other good is by nature as great as that of their children and their care of them.

810. This affection, by which nature unites parents to their offspring to form a single thing, is the source of all that the child's parents do and expend, as if they were doing it for themselves. Whatever the child gains from this care, the parents also gain. No repayment need be made to them therefore because there is no reason to repay what is done or used for one's own satisfaction. This is a law of nature.

811. The child therefore must show gratitude, the duty of respect and of submission. We will discuss these duties later, but there is no question of repayment, properly speaking. There can be no question of debit and credit between father and child, although there can be between child and father.

812. It may be objected that not all parents feel or show this paternal and maternal affection; many in fact abandon and mistreat their children. — This is very true but such parents cannot draw any advantage from their evil action. As we have

said, no right comes to anyone from his own wickedness and depravity of nature.[201]

813. But is the natural feeling of parents a moral obligation? Don't we normally say that feeling and obligation are different things? — In a rational being a feeling becomes an obligation when it is noble and naturally ordered to the advantage of the one who feels it; this is the case with the feeling of parents for their children. The effect of this feeling, and therefore nature's purpose for it, is the union of humanity, and the happiness of this union, and its prosperity and moral development as a result of the aid given particularly by parents to their descendants.[202]

---

[201] Cf. *ER*, 256-261.

[202] I am certain that the grandeur of paternal love pertains to the perfection of human nature in such a way that, if human nature were perfect, parents would be bound to their children by the mysterious feeling called φιλογονια. However, although this grandeur of feelings is, considered in itself, a perfection of nature, the grandeur could indirectly damage the development of nature itself, if nature did not find in *reason* a corresponding force capable of dominating the grandeur and subjecting this feeling to other feelings of greater dignity. A perceptive *History of Humanity* would have the task of recording the variations of parental affection towards their offspring and descendants. This affection is expressed with more intensity and grandeur in the east than in the west, and more in ancient times than in modern. The west is populated with adventurous young members of families who have broken their bonds with their parents. This spirit of adventure, which tore apart ancient families to establish new families elsewhere was, if we consider its consequences *in toto*, helpful to swifter, fuller development of humanity (cf. my observations on this subject in *SP*, bk. 3, cc. 6-9). In my opinion, we owe the character of the European peoples to this: individual activity is paramount, and the union between parents and offspring is less close. It also explains the tendency of modern European laws to gradually curtail *patria potestas* and favour freedom. However another cause must be added: the progress of knowledge with its consequent development of understanding. Reason is naturally individual, and the more it becomes active in every sense, the more the individual must acquire freedom in fact and by right. — If we consider the special providence of God towards the Hebrews, we can easily see that it aimed at two things relative to philogony: not to destroy this affection, and to subordinate it to the love of God. The sacrifice imposed on Abraham of his son, and the law by which God reserved for himself all the first-born are the principal means used by God to temper the excessive love of parents and hold it within the limits imposed by the primary affection, that is, the love of God to which all other affections must be subject. Moses' separation from his family, the sacrifice of Jephthah, the generous

[813]

8

<u>814.</u> The duty is deduced as follows.

Human nature must be acknowledged and respected for what it is worth. This practical acknowledgement and respect produces a corresponding love, which becomes the measure of the care we must each assume for the advantage of humanity. Human nature, as realised in parents, has the love of children as one of its elements, as we have said.

Fathers must respect this love for what it is. Otherwise, they harm within themselves the human nature of which that love is the noble part. Hence, a good father respects and values this love; an unnatural father spurns and rejects it.

A father who does not act according to natural paternal love offends against the respect due to the human nature which is in him and bound to the nature in his children. Consequently, the child's nature, too, is violated.

815. In fact, paternal feeling and affection bind together generations and unify the whole of humanity, giving it the greatest strength and perfection. This affection (of those who beget) is the font of all development, increase and striving in humanity. Those fathers, therefore, who reject their natural affection for their children offend in reality against the whole of humanity in so far as humanity is shared by all individuals on earth.

Article 4.
Modifications affecting rights arising from the title
of occupancy when it is joined to the title of generation

816. The title of occupancy gives the first occupier the right to draw from the child all the good he can for himself with due respect for the moral, intellectual and physical rearing of the child. But we have seen that this good which the occupier can draw from the child for himself lasts only for the time the child

friendship of Jonathan, were examples intended to instruct the people of Israel and to moderate excessive and over-exclusive love of parents for their children.

[814–816]

is subject to him, that is, the time necessary for rearing him. The occupier must gradually allow the child government of itself: first in some acts, then in others, and finally in all.

817. This applies also to true fathers, who have the primary right to occupy and rear their children.

818. In the exercise of the father's right to *rear* the children, the children are the end, and the aim is the childrens' good. In the exercise of their right to *occupy* their children, the end is the occupier, the fathers' good.

819. The fathers' intention of drawing good for themselves from the children does not, as we noted, exclude natural love. In many poor families the children are put to work not only to educate them but more importantly to gain something for their parents. No one can say that the parents are not justified in using their children in this way. It would be absurd and contrary to common sense to wish to restrict all the rights of those who have given children their existence to the sole right of benefiting them by education without the parents being able to draw any good for self from their offspring.

820. But if we make occupancy the only source of the fathers' right to draw good for themselves from their children, it is clear that such a right can last only as long as the children remain occupiable, so to speak. Occupiability ceases in the children as they gradually take possession of self.[203]

However, when the *occupancy* has ceased, *generation* remains. In my opinion, this gives fathers the right to keep their children with them, not as previously in a state of mere *submission*, but in what we call the state of *parental society*. Children never have *per se* the right to leave this society without their begetter's consent, except when the latter constantly abuses his authority, or for the sake of cleaving to a wife and so forming a new family.[204]

---

[203] Prior to this, others can draw benefit from the children as they can from land whose absent owner cannot cultivated it. But fathers have primary preference through the title of generation, so that no one may occupy their children in this way when their fathers intend to occupy them for themselves.

[204] Not least, it seems to me, among the fine qualities of the code of the King of Sardinia is that it supports filial piety far more than any other European code I know. The continuity of *patria potestas* which, I maintain, is perpetual according to natural right, is one of the principles solemnly upheld by the

821. This last reason for offspring to leave their fathers is recognised as lawful by divine Scripture, which says: 'A man shall leave father and mother, and shall cleave to his wife: and they shall be two in one flesh.'[205] These words, spoken by the first man at the moment of contracting matrimony, show the kind of spirit that the paternal bond should have. They show that the marital union which constitutes a new family is so intimate that, if the new (marital) society cannot exist with the previous (parental) society, the former must be preserved by the sacrifice of the latter.

822. A son therefore can leave his father and join the family of his spouse, if he could not have his wife in any other way. For the same reason, a wife can go to the family of her husband. Both husband and wife can leave their fathers (provided the parents have no need of them) if this is required by ownership of the new family they form. On the other hand, if these conditions are absent and the married son can remain with his father

Albertine code. According to this code, neither the age of majority nor any other age, nor even the marriage of offspring causes *patria potestas* to cease. The only reasons recognised as valid for cessation are: '*Patria potestas* ceases not only through death and judicial condemnations to which the law has attached cessation, but also through the declared absence of the father and during this absence, and through emancipation' (Art. 237). Emancipation is effected 1. through the expressed will of the father: 'The emancipation is effected through a spontaneous declaration of the father and the acceptance of the son, provided the latter has completed his 18th year' (Art. 238); 2. through the presumed will of the father, as in the case expressed in article 242: 'Those sons are considered emancipated who have been living apart from their father for five years after attaining the age of majority and control and administer their own interests, provided the father knows and does not oppose the fact'; 3. through a court sentence dependent upon the faults of a father who abuses his authority: 'Emancipation is also effected through a sentence of the courts whenever the father seriously mistreats the person of his sons or abuses his *patria potestas* in any other way' (Art. 239). I consider all this very much in harmony with natural Right. But we must note that, although the Albertine code never makes *patria potestas* cease of itself, the authority is continually being limited to allow for the development of the son and his future family. Thus, after 25 years he can leave the paternal home, according to the ruling of articles 212-213.

[205] Gen 2: [24 Douai]. — This law was confirmed by the Gospel: Mt 19: 5; Mk 10: 7.

who requires this, I think the son has the jural obligation to obey his father's will and not abandon him.[206]

823. Here we see a difference between those who simply foster children and true fathers. Relative to the former, occupied children are completely free as soon as possession of them has ceased. The children cannot be forced to remain in society with their benefactors. True fathers, even though they lose the superiority over their children which comes from occupancy, do not lose all superiority; they still have enough to constrain the children to remain in their society.

824. *Parental society* therefore is not the kind of society that requires the consent of the parties for its constitution. It is established and endures solely by the father's will. The children have the jural duty to submit by *consenting* to the paternal will.

825. Let us now examine the *end* of this society and its administrator or *governor*.

§1. *The end of parental society, and the laws deriving from it*

826. Fathers, children and all descendants, even those who do not yet, but will exist, must be considered as a collective person.

827. It may be objected that we cannot conceive a society of still non-existent persons. This objection however contradicts human consciousness. We need to keep in mind that, in the opinion of the human race, a communication of rights and between those who are alive now and those yet to be born.

828. Human beings, through acts of their intelligence, are certainly in touch with the past and the future. They can relate to persons and things which, although they do not exist now, will exist. For example, am I not the owner of the produce that my land will give me in the future? Don't I have an absolute right to it, so that it is even now bound to me by a bond of ownership? I can certainly calculate the produce and plan for it in the future, although it does not yet exist.

I can also make a contract that will bind future generations. I

---

[206] Thus nature teaches children to ask permission if they wish to live apart from their fathers. The Prodigal Son himself is proof of this.

grant that this kind of contract could not take place if the consent of those to come were their own free decision, but it could if the consent were obligatory. In this case they must consent to and thus conclude and ratify the contract drawn up by their predecessor who may also have accepted for their benefit some kind of deposit from the other contracting party.[207] This is precisely the nature of agreements between families and between nations.

Finally I can provide simultaneously for my own good and that of all my descendants. This is a bond of society, which I form with them. It is a society in which every member who arrives thereafter into the world contributes to the common good. Each shares his work and profits in common, providing for the good of the future members, and performing filial duties towards the departed by respecting their memory and honouring their tombs. Only the materialist mocks a religion which honours the dead and breaks the bond which holds generations together. For the believer in immortality the *person* does not perish; divested of its body and made invisible, the person co-exists with members of the family who come to live upon the earth. The human race believes this and has a profound understanding of it. This truth gives rise to customs, religion, literature, laws and art which speak both to and of future members. They do not yet exist, but they are protected and represented; they receive rights and duties, and a heritage of memories, teachings, support and riches produced by the arduous labour of others. The end of this society of descendants therefore is all the good that it brings to all the new members, everyone of whom must share in this good.

829. This explains why the government of family society tends naturally and reasonably to the good of its future rather than its present members.

830. The reason why this tendency inclines more to future generations than present members (clearly demonstrated by fathers and by the civil laws which protect domestic society) is

---

[207] By their will, fathers can impose obligations on their descendants because of the honour owed them by the descendants. — Testators who are not fathers can impose obligations on their heirs but only on condition that the inheritance is accepted.

that future generations taken together are always in the majority compared with the few persons who form the present generation, conscious as it is of its paucity. The *greatest possible good* therefore is obtained for the whole family when dispositions are made for its extension into the future, that is, for all its descendants. In any case, the *end* of anything is normally esteemed more than its principle, and what is to come is valued more in human eyes than what has already come and is now passing away.

831. The natural tendency of parents towards the good of their descendants must therefore be seen as a kind of intelligent feeling, a part of that sense or touch, so to speak, which human intelligence maintains in constant alert and with which it so wisely but unconsciously discerns what is best, although it is unable to account for the hidden mental calculation directing it towards the discernment.

832. Another consequence is that fathers see, and according to reason must see, in their children's good the good of all the descendants who are comprised in their own children. Thus, they must place their children's good before their own in this society. They must not be content simply to avoid obstructing their children from acquiring all moral, intellectual and physical good possible, but must want to help towards this acquisition with all their power.

833. However, this kind of paternal instinct can be blunted and checked by evil, which struggles powerfully against reason and good nature.

834. We see once again why the good of the offspring and of their new family often requires separation from their father, who must release the children and dissolve the 'living-together society' by emancipating them.

§2. *The governor of parental society,*
and the nature of his government

835. The administrator and absolute governor of family society is always the father.

836. Some writers have seriously questioned the reasons for this authority, which according to natural, rational Right is

always the father's. They were guided by their observation that a father lacks the force to make his adult child obey when the child realises the full vigour of his age and the father weakens.[208] But I must repeat, one of the most basic errors is that of always substituting force for right, or seeing the title of right in force.

837. It is true that the government of patriarchal societies deteriorates; the aged father has to tolerate many disorders in his children. The patriarchs of the Hebrew people sometimes limited themselves to secretly deploring the serious disorders of their children, feeling they did not have enough strength to control them.[209] This weakness of government can sometimes be a reason why a father allow his child's autonomy by emancipating him.[210]

838. But the contrary can also happen. Good children feel a duty to obey and submit to a father who uses his authority very well to direct the home. In this case the only force with which he exercises his right is the great respect and love shown him by his children.

839. However, when the children who remain with their father are basically intelligent, the father is morally bound to use their knowledge and ability to improve the government of the family. The adult children are the natural *ministers* and the

---

[208] It seems that Gabener explains *patria potestas* as the prevalent force of the parents at the time the children are small. But prevalent force is not the *title* of *patria potestas*; it is only the *means* which in certain cases makes the exercise of the force possible.

[209] For example, the crimes of Reuben and Simeon who were punished by their father on his death-bed.

[210] Adult, married children have the right to separate themselves from their father when their family good requires this. They also have other rights proper to them which their father must respect. Wherever a father maintains the prevalence of the physical force he had over his child as a baby, the adult child's rights and those of his family are often endangered by the father's evil and violence. We see nature's providential purpose in making the children's strength increase with age and the fathers' diminish. By this law the author of nature provides for the preservation of the children's rights as they become independent and begin families, in which the hope of future generations lies. At the same time he leaves intact the *moral ties* between adult children and their aged begetters, because the good resulting from the union and submission of the children at such a time is, almost without exception, moral.

consultors of their aged parents who willingly cede part of their authority.

840. But if the children find in paternal government too little provision for the social good, how long must they be subject to their father when opinions differ as to the good of his person and of the family? In domestic government the father has the same right as a *competent judge*, that is, his judgment must be accepted whenever there is doubt (cf. 611, 612).

841. When the adult child clearly sees that paternal judgment is seriously harmful, or generally obstructs the good of the actual or future family, he can reject the judgment but always with respect and moderation.

842. If the father, moved by unnatural waywardness, then tries to harm the child and the child's family, they can separate and even seek refuge from him.

843. But the adult child can never defend himself and his family against his father's violence to the point of blows and injury.[211]

Article 5.
Particular rights arising from the title of generation

844. Fatherhood has a natural right not to be violated or

---

[211] It would be a different matter if it were a case of using force to restrain the father from his excesses, without striking or injuring his body, and for his own good. There can in fact be quite extraordinary cases where common sense has always recognised that it is lawful to have recourse to exceptions to the ordinary rules — Let us consider the sad circumstances in which Conrad found himself relative to his unnatural father, Henry IV of Germany. This wicked man wanted to force his son to do violence to his wife Adelaide, Conrad's own mother. When Conrad refused, he was vilified and persecuted by his father. Moreover, Henry's wickedness would have done immeasurable damage to public morals, religion and society. The only way of halting this human beast was to oppose force with force. Conrad sided with the opposing faction in defiance of his father's armies and the unjust war with which his father was laying waste the world to his own ruin. None of Conrad's contemporaries judged his action rebellion, but rather an act of singular justice and filial piety on the part of a son. His behaviour redounded to the good of the emperor himself whom he could help only by impeding his mad, devilish fury. Cf. *Amico Cattolico*, May issue, 1842, pp. 329 ss.

harmed by the offspring, who must forego their own right rather than harm their fathers. Morality sets this limit to the children's right which then ceases because of the limit. As the right ceases, the purely moral obligation which children previously had becomes jural.

845. Furthermore, fathers have a superiority and authority over their emancipated children which can never be destroyed.

846. The reason for this permanent superiority is that the children are always a production of their fathers by generation.

847. If the children were merely things, they would always remain in their fathers' ownership. If they withdraw from this ownership, it is solely for the development of their person. Thus, their withdrawal from submission to their fathers takes place according to the demands of their personship. On the other hand, the degree and mode of *patria potestas* which does not harm but helps the personal dignity and good of the children and their families cannot be a reason for the cessation of *patria potestas*.

848. Such authority certainly exists in nature. The honour, deference and obedience of adult children towards their aged fathers, far from being contrary to personal dignity, ennobles and embellishes it. All virtue elevates personal dignity, and is moreover very helpful for union among the descendants, for greater wisdom and counsel in what they do, and for the ability to establish and preserve family practices. Respect for the wisdom of our elders bestows all these good things and their causes on families.

849. This authority of fathers over their children of whatever age and condition is not only moral but also strictly jural, precisely because it is what remains of the paternal dominion over the offspring.

850. We must note however that this residue of paternal dominion is to be exercised temperately and prudently.

851. Moreover, the principle on which it is founded is the same as that for paternal dominion over a baby, that is, 'children are the property of their fathers in everything except the personal element and in the freedom necessary for the descendants' good.' The reasons why parents' dominion is limited are therefore:

    1. relative to their acts the personal element of the children increases with their age;

2. paternal dominion must be withdrawn whenever it prejudices the free, prosperous development of the children's descendants.

852. However, as we have said, these two reasons do not necessarily and radically remove all paternal dominion. In fact this remains in such a way that the fathers could not of themselves entirely secede from it;[212] the children would always have at least the obligation to honour their fathers, even if these were evil, or so unnatural that they had sold the children.

853. Aged parents therefore need wisdom and prudence to exercise their *patria potestas* within just limits over their adult children.

854. The authority shows itself particularly in two cases:

1. in favour of the children themselves, when they are evil and harm their descendants;

2. in favour of the fathers if they need the children's goods in order to live.

A comment on these two particular rights will be helpful.

§1. *The right to correct and punish wayward children*

855. According to natural Right, the authority to correct and even to punish wayward children always remains with the fathers, whatever their children's age and condition.

856. We have already given the reason: this authority does not in any way detract from the children's personal dignity, but helps them and their present and future families.

857. This authority, although recognised by all peoples, is evidently denied by some authors. The reasons why they deny it and omit it from their treatises seem to be reduced to two.

1. The fear that fathers, if granted such authority, will perhaps abuse it. — But this is not a valid reason. I admit that the right to correct and punish perverse adult children is

---

[212] A father can renounce it in part and make promises and obligatory contracts with a child. For example, a father must keep his word if he promises not to involve himself any more in the administration of the child's goods.

difficult to exercise wisely and fruitfully, but I do not think I am obliged to deny its existence. The possibility of its exercise on only one occasion would be enough to require its acceptance and recognition.

858. 2. The necessity of force which the right to punish perverse children requires for its exercise; weak, aged fathers do not generally have this force against their young, healthy children. — But, as we have said, force does not form the title to rights; it is only the means with which they are exercised when obstructed. Hence, lack of force does not prove the lack of right (cf. 809-811).

Moreover, we know of fathers who have been able to punish their wayward adult children by imposing penalties. The children did not revolt because they were restrained by the authority they knew their fathers had, or by their feeling of filial respect which sometimes exerts itself even in perverse spirits, or by fear of being deprived of their inheritance, or by some other accidental circumstance.

§2. The right to dispose of the children's goods in case of necessity

859. Fathers never lose their right to be helped and cared for by their children nor, in case of necessity, to use on their own behalf the goods of their children in order to live.

860. As long as fathers live united with their children, the case is clear. They are the administrators of all the goods of the family whose head they are. If it is true that every member of a domestic society must live off the common assets, it is even more true of the head.

861. Children can acquire goods through their own personal individuality, but while they live in their fathers' house, the goods must be administered by the fathers and disposed of for the children's good.

862. When the children live separately, poverty is the only case where fathers retain the right to use the goods given to their

children and the goods acquired separately by the children. They have a right to enough for their maintenance.

863. This right does not stem from repayment owed by the children who have been cared for by their fathers, but from the residue of *patria potestas* which never entirely ceases and is rooted in the father as begetter of his offspring. The children must refer their own existence to their father, and with their existence all that they are and have.[213]

CHAPTER 7

The preservation of rights of ownership acquired through occupancy, and their extinction

864. We must now see how ownership, acquired through

---

[213] The code of the Canton Ticino, more than the French, Austrian and Piedmontese codes, favours fathers in the matter of usufruct of goods of children under *patria potestas*. According to this code, *patria potestas* has joined to it the right 'to make the children's possessions its own, including those goods acquired by military service and by the liberal arts', and also the right 'to administer and have usufruct of the goods disposed in favour of the children by living persons or last testaments, if the disposer's will does not oppose the right' (§103). — Article 384 of the Napoleonic code grants to the father, and to the mother if she survives him, the usufruct of the children's goods up to the completion of their 18th year. In the session of March 12th 1803, the Councillor of State, Real, apparently gave as the reason that the legislators considered this advantage granted to the fathers as an indemnity due to the hardship and care experienced by the parents in rearing the children. In my view, this reason would not have been accepted if paternal feeling had been preserved in all its natural vigour. When this feeling is complete, as it would be in perfect human nature, it does not require indemnity, although it does require authority. Whenever paternal feeling has weakened in nations or in humanity, indemnity is spoken about and accepted as right. The father in this case thinks and reasons as a mere upbringer or supplier of food. In this way the varying force which *paternal feeling* expresses must modify Right among nations, as I have observed relative to the varying force of the *marital feeling* (cf. *ER*, 81-82). The same can be said about every other natural feeling, because *every natural feeling furnishes matter for Right*, which establishes itself in a particular people.

occupancy and the other ways we have examined, may be preserved and lost.

Does the preservation of ownership require the continuation of the conditions we have laid down for occupancy? If this were the case, would ownership be lost when one of the conditions — for example, the commencement of useful work on something — ceased altogether? Is ownership such that, once acquired, it cannot be lost through inaction on the part of the owner?

865. As we have seen, ownership is the result of a moral-physical bond (cf. 397). If this bond is formed by nature itself and not by some act on our part, it is unbreakable by us, and breakable only in certain cases by nature, which formed it. For example, ownership of our body could not eliminated by any act of our own. Only nature, through death, can remove the body from our power by separating it from our personal principle and thus destroying it as an object of right.

866. What belongs to us through a bond formed by nature cannot therefore pass to the ownership of others by any kind of prescription or usucaption. This explains why civil laws themselves acknowledge that such titles are inapplicable to certain objects.[214]

867. But if the bond of ownership is not formed by nature, so that we are dealing only with acquired rights which are not contemporaneously moral obligations, the bond that we make may also be dissolved by us.[215]

---

[214] Cf. the Austrian code, §§1451, 1452, 1455, 1459, 1481, 1483 — the Albertine code AA. 169, 2361.

[215] Amongst our acquired rights it is possible to find ownership which depends simultaneously on an act of ours and upon nature which intervenes to sanction this bond of ownership with moral obligations inherent to the acquired rights. For example, marital rights draw their origin from an act of ours although nature intervenes to form and consecrate the marital tie. Consequently, the relationships between husband and wife, like those between father and son, are unalterable. This is true even though we can say that their origin, relative to their real subsistence, springs from some willed act of ours. *Connatural* rights are not the sole category of rights over which prescription and usucaption are unable to prevail; acquired rights in the formation of which nature intervenes are also free of all prescription and usucaption. Because of nature's intervention they belong more to nature than to ourselves, and are sanctioned in their very being by moral obligations.

868. There is no doubt that in such a case our ownership ceases first of all as a result of a simple act of our will which renounces that right. The act of will is the first necessity in possession and dominion and, as such, is the principal element of the moral-physical bond.

869. Granted, however, that we have not willingly renounced ownership of anything, could ownership cease as a result of some deficiency in the conditions necessary for occupancy? Let us examine the matter carefully. One of the conditions was the usefulness of the object for the occupier.[216] Now it seems clear that if an object becomes evidently and perpetually useless to me and mine, rational Right requires that it be considered no longer as occupied by me, but free.

870. This object could, therefore, be occupied by another provided that the new occupier shows the necessary moral regard due to the person who wrongly wishes to continue his occupation. In other words, the new owner must provide a clear explanation of what he is doing so that the other person does not suffer reasonable displeasure.

871. It may be objected that the right not to make use of something is included in its ownership. — This right not to use something that is one's own is generally acknowledged by authors. I acknowledge it also, but I think that more careful consideration is required if it is not to be misunderstood.

872. Let us imagine that a person declares and obliges himself not to want now or in the future any use or profit for himself or his family from some given thing which, however, he retains as his own to prevent its use by others. I am sure that every person of good sense would see this as unreasonable and therefore against right. The thing under discussion would be considered as free, and as such could be occupied by others. It could even be removed from the unreasonable occupier by force if he tried to retain it by force. In the state of nature this would be idle retention, and in our case declared so by the occupier himself.

873. But why is this the only limit placed upon the non-use of something by its owner? — The reason is as follows.

If we consider human beings in the state of nature, we start by

[216] *ER*, 252-255.

mentally conceiving them as isolated, without any relationships amongst themselves. In these circumstances, our first question is: 'What are the duties and rights which have their foundation in nature alone?'

Strictly speaking, there are no rights except in relationship with others. Nevertheless, the *roots of rights*, that is, the faculties for doing forcefully and lawfully all that one pleases, are found in every isolated individual of the human species considered without reference to others. Solitary individuals think only of themselves, but not as a result of selfishness or lack of benevolence towards their fellows. Others do not yet exist for them; they suppose others not to be, and abstract completely from their existence.

The freedom of such individuals cannot therefore be limited by relationships proceeding from others who have been totally eliminated from the calculation. An individual's thoughts, affections and actions are subject to certain moral laws, but not to anything else. In such a hypothetical state, personship develops with all its force; it can only believe that no obstacle will impede whatever it wishes to do; when anything does impede its action, personship can only feel pain and indignation. In these circumstances it emerges in all its freedom wherever it pleases, carrying out once and for all whatever it wishes. Everything is affected by the real force which the human person possesses and with which the person refers everything exclusively to itself. Taken up with itself as it is, the human person cannot refer things to any other end, which is still unknown to it.

874. Human personship is also naturally inclined to this absolute dominion over things for other reasons:

1. because of its own excellence which is such that it cannot subject itself to anything except the truth;

2. because it does not as yet know any other personship which merits the same esteem as that attributed to itself;

3. because nature has joined to personship certain things, such as its own body and the faculties available to the person, with a bond that is of itself unbreakable and inviolable.

875. Imitating the natural dominion that it possesses and exercises over the inferior powers and over its animal body, human personship also reaches out to dispose of everything that can be useful to it. It draws everything into the whirlpool of its

existence without regard or consideration for others to whom it reacts with irritation and displeasure if they place any obstacle to its activity.

876. Such absolute dominion of personship over things could never be blameworthy if human beings always did what was good. If this were the case, dominion could be loved and willed by personship only for the sake of some real advantage.

877. Human depravity, however, is such that personship delights in its dominion over things not for the benefit and justice accruing from dominion, but solely for the sake of naked dominion and the pleasure of feeling its own superiority. The more dominion is exercised capriciously, the more pleasure is felt as absolute and free from any limitation exercised by reason. When ambition and longing for seigniory over things has entered corrupt, human spirits, it is clear that any attempt to disturb their pretended seigniory is going to cause great offence; anyone occupying something already possessed by another is going to cause trouble whether the thing is held according to a reasonable state of satisfaction or simply for the power that possession brings with it. Consequently, it was thought that in both cases some injury would be inflicted as a result of the disturbed possession and its ensuing discomfort, and that the first occupiers of a thing had the right of ownership over it even if they held it only for the sake of dominion. Finally, it was also thought that this right extended to any use whatsoever, however capricious it might be, and even to non-use intended to prevent the thing's use by others.

878. But careful consideration will show that this is not human nature's natural Right; it is not rational for a rational creature to act against reason. Antiquity was very clear about this when it placed the foundation of Right in the law of probity which is as natural to humanity as reason itself.[217]

---

[217] 'Those who have received reason from NATURE have also been given right reason. They have therefore been given law, which, as right reason, commands and prohibits; but if they have been given law, they have also been given RIGHT' (*De leg.*, 1, 12). — Hence, *right* has its source in the *moral law*, the moral law in *reason*, and reason is given by *nature*. According to Cicero, *natural right* is the child of reason and of the moral law. This is not the so-called right shared with animals, but 'the right proper to human nature', as we have said.

[876–878]

It is true that we all have to abstain from causing others displeasure when displeasure is natural to human beings, that is, when displeasure is rational, as in the case of harm to just ownership; but there is no moral obligation to do this when displeasure is unnatural because irrational. In this case, the discomfort arises from a vitiated, capricious desire to prevent others' using things which, according to our hypothesis, the present occupier cannot and does not wish to use either now or in the future.

879. Let us move on now from consideration of the isolated individual who appropriates things without regard for his fellow human beings to a reflection on the same individual who has made some progress in the state of nature. He now co-exists with other human beings to whom he is related through his intelligence and moral status. When he makes things his own, therefore, he has to take others into consideration. Mere caprice can no longer provide a good foundation for the right of ownership. Moreover, the person at the first stage of the state of nature has still not acquired ownership by right, although a material ownership has come into being; he has united things to himself instinctively, almost in the same way as an animal appropriates its lair and the food it requires for itself and its offspring. A physical bond exists, and pain when the bond is broken; but right, the moral form, and jural resentment arising from its violation, is not yet present. This begins only in the instant that the physical bond becomes a source of moral obligation forbidding others from doing harm. However, the physical bond, which is not morally worthy of respect because it is not reasonable, is only an abuse of power and freedom entailing contempt and damage for others. It neither requires reverence nor is it informed by law. It is a fact, but it is not yet a right.[218]

---

[218] The same principles resolve the question: 'Does ownership cease in the case of necessity?' It is certain that if an owner, even in the state of nature, has to consider others, he also has the *jural* obligation to allow others to use what is his when this is necessary for the preservation of their existence, provided it is not necessary for his own existence. Whoever uses another's property in these circumstances should, however, make known to the owner the dire need in which he finds himself. If the goods were just as necessary to the existence of the owner, no one could take them from him. — Finally, the person in need may find it possible to take what is necessary as a loan rather

880. Our question has been decided, therefore, solely on the basis of the rather improbable supposition that someone capriciously retains things for the sole motive of having them or excluding others from enjoying them. The supposition is not, however, impossible, nor could we do without it as a means of first offering a general solution to the essence of the problem, considered bereft of its accidents. But we can now go on to consider the accidents which may accompany the problem and solve it with reference to them and the changes they may bring about.

881. In fact, it is hardly likely that anyone will go so far as to declare that he has no wish either now or in the future to use something he possesses for himself or his family. If he does not make such an unusual declaration, it cannot be presumed, nor can frivolous arguments be employed to establish it. Indubitable arguments in its favour have be present before it can be used as a basis for action. Such proofs are, however, very difficult to procure.

882. If it is difficult to find such a case in practice, others can be found. For example, there is no doubt that if I were present when someone in a furious rage was about to smash a precious vase, and I managed to save the vase from certain destruction (if I caught it before it reached the ground), it would now belong to me, not to the previous owner,[219] who has shown only too clearly that he never wanted to use it again.

than in absolute ownership. If this is possible, it must be done, and the loan restored as soon as possible. His need to preserve his existence gives him the right to use the property of another only for his own preservation, and with the least possible disturbance to the owner.

[219] If, for instance, some wood is swept away by a river, and its owner does not come after it, what I save from the water and collect belongs to me. In this case, it is mine under the title of *salvage*. The difference between the titles of *salvage* and *occupancy* is this: in occupancy, I can hurry, along with others, to be the first to occupy and take possession of what is free; in *salvage*, I must give precedence to the person who has lost what is his (provided he wishes to save it); I can save it only if the owner shows that he does not want or is not able to save it. There is another difference in rational Right: if the owner does not save something because he does not *want* to do so, he has no right to restitution. If however he does not save it because he *cannot*, but I save it, I must in equity give it back to him. Compensation is due for my expenses and effort; if the favour I do has cost me no effort (for example, when I have found

883. It is certainly not correct to conclude from temporary non-use of anything that its owner has no intention of ever using it again. Nor can another person's ownership be disturbed if he makes little use of what he owns and draws less benefit from it than he could. An owner has to be granted full power of decision about the quantity and quality of the use of the things he owns, provided that he makes some use of them.

884. At most, lack of understanding, power or will in the use of some given thing authorises others to complain to the owner, according to rational Right, if they suffer harm from the privation of some good that might accrue to all from better use of the thing. They may come to some agreement with him about better use of what he owns, and even put pressure on him with due moderation if he evades the agreement, and resultant harm is serious, evident and common.[220]

885. If this right did not exist in nature, there would be no foundation in natural Right for the laws with which civil society places wastrels under supervision. It is just and in accordance with reason for the rest of the community to appeal in favour of minors or the public, or even of private good. This kind of natural limit is contained in the right of ownership.

886. If the simple temporary non-use of something is insufficient to prove the owner's desire never to use it, lack of adequate defence of the thing provides still less proof that it has been abandoned to occupancy by others. Some kind of force, although always present in the case of occupancy, entails use of the thing, but does not form the physical bond (cf. 469).

887. Generally speaking, the defence of private ownership is always present when civil society has been constituted. If the private owner himself is incapable of defending what he owns, society itself undertakes this responsibility.

888. In addition, we know that human nature has to be handled with respect even when necessarily subjected to

something), some reward seems appropriate from an equitable, moral point of view. I have only a *moral*, not a *jural obligation* to save the lost property of others if I can do so.

[220] Common sense is inclined to excuse thefts against people who do not know how to benefit or profit from what they have, and to look favourably upon well-maintained fields and houses, etc.

unpleasant treatment (that is, to what defective human nature sees as harsh treatment) (cf. 457). This is even more to the point when proof that something has been abandoned is still uncertain.

889. This uncertainty provides us with no right except that of verifying the proof.

890. One way of doing this is to ask the owner about it. At times, it may even be possible to attempt, in the presence of the supposed owner, to use the thing or the right whose use has apparently been abandoned. If the owner is silent, and refrains from complaining, we have a sign that he is not displeased. This proof can be considered satisfactory because damage to owner-ship would provoke pain or complaint on his part as a definite natural symptom of the damage.

891. It may be objected that it is impossible to begin to use something which could belong to another. — Yes, but there would not seem to be any injury or harm done if such use, intended simply as a proof, were done without damage, and if accompanied by a readiness to withdraw when the doubtful owner insisted on his right. This in fact is what normally happens.

892. On the other hand, this is the usual reaction of anyone who doubts whether he owns something. If a doubtful owner of something remains silent when I use it freely under his eyes, a reasonable persuasion arises in favour of my ownership and against that of the other person, provided that the silence cannot be explained in some other way. For example, as a sign of fear, ignorance about one's own titles, and so on.

893. Civil laws often have recourse to this proof when dealing with doubtful rights. Prescription and usucaption, which pos-itive law considers as titles or modes of acquisition, are examples of such proof. However, they are not recognised as means of ascertaining rights unless the apparent owner has failed to complain, when he could have done so, against the use he sees others making of the uncertain right.[221]

[221] Cf. §§1459, 1478, 1482, 1483, 1487, 1490, 1495-1497 of the Austrian Civil Code. — This code first recognises the right of an owner not to make use of the thing he owns (§1456, 1481). — Simple non-use of a right does not invalidate that right. Some other sign is needed from which it may be inferred

894. All this clearly shows that the principal questions arising about rights are normally concerned with the *signs* that make rights known and publicised, rather than with the matter of right itself. In other words, we are dealing with that which imposes the obligation to respect rights.

CHAPTER 8
Analysis of the right of ownership

895. As far as I can see, we have now arrived at a point where analysis of the right of ownership will be both clear and useful. Summarising what has been said, the analysis will throw new light upon it by ordering and completing it, and thus serving as a foundation of all that remains to be developed under the heading of rational Right.

896. With this in mind, we need to start at the highest level by reconsidering the concept of the *state of nature*, and comparing our understanding of it with that of writers whose opinions we

that the possessor of the right considers it as abandoned and conferred upon someone else. One such sign is seen in his not complaining when others use the right, or in his not making use of it when there was an occasion for doing so and circumstances would lead people to believe that he would use it if indeed he believed he possessed it. Another sign would be his failure to prohibit its use. — Notice that in the state of nature prescription and occupancy serve as *signs* for recognising if the rights of others are extinct, and hence if it is lawful to dispose of the objects of these rights. Under civil law, prescription and occupancy are also used as *penalties* against negligent owners in order to make them more vigilant in the administration of their goods, and as a *means* for resolving disputes. Nevertheless, the principal concept under which civil laws consider prescription and usucaption is always that of signs indicating where right exists between two parties. For instance, if someone has paid a debt without appealing to prescription, he loses the right to appeal to it. He has acknowledged the debt in paying it (§1497 of the Austrian code). For the same reason, a judge is under no obligation to consider prescription unless the parties to a dispute have spoken about it. Prescription is a means of ascertaining the persuasions of the parties; it has no other purpose (§1501 of the Austrian code).

do not wholly share. If this concept is not well defined, the following question will not be clear either: 'What right is present amongst people in the state of nature?', nor the rather more restricted question: 'What is ownership in the state of nature? What elements does it include?' Again, it will be impossible to judge writers whose opinion we do not accept, or explain their errors, if we are ignorant of their concept of the state of nature.

897. There is no doubt that the nature and the constitutive elements of the right of ownership necessarily vary according to the concept expressed by the word 'nature'. However, I shall not indicate all these meanings here, nor describe their history. I shall restrict myself to pointing to the three principal meanings which are most useful for our purpose and give three different values to the expression 'the state of nature'.

Article 1.
The threefold meaning in which the word 'nature'
has been understood by writers on natural right

898. The first meaning in which the word 'nature' was taken by authors on Right contradistinguishes *nature* from *reason*. Taken in this way, *nature* was understood as the complex of animal inclinations. This meaning is found, for example, when we say: '*Reason* teaches us to conquer the fear of death; *nature* is always fearful of death.'

899. The second meaning is used to indicate an isolated individual, cut off altogether from his fellows and left to himself. In this sense, *nature* is the opposite of *communal living*. A person in this condition is not strictly speaking deprived of reason, but he is cut off from all association with his fellows, and with all society — which is much more serious.

900. Finally, the third meaning is that which contradistinguishes *nature* from *society*. In this sense, the human being in nature is not only furnished with reason and morality, but also with relationships towards his fellows relative to whom he must use his reason and observe the moral precepts.

901. We take the word 'nature' in this final meaning in our examination of the rights which exist between people in the *state*

of nature. It would seem that in wanting to define such rights by forming for ourselves a more abstract concept of the state of nature, we run the danger of losing ourselves in a mass of useless subtleties which lead only to harmful mistakes.

902. The sophist Rousseau took the word 'nature' in the first of the three meanings. Consequently, natural Right, from which he excluded the effect or requirement of reason and morality, was for him an animal, not a human right. It was a Right that was not Right.[222]

903. The second meaning of the word 'nature' expresses the concept of what is innate in the human being (cf. 283). It includes, therefore, his rational as well as his animal part, but excludes his relationship with other people precisely because they are not contained in the simple concept of the humanity of an individual. But holding strictly to this concept of human nature would mean leaving aside all external things as well as other people. Those professing this meaning of 'nature' would also have to reject all human actions that do not begin at birth.

904. In this case, no effective natural Right would be possible. Only its potentiality would remain or, as we have already said, certain roots of rights (cf. 873).

905. This would also entail a very demanding and tiring kind of *abstraction* without any consequent benefit for knowledge or human life.

906. Most writers of this class do not, however, strictly maintain the abstract human nature on which they have based their Right. They are satisfied with the individual human being, surrounded by beasts and material things, but cut off from his fellows. The system of natural Right arising from a method of this kind is not *animal*, but totally *selfish*.

907. In this system, the human being taken in isolation is granted an absolute ownership together with strict, inflexible rights, simply because these rights are established without the least regard for other co-existent human beings. Rights conceived in this fashion are inevitably false because they are not derived from human beings as human beings are and must be. These are not true human rights, which are *moral relationships*

[222] Cf. *SP*, bk. 1, c. 4, for my opinion of Rousseau's system of natural Right [App., no. 4].

between several individuals, not simply *qualities* inherent to the nature of the individual. True human rights spring from common human nature existent in each human being. On the one hand, therefore, this method endeavours to promote the derivation of rights; on the other, to eliminate that *relationship* in which right consists.

908. Some comment is needed here.

There are authors who maintain that they consider human beings in relationship with their fellows, and derive the nature of rights from this relationship. However, having begun their treatises in this admirable way, they go on to propose the crudest and most inexorable right of ownership which they declare lawful even while admitting its essentially immoral character.[223]

909. These authors are not consistent. Ownership which remains intact even when detrimental to other people can be derived only from the suppression of intellectual and moral relationships between the individual to whom ownership is attributed and his fellows. Ownership of this kind can only be understood without reference to these relationships. It vanishes, considered as right, when the relationships emanating from human nature are reinstated as part of the calculation from which they had been unlawfully excluded.

910. One meaning given to the word 'nature' depends upon considering it in opposition to *freedom*. Necessary activity is attributed to nature; and the human will itself, if it acts necessarily, is called *nature*.[224]

---

[223] As we have seen, Zeiller, an otherwise excellent author, agrees that right involves some relationship with other human beings. In a note to his *Manuale*, he expresses the matter very well: 'If only one individual existed on earth, the idea of ownership, which always has reference to the exclusion of others, would not exist. In the literal sense of the phrase, we do not have "a right to anything", but only a right to exclude others from it in so far as it belongs to us' (Note to §77). Here Zeiller sees that right supposes the faculty to exclude, but does not observe sufficiently that the right to *exclude* arises from the *moral obligation* of others to allow themselves to be excluded. If this obligation did not exist, our right would no longer exist.

[224] The human will sometimes acts spontaneously but *necessarily*, and sometimes *freely*. Consequently, metaphysicians have distinguished two kinds of willed acts which they call *will as nature*, and *will as will*. — Cf. St. Thomas, *S.T.*, I, q. 83, art 3, ad 4; III, q. 18, art. 3.

911. Consequently, that which pertains to *art*, considered as an effect of free human activity, is contradistinguished from *nature*, as we see in the following phrases: 'in poetry, nature is more effective than art', 'as a speaker, he is too artificial and insufficiently natural', and so on.

912. Society is presumed to be a work of human freedom, and people are presumed to form societies because they freely wish to do so. It cannot be denied that any society whatsoever is bound together by means of willed acts.

913. According to this meaning, the *state of nature* came to be called that in which the many inhabitants of the earth were found together but not yet associated amongst themselves. Indeed, my co-existence with others, granted that they are not my descendants (as Adam and Eve are not) is not the effect of free will on the part of any individual. It is therefore a condition posited by nature. This is the natural state in which I normally consider human beings when I ask: 'What Right has one human being towards another in the state of nature?' and more particularly: 'What is the nature of the right of ownership in the state of nature?'[225]

---

[225] What has been said in this article does not prevent the division of a treatise on *rational Right* (after the distinction between *individual Right* and *social Right*) into two subdivisions of *individual Right* called natural Right and *contractual Right*, that is, willed right. This is precisely the division of rational Right proposed in the Introduction to this work. In this division, the title 'natural Right' does not mean 'the Right of human beings in the state of nature' but 'the Right that springs from the elements of human nature, not from acts of free decision on the part of individuals'. Natural Right, considered in this way as a part of individual Right, is not subject to the defect we have noted in excessive abstraction. The basis of our natural Right is not an hypothesis concerned with isolated individuals, but supposes that human beings are already in full communication with one another. Our single reservation is that in the accumulation of rights possessed by people who co-exist and communicate with one another in a state anterior to civil society (state of nature), we distinguish rights which have their TITLE in human *nature* itself from those whose TITLE depends upon *agreement*, that is, upon a contract established between human beings as a result of free acts of will. In my *Society and its Purpose*, I have called the whole of *individual Right*, 'natural Right'. It can indeed be called this; what is necessary is that we state clearly the meaning in which we use words.

[911–913]

Article 2.
Three other meanings given to the word NATURE
by writers on natural right

914. Before replying to this question, we have to justify more adequately the sense we give to the phrase 'state of nature'. What we have said so far justifies it relatively to the first two meanings of the word 'nature'. The first meaning is confined to expressing an animal condition from which no right can be derived; the second, by isolating human beings from one another, also makes Right impossible (Right can only be furthered on the basis of mutual relationships).

The third meaning on the other hand retains both human beings and their intercommunication; only the positive laws of civil society are excluded. Given the totality of natural conditions,[226] this third meaning expresses the rights proper to each individual.

915. But we have to defend the suitability of understanding the phrase 'state of nature' in this sense against other meanings, which go to the opposite extreme to those we have already criticised. While the first two meanings detract excessively from human beings in nature, the other meanings, of which we are about to speak, grant them too much.

916. Some writers, in opposition to those about whom we have spoken, maintain that domestic society should be included in the state of nature. The bonds of this society are natural in so

---

[226] Note carefully that we are speaking about what is given by *nature*, not by human *free will*, and that nature forms the *conditions* in which natural rights are found, not the rights themselves. In our system acquired-natural rights often have as their cause and title a free action on the part of the human being who acquires them (cf. 293 ss.). The *condition* in which this person finds himself, however, is *natural*, not *artificial*. We call this natural condition the 'state of nature'. According to us, therefore, the natural condition which forms the state of nature is the *individual* in relationship with other individuals. The *individual* state of the human being is the state of nature, a primitive condition which changes with the formation of society. At that moment, several individuals make up a single artificial individual normally called a 'collective person'. This is a new condition and a new state, the *state of society* as opposed to the state of nature.

far as only the inclinations of nature, not free will, seem required to bring them about.

917. Other writers, for a similar reason, want the *state of nature* to include civil society taken in general. According to them the human being, drawn and led by nature itself to found civil communities, is naturally social [*App.*, no. 5].

918. Finally, others go so far as to consider that the various forms of government and even positive legislations pertain to the state of nature. According to these authors, human beings exceed the state of nature only when they do evil; all governments, and even the laws which appear as determinations willed by human beings, are simply the development of the natural human being. Like a great tree, which grows from a humble shoot to become a sturdy trunk and rich foliage without losing its nature as a tree, human beings do not abandon but extend and perfect their state of nature when they use and develop their faculties through associating with one another in so many different ways. C. L. Haller employs something akin to this kind of reasoning.

919. We do not want to argue about the use of words, and we willingly grant that in so far as anything is reasonable for human beings it is also natural. It is also true that society is a natural development for humanity. We simply reply that in the treatise on rights it is a useful part of method first to consider human individuals as co-existent but not yet associated, and then as associated; we examine separately the rights resulting from relationships between individuals and individuals, and then those proper to members of a society. We maintain that the state of individuals and the state of associates have to be suitably distinguished, and that this can be done conveniently by using the phrase 'state of nature' for the former and 'state of society' for the latter. People are first born as individuals, and then become members of artificial society; they cannot be considered as associated in society before they have consented to its existence. Association only begins with an act of one's own will.

920. Those who maintain that family bonds are formed solely by nature have confused the physical juncture and gregarious living common to animals with the juncture which is the characteristic of society proper to human beings alone. Society is not mere physical togetherness, but a union of intelligent wills

aiming together at the common good. This is the *form* of society; physical togetherness provides only a material rudiment of society.[227]

Article 3.
The distinction between ownership and the right of ownership

921. The distinction we make between *ownership* and the *right of ownership* is somewhat similar[228] to that between physical *togetherness* and *society*.

922. Union, nothing more, is included in the concept of *ownership* — or possibly unification of something with a person in such a way that the person believes the thing to be *his*, to pertain to himself as an appendix of himself.

923. For the person to be persuaded of this, a *physical* and *intellectual* juncture between the thing and the person is sufficient. The moral bond in all its fullness is still not necessary.

924. The existence of the person[229] and something useful, and

---

[227] Cf. the notion of society developed in my *SP*, bk. 1.

[228] 'Somewhat similar', not 'equal', because animality is sufficient for gregarious living despite the lack of the intellectual and moral element. To form *society*, the *intellectual* element is also required, although nothing more; for the formation of *ownership*, both animality and the intellectual element are required; for the formation of *right*, however, the *moral* element is needed more.

[229] Person is not present in animals. External things are joined to the animal feeling by means of a physical or animal bond, but the animal knows nothing of its own self, does not think, does not believe anything. The SELF attributed to animals is bestowed upon them by our imagination, nothing more. — If, therefore, no MYSELF and no owner exists, there is no *ownership* and nothing of *one's own*. Ownership (and hence *a fortiori* right) is not found in animals; only a juncture of feeling is present which simulates human ownership. — This observation will be very clear to readers who have accepted the concept of animal which we developed at length in *AMS*. — Note finally that the first of the two intellective acts forming the physical bond (cf. 386) is sufficient to form *ownership* (but not the *right of ownership*). The second element could be lacking provided that the intellect posited no contrary act by judging that the thing in question was not lawfully occupiable. In this case, the individual would be conscious that the thing is not his and that he would not have ownership of it.

their mutual bonding with the ties we have indicated, is sufficient to place in being the first two junctures, physical and intellectual, and to allow the person to *believe* that a given thing is *his*.

925. If there were only one individual on the earth, therefore, *ownership* would exist. Everything that the person intended to use and enjoy in perpetuity would be his.

926. The *right to ownership* would not, however, exist, because this right involves in addition a relationship with other people which consists in their moral obligation to respect the ownership of those who have it. Ownership is elevated to the dignity of right only in so far as moral obligation seals and informs it.

Article 4.
Ownership is in some way unlimited;
the right of ownership is limited

927. The distinction between *ownership* and the *right of ownership* enables us to explain how a great number of authors on Right have formed an absolute and totally unlimited concept of the right of ownership. Zeiller says:

> By power of the right of ownership, that is, of the exclusive and arbitrary disposition of the very substance of anything, the owner can give to that thing an altogether different form (specify it), use it up or destroy it as he wishes, even though that may be contrary to morality.[230]

928. After that, it is not surprising to find the same author maintaining, as we have seen, that the harmless use of what belongs to other people is an injury to right if such use is against the will of the owner, even though the owner's will is evidently irrational and insane. It is very clear that authors like this confuse *ownership* with the *right of ownership*.

929. Civil codes normally put a limit to the right of ownership by defining it as 'the right to dispose of and enjoy what is owned

[230] §80.

in any way whatsoever provided the use made of it is not forbidden by laws and ordinances'.[231] These laws and ordinances are intended to prevent owners from using what they own in a way injurious to others or to the commonalty, but can do this only by acknowledging that there is no right to such use. Legislators, therefore, reveal in practice that they share the opinion we defend (ownership as a right has limits), although they do not say so directly.

930. But perhaps the legislators decree laws arbitrarily, or with the tacit consent of owners? — Maintaining that positive laws arise from caprice would be to deny their quality as law. If human prescriptions are to be laws, they must be reasonable and just.

931. It is gratuitous to maintain that in the formation of laws on ownership, owners have tacitly renounced the fullness of their ownership. The renunciation of the right to ownership, or of part of it, should be expressed. If owners keep silence, they approve common sense which acknowledges that ownership receives limitations from reason and from morality. It is certain that owners would not have allowed their ownership to be curtailed if they were all persuaded of their right to unlimited ownership; if someone had allowed this, he would have performed an act of generosity, which would not be obligatory for all other owners.

932. We can see this better if we consider more carefully the inner feeling of legislators and in particular — to avoid interminable quotations — that of Roman legislators whose work has provided the source of all our modern legislations.

In Justinian's *Institutes* under the title *The division of things and how their dominion is acquired*[232] we read:

> According to natural Right, the following are common to everyone: air, running water, the sea and the foreshore, as an extension of the sea. No one can be forbidden access to the foreshore, provided they keep away from houses, monuments and buildings which are not part of the law of the peoples in the way the sea is. All rivers and ports are in the public domain and, therefore, the right to fish in ports

---

[231] Albertine code, §439.
[232] Bk. 2, tit. 1.

and rivers. — The use of river banks is also in the public right as a result of the law of nations, along with the use of the river itself. Anyone is free, therefore, to draw up to the banks of rivers, to tie ropes to trees growing in the rivers, and to carry cargoes on the rivers, just as they are free to navigate on these waters. The ownership of the banks, however, belongs to those who own the adjacent fields; and the same is true for the ownership of trees.

This is sufficient. I am not quoting this passage in order to discuss problems that may arise from it, but simply to present the feelings of its authors about the claim to the so-called unlimited nature of ownership.

933. First, we must note that the text is not a law, but a doctrinal exposition; it does not express the will of the ruler, but the reason for things. The language is that of natural Right, that is, the Right of nations.[233]

934. According to this rational Right, therefore, limits are placed to private ownership. But the reason this passage of Justinian disallows appropriation of certain things by human beings is the respect that we should have for our fellows. We are forbidden to take possession of the foreshore, which has to remain public, or to defend it forcefully although we could use it for our own purposes and advantage. Private ownership must observe certain responsibilities of equity and benevolence towards others if it is to be just and moral. If not, the good sense of nations will refuse to acknowledge it as a genuine right.

935. It is true that private citizens are permitted to appropriate the banks of rivers, but only on condition that ships are allowed to draw up to them, and that mooring to their trees and unloading of cargoes is permitted. In a word, navigation is to be free. A right of ownership over beaches is acknowledged, therefore, but it is restricted by the rational Right accepted by all nations. The owner must respect other living people.

936. The opinion held by Roman jurisprudence is clear: no right of ownership is conceived as a crude faculty for untram-

[233] The *right of nations* is still a natural Right according to Justinian. His concept of it is expressed as follows: 'That which NATURAL RIGHT has established amongst all human beings is equally preserved amongst all peoples. It is called THE LAW OF NATIONS, and all nations use it as such' (1, 2).

melled use of what has been appropriated without reference to others. The right of ownership has to be founded in certain moral relationships with other human beings.

Separating right from morality under the pretext that *morality* and *natural right* are different things, means sacrificing the truth to abstract knowledge which, of itself, evaporates. For myself, I would prefer to hold to the uniform feeling of people throughout the ages; I would prefer the truth of Cicero's affirmation about the proper, original essence of human right, which he expressed in a manner worthy of the light of Christianity: 'The foundation of RIGHT is found in the inclination we all possess by nature to love our fellows.'[234] This is the constant opinion of a man who had drunk at the sources of all ancient philosophy, who held first place in one of the greatest civilisations, who was an excellent jurist and a most eloquent and moving interpreter of human nature.

937. The limits of mutual ownership have provided some of the most difficult and delicate questions of jurisprudence amongst private individuals as well as nations. It is these questions which witness to the universal, constant opinion that the right of ownership must have moral limits. If moral limits did not exist, there would be no litigation to determine them.

938. We have seen that according to Justinian the sea is free, and the foreshore is public. He drew this limitation of the right of ownership from the human, moral principle that the common good of free navigation should not be impeded. In modern times, this right over the sea has been restricted by jurists and it has been almost universally recognised that the part of the sea around coasts belongs to the country whose coasts they are.

939. The extent of this dominion has, however, been disputed. The lawyers' reply is that it extends as far the sea can be defended, that is, within cannon-range.

---

[234] *Nam hae nascuntur ex eo, quod natura propensi sumus ad diligendos homines,* QUOD FUNDAMENTUM JURIS EST (*De Legib.*, 1, 15). Cicero touches the true principle of Right with this principle. As we have said, it consists 'in the obligation that others have of not causing us harm' by disturbing our freedom and our ownership. This obligation is nothing else than a branch of our duty to love our fellows, a duty imposed by nature. Certain modern authors vainly claim to have discovered a *Right* without any relationship whatsoever with *morality*. Morality will always be the sole source of Right.

[937–939]

940. This reply shows that the question has not been considered as one of *private ownership*, but as of *sovereign dominion*. There has never been any argument about the right of the inhabitants of a region to come and go as they please, and to use the sea where it touches the shore provided the government does not forbid them.

941. The reply is equitable precisely because there is no question of private ownership, but of sovereign dominion. It is necessary for the ruler to be able, normally speaking, to defend any place in order to say it belongs to his dominion.

942. Nevertheless, many modern States have abandoned such a decision. Denmark lays claim to the sea for seven leagues around Iceland; England wants to prevent herring fishing by the Dutch within 30 English miles of the North Sea coast. Certain stretches of the sea have been declared the exclusive dominion of a nation: the Irish Sea between England and Ireland has been claimed for the British Empire; the Hellespont, the strait of the Bosphorus, the sea of Marmara, the Aegean and the Black Sea for the Ottoman Empire; the Strait of Messina for the King of Naples; the Zuiderzee for the Low Countries. the Sound and the two Belts for Denmark, and so on. The question of dominion over the sea by Venice, and the English dominion of the sea around its shores, has been much debated in the schools. There was even question of the exclusive right to navigate certain seas for trade. The Hanseatic cities complained bitterly about Dutch vessels landing at Bergen which until that time had been visited only by Hanseatic boats; the Portuguese and the Spaniards were in conflict over mutual claims to exclusion from seas they had navigated and lands they had discovered. This dispute was settled by the supreme Pontiff in 1506.

943. It is clear therefore that in the common feeling of nations the right of ownership is often limited by circumstances, all of which are reduced finally to a moral principle, that is, to appropriating things in a way that preserves due respect for others.

944. On the contrary, there is no limitation to *ownership* when it is a *fact* of human nature.

945. This extraordinary fact of human nature called *ownership* consists in the inclination and the power possessed by the human person for uniting to himself, with all the forces at his disposition, whatever he considers as good. The person immediately thinks of

these things as parts of himself, as his own; this act is called *appropriation*.

946. If appropriation consists in the act with which *the person* makes things part of himself, in his feeling and persuasion,[235] we should not be surprised if *ownership* shares in the very characteristics of person.

947. These characteristics are principally: 1. *exclusiveness*: person, to whom incommunicable being is attributed, is essentially exclusive in its relationship to everyone else. Consequently, one person's *ownership* also excludes all other persons from participation.

948. 2. *Perpetuity*: person is identical, unchangeable and perpetual. Consequently, *ownership* also supposes perpetuity, that is, what is mine is always mine; it forms part of me for as long as I am.

949. 3. *Unity* and *simplicity*: person is one and simple. Consequently that which belongs to person also shares in its prerogatives of unity and simplicity.

950. It follows that in *ownership*, which includes the right to innumerable different actions, all actions depend upon a single, extremely simple concept, the concept of *ownership*, in which they are all included.

951. Again, we have here the explanation why legislators and philosophers consistently conceive and speak of ownership as a very simple concept. Analysis reveals innumerable elements of ownership none of which, however, taken separately is ownership. Ownership as such is one, simple and indivisible, just as person is. As we have already noted, divisibility does not pertain to ownership as a *fact*, but to ownership as *right*.

952. 4. *Unlimitedness*: person is freedom and cannot therefore be limited in its activity. It would be a contradiction to say that what is essentially free could at the same time be bound. This

---

[235] Note, however, that if a human being knows his fellows and *reflects* on the moral respect due to them, he cannot acquire this *persuasion* of unlimited ownership. The ownership of which we are speaking is a fact which takes place when the human being is either cut off from his fellows (cf. 846) or is so preoccupied with himself that he does not reflect on the moral exigencies arising from this presence.

characteristic is also communicated by person to ownership, which involves the faculty of unlimited activity.

953. This explains the opinion of those who, without separating *ownership by right* from *ownership in fact*, attribute to the latter what is proper to the former. As a result, they maintain that the human being can do what he likes with what is his: he can abuse it, prevent others' from using it harmlessly, destroy it without any motive other than caprice, make it harmful to others and even to himself. It is certainly true that person has the physical faculty to do this; person feels this faculty, and such a feeling relative to the instrument it uses and abuses for this purpose is called *ownership*. But this, according to me, is only the *fact* of ownership, not the *right*.

954. But does ownership considered as right retain anything of the four characteristics we have mentioned? Considered as right, ownership retains a great deal of the nature of ownership considered as fact. The former is simply ownership as fact subjected to the rule of moral reason, which prescribes that 'ownership in fact is not to be used in such a way that the person using it harms others without any advantage to himself.'

955. But how much does the right of ownership retain of the characteristics of ownership in fact? It retains all the characteristics allowing it to act without falling into the immoral activity already indicated in the proposition: 'Ownership must give way as soon as it is no longer of use to the person possessing it, and harms others either by impeding their good or harming them.

956. Note that what we have said does not eliminate the line separating jural justice from benevolence, although incomplete understanding of what we are saying here could give that impression. On the contrary, our position is that this line is to be maintained constantly as an extremely important, true and necessary boundary. Our problem is entirely jural: we want to establish the limit of right, that is, of right in its true, proper meaning.

957. The truth is that what we have said shows the inadequacy of the boundary normally drawn between *jural duty* and *ethical duty*.

958. We shall repeat what has been said, and use this opportunity

for reducing to a brief formula the whole of the teaching already proposed.

When we sacrifice the smallest good that is ours by right for the sake of someone else, we act benevolently. We are not bound under any jural obligation to make this sacrifice either to spare the other person from the greatest possible evil or to procure for him the greatest possible good. Under the moral law of mutual benevolence there is nevertheless [*App.*, no. 6] an obligation to do this.[236] There is always damage to right, always some violation of the moral-jural law, when we force others, as a matter of fact, to make some sacrifice for us or to cause harm to third parties. This is true however insignificant the sacrifice or harm may be, or however great the evil or good that we want to avoid or procure.[237]

Knowingly preventing good to others or causing them harm with actions that bring us no advantage whatsoever, but which we exercise under the pretext of using our ownership, means acting injuriously, invalidly and vainly. This kind of activity is not sanctioned by any moral law. Consequently there is no obligation in others to respect either the freedom of these actions or the ownership on which they rest.

Acting in a way which avoids harm to oneself or obtains some good, without harm to others or impediment to their good, does no injury to another's right, no matter how ownership of fact is employed. Such activity is always jurally lawful and valid, and can sometimes be upheld by force.

959. The second of these four principles flows from the first; the fourth from the third. Taken together, they express the limits of the obligation of right and of benevolence, the limits of *ownership* and of the *right of ownership*.

---

[236] This principle was known to the ancients. — 'One's own utility is to be conserved', says Cicero, 'if it causes no harm to others. You know this very well, Chrysippus. The runners in the stadium have to make every effort to win, but without committing a foul on their opponents. Life, too, is like that. Without doing evil, anyone can try to use what is his own; but he has no right to harm others in doing so' (*De Off*. 3, 10).

[237] Cicero expounds this principle magisterially in *De Off*. 3.

Article 5.
The method for carrying out the analysis
of the right of ownership

960. Separation of *ownership* as a *fact* of human nature from the *right of ownership* immediately clarifies what still remains to be done in our proposed analysis of the right of ownership. The preceding distinction also shows us the way forward in this analysis. It provides the extremely important corollary that the right of ownership can be considered from two points of view: in so far as it retains the nature of ownership, and in so far as it moves away from it.

961. This distinction is the first step in the analysis of the right itself which now stands divided in two: one part springs from the animal-intelligent nature of the human being, the other from the human being's moral nature. We have to consider both these parts and submit each of them to further analysis.

Article 6.
Analysis of the RIGHT of OWNERSHIP in so far as
it is ownership itself

962. *Ownership* does not change its nature when it becomes a right, but retains its four important characteristics of *exclusiveness*, *perpetuity*, *unity* and *unlimitedness* (cf 946-952).

963. The same thing can be expressed as follows: my right of ownership over anything ceases when this right is no longer exclusive, perpetual, simple and one, and unlimited.

964. The fact that this right is one and simple, as person is, does not prevent its analysis. Person itself in its simplicity acts in multiple ways as we shall see in examining the act of appropriation.

965. Through this act, free personal force takes seigniory over something. In doing this, the person does not merely apply his spiritual force, with which alone he could know, desire and want the thing in question without producing any real effect on it; the thing would remain unthreatened, as it were, by any real action. The person, therefore, uses his corporal forces to dominate the

external thing and to dispose it for his own use — or at least he prepares himself for this. Bodily forces have necessarily to intervene in order to ensure benefit from a bodily thing. And this is what brings about possession,[238] occupancy, appropriation.

All the person's forces are therefore applied to the thing he wishes to occupy in so far as these forces are necessary. He applies whatever is needed to draw all possible advantage to himself from ownership of that thing.

966. Personal force is first exercised over the thing in order to enjoy it.

If, however, enjoyment is not immediate, the same force is applied to cultivating and improving the thing to produce the desired fruit.

Thirdly, personal force is applied to ensure tranquil possession of the thing, and defend it.

Fourthly, force is applied to drive off aggressors who wish to take the thing into their own power.

Fifthly, it is applied to regain repossession of the thing if it has been taken.

In the sixth place, it is applied in order to obtain compensation for an injury or harm suffered through aggression, and through deterioration or total loss.

Seventhly, in order to extract a guarantee or pledge of security from wayward people threatening what is owned.

Eighthly, in order to cede to others wholly or in part dominion over the thing.

These are the ways in which the right of ownership is exercised. They consist simply in the use of our personal force, with which we make a thing our own through occupancy, and dispose of it in such a way that all impediments to our free use of it are resisted.

967. All these acts, or different ways of disposing of things,

---

[238] We have already distinguished *possession* from occupancy in this respect: possession means retaining the thing with the intention of having it as one's own. This is not sufficient for acquiring the right of ownership over something: a thief intends to hold and use as his own something that he has stolen. We rightly have to distinguish between *possession* in good and bad faith. *Occupancy*, however, is understood as a title which lacks nothing for producing right of ownership over something (cf. 483).

possess perfect unity in personal force which works in us all but in different measures according to need. The aim is always the same: there is no difference in the nature of the agent, only in the circumstances which modify the agent's action. Considered under this aspect, the right of ownership is one; the eight ways of exercising it are not eight different *species* of rights, but properly speaking *modes*, actions, applications, *functions* of right itself.

Article 7.
Analysis of the RIGHT OF OWNERSHIP as RIGHT

968. *Ownership* as a *fact* is brought into being by the person furnished with all the forces he finds at his disposition in the human nature adhering to him. Intervention on the part of the intelligence is provided only in so far as this is necessary for apprehending the thing in question. This constitutes the intellectual-physical bond.

Ownership becomes a *right* when the intelligence *reflects* on the fact of ownership and begins to consider it from a *moral* point of view, submitting it and restricting its title[239] to the laws of morality revealed in human relationships, that is, to the law forbidding others to be harmed. In a word, the right is formed by the moral bond.

969. In simple ownership the *subject* dominates; in the right, the subject's natural activity is submitted to the moral exigency of the *object*.

970. The subject, one and simple as it is, produces ownership as a unique, almost 'compact' thing. When this ownership is then considered in relationship with other people, it is multiplied and transformed into as many different rights[240] as there

---

[239] The 'title', because it is the *title* which must be moral in the establishment of a right, as we have noted elsewhere. Immorality, which does not infringe the title of right, does not destroy right.

[240] These rights are all of the same species, as we said (cf. 967). But *species* itself takes two principal *modes* (cf. *OT*., 648-652), that is, the *full species* and the *abstract species*. Both species have many *variations*. When this scheme is

are special relationships with these people and different modifications of ownership resulting from the relationships in which it is considered.

971. The multiplicity of rights over things does not arise, therefore, from the nature of ownership, but from the multiple acts which the moral reason exercises relative to ownership by converting it into right. We have said that a very simple act is a sufficient object for constituting a right.[241] This multiplicity is proper to rights precisely because rights are forged by the *reflective reason* which has power to abstract, analyse and consider the thing under different aspects. In a word, it can render multiple that which in its own reality is one.

972. As a result, what is called 'right of ownership' 'can be considered almost as a complex of innumerable rights', as Zeiller says.[242]

973. The eight functions of the right of ownership that we have listed in the preceding article do not in reality, therefore, split ownership. In each of these functions ownership is exercised in its entirety. The presence of many functions arises solely because ownership is exercised in several modes, not because it is divided into many parts.

974. The same cannot be said about the rights enclosed in ownership, which we must now enumerate. We consider each one of these as an exercise of a part of ownership, not of all ownership. They are parts of ownership which stand on their own, separate from one another.[243] Here multiplicity arises from the moral reason which puts various real limits, according

applied to rights, the eight functions of the right of ownership that we have enumerated are seen (cf. 966) to be *variations* of the species (full or abstract) of the right itself. The eight rights, therefore, do not differ simply as one individual to another, but as *variations* of the same *species*. The variations of the species are repeated both in the *mode* of the *full* species and in the *mode* of the *abstract species*.

[241] Cf. 224-237.

[242] §77.

[243] The division that we attribute here to the right of ownership is not concerned with the *essence* of this right but with the *quantity of its exercise*. Hence the logical schema which we have used in ftn. 240 cannot be applied to it.

to circumstances and accidents, on ownership itself or on its exercise.

975. Ownership, together with its exercise, is divided and limited, like right, in two ways. First, it is limited when there is a right to exercise some, but not all the acts of ownership; second, it is limited when the right to exercise acts of ownership is relative to some persons, but not others.

§1. *Division of the complex right of ownership relative to the different acts of ownership*

976. The complex right of ownership can be divided into three groups relative to the acts with which it can be exercised. They are:

1. *the right of predisposition;*
2. *the right of use;*
3. *the right of naked ownership*, or quite simply of ownership.

These are still complex rights, however, which we shall have to call 'groups of rights'.

977. 1. The *right of possession* is foremost among the rights of *predisposition*.

978. Relative to possession, we must make a distinction similar to that which we have made in speaking about ownership: that is, *possession* is one thing, the *right of possession* is another.

979. *Simple possession* is only a fact which consists in retaining something either through one's own forces or through the forces of others acting in our name as though the thing were our own. This fact comes about through the intellectual-physical nexus.

980. But we can hold something as our own in good or bad faith. If we know that it is not our own, but intend to keep it as if it were, we are possessors in bad faith. In this case, *possession* is present, but not the *right of possession* or jural possession.

981. If, however, we think in good faith that the thing is our own although it is not, we have the *right of possession*, but not the *right of ownership*.

982. Others who know that the thing is not ours have a

corresponding jural obligation to respect our right of possession and our good faith.[244]

983. The owner himself cannot take the thing away from us without first proving his title of ownership.

984. If this title is proved incontestably, and we still will not cede, we have lost our right, and only retain simple possession. The thing could now be taken from us by the true owner by force because we would no longer be in good faith.

985. But how do matters stand when no jural and incontestable proof can be given to the possessor, although the owner has no doubt about it? In this case, the owner could repossess what is his, but on condition that he did so without harming the possessor in good faith. In this case, the owner's right to claim the thing as his own is limited by the moral-jural duty of not causing harm to an innocent person, even for the sake of vindicating his right.

986. What if the proof of right is doubtful on both sides? According to rational Right, there would an obligation for both to discuss the matter in a friendly way and come to some compromise enabling the thing to be divided in proportion to the doubt. If the thing is indivisible, some other equitable compromise should be made.

987. Other rights of the possessor in good faith can be seen in

---

[244] The *right of possession* brings with it further obligations on the part of others, for instance, the obligation of restoring the thing to the *just possessor*. Busembaum, followed by St. Alphonsus, writes: 'When goods are certain, they have ordinarily to be restored to the just possessor from whom they were taken or on whom damage has been inflicted, even if this person is not the immediate owner. What has been taken therefore from caretakers, holding agents, carriers, guardians or administrators must be restored to them, not to the owner. Otherwise, some harm would be done to them by depriving them of their right to possession, detention, guardianship or utility. Moreover, damage and pecuniary loss must be compensated. Exceptions to this rule are: 1. if they have no interest in the matter so that no restitution has to be made to the owner for damage or loss of good name; 2. if it is probably thought that they themselves were to carry off or take away the thing with damage to the owner. — Again, if something has been taken from a child, ward, madman, wife or religious who is not entitled to administer what has been taken, restitution is often to be made to the father, guardian, husband or superior' (bk. 3, 596).

the treatises on the matter and in the codes of civil law, whose dispositions normally follow those of rational Right.

988. 2. The *complex right of use* includes all rights to the enjoyment of consumable goods by consuming them, to the use of non-consumable goods, and to usufruct, that is, the right to bring things to fruition for oneself.

989. The first of these three rights became the centre of a great discussion: is this right distinct from the right of substantial ownership of a thing? It is true, of course, that a person can have the right to consume the food he lives on without owning it. Ownership which, in its fullness, would give him the right to alienate food and do what he liked with it, is not necessarily connected with the right to food and drink. This can be a special right, that is, a part of ownership rather than entire ownership. The other two rights of *use* and *usufruct* are sufficiently dealt with by the relevant authors.

990. 3. The *complex right of naked ownership*, which is used as synonymous with 'direct ownership' (to distinguish it from indirect ownership or ownership in use, applicable to the usufructuary in the cases of land) and is called simply 'owner-ship'. The right of ownership (naked, or direct) is normally concerned with what relates to the *substance* of anything.

991. Strictly speaking, however, this is not the case. Substances do not belong to human beings, who can neither produce nor destroy them, but to God, their Creator.

992. Nor can we say that direct ownership is related to the *substantial form* of anything. This can clearly be seen in the case of a direct owner who could not change a vineyard into a pleasure garden without damaging and violating the right of the person holding the right of use over the vineyard.

993. Direct ownership, therefore, is simply a complex of rights which limit the right of ownership of the person called the 'owner in use'; *indirect ownership* is simply the complex of rights limiting the right of ownership of the person called the 'direct owner'. The complex right of ownership is, therefore, divided. The rights which compose it are divided between two owners, and divided in different ways in accordance with what results from the origin of such a division of rights.

994. Sometimes, the *owner in use* is also obliged to certain provisions relative to the *direct owner*. This occurs when, for

example, the origin of the division we have mentioned lies in contracts dependent upon conveyancing, hereditary tenancy, emphyteusis, land rents, and so on.

995. One of the modes and titles of acquisition of ownership of material things is *accession*, which may be *natural, artificial* or *mixed*.

996. *Accession* is the name given to everything that arises from the thing, or is joined to it, without its being given to the owner by others.

997. If the right of ownership over a thing is simply divided between the direct owner and the owner in use, accession itself, which is concerned with non-fungibles, is divided between the two owners in the same way as the right of ownership over the principle part of the thing.

998. But the two owners, besides sharing as we have said in the right of ownership, may also have other rights and obligations arising either from the contract which originally stipulated the division or from other agreements. For example, the owner in use may have to pay a share of his produce as a quota. In such cases, prestation increases as the amount of land increases through accession.

999. The same is to be said every time the division of ownership takes place through a contract by which the person having full ownership over land transfers its dominion of the use for a suitable consideration. The contract can in fact only refer to existing land; in other words, that which is united through accession either belongs entirely to the direct owner, or gives him the right to receive from the owner in use some recompense proportioned to the return on the new land. But we shall continue elsewhere this analysis of the right of ownership.[245]

---

[245] Bk. 3, c. 5.

§2. *Division of the complex right of ownership relative to different persons who have a jural obligation to respect the right*

1000. Jural reason, as we have said, also limits ownership from the point of view of persons. For example, someone receiving an article in deposit has the right to look after it. This is classed amongst rights of *predisposition*, as we call them. But the right to look after a deposited article received from its owner is relative to other persons, not to the owner himself who at any moment can demand the return of what he has deposited.

1001. In the same way, a right entailing a pledge (which also pertains to the class of rights of *predisposition*) is limited according to relationships between determinate persons. The person holding the pledge has the right (and the obligation also) to take care of it relative to any other person except the owner himself, to whom it must be returned when he liberates it by paying his debt.

1002. Examples may be found in predial servitude such as pasture for cattle, cutting wood, fishing, hunting on others' land, and so on. The owner has full dominion relative to all other persons except the one who has the right to the predial servitude we have indicated. This example is also relevant to the second group of rights, that of rights of *utility*, into which ownership is subdivided.

1003. Finally, we give an example taken from the third group of rights, that of *naked ownership*. Here we can examine the right of *co-ownership*. Let us imagine that the naked or direct ownership of a plot of land belongs to several persons. Each has the right to such ownership without limitation relative to all persons outside the group which owns the land; at the same time, each one's ownership is in reality limited relative to his co-owners. This limitation comes about through acknowledgement of the same ownership in them, and through their being allowed freedom to exercise it equally with him. But this analysis also will be continued elsewhere.

Book 3

THE TRANSMISSION OF RIGHTS, AND THEIR CONSEQUENT MODIFICATIONS

INTRODUCTION

THE SUBJECT OF THIS BOOK AND ITS CONNECTION WITH THE PRECEDING AND FOLLOWING BOOKS

1004. So far we have discussed *connatural* rights and the formation of *acquired* rights. But acquired rights change, and when changed are even considered as new rights. In this sense there are acquired rights whose formation we have not discussed. We must now see which they are and how they differ from those which formed the subject of the preceding book.

I.

The classification of rights according to the level of reflections of the human mind

1005. Before all, we must distinguish *rights at the first level*, which are acquired by the use of our *natural freedom*, not *our acquired freedom*, that is, not by the exercise of another, previously acquired right. Thus, occupancy of a piece of unoccupied land is effected by an act of *natural freedom*, which does not presuppose a right already acquired.

1006. We then have *rights at the second level*, which are acquired only if rights have already been formed at the first level. For example, I cannot acquire the right of pledge over some movable or immovable thing unless the thing has an owner who pledges it to me. The owner is invested with a right which precedes my right of pledge; his right is at the first level relative to the pledge which I acquire later.

1007. *Rights at the third level* follow next; their formation requires as a necessary condition rights already formed at the second level. An example would be the right acquired by the owner of a pledge if I wrongfully sold and destroyed the pledge. Here a right of repayment presupposes the right of pledge, just as the right of pledge presupposes the right of ownership of the thing pledged.

1008. Obviously this is not the final level of rights; there can be as many levels as we wish, but all must be determined by the same formula: 'As a condition of its existence, every right belongs to a higher level than the rights on which it is founded.'

1009. Such is the hierarchy of human rights. It is rooted in the limited nature of human activity, which is modified and increased by its own acts, and uses its preceding acts to perform new acts.[246]

1010. The principal seat of this hierarchy of rights is the particular human activity called intelligence, which is itself subject to a similar law and performs acts divided into what I call *levels of reflections*.[247]

1011. The division of rights according to the hierarchy of the levels of reflections is not a useless activity but a highly productive classification. The truth of this can be seen by anyone who undertakes a *History of the Philosophy of Rights* and highlights the stages of progress of nations at different periods of their political life by the higher or lower levels of rights which individuals in those nations attain.

1012. Meditation on the art of the government of nations will show that different levels of rights binding peoples together change the state of civil society; this in turn requires a corresponding change in legislation and politics, that is, in the way of government.

1013. But I cannot pursue such important considerations. I must leave them to thinkers willing to apply their mind to the matter. We must ask ourselves: 'What is the level of the rights whose formation I presented in the preceding book? And what is the level of the rights whose formation I must now indicate in this and the following books?'

---

[246] I spoke of this law of human activity in *SP*, bk. 4, c. 6.
[247] Cf. *CE*, 1258-1263; *CS*, 162-174.

II.

Rights at the first level are posited in being either by the act of one person or by the acts of many persons.

1014. The preceding book dealt with the formation of some but not all first-level rights.

1015. These primitive rights can in fact be generated in two ways: either by the act of a single person who acquires the right, or by the acts of two or more whose corporate action results in the right. For example, if two or more persons form a society, they have new jural obligations and entirely new rights. Because these rights are new, they are primitive, first-level rights. Thus, before two persons of different sex form the marriage contract, the right of cohabitation for the procreation of children does not exist — it is therefore a primitive right.

1016. In the preceding book I have only spoken about those rights at the first level which acquire their subsistence as a result of the act of a single person. It is true that in passing I mentioned a case where, in the very act of acquiring a first-level right (e.g. occupying unowned property), an obligatory contract was, as it were, implicitly introduced which modified the rights arising from occupancy (cf. 521-527). But this fleeting reference did not contain all the elements I consider necessary to elucidate the jural effects resulting from the concerted action of two or more persons.

1017. We must therefore discuss:

1. which first-level rights are posited in being by the acts of two or more persons;

2. the formation of rights at higher levels.

III.

The acts of two or more persons can influence rights either by modifying existing acts or by producing new acts, or by doing both these things

1018. Before dealing with first-level rights which result from the concerted acts of two or more persons, we must carefully consider all the jural effects that can follow from such action.

1019. Without this consideration we could not obtain full knowledge of the jural effects resulting from the acts of two or more persons and could easily fall into error, believing that such acts produce new rights every time they influence rights. This, however, is not the case. If we thought it were, we would harm the science of Right by confusing its ideas and preventing its exact, scientific and orderly progress.

1020. We must therefore distinguish the jural effects which arise from the concerted acts of two or more persons by dividing them into three classes. Sometimes the concerted acts of two or more persons really produce *new rights*, such as the right to procreate in the marital contract; at other times they simply produce a *modification* of pre-existing rights. Finally, they sometimes produce simultaneously *new rights and modifications* of pre-existing rights.

1021. We can see this mixed effect of the production and modifications of rights in all associations, including marriage, where the previously mentioned conjugal debt is a new right simultaneously modifying and making the spouses' external ownership common to both parties.

IV.

The concerted acts of two or more persons produce new rights only in the case of association

1022. The discussion of social Right must therefore be placed after the discussion on the production of rights and their modifications; the elements of the discussion must be clarified before we can deal with the complex teaching on the acts and effects of association. What is complex cannot be seriously discussed before we examine what is simple. Thus, after we have dealt separately with the production of rights and their consequent modifications, we will be better equipped to discuss the acts of association by which new rights are created and pre-existing rights are simultaneously modified.

1023. We must note however that the concerted acts of two or more persons produces entirely new rights only in the case of association. In all other cases the 'new rights' can be considered *modifications of pre-existing rights*.

1024. Consequently, what was said in the preceding book about the simple production of rights, and what we intend to say later in the book on social Right, will be sufficient. Our present intention is to limit ourselves to an extensive treatment of the teaching about the *modifications* these rights undergo.

V.

The modification of rights has its origin either in the act which produces them or later

1025. The teaching on the modifications of rights is very extensive and requires careful indication of its extension and its limits if every part of it is to receive at least a mention.

Let us first consider the various accidents which can occur in the modification of rights. This will allow us to arrange our discussion in an orderly way.

1026. In the first place, the acts which modify rights are sometimes contemporaneous and, as it were, elements of the way in which rights are acquired. This was the case in our example of the two hunters who simultaneously shoot the same animal (cf. 522). The accidental presence of two hunters rather than one modifies the right of ownership of the animal and gives rise to the obligation to divide the animal between the two parties.

1027. On the other hand, acts which modify rights sometimes occur when rights already exist; if, for example, a hunter sold the animal he had trapped. The sale would modify the right of his ownership of the animal.

1028. But this circumstance needs no further comment (cf. 521-527). The modification undergone by the right remains the same whether the acts producing it are mixed with the manner of its acquisition or posited afterwards.

VI.

The modifications of rights are produced both by the acts of two or more persons and by the act of a single person

1029. We must carefully note that the *modifications* of rights do not occur solely through the acts of two or more persons but also through the act of a single person, as in the case of the violation of another's rights: the violated rights are modified and from that moment require satisfaction and restoration.

1030. Just as first-level rights are produced either by the act of a single person or by the concerted acts of two or more persons (I will deal with this when I discuss social Right), so it is with their modifications. Our discussion of these modifications would be deficient if we did not consider them both as effects of the acts of two or more persons (as we intend to do in this book) and as effects of the act of a single person (the topic of the following book, 'Violated rights, and their resultant modifications').

VII.

The modifications of rights either consist solely in changing the subject of right or alter the form of right itself

1031. Modifications of rights are of two kinds.

1032. Some consist in altering the subject of right without any alteration to the right itself. For example, a donation changes only the owner of the thing donated; the right of ownership remains the same.

1033. Strictly speaking this change is not a modification of rights themselves, that is, of their form, but a change of the

[1029–1033]

person in whom the rights adhere. It is not a modification of what is contained in the *idea* of right, but of the *subsistence* of right (because this ceases to subsist for one subject and begins to subsist for another).

1034. Other modifications alter the idea, that is, the form of right itself; they splinter it, limit it and add new relationships to it. When a house or section of land is mortgaged, for example, the right of ownership of the house or land has undergone a change of form; the right is reduced in proportion to the quantity of the right conceded to the person in whose favour the mortgage was established.

1035. We have therefore modifications both in the *subsistence* and in the *idea* of right (one specific idea is substituted for another), that is, in the formal essence or, if preferred, in the form of right. The first kind of modifications exists solely in the *real world*, the second belongs to the *ideal world*.

1036. I call this second kind also 'variations' of rights (cf. fn. 240).

VIII.

Only first-level rights are true rights — those at higher levels are, properly speaking, only modifications of rights

1037. These *variations* are in reality the same as the rights we have called second, third, fourth-level rights, etc.

1038. In fact, higher-level rights are simply first-level rights modified in different ways. If this were not so, they would be completely new and therefore primitive rights, because they would belong to the first level.

1039. Thus, our discussion of the modifications of rights will explain the origin of all rights higher than first-level rights, and will enable us to accomplish what, as we said (cf. 1014-1017), remains to be done.

[1034–1039]

IX.

Conclusion regarding the order of matters to be discussed in the remaining books

1040. Our previous considerations indicate the order to be followed in the remaining books. Two things clearly present themselves to be discussed in order to complete our tract on rational Right: the first concerns the nature of the principal modifications to which rights are subject; the second, the nature of the rights arising from associations.

1041. The latter pertain to social Right, the former to the completion of *individual Right* and as such furnish the matter for this and the following book. Hence, in these two books we will deal with the modifications which rights undergo, and the various forms they take when humanity is considered in a single social state.[248]

1042. The matter of the present book will be those modifications of rights which arise from the concerted acts of two or more persons.

1043. These acts always imply a transmission of rights from one person to another. The title I have therefore given the book is: 'The transmission of rights, and their consequent modifications.'

1044. The next book will deal with the modifications which arise from the act of a single person. These modifications take place when the rights of others change. Thus the book is entitled: 'The changes in others' rights, the resultant obligations and other jural effects.'[249]

---

[248] 'A single social state' because variation in the social state of humanity is matched by variation in *rights of the first order* to which are joined the *modifications* discussed in the third and fourth books of *individual Right*. First-order rights have *modes* arising from the difference of feelings, in which they are rooted (*ER*, 81; and cf. 576, 651, 943). After *derived Right* I will discuss these modes which affect rights and are caused by changes in mankind, particularly by the different levels of civilisation nations have attained. I will trace the *History of Rights*, which I have already mentioned. It will indicate for civil legislators the many circumstances they must consider in order to adapt the laws to different periods in the life of nations.

[249] It may seem at first that *contracts* dealt with in this book and *harm*

CHAPTER 1

The two ways of transmitting ownership: abandonment of what is owned and its occupancy by someone else, and contract

1045. There are two ways of transmitting ownership:

1. When I free something of my own and someone else occupies it, making it his own.

2. When I free something of my own free in favour of someone else who, under certain conditions or without conditions, accepts and takes it immediately as his own; this is called 'contract'.[250]

Article 1.
The first way of transmitting ownership: the abandonment of what is owned and its occupancy by someone else

1046. The first way is accomplished by two entirely distinct acts, one of which precedes the other: the act of the owner and the act of the new occupier. The owner abandons what he owns either with or without the intention that it be occupied by someone else; it is in fact occupied. Thus, ownership has passed from one person to another, although we cannot say that the

discussed in the next are totally separate things. But they have a very close affinity in that they both cause *modifications* of rights and *new obligations*. Roman legislators took the same view of *contracts* and *harm*. The *Justinian Institutes* speak about harm immediately after contracts, just as I do: 'Obligations arise from contracts or quasi-contracts, or from malfeasance or quasi-malfeasance. We must first consider what concerns contracts' (Bk. 3, tit. 14).

[250] Roman laws show traces of these two ways in many places, for example: 'The dominion of things is transferred by CONSIGNMENT and USUCAPTION, not by mere agreements' (*Cod.*, bk. 2, t. 3, 20). Consignment presupposes a *contract*; usucaption is a kind of abandonment of something owned, and its possession and dominion by another.

first has transmitted it to the second. The first simply abandoned it and the other appropriated it.

1047. This first way of transmitting ownership takes place in
three general cases, each of which can be subdivided into many
others:

1. The owner renounces his ownership which, being free, is
honestly occupied by someone else (dissolution of the moral-
intellectual bond).

2. The passage of time and forgotten historical records allow
the possessor to consider himself the owner even though, if the
past were known, he might discover that his ownership began
with usurpation (*natural-positive prescription*).

3. The disuse of the thing, with its ownership forgotten and
further dimmed by the passage of time, dissolves the *physical
bond*, that is, it destroys the *ownership*, which is the matter of
right. At the same time another person appropriates the thing in
good faith or obtains it in good faith from the one who had
appropriated it. Thus, a new physical bond has been effected
which supplies the matter for the right of ownership of a new
owner (*usucaption*).[251]

1048. In the first case the owner expressly renounces what
he owns. Generally speaking, this renouncement cannot be
presupposed, because renouncing what is good is contrary
to human nature — the renouncement has to be proved (cf.
881-893).

Proof is the *words*, *facts*, and *non-facts* of the owner, which
must clearly indicate his intention, and *circumstances*, when
these are such that human beings must reasonably give up their
intention to keep the thing as their own or their persuasion that
it is theirs. This last proof produces a particular persuasion.

We do in fact, under certain circumstances and despite ourselves, sometimes reasonably abandon our intention to possess
something. This happens when it is not so much the owner who
abandons the thing as the thing which abandons the owner: for

---

[251] To make myself clear, I distinguish natural *prescription* from *usucaption*.
The title for possession in prescription is *presumed*; it is considered forgotten
in the passage of time. The title for possession in usucaption is not presumed;
it is *supra-occupancy*, that is, the gradual occupancy of a thing by others as
little by little the *physical bond* uniting the thing to the first owner ceases.

example, when something goes astray, a bird escapes, or firewood is washed out to sea when a dam bursts. These things are now free and occupiable by anybody, because the owner can never have them back for himself, or no longer thinks about recovering them, or is unknown to their finder.

1049. In the case of positive prescription, three conditions are required for the transmission of ownership: 1. the thing is prescribable, 2. its possession has continued peacefully from time immemorial, 3. the present owner is in good faith. These three conditions must be present in such a way that a critical examination results in the probability that the just transfer of ownership from the former to the present owner has indeed taken place, although it is now lost to memory. On the other hand, if the history of the ownership was clearly preserved and it could be proved that the original transmission was unjust and no other title had ever been applied, the prescription, according to rational right, could not have taken place — the passage of time alone does not constitute any just title.

Hence it is more difficult to confirm the case of natural prescription relative to empires than relative to private ownership, because the memory of the latter is preserved much longer than that of the former.

1050. Finally, *usucaption*, as I have described it, has its root in the intimate nature of the physical bond, that is, in the matter of Right. This matter consists in a FEELING, as I have explained many times, by which human beings appropriate things to themselves and, as it were, assimilate them. But with disuse and oblivion *time* can obliterate the feeling of ownership in the human spirit, and without this feeling, right is not possible. Thus, the feeling of ownership which binds a person to an object can be extinguished in the person, while a similar feeling is formed in someone else by the factual use of the forgotten or disused object. This second feeling takes on the quality of right as soon as the first ceases.

If the first owner should awake, as it were, and claim the object, his claim would be invalid. If the feeling of ownership has finally perished in him but awoken in another, he can no longer claim the thing, because it now belongs to another. He can no longer establish a physical bond with the object that now belongs to another.

But we must move on to our principal argument, contracts.[252]

Article 2.
The second way of transmitting ownership: contracts

§1. The limits within which contracts are part of rational Right

1051. Contracts are part of rational Right in so far as they are subject to the laws of reason, and part of positive Right as subject to positive, freely-chosen dispositions and conventions.

1052. In fact, in the state of nature in which we are now considering human beings, we must distinguish several stages. Contracts take place only in some of them.[253]

The *first stage* is present when we are born. At this stage we have not only made no contracts, but have done nothing and therefore have not acquired rights. We are endowed with innate and strictly *natural* rights (cf. 283).

1053. The *second stage* is when, by our action, we acquire rights without dealings or contracts with our fellows. These primitive rights were discussed in the preceding book.

At this stage we have only a negative relationship with our fellows, which consists in their duty not to encroach on the sphere of our acquired rights, and in our duty not to encroach on the sphere of their acquired rights.

1054. In the *third stage* people are considered as coming together and entering into a mutual relationship by the use of language. The moral need to understand each other's rights manifests itself as soon as some obscurity or conflict arises about rights. The moral-jural law, written on the hearts of us all, requires a peaceful solution to disputes (cf. 501).[254] This is the origin of contracts.

---

[252] Further reading about this first way of transmitting ownership can be found in chapter 4, bk. 2 of Grotius' *De T. B. et P.* Grotius was a great man, treated very unjustly by the sceptics of the last century.

[253] Cf. *SP*, bk. 1, c. 4.

[254] Agreements of this kind, invented to settle disputes in the state of nature, were excluded by Hobbes and Spinoza, who consequently posited war as the state of nature. It is clear that if we begin with the definition, 'The state of nature is the opposite of every accord and agreement; it is the state in which

1055. These contracts are morally and jurally necessary; others, which are free and not morally necessary, are made between human beings sometimes for the purpose of obtaining some good or avoiding an evil in the eudaimonological order, and sometimes for the sake of exercising an act of moral virtue.

1056. Among both *obligatory* and *non-obligatory* contracts we can often find freely-chosen agreements, that is, agreements which are not determined by principles of justice and equity or by the moral law.

These principles sometimes require a dispute to be settled, but leave the parties free to bring this about in one way or another. Or, in the case of non-obligatory contracts, the same principles prescribe some conditions but leave many others to the free choice of the contracting parties.

Agreements become obligatory laws for the contracting parties. Hence, freely-chosen agreements, that is, everything determined by free choice and not imposed necessarily by rational law constitutes a *positive* right, which is not part of rational Right.

In a treatise on rational Right therefore only those prescriptions should be dealt with that are subject to rational law, not those which depend merely on the will of the contracting parties.

1057. There is also a *fourth stage* in the state of nature. At this stage contracts forming societies are made between human beings which give rise to collective bodies.

1058. Contracts forming societies are themselves divided into *obligatory* and *freely-chosen*, and what has been said in general about both kinds of contracts can be said about these: the contracting parties must observe certain conditions required by jural, moral reason. These conditions therefore belong to

human beings think only of themselves and of preserving their goods', we have a state of war. That is true, but it is only a question of words: the state of nature is such because that is the sense given to the phrase 'state of nature'. But this does not give us the right to propound practical, pernicious teachings as consequences of that arbitrary definition. We need only reply: the consequences are as true as the definition. But the definition is arbitrary. Therefore the consequences are arbitrary and hypothetical. — For the moral-jural obligation human beings have in the state of nature to settle their differences peacefully, see *SP*, bk. 1, c. 9.

[1055–1058]

rational Right. In addition, the parties can form agreements and make freely-chosen regulations. These are the positive part of the constitutions of such societies.

1059. In general, human beings begin by contracts to submit to positive Right in addition to rational Right, in so far as the contracts contain something freely chosen. As a result of particular contracts forming societies, men and women begin to move out of the *state of nature* into the *social state*. But the acts (social contracts) which make them pass from one state to the other belong to the state of nature.

1060. Furthermore, because legislative power is normally present in a society, anything this power subsequently lays down as law for a society contains something springing from moral-jural reason and something springing from the legislator's free choice. Here again rational Right mingles with positive Right.

1061. The state of nature, therefore, in my opinion, divides into four stages. In the last two, contracts appear, and positive Right mixed with rational Right begins to show itself.

1062. It seems that one of the sources of error which bring downfall to many writers on rational Right is their inability to accurately distinguish these four stages of the state of nature, which are four different conditions in which human beings are found prior to the state of society.

The expression 'state of nature' has many meanings. By restricting rational Right to Right presiding in the state of nature, different concepts depending on the narrowness or breadth of the concept of nature are necessarily produced.

1063. Some writers excluded the fourth stage from their state of nature. Others excluded the third as well, and finally some acknowledged as the natural human state only that in which the human being is born, a state anterior to all jural action.

1064. This gave rise to disagreement about the definition of *natural Right*, which they confused with *rational Right*. As a result, they could not agree about the solution to problems on natural and rational Right.

The best way to bring these writers closer in their opinions and to establish agreement on many points is, it seems to me, to call their attention to the different concept they have of the natural state, in other words, of the different *hypothetical*

[1059–1064]

condition from which they start in order to find the right for which they are searching.

1065. It may be asked how I can include freely-chosen contracts in natural Right. I do not include them in natural Right; I only ask that *natural* Right be distinguished from *rational* Right, and that the former be made a part of the latter (cf. 283). Thus, the exclusion of freely-chosen contracts from natural Right does not exclude them completely from rational Right which must consider them as follows.

1066. The fact that contracts are freely-chosen in so far as there is no obligation to make them is not the same as their being freely-chosen in so far as they include freely-chosen agreements and dispositions. Agreements and dispositions not dictated by reason but added by the will of the contracting parties are extraneous to rational Right. It is also clear that if the dispositions determining contracts are dictated by reason, they must be considered in the science of rational Right, even though those who draw them up are not forced to do so by any natural law.

1067. *Rational Right* is, after all, the opposite of *positive Law*. But in the contracts we are discussing, which are drawn up by human beings who are under no jural or moral obligation to do so, the only positive, freely-chosen element in them is the *fact*, that is, the decision to enter into the agreement. On the other hand, the *right*, that is, the law which governs the agreements, granted they are made, is by no means freely-chosen. Hence writers on *rational Right* are necessitated by their argument to speak about all that Right which proceeds from reason, even if this Right presupposes a freely-chosen fact, from which the Right draws its possible existence.

1068. If therefore all freely-chosen facts had to be removed from rational Right and only natural facts retained, the sphere of rational Right would be too limited. Everything would be reduced to the Right of that short period of time we have called 'the first stage of the state of nature' (cf. 1052) where the baby exists without having posited any act capable of acquiring rights for itself. We could certainly call this *natural Right* but not *rational Right*.[255]

---

[255] There are therefore five *jural states* of human beings. The first four, I have said, are those of the *natural state* (the opposite of social state); the fifth

§2. *The definition of contracts in general*

1069. I define a contract as: 'The concourse and jural effect of corresponding acts of two persons, of whom one, an owner of a simple or complex right willingly dissolves the jural bond of the right with or without certain conditions, so that the other may become the owner, if he wishes. The second owner brings into effect the act of acceptance and, after satisfying any attached conditions, appropriates the right.'[256]

1070. We have seen what the jural bond is and how, granted the necessary conditions, it is formed by a moral-jural act with which a person wills to reserve to himself something to which he is joined by a physical bond (cf. 383-401). An act of will contrary to that by which the jural bond is formed dissolves the bond according to the relationship between contraries.

1071. Here we see why two 'acts of ownership' must be present in every transmission of ownership from one person to another: the act by which the owner abandons his right (*act of disappropriation*) and the act by which the other joins the same right to himself (*act of appropriation*) (cf. 1045).

1072. In contracts these two ways are co-relatives, the first

is the *social state*. *Rational Right* (the opposite of *positive right*) deals successively with all these five stages, expounding the *Right of each*. The Right of the first stage is *natural Right* in the strictest sense (the opposite of *acquired right* (cf. 283)). The Right of the first and second stages is *natural Right* in a less strict sense (the opposite of *agreed right*). The *Right* of the first three stages is *natural Right* in a wider sense (the opposite of *social right*). The Right of the fourth stage is the introduction to social Right, that is, the Right of actions which form the passage of human beings from the *state of nature* to the *state of society* — I make this part of *social Right*. Finally, the Right of the fifth jural stage of human beings is *rational social Right* itself.

[256] Many define contract as: 'A pact or agreement made between two or more'. Saying that a contract is a pact or agreement does not seem to define anything but substitutes one word for another; we still need to know what a pact or agreement is. Furthermore, the phrase 'between two or more' seems to complicate and confuse the definition unnecessarily. Two persons means *jural persons*, who can be either *individuals* or *collective*. And if we understand that the *jural persons* making the contract are more than two, it would not be one contract but several contemporaneous contracts. Again, in the definition of a contract in general we should exclude the complicated case of several contracts, which we will discuss later.

being the condition of the second, that is: one person abandons his right on condition that the other accepts it for himself. Hence the latter's act of appropriation is called 'acceptance' and is essential to the nature of contract.[257]

1073. If a person abandons his right without the condition that another appropriate it, and if the other appropriates it simply because the first leaves it vacant, without any understanding between them, the right would pass from the first to the second by means of two separate and independent acts, which consequently would not constitute a contract. This would be the first of the two ways we described for the transmission of rights (cf. 1046).

1074. The act by which an owner dissolves the bond binding a right to him can be considered either before the act is accepted or in the act of acceptance itself by the person in whose favour the act is posited. Before acceptance the act is complete relative to the person positing it, but conditioned, that is, its efficacy is dependent upon its acceptance. As soon as this is given, the act becomes efficacious because the essential condition attached to it has been fulfilled.

1075. To understand clearly how the act can justly be called complete, although dependent on a future condition, we need to consider the particular way human intelligence and will act.

Our intelligence can know a particular object, and our will desire it, even if it is a future and conditioned object. The condition becomes a quality of the desired object so that the object without the condition would be something else, not that which is desired. The desire for a conditioned object therefore can be absolute and certain, not simply provisional or doubtful.

1076. When acceptance is added, the bond of ownership is

[257] Zeiller says: 'Consequently, *mediate acquisition*' (acquisition by contract) 'substantially accords with *immediate acquisition*' (acquisition by occupancy) 'and both are grounded in the same principles of Right. — Immediate acquisition is directed to obtaining something which, relative to all, is vacant (free); a declaration or indication is necessary which can be recognised by all. On the other hand, mediate acquisition refers to something declared free solely in respect of the person to whom it was promised and on condition that he is willing to accept it. No one else can appropriate it to himself, and it is sufficient for that person to have revealed his will to the promiser to whom the exclusive right over the thing belongs' (§94).

dissolved not by a new act but by virtue of the act itself by which the relative dissolution was revealed to the other person and proposed for his acceptance.

1077. We see therefore that a contract is not always a promise which simply concerns the future. It is a moral-jural action of a fully present will. This is so true that until there is acceptance, there is no contract; as soon as acceptance is obtained, the contract is completed, mutual obligation begins and the right has passed from one to the other.

1078. The reason why all contracts were considered promises[258] — later we shall see how promises are contracts of a determined kind — was, I believe, the confusion between the *right of ownership* of a thing and its *possession*.

1079. The right of ownership is formed and lost by a simple act of the intelligent will (moral bond), granted the necessary conditions. For example, I say it is my will that a certain object is no longer mine and is to belong immediately to John. As soon as John has made an act of will corresponding to mine and says he wishes the object to be his, he has become the full owner of it, although its consignment has not been carried out.

1080. Possession is an element of the physical bond. It consists in placing a thing or right under my physical power or under an equivalent symbol, protected by force. This force declares that the thing is mine and that I can physically do with it as I wish without my being impeded by greater force.

I have already noted that the symbol belongs to the moral bond in so far as it serves as an indication of ownership to all and causes in them the moral obligation to respect it. This obligation is not present as long as others are ignorant of the ownership (cf. 508-509). The indication is already present, however, in our case where we are dealing with something which has an owner (cf. 450-451). It is simply a question of indicating that what is owned must now be to someone else's advantage. The sign no longer indicates that ownership pertains to the first person. Nothing else is needed because the transmission of rights is known to the two contracting persons.

Real or symbolic possession therefore is not necessary in

---

[258] Zeiller also considers them *promises* in his *Diritto naturale privato*, §93. — Cf. Austrian Civil Code, §861.

rational Right for the transmission of ownership from one person to another.[259] The only thing necessary is that, as a consequence of the transmission, the one who cedes ownership understands he is leaving its recipient free to take possession of it.

[259] Positive laws often require the *consignment* of a thing, before they acknowledge transmission of ownership. Thus, the Austrian civil code, after saying that 'the title of mediate acquisition is founded in a contract, etc.' (§424), adds in the following paragraph: 'Ownership is not acquired by title alone. With the exception of the cases determined by law, ownership and all real rights in general can be acquired solely by legitimate consignment and acceptance.' This regulation is a necessary consequence of considering all contracts as 'accepted promises' (§861). The promise of giving is certainly not actual giving; if the ownership is to be really handed over we need to add 'the consignment of a thing'. I do not consider a contract as a promise to give, but as a true jural consignment (a consignment of the right), although the recipient may not enter into possession, and the physical consignment may be lacking. According to me, the promise present in every contract refers only to this physical consignment.

Furthermore, if we consider the matter carefully, we will see that even in Austrian legislation 'the consignment of a thing' is required more as a sign to reveal clearly the intention of the contracting parties (indeed, without a sign of the transmission of ownership, civil law could not acknowledge and sanction it) than as an element intrinsic to the completion of a contract. As proof of this, the laws themselves are satisfied with a *declaration* of the parties or a *symbolic consignment* of some thing, in place of a real *consignment* (§§427-428, 431-440). This is because a declaration or a symbolic consignment clearly reveals the internal act of the contracting parties' will, in which the transmission of the right properly consists. If this were not the case and it were not acknowledged by Austrian civil laws, these laws would not be satisfied with certain signs testifying to the act but unaccompanied by a real consignment of a material thing — a symbolic consignment or a declaration is not in fact a material consignment. The relevant paragraph in which the declaration of the parties is considered sufficient states: 'The consignment of a thing is done by *declaration* when the alienator manifests in a demonstrable way his will that for the future he will retain the thing in the name of the accepter, or that the accepter can for the future possess by real right the thing which he previously retained without such right' (§428).

§3. *The distinction between promises and contracts*

1081. Not all contracts are simple promises, although all accepted promises are contracts.

1082. The difference between *promises* and *contracts* is that in the case of accepted promises only a *right to the thing* promised, but not given, passes to the other person, while in the majority of contracts, that is, in all those which are not simple promises, the ownership itself of a thing, the *right to it*, is transmitted, even though it is not yet possessed.

1083. *Promising* and *ceding* something to another are, therefore, different acts. Although both are internal, manifested by external signs, and both are contracts when acceptance is added, they have different objects. The object of the first, as we said, is merely a right of appropriation; of the second, ownership itself.[260]

1084. One of the reasons why people believed that all contracts were promises is this: in the majority of contracts the *possession* of a thing is not, in reality, immediately transmitted. The *ownership* however is transmitted in the act by which the contract is completed. Hence, the promise to transmit the material possession itself of the thing is always carried out in either a tacit or expressed way together with the act of contract, in virtue of which ownership of something is transmitted.

1085. But we can easily see that a promise which is always

---

[260] In order to explain how a contract is obligatory, Tittel has recourse to 'a tacit agreement of the human race, which laid down that a contract must be a symbol of a real translation' (cf. Feder's *Schiarimenti al Diritto naturale*). This way of explaining the obligation produced by a contract shows that the author did not know the nature of the *act of appropriation* by which a human being establishes and dissolves the bond between a thing and himself. The nature of this act, in my opinion, has been generally missed by authors. In the second place, ownership does not pass from one person to another by a *real consignment* of things but by a *moral consignment*, by which a person dissolves the bond of ownership uniting the thing to himself so that another may establish it. A mere external symbol of the real consignment is, therefore, much less capable of transmitting rights. Finally, recourse to an agreement of the human race to explain the obligating force of contracts is a vicious circle because one has recourse to the obligating force of a contract to explain the obligating force of contracts!

joined to contracts *de faciendo* and *de dando* does not form the essence of a contract; it is purely an element and consequence of a contract. Thus, whenever this kind of promise is not expressed, and particularly when someone who sells or gives me something has no intention of giving me possession, I would still have acquired ownership of the thing according to rational Right, and I could even take it with force despite the opposition of the vendor and donor.[261]

1086. Similarly a contract would be complete if the vendor added no promise of giving me possession of something, or even if he expressly excluded a promise and, for example, ceded to me something he owned on the understanding that I took it of myself.

1087. A promise to give me possession of a thing (a promise of consignment) does not, therefore, constitute transmission of ownership; it gives me only the *right of action*, to which the owner is obligated when he promised to give me the possession and, more generally, the *right to take possession*.

---

[261] The moral act of cession of ownership was called 'consent' by Roman laws (*Institut.*, bk. 3, tit. 23). They distinguished between obligations arising from *mere consent* and obligations coming from a *verbal promise, written consent* or from the *consignment* of a thing. Relative to obligations we read: 'Obligations in buying, selling, letting, hiring, partnerships and mandates are effected by consent. In these ways the obligation is said to be contracted by consent. In order to substantiate the obligation there is no need of anything written or physically present, nor need anything be GIVEN; it is enough that those negotiating consent' (bk. 3, tit. 23). — There was certainly a rule that 'dominion over things is not transferred by pacts but by traditions' (bk. 20, c. *De pactis*). However, as I have observed, exceptions to this rule are found in Roman law itself, e.g in the last section of *S. De off. jud.*, and in the last book of *D. De serv. leg.* — This rule certainly applied to *undetermined contracts* and perhaps also to all *bilateral-promissory* contracts, where the transmission of ownership is taken as contemporaneous. — Höpfner (*Diritto naturale*, §80) refers to the principal authors who discussed the question whether the consignment of a thing is a necessary condition for the transmission of ownership.

§4. *The morally and jurally obligatory force of accepted promises and other contracts*

1088. An accepted promise is a contract in virtue of which I oblige myself to an action in favour of another (that is, to be the recipient or doer of an action, to lend or to give).

1089. By the contract the right over my action (cf. 1087) passes to the accepter. The right can be exercised by the use of force in order to constrain anyone who reneges on his promised action, but not for any other purpose.

1090. I am obliged to keep the accepted promise because my promise has given the other person a right, which he has accepted, to my action. Hence, if I do not perform the promised act, I harm the other's right, refusing to give him what is his.

1091. Similarly, *not honouring* other contracts is reduced to not keeping the promise attached to a contract which grants or allows possession of a thing whose ownership I have transmitted to another by the act of contract.

1092. Thus, every violation of an agreed contract consists in the failure to keep the promise attached to the contract.

1093. However, if no promise has been attached — for example, when an object has been alienated provided that the accepter himself obtains possession of it — violation of contract is impossible. Damage to the other's ownership independently of the contract would be possible only when I impeded with force his taking possession of an alienated thing, or if, after the receiver has obtained possession, I steal what is legitimately possessed, or in any way disturb the owner in his possession or legitimate use of the thing.

1094. In any case, the reason for the obligation is the same as the reason we gave when speaking about damage to others' right in general; it is the moral precept: do not harm another by attempting to deprive him of his ownership (cf. 368-449). Promises must not be left unfulfilled, therefore, precisely because failing to keep them really deprives a person of what has already been joined to him by the bond of ownership.[262]

---

[262] Authors like Fries (*Dottrina filosofica del Diritto*, Jena 1830) are mistaken

1095. The obligation resulting from a simply accepted promise, however, differs from the obligation arising from a contract which transmits the ownership of a thing, even relative to the time during which the promise or contract must be honoured.

1096. Let us suppose that in one case we are dealing with a promise to donate a book, and in another with the actual donation of a book; the promise and the donation have been accepted and both contracts concluded. In the first case, when must the promise be fulfilled? In the second case, when must the donor present the book if he had included this obligation in the donation?

In this second case, because no time is fixed, the consignment must be made immediately or as soon as possible, if the new owner so requires. In fact, if there is delay, the donor can take the donated book for himself as something he owns.

On the contrary, in the first case, where the promiser has not fixed a time for fulfilling his promise, he can execute it whenever he wants; he has the responsibility of determining the time. The promisee has no right to force him to fulfil what he has promised, because the promisee has in no way acquired any *real* right — 'the act of ownership' transmitting the dominion has not yet been carried out.

1097. All we have said so far concerns an *accepted promise* and any contract to which this kind of promise is attached. But what

when they try to extract the duty of keeping promises and honouring contracts from the law of truthfulness. A promise is not an affirmation but 'an act of ownership' or, in other words, an act by which a right is made to pass to another and a duty is accepted. If the promiser had no intention of keeping his promise, it would be a kind of lie, because to promise something is a way of making another believe that the promiser will keep his promise. Nevertheless the promise would be just as valid, provided the promiser were persuaded that he was obligating himself. However, if he intended not to obligate himself, it would be a lie but not a valid promise. The lie does not consist in failing to keep a valid promise but in depriving a material promise of its validity, which comes from internal consent, and thus from the truthfulness of the words expressing the consent. The person who accepts a false promise acquires the right to have it upheld, if the falsity, that is, the lack of internal consent, remains uncertain for him. If he is certain about the lack of consent, he nevertheless retains the right to restitution if, while acting in good faith, he was harmed by the false promise.

[1095–1097]

about a promise that has been made but not accepted or rejected?

First, a promise, at this stage, is not a contract. Nevertheless it is a promise and therefore a new reason for distinguishing the notion of *promise* from that of *contract*.

1098. Does this kind of promise entail obligation, even though it does not have the nature of contract?

It is certain that whenever a person promises something to another, he intends to obligate himself by his own words, granted the other's acceptance. In fact, the acceptance is usually presupposed; our acceptance is taken for granted because a promise concerns something we desire. For example, if someone says to his employee, 'I promise you £1,000', he has no doubt at all that the employee will accept. But the meaning of the promise is: 'I obligate myself to cede to you this right, provided you accept it.' The obligation resulting from the promise is indeed conditioned, but it is of its nature irrevocable. After its communication to the promisee, moral and jural reasons require that it be maintained at least for the time necessary and suitable for its acceptance or rejection, or within the fixed terms of the promise.

1099. A promiser always presumes in his promise a tacit condition that the promisee will express his acceptance as soon as possible, or at least without too long a delay. In fact when we make a promise, we do not intend to bind ourselves to fulfil it if we have to wait indefinitely on the response of the promisee; we want the contract concluded quickly and not left indefinitely open and suspended.

1100. At the same time, however, the promiser, by the very fact of his promise, obligates himself to allow some reasonable time for its acceptance. Civil laws generally define this time.[263]

1101. This shows that in the opinion of civil legislators even

---

[263] 'If the acceptance of a promise is verbal and no time has been agreed for its acceptance, it must be accepted immediately. In the case of a written promise we must distinguish whether both parties are in the same place or not. If they are in the same place, the acceptance must be acknowledged and notified to the promiser within 24 hours; if in different places, within the time necessary to despatch the reply twice. Otherwise, the promise is no longer obligatory. Before expiry of the fixed period, the promise cannot be revoked' (*Austrian civil code*, §662).

a person's simple act transfers the right,that is, the right to acceptance of the promise, to another person.[264]

1102. We cannot object that acceptance is simply a lawful action, not the exercise of a right. If this were the case, anyone who withdrew a promise before the promisee could reply would not offend the promisee, which is contrary to the supposition of all civil laws.

1103. The irrefutable proof that offence has really been given is in human nature. If human nature has been seriously promised something it desires (a good), it naturally feels upset when the promise is suddenly withdrawn before its acceptance could be expressed. A disturbed feeling like this is the indubitable characteristic of harm; it shows that the moral law, the foundation of right, has been transgressed: 'Do not upset human nature by taking from it the good it had naturally appropriated to itself.'

§5. *Certain contracts transmit ownership of a thing only in the act of its material consignment; prior to this they are simple promises*

1104. We must note that certain contracts remain simple promises until they are executed, that is, until one or both of the parties carries out the actual consignment of the thing. This happens when the object of a contract is not sufficiently determined; the contract concerns only the obligation to determine the object. The contract is made solely by a promise, not by a transmission of ownership, because ownership of an undetermined object cannot be transmitted.

1105. The three contracts of exchange, sale and loan will serve as examples.

In exchange the objects to be exchanged are determined. Thus, once the contract is made the ownership of the two objects is reciprocally transmitted and exchanged.

---

[264] Donation is another example. Before a *donation* is accepted, it gives the person to whom it is made the right not to be prevented from knowing the proffered donation (cf. 32).

1106. This is not true for a sale's contract. On the one hand, the object to be sold and bought is determined in this contract; on the other, only the price is determined. The fixed price is not a materially determined object; it is simply an ideal being which determines in a particular way the measure of another real being (money), but not the real being still to be determined by the buyer. As long as the money is not present, the contract is a promise which means (for the seller): 'I bind myself to transfer to you the ownership of this object on the condition that you determine the quantity of money (whatever it is) to be given me in exchange'. For the buyer it means: 'I bind myself to determine the quantity of money and to give it to you in exchange for the object you are selling me.' The object of the contract is therefore, clearly determined for one of the parties; for the other there is no determined object, because the object is replaced by a promise to determine it. Hence, while this situation obtains, the ownership of both objects is not exchanged; only the promise of their exchange is given, and without the determination of the object its ownership cannot be given to another.

1107. It is the same for a contract for a loan. In buying and selling, as we have seen, the object is determinate only for the seller and remains undetermined for the buyer, as long as the latter does not present the money for the desired purchase. Similarly, in a loan the borrower merely promises to restore an equal value. He is simply making a promise to transmit to the lender the ownership of an object at the moment of repaying the loan.

In contracts of this kind, therefore, rational Right requires that ownership be transmitted by the material consignment of the thing, or at least by its determination. Consequently, in contracts of exchange, ownership is transmitted at the moment the exchange is made.

§6. *When* promissory contracts *must be effected*

1108. I call these contracts *promissory* to distinguish them both from contracts in which ownership is transmitted and from simple or gratuitous *promises*.

1109. We have seen that a *simple promise*, even though

accepted, gives only the right to the promised action, not to ownership. But if the promiser has determined no time, he cannot be forced to determine it. His promise is gratuitous and unilateral, and therefore must be considered as a free gift which does not give the other the right to ask for its execution at a stated time, unless the time of execution is contained in and forms part of the promise itself.

1110. But this is not the case with *promissory contracts*, in which both parties bind themselves and undertake to lend something with a view to some advantage. Here, each contracting party has acquired a right to the benefit which necessarily comes to him from the execution of the contract; each can therefore claim it as his own. Hence, if the time for the execution was not agreed in the contract itself, one party can require from the other that the execution take place as soon as possible.

1111. Furthermore, some codes consider the promise of this kind of contract as the contract itself. Because the contract is a promise, and a promise which requires immediate execution, the difference is more of words than of things in the following two ways: 'I promise to sell' and 'I sell'.[265]

§7. The nature of consent in contracts

1112. In order to be jurally effective, the consent by which contracts are formed must:

    1. concern a thing capable of being the matter of a contract;

    2. be given by persons jurally able to give it;

    3. not be produced by an injustice of one contracting party to the other;

    4. be expressed in such a way that it must and can be considered a true, certain consent.

---

[265] Art. 1589 of the Napoleonic code says: 'The promise to sell is the same as a sale when there is a reciprocal consent of both parties regarding the thing and the price.'— M. Portalis, speaking about the motives of this law, says,: 'There is in fact present in this case everything concerning the substance of a contract of sale'; he quotes Cochin, t. 6, p. 160 *Séance du 7 ventôse an. 12.* — The Albertine code enacts the same in art. 1595.

A.

The first condition: the thing must be capable of being the matter of a contract

1113. In order to be the matter of a contract, a thing must be alienable, and if it is by nature alienable, alienation must be possible.

1114. The following are inalienable:

a) divine things (any attempt to make them otherwise is the sin of simony)

b) rights which are simultaneously duties and concern truth, virtue and happiness (cf. 52, 89-93).[266]

1115. Hence, no action that is substantially and without exception evil can be the object of a contract.[267]

1116. However, if the thing or action alienated by someone is of its nature alienable and honest, the contract would be valid even if the circumstances of the alienation were forbidden by the moral law. The contract is rendered invalid not by the

---

[266] Zeiller says: 'A contract by which a human being subjects himself to another without condition and is obliged to perform, omit or suffer everything the other wishes would lower him to the level of a mere thing, a purely feeling being (an animal). No one can acquire this kind of authority as a right over a rational being. Anyone who really subjected himself to an unlimited authority, would be acting like an irrational creature which is unable to conclude a contract. Moreover, he would be obliged to serve the other as a mere thing and thus deprive himself of personal dignity. His renunciation of the right to act as a reasoning, moral being would mean that in future he would no longer be a subject of moral obligation and legal duty. What a contradiction!' (§103). And in the footnote to §104 he says: 'The promise to obey indiscriminately all the commands of a superior, to become drunk by immoderate drinking, to become a victim of licentious behaviour and unnatural vices, to rob, assassinate and murder cannot produce a right or a duty. Papinian says all too accurately: "It is unthinkable that we can perform actions which offend our piety, esteem, modesty and, generally speaking, decent mores"' (bk. 15, *De condit. instit.*).

[267] Anyone who causes a crime to be committed against another is not, in my opinion, obliged to pay for an act which is substantially and not accidentally criminal, even if the amount is agreed. But in conformity with the amount of influence he had over the criminal's action, he has the duty of restitution for any calculable harm sustained by the delinquent as a result of the crime. Similarly he has the duty of restitution or of renouncing the benefit he may have gained as a direct effect of the crime.

wickedness of the action of the contract (provided the contract is just) but by the wickedness of the *object* or matter of the contract. Thus, anyone who has sold some books must consign them to the purchaser who has paid, even though by the sale he has failed in his duty to his children who need the books for their education. Although the sale was morally unlawful, the object (the books) is alienable, honest matter. Hence, after the sale it is still lawful and obligatory to consign them to the purchaser. To give another what is his is both lawful and obligatory.

1117. Furthermore, according to Right the purchaser cannot be obliged to give up the books after the completion of the contract, just as he cannot be jurally obliged to give an alms. Even if he knew for certain that the seller was failing in his moral duty by selling the books, it could not be said that in buying them he sins against moral-jural duty in such a way that he is obliged to restitution. When a contract is made by the two different acts of alienation and appropriation, appropriation is always just (although not always lawful) when it follows alienation; the acquirer appropriates things left free by their owner. The moral law is therefore violated, but not the jural law which imposes respect for another's ownership.

1118. Alienation of the thing that forms the object of the contract must be possible in addition to its being alienable by nature (cf. 1113). According to Zeiller, alienation or loan of the object of a contract

> is physically impossible, when it is beyond the natural powers of human beings in general, or the powers of the promiser in particular. In this case the will cannot intervene. Consequently, the legal use of freedom or moral necessity is not possible, and therefore no legal obligation can exist.
>
> When the impossibility is clear to both parties, the declaration of the will can be the result only of play-acting or mental alienation. But if the impossibility was kept secret from the promisee, a proportionate possible loan or restitution can be required.
>
> *a*) Hence, if someone has too much confidence in his own powers (for example, an incompetent artisan) and promises more than he can really give, he can be obliged to have the task completed by an abler man.

b) If a person promises something absolutely which involves a third person (that is, does not simply undertake to persuade the third person to be forthcoming), he is responsible to the deceived person for damage resulting from unfulfilment of what has been promised.[268]

c) If the loan of the object was possible at the time of the contract but later was rendered impossible (for example, by the owner's careless neglect of what had been promised or by his squandering borrowed money), he must reimburse its value with money or labour.

d) Those who fraudulently extract money, by engendering false hopes in uneducated people, as quacks and impostors do, are held to pay indemnity.

Moreover, if any difficulties arise greater than those that were, or could have been present at the time of the promise, they cannot in any way reduce the right of the accepter.[269]

B.
The second condition: those who give or receive consent must be jurally able to do so

1119. No one can give valid consent unless he is able to use his understanding and free will. Those incapable of perceiving the thing to which they must assent either through lack of intellective development, or through mental alienation, drunkenness or any other accidental mental state, are incapable of consent.

1120. According to rational Right, those who do not see the

[268] Cf. Höpfner, *Commentario sulle Istituzioni di Eineccio*, §76.

[269] §104. — Concerning the last observation, I think that eventual difficulties do not reduce the right of the accepter if they are virtually understood although not foreseen in the promise; this is not the case if they result from an extraneous, accidental cause. If, for example, I have made a contract with a well-digger, he is obliged to complete the work even if he encounters ground much harder and more resistant than he had imagined; he must sustain any loss. But he is not obliged to pursue the work in the event of war when the battlefield is so close that the work could be dangerous; this circumstance is not included in the promise, even virtually. It would be the same in the case of a landslide which covered the site of the well; the expenses for clearing the obstruction could not be the responsibility of the person who had promised to dig the well and nothing more.

proximate consequences of their consent are incapable of consent, although they need not see the remote consequences nor understand everything virtually contained in the obligation they assume.[270]

1121. Consequently, some are capable of giving their consent in simple matters but not in more complex matters, where it is more difficult to conceive the nature of the contract and even its proximate consequences.

Generally speaking, civil legislation requires a lower age for giving valid assent when accepting benefices than when contracting obligations.

1122. Those who cannot express their consent clearly are also incapable.

1123. If, in order to conclude a contract, one person's will depends on another's, the jural freedom necessary for the contract is lacking in the first, when consent is not given by the second on whom the first depends.

C.
The third condition: the consent must not be produced by an injustice of one contracting party to the other

1124. If the action of the contract is unjust towards the person with whom it is made, it is clear that it cannot produce a right against that person.

1125. Höpfner, together with Zeiller,[271] Grotius[272] and Bodin,[273] restricts the *injustice* which renders contracts invalid to these limits.

1126. But many distinctions are necessary:

1. If the contract itself is an injustice, it obviously cannot be binding.

2. Similarly, if injustice was the *cause* of a harmful, unwanted contract to the party who has suffered the injustice, this party

---

[270] If this were necessary, a contract could never be made to the advantage of one of the parties. The party with no advantage could always rescind the contract on the grounds of not having foreseen the consequences.

[271] §1004, footnote.

[272] *De jure B. et P.*, pt. 2, §9.

[273] *De conditione turp. implet.*, c. 2, §3 ss.

[1121–1126]

must at least be compensated and satisfaction made, although the contract is just in itself.

3. Injustice which was neither in the contract nor in its efficient cause, but was the cause of its execution, is an evil which does not render the contract invalid.

4. Injustices which are only accidental and inessential to the contract require restitution and satisfaction for damages, but do not nullify the contract.

5. If there was some accidental injustice in the contract against a third party but not against the contracting parties, no. 4 applies.

6. If the act of contract was just but immoral, a similar distinction would have to be made:

Immorality affecting the acts of alienation and appropriation which are present in every contract annuls the contract.

Accidental immorality does not nullify a contract which is substantially upright, but, like all immorality, produces an obligation to expiate the fault.[274]

1127. Violence and fear can be great enough to remove the use of intelligence and free will, and thus render the person incapable of giving valid consent to a contract for lack of the second condition I have given (cf. 1119).

1128. Violence and fear, when insufficient to remove intelligence and free will, are nevertheless unjust and require reparation. If the injustice becomes the cause of a contract by extorting consent, it can certainly make the contract invalid. This happens whenever someone is induced to make a contract in order to avoid the greater evil unjustly threatened by the person wanting the contract, even though the contract is in itself upright.

1129. We must note in the above case that the contract is not invalid because the person making it is induced to do so through fear of an evil, but because 1. the evil is unjust and 2. it is threatened by the contracting party to force the conclusion of the contract. On the other hand, the consent is valid if a person is induced to make a contract in order to escape an evil evidently caused by accidents independent of human beings, or justly

---

[274] All these cases can be reduced to the general principle that 'there can be no injustice or immorality in the TITLE which posits a right in being, nor in the ACTIVITY constituting it.' Cf. *ER*, 256-261.

dependent on human beings, or unjustly dependent on a third party not involved in the contract.

1130. He has only the right to restitution by the third party who caused the fear and thus forced him to make the harmful contract.

1131. The fear in each case however must not be panic nor be such that the person could have easily escaped it.

1132. Fear, even though not strong enough to prevent reflection, can render a contract invalid. Nevertheless, in this case it must be such that the person must have reasonably let himself be moved by it to make the contract.

1133. Fear is always of this kind whenever it arises from the threat of a definite future evil if the contract is not concluded, and of harm greater than that inherent in the contract, whether this harm is real or a sacrificed affection, which also has value.

1134. If the feared evil, however, is not certain, it must be calculated according to its degree of probability, and the resultant evil must be such that the conclusion of the contract is rendered less obnoxious than its omission.

1135. Anyone who abuses the weakness of a credulous person or of a person subject to fear acts unjustly.[275]

1136. If however this kind of contract can no longer be cancelled, the restitution must be equal to the total of the *real harm*, the value of the sacrificed *affection* and the *evil caused by the fear*.

1137. It may be objected: 'Surely the promise to give a murderer a sum of money, or any contract imposed under threat of death, removes the duty of truthfulness which your words must have? A person who has not lost the use of reason is always free; he can refuse to promise, and be ready to die instead.'[276]

If veracity is the point at issue, I refer to my earlier opinion that an unjust person who seriously misuses words for the sake of harming others has lost the right to their use because words

[275] 'Deception is a cause of nullity of an agreement when the deceit employed by one of the contracting parties is such that without it the other party would clearly not have made the contract' (Albertine code, art. 1203).

[276] This objection is supported by Cr. G. Schwarz, *Sylog, problem. jur. nat.*, Altorff 1738, 38, and by K. H. Heidenreich, *Sistema del diritto naturale*, Leipzig 1894, 1.

no longer mean anything to him (cf. 106-112). Properly speaking, however, it is not a question of truthfulness: the validity of a promise is not founded in the moral law requiring us to speak the truth, but in the internal act manifested externally of the transmission of what is possessed. In our case the internal act can be missing. Thus the murderer, a human being endowed with reason (without reason he would not be capable of rights), knows or should know that the promise or external contract is not the expression of an internal will, but simply a means of avoiding a greater evil.

1138. Even if we suppose that the internal act of transmission of ownership has taken place, the right to restitution of the equivalent value of what has been lost always remains along with the value of the affection for it, the usefulness and enjoyment corresponding to the time of its absence, the cost of the evil of the fear inflicted. All this is due, over and above the satisfaction required for the harm done.

1139. If this kind of just restitution is denied me, I can, according to rational Right, obtain it myself with the use of force, as I can every other right.

1140. What has been said about unjust fear applies equally if a false hope of gain is used to make me accept a contract.

1141. But if the hope enkindled in my spirit originated solely from my irresponsibility or waywardness — for example, the hope was unjust or an unjust gain was promised me — I no longer have any right to claim that the contract is invalid.

1142. Nor has the person who deceived me acquired a right to any utility resulting from such a contract. Each of us must expiate his own fault.

1143. However, relative to me the hope may be unavoidable, that is, invincible; in particular a falsely promised good may be honest and such that it renders the contract a good and even reasonably necessary undertaking for the person making it. In this case the deception concerns either the object of the contract or its consequences.

1144. If a mistake was made about the *object* of the contract because the object appeared substantially different, the contract is null for lack of consent — the consent referred to another object.

1145. If the deception concerns only some accessory quality

of the object of the contract, it does not render the contract invalid but simply gives a right to restitution for the damage done.

1146. If however the hoped-for gain, engendered by false, deceptive information, concerns the promised consequences, it is my belief, contrary to the opinion of other authors,[277] that the contract is invalid. It is clearly reasonable for me to make a contract which will bring me great gain and save me great loss. Hence, the person who offers this kind of motive to a reasoning being is the efficient cause of that being's action and, if the motive is deceptively false, of any harm to him.

1147. False hope is a cause similar to that of an unjust threat of harm. Such causes, although not mechanical, have a near infallible effect on reasoning beings and are therefore equal causes of harm. Thus, stock-jobbers who disseminate false news, or dealers who falsely put it about that a certain food product or merchandise is in abundant supply so that the price will drop when they want to buy, or is very scarce when they want to sell, must be considered as real robbers of the possessions of others and are bound by the obligation of restitution.

1148. Some codes require that a contract, to be valid, must be seen to have a just, upright cause precisely because knowledge of the contract's cause can indicate whether deception is present or not.[278]

[277] For example, Zeiller, §101.

[278] The French code, followed by the codes of the Canton Ticino and the Kingdom of Sardegna, requires a cause for contracts: 'An obligation without a cause, or founded on a false or unlawful cause, can have no effect' (art. 1131); the next article states that the cause need not be expressed in the contract, provided its existence can be proved. The Austrian code does not impose this condition for the validity of contracts; gratuitous contracts and testamentary dispositions would still be valid even in the case of a false cause, 'unless there is proof that the testator's (or donor's) will was dependent solely on this erroneous motive' (§§572, 901). This comparison is itself sufficient to indicate the different spirit of the two original legislations, the French and the Austrian. The former is keen to discover and punish deception wherever present; the latter to see that the will of honest people produces its effect. It is easy to see that civil legislators have to avoid the two hazards of not punishing false dealing and of placing an obstacle to a just will; they can be happy if they avoid both. In fact all measures to uncover fraud bring with them the great evil of rendering many conditions or just desires useless through lack of

D.
The fourth condition: the consent must be expressed in such a way that it can be taken as true and certain

1149. Reciprocal consent which renders a contract valid must be seen as true and certain. It must therefore appear as internal, serious, determined, free from error and intelligible.

1150. I say it must *be seen* to have these qualities because the cause of the right acquired by the parties through the contract must be something externally visible, not internal in the spirit; what happens in the spirit is hidden and cannot constitute any title to right.

1151. Anyone who pretends to give consent without doing so is certainly aware of not giving it. For this reason some philosophers believed that although the person sinned by lying, the lie did not impose a jural obligation to execute the contract.

1152. In my opinion they are mistaken, as the following argument demonstrates. No one can acquire a right through a contract without the aid of an external sign manifesting the mind of the other contracting party. An external sign, therefore, whose meaning cannot be doubted, is the sole possible title to the acquisition of rights by transmission. Thus, if one party undoubtedly acquires a right by such a sign, the other party contracts the jural obligation corresponding to this right. This proof seems clear to me. The only exception is when through our own fault we lose the right to the truth of language.[279] This

formal requirements. However, although the omission of such measures may uphold the validity of many agreements and desires of honest people, it leaves the door open to deception of the unfortunate. The desire to defend ourselves excessively from deception impedes honest wills and hampers trade between upright citizens. In any case, it is all too clear that the spirit of the Austrian legislation, which leaves the will more free and protects acts more precisely, is more *liberal* than that of the French, which is totally directed to defence against deceivers. When we concern ourselves too much with defence, we are obviously restricted in our position and not free; on the other hand, many measures against human wickedness not only protect the good, but make the wicked more cautious. While the law remains majestically stationary, the wicked progress.

[279] Some authors deny that a person has a real right to the truthfulness of

happens, as we have said, when one person forces another to use words in such a way that the latter can be despoiled of his possessions (cf. 1137, 1142). The unjust assailant must know, as a reasoning human being, that the words he forces from the other are not words, because by his wrongful action he has lost the right that they should be such for him.[280]

1153. The requirements for the validity of a contract, therefore, must be external, and when external indications give no reason for doubt, internal consent must be supposed. The contracting parties are obliged to give this internal consent when they express it externally. If they do not give it at the moment of agreement, they have a jural duty to add it later, or at least a duty such that the withholder of consent loses any right given by the law of ownership. He may still have *ownership*, but he has lost the *right of ownership* (cf. 922-923).

1154. Hence it is clear that the consent must be expressed seriously:

The following have no jural effect: preliminary discussions,

others. I reply: there is no right to the words of others, but there is a right to the truthfulness of the words. This right is particularly evident when displeasure or harm is caused to others by deceptive words, because we all have a clear right not to be upset or harmed. Speaking only about harm, I affirm I may not in any way be a cause of harm to another; but every time I posit a fact (words are also a *fact*) which is a reasonable motive for others to inflict harm on themselves, I am the cause of that harm. If I make a promise to a business colleague and then retract it before he replies, I must indemnify the harm caused him. My promise gave him a reasonable motive for action (for example, to buy a quantity of silk if I have promised him a loan). After acting reasonably, he does not have to bear the resultant harm — that is my responsibility, because, by withdrawing the stimulus which made his action reasonable and useful, I have rendered the action harmful to him.

[280] These observations and those that follow indicate to what extent those authors are right who on the one hand deny the necessity of internal consent for the validity of an agreement — Vasquez, Turrianus, Pontius, Pallavicino, Dicastillo (who refers to the first four in *De jur, et justit.*, bk. 2, tr. 3, Disp. 1, n. 461 ss., and others) and others are examples — or on the other hold that *internal* consent is necessary — Sanchez (Bk. 1, *De matrim.*, Disp. 9, num. 3), Molina (t. 2, Disp. 352), Card. de Lugo (*De jur. et just.*, t. 2, Disp. 22, Sect. 4, n. 45), Beuch (*De pactis et contract*, Tract. c. 1, Sect. 2). — If internal consent is involuntarily and innocently absent, the contract is null and void; if it is deliberately and maliciously withheld, and all external evidence indicates that it should be and is present, the contract must be upheld.

the offer and the reply (which simply reveal the parties' intention and will before the contract is concluded, or make use of offers as a means to conclude the affair), imperfect promises (*pollicitatio*)[281] — these lack the intention of conceding any right at the time and simply make known the intention of being ready to transfer a right at a future date — any clearly irresponsible statements and expressions, acts which are merely apparent, and any excessively complex declarations.[282]

1155. The consent must also be *precise*. Thus, if it was not known which object was meant, or if each party gave consent for a different object, the execution of the contract would be impossible.

1156. The same applies in the case of substantial error about the object where I think I am contracting for one thing but am actually contracting for another.

1157. If my mistake concerns only the motive for making the contract but not its object, the contract is valid, provided the harm done to me is not the result of the other party's deception, and provided the motive for the contract is not an essential condition of the contract itself.[283]

1158. Finally, the consent must be clear.

1159. This clarity relates either to the parties or to the judge who must adjudicate their disputes.

1160. It could happen that the parties clearly understand each other, although the contract itself is unclear, equivocal and false. In this case, they are morally and jurally obliged to the contract.

1161. If one party has understood one thing, and the other, something else, the party who has understood the spirit and letter of the contract has the advantage, and can presume that the

---

[281] Ulpian says: 'A contract is the consent and agreement of two persons, but pollicitation is the promise of someone merely making an offer' (bk. 3 ss., *De Pollicit.*).

[282] Zeiller, §96.

[283] The Austrian code says, 'When the motive or purpose of a consent is expressly stated as a condition, it is considered to be like every other condition' (§901). Zeiller justly adds that the contract's purpose could have the nature of a condition even if it were not expressly stated but understood according to the circumstances 'in a way that it is impossible not to be known' (§101, *Diritto naturale*).

other is not acting sincerely. But if the circumstances and the known honesty of one party persuade the other that the first is in inculpable doubt, the other must retract and the contract be considered as null.

1162. Whenever one party reasonably doubts the other's sincerity in understanding the contract, the former can have recourse to a judge.

1163. The same applies when both parties are uncertain about the other's rectitude, or if neither wants the contract annulled, although both are aware that in its expression and thought it lacks clarity and precision. In these cases they can either agree among themselves or seek the opinion of the competent judge or tribunal.[284]

1164. If the judge or competent tribunal finds the contract unintelligible and vitiated, they can declare it void and assume the office of mediator in drawing up a new contract, provided the parties agree. Alternatively, they could find that the contract needs to be submitted to interpretation, in which case they could interpret it, using the rules of hermeneutics.

1165. This interpretation or clarification is made when the contract can be understood in its substantial part. As regards the other parts, it will be sufficient for the judge to give the most probable interpretation, which is often reduced to an equitable transaction.

§8. *Rules for the interpretation of contracts*

1166. The rules for the interpretation of contracts according to rational Right will certainly be the same as those determined by Roman wisdom and fully accepted by modern legislators.[285]

---

[284] According to rational Right, the conscience of each contracting party must clarify their own obligations and interpret those of the other party. Generally speaking therefore it seems that Huffeland was close to the truth (*Principii di Diritto naturale*, §327), in maintaining that rules of interpretation are solely for the use of a third party, a judge or referee. However the parties themselves, especially in the case of an ancient contract, may have to resort to the same rules to interpret the contract.

[285] After the State Councillor, Bigot-Préameneu, had stated the rules of

They are in fact precisely *logical* rules, and pertain therefore to *the logic of Right* and of *morality.*[286]

1167. The aim of the interpretation is to know the intention of the contracting parties.[287]

1168. The following rules are helpful for this purpose:

1. The sense given by the whole act must guide the understanding of both parties to the contract.[288]

1169. A contract therefore must be interpreted in such a way that

a) the parts and clauses of the act contain no contradiction;

b) the contract has effect.[289]

1170. 2. If this is insufficient, recourse must be had to the region and time when the contract was stipulated.[290]

1171. According to this usage therefore:

a) ambiguous clauses or those with double meaning must be interpreted;

b) unexpressed clauses must be understood.[291]

1172. 3. If doubt still remains, we must require the obligation to be proved; as long as the obligation remains doubtful, it does not exist.[292]

interpretation of contracts in Roman law, he added: 'Axioms must be invariable, like the justice that has dictated them. They were simultaneously the embellishment and foundation of Roman legislation and had to be inserted in the civil code' (session of the 7 Pluviôse, year 12).

[286] Cf. *Preface to the works of moral philosophy* and the schema of the distribution of this science [*PE, 1-14*].

[287] 'In agreements between contracting parties, desire is given more importance than words' (L. 219 ss., *De Verb. signif.*) — 'Applying equity without concern for the words' (Cic. pro Caecin. 13).

[288] 'It is irregular to judge or respond to any single proposition without considering the total law (the total agreement)' (L. 24, D., *De legib.*).

[289] 'Whenever there is ambiguity in determining customs, it is most fitting to accept whatever guarantees the matter in question' (L. 8 ss., *De verb. oblig.*).

[290] 'In stipulations and other contracts we must follow what has been enacted. If the enactment is not clear, we must follow what is normally done in the region in question' (L. 34 ss., *De reg. jur.*). — 'Whatever is inserted in contracts to remove doubt does not harm common right' (L. 81 ss., *De reg. jur.*).

[291] 'What pertains to custom and practice is tacitly understood in contracts'.

[292] 'It is unjust to remove by agreement information which has not been passed to us' (L. 9 ss., *De trans.*).

1173. Hence, in unilateral contracts, the person supposedly has the desire to accept the lighter rather than the heavier burden.

1174. 4. In bilateral contracts, where the burden cannot be reduced for one party without increasing it for the other, reason requires that ambiguous expressions be interpreted against the one who used them.[293]

1175. Finally, an obligation can also be tacitly contracted by positing a fact which reasonably indicates consent. For example, the person who uses a hired vehicle must pay for it without any previous agreement; the fact proves that he has the intention either to pay or to abuse the other's possession.

1176. On the other hand, a jural obligation is not contracted by silence without external facts, unless the person remaining silent has the jural obligation to speak and his silence is the cause of harm.[294]

§9. *How obligations arising from contracts cease*

1177. Obligations arising from contracts cease with:

    1. the execution of what is agreed in the contract;

    2. the acquisition of the creditor's right;

    3. the impossibility of executing the contract;

    4. the non-verification of the condition applied to the contract;

    5. a new contract or reciprocal agreement;

    6. the fault of one of the parties, so that the other party is freed from the obligation undertaken.

---

[293] 'The interpretation is to be made against the one who could have stated the law more clearly but did not do so' (L. 38, §18, *De verb. obligat.*).

[294] In the opinion of Zeiller (*Diritto privato*, §96, footnote), 'Wolff goes too far when he maintains that the person who does not reply to a letter in which some business is entrusted to him must execute the task' (*S. N.*, t. 4, §792). — Nevertheless, the writer can reasonably believe that the commission will be carried out, despite the lack of a reply if, for example, he had added that he would consider the commission as definitely fulfilled if he had no reply. Thus, if his friend culpably fails to reply, there is a *moral* cause of harm and perhaps also *jural* harm. Friendship *in this particular case* seems to become a *jural title* giving the right to a reply.

1178. The *execution* of what is agreed is carried out by;

a) consigning to the creditor what is owed him at the time and in the place and manner agreed;

b) consigning to him an equivalent with which he must be reasonably content, as if he were being paid an equal debt (*compensation*);

1179. The acquisition of the creditor's right by the debtor takes place by:

a) the tacit or expressed remission of the obligation by the creditor;

b) any other means of acquiring ownership; for example, by buying the useful dominion of a field owned by direct dominion, by inheritance and so forth (the *intermingling* of credit and debt in the same person).

1180. The *impossibility of the execution* of the contract arises from

a) the loss and destruction of what is agreed;

b) a greater force preventing the execution of what has been undertaken;

c) oblivion of the agreements, doubts arising about the existence of the contract, or long-lasting mutual negligence to execute it (*prescription, antiquation*).

1181. We must note however that if one of the parties is the culpable cause of the impossibility of the contract, they are held to make good the harm to the other party.

1182. The same applies if one party has used unlawful influence to obstruct *the verification of a condition* present in the contract, intending to annul the contract, with consequent harm to the other party.

1183. The *new agreement* between the parties which terminates the obligation of the previous contract is made by:

a) altering the intrinsic, essential agreements of the contracts, which is the same as nullifying the previous contract, and forming a new one (*novation*);

b) rescinding the contract by agreement without substituting another (*restitution*);

c) substituting another debtor for the first, who is freed from his debt (*substitution*).

1184. Moreover, the creditor can alienate his right without consulting the debtor. In this case, the debtor's obligation to the creditor ceases, but continues towards the person to whom the right was conceded.[295]

§10. *Equity*

1185. Equity must sometimes be applied in the fulfilment of obligations arising from contracts. We must therefore say something about this difficult and controversial matter.

1186. Authors are uncertain whether to place *equity* among acts of strict justice or among the virtues of beneficence.[296]

1187. 'Equality', the original meaning of 'equity', is a cause of this uncertainty of opinion. Because 'equality' can be and is applied to both physical and moral matters,[297] we are left uncertain about which it applies to.

1188. Thus, when it refers to moral things, it sometimes expresses evenness of spirit,[298] and sometimes the balance between giving and receiving as practised by human beings.[299]

[295] 'Heidenreich (*Sistema del diritto di natura*, 2, p. 238, Leipzig 1794) and Grotius may object that in contracts the parties unite their will in perfect accord so that a contracting party who alters the contract against or without the consent of the other commits an injustice against the other. I would reply: the person to whom the right pertains can, by custom, freely dispose of it. The acquisition by contract of only a personal, untransmissible right is not, therefore, a custom but an exception. If Grotius then maintains, for the reason just given, that the necessary compensation cannot be known by natural Right, we must reply that a contracting party must clearly permit any novation whatsoever of the contract, which relative to his right is truly indifferent. Or, as Bauer says (*Diritto di natura*, p. 174): in accepting an obligation in compensation there is a tacit remission for the one who now acquires the right of the obligation existing up to the present' (Zeiller, *Diritto naturale*, pt. 1, §119, footnote).

[296] Cf. Grotius, *De Aequitate*. — Klein, *Annali della legislazione*, 3, Berlin, 1788.

[297] Seneca applies it to physical things in the following fine passage: 'Nature deals with its parts, as it were, according to their weight. If the equity of the portions were upset, the world would overbalance' (*Quaest. nat.*, 3, 10).

[298] Plautus uses it in this sense: 'An even spirit is the best condiment for hardship' (*Rud.*, 2, 3, 71).

[299] Cicero properly distinguishes two kinds of equality between giving and having, and therefore two forms or acts of *equity*: first, the equity between

1189. In this last sense 'equity' is a part of strict justice, which usually consists in equality between giving and having.[300]

1190. But even in this last sense it sometimes means a softening of strict justice, that is, when strict justice is no totally in harmony with *equality* in giving and having, but rather falls away somewhat from equality.[301]

1191. There is therefore a way of acting called *strict justice*, which brings about *equality*, and another way, also called *strict justice*, which does not bring about *equality*. Hence, *equity* is needed to restore the balance.[302]

1192. Properly speaking, this is the meaning we give to the word 'equity', understood as a virtue completing justice.

1193. However, before discussing this concept further, we must identify all those other functions of moral reason which resemble equity and can be easily confused with it.

1194. The first is the *interpretation* of positive laws. This interpretation has its own rules for enabling us to know the legislator's mind in obscure cases.

1195. The second function is called in Greek επικεια.[303] This

---

what is owed and what is given by strict right, and second, the equity by which kindnesses and offences are reciprocated: 'Equity has a double meaning: one meaning is dependent on what is direct, true, just and, as we say, fair and good; the other pertains to the reciprocity in the favour to be bestowed. This is called 'favour' in the case of kindness, 'revenge' in the case of an injury' (*Partit.*, c. 37).

[300] Cicero very often uses 'equity' where he could have used 'justice'; for example, in *De Officiis*, he says: 'What kind of equity allows a person to take possession of a field he does not own, while the person who owns it, loses it?' (2, 22).

[301] In this sense Cicero employs the form: 'To speak in favour of equity against right' (*De orat.*, 3, 56).

[302] This opposition between strict justice and equity results from the fact that what we call *strict justice* holds to the letter of positive laws, which in many cases are a long way from justice. Thus when positive laws truly harmonise with justice they are called 'fair' ('fair rights', Cic., *pro Quintio*, 14 — 'law which is fair and useful for all', *Ibid.*, *pro Cornel. Balbo*, penult. c.). In this case 'equity' means 'natural justice', and 'law' or 'right' means positive justice. However, when Cicero says: 'What is true must be judged by what is fair and good, not by what is clever and shrewd' (*pro Caecin.* 23), he means we must not keep so close to the *words of positive law* that we abandon the prescriptions of *rational law*.

[303] From επι and εκω.

is the faculty enabling us to know those natural exceptions in which the law loses its obligating force. The legislator could not have foreseen these cases, and their scrupulous observance would harm their purpose — keeping the law would be entirely unjust or immoral or harmful to public good. Alternatively, its observance would certainly be a greater burden than that intended by the legislator for his subjects, so that if the legislator were present, he himself would dispense from it.

1196. A third function of moral reason is related to the art of applying positive laws to particular actions. It becomes effective when the obscurity of the law cannot be clarified in any way by the rules of interpretation. In this case the obligating force of the law has to be determined in another way, that is, by the so-called rules of conscience (*formation of conscience*).

1197. The *equity* we are discussing is not involved in these three functions (interpretation, epikeia, conscience). On the other hand, because they concern the art of applying positive laws, they pertain, properly speaking, only in part to the rational Right under discussion.

1198. *Equity*, taken in the sense we give it, manifests its exigency in contracts.

1199. Agreements and pacts, by which contracts are formed, are a kind of private positive law mutually imposed on the contracting parties,[304] and accepted by them.

1200. Hence, moral reason also exercises the three functions in the matter of contracts: *interpretation* (cf. 1166-1176), for discerning the intention of the contracting parties; *epikeia*, for rectifying badly expressed clauses which, understood to the letter, would destroy the effect of the contract;[305] finally, *conscience*, for determining the obligating force of these clauses when the clear, certain meaning cannot be completely

---

[304] The Romans took to an extreme the principle: 'What language dictates, right dictates'.

[305] For example, the following regulations of the Austrian civil code: 'The regulation is valid when it is evident that the thing enjoined or the person in whose favour the regulation was made was erroneously named or described. — The regulation also remains valid when the testator has added a clause which is found to be false, unless it is proved that the testator's will was based solely on this erroneous motive' (§§571, 572; cf. §901).

determined. I repeat (cf. 1194), however, this is not the *equity* we seek in contracts.

1201. Such *equity* is precisely what the Roman legislators acknowledged as necessary when they divided contracts into two classes: those called 'in strict right', and those called 'in good faith'.[306]

1202. Because this division truly pertains to rational Right, we must demonstrate its basis and nature.

1203. As we have said, agreements and pacts are positive laws which the contracting parties impose on themselves (cf. 1199). But rational laws, to which all legislators and their laws are subject, exist prior to all positive laws. Private legislators, that is, parties to a contract, must therefore draw up pacts and contracts which, if they are to be binding, must not offend rational laws.

Thus, obligations resulting from contracts must be judged according to two codes, as it were: a code of rational laws which pre-exist contracts and to which contracts must conform, and a code of positive laws, that is, of agreements made by external signs between the contracting parties.[307]

A contract can conflict in two ways with the laws of the first code of jural reason to which agreements must conform: the contract is vitiated either in its very formation or because of new circumstances arising at the time of its execution in accordance with its terms.

A contract may be vitiated in its very formation because its cause is immoral, or because the agreed pacts are damaged by deceit and bad faith, or finally because its effects are harmful to the right of third parties. In these cases the contract is null, according to rational Right, and a referee or judge must declare its rescission.

[306] Bk. 2, *De act. empt.* - Bk. 22, §2, ff. *De usur.* — Bk. 54, ff. *De O. et A.*— Canon law acknowledged and permitted this division as just, c. 1 and 2 *De N. O. N.,* — c. 6, § *ad haec, de except. c. fin. de deposito.*

[307] Positive civil laws are either in harmony with rational laws and as such cannot be ignored, or they are simply positive, that is, freely-chosen and designed to regulate contracts in areas left undetermined by the wills of the contracting parties. It is only to this second part of civil laws regarding contracts that our two proverbs apply: 'Where there is agreement there is no deception' and 'Agreements break laws'.

Although a contract may be formed on a sound basis, unforeseen accidents can be such that its execution would be impossible without harm to the rational laws which govern just contracts. In these circumstances two cases could occur: 1. the execution does not allow emendation; for example, if the object of the contract had become immoral without the parties' fault. In this case the contract is dissolved and the parties' obligation ceases, apart from restitution if one party had already fulfilled its obligation and the other had not. 2. The execution of the contract is emendable and, by means of non-substantial modification, can be reclassed within the laws of justice. It is these modifications, made to contracts of this kind, that are precisely the object of the EQUITY we are discussing and are the task of a tribunal called to judge *de bono et aequo* [what is good and fair], as the law says.

1204. This is indeed what the Romans, the wisest legislators of pagan antiquity, understood when they expressed the first rule for judges in the fine words: 'In all things the ruling principle of justice and equity is more desirable than that of strict right.'[308]

1205. In my opinion, therefore, *equity*, strictly understood, has its seat in the execution of contracts. It is that 'function of the moral-jural reason which modifies their execution in such a way that, while this may depart noticeably from what has been agreed, it draws nearer to the law of rational justice to which all contracts must be subject.'

1206. The distinction I have made (cf. 921 ss.) between *ownership* and the *right of ownership* should make this definition clearer.

1207. In fact some authors would totally exclude *equity* from *right*; they see equity as releasing human beings from the word they have given in agreements. They say that we are all masters of our rights and that from the moment we transmit them to

---

[308] Bk. 3, c. *De jud.* — Papinian also thinks that 'anything equitable and good is to be defended, even when subtlety would seem to impugn it' (*Digest.*, bk. 28, tit. 3, leg. 17; Celsus, speaking about strict right, says: 'Many have perniciously erred in this matter, invoking the authority of the right of knowledge.'

another by contract, the rights are alienated and our word can no longer be revoked.

1208. Their mistake lies in beginning from the concept of *ownership* rather than from the concept of the *right of ownership*. As we have already observed, *ownership* is something absolute and entirely restricted to the owner; it is totally unrelated to any other form of life, even any other intelligent life, outside the owner. If all this perishes, the owner is not disturbed, nor need he know of the destruction. *Ownership* is indeed natural but it is not *right of ownership*; moral reason has not yet spoken in all this, and right is a statement of moral reason. Moral reason limits bare ownership and even compels an owner to renounce part of it so that what he has left may be raised to the sublime dignity of right, and be as it were consecrated. The truth of this will become clearer as we continue to clarify the proposed concept of equity.

1209. We have said that 'equity modifies the execution of contracts when, because of some accident, their strict execution would deviate from natural justice and, more properly speaking, from commutative justice, as I should have said.'

We need therefore to investigate when this takes place, to indicate what this *commutative justice* requires and the law it imposes on contracts, and finally to give a definite rule telling us in which contracts and cases *equity* can and must intervene.

1210. In speaking of commutative justice I have already indicated the contracts in which *equity* is seen to be necessary. Donations and, in general, gratuitous contracts do not properly speaking pertain to commutative justice[309] which presupposes a kind of equality (cf. 1189) between giving and possessing. Donations are not measured or equated against any debt but solely against benevolence and liberality, which are freely-chosen and therefore not susceptible of any assignable measure, except that of the donor's large-heartedness represented in the gift itself.

There is no law of natural justice therefore that can modify the

---

[309] St. Thomas says: 'If a person simply transfers what is his to another without incurring any debt, as in donation, it is an act of liberality, not of justice' (*S.T.*, II-II, q. 61, art. 3).

execution of a contract of donation which, if unconditioned, is also irrevocable by nature.

1211. Hence, although according to the spirit of Roman legislation gratuitous contracts were considered 'of strict right', nevertheless Justinian placed among actions 'of good faith', which they certainly are, all actions 'dealing with something of value' and any action which 'comes about through exchange'.[310]

We see therefore how the law of equality between giving and possessing in commutative contracts is that which forms the natural justice of these contracts. Agreements cannot alter such contracts without changing their nature from being onerous to partly gratuitous. We see how *equity* must be applied to restore and strengthen the lost balance whenever equality is upset by some accident independent of the acts of the contracting parties.

1212. Sales contracts are the commonest of commutative contracts. Our discussion therefore will proceed more clearly if we consider the nature of this kind of contract rather than the nature of a commutative contract.

A sales contract presupposes and requires equality between what is given and what is received, between the thing sold and its price. When this equality is present, the price of the thing is said to be just.

1213. The intention of the two contracting parties is as follows: the purchasing party does not wish to pay more than the thing is worth; the party who is selling does not intend to consign it for a price less than its value. Neither of them has the intention of donating what he has; they intend to give the least they can. But if one tries to give the other the lowest price he can, he is not asking the vendor to give him a part of the thing as a gift; he is simply trying to persuade the vendor that the thing is not worth more than he is offering. Similarly, the other party tries to persuade the buyer that the thing on sale is worth more than the buyer estimates but he is not in any way asking him to

---

[310] *Instit. de action.*, §28. — Cf. Beuch (*De Pactis et Contract.*, c. 2, sect. 2, §4) where he shows that Roman laws did not however restrict actions of good faith solely to these two classes. All contracts formed by mutual agreement were considered contracts of good faith and so too were some real contracts: commodation, deposit, pledge, precary and unnamed contracts.

pay more than the thing is worth, which would be futile and irrelevant.

All discussion between the parties is therefore an attempt to establish a just price, and their differences consist solely in this: one is trying to show the other that the just price is more than the other is offering; the other is persuaded that the just price is lower than that asked by the first.

1214. Finally both parties agree on the just price, having attained it gradually or 'worked round it' (if we prefer the Roman law expression). The party with the greater advantage is the one who has succeeded in persuading the other to accept his estimation of the just price. Because no norm exists for establishing the just price for the thing, both parties are able to range between two extreme, just prices. Within this range they finally find a price they agree to, a price which can vary between the lowest and highest. The decent, limited gain obtained by one of the parties depends on the degree of advantage obtained in the sale.

1215. It is true that some deny the existence of a *just price*, because, in their opinion, a just price cannot be rigorously determined.

1216. But the inability to determine rigorously a just price simply shows that the just price oscillates between two extremes, outside of which we can certainly declare the price is unjust.

1217. A just price results necessarily from various elements, some of which however can be eliminated by particular circumstances.

1218. These elements are:

1. the quantity of goods being traded in a particular city, province or region where commerce is pursued;

2. the quantity of money in circulation;

3. the desire for goods, which in varying degrees will be stronger than the affection for money. This desire for goods is principally produced in our spirit by natural needs and by needs which the goods themselves generate.

1219. It may be objected: 'How can we deduce a price from such complex elements?'

But every day we see in the press the average price of certain

[1214–1219]

foods. This demonstrates the common belief that such a price can be known.

1220. It is in fact buying and selling that reveals this price. The would-be buyer tries to acquire merchandise for the least possible price, as we said; the vendor, on the other hand, tries to push the price as high as possible. It is this bargaining which produces the just, that is, the current price of the merchandise. A vendor acts carefully to draw buyers to himself and away from others, and is thus induced to lower the price of his goods so that other vendors cannot undercut him.

Vendors therefore by reducing their prices compete for customers. The reduction however finally reaches a limit (we ignore for the moment another limit determined by the price which the trader himself paid for the goods) determined by a relationship of equality between the saleable *quantity of goods* and the *quantity of desire* purchasers have for it.

1221. Let me explain. The quantity of goods is balanced against the quantity of the purchasers' desire in the measure that the price is determined. Obviously, great desire is not compatible with buying at a low price. Generally speaking therefore the price is reduced to the level where the desire of the buyers embraces all the merchandise on sale or at least all that can fully satisfy their desire; anything over and above, if there is any, has no value whatsoever. The vendors have no reason for reducing the price below this limit because, once this price is arrived at, they are able to sell all their saleable merchandise. But they must *all* arrive at this amount; if one of them wanted to keep a higher price, he would alienate the buyers and be left with his goods unsold.[311] Thus a uniform price emerges, called the *current* price, which is the *just price*.

All purchases and sales below and above this price are

---

[311] If the *goods* cost the vendor more to produce or get to market, this circumstance would reduce their production or manufacture. But in the case of existing goods, he would have to be content with selling them at a loss rather than keep them unsold without any hope of a better sale. Hence, the expenses necessary for the manufacture of the goods and for putting them on sale are the reason why the quantity of goods is not, generally speaking, so abundant that the price must be reduced below the expense sustained by the farmer, manufacturer and vendor.

exceptions which, like the smallest parts of a whole, are swallowed up in the multiplicity of transactions.

1222. It is true that, granted equality between the quantity of saleable goods and the quantity of the purchasers' desires, the current price can fluctuate at different times and places. This would depend on the *quantity of money* in circulation. But this simply means that the current price varies at different times and places. The current price at a particular time and place is always the just price.

1223. Such is the theory of *price* relative to our discussion. Let us now look at two special cases of the theory where the price is exceptionally high.

In the case of necessary goods, an exceptionally high price can be caused 1. by the *shortage of goods*, and 2. by the *shortage of vendors*.

1224. Purchasers' desires are not in fact all freely chosen; some are founded on needs of varying intensity. The most intense and unavoidable needs of all are those connected with existence. We will therefore consider these alone: the arguments advanced concerning the extreme need of existence can be equally applied, with due proportion, to the alterations in price produced by other needs.

1225. If basic goods are scarce, their price must obviously increase and be fixed by buyers who have more money. People who have more money draw necessary goods to themselves and thus deny them to others with less money; the rich give as much as is necessary for securing the goods.

1226. In these cases the price of necessary goods can increase until the total quantity of saleable goods is equal to the total quantity of existing money or anything else making up the price.

In difficult times the price is fixed by the relationship between the quantity of necessary goods and the quantity of things exchangeable for the goods. Thus, if the head of a donkey was sold in the famine of Samaria for about 80 shekals per head, we could deduce solely from this amount the total quantity of remaining food, granted we knew the total quantity of wealth in the city.

1227. The exceptional increase in price which results from the

[1222–1227]

scarcity of goods also takes place whenever dealers have no opportunity to compete in reducing the price.

1228. This happens whenever dealers are few in number and form a cartel themselves, or when a single dealer controls all the goods; he can do this either because he is in fact the sole owner of all the goods of a region, or has created a monopoly by cornering the market.

In these cases, the buyers who need the goods have to pay the dealers' price which is determined solely by necessity (which cannot be satisfied in any other way) and by the wealth of the purchasers. It bears no relationship to the quantity of goods, because circumstances exclude this relationship.

1229. It would be impossible to demonstrate, in the light of rational Right, that this last case (in which all necessary goods are held by one dealer) is contrary to justice, unless the monopoly or some other action depended upon fraud or violence.

1230. The owner of these goods would, of course, be free to impose whatever price he wished, and could do so entirely free from control by the laws of commutative justice, which could not be applied.

1231. However, if the owner's capricious refusal to sell necessary goods meant that people would die of hunger, he would certainly be exceeding the limits of his right of ownership (cf. 921-957).

1232. Again, if he raised the price of the goods so high that it exceeded the balance between all the goods and all the existing wealth, he would exceed the limits of his right, because a quantity of useless, unsold merchandise would be left.

1233. In the third place, if the price increase did not reach this balance but was high enough to leave some goods unsold because few people had sufficient resources to buy them, he would again exceed the limit of his right of ownership.

1234. But if the imposed price, although very high, were such that sufficient buyers were available to purchase the entire quantity of goods at that price, he would not exceed the limits of his right of ownership, because all the goods would serve the advantage of his fellow human beings.

1235. Poor people and those with limited resources would only have the same right of sharing in the goods as a person in danger of death through starvation.

[1228–1235]

1236. Moreover, the law of humanity and of charity would oblige a dealer not to sell the rich more than they needed. In this way, goods necessary for the existence of other human beings would not be uselessly removed either by excessive consumption on the part of the rich or by an excessive fear of future needs which could persuade the rich to lay up a superfluous quantity of goods. The injury to right resulting from this failure to care for humanity would depend more on the rich who had removed goods necessary for others but superfluous to their own needs.

1237. We may now consider the case of someone like Joseph in Egypt who owned all food supplies, and used his position to acquire the wealth of his compatriots, and seigniory over them after they had handed over all they possessed. In our hypothesis however no one has died; food has been provided in exchange for what the people possessed, or given freely to those who had no means of payment. According to the laws of simple rational rights, no injustice would be done in such a case.[312] However, there would soon be almost no occasion for the application of the rules of commutative justice. As I said, relationships between such an owner and his fellows would shortly have to be regulated by humanity and benevolence on his part, and submission and gratitude on theirs. All this must equally be applied in the case of extreme famine when the price of food exceeds all limits of normal trading.

1238. We must therefore acknowledge a just, *ordinary* price for goods and an *exceptional* price which also is just, because both result from the same laws which control how the price is determined.

1239. Moreover, it sometimes happens that a common *price* cannot be determined because of the extreme mobility of the

---

[312] All legislators agree that the sentimental value of a thing is just. One instance of this may be found in cases of a single vendor who prefers to keep something which he treasures rather than sell it. He has to be offered a high price to convince him to sell although the buyer would pay less if there were other sellers available. However, others may not have anything similar for sale, or the buyer himself may want to buy that single object only. In this case, there is one sole vendor who as a consequence of his right of ownership sets the price justly. No harm is caused to the buyer whatever price he is forced to pay for the object of his affection.

elements causing it, for example, objects of fashion. Here, the desires of purchasers are an unstable element to which laws cannot be applied in practice.

1240. For this reason legislators do not acknowledge any claim arising from injury in the case of buying and selling of chattels,[313] but do acknowledge as *just* the price current at the time of the sale, or rather, any price whatsoever agreed by the contracting parties in the sale.

1241. If we encounter difficulty in determining the approximate just price of something, we will certainly have greater difficulty in determining the price for a limited period of time, for example, for a particular month, day and hour.

1242. The reason is that the number of sellers and buyers is reduced in proportion to the limitation of time: there are obviously more buyers and sellers in a year than in a month or a day or an hour. As we have seen, reduction in the number of contracting parties leaves the price more undetermined and open to fluctuation (cf. 1223). Hence, anyone forced to sell at a particular time is the most disadvantaged, because he generally has to accept the level determined by the few buyers available within that short time. Similarly anyone who has to buy at a particular time is disadvantaged; he has to submit to the level established by the few sellers with whom he has to deal.

1243. However, according to commutative justice, we cannot say that a person does wrong either by buying at a low price from someone who has to sell, or by selling at a high price to the person who at that moment must buy. In these circumstances, a price either much higher or lower than the normal price is determined by the same general elements and causes which

---

[313] Portalis says: 'It states that the sale of chattels does not involve this claim in any way. The frequent movement of chattels and the extreme variation in their price would render a rescissory system impossible because of the harm to the sale and purchase of similar objects, unless we wished to cause universal upset in all commercial relationships and halt the course of daily business in life. In these matters, we must allow more for public freedom of trade than for the particular interest of a few citizens' (*Exposé des motifs de la loi relative à la vente*). — However, according to rational Right, there can be *injury* in the sale of chattels. Even granted that the price changes very frequently and very notably, we can know more or less what it is at the time the parties make their contract. This price must be the norm for the contract.

determine the price of things in all other circumstances. Cases of this kind therefore must be regulated more by the laws of human kindness than by those of justice.

1244. Hence, civil laws exclude the right of injury in the case of sales by public auction, but allow it in the case of private sales arising from the great needs of sellers and buyers.[314]

1245. Sales by auction and (in case of urgent need) private sales take place at a determined time. The only difference between them is that in a public auction, the desires of all the buyers are publicly expressed at the place of auction at a stated time; this is not so in the case of private purchases and sales at a time of urgency. Thus, the price determined by competing buyers at the time of an auction is considered just, even if the goods could be sold at more than double the price at another time. On the other hand, if a price in a private sale is excessively low, an obvious injury is done because it is not known whether it was determined by all the buyers available at the time, or rather by the greed of one of them, who by his purchase profited from the simplicity or shame of the needy, or sold and profited from the buyer's simplicity or desire or urgent need.[315]

---

[314] The injury can be caused by either the *seller* or the *buyer*. But the French code admits this claim only for the seller because, like Portalis in his exposition of the motives for the law, it considers that a buyer is never forced to buy. This however is false. If a buyer is rarely forced to buy because of necessity, his passions and the clever seductions of others lead him to buy. I find the regulations of the Austrian code more just than those of the French code in this matter. I readily support the Austrian civil legislation because it seems to me very deserving of merit and is more *liberal* than the French. The Austrian code is more reluctant to impede private freedom but more favourable to the natural *equality* of the human race. I readily quote its regulations on injury:

'If one of the parties to a bilateral contract has not received half of what he gave the other, according to its ordinary value, the law grants the offended party the right to request the rescission of the contract, and to restore things to their former state. —

'This remedy in right has no effect 1. if one of the parties has expressly renounced it or declared that the thing has been accepted at an exceptional price because of some particular affection for it; 2 if, despite knowledge of the true price, consent is given to an exorbitant price; 3. if personal relationships necessarily induce the presumption that a contract of both onerous and lucrative title was desired; 4. if the true price can no longer be ascertained; or finally, 5. if the judge has sold the thing by auction' (§§934-95).

[315] This explains why modern codes do not accept private auction or pure

1246. If we take all these circumstance into consideration, we can form according to commutative justice the concept of *just* price. These circumstances can greatly change this price but its determination always depends on the same principles and elements.

1247. The concept of a sales contract and of all commutative contracts in general can be based on this price once it is determined.

1248. We said earlier that neither contracting party intends to give anything of his own to the other. Their intention, will and understanding is to exchange money for goods according to equality of values, or to exchange goods for the *just price*. Thus, when one of them eludes the will of the other and sells at a higher price or else buys at a lower price than the just price, commutative justice is injured.

1249. Nor can it be objected that the agreement is entered into willingly. On the contrary, the will of the one who suffers the injury is truly deceived; if he knew he could have sold at a higher price, he would have done so because there was no wish to donate anything. From what we have said, we see how the excess above the just price comes about: one of the parties has the chance of a better bargain because of the competition possible at the time, but he is made to accept (or does so, because he is foolish or deceived) a worst bargain. He does this either by selling to someone who offers too little or by buying from someone who demands too much compared with the price which the wills of the other buyers would have determined.

1250. Hence, legalists correctly apply to cases of injury the dictum: 'Consent given to someone mistaken or deceived is null and void', and Roman laws call the injury 'fraud in the act itself'. Even if no pretence has been used to conclude such a contract, its very acceptance is a kind of deception and fraud.[316] Thus, the

---

licitation in the division of an inheritance, but require public auction. In private auction the price is not decided by the competition of all the buyers available at the time of the auction. — Cf. the Albertine code, art. 1062.

[316] Jurisconsults use these expressions: 'It is not injury but rather deception, and the deception extends to more than half of the contract' (cf. Dumoulin, *Tract. De usuris*). Portalis states that in the statutes and practices of various French cities the expression used is: 'Deception beyond half'.

same Roman laws very aptly say: 'By a law of nature no one can justly become richer to the detriment and harm of another.'[317]

1251. We had to deal with these teachings about a just price and injury in contracts so that we could clarify the nature of *equity* considered as part of commutative justice. Equity is not avoidance of injury but of what positive law calls injustice.

1252. From what has been said therefore we see that *equity* consists in the *just execution* of just agreements.

1253. A commutative agreement or contract is just if the agreed price is just. But an unforeseen accident which puts the price beyond just limits can occur between the formation of the contract and its complete execution by both parties.

In the case of an *absolute contract*, where ownership is transmitted at the moment agreement is made (contracts of exchange are an example), equity is no longer present. Because the contract is finished and what happens afterwards no longer pertains to the contract itself, equity can only suggest the human, moral duty to give some compensation.[318]

In the case of a *promissory* contract (for example, a sales contract, or any other contract involving money) rational Right teaches that ownership is transmitted solely upon the actual payment of the agreed price. Hence, *equity* can be involved, in the following way.

1254. The thing sold must be paid for at the just price current when the contract was made. If in the meantime the just price has altered, there would be no occasion for exercising equity, but at most humanity. But equity could be exercised 1. if the means used for calculating the price at the moment of the contract were still valid, but the present value of the article were now known to be different from its earlier value; 2. if the article were to suffer some unforeseen and uncalculated modification which, if foreseen, would have been calculated by both parties

---

[317] Bk. 206, § *De R. I.* — Grotius (*De I. B. et P.*, 2, 12, §8 and 12) and Wolff (*I. N.*, t. 4, §926) acknowledge that injury is also found in *natural Right.* — Grundling (*I. N.*, c. 23, §24) and Zeiller (*D. N. Priv.*, §§129, 133) hold the contrary opinion. It seems to me that what I have said shows that the first two are correct.

[318] Hence, rescission as a result of injury is not admitted in a contract of exchange. Cf. the French code, art. 1706.

as part of the agreement and would have influenced the price; 3. if anything else occurred which would be recognised as having seriously influenced, relative to the value justly put upon the article when the contract was made, the price fixed for the act of execution of the contract. Equity is therefore reduced to acting in such a way that 'the article sold really attains the just price that would have been assigned to it at the moment of the sale, if at that moment the article had been known for what it was, or if it had been known that when consigned it would have undergone the modifications that had in fact affected it.'

1255. In this way, the defective and obscure expression of the contract, that is, its form drawn up with insufficient foresight, is emended, and the true, formal and virtual will of the two parties is carried out.

1256. A few examples of what I am saying will clarify the matter.

Suppose a house has been sold with *all* its chattels for an inclusive price. When the moment arrives for the execution of the contract, the seller discovers that some chattels have not been calculated in the price of the house. These articles are so precious that the just price for the house should have been notably higher than the stated price. Equity requires that the buyer renounces the valuable articles or pays for them separately at exactly the just price current when the contract was made, whether the price has increased or decreased in the meantime.

1257. A worker's wages are agreed according to a determined currency. Before payment however this type of currency is no longer valid. Equity requires that his work be paid for in another currency equivalent to the just price at the time of the agreement; otherwise, the thing sold (his work) would remain without its just price because of the unforeseen event.

1258. Excavation work is to be done at a fixed price per cubic metre. The extraordinary hardness of the earth makes the work so slow and difficult that the workmen are unable to earn their living, no matter how hard they apply themselves. The equity of the hirer must supply for this morally difficult situation by paying what an unbiased judge would estimate for the work in the absence of agreed compensation. Otherwise, the quantity of effort and work of one party would not be met by a just price paid by the other.

1259. We are reminded at this point of the contract of chance, and the question is asked: 'Is it true, as some maintain, that injury is not possible in a contract of chance?'[319] To answer the question we need only know that the cost of the *expectation* of an event can on many occasions be calculated much more accurately than the cost of goods sold on the market. This can be verified by knowing exactly the number of events which favour one or other of the parties with equal probability, and the total cost of a favourable chance — the problem is well known in mathematics. In my opinion, therefore, injury can be done even in contracts of chance just as in any other sales contract, and equity can always be present. But I must add a note of warning: the injury can never be judged from the event, and the compensation required by equity does not depend on the event. In both cases restitution has to be obtained by investigating whether the value of the expectation of both parties was accurately calculated at the time of the contract and whether this value was equal for both.

1260. If one of the parties has bought an *equal expectation* at a higher price than the other party and this fact is known by the party who has the advantage, there is *injury*. But if both parties are acting in good faith and ignorance, or if the equality of the cost of the expectation was altered by some unforeseen accident taking place after the contract, *equity* must be applied.

1261. From all this we must conclude that *equity*, understood in this strict sense, is a part and *function of commutative justice*. This is precisely how the Romans considered it.[320]

1262. The reason why people doubt this and have a strong inclination to accompany equity with beneficence is the common mistake of thinking that agreements are the only laws governing commutative justice. But the opposite is true: if agreements are laws of justice, and if these laws are to have any value, they must, as we said, be drawn up according to the norm

---

[319] The Austrian code does not recognise injury for contracts of chance, §1268.

[320] According to Ulpian, Celsus correctly defines jurisprudence as 'The right and art of what is good and equitable' (bk. 1, tit. 1, c. 1).

of preceding laws. Thus, *equity* emends agreements when they were made in good faith and without deceit and in such a way that they could be executed without departing from the primitive laws according to which they had to be made.

CHAPTER 2

Transmissions of rights which change their subject but not their form

1263. We have already said that the modifications of rights are sometimes reduced simply to a change of subject possessing a right; at other times, they consist in a change in the form of the right itself. The modifications which consist in the change of a subject of right and those which affect the form of right take place on the occasion of the transmission of rights.

In this chapter, therefore, we shall speak of the ways by which rights are simply transmitted from one subject to another without any change in the form of these rights. We shall deal later with the variations which take place in the form of right.

1264. The transmission of rights occurs in two ways, as we have seen: 1. when one subject abandons his right and another occupies it; and 2. through contracts. Let us see how rights can be passed from one subject to another in both ways while preserving their integrity and form.

Article 1.
How rights pass without any alteration from one subject to another through abandonment and successive occupation

§1. *Right when simply abandoned and reoccupied*

1265. It is clear that if someone abandons part of his ownership, whether willingly or not, the right of ownership has to this extent simply changed its master without sustaining any division or alteration.

1266. This way of changing one owner for another takes place first of all in the cases we have listed above. It often occurs with nomad tribes and in colonies where people, having dwelt in a place and half-cultivated it, abandon their land for something better. It also occurs when rich people dispose of what is useless to them, but helpful to the poor. Another case in point is that of animals who have lost their master and regained their freedom, or of things whose owners cannot be traced. In all these cases, the object changes owner in the way we have described.

<h3 style="text-align:center">§2. Right as transmitted within a moral body
when the individual members enter or leave the body</h3>

1267. If an owner is a collective, perpetual body, it is clear that, as individual members enter or leave the society, the ownership continually adhering to that body devolves upon differing numbers of members.

1268. This is the case with communal goods in Communes, and with all rights pertaining to members of States, provinces or districts; it is also the case with ownership in religious societies, relative to the use of and benefit from such goods. By entering these bodies, members acquire the rights connected with them, just as they lose them as soon as their membership lapses.

1269. The same is to be said in the case of a lifelong contract by which several persons agree to enjoy together a certain quantity of substances and rights with the entire benefit devolving successively upon the survivors until the death of the last.

1270. It is true that in all these cases we are dealing with a social contract or quasi-contract. To this extent, the transmission of rights under consideration could be regarded as part of the second manner of transference of ownership, that is, by contract. But we think it better to mention it here, while we are dealing with the first manner of transmission, because the social contract, or quasi-contract, is only the remote cause of the transmission of rights. It is in fact an occasion rather than a cause of transmission. The proximate cause on the other hand is, properly speaking, people's entry into the collective, owning body, or their departure from it.

§3. *Intestate succession*

1271. The family itself, according to the Right of nature, is also a collective body in possession of rights.

1272. In the family, man and woman are simply two portions of a single human being. Love unifies their life, their souls, their bodies. In this single being, the man is by nature the head, the ruler;[321] the child is the offspring of the union. Love, the principle of this union, flows down to the child which it holds indivisibly united to the twofold root.

1273. In order to know the nature of this natural unification of three persons in a single being, we have to abstract from whatever occurs outside or contrary to nature. We cannot reach any clear knowledge of the nature of family if we mingle within its concept the divisions and rifts springing from the free activity of its members. This, of course, is true of anything: we cannot know its genuine nature if we either destroy it or examine it in the light of deformed and corrupt reflection.

1274. This, I think, is the principal reason why many legislators offer such a poor definition of what composes family society. They fix their attention only upon the ignorance and weakness, the internal divisions, and all the abuses that can be perpetrated freely by each individual who forms part of a family, but usurps what belongs to others and tears the family apart. All this must be taken into account by legislators whose obligation it is to help diminish or heal such evils. Nevertheless, such deficiencies must be ignored from the outset when we are endeavouring to establish the theory of family right. First, we have to know what the family is in itself according to nature, and then concentrate on its natural, original Right.

1275. In considering this society as a collective, owning body,

[321] I hold that polygamy, and even more polyandry, is contrary to rational Right when human beings are considered in an uncorrupt state. I shall demonstrate this in bk. 3 of *Social Right*. My only hypothesis, therefore, concerns the married union between one man and one woman.

we find ourselves faced with the question: 'Is there natural succession in families in such a way that ownership is transmitted naturally as people come into ownership through birth and relinquish it through death?' This is our question. First, I shall state my opinion, and then resolve the difficulties that arise.

1276. When we look at the origin of mankind, we see a single family, composed first of two individuals, husband and wife, and then of children also. As we said, this family is a society possessing the greatest unity that can exist between individuals of the human species: the father has the responsibility of governing and representing the family; the mother, subject to the father and superior over the children, acts as quasi-mediatrix between father and children. She puts them in touch with the father's commands, which she adapts and moulds for them, and fills out with her own authority whatever the father has left her to determine and decide.

In order to see what kind of transmission of rights must take place in this society through the death and birth of its individual members, we first consider the family in parents without offspring; we look at the couple's co-ownership and their mutual succession. Later, we consider the family enriched with children.

A.
Succession within marriage

1277. Woman, when joined to man in an indivisible society, subordinates herself to him and consequently cedes to him all that she owns.

1278. This subordination and natural secession to her husband of what she possesses, although a transmission of ownership,[322] is however a *relative* and *incomplete* transmission.[323] In other

---

[322] Cf. *ER*, 326-327.

[323] In fact, this transmission arises from a contract, that is, from the contract that takes place with marriage. We should speak about it, therefore, in the

words, the woman loses her ownership over all that she has relative to her husband with whom she forms a single indivisible unit, but not relative to other persons, for whom she remains the owner she was before her marriage. On the contrary, she now becomes the owner also of all the goods of her husband, with whom she is associated as co-owner.

1279. The nature of *relative ownership* springs, as we have said, from the following principles: 1. Whoever has *full right* of ownership over something belonging to another by right of *relative* ownership can use what is owned and even consume it, but only in a reasonable way. Outside this limit, he injures the right of the relative owner.

1280. 2. There may be co-ownership, as a result of association, between a person who has *full right* over something and another who has a right of *relative* ownership over the same thing. In this case, the former must use the goods held in common for the ends proper to co-ownership and to society. In the case of husband and wife, therefore, these goods must be employed for family expenses in proportion to their respective quantity.

1281. It is the responsibility of the absolute owner, that is, of the husband, to judge what is to be spent not only for family necessities, but also for the moral and physical benefit and betterment of the family and for decent pleasures. In carrying out this responsibility, he must not consume in a matter of days what he possesses for his own support and that of others, but take into account the continuation of such benefits for all the family.

1282. 3. As we said, the nature of the *relative owner* is such that his right of ownership is limited relative only to the person of the *full owner*. Consequently, the relative owner has preference with respect to all other persons in the use and dominion of these goods, and takes full possession of them when the *full owner* relinquishes them.

1283. This does not mean that the relative owner can limit the full owner's use and consumption of the goods, provided that they are used up reasonably and with the qualifications we have

following chapter. But the connection of ideas and the need to unite under a single heading all that concerns the natural transmission of ownership in domestic society forces us to deal with conjugal transmission here.

indicated. But the relative owner certainly has the right to require that these goods should be identified and distinguished from all other belongings of the full owner. What remains at the full owner's death will then pass entirely to the full ownership of the relative owner.

1284. In our case, if the wife's goods are found to be indicated in this way at the death of the husband, she can take possession of them immediately.

1285. It is true that the wife naturally succeeds to what belongs to her husband. However, others may have some *relative* ownership of those things of which she has now become *full* owner. A case in point is that of children, if the husband has left living offspring.

1286. The *relative right* that children have to the goods left by their father impedes the widow's *full* right over these goods except in so far as she is head of the house. As long as she lives in domestic society with her children as mother and ruler of the household, she dispenses all the family goods as the father did during his lifetime. But she dispenses them solely by this title; if she ceases to be head of this society, her power to dispense the goods left by her husband to his own family also ceases.

1287. The widow could cease to be head of the house of her dead husband because she retains her right to remarry and enter the house of another man after leaving her former house. In this case, she could not bring to her new family, of which she becomes a part, the goods of her husband, but only those which belonged to her originally. Her husband's goods belong by nature to the children who continue the family of which the widow has ceased to be head.

1288. However, if the children of the first husband lack what is needed for their support and education, she would have the natural jural duty to provide for them with her own goods, which she would not be able to bring in their entirety to the family of the new husband.

1289. If she is a widow without children, she may continue to live as a daughter in her father-in-law's house until her death, if her husband had not separated from him to form a household of his own. In this case, the father-in-law should succeed to all the goods of the intestate widow of his son. She has in fact continued to be part of the son in his affection, which is the moral foundation of ownership.

1290. If the widow remains without children and father-in-law, she forms a family on her own. What originally belonged to the husband would naturally fall to his descendants; what originally belonged to her own paternal family, to these descendants [*App.*, no. 7].

1291. If the wife were to predecease her husband, he would succeed to all her goods (unless some other agreement had been made with her father or family before the marriage — but we prescind from that here) and become owner to the fullest degree without having to hold separately from his own goods what had belonged to her.

1292. If the husband has had children by the widow and remarries, the new wife, on entering the household, ought according to nature and reason form a single family with the husband and his children. On her death, whether she has children or not, what she owns is entirely her husband's. However, what remains of her goods should, at the death of her husband, be transmitted to her surviving children. These succeed to their mother as *relative owners*, while the widower continues as their *full* owner.

1293. Hence the husband should provide an exact account of all that belongs to his first and successive wives so that their offspring may, at his death, come into ownership of their mothers' remaining goods.[324]

We must now consider natural, consanguineous succession.

---

[324] Roman legislation shows clear traces of this succession indicated by natural Right. It prescribes that when a spouse remarries, the goods obtained from the other deceased spouse (except those that come to him by law) are to become the property of the children of the deceased spouse with the condition that the remaining spouse should continue to enjoy their usufruct (*L. feminae 3. Cod. de secund. nupt.* — Cf. Voet. *in pandect.*, bk. 23, tit. 2, n. 101. — Somereu, *De jur. nov.*, c. 13, n. 5. — Wesel. *ad novell. const. Ultrajectin.*, art. 11, n. 25 ss. and n. 36. —Sande *Decis. Frisic.*, bk. 2, tit. 3, def. 3). If a child of the first wife dies intestate after his mother, the father enjoys the usufruct, and his blood-brothers and sisters the ownership of what the son has inherited from the mother. Such dispositions are maintained against attempts of evasion by multiple laws. Cf. Jo. Devoti, *De notissimis in jure legibus*, bk. 1, 1826 ed., p. 59 ss.

B.
Succession in the case of sons and daughters

1294. In deducing this succession, and the previous one, we always have to begin from the principle of a permanent, co-owning society. Note carefully that an *unequal* society composed of superiors and inferiors does not render co-ownership impossible, but simply ensures that its various members enjoy an unequal right of ownership.[325]

1295. Granted this, we go on to note that if there are children in the family and the father dies, the family continues to exist and possess what it already has. The sole difference is that the mother has become the head of the family. It is understood that the laws of wise government which are obligatory for the father are equally binding on the mother. However, this does not diminish the authority that the mother possesses by nature.

1296. If the mother dies, the body of the family still exists. All the siblings together have co-ownership of the paternal and maternal estate.

1297. They can enjoy it in common, but in doing so have necessarily to set up amongst themselves some agreed administration. By natural Right, none of them is superior to the others, provided they are all adults.

1298. If the survivors wish to divide the estate, there is no reason why family goods have to be shared in unequal portions,[326] why daughters should have less than sons or be excluded from inheritance [*App.*, no. 8]. All receive an equal part, therefore, in the goods possessed by the moral body, called family, to which they belong.

[325] It seems that normally the right of ownership is considered as something simple and absolute without any middle way between absolute ownership of an object on the one hand, and complete non-ownership on the other. This, I think, is a mistake which has its roots in the lack of a clear distinction between *ownership*, which is absolute, and the *right of ownership*, which is subject to degrees, divisions and limitations (cf. 966-1003).

[326] In France, primogeniture was introduced under the third dynasty. 'This ancient right', says Chabot de l'Allier, 'was handed down under Geoffrey, count of Brittany, in 1185: "The first-born should have the entire dominion, and should as far as possible provide the younger children with what is necessary for a decent living".'

[1294–1298]

1299. Here we need to reconsider the nature of domestic society. The family is a collective body with its own proper nature. It is composed of individual persons, although everything personal is incommunicable and thus outside the society.

1300. Consequently, the head is a governor who cannot sacrifice the good of the society to his own individual good, but can nevertheless enjoy the society's goods provided its greater good is safeguarded.

1301. Again, the head must acknowledge and respect the bond of ownership which, although conditioned, has been contracted and is contracted with things by the individual members of the family.

1302. As we have said, the wife has a right to claim that the goods she brings to the husband's house should be identified so that she may take possession of them after his death. In the same way, any ownership acquired by the wife herself or one of the children through their own work belongs in the state of nature to the father or the surviving mother, but in such a way that of its nature it remains with the member who has earned it when the head of the family is no more. It is understood that this member has not renounced the ownership by willingly placing it in the common substance.

1303. The father, therefore, and after him the surviving mother, is master of all that belongs to the single members of the family within the limits of certain laws. One of these states that 'what remains at the death of the parents' is divided into that which belongs to all, and that which belongs to the individuals who have acquired it, say, by their individual work. The two kinds of substance have to be kept distinct and as such reserved for the individuals until the death of father and mother.

1304. If, therefore, a subject-member of the family acquires some new ownership through his personal work, it is just, despite the ownership that the head of the family has over the thing as long as he lives, that it should be identified at the request of the person who has acquired it. This ownership can then be distinguished when the head of the house and his right is no more, and the right of ownership restored to the one who would have acquired it if parental power had not impeded its full acquisition.

1305. The father or the surviving mother has the ownership of these goods but also the obligation to harmonise their right of ownership with that other right of ownership which the member acquiring the goods retains relative to all other human beings, and which he loses relative only to his parents and for the duration of their lives. At the death of the parents, these goods pass by that very fact to the member of the family who acquired them.[327]

1306. As long as one of the parents is alive, the subject-member of the family is not the owner, except in relationship to other people. As head of the house, the father is the full owner of every material substance that enters the house in any way whatsoever and is free to dispense it provided he does so in a reasonable manner. *Reasonable* here means at least that all the members of the family society can live off the substance which he can dispense.

1307. In fact, the members of a society of owners, such as the family in which there is perfect communion of goods, have the primary right to live off the common substance.

1308. Despite this right, however, members have an obligation to work for the common maintenance, as far as they can. Their right to eat is conditioned by this jural obligation of work in proportion to their forces.[328]

1309. If something remains from what a member of the family has earned with his own effort after the head of the family has dealt with expenses, it must all be marked and set aside so that it may be acknowledged after the death of the father and the last parent. Thus the person holding the title of acquisition over it will be its owner. The title, which was null relative to the father and the mother, is alive and effective relative to siblings.

1310. The entire family, in the person of the head, is heir if another member dies before the head.

1311. These successions of rights at death which have been examined up to this point pertain to rational Right, and I think this can be proved rigorously. Such rights have not been deduced casually. Before we began to deduce them, we set out

---

[327] The portion of these goods used up by the father's disbursement from the common substance must be subtracted from them.

[328] St. Paul expresses this jural duty in the celebrated words: 'If anyone will not work, let him not eat' (2 Thess 3:10).

the principle from which all rights are deduced as logical consequences. We called it 'the principle of the determination of rights', and it should be familiar to those who accompany us in our study so that together we may apply it to the deduction of particular rights (this is the work we have undertaken). Such a principle is undoubtedly the only leading thread in the deduction of rights regarding natural succession. As we have said, it consists *in the characteristic of ownership.*[329]

We also said that the characteristic and nature of ownership as right springs from two elements: from a law issuing from human nature by which human beings bind things to themselves spiritually and intentionally — this is the *matter of right*; and from a consequent moral duty arising in others to respect that right — this is the *form of right* and a branch of the general duty not to cause disturbance to other persons. Such is the right of ownership, which enables us to state that whenever we can prove the presence of these two elements constituting the matter and form of right, we also prove the subsistence of a right.

But in every succession so far described, the first of these two elements stands out as an undoubted fact, obvious at all times and in all places. The members of a family have always assigned family goods to themselves at the death of one of their members, and have always felt themselves injured (a symptom of ownership) if strangers usurped what should have gone to the family. In the same way, any members of the family who either brought goods when entering it, or earned enough by their own efforts to accumulate some estate, always considered they had a right to what they had obtained for themselves or had devolved upon them (provided that these things were still in existence when the head of the family died). Placing such things in the common holding, so that everything in it became one, was always looked upon as an act either of no consequence or of affection and liberality towards the family itself; it was never regarded as a jural duty. This undeniable fact gives rise, therefore, to the duty of respecting the feeling founded in human nature if we are to avoid inflicting harm or pain on individuals. It is an obvious consequence of the precept: 'Do not inflict harm on intelligent

[329] Cf. *The Principle of the Derivation of Rights* (*ER*, 318-360).

beings.' Hence each of the successions we have indicated is a rigorous natural right.

1312. The following successions also spring from the same principles of natural reason.

Both sons and daughters have a natural right to marry at the appropriate age.

1313. This right can be exercised by all the children if they so wish. They must however act in such a way that the rights of parents are safeguarded, and both jural and moral obligations are observed.

1314. They should certainly listen to the advice of their parents when choosing a spouse, although the final choice is theirs by right. It is understood that this does not give rise to a right to make a hare-brained choice, but only to a reasonable, wise option.

1315. Granted this, we can now reflect on the world's first family. The daughters had necessarily to choose brothers as husbands, and as a result were not obliged necessarily to leave the paternal family. The father could keep them, even married, at home. Everything was done in the house; they were still parents and siblings.

1316. But when both heads of the house had died and the children had split up[330] into different families (the bond tying siblings in a single family would have sprung from agreement, not from nature), the daughters of already separated families were able to choose a husband outside the family even of their living parents. In this case, they entered a new family and ceased to form part of the paternal family. Their sole remaining duty towards their fathers was that of respect.

1317. Because the daughters have this natural right, the father is obliged not to impede its exercise, but to help them exercise it to their best advantage. If necessary, therefore, he must give them the part of the substance which, in proportion to the family wealth, will ease their way to an advantageous settlement.[331]

---

[330] As we said, according to natural law daughters have an equal portion with their brothers in succession to the family fortune when no will has been left (this is not the case with *peculia*). When daughters marry, they must bring this portion to the husband's family, in which they enter.

[331] The father's natural obligation to provide a dowry for his daughters was

1318. The substance that the father has to assign for the sake of an adequate settlement for his daughters varies according to the different periods and conditions to which the human race is subject. But the sole reason for the father's obligation is the best possible settlement for the daughters. When that has been achieved, no further reason for the obligation is present.

1319. In the period of society when the *substance*[332] of public power was formed by *physical force*, and consequently by *population*, the advantage lay with larger families. In this case, there was no need to provide wedding dowries for the daughters. On the contrary, it was the family of the bridegroom which had to provide the bride's father with a price. Examples of this are frequent in very remote antiquity not only in the East,[333] but also amongst the Greeks.[334]

part of Roman civil law (L. Capite, 19 ss. *De ritu nuptiarum*. L. *ad exactionem Cod. De dot. promiss.*). The oldest laws on the point are those of Metellus Numidicus and of Augustus, called the Julian and the Papian laws. The last named established various punishments for parents who withheld dowries from their daughters. Dionysius of Halicarnassus and Livy mention the law of Metellus, while A. Gellius (*Noct. Act.*, 1, 6) has saved for us a fragment of the address in which Metellus proposed his law. — On the obligation of fathers to constitute a dowry for their daughters (an obligation upheld by Roman laws), cf. Voet (in *Pandectas*, 1, 26, tit. 3, n. 11), and Cuiacius (Quaest. Papin., 1, 29, ad 1, 6, *Cod. De Usar.*) who believes that the Papian law also forbade the dowry for daughters to exceed one million sestercii.

[332] I have shown that the *substance* of the State, that is, its prevalent force, changes place in different *social ages*. Sometimes it is found in *physical force*, sometimes in *riches*, and sometimes in other objects. Cf. *SC*, c. 26.

[333] Amongst the Hebrews, the bride was bought, as the saying is. When the marriage was being arranged, gifts were made to the brothers of the bride, and her father received a price for her (Cf. Gen 29: 18, 27; 34: 11-12; Jos 15: 16; 1 Sam 8: 23, 26; 1 Kings 3: 4). The bride's price varied at different times because of the variation at different periods of society in the great number of members composing the family. I shall show this more at length in *Della naturale costruzione della società civile*. It would seem that at the time of Moses, the minimum price of brides was thirty shekels (about fifteen scudi) and the maximum fifty (twenty-five scudi) (Cf. Ex 21: 32; 22: 15; Hosea 3: 1-2; Deut. 22: 29). The bride was sometimes given away if the family was rich (Gen 16: 1, 3); sometimes, but this was exceptional, she also received a dowry from her father (Jos 15: 18, 19; Jud 1: 14-15; 1 Kings 9: 16).

[334] Plutarch, *Apophthegm. Lacon*; Aelianus, *V. H.*, 6: 6; Justin, 3: 3. In Greece also, the disbursement for a wife first varied from high to low at different times, before dropping to nothing. Finally, a dowry was required.

[1318–1319]

1320. The wedding dowry which, when first required, was rather low,[335] gradually grew.[336] According to Montesquieu,[337] one reason for the increase is the monarchic form of government; a stronger reason is that *artificial riches* have much more weight in given periods of society than *natural riches*. In this case, the State is normally brought to a monarchic form and to the superior well-being which impedes numerous children.[338]

1321. The father's only obligation is to make the best possible settlement for a daughter who wishes to marry. He satisfies his jural duty according to times and circumstances either by receiving a price for the child on her marriage or by giving her away without a price, or by bestowing upon her a large or small dowry sufficient to procure her decent settlement.

1322. According to rational Right, the daughter, after being settled and leaving the paternal house to enter the household of her husband, no longer has any succession with her siblings in the inheritance of their parents. She has in fact ceased to be a co-owner with her brothers and sisters.[339]

---

[335] According to Strabo (bk. 4), the republic of Marseilles had fixed the *maximum price* for a dowry at one hundred scudi in cash, and five in clothes. If Montesquieu had considered this regulation as we do, he would not have said that 'Marseilles was the wisest of the republics of its time'.

[336] Cf. Aris., *Polit.* 2, 6, 11. As usual, Montesquieu's description is factual rather than about right. He says: 'Dowries have to be substantial in monarchies so that husbands can uphold their grade and their accustomed luxury (Would it not be better to curb the excesses?). In republics, where luxury does not hold sway, they must be at a lower level. Finally, they must be reduced to practically nothing in despotic States in which women are already almost slaves' (*L'Esprit des Lois*, bk 7, c. 15).

[337] *L'Esprit des Lois*, 27.

[338] The Papian law, established under Augustus to remedy the scarcity of the population, was the first to restrict the Voconian law and favour women in succession, and relatives in the female line. From then on, women were gradually more favoured up to the time of Justinian who completely overthrew the ancient right regarding succession on the part of women (Leg. 12, Cod. *De Suis et legitimis liberis*, Novell., 118, 127).

[339] 'It is almost universally accepted that a woman moves to the family of her husband. A contrary custom, which causes no harm to anyone, is found in the island of Formosa, where the husband forms part of the wife's family' (*L'Esprit des Lois*, bk. 23, c. 4). Montesquieu's judgment is rather facile here. Is it true that this practice causes no harm to anyone? This is one of the many rash judgments found so frequently in this otherwise admirable author.

1323. As far as I can see, one reason why many laws deprived women of the right to inherit was the underlying supposition that women would marry and thus, by separating from their original domestic society, loose their natural right to succeed to their parents.[340]

1324. If we continue to abstract from evil conduct on the part of parents, we shall easily see that the condition of women who marry, despite their disinherited status, is in no way inferior to that of their brothers. By entering another household they contemporaneously lose one co-ownership and gain that of the husband's house.

On the other hand, although a father or surviving mother can in certain periods marry off the daughters without providing a large dowry, or perhaps any dowry at all, there will be other periods when marriage becomes more difficult. Large dowries, equivalent to the daughters' share of the inheritance (and perhaps even greater) would be necessary.[341]

1325. In the light of the conditions we have described, no harm would be suffered by depriving of their heritage daughters who marry. Their marriage would not be rendered more difficult, but rather assured, and the general effect in the division of

---

[340] We should reflect that in antiquity all daughters took husbands. Virginity was unknown to the Hebrews. According to the Mosaic law, girls inherited in the absence of males. But in this case, they then had to marry a close relative, a man of their own tribe, to prevent the inheritance passing to another tribe and family (Cf. Num 27: 1-11; 36: 1-12). From this point of view, the Voconian law of which we have spoken provided girls with an impetus to thinking about settling in marriage. If they did not marry, their situation was very precarious. — Christianity, after bringing virginity into such great honour, had to provide for women who wanted to remain in this state. Light came to the law-makers when they realised it was against the natural law to deprive women who did not leave their families of their parental inheritance. Justinian himself declared that the right enjoyed by males to succeed in preference to females was barbarous (Novella, 21). One of Marculf's formulas speaks of the custom depriving daughters of succession to their fathers as *impious* (bk 2, c. 12). Barbarian laws did not disinherit daughters (Cf. Lombard laws, bk. 2, tit. 14, §6-8), although the feudal laws left them seriously disadvantaged.

[341] This change in the right of female children to a dowry is another example of those different *modes* in which *specific rights* come to be presented during the different ages of nations.

goods would be the same. If a small dowry were required for the marriage of a daughter, her own family would not lose a great deal, and the family of the husband would not gain excessively. Whatever the dowry, there would be a general levelling as dowries leave and enter families.

1326. It is true that there would be less movement of owner-ship, but this would in fact be beneficial. Change of ownership without profit is a costly nuisance.

1327. All this is valid in general terms, that is, from the point of view of the individual families. The position is the same for them all because anyone of them could have a disproportionate number of daughters or sons. However, when we consider what actually happens in particular, we find that giving an equal share in the heritage to women and men alike, including women who marry, produces a notable and unreasonable change in family substance — some families get richer, others poorer.

In fact, families with a large number of daughters and few sons either have to prevent the women from marrying (blameworthy greed and cruelty on the part of parents is quite capable of this) and thus violate their sacred right, or leave the sons in a very reduced state. If, for example, six daughters take six shares of the paternal heritage (we are speaking only about lawful shares), it is clear that the one remaining son will have a substance entirely out of proportion to that held by his father in the house in which he was raised. This single male child will have in exchange only one woman who, granted the boy's poverty, will probably be poor herself.

Here I would point out that insurance is bought against fire, shipwreck, hail and other disasters in order to rescue families from the fear of repeated misfortunes of this kind. Many families, in fact, make a regular payment in order to assist the comparatively few families who would suffer in this way. Why, then, does the law provide that married women should have equal shares in the inheritance with the males when it is possible for certain families to be impoverished by having a swarm of daughters and very few sons, or even only one? Does it prefer people to use immoral means to avoid this kind of disaster? I think it would be better for positive legislation to follow rational Right here by ensuring by inescapable, rigorous obligation that parents give their daughters all that is necessary for a good marriage settlement. On the other hand, daughters should inherit in their own house, not outside it.

1328. It is true that laws which grant equal succession to daughters married or not — French law is one example — are advantageous in the sense that they eliminate the need for many minute dispositions and at the same time protect daughters against the cruel self-interest of parents. However this is one of those inflexible laws which attempt to submit various conditions and needs of different periods to a single rule. Inevitably, such laws will sometimes harmonise with the needs of periods of social life, and sometimes seriously contrast with them. The size of the necessary marriage dowry will vary from period to period so that the stable dowry fixed by law will sometimes be excessive and sometimes insufficient.

1329. When daughters are provided with more than they need to marry decently, we find useless movement of ownership, and boldness on their part proportioned to the amount these women acquired over and above the needs of the times. This boldness reduces their subjection to their husbands and union in their families; and evils habits increase with luxury.[342]

1330. We must now examine the question of primogeniture. I maintain that this is a right in nature, but only in certain periods of society. In others, it ceases to have effect.

1331. Natural affection on the part of the father brings him to give his first-born some share in his authority, to use his assistance in rearing the younger children, to treat him with greater trust, to see in him the shoot which assures the conservation of the line, and to view him as the desired fruit of his first love. However, while these affections are very strong in certain periods, as we said, it would seem that they diminish and peter out in others.

1332. I do not think that the principal reason for the rights of primogeniture, upheld throughout the whole of antiquity, is simply that of greater age. It is not this which gives the first-born preferential right to succeed the father, although I do grant

[342] Solon did not deprive of their inheritance the women who remained at home, but did forbid the grant of a dowry when they married. He decreed that the bride 'should have no more than three woollen mantles and other drapes of little value.' Cf. Plutarch, *Life of Solon*.

that being first to enter the house and first to take possession of the *relative ownership* proper to the children seems to give rise in younger children to the concept of the need to respect the feeling already aroused of hoped-for seigniory over the paternal estate.

1333. As far as I can see, the principal reason favouring the rights of the first-born is that fathers, to avoid excessive burdens and divisions of ownership, sent or seconded younger children to industry and business outside the house. And precisely because they were separated from their parents' family, they lost the family heritage in the same way as the married daughters.

Nevertheless, something was given to the son who left, and in this sense the condition of daughters and cadets was the same. In both cases, the principle was that they ceased to be co-owners when they left the domestic society, and that fathers had the right, recognised by the whole of antiquity, to send the sons away from the house to seek their fortune. Naturally, the person who remained in the house received the paternal heritage.[343]

The contrary could also be maintained: that is, that the cadets were encouraged to turn to honest business and wholehearted enterprises because they knew they would be excluded from the inheritance. It seems that certain law-givers, such as Lycurgus, aimed to stimulate this attitude — if it is true that only the first-born was heir in Sparta, and housed and governed his brothers in place of the father.[344]

---

[343] Thus Esau was Isaac's heir, although Jacob had acquired from his father the first-born's blessing. When he left the house, he could no longer make his right prevail.

[344] Procul's annotation to Hesiodus (*Le opere e i giorni*, vs. 374) indicate that according to Lycurgus it was necessary to have a sole heir δειν ενα κλερονομον κατακιπτειν. — Where polygamy is practised the father chooses one of the children from his different wives to be the principal heir and ruler of the others. His choice falls either on the best of the sons, or the one born from the dearest of his wives and therefore the fruit of his most cherished love. These are the reasons indicated by Scripture when it describes the succession of Abia, the son of Roboam: 'Roboam loved Maacah, the daughter of Absalom, above all his wives and concubines. — and he put at the head of them [the other brothers] Abia the son of Maacah to be the chief ruler over all his brethren: for he meant to make him king. Because he was wiser and mightier than all his sons, and in all the countries of Juda, and of Benjamin, and in all the walled cities' (2 Chron 11: 21-23). — David chose

C.
Succession further extended as long as a family society exists

1334. Does natural succession in the case of intestacy stop at the parents and children, or does it extend further? In my opinion, it extends much further, and must be considered relative to two circumstances, that is, relative to blood relations who together form a family, and relative to blood relations who have already left the family. Here, we want to examine what happens in the first of these two circumstances.

1335. We have said that the father inherits in the case of offspring who die in the house. If there is no father, the mother inherits. But it could happen that a paternal grandfather lives in the house and with him the spouse and children of the dead offspring. What is the natural succession in such a case? The right of *full* ownership in all these cases always resides with the head of the house who, in our supposition, would be the grandfather.

1336. But together with such a right of *full* ownership, there would co-exist the right of *relative ownership* for other members, who would succeed in the following way:

The grandfather inherits the right of relative ownership so that at the death of the father he inherits what remains of the children's estate.

1337. If the father dies leaving a widow, she inherits the right of *relative ownership*. Consequently, the residual substance of the husband falls to her at the death of the father-in-law.

1338. But if the widow has children when she becomes full owner at the death of her father-in-law, the children succeed at the same time to the right of relative ownership of the same estate. They acquire the full right either when the mother dies, or when she leaves the house and separates herself from them.

1339. It is clear now that this distinction between the *right of full ownership* and the *right of relative ownership* offers the possibility of deciding in the same way all cases of direct succession within the limits of a family, whatever the

Solomon to succeed him for the same reasons (1 Kings 1 [Douai]).

extension of the ascending and descending line. We can summarise what has been said as follows:

1. Succession to the right of *full ownership* over all the goods of the members of the family will always fall to the head of the house, that is, to the oldest of the ascending line or, in his absence, to his wife.

2. Succession to the right of *relative ownership* always falls to:

a) whoever remains as head of the family when the oldest person in the ascending line dies; then

b) to the spouse; then

c) to the children.

D.
Succession amongst blood-related families

1340. Everything said so far is founded on the concept of the family society, which is an owner.[345] The family does not cease as one member departs, nor does it become another family as it acquires a new member. The owner, therefore, that is the family, cannot even *succeed*, properly speaking, through the death of a member because it remains an owner as before. Only the rights to common ownership, held by the various members of the family, change. And the changes take place in the way we have described.

1341. However, another question arises: does succession between related families exist in nature? Once more we have to turn to the principle we have established about the determination of rights, and verify a natural *fact* on which depends the *right* of ownership.

'Abstracting from positive laws, agreements and customs, is it natural for members of a family to expect possession of the estate of a closely related family when this family ceases to exist, or to look forward to inheriting in this way, or to feel pain

---

[345] Schlettwein, who opposes wills, but nevertheless admits natural succession in families, turns to co-ownership to explain his ideas on succession (Cf. his *Diritti dell'uomo*, Giessen, 1784, §141-258).

when others occupy the abandoned patrimony?' This is the fact we have to verify. If this feeling arises of itself in human nature, without being provoked by the laws of civil society, the foundation of such ownership exists. In other words, a physical bond is formed from which the moral bond follows of its nature. This obligation states that all other human beings have 'the duty not to offend this kind of natural feeling', and consequently that such an offence is already an injury to the right of ownership.

1342. For myself, I think it certain that such a feeling is natural to human beings. I deduce it from my observation that people are of their nature furnished with minds that have long memories of parental unions, and with spirits that live joined for a long time with those who no longer share the same roof. Moreover (although I am not so sure about this), there also exists a life instinct secretly drawing together and as it were attracting close blood relations. I also deduce the feeling from the same fact of succession established in all laws, and primarily in all customs. Such laws and customs are not sufficiently explained by the views of legislators about the body politic. These views, which arose only after customs had been formed, are first and foremost simply the written expression of the customs. Succession can only be explained by the feeling in human nature which produces of itself the customs we are considering.

1343. I admit, however, that this feeling varies as a result of the different states of perfection of human nature found in various individuals, and of the consequent variety in the strength, intensity, limitation and preciseness of feelings.

There is no doubt that the explanation for customs and various legislations must be derived from these feelings. In particular, we find in them the reason why succession in the case of intestacy is extended by some customs and laws to further degrees of relationship than by others. The right of succession finishes precisely at the point where the memory and feeling of a given population ceases to accompany close, lineal relationships. Persons exist whom no one remembers as blood relations, and towards whom there is no longer any affection of relationship. No one considers them as belonging to himself, or himself as belonging to them, nor lives with them in that society of feeling which denotes a trace of domestic society still extant in their spirits. Finally, there is no one who, as a natural consequence of such memories and feelings, expects to succeed to their estate. Such people are already lost to sight and have mingled with the common mass of mankind like a drop of water in the ocean. Their sole relationship with others is likeness in a common origin. Every particular proximity has been annulled, and as they die, their estate, which remains without any master, belongs to the first occupier.

1344. But it is not true that less isolated persons, who still live in harmony with the memories and affections of their kindred, leave what they have to the first individual who occupies their estate. Even when these persons do not live in the same house, and hold nothing material in common with related families, their blood relations have a natural preference, which must be respected by others, in the occupancy of these goods. The strength of the preference, and consequently respect for this preference, depends upon the closeness of the blood relationship. In other words, people of this kind have a natural right to succeed to the goods left by their close kindred.

1345. Nevertheless, I think that relatives who together form a family in the strictest sense must, according to nature, be preferred in succession to closer relatives who have, however, separated from the family.[346]

1346. I see no reason for preferring males to females amongst those who have separated from the family. But natural succession amongst the separated relatives would mean in the first place that the spouse who separated would succeed to the partner who leaves no children or has no family. If there is no separated spouse, the father succeeds if united with the mother; if not united, each of the separated parents succeeds to half the estate; if the mother alone is alive, she succeeds. But if both

---

[346] We are speaking, as always, of natural domestic society, not of society formed by agreement. The society amongst siblings, in the absence of parents, would depend on agreement. Consequently, if one of the parents survives, he or she would be the heir of offspring who died without spouse or children, even if this offspring lived in common with other children. On the other hand, the spouse who has separated from the family could not succeed the one who has family united to him in the ascendant or descendant line, although the united spouse succeeds to the spouse with whom he forms a single person.

[1344–1346]

parents are dead, their offspring and the offspring of others in the ascending line should succeed in such a way that the closest relative inherits everything, while equal relatives inherit in equal shares.

1347. Nevertheless, as I said, no natural limit could be assigned to this succession, which would have to be extended more or less indefinitely. The actual extent would depend upon the degree of social quality, affection, memories and other accidents which, by keeping people united, produce in the spirits of some, the feeling that they have to succeed when others are no longer present,[347] and as it were represent them on earth by occupying their portions.[348]

[347] It will be objected that this means making the right of ownership depend upon a state of feeling, and upon changeable persuasion of mind. But although such an affirmation seems totally new, it is in fact shared by common sense and by law-makers. As a proof of this, I can appeal to the authority of Roman laws (to take one example from innumerable others). I leave the comment to one of the most accurate and careful authors on right. He says (and this needs to be considered carefully): 'A person who loses something he owns, does not lose his ownership until he considers the thing as abandoned. He does this either freely, by ceding it to the one who occupies it, or necessarily, if it is morally impossible for him to recover it.' Notice how ownership depends here, according to this famous jurisconsult, on the judgment pronounced by the spirit of the owner: 'unless he considers it abandoned.' This is confirmed by Roman laws §47, *Inst. de Reg. Div.* — bk. 2 ss., *pro derelicto*. He goes on: 'Even the person who finds and keeps it does not acquire dominion over it, "unless he desires it as his own". This consequence is proved textually (bk. 1 ss., *pro derelicto*): "things cease to be our own in the same way as they are acquired." But they do not cease being ours except through an act of will, "only by an act of will with which we desire to have something as our own"' (William Beuch, *Tract. de pactis et contractib.*, c. 1, §23). This is the common opinion of writers on law. It implicitly supports my theory which makes ownership depend upon *the spirit*. In other words, I have only followed my normal custom: of expressing *explicitly* what others will always have said before me, but *implicitly*.

[348] According to Baroli, 'Some writers assert the necessity of conceiving a kind of species of *ideal condominium* in hereditary right. This condominium would be conditioned by the life of the person whose estate was in question, and would cease with his death when the heir would acquire the right of full dominion over the patrimony of the deceased' (*Diritto naturale*, §205, *1).
This consideration is correct when confined to natural successions. We have to keep in mind, however, that every dominion and condominium can always be called *ideal* in so far as all rights originate from intelligences and their ideas,

[1347]

1348. It may be asked whether such protraction of people's expectation of succeeding to their relatives accords with any state of perfection in the human race. I think it does. First, because breadth of feeling appertains to perfection; second, because it shows a greater degree of the intelligence by which human beings rule;[349] third, because the act of bringing the human race to perfection requires a genuine bond between people. In fact, the ideal perfection of humanity supposes and holds that all individuals in the human species be considered more or less as brothers. We must not forget that all human beings are related by blood as a result of their common origin.[350]

In this way, therefore, succession in the case of intestacy would never be lacking; it would be determined for every possible case, and the revenue-authorities would have no pretext for claiming succession.[351]

which alone can unite persons and things (the bond of ownership).

[349] We have given four *rules* according to which the actual *quantity of intelligence* in nations can be measured. Cf. *SP*, bk 3, c. 5.

[350] Successions, therefore, are unlimited, and in ruling families are infinitely extended. Here civilisation is at its highest level, while the greatness of the heritage keeps the memory fresh and serves to bind more closely succeeding generations.

[351] It is clear from what we have said in this paragraph that we cannot agree with Zeiller and other jurists who maintain that 'succession in the case of intestacy is founded on the presumed will of the testator to leave the inheritance to the nearest relative' (*Diritto nat. privato*, §140). On the contrary, we find the foundation of succession in intestacy to exist in the will and the feeling of relatives who appropriate for themselves the right to adhere to the heritage in the same was as they appropriate any other right of ownership, that is, by means of the moral-physical bond we have described when dealing with the principle of the determination of rights (cf. 321 ss.). It is not the deceased, but the natural heirs who would be offended if someone else were to make himself master of the heritage. The question of an injury to the deceased depends upon our answer to the problem about the efficacy of his will after death, and our verification of a fact: 'His will has been, or can be presumed in favour of the natural heirs.' If not, these heirs would not be less injured by the persons who relieved them of their heritage in the case of intestacy. — Other authors deny that succession in intestacy resides in natural Right. They begin, however, from the mistaken supposition that succession can only be explained through the presumed will of the person who dies. According to them, this will cannot be presumed without a supposed jural duty to do good to one's relatives. Nevertheless, this duty is only moral. The person who dies, therefore, is not jurally obliged to leave them his estate. It

§4. Succession through an act of will on the part of the one who dies

1349. We have dealt with succession in the case of intestacy. According to rational Right, can this kind of succession be changed by the will of an owner who dies?

Before examining the question, we need to explore the territory it covers to see if perhaps we are being drawn away from the scientific terrain, as it were, to which this article is limited.

We want to know how 'rights can pass without alteration from one subject to another through abandonment and successive occupation.' As long as we are dealing with succession through intestacy, rights pass from one subject to another through abandonment, as the dying person leaves them behind, and through successive occupancy on the part of the heir. Now, however, we have to take into account the acts of the dying person's last will, which determine who shall succeed. The transmission of rights, therefore, is no longer caused by simple abandonment and successive occupancy, but by the force of the act of will which determines the successor (we shall see later if this act of will is valid in the state of nature).

1350. It is true that the act of last testament, granted its validity, can give the destined heir only the right to claim the inheritance; it cannot bestow the inheritance itself, the occupancy of which depends upon acceptance. But the right to claim the inheritance is nevertheless a right, and a right with a new form (if indeed we do not wish to call it a new right). This right, therefore, would at least have its form altered and be transmitted not through the intervention of acts by both parties, but by the act of one party alone. Such a way of originating rights in a new form will be examined in the following book.[352]

1351. It is true, if we speak about the right to the inheritance which the heir acquires through accepting the legacy, that the

follows, they conclude, that the will of the deceased cannot be presumed unless he has manifested it. We need waste no words demonstrating the weakness of such an argument.

[352] The right *to claim the inheritance* is properly speaking a right of transitory form. We shall speak about the *transitory* form of rights in the following chapter, article 1.

rights held by the deceased do not necessarily change in transmissions of this kind. But it is also true that they could change because this depends upon the will of the deceased who can split them as he wishes, and condition them as he wants. From this point of view, these kinds of transmission would belong to the next chapter. However, I think our argument will be made easier if we avoid excessive fragmentation of the subject and continue, immediately after the work on natural succession, with our discussion about succession through dispositions made by a person's last will. I hope that this note about the many places where our present material could be found will be sufficient to enable the reader to refer the material mentally to the places in this treatise where it would be seen if the scientific order were followed. In this way, the series of discussions on succession will not be broken up, and systematic distribution will not be lacking.

Our question, therefore, was as follows: 'Can natural succession be changed by the will of the testator?'

1352. The question contains several others. The two principal are as follows.

1. Given that a person has no relatives within the degree to which natural succession extends in the case of intestacy, and that his estate would not pass naturally at his death to one person rather than another, can he determine, through an act of his will, the persons to whom such goods should pass?

2. Would his act of will have jural force even within the limits of natural succession?

We shall deal briefly with both questions, starting with the first.

A.
The right to decide who should possess one's goods after one's death in the absence of a natural successor

1353. The right to dispose of one's own goods at death can be conceived, and has in fact been conceived in various ways according to which it changes its nature and therefore becomes another right.

First, we have to distinguish the different ways in which such a right can be conceived, and then examine the question we have proposed relative to each of them.

1354. There are two principal ways in which we can think of the transmission of goods after death to a chosen heir:

1. as a form of bilateral act by which one person gives and another receives;

2. as a form of unilateral act.

I.
Successory pacts

1355. The first of these two ways would be a contract. In fact, many authors consider wills solely as donatory contracts which testators make on condition of their death and of unrevoked wishes. The following have considered wills in this way: Grotius,[353] Daries,[354] Martini,[355] Rasp[356] and others who defend their validity in the state of nature, and Egger,[357] Zeiller[358] and others who attack this validity.

1356. We admit that the *successory pact* can be called a contract when it is made known to the heir and accepted by him during the donor's lifetime.

We should deal with the transmission of ownership by way of contract only in the following article, but think it would be helpful to insert brief considerations about the matter here, granted its connection and affinity with our present subject.

We must, however, be brief because we have to return to the question of testamentary succession. Therefore: are successory pacts valid?

[353] *De J. B. et P.*, 6, §14.

[354] *De acquir. haered. secundum jus nat.*, Jen. 1746.

[355] *Positiones de lege naturali.*, Vienna, 1772, §788.

[356] *Dichiarazioni del sistema del diritto naturale*, Vienna, 1795, §788 *ss.*

[357] *Dottrina del diritto privato di natura comune, e del diritto prussiano*, P. 1, Berlin, 1797.

[358] *Diritto naturale privato*, §140-142.

[1354–1356]

1357. Zeiller, following Egger and other authors,[359] denies this. He says:

> If this were so, the testator would in substance declare that he renounces his right at the moment when the sphere of his rights is already being brought to a close in this world. Either his declaration is not serious, although it should be, or there is no legal possibility of his attaining his purpose.[360]

1358. But how can the successory pact lack any possibility of attaining its purpose if it is valid? It has no other aim, in fact, than to ensure that the rights of the donor pass after him to the donee. There is no reason to prevent this from happening.

1359. Nor can it be said that the declaration is not serious, just as it cannot be said that the necessary seriousness is lacking to a donation made by an emigrant who gives a friend his house or anything else, as he leaves his country with the firm intention of never returning. The fact that the emigrant is incapable of benefiting by what he gives does not mean that he has no right to give it to anyone he wishes. This argument is particularly strong in Zeiller's case because he concedes that an owner, without losing ownership of something he holds, has the right not to use it. On the other hand, giving is itself an exercise of ownership, although it is true that in every donation the donor can no longer make use of what he has given.

1360. To say that the donee does not begin to benefit by the thing until the donor naturally loses his rights through death does not prove the nullity of such a donation. The donation is made and received during life; as soon as the donee has accepted, he has acquired the right *ad rem*. This right is admittedly not exercised until the donor dies and we might say, ceases to have rights, but no objection can be based on this. The donee-heir,

---

[359] Schaumann, *Diritto naturale scientifico*, Halle, 1792, §321, note 2 — Schmalz, *Dichiarazione dei diritti dell'uomo e del cittadino*, Königsberg, 1798, c. 2. — Heidenreich, *Sistema del diritto naturale*, Leipzig, 1794, tom. 2, pref. — Klein, *Principi della scienza del diritto naturale*, Halle, 1797, §296 *ss.*

[360] Zeiller makes this objection against wills in general because he supposes that they are always contracts. I do not accept this supposition, and consequently consider the objection as restricted to *successory pacts* against which it does appear to have some force.

whose root of right was formerly founded in the donation, continues to live, and has a capacity to exercise his rights. At the death of the donor, he simply obtains the benefit dependent upon the fulfilment of the condition. In a word, he exercises his right at that moment; he does not acquire it. There seems nothing absurd in this. In fact, in every donation the donee enters into possession of the thing in question at the instant the donor leaves it. Could one person become the owner of something as long as another had not ceased to be its owner? Any moment can be established for transmitting ownership, so death can be that moment. — But could it not be insisted that at the moment of death the dead person loses all his rights? — That is true, but the heir, who is alive, already has the right to enter into possession of the dead person's rights, and thus reasonably takes possession of them.

1361. One reply to this difficulty ran as follows. If you are not happy that the donee-heir should enter into possession of the estate after the donor has already left it, anticipate the possession by an instant, and let the last moment of life of the donor be the agreed point in which the other person becomes owner.[361] Solving a difficulty by hair-splitting of this kind shows the inconsistency of the objection.

1362. Another way of proving the weakness of the difficulty is to render the donation unassailable by changing its form while leaving its substance intact. John gives what he has to William, who accepts the donation, but William contemporaneously leaves the free use of these goods to John for the length of his life. The two pacts coalesce, and withstand every objection.

1363. Again, all contracts made between human beings suppose the following principle: 'The will of each of the contracting parties produces an effect which lasts beyond life.' If I give something today, and tomorrow die, the person to whom I have made the donation keeps it as his own even after my death in virtue of the act of will that I made while alive. It is totally indifferent whether the act with which I make the gift comes into being shortly before my death, or a long time before it. The effect of my act is perpetual of its nature, as all mankind agrees.

---

[361] Baroli, *Diritto naturale privato e pubblico*, §205, *1.

[1361–1363]

1364. Similarly, I can give an object to another person while reserving its use for myself for a year. In this case, the donee becomes the lawful owner of the object after a year, although I could die before the year is out. The accidental intervention of my death does not invalidate the right which has been acquired.

II.
Wills

1365. We come now to those dispositions of last will which are properly called 'testaments'. They are made solely by the testator; acceptance by the heir takes place after the testator's death. These, too, are treated by many authors as though they were contracts, although under the name 'quasi-contracts'.

a) Quasi-contracts in general

1366. The name 'quasi-contracts' is inexact and absurd because it is impossible to conceive of anything halfway between a contract and a non-contract, between making an agreement and not making one. The word has therefore no place in a treatise on *philosophical Right*.

1367. To understand this truth better, we must examine the origin and nature of the acts called 'quasi-contracts'. This will enable us to arrive at the concept of testament, and answer the questions which arise concerning it.

Quasi-contracts appertain to positive law.

Legislators introduced this term, and many other illogical names, because they found it convenient to persuade people of the existence of an *obligation* which is as binding and urgent as that resulting from contracts, although there was no question of contracts. Most people, even when society is still in a primitive state, understand perfectly well the force of obligations arising from pacts and contracts, but are not clear about obligations which come into being irrespective of contracts. As a result, legislators imagined *fictitious* contracts where contracts did not really exist, and from these fictions deduced the kind of jural obligations which do not spring from true contracts.[362]

1368. Vinnius defines the quasi-contract as: 'an upright fact by which one person is obligated to another, or the second to the first, or both to one another WITHOUT ANY AGREEMENT'.[363] This is the true definition of quasi-contracts introduced into Roman laws. They are not contracts at all because they contain no agreement of any kind.[364]

1369. Hence, under the name 'quasi-contracts', we have to distinguish both *expressed* and *tacit contracts*.

1370. Tacit contracts are those in which the consent of the parties, although acknowledged only indirectly, is nevertheless *certain*, or at least *probable*.

1371. Consent which is only probable, but such that at the same time it has to be considered *certain*,[365] is called *presumed*

---

[362] It is possible, however, that some of the legislators themselves thought that there could be no obligation which was not deduced from a contract. Such a supposition would depend on the difficulty that the mind found in conceiving how a jural obligation could originate from a simple law applied to a fact. This does indeed seem to have been the opinion of the jurisconsult Pedius, an opinion approved by Roman law which states: 'As Pedius neatly says, there is no contract, NO OBLIGATION, without an accompanying AGREEMENT expressed in fact or verbally' (bk. 1, §3, *ff. De pactis.*).

[363] *Comment. ad Instit. Tit. De obligat. quae quasi ex contractu.*

[364] Baroli (§202) and others are deceiving themselves when they call quasi-contracts *agreements*.

[365] Probable consent can be taken for certain:

1. when there is no burdensome consequence for the person presumed to have given his consent;

2. when consent is obligatory for the other party. In this case, we apply William Beuch's observations: 'Because what is false cannot possibly be true, jural fiction cannot be converted into presumption; however, presumption, which is concerned with what could be true, can be changed by the ruler or the legislator into fiction' (*De pactis et contractibus in genere*, c. 1, n. 41). This decision was first enunciated by Ludovic de Sardis and by Müller (*ad Stronium*, Exercitat. 28, thes. 20). We add that in our case, this may be done by anyone, not only by the law;

3. when probable consent reaches *maximum* probability, or *legitimate probability*, according to the table of probability I have indicated in *CS*, 812-815.

consent. It takes the form of a true contract, the essence of which is the consent of the parties.[366]

1372. In quasi-contracts, however, consent is altogether lacking. Their obligation comes not from consent, but from elsewhere. The law *imagines* consent and, through this fiction (*fictio juris*), presents an obligation to the people, while authorising itself to invent the expression *quasi-contracts.*

1373. The obligations which quasi-contracts were invented to explain arise immediately from the force of natural law. Granted certain facts, this law obliges us to certain undertakings and, in so far as it does not result from agreements or remains unwritten, or is contrary to what has been written, is also called the law of *equity.*[367]

1374. Because of this, some authors define the quasi-contract as 'an upright fact from which, without any agreement, obligation arises for reasons of equity.'

1375. Hence William Beuch says that quasi-contract was always acknowledged, even before its establishment by Roman law, because it pertains to natural law.[368] This is true if we

---

[366] Beuch's usual accuracy has deserted him here. It is not true that so-called quasi-contracts can be considered a kind of tacit agreement (*Tract. de pact. et contract.* c. 2, n. 80).

[367] That which arises from agreements between human beings (these pacts are defined by the Roman legislators as *private law*, cf. bk. 51, *ff. de action. empt.*; bk. 1, c. *de pactis*; bk. 23, *ff. de R. I.*) or springs from the letter of *public law*, is referred to as *strict right*. That which springs from the *natural law*, and is not included in positive laws, is referred to as *equity*, which can be divided into two parts, *equity of contracts*, of which we have spoken (cf. 1185-1262) and *equity of judgments* in the application of the laws which we are discussing here. The equity to be used by judges in interpreting and correcting laws whose defects depend upon the legislator's incapacity for considering all possible cases, or even certain cases which he should have foreseen, is little by little consigned to writing. This forms a body of more recent legislation which in part is contrary to ancient legislation, relative to which it bears the title 'equity'. This explains why the jurisconsult Celsus defines the art of Right as *the art of what is good and equitable.*

[368] 'For a quasi-contract is at least a fictitious agreement' (he says 'at least fictitious' in order to embrace within the definition the case of presumed consent, changed by the law into *certainty* through a fiction of the law itself to eliminate any contrary proof when judgment has to be given) 'whose power of effecting action is never denied, and whose efficacy pertained to natural right, before it formed part of Roman right, precisely because natural

consider only the *obligation* posited by positive law in what is called quasi-contract and fictional contract. But it is not the case if it refers to the expression or fiction, which certainly does not exist in simply natural Right.

1376. As a result, *fictitious consent* in law has much more force in judgment than *presumed consent*. In fact, presumption of consent can in certain circumstances be impugned with the resulting annulment of the obligation, which depends on consent as an effect depends upon its cause. On the other hand, it would be totally useless to prove with even the clearest evidence that in fact there was no consent in quasi-contracts because the law not only does not presume this consent, but goes so far as to invent it. In this case, the obligation would remain equally stable because it does not truly follow from consent but solely from *equity* which has been clothed with the juridical phrase of fictitious consent.[369]

b) Wills

1377. We return now to the question of wills, to which we must apply these teachings. First, we have to affirm that testaments have no force as contracts. Calling them 'quasi-contracts', therefore, simply obscures their concept. Indeed, I think that the immense difficulty experienced by authors in accepting wills as acts pertaining to rational Right springs from this very

right has to favour equity' (*De pactis et contrib. in genere*, c. 2, n. 81).

[369] This explains why, in judgments, laws do not permit any proof against *presumption*, which they change into *fiction* (bk 23, c. *Ad SC. Velleyanum*, bk. *fin*, c. *Arbitrium tutel.*), although this is admitted against simple *presumption* provided it is what jurisconsults call *indirect* presumption; in other words, it is directed to show that, in a particular case, presumption does not exist (Cf. Menochius, *De praesumptionib.*, bk 1, q. 61 ss.). Legal practitioners also say that 'in a fictitious case, fiction effects what truth effects in a true case' (c. 14, *ff. De Cler. non resident.*, *l. un. in princ. de Rei. Ux. vind.*) and 'fiction is about something certain, presumption about something doubtful' and therefore 'fiction is taken absolutely and unconditionally for the truth, not conditionally, as presumption is.' Finally Menochio says that legal *fiction* cannot be impugned in any way except by demonstrating that in a given case *equity*, on which fiction is founded, ceases (bk 1, q. 6, n. 14).

point. This would explain the crowded ranks of those who, having despaired of showing that wills belong to natural right, have forced themselves to conclude that testaments are a merely positive institution and a creation of civil laws. This is certainly the case with those who call wills quasi-contracts, because, as we have seen, the quasi-contract is a fiction of law.

1378. Some authors attempted to make testaments contracts, but this was soon abandoned as unsustainable because a contract requires the simultaneous consent of stipulator and accepter.[370] In a will, however, the heir does not accept until after the death of the testator. Finding it impossible, therefore, to make wills natural through lack of contractual qualities, these authors saw no other way out of the dilemma than that of considering wills as a product of positive law.[371]

1379. But if nature did not speak so clearly to them, as it speaks to us, history could have educated them — if they had wished to listen. Only that which is natural[372] can be universal,

---

[370] We grant the necessity of simultaneous consent in contracts. We cannot in any way favour the opinion of certain modern authors who deny this.

[371] An incredibly deep impression is made upon peoples by long lasting legislation. As a result, positive legislation — up to the present, far more restrictive than rational Right — has also restricted intelligences which for a long time have been incapable of seeing anything legitimate and just outside the written law which, in turn, has served as the source of a debased rational Right. Although freer minds come to realise that it is now time to enlarge the boundaries of thought and destroy the barriers arbitrarily erected by ancient legislators around societies in order to defend them from danger, restricted legislations continue to exercise their secret influence on normal thinking and even on those who have realised what legislators have done, and seen how ancient laws have generated prejudiced opinions and errors. Blackstone is a case in point. No one was more persuaded of the defects inherent in Roman legislation and of its unhappy influence on modern nations. Nevertheless, Blackstone himself was subject to its pressure. Unable to reduce testaments to natural contracts, he did not hesitate to declare that the right to make a will (along with the right to inherit) was simply an effect of positive law. Another contradiction in the same sense can be observed in his *Commentaries on the Laws of England* in which he acknowledges testatory acts as a universal institution and custom, but goes on to deny that wills are natural. It is almost as though he wanted a more certain sign than *universality* of place and time by which to recognise nature and human reason (Cf. Blackstone, t. 2, p. 312 ss., French ed.).

[372] 'Haller ... notes the present sad condition of the writer on natural Right

and present at all times and in all places; and the practice of making wills is indeed immemorial and universal.

1380. Nevertheless, this historical argument, although finally permitting us to know something originating from human nature, does not offer any reason for the information it provides. Searching for this reason is our next task.

As long as we were dealing with natural succession, we found its moral-jural foundation in the natural feeling of our nearest kin, in their affection and in their natural persuasion that the ownership held by blood-relations and in-laws whose eyes they closed should devolve on themselves and not on others. In the present case, however, in which we are no longer dealing with natural heirs, we cannot appeal to natural inclination and volition. The reason for the efficacy of such a testament can be sought only in the validity of the will of the testator. Everything depends upon whether this will should be respected by others and is capable of imposing a jural obligation upon them. If it can be shown that the will of a testator is authoritative and holy, and able to posit a jural obligation that the survivors have to uphold, it is clear that there is a right in nature to make a will

who is every day obliged to prove the most obvious elements of his science without ever being allowed to suppose certain principles as impregnable and universally accepted. Everything is doubted; everything is brought under attack. This scepticism and spirit of destruction has not spared what was universally admitted; it has dominated in recent times even in the sciences. As a result we now have to use the force of reason to uphold a principle which at other times was admitted of itself as an obvious truth.

'We must first reflect that the ordinary reason of the human race (the reason that judges about concrete things) is altogether opposed to the assertion that dispositions of last wills have no value without a positive law. The opposition between ordinary reason and this assertion must arouse serious doubt about the truth of the latter. Anyone claiming that hereditary succession is opposed to natural Right, or at least that it does not derive from, nor have its lawful foundation in natural Right but in civil-positive law, has to prove why it is present at all times and everywhere. No one in good faith can ignore this. But does not this show that it is founded in the natural law? This universality is indeed a shining confirmation of the dictate of ordinary reason relative to the matter in hand. It is impossible for positive legislators to have introduced it, and with it removed the pretended right of occupancy from others. Finally, why is it held in honour even amongst independent persons who live without subjection to positive laws in the so-called state of nature, or extra-social state?' (Baroli, *Diritto naturale privato e pubblico*, §205).

[1380]

1381. This is what we maintain, and we intend to prove it with two reasons which follow as consequences from the same principle that we have posited as the foundation of all rights. This principle is invariably the extremely simple, ethical maxim: 'Whatever naturally displeases a human being is to be avoided; the bond of feeling with which the human being naturally attaches things to himself is not to be severed; in other words, ownership must not be taken from others.' Our conclusion was that ownership (the bond of natural feeling we have described), considered in relationship with the obligation existing in other people, is that which constitutes the right of ownership.

Granted this, it is clear that the right has the same extension as the obligation, and that the obligation extends as far as the natural displeasure which others cause by attempting to disunite a person from the things which he has united to himself in the feeling we have described.[373]

1382. This principle provides two consequences which are clear reasons proving the right to make a will.

First reason. Human beings naturally make acts expressing their final will and want them fulfilled. Precisely because we are persuaded that we are able to dispose of our goods after death, we insist that others put our dispositions into effect. If we knew that our directions (indicated by the use of the phrase 'I will' in reference to what has to be done with our estate after our death) would be totally ignored, we would, while still alive, experience a sense of sorrow. In a word, it is naturally painful for us not to dispose efficaciously of our goods after our death. The hurt arises from our desire that such an act of ownership on our part should produce its effect, and from the affection that we bear towards those we have chosen as our heirs and have made one person with ourselves.

All our surviving neighbours, therefore, must agree to respect this inclination of nature and maintain the dispositions that the dead make about what belongs to them. They have to agree not to violate these dispositions, and this has always happened in

---

[373] Not all displeasure caused to others is *jural injury*, but only that which consists in removing or attempting to remove from the person the thing he has united naturally to himself with the feeling of ownership (Cf. *ER*, 332-339, 360).

fact, in order to avoid harming living testators who may anticipate lack of respect for their wishes. The inclination to dispose of ownership after death is as natural and normal to people as the inclination to own many things during life, and the former must be respected in the same way as the latter.[374] If all do, in fact, respect it, everyone will benefit; all can enjoy the satisfaction which human nature offers of being able to pass beyond the grave in thought and desire, and foresee that each person's dispositions are carried out and respected. A lasting trace of one's own power and a naturally attractive extension of ownership is left in the world. If this were not the case, a natural, human propensity would be sacrificed. But everything which leaves human nature devoid of some natural inclination, of some inborn feeling, is against natural Right.

1383. The *second reason* is based upon an observation by Leibniz, Germany's greatest philosopher. This great, generous-hearted

---

[374] Genovesi (*Diceosina*, vol. 2, f. 57) denies that donations *mortis causa*, testaments, legacies and succession in the case of intestacy are valid in primitive natural Right. He simply asserts that they are facts common to all nations. The reason for his claim is that the right of ownership springs from a *right to use*, which in its turn depends upon the needs of the present life. But this shows that he has not considered human nature in all its extension. Human nature's needs and exigencies, dependent upon its natural feelings, are not limited to the simple use of things. Ownership or dominion satisfies a deeper need, rooted in the essence of human beings. This, I maintain, is the need to feel powerful, to feel one's own greatness and to feel in possession of an effective will. Moreover, because human beings have intelligence and affection, they draw close to their neighbours; they are made for friendship and society. And perhaps there is a secret bond uniting individuals of the same species more closely than we imagine (Cf. what we have said about human instinct in *AMS*, 683-686). It would be impossible to explain the miser's insatiable desire to accumulate rather than enjoy unless he considered dominion as a kind of means for satisfying his need of greatness. Again, by means of their affections, human beings do not acquire goods for themselves alone, but for all those whom they hold dear, relatives and friends alike. Their sense of ownership allows them to attribute these things not to themselves alone, but to all those who are joined to their person through affection, and outlive them. Genovesi's ideas would perhaps be correct if human beings were constrained by nature to withdraw within themselves. His teaching supposes that they are essentially egoists. It is, therefore, essentially sensistic because it sees in human beings only the senses and what is good for the senses, all of which perish with the body.

[1383]

man noted that the tendency and right to make a will is a consequence of the immortality of the soul.

1384. This noble idea was rejected, but unworthily. The 'republic of souls', to use a phrase employed by this great man, is not a chimera. Granted the immortality of souls, it is impossible to believe that once deprived of their bodies, they are denuded of all the relationships they have naturally acquired with other persons of the same species. Nor can we believe that they lay aside what is natural to them, such as the desire to see their will esteemed amongst their fellows. Human beings naturally desire power, and all their power consists in the efficacy of their act of will in obtaining what it commands and desires. It is therefore an affront to the natural desire of the human person, which does not perish, and a lack of respect for personal will when what it decides about the things it has taken as its own 'with the intention of using them in life and disposing of them after death' is set aside. It is A FACT that all this is contained in the single, moral-physical act of the appropriation of things, and it is there for all to see.[375]

1385. Moreover, the right to make a will arises so intimately from the union between the living and those who come in the future that if it were not accepted it would be impossible to understand how civil society would have the right, or even the idea of instituting wills and making laws about them. These laws are intended solely for the benefit of those who are to come. Legislators start, therefore, from the principle that human beings, although succeeding one another on the stage of this world, form a single, continuous whole. The same principle which makes us think of those to come also dictates our respect for those who have preceded us (cf. 1383-1384).

1386. It is impossible, therefore, to take as true the affirmation

---

[375] Roman laws without exception acknowledge that the transference of goods according to the will of their owner is a principle which conforms with equity, that is, with natural justice. 'Nothing is more fitting to NATURAL EQUITY than that the WILL of an owner should be ratified when he wishes to transfer what he has to someone else.' If Genovesi were correct in maintaining that the right of ownership comes from a *right to use*, how could he possibly explain the right to donate one's own goods? What is given away is clearly not used by oneself, but disposed for the use of others by the owner who deprives himself of its use.

of many authors that all rights perish together with the present life. Just as we have sacred duties to fulfil towards those who have preceded us — duties accepted unanimously by all mankind — so we have to acknowledge that rights subsist corresponding to those duties, even if the active exercise of these rights has been blocked and suspended for our predecessors. It has not been blocked for the living, whose respect they gratefully receive. In this passive manner the dead come to exercise their rights by approving, as we must suppose, the reverence paid to their person and will by their survivors.

1387. It is possible that some will deny jural, but not ethical value to duties binding the living with those who have passed to the next life. They will argue that the dead can no longer exercise rights or impose sanctions on this earth. But it is not good for those who believe in the immortality of the soul and in a just God to affirm so easily and indubitably, as they do, that the injustices carried out against the persons of the dead pass without punishment of any kind whether applied in a hidden way by the dead themselves, or by God and his Providence, who may punish on behalf of the dead.

I repeat, relative to the exercise of rights (and ignoring that right is one thing, and its exercise another), that the deceased exercise their rights very well when their surviving heirs enjoy on their behalf the ownership they have left in virtue of their will. This enjoyment is a virtual exercise of their rights because it is the efficacious effect of their last wills. If these desires are not observed, their exercise is lacking, but only in the same way that an owner cannot exercise his right to use something stolen from him by thieves. In a word, the deceased have some rights not *per se*, but by means of their dear ones. They exercise these rights through their heirs if the survivors allow them the exercise.[376]

1388. Nor would the same reasoning be sound relative to the heirs if duties towards the dead were considered simply as *ethical* because of the condition in which the deceased found themselves, that is, beyond the senses of those who live on earth. The heirs *can be* seen; they eat, drink and dress. If the duty of

---

[376] Nature itself suggested the sentiment expressed by Roman laws: 'the heir forms a single person with the testator' (bk. 59, *De R. J. et Nov.* 48 pr.).

respecting the will of the dead were only ethical relative to the dead, it would nevertheless be jural relative to the living who, in virtue of that ethical duty, are called to succeed; that right is jural whose infraction harms a person's ownership.[377] But those named as successors already consider themselves in the place of the dead testator and intend through natural affection to be substituted for this person, holding the same bonds of ownership as he held. This natural affection and expectation establish the right of ownership which, as we endlessly repeat, has its root always in affection.[378]

1389. It may be objected that heirs cannot have this feeling if the contents of the will have been kept hidden from them, nor be owners of the bequeathed estate until they have accepted the inheritance. My reply is that the will of the testator confers on the heirs the right 1. to know the will; 2. to accept it if they wish to do so. Thus, they would be harmed in their rights if anyone wished to conceal the will from them or occupy the inheritance before they declared their non-acceptance of it.

1390. As we have said, there are rights *ad rem* which are acquired without need for acceptance or consent. The right to give and deny acceptance is one of these rights.

1391. I would be offended jurally if a donation made me were concealed to prevent my accepting it. Anyone doing this would steal what was mine in the sense that he would impede me from making my own that which I have the right to appropriate before anyone else does (jural freedom). The same would be true if a testamentary disposition were hidden from me or a legacy withheld from me. The inheritance must be made known to the named heir, and once made known, restored as soon as he claims it. If it is not restored, he can vindicate it forcefully.

---

[377] We need to keep in mind that an *ethical* duty can give rise to a *jural duty*, and does so whenever the violation of an ethical duty causes harm to the *feeling of ownership* in another (Cf. *ER*, 275-292).

[378] Roman laws express this very well: 'Account is to be taken of the AFFECTION of the possessor in questions about loss of possession' (bk 3, §6, *ff. de acquiren. et amit. poss.*). — 'He has lost possession immediately if he HAS NOT WISHED to possess' (bk. 1, §4, *ff. de acquir. et amitt. poss.; bk. 1 and 2, ff. pro derelicto*). The same is substantially true in the case of acquisition, according to the known rule: 'Things cease to be ours in exactly the same way as they are acquired' (bk. 1, *ff. pro derelicto — R. Jur. Can.*, c. 1).

1392. The matter becomes even more clear if we consider that the virtual consent to the acceptance of an inheritance must be presumed in accordance with natural equity. 'In the natural act by which human beings desire what is good they virtually accept all favourable conditions; such acceptance must therefore be presumed unless the contrary is proved.'

1393. No presumption is more reasonable and fairer than this; and even presumption of consent, when reason indicates this, is a jural duty whenever the contrary would place in danger the right or substance of another person. As we have said, and must repeat, moral duty is always jural if it 'can be the cause of disuniting our fellow human beings from that which is united to them with the feeling of ownership.'

B.
The right to decide who should have one's goods after death in the case of heirs who otherwise would naturally succeed

1394. Does the right to make a will, which we have defended in the preceding pages, still hold even to the detriment of heirs who would naturally succeed? This is a serious question that needs to be dealt with separately. In fact, it seems to me that the confusion of ideas often apparent in authors on natural Right when they discuss testaments depends on their failure to distinguish this question from the preceding one.

I.
Historical considerations

1395. Baroli writes: 'In right, testaments have been given and must be given precedence over hereditary succession through intestacy because they are founded solely on the presumed will of the deceased.'[379]

What we have said so far shows that in the case of intestacy succession receives its value not from the presumed will of the deceased, but from natural human feeling. Consequently, this

---

[379] *Diritt. Nat. Priv. e Pubbl., Diritto Privato*, §205.

kind of succession is proper to natural Right and is prior chronologically to testaments which are acts of will. History confirms what reason indicates in this matter.

1396. As long as only one family existed on earth, the abundance around them together with their few natural needs prevented their feeling the necessity of separate ownership. For the same reason, testaments had no place. Rather, successive generations succeeded one another in the ownership common to all.

1397. A century after the Flood, however, when the number of human beings had greatly increased, families and their ownership, especially their land ownership, had to be divided. The Bible speaks about this as taking place under Peleg, who lived to the age of 239. It would seem that the construction of the tower of Babel, which preceded the division of the families, began when Peleg was 14 years old. The division, decided upon by others, was perhaps carried out in great part by this man.[380]

1398. It was natural, after families and ownership had been divided, that each family would think of itself, not of others. It was also natural for fathers, when they began to make wills, to limit the division of goods to their own children and other members of the house without leaving anything to other families. In fact, remotest antiquity provides no example of goods being left to another family. As time went on, such dispositions came substantially to follow natural succession, which it further helped to strengthen.

1399. It was clearly recognised that fathers had the right to send away from the house one or more members of the family. In this case, the person who left lost the right to inherit and formed a new family. This happened not only in the case of daughters who were given in marriage, but also with male children and any other member of the house. Thus, Abraham sent away Agar and Ismael. Jacob himself left Isaac's family, and was totally deprived of the paternal estate which fell to the hands of Esau, who had remained at home. All Jacob's sons

---

[380] Scripture says that he was given the name of Peleg, which means *division*, because the land had been divided up in his days. 'To Eber were born two sons: the name of the one was Peleg, for in his days the earth was divided' (1 Chron 1: 19). Why did he, rather than one of his contemporaries, bear this name unless he played a great part in carrying out the division?

inherited, however, because they were all at home at the death of their father, who in making his will mentioned Joseph in particular, adopting his two sons as his own and assigning them an equal share with his very own sons. As we said, there is no example of any inheritance leaving a house. Natural succession was substantially maintained.

1400. This principle explains almost all ancient legislation about succession. The laws were intended to preserve *natural succession* in its substantial part in so far as 'the members of a family should succeed to the estate of the same family', that is, 'patrimony was not to pass from one family to another.' Everything differing from this principle was introduced later by civil law, and as an exception.

1401. As we know, Hebrew laws took great care to ensure that every tribe and every family should retain the same portion of land assigned to it in the first division carried out when Palestine was conquered. No one could sell or in any way transfer to others the full dominion of the lands belonging to his own family.[381] The land always had to be recoverable; if it was not bought back before, it was returned to the first owners not later than every 50th year. Daughters who inherited had to marry a man of their own tribe so that the inheritance would not be lost to the tribe. The brother of a man who died without leaving children had to marry the widow and consider any children he might have from her as successors to his brother, whose family thus continued to exist as part of the feeling amongst the living, and before the law.[382]

1402. The first division of land carried out by the Hebrew conquerors of Palestine and the laws they established for preserving the division as far as humanly possible are to be found in all the conquests of ancient colonies which entailed the expulsion of the former inhabitants and the establishment of a new people.[383]

[381] The usufruct was sold, for the years remaining until the jubilee year, but not the dominion (Cf. Lev 25).

[382] This law of Moses is somewhat similar to Solon's law at Athens which permitted an heiress to marry one of the near blood-relations of her impotent husband (Cf. Plutarch, *Life of Solon*).

[383] Aristotle notes that it was easy to establish equality amongst patrimonies

The Carthaginians, who could have been the Canaanites defeated by Josuah, had similar laws. Phales, their legislator, wished especially to establish and preserve equality amongst family patrimonies.[384] The Locri, like the Hebrews, were also forbidden to sell ancestral possessions. This was intended, says Aristotle, 'to preserve ancient heritages'.[385] It is said that Oxylus, king of Elis, promulgated the same law. When the Dorians took possession of Laconica, they divided the land into equal portions, as the Hebrews did with Palestine; Plato called Sparta fortunate because it was able to establish a certain equality amongst the patrimonies.[386]

1403. Aristotle, however, considers Spartan legislation unfavourably because it did not attempt to maintain the equality which had been established. According to him, the cause of distortion of the equality introduced into ownership was that

it had been badly protected by the law which, although it had done well to render unlawful the buying and selling of what was owned, had nevertheless permitted estates to be donated and left in wills. This amounted to the same thing as freely buying and selling them. In fact, women possessed almost two fifths of the country as a result of heritage, and owned great dowries which would better have been set at zero, or at a small or mediocre figure. Instead, it is lawful to leave anything in one's will to anyone, or make donations through legacies if no heir is wanted. As a result, this region, which was capable of feeding 1,500 horsemen and 30,000 footmen now has less than 1,000 in all.[387]

1404. The laws of Sparta did not change after the time of Aristotle. The law of Epitadeus permitted everyone to will

when peoples were first constituted, but more difficult after they had been established. He suggests a curious remedy for the situation. According to him, the rich should be obliged to endow their daughters, but to marry daughters without dowries; the poor should receive as wives girls with dowries, but not give dowries when their own daughters married. — This great man had seen the difficulty we have mentioned (cf. 1293) (*Polit.*, 2, c. 5).

[384] Aristotle. *Polit.*, 5: 2.

[385] *Ibid.*

[386] — ισοτητα τινα της ουσιας in *Laws*, 3. — Müller notes that the Spartans are called ομοιοι, that is, *equals*, as though it were their characteristic.

[387] *Polit.*, 2: 7.

their fields to people indiscriminately, or to donate them *inter vivos*.[388] As a result, riches accumulated in a few families so that the 700 families who possessed land in Lacedaemon had fallen to only 100 at the time of Agis III.[389]

The Thebans also had laws (the work of Philolaus of Corinth) dedicated to preserving a certain number of inheritances. Aristotle notes, however, that this legislator did nothing to remove inequality in patrimonies.[390] The inhabitants of Calcide were provided by king Andradama with laws regulating heritages.[391] The ancient laws of Athens did not permit citizens to make wills, but preserved natural succession in all its vigour. Solon later permitted it, but only to persons who had no children.[392] This shows that the legislator did not believe that

---

[388] It seems, according to Plutarch, that this law of Epitadeus was formulated after the time of Lysander. However, it could not have been totally new in Sparta, and may simply have confirmed an existing custom which had arisen despite the laws of Lycurgus. And it would seem reasonable for people to have complained about it after they have seen the damage caused by this freedom to hand over and accumulate patrimonies. The possessors won, however, and succeeded in sanctioning through law what they had previously done through abusive custom.

[389] However, as Cantù notes, the loss of Messenia, which the Spartans suffered after the battle of Leuctra, must have contributed considerably to lowering the number of those holding possessions. — Aristotle had already foreseen this in a certain way. He reproves the admission and provision on behalf of the commune of a great number of new men in an attempt to make up for the scarcity of population (he may be alluding to the distribution of lands carried out especially after the conquest of Messenia at the time of the king, Polidorus). 'It would have been better', he says, 'to fill the city with men by satisfying passion.' (*Polit.*, 2: 7).

[390] *Polit.*, 2: 9.

[391] *Ibid.* — We note that κληρονομος, 'heir', presupposes a division in equal shares drawn by lot amongst siblings. The word comes from κληρος and νεμω. It was used, therefore, to indicate natural heirs. The Romans used *haeres*, or *haeres suus*, for the same purpose.

[392] 'Solon acquired a good deal of credit for his law about wills. Previously, testaments had been forbidden. The wealth and everything of value possessed by the deceased had to remain in his family. Solon, however, allowed anyone without children to dispose of his estate and give it to whomsoever he pleased. He put friendship before relationships and favour before necessity. In this way riches were totally at the disposition of the will of their possessors' (Plutarch, *Life of Solon*, from Pompei's translation).

one could or should overthrow the order of natural succession in the case of children.

The laws regulating succession in Rome contained the same spirit, and were as far as possible directed to defend natural succession against free choice by testators.

1405. Montesquieu notes that these laws sprang from the division of lands carried out by Romulus and his companions.[393] This is precisely what we have observed in the various oriental and Greek legislations that we have glimpsed so far. He says (*L'Esprit des Lois*):

> The law governing the division of land required that the goods of one family should not pass to another. Consequently, there were only two orders of heirs established by law, the children and all the descendants living under the *patria potestas*, who were called *his heirs*, and in the absence of these all the nearest relatives on the male side, who were called *agnates*.[394]
>
> Another consequence was that relatives on the female side, called *cognates*, were prevented from succeeding because they would have taken their goods into another family. Yet another consequence was that children had to be prevented from succeeding to their mothers, and mothers to their children, because this would have inflicted damage by one family upon another. They were, therefore, excluded by the law of the XII Tables which provided for succession only by agnates and children. Mothers were not amongst the heirs.[395]
>
> It was of no consequence whether the heir, or in the absence of the heir, the nearest agnate, was male or female. Because relatives on the maternal side did not succeed, any estate re-entered the family if an heiress married. This explains why the law of the XII Tables made no distinction between male and female in respect of succession.[396]

[393] Dionys. of Halicarnassus, 2: 3. — Plutarch, *Comparison between Numa and Lycurgus.*

[394] 'But if anyone dies intestate, without any HEIR of his own, the next in the family line will be considered as the AGNATE' (*Fragment of the XII Tables*, in Ulpian, tit. ult.).

[395] Cf. Fragments of Ulpian, §8, tit. 26. — *Instit.*, tit. 3, *in proem. ad S. C. Tertullianum.*

[396] Paul, bk. 4, *De Sentent.*, tit. 8, §3. — This shows that although the

Yet another consequence was that grandchildren in the masculine line succeeded the grandfather, while grandchildren in the feminine line did not. The agnates were given preference over the latter to prevent the estate passing from one house to another. The daughter succeeded her father, but the daughter's children did not.[397]

1406. All this is true. We differ from Montesquieu only in the point of view from which we regard the laws regulating succession.[398] Montesquieu stops at the division of lands, which

Romans had a clear idea of paternal authority, they nevertheless lacked the right idea of indissoluble union in marriage. But this is true of all peoples, not only the Romans. It was Christianity which restored honour, dignity and force to the weak sex, and reconciled the two beings, man and woman, who although made for one another, had been separated through the discord resulting from overwhelming force on the one hand, and baseness of spirit on the other. Christianity made a single being of the two, restored them to their original state and made them happy in their unity. This was how Christ brought about the restoration of marriage, after which the possessions of each of the spouses were necessarily the possessions of them both, and one naturally succeeded the other.

[397] This law, and others in the XII Tables which restricted natural succession in the female line, made force the arbiter of weakness. In Christian times Justinian declared these laws to be *against nature*. He says: 'The old law favoured descendants on the male side by allowing succession only to male or female grandchildren who descended on the male side, and by giving them precedence over the law of agnates. The daughter's grandchildren, and the children of female grandchildren, were numbered amongst cognates and called (when there was a question of succession to the grandfather, or the maternal grandfather, or the grandmother or maternal grandmother on the paternal or maternal side) to succeed by law after the line of agnates. But wealthy princes did not allow such an injury AGAINST NATURE to continue without emendation, etc (*Instit. Just.*, bk. 3, t. 1, 15 *ss.*).

[398] Montesquieu claims that Roman laws about succession were not numbered amongst those which the legates of the Greek cities brought to Rome because, as he says, 'they were a natural consequence of the constitution and derived from the division of lands.' But what we have said about oriental and Greek laws shows rather that the constitution itself, the very division of lands amongst families, was an imitation of what had first been done in Greece, or rather wherever colonisation had taken place, and even throughout the whole world, beginning with Peleg and continuing through Indian and Egyptian castes down to the laws of Moses, the Phoenicians, the Carthaginians and the Greeks. It may indeed be that the division of lands carried out by Romulus preserved some faint consignment or some suggestion dependent upon the nature of things. Nevertheless, it is certain that there is a great likeness

he considers as a merely civil law, and concludes that the order of succession amongst the Romans was simply the consequence of a civil law.[399] Our own view is that we should not confine ourselves to what the Romans decided about succession, but consider the substantial uniformity and similar tendency found in all previous legislations. It is true that we find land divided everywhere, but we should go beyond this and not take it as the first reason for laws about succession. We have to arrive at a more elevated principle which explains both the division of land and the laws of succession. This principle is neither political nor civil, but *natural*; it is the principle of 'separation between families, and the unity of each family'. Land is divided because families split up; laws were made with the intention of maintaining succession in families precisely because this is the *natural order* emanating from the unity of each family society.

1407. Montesquieu, in taking the Roman division of land as his starting point and considering it as a merely civil law, encountered irreconcilable contradictions in Roman laws. On the one hand, we have the laws already mentioned which were intended to maintain ownership in families, and on the other, ample power to make wills in favour of any citizen, even outside the family.

Such contradictions vanish in face of our principle of the natural constitution of the family. If succession is intestate, it

between this division and divisions of land made by other peoples before Romulus, and between the Roman laws of succession and those of more ancient peoples. And we have to remember that, according to Dionysius of Halicarnassus, the greater part of the Latin cities were Spartan colonies, and that the Decemviri went in search of laws not only in Greece, but throughout the various cities of Italy.

[399] I think that Montesquieu is mistaken when he writes: 'The law of nature requires fathers to nourish their children, but does not oblige them to make them their heirs. The division of goods, laws about this division, succession after the death of a person holding a portion of goods, can be regulated only by society and consequently by political and civil laws' (*L'Esprit des Lois*, bk. 26, c. 6). But according to the order of ideas occupancy carried out by single individuals precedes the division of lands. Ownership, the family, natural succession in the family, paternal authority which modifies natural succession: all these pre-exist political and civil laws. Civil, political dispositions can only follow and modify customs which have already been formed according to the light of reason and natural instinct.

follows naturally the thread of generations; if it is the result of a will, it must be as extensive as the concept of *patria potestas*. The principle governing the *division* of families gave rise to laws about intestate succession which are intended to restrict every family within its own limits and conserve its goods; the principle of the *unity* of every family as dependent upon the unity and full power of its head gave rise to the laws that allowed the head to make his will freely.

1408. It was an established principle of Roman legislation that anyone subject to the power of another was unable to make a will. Power over a person involved power or dominion over the things belonging to that person. As a result, wills by children still living under their fathers' power were not permitted.[400]

It is clear from a complete study of ancient Roman legislation, which Montesquieu interpreted badly by subjecting it to his own system, that the right to make a last testament was a consequence of the Roman concept of *patria potestas* and derived, therefore, from natural Right. Civil and political Right added at first only a sanction and differing forms to natural Right.

1409. Because wills were formulated imperatively, Montesquieu wished to deduce that wills were acts of political authority on the part of the people.[401] The contrary was, in fact, the case: it is clear that a testament, as the word indicates, was always held to express an act of will[402] and power on the part of the testator.

---

[400] 'Those subject to the rule of another have no right to make a will. Even if they are allowed to do so by their parents, such wills are invalid according to law (*Inst. Just.*, bk. 2, tit. 12). The inability of fathers to allow their children to make wills would seem to have been a political decision. However, it is more truly a consequence of the different notion, prevalent amongst the Romans, of *patria potestas*. It seemed contradictory to the Romans that a child could be subject to this power and still retain the faculty of making a will.

[401] 'As I have said, wills were a law of the people. They had to be made with the force of an imperative as "direct commands"' (77).

[402] Ulpian defines a 'will' as follows: 'A testament is a just decision of will which a person wishes should come about after his death' (*Digest.*, bk. 28, tit 1, leg. 1). The jurisconsult Sulpician falsely held that *testamentum* originated from *mentis testatio*. This etymology was inserted in Justinian's *Institutes*, where we read (bk. 2, tit. 10): 'A testament is given that name because it testifies to the mind of a person.' A. Gellius is correct in finding fault with this etymology (bk. 6, c. 12) because 'testament' is a manifestation and

It was not the people but the testator who used the imperative form in establishing his heir.

1410. When, therefore, a bond-servant was made an heir, it was understood that he was thereby free; the testament was always thought to transmit some *authority* and *dominion* from which the right of ownership flowed as a consequence.[403]

1411. The same principle explains the form of testaments *per aes et libram* [by money and weight], and phrases such as 'selling the family' and 'emancipation of the family', which were used to indicate the establishment of an heir. In other words, the testament made under this form was considered as an act by which a person sold his *own family*, that is, the power or dominion he had within his own family, and consequently ownership over all the goods pertaining to the family. This was called *emancipation* precisely because it was intended to free the family from one's own authority and make it pass to the authority of someone else.[404] Here, too, the right of *ownership* appears indivisibly joined to that of *seigniory*. 'Testament', therefore, is an act of one's own natural power.

1412. Error will always result when legislation is judged on

prolongation of *testamen*. Nevertheless, the false derivation of the word indicates the nature of the Romans' concept of a testament, and shows that they considered it AN AUTHORITATIVE ACT of the testator's will. And this is precisely the notion that natural Right gives of a testament.

[403] 'According to the opinion of many, it was once lawful to establish justly (as heirs) one's own (bond-servants) who by that very fact received their freedom — the bond-servant who had been established as heir by his master was freed by the testament to become the heir desired by the testator' (*Instit. Just.*, bk. 2, tit. 14). A later disposition of Roman law allowed a bond-servant remaining in servitude to inherit. But, as we shall see, he acquired only a certain *relative ownership*. In any case, this was a step towards the distinction between *dominion over persons* and *ownership of things* which the ancient Romans united very closely. It was also a step towards the acknowledgement of human dignity which was gradually gaining ground relative to bond-servants through the light shed by Christianity. The bond-servants to whom Justinian gave the right to inherit were already different from those to whom ancient laws had forbidden such a right, although the word 'bond-servant' had been retained.

[404] According to Festus, '"emancipate" may be understood in two ways: as the condition of those who have ceased to fall under paternal right, and of those who are within the dominion of others. [Freedom] for both depends upon "emancipation".'

the basis of arguments which presuppose that the first customs and laws of nations are political or civil. This is not the case. The first laws of nations (with the exception of those imported from mature or ancient peoples) are founded in natural laws; they are never political or civil.

This obviously does not mean that such laws, dictated to primitive peoples by reason and nature, are of necessity always correct. They are in fact the expression of what, 'according to the people, conforms to natural Right.' Consequently these laws follow the sometimes erroneous opinions of the people who form them, and depend in part upon their traditions. Nevertheless, these opinions are concerned with what is just and unjust considered in nature according to the power and development of minds, and the conditions of spirit which have such an influence on judgments passed by understanding.

At the beginning *politics* is involved only in so far as obvious, urgent necessity requires, and no further; *free choice* and *civil foresight* also play little part. In a word, the positive aspect of such laws is concerned with the *words* in which the opinion or custom is clothed; very few *forms, modifications* or *cautions* are introduced by civil and political prudence.

This prudence gradually intervenes more strongly as abuses manifest themselves; the desire to abolish all abuses, the presumptuous hope that this can be brought about by the multiplication of laws and dispositions, the open frivolity with which the legislature thinks it can obliterate the primitive traces of nature without causing harm (the interests of special classes who have reached power and form laws for their own benefit are not considered here) — as time goes on, all these causes act together to increase deviations from rational Right within codes of law. Dispositions pile up one upon another which may not be totally arbitrary, but are certainly the fruit of false human prudence rather than the wisdom of nature. In the end, the natural element, constantly decreasing, is rendered almost invisible, indiscernible and weighed down under the burden of the commandments of the infallible, supremely wise power of human legislators.[405]

---

[405] Cf. *SP*, where I distinguished between a nation's early and later legislators, and between laws originating from the good state of nature at

1413. But leaving this aside for now, we shall offer only a few examples which serve to illustrate our point. They show how *political* and *civil* laws — in the proper sense of the phrase — are gradually introduced amongst nations which in their customs and written laws originally followed laws believed to be in conformity with rational Right.

Naturally enough, *patria potestas* was of overwhelming importance in the opinion of the Romans. Fathers could dispose even of their children's life. For this very reason, political laws limited themselves to regulating relationships between families which had to be bonded into civil society itself. These laws did not, however, affect the internal constitution of the family. Inside the house, the father was everything, in accord with what he was thought to be by nature. In such a state of legislation, the offspring ceased to fall under the *patria potestas* only through an act on the part of the father. In fact, to show that the father was as much *owner* of the child as he was of everything else he possessed, the child was emancipated under the form of sale; and to show that the child was the father's property even more strictly than other things were, this sale was repeated three times. Emancipation through the will of the father was, therefore, the primitive law, entirely conformed to natural Right as it was understood at the time.[406]

If we want to see what happened as civil and political laws succeeded one another, it is sufficient to note how emancipation was brought about in many different ways: for example, through imperial rescript,[407] through privileges attached to great

the beginning of societies, and laws destined to impede abuse in aging societies (bk. 3, c. 13).

[406] Before the formation of civil society, the *patria potestas* contained what was later to be *civil power*. At the origin of civil societies, therefore, laws respected fathers, whom they found in possession of such power, which was abrogated only a little at a time. Thus, when well understood, the distinction between the *state of nature* and the *state of civil society* is not a chimera, but an historic fact. It provides the necessary explanation on the one hand of the gradual development of nations, and on the other hand of the laws imposed upon them.

[407] 'Emancipation came about in the first place through the ancient observance of law which was carried out through imaginary sales and appellant

dignities such as the patriciate,[408] by judges and magistrates[409] — these were all political and civil laws which followed upon the primitive, natural law of emancipation.

1414. The same is to be said about the laws regulating wills. Such laws are *natural* in the first instance; later they became *political* and *civil*.

1415. At this point, Montesquieu may object that the first form of testaments amongst the Romans was that made at gatherings of the people (*comitiis calatis*, as they said). This, however, does not mean that wills were made by an act of political authority. On the contrary, this form of testament expresses, I think, the true nature of testament according to the natural law, for which a last testament is neither an act of public authority nor even a contract. It is an act of will on the part of a testator; and it is an authoritative act of will in so far as the testator possesses dominion and ownership. A master, an owner, can make laws about his own seigniory and about what belongs to him.

This natural principle was accepted by the ancient Romans; it followed that the testator was in charge. A will made in favour of his children, or descendants, or servants had to be accepted by them, because they were subject to his power. Such heirs were, therefore, called *necessary* heirs.[410] If on the other hand the heir was not subject to the power of the testator, the latter could not oblige the named heir (the *extraneous* heir, as he was called)

manumission, or by imperial rescript' (*Instit. Just.*, bk 1, tit. 12).

[408] 'According to our constitution, the great dignity of the patriciate, dependent upon imperial decisions, frees the son from *patria potestas*.' The reasoning behind this statement is as follows: 'A father is allowed to liberate his son from his own power by way of emancipation. It is, therefore, even more proper that the imperial majesty should be able to free from the power of another the person who chose him as his father' (*Instit. Just.*, bk 1, tit. 12).

[409] *Instit. Just.*, bk. 1, tit. 12.

[410] 'Necessary heirs are those who, in accordance with the laws of the XII Tables, are heirs whether they want to be or not, both in the case of intestacy or of a will' (*Instit.*, bk. 2, tit. 19). The unity of the family was so great amongst the Romans, and the child considered to be so at one with his father, that (it was claimed) the child had to take on the person of the dying father and all his obligations. Money lenders, for example, lent not to the father alone, but to the family as a whole; and it was the family which was obliged in every way to restitution after the death of the father.

to accept the inheritance. If, however, he did accept the inheritance, he came under the law of the testator and was obliged to carry out his dispositions. Whatever happened, the will of the testator was acknowledged as something to be respected, as is the will of any owner when he makes use of what belongs to him. In this sense, such a will is a law for all mankind.[411]

The Roman people, when gathered in their assemblies, carried out two apparently opposite functions, that of receiving the law and that of confirming it. The people received the law which the testator promulgated in the assembly and gave it their public testimony;[412] at the same time, they took it upon themselves to maintain, defend and sanction this law with their own power. Receiving the law was proper to all human beings considered individually and in the state of nature; guaranteeing and defending it physically was, even when individuals found themselves in the state of nature, proper to an assembly which acknowledged right and justice in what had been resolved. But sanctioning it as public, inviolable law was a political element added by an assembly already bound together by social ties.

1416. The testament made during assemblies of the Roman people and the testament *per aes et libram* are, therefore, two forms which show the concept of testament the Romans instituted for themselves according to the principles of rational Right.

Other forms of testament differ from the first (which consisted in a testament made in the presence of the people) only in the manner of their promulgation. Because assemblies of the

---

[411] In so far as it is imposed on others that they 'should not occupy the inheritance, but leave it to be occupied by the heir.'

[412] The word *testament* itself, that is, *testamen*, comes from *testor*, which means *I affirm, I profess*, as well as *I call* or *use witnesses*. But both in affirming something and professing anything, and when calling others as witnesses, some kind of assembly is needed, or at least the presence of several people. Not only testaments, but sales contracts were done in public in antiquity, as we see from the story of Abraham when he bought the field with the double cave (Gen 23 [Douai]). The people served as witnesses for one another about the promulgation of the natural law which each person received and acknowledged. As a sale was an act of ownership carried out in public, so too was a testament amongst the Romans.

[1416]

Roman people were held only twice a year, it was not always possible for testaments to be declared so publicly and solemnly as on those occasions. The promulgation of the testator's will was, therefore, rendered easier by the need for a smaller assembly and a lesser number of witnesses.

First, soldiers leaving for war were allowed to testify in the presence of their companions; this was called a will *in procinctu*. Later, *praetors* allowed wills in the presence of seven witnesses who had to put their signature to the act recording the testament. Later still, *civil right* was content with the presence of seven witnesses, without seal or signature [*App.*, no. 9]. Finally, the imperial Constitutions required the testator and witnesses to sign, and either testator or witnesses to write the name of the heir. All these later dispositions certainly pertain to *positive* Right, that is, to praetorian edict, to civil and imperial right, as Justinian expressly declares.[413]

1417. The Voconian law, which deprived women of the right to inherit in order to curb effectively the luxury and influence they had attained, pertains to political Right. It was in part one of the laws dealing with expenditure, and as such vigorously defended by Cato the Elder.[414]

1418. The difference between *civil* and *political* laws is this. Civil laws are not normally opposed to natural law, but clothe it with formalities to protect it from fraud. However, when the

---

[413] 'Gradually, as a result of custom and amendments of the Constitutions, civil and praetorian right began to merge. It was then established that seven witnesses should be present contemporaneously (this was the requirement of CIVIL RIGHT) and that seals should be placed on the testaments by the signature of the witnesses (this requirement was found both in the CONSTITUTIONS and in the PRAETORIAN EDICT). This right thus took on a THREEFOLD aspect: the witnesses, and their contemporary presence for the sake of the will, was due to civil right; the signatures of the testator and the witnesses depended upon the observance of the sacred constitutions; the seals and the number of witnesses sprang from the praetorian edict. And we have added in our constitution, to ensure the sincerity of the witnesses and avoid fraud, that the name of the heir should be expressed in writing by the testator or the witnesses' (*Instit.*, bk. 2, tit. 10: 3, 4). Justinian continues to maintain that the heir is at one with the ancient 'buyer of the family': 'because he takes on the image, found in antiquity, of the buyer of the family' (bk. 2, tit. 10: 10).

[414] A. Gellius quotes a brief passage from Cato's speech (N. A. bk. 22, c. 6. — Cf. *Epit. Titi Livii*, bk. 41).

formalities grow too numerous, they no longer attain the end in view. Natural laws become submerged in formalities with the result that acts which would be totally valid in natural law are now invalidated through lack of one or other of the formalities which have been positively commanded.

1419. Political laws on the contrary often contradict natural laws not only indirectly and by accident as, for example, when legislators lack foresight or act against their own intention, but directly. Montesquieu himself affirms this in the case of the Voconian law.[415]

1420. As a result, people are always more eager and ingenious in avoiding political laws than merely civil laws. And sooner or later, they almost always succeed. This seems to have been the case with the Voconian law which was easily avoided by not having one's name inserted on the register, or by not including in the census those properties which persons wished to leave to daughters.[416]

1421. When political law opposed to nature comes to be frequently avoided by human nature's own cunning, the law undergoes another slow, corroding action dependent upon *interpretation* by legal practitioners. *Epikeia* and *equity* on the part of magistrates and judges then intervenes to weaken political law; these functions of jural reason eventually amend

---

[415] 'It is an unhappy part of the human condition that legislators are obliged to make laws which oppose natural feelings. Such is the case with the Voconian law. What happens is that legislators take more account of society than of the citizen, and more account of the citizen than the human being. The law sacrificed both the citizen and the human being; its only consideration was the republic' (*L'Esprit des Lois*, bk. 27). This is without doubt the wisdom claimed by political legislators. Their wisdom, however, is false because opposed to the greater wisdom of nature. The author of *The Spirit of the Laws* has a very poor understanding of this great truth. For the most part, natural justice is overshadowed for him by the false splendour of human cunning. He believes in the boldness characteristic of his century and the prostitution to which men of State subject themselves. How mankind suffers!

[416] It may be objected that all Roman citizens had to be registered. — Montesquieu thinks that in the Voconian law 'registered' means inscribed in one of the five classes of the people, but not in the proletariat, the sixth class. — Perhaps the following observation could be added to Montesquieu's conjecture: not all goods were subject to registration, but only those pertaining to *Italic right alone*. Cf. Cicero, *Pro Flacco*, c. 32.

the law in a way unknown to public consciousness. Finally, if the nation is capable of being healed, the legislative power itself undertakes the unanimously desired correction of the law — until everyone realises that correction is useless. At this point, it becomes obvious that the law, contrary to nature, has to be abrogated, and another put in its place in order to re-establish nature. The legislator who arrives at this final point congratulates himself on having remedied the crudity or harshness of his ancient predecessors and, as rights are restored to humanity, attributes to himself the painstaking work proper to humanity. And this is indeed the history of the Voconian law.

1422. The word 'registered' used by this law was soon interpreted as referring to a person having goods which had been registered, rather than to a person listed on the register of citizens. According to Cicero, the praetors favoured those who had chosen to elude the law in this way.[417] Then the legislators began first to attack the law indirectly, as did Augustus for example, by the institution of *fidei-commissa.*[418] This was followed by a partial, but direct attack from the Julian and Papian laws,[419] and from the Tertullian[420] and Orphitian[421] decrees. Finally, the Voconian law was totally eliminated by the reform under Justinian who was happy to announce, with a certain degree of truth, that he had purged Roman legislation of many difficulties, and brought it back to nature.[422]

1423. We must now draw together the threads of our argument. We said that the natural law constitutes the primitive fount of positive laws; the older these laws, the more they retain of the characteristics of natural Right. Time passes, and this Right is gradually modified by civil and political prudence as the number of dispositions increases. People thus withdraw further from their natural state and eventually find themselves in very distressing circumstances. Nature itself, however,

---

[417] In *Verrem*, 2.

[418] *Instit. Just.*, bk. 2, tit. 23.

[419] These laws began to encourage marriages and the rearing of offspring.

[420] The law instigated by Ovidius Tertullus under the Emperor Hadrian (Cf. *Instit. Just.*, bk. 3, tit. 3).

[421] The law instigated under the consuls Orphitius and Rufus (cf. *Instit. Just.*, bk. 3, tit. 4).

[422] *Cod.*, bk. 6, t. 55; 12. — *Novell.*, 118, 127. — *Instit.*, bk. 3, tit. 3.

rebels against these repugnant conditions and frees itself from them either through peaceful reform (if legislators act when need arises) or violent reform (if the people undertake the work).

Again, we said that if we apply this principle to succession, we do indeed find both natural succession and succession established by the free choice of the testator. Primitive legislations, therefore, had first to determine natural succession, by ensuring either that it took place, or that is was not unduly disturbed. This is in fact, without any exception, the spirit of all ancient legislations about inheritance. Nevertheless, as we saw, legislators recognised the power and the authority of the will of the person who made the testament, which they conceived not as an act of political or civil law, but as a natural act on the part of the will of the testator and an exercise of his right of ownership.

We showed that the first political and civil laws simply sanctioned and guaranteed such acts of will which it required to be public. Sometimes this was done in the presence of the sovereign authority of the people, as at Rome; sometimes in the presence of a certain number of witnesses and furnished with other precautions which, in case of need, would provide testaments with the vigour they required to attain their desired effect. Such acts of will were not considered as contracts, except in the case of donations *inter vivos* or of successory pacts such as that carried out by the Romans *per aes et libram*, none of which was a true testament. A testament was considered a private law, which imposed on all and sundry the obligation not to occupy the estate left by a deceased person; it gave the *jus ad rem* only to the heir. If the heir was able to accept the testator's law, he was also obliged by it to accept ownership and enter into possession.

We concluded therefore that a true testament was not considered a donation (it differed from a legacy which was expressly called a donation)[423], but presupposed the establishment

---

[423] 'Making a legacy before the heir has been established is useless. Testaments take their force from the establishment of an heir. Consequently the head and the foundation of the whole testament is the establishment of the heir.' (*Inst.*, bk. 2, tit. 20: 34).

of an heir who had to carry out the legacy;[424] the testament was not a bilateral, but a unilateral act whose efficacy was found to reside solely in the will of the testator.[425]

1424. Natural succession and the force of the testator's will were, therefore, the two elements which attempted to preserve and reconcile all legislations. Our next step is to see the extent to which the testator's will can derogate from natural succession, and the extent to which it can not.

II.
The extension of the right to make a will contrary to the order of natural succession

1425. We have distinguished three kinds of natural heirs:

1. those who live in a family which has its own natural head, but have their own *peculia*;

2. those who live in a family, but have no *peculia* of their own;

3. separated relatives, to the degree determined by the relationship of feeling in force amongst families still in the state of nature.

a) Relative to *peculia*

1426. I call *peculia* those goods which a member of a family would possess exclusively under a good title if it were not necessary for every ownership entering a family to devolve on the head of the family. The member furnished with a title making him owner of goods has the ownership of these goods

---

[424] 'A legacy, therefore, is a DONATION left by a deceased person which has to be carried through by the heir' (bk. 3, tit. 2 , c. 20: 1).

[425] This is Justinian's starting principle; his laws are always aimed at supporting the will of the testator: 'We desire the will of the deceased to be given more weight, and we favour their will rather than their words' (*Inst. Just.*, bk. 2, tit. 20:2). 'Following what has been written as a norm while spurning the will of the testator is, we think, opposed to what is civil' (*ibid.* 34). Declarations of this kind are constantly being made by Justinian.

[1424–1426]

relative to everyone else except the natural head of the family [*App.*, no. 10].

1427. I said that the natural head of the family can make use of all the goods of the family for as long as he lives, and consume then as he pleases, provided he does this *reasonably*. But he cannot make a will about *peculia* because at his death there is already a title of ownership in favour of the member whose *peculium* it is. This member, as owner of the *peculium* relative to all other human beings and to the other members of the same family, now becomes the complete owner through the act of cessation on the part of the natural head of the family.

1428. Consequently, whoever steals the *peculium* commits an injustice not only towards the head of the house as representative of all the family, but also towards the relative owner of the *peculium* who has the right to use in his own name forceful means to gain restitution.

1429. The natural principle about *peculia* is present deep within Roman legislation although associated and clothed with positive dispositions. The more ancient laws started from the principle that everything acquired by a child or servant was acquired by his parents or his masters. An exception was then made first for the *peculium castrense*, and secondly for the *peculium quasi-castrense*. Finally Justinian recognised relative ownership of the children with regard to all the goods which came to them not from their father or from the goods of their father, but from elsewhere (*bona adventitia*). He decided that the father should have the usufruct, but not the ownership of such goods.[426]

---

[426] 'At one time, whatever came to your children of either sex while they were still under the power of their parents, was acquired by their parents indifferently (with the exception of *peculia castrensia*). It belonged to the parents in such a way that they could give it, whether it belonged to a son or a daughter, to another child or to an outsider; they could also sell it, or indeed apply it in any way whatsoever. To us, this seems inhuman, and we have set forth a general constitution which will spare children and retain the dignity due to fathers. We have indeed decided that if anything has come to a child from its father, it is, according to ancient observance, acquired in its entirety by the parent. There can be no cause for envy if what came from the father should now revert to him. But if the child has acquired anything for himself in some other way, the usufruct of this is acquired by the father, while the

[1427-1429]

1430. This disposition contains one element pertaining to the law of nature, and another pertaining to the positive law. In accordance with the natural element, the offspring has relative ownership during the father's lifetime, and full ownership after his death; in accordance with the positive element, which is dependent upon civil prudence, the living father is deprived of full ownership, and left with only the usufruct. This is to prevent the father's violating the relative ownership of the offspring by disposing of it unreasonably.[427]

1431. My opinion is that according to natural law, the father (or more generally the natural head of the house) is full owner and, as such, can during his lifetime dispose even of the *peculia*. But this law makes him the *full* owner provided he uses this ownership *reasonably*.

The positive legislator *cannot*, or better does not *see* how to take and determine this natural limit in order to render it effective. To preserve it, therefore, he takes ownership from the father and leaves him only usufruct. This is the way in which the human legislator goes about his work.

dominion of it remains with the child. In this way, what the child has obtained through its work or good fortune will not pass to others to the child's detriment (*Inst. Just.*, bk. 2, tit. 9: 1).

[427] According to the ancient Romans' concept of filiation, family members in direct line, ascendant or descendant, formed a single, undying person. In this way, all members of the family were together under an obligation to creditors. As time passed, this family *solidarity* appeared excessive, in accordance with a law governing the course of humanity, that is: 'The *individual* element, first absorbed by the *species*, gradually emerges and asserts itself.' As a result, the praetors, who were responsible for so many deviations from the laws of the XII Tables, successively permitted offspring not to accept the paternal heritage when it was overburdened with debt. 'They are called "necessary heirs" because the law of the XII Tables makes them heirs whether they like it or not, both in cases of intestacy and when a will has been left. But the praetor permitted those wishing to decline the inheritance to do so in order that the goods of the parent, rather than his own, should be seized by creditors.' (*Inst. Just.*, bk. 2, tit. 19: 2). Equally it was permitted that a bond-servant should be established as the heir so that creditors should distrain the bond-servant's goods rather than the testator's (*Inst. Just.*, bk. 2, tit. 19). As a result, the bond-servant could have *ownership relative* to everyone else, as far as the Romans were concerned, but not *full* ownership as long as he remained in servitude when he, too, was considered as belonging to the master.

[1430–1431]

Our study, however, has only rational Right as its object. We have to restrict ourselves to determining what is meant by *reasonableness* relative to the disposition made by the head of the house about the goods he possesses and administers.

1432. The head of the household, the full owner, is therefore the *competent judge* of the reasonable use he makes of what is his own. No other judgment is valid against the competent judge except that which is formed with the utmost consideration and maturity, and gives full *certainty* to the spirit (cf. 611, 612). Neither the family nor any of its members can oppose the use of the family-substance made by the head of the house unless there is complete certainty that he is consuming it unreasonably.

1433. Such *unreasonableness* in using up domestic resources is known when there is proof either

1. that he uses them *immorally*, for *immoral* and guilty purposes, or

2. he uses them *stupidly*, that is, aimlessly (in this case he is called a wastrel), or

3. he uses them *capriciously* by depriving the family of necessary sustenance or the children of education in order to satisfy some frivolous, superfluous purpose.

1434. The unreasonable use of the family substance (a use to which the owner has no right) consists in these three abuses. Such abuse gives the co-owning, oppressed family, or whoever acts on their behalf,[428] a just title for effectively opposing the head of the house in the most peaceful, least violent way.

---

[428] Civil society, if already instituted, has to undertake the defence of the family. The history of primitive nations shows that grown-up sons were called to govern the family with the father. This came about *on the father's part* because he naturally desired, and had to desire, to be helped in the government of the house by the wisdom of his sons, and wished to have them as witnesses to justify his administration. It came about *on the part of the grown offspring* because they wished to see some achievement of their own, and felt that they had the forces necessary to make their achievements prevail in the house. Daughters, who lacked such a force, remained in an inferior condition. We have an example of this amongst the Hebrews where the father invariably married off his daughters with the consent of their brothers (Gen 24: 50; 34: 5 ss.; 2 Sam 13: 20, 29). Giovanni Jahn, in his *Archeologia biblica*, defines betrothal amongst the Hebrews as: 'A pact between the father and the brothers german of the bride, and the father of the bridegroom.' Again: 'In

1435. But if these abuses are set aside, the father, or the mother in his place, can dispose during his lifetime of all that the family possesses, not only for the family's immediate good, but also in the exercise of beneficence and any moral virtue or decent and useful end whatsoever. But in death he cannot dispose of the *peculia* because those who possess the title of ownership, whose effectiveness remains suspended by the authority of the parent, are already owners. The father cannot attribute to others the substance which, at his passing, already has a master.[429]

1436. Equally, a member of the family who has a *peculium* cannot leave it in a will during the life of a predecessor in the direct line, in whose power and family he resides, unless he has descendants. If he dies, his *peculium*, now naturally free, falls to the head of the house.

b) Relative to other goods of the head of the household; to the disadvantage of other members of the family

1437. The association or non-association of members in a natural family does not depend simply upon their being united physically, but on the power of the father, or of some other person over them in the direct line, who governs them and administers the common patrimony.[430]

the betrothal were established not only the marriage but also the gifts which were to be given to the brothers german of the bride and the price of the bride which was to be presented to her father' (§153). Moreover, at the father's death the daughters themselves belonged to the inheritance of the brothers, who sold them as wives.

[429] According to natural Right, the *patria potestas*, springing from the title of generation, is the reason why the father disposes during life of the *peculia* (cf. 781-790). But this power cannot, as something personal, be transmitted as an inheritance. The same applies to the father's ownership of the *peculia*. Roman laws themselves, which gave fathers the right to sell their children and even put them to death, recognised that the *patria potestas* was personal and could not be handed on through testament. Hence 'those who are under the *patria potestas* become *sui juris* at his death' (*Inst. Just.*, bk. 1, tit. 12).

[430] The Romans, too, recognised this. Their laws prevented the loss of

1438. Although descendants in the direct line are always dependent upon the predecessors who authored them, they cease to be members of the same family, strictly speaking, when they form another family and no longer depend upon the predecessors as governors of the family and dispensers of its ownership. In this case, they depend upon the predecessors simply as authors of their life.[431]

1439. The predecessor in the direct line may have a reasonable cause for depriving a descendant, who is with him at home, of all or part of the inheritance. If so, he has the right to do it.[432] But if there were no cause, he would seem to violate the law of nature by doing this.[433]

---

rights on the part of a person who was taken as a slave by the enemy. This was called the *jus postliminium*, and enabled the captured person to be considered as present: '*Postliminium* is a fiction that treats the person taken captive as though he were always in the city' (*Inst. Just.*, bk. 1, tit. 12: 5).

[431] Thus the emancipated offspring themselves were called *extraneous heirs* by the Romans. 'So our children also who are no longer under our power are considered as heirs established by and extraneous to us (*Inst. Just.*, bk. 2, tit. 19: 3).

[432] Roman laws, too, declared *inoperative* any testament which disinherited the son without cause. 'Often parents disinherit or omit their children from their wills without cause. Hence, we give leave for an action to be brought by children who complain that they themselves have been wrongfully disinherited or excluded. For instance, they might claim that those who drew up the will were not *mentis compotes* at that moment. This is said not because the testator was out of his mind, but because the will, although correctly made, did not result from THE DUTY OF PIETY' (*Inst. Just.*, bk. 2, tit. 18). I wanted to offer this quotation here to show once more how Roman common sense founded *right* on *moral obligation*, as we do constantly. Another point to notice is that the same cause (the need for a valid reason if offspring were to be disinherited without injustice) impelled Roman laws to require that the disinheritance be expressly declared in the will. If it was passed over in silence, the will was invalid. This was first required for male offspring alone, then required by the praetors for female offspring. They made an exception, however, for already emancipated offspring who did not form a single family with the father. 'It is not necessary to establish or disinherit emancipated offspring by civil right because they are not HIS heirs (*Inst. Just.*, bk. 2, tit. 13: 3). This shows how much force was attributed to co-ownership in the family society.

[433] Domat (*Lois civiles*, c. 11, §16) teaches that the obligation of fathers to leave their goods to their children pertains to natural law. According to Montesquieu fathers are obliged only to feed their children (*L'Esprit des*

1440. A reasonable cause can only be one of the two following:

1. some grave fault on the part of the children or other descendants which merits such a punishment; or

2. the exercise by the father of some great act of virtue such as gratitude willingly shown towards a friend and benefactor of the house in reduced circumstances who can be recompensed by a legacy or by part of the inheritance. Another example would be public beneficence, which draws a person to leave something for works of general assistance, and so on.

1441. But only the first of these two causes would be sufficient to authorise the parent or predecessor in the direct line to deprive the offspring of the entire inheritance, except perhaps for the part needed for their maintenance or education.

1442. If on the other hand the offspring had sufficient *peculia*, the father is free to dispose in his will of whatever is his own for either of the two causes we have indicated.

1443. It would seem that the father is, according to natural Right, entirely free to prefer one child in preference to another provided he does so in such a way that the necessities of life are not withheld from anyone without fault, and that there is a good reason for acting in this way.

1444. Nevertheless the testator cannot invert the order of personal power. A grandfather can make a grandson his heir, but cannot deprive the grandson's father of the *full* ownership of such an inheritance, which thus becomes the *peculium* of his child.

1445. The substance of the question is left intact whether the inheritance passes directly to the heir required by the law of nature or by means of a trustee, provided the *fidei-commissa* is put into effect, and is required by some necessity or utility.

1446. The principles we have explained show that the perpetual bonds placed upon family resources, unlimited *fidei-commissa*, and the total right to inheritance of the nearest of kin are the invention of political and civil jurists. Such laws do not result from natural Right, but are opposed to it because harmful to the personal authority of the head of the family.

Lois, bk. 26, c. 9).

[1440–1446]

1447. Let us imagine that a testator obliges his descendants to hand on some possession from first-born to first-born without their being able to alienate it. In doing so, he reduces the fullness of their *patria potestas* which requires that during the father's lifetime he may dispose as he pleases of all the goods of the family itself, and even of his children's *peculia*.[434]

1448. It is true that the predecessor in the direct line can make successory agreements with his linear descendant, but in this case the bond arises from the free will of the latter, and is confined to him. The recommendations left by the predecessor to his linear descendants would not constitute jural duties. Nevertheless, civil laws should be careful not to place the least impediment to their spontaneous execution on the part of the successors.

c) Relative to kindred who are not in the family

1449. The will of the testator is entirely free relative to kindred who are separated from the family and thus no longer hold any co-ownership. Moral duty will indeed require the testator to follow what is suitable, but separated kindred can never reasonably infringe his dispositions.

---

[434] The reason for believing that the head of a family can bind all his descendants in their use of the goods he leaves is the *patria potestas*, which first presents itself to the human spirit as something absolute and unlimited. We have seen this occur relative to *ownership* (cf. 921-953). Such persuasion arises in the parent or owner because persons are from the beginning totally intent upon themselves alone and place themselves at the centre of everything. As a result, persons consider all that is within their power as their very *own*. Only later do they come to realise that there are other persons outside themselves, equal to them and essentially respectable. The reverence due to them puts limits to their own power and ownership. At that point, ownership takes on moral limits and changes into *right*. In the same way, the *power* of parents becomes *right*, authority, moral power when it is enclosed in restrictions dependent upon the respect due to the offspring as persons. We have to distinguish, therefore, between *patria potestas* and the *right of patria potestas* as we have distinguished between *ownership* and the *right of ownership*.

Article 2.
How rights pass from one subject to another without
undergoing any alteration by way of contract

§1. *Various possible alterations to rights*

1450. According to the principles previously established, the human person is an inviolable activity. Persons can *enjoy* and *suffer*. Whoever makes a person suffer when there is no just cause to do so, violates and offends that person.

1451. Human beings enjoy:

1. what is joined to them by nature;
2. their own activity;
3. what they join to themselves by their own activity.

No one can detach from human beings, without injuring them, what they have joined to themselves with a jural bond; no one can directly impede the activity of human beings if this activity does not attempt to detach what others have joined to self by means of a jural bond, nor attempt to cause others suffering.

1452. The primordial rights of human beings are the faculty of enjoying that which is united to persons by nature, and the faculty of joining to themselves that which is not joined to others (cf. 246-262).

Activity is necessary both for *enjoying* and for *doing*. Right, therefore, which relative to its form is a *moral* activity, supposes prior to itself a *real* activity or faculty for acquiring and disposing of the object of right.

It would be madness to assert that anyone has the right to do those things which are and always will be completely outside the sphere of the capacity of his nature; it would be insane for anyone to say that he had the right to carry on his shoulders a weight one hundred thousand times greater than his strength, or that he had a right to walk on air, or dance on the tip of a church spire.

1453. But if a right, a faculty, cannot be conceived without some *real* faculty, it is not however necessary that such a faculty extend as far as the moral faculty, nor that it be a direct faculty.

It is sufficient for it to be a real, virtual faculty. This needs explaining.

Relative to enjoyment, although I may not have the physical faculty for drinking all the wine in my cellar, or eating all the grain in my barn, my right still extends to all the wine and all the grain. I can in fact consume by means of others the part I find impossible to consume for myself. I have the moral-physical faculty to have these foods used and consumed. And that is sufficient for me to possess the right of ownership over them.

Relative to doing, if I do not have the direct physical power to do one particular thing, but do have the power to do another, and with this done, the power to do another and so on until I arrive at the last thing, which is what I set out to do in the first place, I can justly say that I have the faculty for doing the last thing of all, although my power to achieve it is not direct. This chain of faculties or varied length of means, is present in practically all operations of some importance. I cannot, for instance, build a house in the bat of an eyelid; I have to pass through a long series of operations which gradually lead to the completion of the house or even of a palace. I can, therefore, say that I have the physical power to do this, even though the faculty is not direct. An indirect physical faculty is sufficient to constitute the *matter* of rights.

1454. Two physical powers correspond to the two primordial rights: the power to enjoy what is joined[435] to my person (ownership); and the power of joining to my person other things which are free, in other words of making them my own (freedom).[436]

1455. Both these powers can be direct or indirect. I have the direct physical power of enjoyment if I find the pleasure I am seeking in an operation which I myself do. I have the direct physical power of making something my own if I can unite

---

[435] The mere faculty of acting when the action is not aimed at enjoying anything, or at joining anything to the person, has no reference to any right. But in so far as the pleasure joined to the activity is kept in mind, mere activity is also included in the physical power or faculty for enjoyment, and is referred to ownership, the first of the two primordial rights.

[436] By 'joining something to a person' I always mean 'uniting it with the bond of ownership'. This bond has been the object of lengthy analysis in the preceding books.

anything to myself by the bond of ownership. On the other hand, I have only indirect power to enjoy something or make it my own if, in order to reach the enjoyment I seek or make something my own, I have to perform successive operations or make others do them.

1456. The state of my rights can, therefore, be altered in two ways: either relative to the *matter of right* or relative to the *form of right*. The matter of right is the physical activity or power; and the form is the moral faculty or power.

1457. The physical power of right varies

1. according to the aim to which the physical power is referred (making something one's own, or enjoyment);

2. according to the nature of the physical power itself (direct or indirect, more or less indirect, in a variety of ways and degrees).

1458. Therefore, in order to say that a right passes from one subject to another without undergoing any alteration (in other words, the only modification is the change of subject), we have to be able to affirm that nothing, either in the *physical power* or the *moral power*, changes in the right.

1459. We say 'in the *right*' because we are consistently dealing with the power which constitutes right, not with a physical power which can vary accidently in the persons forming the subjects of rights. The physical power accidentally adhering to persons is relative to the *exercise of right*, not to the *right* itself in its substance. Thus, if I sell my horse, the buyer acquires through the sale a right over the horse exactly equal to the right that I had. It is of no consequence that I can ride the horse because I am well, and that he cannot because he is sick. My physical power, as inherent in the right, has passed to him; he has the horse in his possession and can use it as I used it, even though he is forced to exercise this faculty by means of others.

If, however, I sell my horse, receive the price for it, but do not consign it to the buyer, he does not have the same right over it that I had. Before being able to make use of the horse as I did, he needs another fact, that is, he has to enter into possession of his horse. In this case, his physical faculty differs from that which I had in using the animal. This difference is inherent to the state of the transmitted right, not accidental to the person. In other words, limitation of the physical power proceeds from the right, from the incomplete act of transmission, not from the conditions of the person to whom the right has passed.

§2. *What is needed in order to say that a right has changed its subject without undergoing alteration*

1460. To be able to say that a right, in passing from one subject to another, has not undergone alteration, the same right, when found in the second subject, must be in the exact state in which it was found in the first. This applies both to the moral faculty and the physical faculty supposed by the right.

1461. If the act of transmission remains doubtful or defective in any way, the second subject will lack the full jural faculty present in the first. If the first subject had not only the right of ownership but also possession of the thing in question, and this possession is lacking in the second subject, it cannot be said that the transmitted right is the same as it was in the previous state.

1462. Hence contracts, by which an entire right passes from one subject to another, have to be put into effect in order that the right in question may be passed without alteration.

§3. *Contracts by which rights are transmitted without alteration.*

1463. There are, therefore, two species of contracts, one of which transmits rights from one person to another, but with certain alterations to the rights; the other transmits rights which remain unaltered, although they do undergo alteration during transmission and until transmission is complete.

1464. To discover which rights are transmitted from one person to another without alteration, we have to compare the state of the two persons before the beginning of the contract and after its fulfilment. The comparison will show that contracts which of their nature transmit rights without altering them are:

1. Amongst gratuitous contracts, *simple donation* which aims merely at passing the gift from one owner to another.

2. Amongst onerous contracts, *barter* and *sale*. Barter aims at passing something I own to the ownership of another, and something he owns to me; a sale also does this, but one of the parties, instead of passing some thing into the other's ownership, passes instead the money-value of what he receives.

Article 3.
How obligations corresponding to rights change their subject

1465. We need to note that not only rights, but their corresponding obligations are transmitted from one subject to another. First, it is clear that when a right is transmitted from one subject to another, the obligation to respect the right has also passed between the subjects: the person having the right prior to its transmission acquires the obligation to respect the same right in the person to whom he has transmitted it; the other person, who had the obligation, now acquires the right in exchange.

1466. Another change arises in the jural condition relative to all other persons. Previously, they had to pay the respect owed to the right to the subject originally possessing it; now, they are obliged to devote the same respect to the subject to whom the right has been transmitted.

1467. These changes in the subjects of the obligations correspond exactly with the changes in the subjects of the rights, and are their consequence. But we have to note that changes can arise in subjects of jural obligations without change in subjects of corresponding rights. In other words, changes in subjects of jural obligation may take place differently from changes in subjects of corresponding rights.

Mankind, for example, changes every time new people are born and old people die; subjects of obligation change, but there is no change in rights corresponding to them. All have to respect the rights of each so that as people are born and die, the number of subjects to be respected increases or decreases; but my rights, and those of every other person who is the object of such a duty, are not necessarily changed.

1468. We have spoken about rights relative to different

persons; we have said that right is always a relationship in which the terms, that is, the person having the right and the person having the obligation, can change; we have said that rights can cease relative to one or several persons without their ceasing relative to every person or to other persons; and rights towards new persons can come into being in the same way. All this shows that subjects of obligations can and do change without difficulty, independently of change in the subjects of the rights corresponding to these obligations.

CHAPTER 3

Rights whose form is changed by transmission

1469. Let us now consider rights in the various forms they take when transmitted. We said that these forms are changed either at the moment of transmission (*transitory alteration*) or as an effect of completed transmission (*final* or stable alteration).

1470. Both kinds are seen in the two modes of transmission we have discussed: 1. abandonment and occupancy; 2. contracts.

Article 1.
Alterations which take place in forms of rights when these are transmitted by successive abandonment and occupancy

1471. The simple abandonment of a right is not its transmission. The only necessary effect of the abandonment of right is the cessation in others of the corresponding *obligation*.

1472. If the right in question involves external ownership, a second effect arises in addition to the cessation in others of the obligation to respect that ownership. This effect is the freedom we all acquire to occupy an object which has no owner. But according to the distinction we made between what is *lawful* and what is *of right*, this freedom is not in itself a right;[437] it takes on the nature of right only in relationship to the person who capriciously disturbs my freedom (cf. 284).

1473. Moreover, if the abandonment of my right is not universal, but relative to only one human being, then this individual has the faculty to occupy the thing abandoned to him. He thus truly acquires a right *ad rem* (a third jural effect of abandonment); he alone can lawfully appropriate and use the thing ceded to him. The same happens in wills: the testator determines the heir by his will and, as we have already noted, the heir acquires the right to have the heritage in virtue of the act of the testator's will. This right would be injured if another person occupied the heritage without waiting for the heir's declaration of acceptance or renunciation.

1474. These rights of *acceptance* or renunciation of what has been abandoned and offered possess a *transitory*, not a *final form*. The concept of right to the occupancy or appropriation of a thing contains only a kind of principle regulating the appropriation, although appropriation is its end.

1475. The *final forms* which rights can assume by this first mode of transmission are as innumerable as the *limits* within which the abandonment took place and as the *conditions* of the acceptance.

Because these forms, as divisions of rights, make an appearance when rights are transmitted in the second mode, the explanation we will give of their principal forms and divisions in the following article will be valid for both modes.

Article 2.
Contracts can alter the forms of rights

1476. We will first speak briefly about the *transitory forms* assumed by rights as a result of contracts, and afterwards about the *final forms*.

[437] *ER*, 324-325.

§1. Transitory *alterations in the forms of rights which take place between the initiation and conclusion of a contract*

1477. During the time between the initiation and finalisation of nearly all contracts the words and mutual acts of the contracting parties can change the reciprocal rights of the parties.

A.
Alteration of reciprocal rights in promissory contracts caused by acts of the parties

1478. The acts which initiate but do not finalise a contract can produce alterations in the mutual rights of the parties. These alterations are of many kinds, but the principal kind is found in those contracts we have called 'promissory',[438] *and consist of:*

1. the *promissory part*, which is distinct from the *executory* part and includes the *conditions* for the execution of the contract;

2. the *guarantees*, arbitrarily assumed or agreed relative to the execution of the contract;

3. the *facts opposed to the contract's execution*, which render it impossible, or extend the agreed time, or indicate reluctance about the execution;

4. the *coercive means* used by one of the parties to obtain from the other the execution of the contract;

5. the *problems* which arise concerning accepted agreements, or concerning acts performed or to be performed in order to effect the agreements;

6. the *acts* which deal with and solve these problems, the *transactions*, etc.

All six kinds of acts, which the parties can posit in the time between the agreement and its full execution, cause changes in the state of the parties' reciprocal rights.

1479. A little reflection upon each will easily persuade us that they alter the form of reciprocal rights.

---

438 Cf. *1081-1107.*

1. The *promissory part of the contract*. A serious promise that has been accepted is enough to make the claim to what has been promised pass to the accepter, and the corresponding obligation to the promiser.

1480. The same is true for all contracts containing a promise: their execution is not accomplished by one or both parties in the act itself but takes place at a future time. In these cases, before the contract is finalised and executed, the form of reciprocal rights is changed. The party that has either not, or only partly executed the contract remains bound by the jural duty to do so, and the other party reciprocally contracts the right to demand its execution.

1481. These promises can concern a thing or an action. They can be absolute or conditioned, and can vary in a thousand ways. Consequently, the form of the rights and obligations affecting the two parties takes on corresponding differences.

1482. The *conditions* applied to promissory contracts deserve our special attention. They can be of different kinds.

Some are called *suspensive* because the validity of the *obligation* assumed with the contract depends on the actuation or non-actuation of a given event.

Others, called *resolutive*, denote an event whose actuation or non-actuation terminates the right or rights which the contract attributed to one party or reciprocally to both parties.

1483. If the effect of the condition is bound to the actuation of the event, the condition is *positive*. If the effect is bound to the non-actuation of the event, the condition is *negative*. Finally, the condition is respectively *positive* and *negative* if both the actuation and the non-actuation of the event make a right pass from one party to the dominion of the other.

1484. This last case is verified in contracts of chance. Chance is usually an event which, no matter how it happens, produces a transmission of rights. Thus, gaming and contracts of chance are 'contracts binding under conditions which are respectively positive and negative.'

1485. The conditions which bring about wins and losses in gambling and other contracts of chance cannot be accurately classified among *suspensive* or *resolutive* conditions. We therefore make them a separate class and call them *attributive conditions* because they always attribute to the parties a win and a loss respectively.

1486. 2. *Agreed or freely assumed guarantees.* If guarantees are agreed, they pertain to the promissory part of the contract; if freely assumed, they produce various rights and obligations in both parties, according to their nature, that is, whether they are assumed reasonably, unduly, etc.

1487. 3. *Reluctance, delay in execution*, etc. These are acts offensive to the other party which oblige the reluctant person to make satisfaction and restitution according to the circumstances and corresponding rights in the second party.

1488. 4. *Coercive measures.* Coercive acts are an exercise of rights acquired by a party injured by another's reluctance to execute everything agreed. These acts can cause various changes in the state of mutual rights, and various reciprocal jural attitudes, according to their quality, quantity or modality, and in so far as they effect execution of the promises contained in the contract.

1489. 5. *Problems and disputes about agreements and about their fulfilment.* The obscurity of agreements, the uncertainty of fulfilment — in a word, doubts of every kind that can arise after agreements have been made, whether the parties act in good faith or not — also alter the state and form of the parties' rights and their jural relationships.

1490. 6. *Negotiations regarding settlement, transactions*, etc. Finally, negotiations and adjustments by the parties are accidents which place the parties in different positions relative to rights. Every phrase or word, as it were, of one of the parties imposes on the other a jural duty of responding in one way or another.

B.
Executory contracts

1491. We must note with particular attention that all these different kinds of intermediary acts posited between the initiation and execution of a contract can be formed into special contracts, called 'accessory' by some authors precisely because they are understood as completing another contract which, relative to them, is called 'principal'.

1492. We call these contracts 'executory'. The following are some examples: 1. *Contractual penalty*, by which both parties, or only one, oblige themselves to make compensation or undergo some penalty if they do not execute the contract, or if they withdraw from it.

1493. A penalty stipulated for the party *who does not execute a contract* which continues to subsist, is a true *contractual penalty*.

A penalty stipulated to allow withdrawal from the contract, is a kind of restitution or substitution (*mulcta poenitentialis*).

An article of value is called a 'pledge' if the party held by a penalty hands it over to the other with the intention of forsaking it in the case of non-fulfilment of the contract. A pledge given as proof and sanction of the contract, is a so-called *probatory pledge*; given in compensation for the possibility of withdrawing from the contract as a result of a change of mind, it is a *penalising or liberating pledge*.[439]

1494. 2. *Guarantee on the thing sold* against appropriation or defects discovered in it, which gives the purchaser the right to restitution from the seller.

1495. 3. *Indemnity*, by which a person assumes an obligation to give or do something for someone else, if the latter does not give or do it. This contract gives a creditor the right to demand what has been promised from the indemnifier provided the principal debtor has in fact failed to fulfil his obligation.

1496. 4. *Pledge*. By this contract a debtor consigns something

---

[439] Although in the state of nature a contractual penalty without a pledge might seem superfluous, the following reasons show that this si not so:

1. The failure to execute the contract does not entirely originate from wickedness; sometimes there may be simply negligence, forgetfulness, laziness or debility on the part of the offending party. Thus, when the applied penalty is burdensome and particularly well-defined, it helps to recall the obligation and fix it firmly in mind.

2. Because the offended party must first try to apply the *contractual penalty*, it helps him determine a procedure for maintaining his own right. He then can go further if the contract still has to be executed, or stop if it has not.

of value to a creditor to satisfy him if the debtor does not pay by the stipulated time.

1497. If the thing consigned is immovable, the contract would correspond to *mortgage* in civil law.[440]

1498. Whenever a pledge is more valuable than a debt, and there has been no agreement that the pledge should remain entirely the creditor's if satisfaction is not made in time, the contract would contain a mixture of *pledge* and *contractual penalty*. Roman law calls this kind of pact 'commissory law'.[441]

1499. If a pledge increases in value, the increase is understood to belong to the creditor and reduce the debt. In this case the contract is called 'antichresis'.

1500. 5. *Preliminary transactions*, which prepare the way for final transactions to a dispute, are also executory contracts.

1501. One example is *contractual sequestration*, in which the parties agree to consign the disputed thing to the care of a third party until the dispute is solved.

All these and similar contracts arise during the time between agreements and their execution and fulfilment. During this interval they alter the jural relationships of the parties and thus produce reciprocal rights and obligations.[442]

---

[440] In civil law, real consignment of what is immovable is not necessary; a *symbolical* consignment is sufficient, that is, some record in registers of public mortgages. Social pressure makes the registration effective, and more effective than consignment of what is immovable. But could a mortgage pact have any jural effect in the state of nature? It could have the effect of determining the creditor's procedure whenever he had to obtain satisfaction by taking over the debtor's goods. In other words he would first of all have to turn to the mortgaged goods; at least this would seem to be the sense of a mortgage.

[441] Ulpian., *Dig.*, bk. 18, tit. 3, law 4; *Cod. Teod.*, bk. *De commiss. rescind.* — Last book of *Cod. de pact. pign.*

[442] If we consider the intimate nature of executory acts and contracts, we find they are always a *different exercise* of the same right. Every right is exercised in many ways, of which we have listed eight (cf. 966). Every act therefore by which a right *is exercised* is the cause of some change in the right itself.

§2. Final *changes in the forms of rights*
as effects of the fulfilment of contracts

A.
Changes which arise from the nature of
momentary contracts and *lasting* contracts

1502. We must first distinguish between contracts of immediate and those of protracted execution. We call the former *momentary contracts* and the latter, *lasting contracts.*

1503. *Donation, sale, barter, assignment, betting* and *games of chance* are by their nature momentary contracts, because they can all be executed instantaneously.[443]

1504. *Lasting contracts,* such as *commodatum, loan, usury, precarium, deposit, pledge, lease, employment, mandate, emphyteusis, rent, life annuity, agistment* and *social contracts* have as their aim something whose execution requires time or a series of successive acts.

1505. What is the difference between *lasting* contracts and what we have called *executory* contracts?

Contracts are called *executory* not because they accomplish what has been agreed, but because their purpose is to initiate the execution or the effective result. Hence, contracts are called *lasting* whose execution does not begin and end in a moment but lasts for some time before their completion.

1506. Consequently, some contracts considered under different aspects can be both *executory* and *lasting;* others, *lasting* and *non-executory;* others again, *executory* and *non-lasting.*

1507. For example, a pledge is an *executory* contract when considered as intended to obtain actual payment of a debt — it

---

[443] I classify *betting* and *games of chance* among momentary contracts because their execution is carried out in a moment, when the event about which the bet has been made takes place, or at the end of the game where there is only winner or loser. Both the time which elapses until the jural event and the time necessary for the conclusion of the game are not part of the execution of the contract; they simply make way for and prepare the execution. This period of time therefore and the players' actions belong to the part of the contract preceding its execution, which we discussed in the previous paragraph.

is not payment, that is, the effect and intention of the principal contract. But considered under a temporal aspect, it can be placed among *lasting* contracts.

On the other hand, *employment* is simply a *lasting* contract. If I engage a person for paid work, whatever he does forms a continuing series during the length of time for which I engage him; he has begun to execute his contract on the very first day he works for me. Thus the contract is always moving forward to its execution and completion.

1508. *Executory* acts and contracts therefore precede both momentary and lasting promissory contracts, whose execution they are intended to accomplish.

1509. The difference between the changes caused by momentary and lasting contracts in the forms of rights is as follows. Momentary contracts accomplish the execution of a contract instantaneously and therefore effect only one change. Lasting contracts, however, accomplish their execution a little at a time by successive acts, and therefore give rise to a series of purely successive changes; every step the parties take in the execution of the contract changes their jural state and their mutual relationships, reducing and altering their reciprocal obligations and rights.

If I let a house for three years, I make a lasting contract. It is clear that when the first year has ended and the rent has been paid, my right has been lessened relative to the tenant, and his obligation and right to me.

1510. Hence, in lasting rights, the time during which the acts of execution are carried out, or an obligation to carry them out is contracted, divides the rights and obligations in different ways, causing a continuous change in the forms of the rights and in the mutual jural obligations and attitudes.

1511. This division of the rights and the progressive change of the reciprocal obligations arises from the nature of the contract, which can be executed and completed only by degrees and after some length of time. But the rights and obligations also split in different ways because of the law they receive from the parties' will, which freely determines the terms of the contract.

B.
Alterations resulting from the will of the contracting parties which determines the terms of the contract

I.
Summary, and connection with what follows

1512. Let us first summarise what we have said so far about the changes taking place in the *forms* of rights as a consequence of the two modes of transmission described earlier. We said that:

1. Some changes in the forms of rights and obligations are produced by the simple abandonment of a right in favour of others who acquire the *right of occupancy* to what was abandoned. Their acceptance also gives them *ownership* of the abandoned thing according to the form and conditions of the abandonment. This form is one that can depend on the free will of the person who abandons his right to others. We will speak about it later.

2. Some changes in the forms of rights and jural obligations are produced by certain acts and contracts done in order to obtain and ensure the execution of (*executory*) agreements. We called these changes *transitory*.

3. Other changes are produced in those (*lasting*) contracts whose execution necessarily takes place gradually within a given period. These changes can be called *successive*.

4. Finally, there are changes which produce some *final* forms of rights. These forms remain in jural relationships between people after the *transmission* of rights is completed and contracts fully executed.

1513. The production of these changes is influenced first of all by the nature of things, that is, the nature of acts and contracts which have their own laws, and secondly by disagreement among the parties, one of whom is not entirely satisfied about the completed agreement. Nevertheless, the greatest influence in determining the forms which rights receive in their transmission is exercised by the unified wills of the parties, when they make the agreements. These unified wills are the theme, as it were, from which spring all the unwilled changes, resulting either from unforeseen accidents or the bad will of one of the parties who fails to fulfil the conditions of the agreement.

We can now indicate the most important of these final forms determined by agreements and the other two causes described above.

II.
The ways in which a right is exercised, and its various forms

1514. We must first distinguish between the *exercise* and the *substance* of right.[444] We must also distinguish between the various *ways in which* a right *is exercised* and the various *forms* it can take. This distinction was discussed elsewhere, when we listed eight ways in which the same right can be exercised. We also said that these eight ways could accurately be called 'variations' of right (cf. 970-974).

1515. The various ways in which a right can be exercised are causes modifying and changing the forms of rights, but they are not the *forms* retained by a right after its modification. We must now list these forms.

III.
Principal forms of rights

1516. *Enjoying* is a form of passivity; *doing*, of activity. When passivity and activity are subjects of our right, they must be respected; we must not be disturbed either in our enjoyment or in what we do. The first two most universal *forms* of rights are: the right to enjoyment and the right to action, that is, *ownership* and *freedom*, to which we have reduced all possible rights and from which all possible rights flow (cf. 59-67). The *right to enjoyment* presupposes the enjoyment of some ownership, and the *right to act* is freedom itself raised to the state of right.

1517. We are able to *enjoy* ourselves, our nature and the things

---

[444] The substance of right is 'a moral faculty'; the exercise, 'an act of this faculty'.

joined to our nature; this is *internal* and *external ownership*. We can also *perform* two kinds of jural actions, that is, we can exercise the rights we already have and acquire new ones; we have *freedom to exercise* and *freedom to acquire* rights. The two primitive forms of rights therefore can be split into four: two kinds of ownership (internal and external) and two kinds of freedom (the exercise and acquisition of rights).

1518. The *act* of acquiring rights can in general be called *appropriation*, a word which includes all the particular ways in which acquisition can be carried out. But in addition to the *act* of acquisition there is the *jural power of appropriation*.

The *act of acquisition* is not always the exercise of one of our rights; it can be a simple *lawful action*, according to the distinction we made between simple freedom to act (innocuous freedom) and a right to act (jural freedom).[445]

The *jural* power of appropriation is a right which gives us a preference over other human beings in the acquisition of some good. We are directed to this acquisition either by the nature of the thing or by someone's authoritative will (this is frequently the case in natural or testamentary successions).

1519. These rights can be called rights of *appropriation*; we do not acquire them by our act but, as we said, by the nature of things or by someone else's act. Rights of ownership, on the other hand, require our act of acceptance.[446]

---

[445] Cf. *ER*, 324-325.

[446] Possession of a thing is simply a fact. The fact, if legitimate, is not the *substance* itself of the right of ownership, but an *exercise* of the right of ownership. When, for example, we are given a donation, we have *a right of acceptance* or *appropriation* (*jus ad rem*); this right belongs to the group of rights we have classified under the title, *Right of freedom relative to action* (cf. 325). As soon as we have accepted and appropriated the gift, we have *ownership* (*jus in re*), that is, we have the right to all possible acts of the object; we can take possession of some thing which has already become ours. This right belongs to the group of *rights of absolute freedom to a thing* (cf. 251-253). Legislators distinguish between obligations arising from *pure consent* and those arising from consent connected with the *handing-over of the thing*. They acknowledge that pure consent sometimes involves a real right (*jus in re*). Ulpian, for example, says about pledge: 'A pledge is contracted not only by handing-over but by pure consent even when it is not handed over' (*Digest.*, bk. 13, t. 7, 1). However, they deny that it produces *dominion*. Reasons for their view can be found in Gomez (*Resol.*, t. 2, c. 15,

1520. Hence right *ad rem*, which consists 'in the power to acquire a right', is a particular form of the very general right of *jural freedom*; but right *in re* is always some kind of ownership.

We must now examine the principal, particular forms into which ownership and freedom are split through agreements.

1521. Agreements themselves are an exercise of our rights. Thus rights are split and individualised by their very exercise.

IV.
The splits in and modification of the right of ownership

1522. Right is a relationship.[447] But relationships are the work of reason. Reason is therefore the cause of rights.

Reason is that which sees and posits various relationships between things, feelings and human beings, each of which is, or certainly contains, an abstraction. Abstraction is inexhaustible, and relationships therefore innumerable. A thing can be considered by the abstracting mind under countless partial aspects, each of which can become the term of a relationship with other things and with their partial aspects. By means of its faculty for abstraction and reference, reason is the cause of the splits in rights, splits which are themselves unlimited. Because our discussion is solely about jural relationships, we correctly call the cause of these relationships 'jural reason'.

1523. Earlier we examined the principal relationships involved in the concept of ownership. We found that they could be reduced to three: 1. a predisposition to the use of the object; 2. its actual use; and 3. pure ownership of the object. We said these constituted the three groups of rights from which full ownership results.[448] These groups can be found or considered as separate. Thus we have the first splits in ownership.

---

n. 23) and Loriotto (*De transactionib. axiom.*, 60). — In my opinion the matter is clarified and simplified by distinguishing, as I have done, between *promissory contracts* and other contracts, and restricting the need for the *real handing-over* of the thing to these alone.

[447] Right is 'a faculty sanctioned by the moral law which prohibits others from violating it.' It is clear therefore that the nature of right consists in a *relationship* between one who has the faculty and others who must respect it.

[448] Cf. 968-1003.

1524. If only one of these groups of rights adheres to a person, the split in right concerns the *form*, that is, the moral faculty. If all three adhere to a person, but because of a defect in the object of right or because of an imperfect transmission cannot be put into act, the split in right concerns the *matter*, that is, the physical faculty joined to right.[449]

Let us briefly analyse the principal contracts to discover how these splits in right of ownership are operative in them.

a) *Contracts involving the* right of predisposition

1525. The first group of rights in the class of ownership is the *right of predisposition*. This right can concern a right not yet acquired, or the use of a right already acquired.

1526. If it concerns a right not yet acquired, it is the same as the 'power to acquire a right', which we described above.

1527. If the *right of predisposition* concerns the use of a right already acquired, it is 'the power to carry out all that is necessary to make full use of some thing'.

1528. Various contracts relate to both these parts of the right of predisposition. We must note therefore that the principal contracts whose object is the right of predisposition are those which depend on *suspensive* or *attributive* conditions, in so far as the right of predisposition is 'a right to acquire a right' (*jus ad rem*).

1529. The *conditions* on which the acquisition of a right depends originate either 1. in the will of the person who has the right; or 2. in the agreement made between the two contracting wills; or 3. in an event independent of, but indicated by the parties' wills as a condition of acquisition.

1530. The following therefore are contracts whose object is a right of predisposition:

1. *Contract of donation*. As long as the donation is proffered but not accepted, the donee has only 'the right to acquire a right', that is, he has the first kind of *right of predisposition*.

---

[449] I say 'joined to right' because the inability to use a right joined to the subject does not, properly speaking, split the matter of right.

The condition for acquiring the right is *acceptance*, which is therefore dependent on the will of someone with a similar right.

1531. 2. *Contract with withdrawal penalty*. In this contract, the parties agree that either may withdraw from the contract on condition that the party who withdraws pays the other a stated fine. As long as the contract is not completed, the parties have no certain right over the object but an uncertain right, which may refer either to the object of the contract or to the fine. Because the matter is not determined, there is no right of ownership but only a right consisting 'in the faculty to acquire the right of ownership'. In other words, a right of predisposition exists, and the condition for acquiring the right of ownership depends on the will of the agreeing parties.[450]

1532. 3. *Contracts of chance*. In these contracts the parties receive only a right to acquire a right. We are still dealing therefore with the first kind of right of predisposition, which concerns an *attributive* condition whose fulfilment depends solely on the case itself, not on the wills of the parties.

1533. Every right of predisposition is something, and has a value; it can also be sold to others. In the contract by which the *expectation* of chance is bought, a right of predisposition is traded. This is the case of lottery-ticket sellers, of a longed-for win in a gambling game, etc, or of those who cede to another whatever eventual expectation they have.

1534. The object therefore of all contracts in which the transmission of rights depends on *suspensive* and *attributive* conditions is the right of predisposition (as I have defined it), that is, the right to acquire a right.

The same can be said about contracts qualified by *resolutive* conditions, but with this difference: because the contract is executed before the condition is fulfilled, two distinct periods exist: one between the contract's formation and its execution;

---

[450] It may be objected that the *condition* even in this contract depends on the will of only one of the parties, that is, of the one who withdraws. This certainly helps the fulfilment of the condition, but the event would not take place unless the other party's will accepts the withdrawal, willingly or unwillingly, from the contract to which he has obliged himself. Thus, although the parties do not contribute equally with their wills to the fulfilment of the condition, they both contribute, one actively, the other passively.

[1531–1534]

the other between its execution and the fulfilment of the condition. Each period has its own forms of rights: in the first, the contract has given the parties only 'a right to the acquisition of a right'; in the second (during which the contract was executed) one of the parties has acquired a right of ownership, which he may lose upon fulfilment of the resolutive condition which restores things to their former state. Consequently, in this second period, the party who executed the contract has 'a right to the re-acquisition of a right', while the other party has a corresponding obligation.

1535. The right of predisposition to acquire a right is of two kinds: it is a right to uncertain or certain acqisition

1536. The first kind is a *right of expectation*; the second, a *right to certain acquisition*.

1537. Because all the above-mentioned contracts are conditioned, their only subject is a right of expectation. We will consider a few examples of contracts whose subject is a right to certain acquisition:

1. *Contract of loan.* As long as the loan is not repaid, the lender has only the right to the certain acquisition of a right of ownership, that is, to the ownership of the sum to be repaid. Because the money lent is the property of the borrower, the lender has only the right to receive in exchange an equal sum of money. it is the borrower who provides the actual, real money for compensating the lender. Hence, as long as this money is not materially determined, the lender does not have any ownership, but only the right to certain acquisition of ownership.

1538. 2. *Sales contract.* As long as there is no payment for what has been sold and delivered, the seller has no ownership over the price. Because this is defrayed with money which is not materially determined, the necessary object of his ownership is lacking. He has only a right of predisposition, a right to certain acquisition of a right of ownership.[451]

---

[451] When one party has executed a sales contract by handing over what has been sold, and the other party has not paid for it within the agreed time, the one who gave the article can freely request the return of the object or payment for it. In this respect, a sales contract has an implied resolutive condition, which is acknowledged by civil legislators. The code of the king of Sardinia says: 'A resolutive condition is always understood as present in bilateral

1539. The same argument applies to all *commutative contracts* where the thing to be given obligatorily by one party to the other remains undetermined. In these contracts, only the right to the acquisition of ownership, not ownership itself, can be transmitted by virtue of the agreement alone.

1540. However, in a contract of *exchange*, the things whose ownership is exchanged are generally determined. The ownership therefore can pass reciprocally from one party to the other by virtue of the agreement alone.

1541. But if one of the parties has taken on an *alternative* obligation, that is, an obligation to give something or other, the agreement gives the other party only the right to the certain acquisition of the right of ownership, not ownership itself.

1542. 3. *Accepted promise of donation*, in which a right to certain acquisition of a thing, but not its ownership, is acquired.

1543. Even this right of predisposition, that is, 'a right to certain acquisition of a right of ownership' has a value of its own and can be an object of alienation. Thus, whenever a credit is ceded in a contract of *cession*, only this right of predisposition is sold. The same happens in the circulation of money drafts, in the buying and selling of gilts, in the case of paper currency, etc.

1544. Let us now consider the other kind of right of predisposition, which concerns *use*. I have defined it as 'the moral faculty to carry out, relative to a given thing, all that is necessary to exploit its usefulness.'

1545. The following is principally what we can do to a given thing in order to exploit its usefulness:
   1. take it physically into our power;
   2. keep it, once we have taken it;
   3. guard and defend it;
   4. work at it to make it usable, if it is not already so;

contracts when one of the parties does not satisfy his obligation. In this case the contract is not terminated with full right. The party for whom the agreement was executed has the choice of either constraining the other to fulfil the agreement, when this is possible, or to require termination together with damages and interest.' — Nevertheless, the resolutive condition inserted into these contracts differs from the resolutive condition established by the agreement of the parties. The latter is obligatory for both parties; the former is only facultative relative to the party who has executed the contract.

[1539–1545]

5. improve its condition;

6. do any work necessary to make it profitable.

These are minor rights, and they result from the division of that kind of right of predisposition which, we said, consists 'in being able to do what is necessary with a given thing in order to exploit its usefulness.'

1546. All these particular rights can be the matter of contracts.

1547. The following contracts have one or other of the above-mentioned rights of predisposition as their matter:

1. *Contract of deposit.* This contract concerns the detention of something. The depositary, relative to everybody except the depositor, has as much right to keep the thing entrusted to him as he has to keep the rest of his property. The depositor, of course, has the right to take back what is his when he wishes, if it was freely deposited.

1548. 2. *Conductio.* This contract can concern my right to guard and defend my goods, if I pay someone to guard and defend them. This person acquires the right to guard and defend these goods relative to everybody except the employer .

1549. The same contract can also concern any work I have the right to do relative to my goods, either in making them usable (if they are not so already), improving them, or making them profitable, depending on which of these rights is the purpose of the contract.

The person employed acquires the right, relative to everybody except the employer, to execute all the work entrusted to him . Thus, if someone prevented him from carrying out the work, his right would be violated .

1550. 3. *Mandate.* This contract can apply to any business entrusted to another, and therefore its matter can be any right of predisposition of the first or second kind.

I shall limit myself to the second kind. If I commission someone far away to send me some property of mine, I am by this mandate using my right to take what is mine. If I authorise him to form a commodatum for me or settle a dispute, I am again making use of different rights of predisposition, because these are acts with which, by means of another person, I wish to defend and take peaceful possession of my rights. The same must be said about other things.

[1546–1550]

b) *Contracts involving the rights of use*

1551. The *right of use* can also be split into minor rights in countless ways. We must always bear in mind the principle that 'pure and simple right concerns only a single act'; other rights are *complexes* of many rights, that is, groups of rights.[452]

1552. The minor rights into which the right of use is commonly split arise from the limitations posited at the time of their use. The limitations can be time, or the tasks themselves, or any other circumstance posited by the nature of the matter, by human beings themselves or by contract. The two largest groups of these rights concern *use* (in the strictest sense), and the *benefit* from things.

1553. The following are the principal contracts which concern the *right of use* either entirely or partly:

1. *Commodatum*, in which we freely cede to someone for a determined time the *use* of something we own. If no time is determined, the contract is called *precarium*.

2. *Location*, in which the use of something is ceded against a price.

3. *Emphyteusis of land*, in which the usufruct of land is ceded to another in perpetuity but the naked ownership retained, whether the usufruct is ceded freely or against some form of payment.

4. *Land rent*, in which the productivity of land is ceded in return for money or something else, or ceded free of charge, although the person renting can free his land from the land rent by paying an agreed capital.

5. *Agistment*, that is, mutual hire. In agistment, one party hires to the other a large number of cattle; the second party hires his work to the first by obliging himself to care for the cattle on condition that he has a share in the offspring of the animals and in what benefits him. The matter of this contract therefore is both *use* (in the strict sense) and *benefit*, that is, the use of the work and the fruit of animals.

6. All contracts whose object is predial servitude involve the

[452] *ER*, 322-323.

[1551–1553]

right of *use*, not in its entirety but divided up in a thousand ways.

1554. The right of servitude limits the use that an owner can make of his land, to the advantage of the owner of other land. Although the use can be limited in various ways, this can be reduced either to having to tolerate something being done on one's own land or having to refrain from doing something oneself.

1555. The land for which the servitude is an advantage is called 'dominant'. When this land is used in a rural economy, the servitude is called 'rustic'. Examples are the right to cross other people's land, to draw water, pasture cattle, cut wood, fish, hunt, excavate stones or sand, burn lime and so forth. It is clear that in all these kinds of servitude only a fraction of the total, complex use possible of a property is involved.

1556. If the dominant estate is not used for a rural economy, the servitude is called 'urban'. Examples are the right to support a building against somebody else's, to introduce a beam into someone's wall, to pierce the wall with a window to obtain light or a view, to construct a roof or balcony which takes up a neighbour's space, to channel smoke through a neighbour's chimney, to drain water onto another's land, to disperse liquids, etc.

1557. Other kinds of urban servitude are not a right to do something on someone else's land, but a right by which a neighbour must not do anything on his land which is of disadvantage to the dominant estate. For example, he may not increase or decrease the height of his house, restrict the light, air, and view of the dominant estate; he may not divert his drainage away from another's estate because it is useful for irrigating the land or providing a water cistern, etc.

All these kinds of servitude involve only particular, possible uses of a thing.

c) *Contracts involving the right of ownership*

1558. In *emphyteusis* useful dominion differs from dominion of naked ownership.

[1554–1558]

1559. Full or varyingly limited ownership is matter for contracts of accepted donation, sale, loan, usury and others.

V.
Splitting of right to freedom

1560. A human being, considered in isolation without any positive relationship with other human beings, can do 1. things that are lawful and 2. things that pertain to him by right. We therefore distinguished freedom into two branches: 1. innocuous freedom; 2. jural freedom.[453] Innocuous freedom can be indirectly limited without reducing jural freedom. But is this freedom, which is proper to right and due to every human being, reduced or split?

a) *Can a unilateral act reduce a person's jural freedom?*

1561. I have spoken about two principal ways of acquiring a jural power over individual human beings: occupancy and generation. I said they are titles to new rights rather than modifications of previously existing rights (cf. 528-863). I now add, however, that *occupancy* and *generation* can be considered as causes which modify *freedom*, at least in their consequences if not directly.

1562. A baby can be occupied only because it does not have free judgment over itself, but must be allowed the exercise of its freedom to the extent that this free judgment reveals itself. Understood in this way, occupancy does not at all diminish the child's freedom because occupancy takes place while freedom is not in act; when it is in act, occupancy ceases. Occupancy therefore produces new rights in the occupier without reducing or splitting the child's rights.

---

[453] Cf. *ER*, 324-325.

When the child first gains the exercise of his faculties, he still has certain obligations towards the person who has occupied him. Truth therefore would not be violated if these remaining obligations were considered as a kind of modification, limitation or alteration of the child's jural freedom.

1563. In addition to early occupancy, the title of generation also leaves important consequences in the child's jural state. Even when his intelligence and personal freedom are in act, he still lives in a domestic society and consequently under *patria potestas*. This continues as long as his father lives and he remains part of the father's family — even when he has left the family, he is still, in certain things, part of it. But can we say 1. that this continuing submission to his father's authority (which is certainly a limit to his freedom) is a diminution of his jural freedom or 2. that the limit of his freedom is the effect of his father as genitor?

1564. The first question must be answered negatively. Relative to the father, no jural freedom capable of being reduced by the father's authority exists in the child. We should rather say that jural freedom, relative to the parent, is limited itself, that is, by the original, natural relationship between father and offspring.[454]

1565. The second question must also be answered negatively. The limitation here is applied to personal freedom, which cannot *in fact* be limited, unless it co-operates with the limitation. We must distinguish between, on the one hand, the power assumed by a parent or occupier over a child who does not yet possess his own free judgment and, on the other, the power of paternal authority over the free judgment of the grown child. The first is exercised over the child in the same way as over a thing; free co-operation therefore is not necessary. The second

---

[454] The same must be said about our submission to God. Properly speaking, this does not diminish but determine our *right of freedom*. The submission is innate, co-existent with the right of freedom which, by its very essence, entails the limitation (if we wish to call it that). — What we say here about the creature's natural, essential submission to the Creator is true whether we consider the Creator in himself or in his witnesses such as (under the law of grace) Christ, the Apostles and the Church.

is exercised over personal freedom itself which, if it must act, must act freely because it is free by nature.

Paternal authority therefore, and any authority whatsoever imposed on the will as a moral-jural obligation, cannot be *exercised* without the will's consent.

1566. Hence, if we are to define paternal authority, or any similar authority, we must say that it is 'a right to the willed obedience of the offspring', or 'the right that the offspring consent to what the father commands.'

1567. The title and foundation therefore of this right is the unilateral fact of human generation, which in a child produces the obligation to submit willingly to obedience. This submission and obedience is posited in being only by the two acts of paternal command and filial consent, a consent which is obligatory and therefore physically, not morally free.

1568. What we have said about the lawfulness 'of helping someone without knowing whether he consents or not, or even when, in certain cases, it is expressly against his consent',[455] justifies according to rational Right the faculty of tutelage, care and, generally speaking, management of others' affairs without a mandate.[456]

1569. Relative to tutelage and care, we must say more or less what we said about occupancy of a baby.

1570. Relative to the management of others' affairs without a

---

[455] We can see that our principle is in substance universally admitted if we consider it in its applications or in particular cases, discussed by most authors, in which the truth of what we are saying is more clearly revealed. One of these special cases is 'the lawfulness of deferring or omitting entirely the restitution of someone's possessions purely for the owner's good'. Moralists generally acknowledge that this is sometimes the case and must be followed. They specify such cases and describe the circumstances. But, surely, they would not hold this opinion without recognising that 'a faculty of helping someone against his will' does sometimes arise? — Cf. on the question Just. Vigler in his treatise *De restitutione in genere*, q. 31 entitled *Quando bonum creditoris excuset a restitutione*.

[456] Although acceptance of this kind of work purely for someone else's benefit comes within lawful actions pertaining to *innocuous freedom*, it is not a right pertaining to *jural freedom*. Hence, anyone prevented from assuming care of another is not injured in his right, but once he has assumed care, has acquired a right and would reasonably feel offended by anyone wanting to be involved in the work.

mandate, we say that this is principally founded on a presumed consent and even more on the 'will for good, which is essential to human nature'.

1571. In any case, these unilateral acts of beneficence do not, properly speaking, limit the right of freedom in those for whom they are exercised. This right, of its nature, does not extend to evil, that is, to harming oneself, and no harm is done if the acts are performed within just limits and with the respect due to the right which, as I have said, we each have 'of judging what is helpful to our own good' (cf. 610).

1572. We must also note a limit and determination to the right of freedom resulting from its intrinsic nature. By this, I mean the limit imparted to freedom by the moral law, when the right is not simply limited but ceases to exist. The submission naturally due to people of wisdom, to benefactors, etc. is of this kind (cf. 675-680).

1573. Finally, we must distinguish between *servitude* and *social dependence*. The latter does not remove our freedom but directs and orders it to its greatest good.[457]

1574. From these considerations we can conclude that the reduction or splitting of the right to freedom can occur only by consent of the parties, that is, by an expressed or tacit contract. The contract however can be obligatory for one party or for both. In this case, a first title exists on which the right is founded prior to the contract itself.

b) *The nature and effects of the splitting and alienation of jural freedom*

1575. Servitude and seigniory originate in the splitting and alienation of natural freedom, which may be innocuous or jural. Through alienation a portion of freedom becomes the object of another's right.

1576. Servitude is not understood as any kind of dependence, but as only that whose direct purpose is the good of the person

---

[457] Cf. my work, *SP*, bk. 1, cc. 6-9, for the distinction between the *dependence* to which members of a society are subject as a consequence of social order, and *servitude*.

served, although in reality there may be some other good which as a consequence of his service benefits the servant.

1577. It is clear that no servile condition can exist without the consent or agreement of the parties. Consequently, according to the order of ideas, the *first state* in which we can imagine the human race is a state without any alienation of freedom and without masters or servants. Oral tradition has preserved a very ancient memory of this state.[458]

1578. Moreover, the bonds of dependence and seigniory must have been formed gradually, so that submission[459] and seigniory, which were not very noticeable in the *second state* of humanity, increased in the *third state*. Consequently, as we go back into antiquity, we find dependences and seigniories fewer and less burdensome. Such must have been the course followed by the

[458] Plutarch refers to the state of primitive equality and independence which, although lost, was still remembered in his time, and which many wise people made an unsuccessful effort to resuscitate. The philosopher-historian says in his comparison between Lycurgus and Numa: 'If anyone would make us place what has been said about the Helots among the political institutes of Lycurgus (which would be very cruel and indeed unreasonable), we would have to reply that Numa's legislation was far more in conformity with the spirit of the Greeks. He made all those considered by everyone as bond-servants enjoy and share the honour of free people; under him, it became a custom for them to be present with their masters at the saturnalia banquets. He also decided, we are told, that those who co-operated by their work in the annual income should share in and enjoy it afterwards. Some people said that this custom was preserved in memory of the equality allowed on the feasts of Saturn, when there was neither bond-servant nor master, and all were considered blood-relatives and equals.' — This and other laws of Numa seem to bear a trace of the Mosaic laws which prescribed that bond-servants were also to be invited to the banquets celebrated with the second tithes (Deut 12: 17, 18). Furthermore, because the Spartans were blood-relatives of the Hebrews (1 Macc 12, 14), it is probable that Numa obtained the idea from the Spartan colonies established in Italy. — Justinian's *Institutes* acknowledge that the state of freedom predated servitude, which was established by the Right of the nations, that is, it is a right subsequent to the right of nature: 'This practice (manumission) took its origin from the law of the nations, because all are born free BY NATURAL LAW. Manumission was unknown because servitude was unknown. But when servitude was introduced BY THE LAW OF THE NATIONS, the BENEFIT of manumission followed' (bk. 1, tit. 5).

[459] The Decalogue which speaks only of paternal authority shows the state of a people in which the bonds of servitude based on consent and on political, civil seigniory are only in their initial stages.

[1577–1578]

natural, progressive development of the relationship of servitude and seigniory among human beings.

1579. We must always note, however, that unpredictable, disruptive and violent causes are at work in the human race alongside the natural, gentle progress of things. These causes explain the exceptions in human history that contradict natural human development.

Let us therefore see what, on the one hand, is violent and unjust, and, on the one hand, peaceful and just in the various relationships of dependence and seigniory among human beings.

c) *Acquired seigniory is just if founded on spontaneous submission*

1580. We say 'violent and unjust' because these two words are synonyms in the case of any servitude corresponding to a real seigniory.

1581. Seigniory is just if submission and dependence on another is spontaneous, consented to and agreed. It is unjust if obtained by force against the other's right of freedom.[460] As we said: the symptom indicating the violation of another's right is resentment. Thus, if someone does not experience a naturally resentment when he knows about another's action, we can say the action has not injured him.

---

[460] When corruption causes the human heart to nurture great hatred, inhumanity and arrogance, any lesser degree of cruelty is normally called 'piety'. When those conquered in battle sold rather than killed themselves, their slavery was considered piety. This kind of treatment, if considered merciful and human, is *a fortiori* taken as even more just. Servitude was therefore instituted by the RIGHT of nations, and manumission was considered a KINDNESS, although at the same time the usual incoherent reasoning of depraved humanity revealed how contrary to nature the matter was: 'Servitude is a constitution of the law of nations by which one person is subjected to another's seigniory CONTRARY TO NATURE (*Instit. Just.*, bk. 1, tit. 3). Montesquieu refers to this when he observes: 'Under despotic governments, where people are subject to *political slavery*, *civil slavery* is more tolerable than in other systems because everyone is glad to have ownership and life. Thus the state of a slave is not much more burdensome than that of a subject' (*L'Esprit*, bk. 15, c. 1).

[1579–1581]

1582. Aristotle defines a bond-servant as 'an animate instrument'. It is clear that if this were the only quality considered in human beings, they would be hurt.

1583. But human beings can be animate instruments to the advantage of others without losing their personal existence and dignity.

If we consider individual human beings from this point of view, it is not at all absurd to find them in a servile state, which can be useful and desirable. Those who make themselves an animate and (I would add) reasoning instrument of the upright aims of others, and thus make a living for themselves, may really desire this state; indeed there may be no better state for them. Those who have sufficient ability to work at a trade, but not to govern and command others or make their living in a profession, can and should consider themselves happy because they are able to serve others with their skills. This can be so true that others in turn make themselves dependent on their ability. Hence, we can say, as Aristotle said (cf. 680), that those who have only the aptitude to serve others [*App.*, no. 9] and for whom serving others is advantageous, are destined by nature to serve.

1584. This natural homogeneity for the servile state is principally connected with two things:

1. With a certain tranquillity, or even baseness, of spirit, and with certain lowly and depressed spirits, which makes people choose a state of submission providing them with happiness; they would not find any pleasure in the thrust and preoccupation of those who command.

2. With a lack of any aptitude or ability except that of earning a decent living or usefully employing their time by serving others.

1585. It is nearly always these two causes that induce human beings to consent to or even procure their own servitude.

1586. The first of the two causes guides a person instinctively to servitude. It is a human condition arising from human instinct[461] and acting in human beings without their noticing it. They find themselves in a state of dependence which they think

---

[461] See what I have said about instinct in *AMS*.

they have acquired by chance, but about which they have in fact made a hidden choice. Moreover, when they reflect on it, they complain about their misfortune because the order of reflection is so remote and separate from that of feeling, instinct and cognition. We could say to such people, as Christ said to his Apostles: 'You do not know of what spirit you are.'

1587. The second cause guides a person to servitude by reasoning and reflection.

1588. Sometimes we react against the dictates of reason, which clearly tells us we must serve for our own good. This happens because the *instinct for domination*, which is given to us and perhaps nurtured by us, opposes the conclusions of our reasoning about our real needs and accidental circumstances. If the instinct is strong, it has its way and we distance ourselves, by tremendous efforts, from the hard condition of servitude to which reason itself would reduce us. Sometimes, of course, our reaction to the conclusions of reason proceeds from wicked pride and great depravity. This kind of reaction is a considerable source of the miseries and crimes that brutalise the world.

1589. The first condition — weakness and softness of spirit — proceeds for the most part from involuntary, natural causes, for example, heredity and climate, although habit also plays a role.[462]

1590. The second condition is principally formed by an education that is excessively narrow and defective from the point of view of method, or slack and unhelpful.

We are obviously speaking here about servitude caused by natural consent; only this kind can be in conformity with Right. We are not talking about servitude imposed by violence, which is a crime of human tyranny.

1591. We said that the origin of the first condition was principally heredity and climate. People throughout history, and all over the face of the earth have certainly believed that there are families capable in varying degrees of ruling or serving. Noah destined Canaan to be the bond-servant to his brothers' bond-servants, and saw in Canaan's people a tendency to servitude.

---

[462] 'Human beings accustom themselves to everything, even to servitude, provided one's master is not harder than one's servitude' (*L'Esprit des Lois*, bk. 15, c. 16).

[1587–1591]

1592. In reference to climate, Montesquieu says:

> There are regions where heat enfeebles the body and reduces courage so greatly that people have no intention of performing troublesome duties unless driven by fear of punishment. In these regions slavery scarcely offends reason. Consequently, because masters are as supine towards their rulers as slaves towards their masters, political slavery runs parallel to civil slavery.[463]

1593. Need, which contributes to the production of the second condition, does not permit our learning anything except mechanical skills, and sometimes makes servitude an absolute necessity.

1594. Moreover, everybody benefits when the less wise and prudent are commanded and directed by those who are able to command and direct wisely.[464]

We see therefore that dependence and servitude can be, and are in fact, accepted by certain kinds of human beings, and even be desired as the best thing possible for them.[465]

1595. Moreover, we see that this dependence and servitude acquires the character and dignity of moral duty, because to serve others is a duty for those who cannot otherwise obtain their living honestly. In this case, servitude is ennobled by morality.

---

[463] *L'Esprit des Lois*, bk. 15, c. 7. — Cf. also bk. 16, where he considers domestic *servitude* relative to climate, and; bk. 17, where he speaks about political *servitude* relative to climate. — *Heredity*, it must be noted, much more than *climate*, can exert an influence; the author of *The Spirit of the Laws*, who went rather far in exaggerating the moral influence of climate, did not note this cause.

[464] Plato himself observed in the first Alcibiades that 'it is more helpful not only for a child but for an adult to be governed by a better person than to govern.'

[465] Among the Hebrews, servitude was not permanent. Bond-servants regained their freedom in the sabbatical year. However, the law had foreseen the case where a bond-servant might wish to remain a bond-servant always. If this happened, the bond-servant's ear was pierced as a sign of permanent servitude (Ex 21: 5, 6. — Deut 15: 16). This law shows and presupposes 1. that there can be people who voluntarily prefer the state of servitude to that of freedom; 2. that, with their consent, no harm is done by keeping them in servitude, precisely because every symptom of injury is lacking, that is, 'the disturbed natural feeling'.

[1592–1595]

1596. If however we consider a higher order of things, we discover an extremely noble dependence and servitude, where the very apex of moral perfection is resplendent. This is *religious obedience*, a kind of servitude to which a human being vows himself. As Count De Maistre noted, the religious of Christian societies have generously taken the place of the ancient slaves; they are the entirely free slaves of Christian charity, just as the others were slaves of violent pagan cruelty.[466]

d) *Degrees of servitude*

1597. Let us summarise all we have said about the degrees of servitude. We distinguished between *dependence*, whose object is both the common good and the order necessary for it, and *servitude*, whose object is the particular good of the person to whom service is rendered. This alone is servitude in the true sense.[467]

We said that dependence, whose object is the common good, is a consequence of association, which can also be jurally obligatory.[468]

Servitude, generally defined as 'an obligation to render service to another', divides into two branches: innate servitude, which does not detract from natural freedom; and servitude which consists in a diminution of innate freedom. The first kind of servitude is that which children must render their parents.[469]

We then showed that the servitude which detracts from innate

---

[466] In my opinion, the origin of servitude cannot be reduced to the sale of children by parents, as A. Granier de Cassagnac maintains in his work *Des classes ouvrières et des classes bourgeoises* (Paris, 1838). Nevertheless I think his work can be profitably read by those who wish to study the question of the spontaneous, natural origin of servitude and the origin of dependent classes in general.

[467] Cf. *SP*, bk. 1, c. 9.

[468] *Ibid.*

[469] We have already noted two elements in the relationship of children to their parents: 1. servile dependence; 2. social dependence. These two elements correspond to the bond of seigniory and of society contained in the concept of fraternity.

freedom cannot take place without the person's consent. We presume that the person has not made himself culpable through his own action, about which we will speak later.

Nevertheless, we considered the case of an occupied baby, and said that as an adult, the child must repay its benefactor's costs (c. 599-636). Although the debt of repayment of the costs is only a real obligation, a person who possesses nothing cannot satisfy it except by his personal work and labour. But the 'obligation of personal work' is itself, according to the general definition we have given, a degree of servitude. To help someone therefore can indirectly, but not necessarily, produce in the receiver a degree of servitude. Apart from this power to subject someone indirectly by an act of kindness, which always requires acknowledgement and often compensation, we entirely denied any faculty to subject one's fellow human beings by violence.

After we had examined our question relative to masters, we considered it relative to the person who becomes a subject. We first said that the latter can in varying degree alienate his own innate freedom but not that part which is intrinsically inalienable (cf. 130).

A question then spontaneously presented itself: can a person contract, even reluctantly, an obligation to serve with his labour? We said this could happen through some kind of indirect consequence.[470]

If the obligation imposed without his expressed will could be satisfied only by 'a personal contribution', the obligation would bring with it a degree of servitude (cf. 599-636). In a broad sense, a personal contribution is always servitude. We will investigate in the next book the obligations which cause injury to others' rights.

1598. We see therefore that servitude can be of two kinds: *direct*, consisting in the obligation of 'personal contributions' made for the sake of others, and *indirect*, consisting in the obligation of 'real contributions' which cannot be satisfied

---

[470] If a person hates us so much that the hatred which has been proved with certainty could cause our death, natural right gives and permits us the exercise of a true *dominion* over our absolute, homicidal enemy for as long as the hatred endures.

except by 'personal contributions', which consequently become obligatory.

1599. Authors have distinguished these two kinds of servitude but perhaps without defining them with the extension we think necessary. For example, Montesquieu limits them as follows:

> There are two kinds of servitude: real and personal. *Real* servitude attaches the slave to the land. According to Tacitus, the slaves of the Germans were of this kind. They had no house duties but gave their master a certain quantity of grain, cattle and cloth; that was the extent of their duty. This kind of servitude however spread to Hungary, Bohemia and many other regions of southern Germany.
>
> *Personal servitude* is service in the house and refers more to the person of the master.
>
> The extreme abuse, slavery, is present when servitude is simultaneously personal and real. The servitude of the Helots among the Spartans was of this kind.[471]

1600. Servitude therefore is not present when human beings are obliged simply to a *real* contribution without personal services. But if personal services have been determined in order to satisfy the required contribution, servitude is present. This is the case of *servi glebae* (bond-servants of the glebe) who must cultivate the land, which they cannot abandon.

1601. Here we must ask: 'According to rational Right can servitude be passed on by heredity?' In my opinion, servitude (taken in our general sense) follows indirectly from real obligations (when often it is not called 'servitude').[472] It can therefore certainly pass to heirs because real obligations pass to them.

---

[471] *L'Esprit des Lois*, bk. 15, c. 10. — Montesquieu makes an excellent observation here: 'Simple-living people have only real slavery because their wives and children perform domestic work. Pleasure-loving people have personal servitude, because their indulgent way of life requires the service of slaves in the house.' — Tacitus in fact, speaking about the customs of the Germans, says that in the midst of the pleasures of life the master could not be distinguished from the slave.

[472] The *executory* part of *promissory contracts* can be considered a personal obligation. On this reflection Kant founded his distinction, later accepted by the Austrian code, between *real rights* and *personal rights over things*. — We must note however that the provision of labour, although personal by nature, is called *servile* only when the work to be done is burdensome, mechanical

1602. But generally speaking, I think that *direct* servitude cannot pass to heirs because its nature is personal.

1603. Nevertheless, it would often seem to pass to heirs for the following reasons:

1. In an underdeveloped nation, many members are like children. In this state they have attained only very little free judgment of themselves. If servitude is introduced, a kind of occupancy of the bond-servants' children would continue in the masters, just as it would in abandoned children who had been taken in, but lacked development and only later (or never) attained dominion over themselves.

2. The *servile spirit* passes from one generation to the next. Families become accustomed to the life; aptitudes and abilities acquired by the children are servile; every thought or desire arising in them is servile. Consequently, their spirit does not find service distasteful; in fact, service is helpful to them, and the only state possible. Each succeeding generation tacitly consents to remain as it is.

1604. This consent however, when servitude is oppressive, can never be presumed. Resentment reveals itself or remains suppressed in the bond-servants, and at this point their service certainly becomes unjust. Montesquieu says:[473]

> The Athenians treated their slaves with great gentleness. At Athens we find that the slaves did not disturb the State as they did at Sparta.
>
> Nor do we have any evidence that the early Romans were uneasy at the thought of disturbances from their slaves. Only when they lost all human feeling for them do we see the beginning of slave-wars, which bore comparison with the Punic wars.[474]

and of some duration. Handing over a sum of money, or any other exchange which requires no bodily effort, is not considered a *service* in the normal sense of the word. On the other hand, ability to have the work done by another does not remove its servile nature, if it is such. It simply excuses the person from providing servitude, from which he thus frees himself.

[473] *L'Esprit des Lois*, bk. 15, c. 16).

[474] Florus says: 'The slave war devastated Sicily more cruelly than the Punic war' (bk. 3). — One injustice produces another: if injustice is accepted by positive laws, then positive law, which has declared just what is unjust, becomes an inexhaustible source of other equally unjust laws, and

1605. What we have said so far indicates that consent to servitude can be either *expressed* or *tacit*.

1606. Consent is tacit when bond-servants neither feel their service as punishment nor show this externally.

1607. If consent is expressed also, it takes the form of a true contract, and is judged according to the rules of contracts.

1608. By means of this contract a person can subject himself to servitude in varying degrees.

1609. We note immediately that any servitude consisting in the alienation of one's *own work* can never include, without contradiction, alienation of the *personal principle*. Because alienation is a personal act, one of the contracting parties, if he intended to alienate his own person, would be non-existent. Granted that one of the parties is non-existent, there is no longer any possibility of a contract. A clear contradiction therefore is present in the concept of a contract by which one claims to alienate one's personship. The contradiction is even more evident if the contract is claimed to be bilateral.[475]

consequently creates a system of laws which protects evil. The so-called right to kill prisoners taken in battle (acknowledged as legitimate by positive Right) was a cause of servitude and persuaded people that human beings could be the property of other human beings. When this monstrous concept had entered positive laws, a master was eventually permitted every inhuman indignity against his slave. As long as masters were aided by the moral feeling of nature, they tempered their use of their extraordinary power. But when customs had declined, the slave became the wretched plaything of his evil master's cruelty. Eventually Rome had to enact the Sillanian senatorial decree and other very cruel laws against slaves under the pretext of defending the masters' lives. These laws, although they appeared just, were in fact extremely unjust, the inevitable consequence of prior injustices permitted and sanctioned by the law.

[475] 'Sale presupposes a price: when a slave is sold, all his goods become part of the property of his master. In this case, the master gives nothing, and the slave receives nothing' (Montesquieu, bk. 15, c. 2). — Permission to be sold, *peculia* granted to slaves, and the laws imposed on slaves after their exclusion from the society for which the laws are made, are the incoherent, involuntary protests of human reason and common sense against the principle of slavery. They are a proof that human beings, and in particular a nation, can never act in coherence with a false principle. To act in this way they would have to be essentially unreasoning, despite the rationality which constitutes human nature. Is it really possible to have a creature, even outside the human race,

[1605–1609]

1610. We ignore such a shameful absurdity. The principal degrees of servitude, therefore, to which a person can subject himself depend on the following conditions:

1. The alienation of the product of his own labour while the *management* of work remains in his own power; the consignment of only the *management* of his work to another's judgment; or alienation and consignment of *management* together. This third kind of servitude is much greater than the first two.

1611. 2. The *product* of one's labour is obtained either by particular actions, that is, by a given skill, or by any other kind of action, in such a way that the person is constrained to earn as much as possible in every way for his master. The same applies to *management*, that is, management over a single determined work or over different works under the master's authority. At this second level servitude is much more onerous.

1612. 3. Any of these kinds of servitude is either permanent or for a determined time, or at the parties' pleasure. The last two kinds are a very light form of servitude, particularly the last.

1613. 4. Finally, there exists a contribution of an entirely free service determined by contract and compensated by a proportionate, agreed payment. Here, we can say, the two parties are in the same state because, while one renders service, the other pays the cost.

The difference between this and other kinds and levels of servitude is so great that even in remotest antiquity they were always distinguished by different names: *bond-servants* and *wage-earners*.[476]

In social Right we will deal with the classification of the different kinds and levels of servitude. What we have said here will be sufficient for the present.

---

who could act in coherence with what is absurd? Such a being would always and in every way be absurd, and less than nothing!.

[476] Hebrew law distinguished the *bond-servant* from the *wage-earner*, and if the bond-servant were a Hebrew, he had to be considered as a simple *wage-earner*, not as a *bond-servant* (Deut 15: 18).

[1610–1613]

Book 4

ALTERATIONS TO
THE RIGHTS OF OTHERS;
CONSEQUENT OBLIGATIONS
AND MODIFICATIONS OF
MUTUAL RIGHTS

INTRODUCTION

SUBJECT-MATTER OF THIS BOOK

I.

Jural effects of acts carried out by a person possessing a right, and of acts of those obliged to respect that right

1614. The preceding book has described the modifications undergone by rights as a result of the correlative acts of more than one person. The present book has already been dedicated to describing the modifications undergone by rights as a result of what is done by a single person.

But the question we have in mind could be divided in two. In fact we know that every right consists in a *relationship* of a special nature between two parties, that is, between the party with the right and the party with the corresponding duty to respect that right. Our questions, therefore, could be: 'What modifications occur in rights as a result of acts done by the party which possesses them?', and 'What modifications occur to rights as a result of acts done by the party who is required to respect those rights?'. It is easy to see, however, that these two questions are intimately bound together, and that it is the second which requires special attention. For the first, it is sufficient to remember principally what we have said in various places as the need arose.

1615. This becomes more obvious as we recall that whoever has a right can do only two things when he acts alone without concurrence from other persons. He can 1. annihilate his right completely or in part by abandoning it or by destroying its matter; 2. offer or promise it to someone else.

1616. The first of these two things, that is, renunciation and annihilation, is not properly speaking a modification of the right. We have in fact spoken about this sufficiently in dealing with the ways in which rights are extinguished.

1617. The second is without doubt a kind of modification of one's right, a portion of which passes to the person to whom it was offered or promised. The offer immediately provides this person with a right to accept. This also has been dealt with, however, and we refer the reader to what has already been said.

1618. Why is this the only modification that a person can make, as a result simply of his own actions, to a right he possesses?

Modifications of a right presuppose that either a part or the whole of the right passes to another subject. However, if this subject refuses to receive it, the right does not pass because no one acquires a right except 'as a result of an act of his own will.'

1619. In the case we have mentioned (donation, or some other contract offered to another person), the person to whom the contract or donation was offered cannot be said to acquire the right to acceptance by the sole fact of the offer. Rather, the offer, through its relationship with human nature, enables him to acquire it. Granted the *essential act inclining human nature to good*, those ways which lead human nature to acquire good must be kept open for it — and the offer is such a way. It constitutes, however, only a right in potency, that is, a power of acquiring rights; it is a right to *jural freedom*, not a right of ownership.

All that is required, therefore, is that we should now examine the modifications which rights can receive from the acts of persons obliged to respect them.

II.

Jurally innocuous acts, and acts injurious to the rights of others

1620. What acts can human beings carry out in relationship to the rights of others? *Right* is a faculty for acting. It is clear, therefore, that a person with a right can act in virtue of this right, that is, he can exercise his right. *Obligation* here consists in a duty to respect the other's right. It is a kind of passivity, a prohibition, a negation, through which we are forbidden to do what injures another's right.

1621. How is it possible for a person with this obligation to modify another's right without injuring it? It is true that harming others' rights through unlawful acts is the principal way they are normally violated by those with an obligation to respect them, but is there no innocuous modification that can be caused to others' rights as a result of these actions?

III.

Innocuous acts which can modify another's right

1622. This can indeed happen, but for the most part it takes place exceptionally. We can see this by making a synopsis of the lawful acts possible to us, and by considering their jural consequences.

We reduced human activity to two species of *freedom*: innocuous and jural. Through *innocuous freedom* we acquire rights; through *jural freedom* we exercise the rights we have already acquired.

We distinguished four classes of acts which can be carried out by *innocuous freedom*. We must now consider the jural effects of each of them.

First class: acts with which we occupy anything which is free. — These acts do not modify others' rights, but simply restrict their *innocuous freedom*.

Second class: acts with which another's goods are used, but without causing the least harm, obstacle or annoyance to the owner. — These acts also do not modify others' rights.

Third class: acts of beneficence without harm to the benefactor. — These acts generate in the beneficiaries moral, not jural, duties of gratitude.

Fourth class: acts of beneficence which cause some harm to the benefactor, but are necessary to supply the needs of the beneficiary. — These acts bring about a jural obligation of recompense in the beneficiary, and thus modify his jural state. Wardship, trusteeship and the administration of others' affairs without a mandate are acts of this kind. We have already spoken of them briefly.

1623. Acts of *jural freedom* can be grouped in two classes:

First class: acts with which one makes use of one's own right. These do not modify another's jural state except with the other's consent, as in contracts.

Second class: acts with which another's right is disposed of, but unknowingly. These are all the acts done by a possessor in good faith. They truly modify another's jural state because they give rise to jural relationships consisting in obligations and rights between the person acting in good faith, and the person to whom the right truly belongs.

1624. The jural effect of such acts consists in obligations arising not from *consent*, but from the *thing itself*. In other words, every time that something is moved, as it were, so that it no longer remains with its master, there is an obligation to restore it to the owner in accordance with the tag: *res clamat ad dominum.*[477]

1625. In this case, the true owner has a *personal* and *real* action allowing him to claim what is his.

1626. The personal action arises from the *obligation*, and the real action from *what is his own*.

1627. The possessor in good faith has the obligation of restoring what belongs to another as soon as he realises that it belongs to the other. This explains why the owner has a *personal action* in his regard; he can claim that the other fulfil his obligation by restoring the thing in question. If, however, the

---

[477] We could mention here the case of accidental harm produced by something we own. Some legislations set a penalty for the person whose beast or cart accidentally kills another person. Even now in England the animal or wagon is confiscated for the poor. This penalty is called *deodand*, that is *Deo dandum*, something handed over to God and through God to his poor. It seems that the ancient British legislators wished to punish any negligence that could have occurred, but considered it more of an offence to God, the author of life, than a jural offence towards the human individual. This offence to God had to be recompensed with the sacrifice that Justinian calls *noxa*, that is *the body that inflicted the harm* (*Inst. Just.*, bk. 4, tit. 8: 1).

possessor is not persuaded that what he holds belongs to another, and cannot be persuaded, or were dead or absent, the owner would still be left with the possibility of *real action*. In other words, he would be able to claim and repossess the thing directly. The thing is his, and he can therefore dispose of it with his right of ownership.[478]

We do not think it necessary to examine such modifications further. What we have said about them in various places as occasion offered would seem sufficient.

IV.

The subject-matter of this book: harmful acts which modify the rights of others

1628. The sole argument of this book is, therefore, the modifications of others' rights when their rights are violated by another person. The book will be a treatise on penal Right, but restricted to the part which concerns human beings in the state of nature.

---

[478] Obligations *ex re* also form part of *contracts (cf. Inst. Just.*, bk. 3, tit. 15).

CHAPTER 1

The nature of the modifications produced in others' rights by harmful acts

1629. Human activity, and consequently jural freedom, has as its term pleasure in the broadest meaning of the word.

1630. But pleasure presupposes an object or some matter which the active principle enjoys through union with it. Hence ownership.

1631. *Ownership* shows itself, therefore, as a condition of *freedom*, which cannot be conceived without ownership; the concept of freedom does not exist if completely deprived of all ownership. Even in 'person', that is, in essential freedom, we find an object, the idea of being, which holds the place of primitive ownership.[479]

1632. The object of ownership is then seized, as it were, by our own personal force. This appropriation, when sanctioned by the moral law which prevents others from disturbing it, becomes a right (cf. 1522-1557).

1633. When human beings have the right of ownership over a given thing, they can lawfully exhaust all their personal force upon it with the intention of gaining all the pleasure it is capable of providing. Every different way of applying one's own personal force can in such a case be called a function of the right of ownership. We have already listed as many as eight of these functions (cf. 966).

1634. We have to take careful note of the difference between *rights* properly understood, and the *functions* exercised relative to right itself (cf. 967). I can defend whatever right I have, repel anyone attempting to deprive me of it, get it back from those

---

[479] Just as we have posited the *essence* of right in freedom, so we have placed the principle of the *determination* of rights in ownership. Of itself, *freedom* is equal in all rights, precisely because it is the essence in which all rights participate. But we then find that right expresses itself differently to the extent that freedom has differing *ownerships* in which to expand and exercise itself. Rights, considered in relationship to *freedom*, are reduced to unity; considered in relationship to the variety of *ownership* which provides their matter, they are multiple (cf. *ER*, 318 ss.).

who have taken it from me, demand reparation for injury done, recompense for damage, and so on. These are all different functions I can exercise in virtue of any right that I possess, of any ownership whatsoever that is mine. Only in a more general sense, as we have said, can each function issuing from the right of ownership, but considered in isolation, be called a right.[480]

1635. Granted this, we may ask what constitutes the modifications undergone by others' rights through harmful acts done to the rights. These modifications consist in certain functions of their rights, functions which are occasioned by a harmful act. If there were no acts of this kind, all rights would certainly remain intact, but their possessor would not be able to exercise his personal force in their regard as he can when harm is done. For example, when a right of mine is under attack from someone attempting to usurp it, I can repel the assault. The function which is exercised would not be activated, however, without some attempted usurpation.

1636. Harmful acts, therefore, provide an occasion for an owner to exercise certain functions of his right over which he certainly possessed moral power prior to the injury, but which depended upon the injury for their actuation.

1637. This is the original modification that harmful acts bring to the rights of others. Other modifications in reciprocal rights descend from it.

1638. Indeed, while the threatened harm gives a right to mount a defence, it also produces in the aggressor an obligation to desist from his evil attack, make reparation for the injury done and recompense the damage, etc. These obligations of his correspond to an equal number of rights in me, that is, to the activated functions of my right. As a result, if the person under obligation does not satisfy those obligations, I can use forceful means against him. I can put pressure on him and make him do what I previously could not make him do.

1639. Such obligations, functions of right and moral powers are indeed innate to every right, but cannot be actuated except in virtue of, or as a result of injury. These functions are the argument we must now discuss. We ask: what are these moral

[480] *ER*, 322-323.

[1635–1639]

powers? What are the jural functions placed in being as a consequence of perpetrated or feared injuries?

CHAPTER 2

**Functions of right actuated as an effect
of an injury received or feared**

1640. The functions of right actuated as a result of an injury already received, or even begun, or at least feared, are reduced to two: 1. *defence*, which includes the right of prevention and a right to guarantees, and 2. *satisfaction*. These functions are normally called *right* by authors who speak of the right of defence, of satisfaction, or guarantee, and so on. We shall discuss each of them, but first lay as the foundation of our treatise certain principles concerning the inviolability of all rights in general. In this way, we shall continue to clarify the concept of the *Right of ownership* under its negative form as the *Right not to be harmed.*[481]

CHAPTER 3

The inviolability of right

1641. The notion of right demonstrates the inviolable quality of right.

Every right is inviolable by force of the moral law which

---

[481] The right not to be harmed can be analysed in various ways. For example, one of the lesser rights contained in that of not being harmed could be expressed as follows: 'The right to have the harm prevented at every moment.' Other examples of these lesser, elementary rights will be mentioned in the course of the treatise.

[1640–1641]

forbids us to cause displeasure to a person; this moral law becomes jural also as soon as we are dealing with some displeasure consisting in the separation from a person of something he has lawfully made his *own*.

1642. Displeasure is of its nature a physical evil for the person suffering it, and a moral evil for the person who, through lack of respect for another's personship, causes the suffering. This is precisely the case in jural injury by which an attempt is made to separate from a person that which he has lawfully attached to himself with the bond of ownership (cf. 922-924).

1643. An infraction of this kind is always a moral evil — at any time, in every place, and in any circumstances whatsoever. If circumstances could exist in which the infraction of a right ceased to be a moral evil, the right would already have ceased to be a right. In the same way, if a law were found to be unjust, it would no longer be law.

1644. People who deny this and admit true collisions of rights, as well as those who maintain that respect for rights is an obligation which ceases as circumstances change, not only err in the way they express things, but actually confuse concepts. According to their way of expressing themselves, right would receive its force and require respect only from outside, that is, from external circumstances. Morality would then be reduced to a calculation intended to solve the following problem: 'Given such and such circumstances, is respect for others' right useful or harmful?' In this system, justice is sacrificed to utility, both private and public. Any government where such a system rules, whatever form it takes, is overwhelmingly despotic.

1645. On the contrary, right depends only on those facts or external circumstances that constitute it. Once constituted, it has an obligatory force independent of all other exterior circumstances not constituting it, and is therefore independent of any relationship whatsoever of utility or non-utility that could accrue to human beings from the respect they give or do not give to it.

1646. The inviolability of right, therefore, is always the same:

1. whatever subject it belongs to;

2. however long the time since the formation of its title, provided the title has not been removed, forgotten or rendered doubtful;

3. whatever circumstances render respect for it useful or non-useful; finally

4. whatever the means with which one thinks that right can be violated with impunity.

We now have to consider each of these four points.

Article 1.
The inviolability of right in every subject

1647. Both individual and social subjects are capable of rights. The social subject is composed of more than one individual subject; the social body has a single will because all the individual persons composing it have a common purpose.

1648. It is clear, however, that the particular *subject* to which right pertains does not render right respectable; this is done by personship in general, which requires such respect, and is found equally in every subject capable of rights.

If we apply this teaching to the two species of subject, individual and social, whom we have mentioned, we can succeed in overcoming a truly pernicious error which is sometimes manifested as deceit, sometimes as prejudice, sometimes as flattery, sometimes as oppression, but always as a source of tyranny. This error is present in those who think that right, when connected with a social body, or in general with a more powerful subject, must prevail over the same right when it is connected with an individual or weaker subject.

§1. *Society is obliged by the same jural laws as the individual*

1649. We must first note that *individual persons*, when they become part of a social person, acquire only an additional relationship without destroying themselves in any way.

1650. When we find ourselves before a society composed of, say, ten members, how should we consider it relative to its rights? Methodologically,[482] we have to consider it as a new

---

[482] I say 'methodologically' because, as I have already noted, only individuals are in fact the subjects of right.

[1647–1650]

15

person, distinct from the persons of its ten members. It will be as it were an eleventh person, to which each of the ten persons has a similar relationship. In this way, the rights of each of these eleven persons will be equally worthy of respect. We will not stop to examine which is the collective, and which the individual person. That will make no difference to us; we will always have an equal duty to respect that which pertains to each of these eleven jural persons.

1651. The nature of personship is to subsist without its being confused with anything else, that is, it exists in a totally independent way. Similarly, the society of which we are speaking presents us with eleven persons jurally *independent* of one another and *equal* (that is, equally worthy of respect relative to their own rights).

1652. How unfortunate was the result of our failure to understand — as we still fail to understand — that respect is owed to a person, whether the person possessing right is individual or collective!

People thought, or seemed to think, that the right pertaining to a *collective person* was greater than that pertaining to an *individual person*. Consequently, it was presumed that the collective person, or society, or whatever other name the people was called, could exercise its own rights by freely sacrificing those of individual persons. Society, or whoever stood for society, then became totally despotic. Individual persons were lost to sight or rather absorbed, as it was thought, by society, and annihilated as they came to form part of the social body. It was as though human individuals could be destroyed or destroy themselves merely by acquiring one more simple relationship such as the social relationship. In a word, a single person, the social person, was all that was wanted. But as we said, this was nothing more than show. If all the citizens are sacrificed to the few who are masters, not citizens, and hold the reins of the State in the name of society, what remains of society?

1653. This is not a new error (what error is new for humanity?). I have already noted elsewhere that things in society acquire an *artificial* value incomparably greater than their *natural* worth, and that human beings sometimes value their *social existence*, to the extent of forgetting and despising their *individual existence* to which they return only when *nature* finally recalls *reason* back to the interior life after its wanderings abroad.

It can be said that the radical vice of ancient civil societies was to obliterate the personal dignity of the individual; the individual was destroyed by means of social despotism. Christianity, and only Christianity, protects the weak against the strong, the individual against the totality, by illuminating the invisible, spiritual interior of the human being and destroying the overpowering illusion which the social mass, like everything great and powerful, produces with its sheer size and materiality. People did not find their greatest good within themselves, but sought it without, externally. Society was everything for them, and they obeyed it as their highest good.

This supposed supreme good thus became the source of pagan justice, which was true injustice. And if the society in question was small, that did not prevent its amassing injustice. A maxim common to all peoples held that their laws did not recognise injustice towards those who found themselves outside society.[483] This was the reality, although a few weak protests were made on behalf of reason [*App.*, no. 12]. The blame levelled at the Spartans and the Cretans[484] could have been aimed at the whole of the ancient world: love of country was the greatest virtue; it created a climate of opinion in which everything could be just or unjust.

1654. This opinion cannot be sustained, as it is today, on the basis that the good of society is of assistance to all, while individual damage harms only a single person. The Gospel has

---

[483] Cf. *SP*, bk. 1, c. 2.

[484] 'Expelling foreigners from Eratostene is a barbarian act' (Strabo, bk. 17) 'and the Spartans are no better in this matter' (Hugo Grot., *De J. et P.*, bk. 1, c. 2, §16). The reasons for the harshness shown by ancient peoples towards foreigners were principally: 1. the lack of *universal love* (love taught only by the Gospel) which left the field open only to *particular love* for relatives, etc.; 2. the natural love of power and dominion over others; 3. the fear of foreigners in whom people saw the same passions as they themselves experienced. As a result, their right of defence was also excessive on two counts: a) in judging others as malicious and offenders without experimental proof and solely on the basis of entrenched opinion about the universal corruption of mankind; b) in neglecting to seek the *minimum harm* to others in the exercise of self-defence — the moderating power of universal love was indeed lacking.

taught us that evil cannot be done to obtain good. Otherwise, it would be lawful to infringe any right with impunity provided that, as harm was done to one person, there would simultaneously be some intention and hope of assisting just two other people. If the principle is valid, it must be universally valid.

1655. Nevertheless, this does not mean that private good must not often give way to public good. It must give way, when 'give way' is understood correctly.

1656. Private good has to cede to public good if all the members of a society are equally burdened in proportion to the advantage that comes to them from the society, and if the imbalance which could be present when the burden is laid upon all is afterwards rectified. In other words, the sacrifice imposed upon one member at a moment of urgent, sudden need[485] will, at the proper time, be evened out as other members compensate him for what he has expended. In this way, it is true that private good has to give way to public good if by private is meant the *good of all the individual members of the society*; it is not true if private good is understood as that of *a single member of the society*.

1657. These comments must be applied to any society whatsoever because, in relationship to right, a collective body is only a jural person equal to any other individual. Between the collective body and its members, and between it and all other jural persons not its members, jural relationships exist and jural questions can arise, just as they do between individual persons. But these questions must be resolved by the principles themselves of universal justice.

1658. Thus it is not lawful even for civil society to absorb its members in itself, devouring them, as it were. It must leave them to live, along with itself, in their natural quality as jural persons, separate from and equal to itself, and worthy to be treated on a par with itself, that is, according to the principles of the same

---

[485] Any physical evil becomes moral evil simply 1. when wrongly inflicted on a person (because a moral evil is always contrary to the dignity of a person or intelligent nature); 2. when inflicted by a person or intelligent nature. It is not always the nature of evil which renders it *moral*, but sometimes only the *relationship* between the person who does it and the person who experiences it.

[1655–1658]

Right. I am speaking here, as everyone will understand, of civil society in general, independently of its form and of the way in which it could be administered.[486]

1659. There is some difficulty, it is true, in separating that which forms the collective person called civil society while leaving intact at its side individual persons who exist *per se* and are, at the same time, members of the collective society. Such a concept requires methodical abstraction because individual persons on the one hand have to be considered without their quality as social members while on the other the social person has to be taken as an aggregate of abstract human beings, that is, human beings taken simply in their relationship as members.[487] This cannot, however, be avoided.

These human beings are abstract in so far as they are considered simply as subjects of rights which arise from their existence as members of the social body and in so far as abstraction is made from their other ties. Nevertheless, despite their existence as subjects of such rights they are and always remain individuals. The abstraction they undergo is indispensable to the science of Right because right itself is only a relationship. If we try to do without it, we shall see that serious errors cannot be avoided.

1660. Wishing to prescind from this abstraction, we would have to suppose that being a member of civil society and being a human being were one and the same thing. It is clear that in such a case the individual would be destroyed, and that nothing would be unjust for society. Only by starting from this supposition can one say with Vattel, for example, that the State is obliged and has the right to preserve itself, and go on to add without further distinction, as Vattel does, that the State has, as a result, the right to all the means that are suitable for this end.[488]

---

[486] The question of political freedom is independent of that of the form of government. 'Democracy and aristocracy are not free States of their own nature. Political freedom is found in moderate governments alone. But it is not always present even in moderate governments. It exists only when power is not abused' (Montesquieu, bk. 11, c. 4).

[487] Government must direct everything it does to the good of human beings as *individual persons*, but must not use them for this end except as *members of a society*. This is the political problem, and it is not at all easy to solve.

[488] *SP*, bk. 1, c. 2, §18-20.

According to this teaching, there are no unlawful means; nothing is unjust for the State when its self-preservation is in question. It could keep itself in being by having thousands of innocents slaughtered if this were necessary. Such teaching is absurd, cruel, brutal and truly sickening.

Neither civil society, nor those who act on its behalf, can ever act unlawfully or unjustly, even for the sake of preserving society. Human beings exist independently of civil society; they are not human beings because they are members of such a society. Belonging to civil society is, as we have said, simply an additional, accidental relationship superimposed on humanity. We must not confuse human beings with a simple relationship; that would be disastrous. Let civil society perish, therefore, if need be, so that individuals may be saved; individuals must not perish so that civil society may be saved. Civil society can be dissolved and reformed, but without necessarily destroying the human individual who will lose for a moment his quality as a social member — or rather, will cease to be a member of one society in order to begin to be a member of a newly formed society. As we have seen the citizen must serve the human individual, not the individual the citizen. Properly speaking, society is the *means*, and individuals are the *end*.[489]

§2. *Jural rights and duties common to individuals and society*

1661. Civil society, therefore, and the individuals composing it must be regarded, relative to Right, as persons who each have a different, independent sphere. Each and everyone of the jural duties which we have explained binds equally the individual and the social person. In the same way, there is no right which cannot equally have as its subject one or other of these jural persons. This is clear of itself, but it is also important, and we shall therefore try to clarify it further by briefly reviewing first rights and then duties.

1662. Civil society, like the individual, can: 1. occupy unoccupied

[489] Cf. *SP*, bk. 2.

goods of any kind whatsoever; 2. defend lawfully occupied goods against any aggressors whatsoever; 3. require recompense for injurious damage sustained by these goods; 4. administer and use its own goods.

1663. At the same time, civil society, in all these four principles and their exercise, must follow the common rules of justice which we have noted; it has no advantage or privilege over its members relative to such rules.

Civil society, and the government acting on its behalf, is bound to observe in its exercise of these general rights the moderation by which such rights are of their nature restricted relative to other jural persons, both social and individual. Hence:

1. It can occupy what it finds unoccupied, but in such a way that others are impeded *as little as possible* from occupying what remains.

2. It can defend its rights against aggressors but in such a way that it does them *as little harm as possible*; in other words, it inflicts only sufficient harm to defend itself.

3. It can require and even obtain forcefully recompense for harm suffered either from a collective or an individual person, although the recompense cannot exceed the harm it has suffered, nor can this harm be used as an excuse to savage others or inflict other harm on them.

4. It can administer and use its goods, but even this has to be done with the *least disturbance* to others, and without inflicting harm on any other jural person, social or individual. The rights of civil society (a jural person equal to, but no greater than any other person) are themselves limited by contact with the rights of others.

1664. It is true that civil society, although considered before the law of Right as a jural person equal to and not greater than other jural persons, is considered, under another aspect, as a person with special characteristics. We shall, however, take its *proper notes* into consideration in social Right when we no longer deal with the notes it has in common with all jural persons. At this point, while considering civil society simply as a jural person, we realise that it is false for civil society, as a jural person, to limit the freedom of other human beings in a way greater than that exercised by any other individual person when co-existing with others. All co-existent jural persons limit one another reciprocally by their possession of rights; in other words, they limit the innocuous freedom of others by impeding both the occupation of things already occupied by themselves and actions which injure their rights. We can say, therefore, that society under its jural aspect limits human beings in their rights in the same way as human beings limit one another.

1665. Rights, and the tempering of rights, which pertain to civil society in its relationships with other persons inside or outside itself, pertain equally to other persons in their relationship with civil society. This is the only way to establish jural relationships between the individual and society, and to resolve the difficulties and complicated questions which can arise between these two jural persons.

§3. *Jural injuries done to individuals by society*

1666. In any case, pure love of truth should lead us to confess that human rights in general have always been oppressed and unacknowledged. This came about because society or social government was always stronger than separate individuals. And by society, or its government, I mean the majority of influential forces, if not always the majority of persons. It is indeed extraordinary to see that the remedy often proved much worse than the evil. Now and again, as oppressed individuals arose, people claimed to free them from oppression. But each of these saviours attempted in his turn to rise to a level from which he could tyrannise society. In this reaction of individuals to society, individuals themselves underwent greater servitude; the oppressor was no longer our tired or enchained society, but individuals who strove to outdo one another in oppression. No one is ignorant of the terrible experience of dominant oppression imposed by the crude, brutish, military force that sprang to the defence of the declaration, proclaimed by the constituent Assembly (1789), of human rights and the citizen. It was not society, but the most daring, rowdy and violent individuals who exercised the greatest tyranny over society itself. An English radical wrote, only too truly, that the declaration treated human beings 'as insane rulers, who had been granted full power on condition that they used it only according to a code of law which regulated the least of their actions.'

1667. Civil society, therefore, injures human rights in all the ways in which individuals injure one anothers' rights. Hence 1. it injures the *rights of freedom* of particular individuals

a) every time it impedes their occupying *actions* and *things*, without lawfully occupying them itself; or

b) restricts in any other way the activity of individuals to a greater degree than required by its own need.

1668. 2. It simultaneously injures the *rights of freedom* and *of ownership* by entering into the rights of lesser societies, or of individuals, and appropriating objects for itself either

a) through foolish pride which, under the title of public authority, thinks it can achieve everything, and uses this title to mask its injustices; or

b) under the pretext of its own advantage and the increase in *common good*, which cannot be promoted if it harms anyone. As we said, if it were lawful to harm unjustly a single human being to the advantage of twenty million, it would be equally lawful to sacrifice nine million nine hundred and ninety-nine thousand to save ten million.

c) Society also harms others' rights of freedom and ownership every time it prevents their owners from using or defending them, or obtaining recompense for them. Harm also results when it renders recompense more difficult, tardy, costly, accidental and so on, than it would be if compared with the use of private means pertaining to the state of nature.

1669. 3. Society injures others' rights again when it does not avoid, in the *use* of its own rights, everything that could offend others, and when it does not employ, within the confines prescribed for it by jural sphere of others, the greatest circumspection in their regard.

1670. 4. Again, it injures others' rights when it fails to temper the *defence* of its own rights, or its demand for recompense.

1671. 5. It injures others' rights again when it *permits* some individual, or body or class of people, to do wrong to another in its name, or when it helps another to do this by providing moral or physical force, or by not preventing another when it can do so.

[1667–1671]

1672. It is true that all these injustices normally contain something *material* and something *formal*, that is, ignorance and lack of consideration on the one hand, and greed and malice on the other. Generally speaking, even an upright will is not sufficient to avoid all acts which are of themselves unjust. In many cases, it is difficult to decide what is just and what is unjust, and the extent of the boundaries of rights. This explains why the greatest experts, legislations, national opinion, tribunals in the same nation and the decisions of identical tribunals are often at variance in their conclusions about cases of jurisprudence.

I certainly have no desire to exaggerate injustices for the sake of rhetoric (we have already had too much of that from deceased demagogues). Let us also grant that many of the injustices committed by society or its government in all ages and throughout all nations must be attributed in great part to the obscurity in which the science of public and private Right was found and still is found, and to an excessive adherence to positive legislation. We could also grant that the concept of civil society has not been sufficiently clarified; it has indeed remained complicated and vague until now as a kind of Proteus of the moral world which, under a thousand forms, slips from your hand when you want to take and bind it — as you would every other determined jural entity — with the thongs of definite rights and duties. In the midst of such obscure, uncertain teaching, self-interest and passions inevitably play their finest tricks.

Nevertheless, decent people came to suspect, and indeed are now certain, that the jural decisions first presented to them are often misleading, or that the difficulty of finding the truth is immensely increased in one's own case. They reflect on the obligation they have to instruct themselves delicately and impartially about the science of justice, and to be very cautious not to injure others' rights in the exercise of public authority. Each person injures these rights when he neglects careful knowledge of the right way, places obstacles to the discovery of truth and, because of his own self-certainty, abhors jural discussion. Civil society has this duty far more than individual human beings because its *peculiar responsibility* consists in making justice prevail, and thus be known.

We have to conclude, therefore, that civil society must take every care to ensure that reciprocal individual and social rights

[1672]

be placed in the greatest possible light for the sake of finding the correct decision in every case, and that society itself bring to an end the danger of infringing others' rights through ignorance.

6. Civil society already offends against others' rights simply by impeding public knowledge of a) moral cognitions and everything that could throw light upon doubtful cases where reciprocal rights and duties have to be determined; or b) by slowing or impeding the verification of the rights of individuals through restriction of their recourse to any action or discussion whatsoever which would serve to unveil injustice of every kind or to defend or vindicate justice in anyone's case. Vain motives of prudence, or claims that the credibility of its authority is better safeguarded, provide no excuse for behaviour of this nature.

1673. Applying the teachings already explained to special cases, we have the following results: 1. The opinion which considers all unoccupied sections of land as belonging to civil society restricts unduly the natural Right of occupation proper to individuals, at least in cases where the public authority, without immediately undertaking the cultivation of these lands, purposelessly leaves them sterile.

1674. 2. All restrictions by civil society placed on the freedom of its members injure their right to indifferent actions which are not *per se* injurious to society. Such restrictions are superfluous, and indicative solely of the vanity of authority.

1675. 3. Patents granted to inventors of something useful are wrongly called 'privileges'. They are simply a defence, provided by civil society, of the inventor's *right*. It is undoubtedly just and fitting that civilised societies should stabilise the existence of ownership whose subject is works of human ingenuity. For example, our own civilisation presents itself in a favourable light when taking the trouble, as it does, to provide a solid base for *copyright* laws. But these dispositions, which spring from common laws about ownership, must not be called privileges. Nor must they be called 'sovereign favours'; that would mean falsifying ideas — falsified ideas are inevitably abundant springs of injustice and calamity.

I cannot see, however, that the same comments could be applied to those true privileges which are sometimes granted to a person who is allowed the exclusive exercise of a trade or craft

[1673–1675]

that he has not invented. If such a privilege is granted, the natural freedom of all other persons is restricted by their exclusion from the exercise of that trade or craft; if public authority favours some person or family, or provides them with some advantage, all other individuals are injured in their rights. This comes about because they find their freedom restricted by means of *words alone*, and not by *lawful fact*. As we have seen, others' *freedom to actions* and to *things* can never be restricted by words, but only by lawful fact, that is, by *prior occupation.* The natural right of a craftsman extends only to the possibility of depriving competitors of their earnings by means of the superiority of his own output and marketing. Such excellence provides him with the lawful fact enabling him to occupy available earnings before anyone else. No one has any cause forcomplaint against him because every person is master of what his ability enables him to occupy before others. On the other hand, if an excellent craftsman or manufacturer is left high and dry as a result of people's ignorance of what is good for them and of their blind attachment to custom, the government may bring this craftsman and manufacturer to the people's attention by informing them of the available advantages. The government itself may even use these workers, and employ its own powers to persuade others to do justice to them. But it may not go further.

This explains why a government which makes some means of income exclusive to a person or family is usually the object of animosity. The people's good sense wants to know why the freedom of many craftsmen should be restricted for the sake of a single worker, who might be worthy of the privilege but would have had no need of it if his own predominance had enabled him to capture business from others. — The people's first feeling, and this is especially true of the other craftsmen, finds such privileges offensive. It seems to them that they have been unjustly restricted in their rights not by prior occupancy, which is the only lawful way of restricting others' freedom, but by mere words supported by governmental force. Insult has been added to injury.[490]

---

[490] 'The sacred laws of the XII tables forbid the establishment of laws for private individuals. This would be privilege. No one tolerates this. There is

1676. The question of curbs placed on trade is in many ways more difficult. If the government decides to impose curbs for the sake of public utility, it will be the responsibility primarily of *political economy* to judge whether such utility will result from the particular fact in question. But everyone knows that freedom of trade is a question which splits economic theorists irreconcilably. If we abstract from the special circumstances of nations and particular States and consider only human beings in one and the same family, free trade is obviously beneficial and moral; restrictions on free trade are a disaster for the human race. But we still have to see if such curbs could be advantageous when considered in relationship to the particular good of a nation or a region, at a determined time and in determined circumstances and external relationships. Here I have no hesitation in accepting the opinion of those who maintain that customs and other curbs of this kind can be advantageous for the special regions for which they are established, provided they are moderate and used for exceptional cases — in other words, they are simply provisional, temporary laws.

But are such curbs fair in relationship to other peoples when it is agreed that they are harmful to mankind as a whole? Are they just relative to all the individuals of the society for which they are established when the immediate advantage of such provisions is enjoyed only by certain determinate classes of persons, owners, traders and manufacturers?

— The question of free trade has scarcely been considered under this aspect of justice, although it is the principal point of view from which it should be examined if indeed it is true that justice precedes every other question and interest. The following reflections may be submitted, therefore, to wise people who may want to resolve the matter by taking it further.

Considered in general, competition through honest means is a *natural right* relative to all kinds of earning. No one can . prevent another from earning except by occupying beforehand, through competition, what the other would have earned. Such *pre-occupancy*, as we call it, comes about through expeditious effort and greater industry. To limit, by an act of will alone,

nothing crueller, more harmful or more intolerable for this city' (Cicero, *Pro domo*, c. 17. Cf. also *De Legib.*, bk. 3, c. 19).

[1676]

others' freedom to earn and in general their freedom to acquire some other good or *occupancy*, is an infringement of Right even if the limitation is supported with force. A private individual could not do this; the government, therefore, cannot do it in favour of an individual. Generally speaking freedom of trade is founded in natural Right and is therefore inviolable.

Applying this general principle primarily to the relationships between nations, and then to individuals of the same nations, we have the following results.

Relative to nations, it seems to me that it is always possible (when nations are agreed in recognising the obligation) to make just agreements or trade treaties which would not be intended to balance materially the burdens variously imposed on the import and export of products and manufactured goods, but to maintain intact freedom of trade by allowing reciprocal compensation and recompense in so far as free trade benefited one or other of the parties. The compensation and recompense could be derived from the right of ownership that each nation has over the territory of the land it inhabits. One consequence of this would be the exclusion of foreigners whose trade would thus be impeded indirectly. If such agreements are possible, they are also obligatory as a means of safeguarding simultaneously the freedom of private individuals and the national interest. Hence, if one of the nations refuses to enter into such agreements based on freedom of trade, the other acquires by the very refusal the right to curb the trade of this nation. Tariffs and curbs are thus legitimated by being brought into the Right of self-defence.

Relative to individuals and different classes of persons within a nation, government can impede the universal right to exercise the same branch of trade or industry by favouring certain individuals or classes if this is helpful to the public good. This, however, depends either upon the willingness of individuals and classes to give their assent to laws which prevent their competing in these activities, or on due compensation. Otherwise, their right of freedom would seem to have been violated.

1677. 4. We have indicated three ways of injuring *natural freedom*. We shall now give some examples of injury to *ownership*.

Extreme injustice is found in that system of absolute

dominion which gives government direct ownership over all the goods of the citizens without some foundation of special fact, such as the buying in of food under Joseph in Egypt. This monstrous system springs from two different sources: one proper to ancient times when nations were still barbarian; the other pertaining to the present, and proper to corrupt nations.

Barbarian nations abused the principle, which is true in itself, that public authority comes from God. Ignorant people, always extremely eager to behold marvels, were led to make of public authority a being which in some confused way could do all, know all and see all — a being which could not be suspected, spoken about or thought of without sacrilege. When reduced to such a deformed kind of concept, public authority not only does whatever it wants but, after deceiving others, deceives itself about its own nature and comes to believe that it can do everything without having any duties of its own. Obvious injustices then become merciful dispositions on the part of the most imaginative authority. This is an example of the fourth kind of injury mentioned earlier.

1678. 5. In modern times, whenever unbelief took the place of superstition, unlimited authority endeavoured to take on new forms and justify itself more subtly. Instead of stating that government can do everything because government comes from God, it was said that it can do everything because it comes from the people, and has the public good as its object. Self-interested flattery gave a philosophical form to theories about absolute monarchy;[491] later, this kind of flattery became the servant of every sort of demagogic passion. The fact remains that not even society as a whole can detach itself from the laws of justice. The principle of common good is valid relative to the *innocuous freedom* of individuals as such (that is, when the government occupies what individuals have not occupied); but it has no validity whatsoever relative to ownership.

Civil society may indeed restrict innocuous freedom by prior occupancy, but not by laws and force. This is a part of common right, and any other person can do the same. The only difference

---

[491] Hobbes' reply, when Lord Clarendon asked him why he had written such a bad book as *Leviathan*, is well known: 'The truth is, I am aching to return to England.'

[1678]

is that civil society, that is, its government, must do this for the common good; individuals as such can do it for their individual good, just as they can do it for the common good.

1679. We have to add only that the purpose for which civil society was instituted gives it a special power, not possessed by individuals as such, over the restriction of the right of an individual's ownership.

Society is instituted for the good of the individuals who compose it. The good of civil society, therefore, can only be the common good of its members. The good of an individual, on the other hand, is his own individual good, and nothing more. Consequently, while the individual person does not possess the right to restrict the rights of others for his own good, civil society does possesses for the common good a part of that faculty relative to the persons who are its members.

An example will help to clarify the matter. Let us imagine that civil society, when disposing of a piece of land belonging to one of its members, provides him with a part in the common good sufficient to fully compensate the harm done. Note that some great common good is insufficient as an outcome; it is necessary that the person who has been harmed should share in that good sufficiently to receive adequate compensation; otherwise he suffers an injustice. But, granted this natural compensation made from the common good or elsewhere for the person who has been harmed, government has every right to commandeer from this person's ownership. We prove this as follows.

We have seen already that each one must use his own rights in such a way that the minimum disturbance and restriction of advantage is inflicted on others. *Modality*, therefore, in the use of particular goods is never the object of true right[492] when the entire *good* which forms the object of right has been safeguarded for the owner. Every owner must be prepared, in accordance with the law of reason, to cede the objects of his rights when this is necessary either to lessen the disturbance suffered by others or to increase their well-being, provided that he is compensated and recompensed to the entire value that his goods can reasonably be expected to have. Government, which is responsible for

[492] Cf. *ER*, 252-255.

[1679]

the common good, can lay claim to others' land for the sake of public good in two cases:

1 when the resulting public good is shared by the owners in such a way that the harm they suffer is fully compensated;

2. when civil society compensates the owners fairly by requiring the person who has benefited to make up to the owners for any incomplete compensation from the common good.

Outside these two cases civil society, and those who govern on its behalf, has no right to use others' ownership.

1680. The first of the two cases is verified when there is danger of some barbarian invasion threatening the life of the citizens, the integrity of their women, religion, civilisation, freedom and every other greater good, even of material ownership. No one would deny that in such straits society has the fullest right to dispose of everyone's wealth. All the citizens are greatly compensated by the defence provided for them by their government. If, however, one single citizen could certainly escape from these calamities, civil society could not commandeer his ownership in the same circumstances without being obliged to compensate him for what it has taken from him. This person certainly has no jural duty to burden himself with arrangements for unnecessary defence. However, other members of the society may need this defence. If so, society's duty is to divide the burden equally between them while compensating those who were disproportionately burdened during the crisis.

The second of the two cases is far more frequent. We may think, for instance, of new roads or other works of public utility. In such cases, the owner is obliged to sell his land or house to civil society which must provide a reasonable price as compensation for his ownership.

1681. Questions could arise about the determination of the price: for instance, does sentimental value have to be taken into consideration? If so, what limit will be placed on it? — of its own nature, affection is extended indefinitely.

We shall find an answer to such questions if we return to moral principles. We reduced morality to a correct judgment made about the worth of things.[493] When we esteem things, we

---

[493] Cf. *ER*, 93-222.

ought not to abandon ourselves to caprice; we have to value them for what they are worth. But there is no place for any right whatsoever outside morality and just esteem. Disordinate affections, therefore, which do not arise from upright human nature cannot provide us with any right. It is true that affection for persons can never be excessive when we consider them absolutely, that is, as persons and not as things. But our affection for things must always be limited. We have to consider them as simple means at the service of virtue and of personal happiness. Two corollaries follow from this:

1. Civil society can never offend persons nor anything such as life and body which is individually joined to persons. Consequently, society has no right to take innocent life, or to inflict bodily injury against a person's will (at least not without adequate compensation — if indeed we are prepared to admit that corporal sufferings are susceptible of being priced as other goods are), even if the entire nation could be saved from extermination by means of such inflictions. The Gospel indicates a tremendous example of such injustice used as a pretext for the death of Christ: 'It is expedient ... that one man should die for the people.' This is an impious, deplorable maxim, although common to all pagan nations. The tag, '*Salus reipublicae summa lex esto*', expresses the same immoral principle, and has as its starting point the radical error whose deformity we wanted to demonstrate, that is, sociality is the principle of all morality. This ferocious principle, which has a thousand disguises and a thousand names, including the title 'reasons of State', never ceases to savage humanity. Machiavelli did not invent it; he popularised it.

2. In the case of things rather than persons, there is always some value to reasonable affection which can be discovered by careful calculation of all the circumstances. In doubt, the benefit has to be given to the owner. The possessor of a right must not be deprived of his right by others, nor be subjected to doubtful loss as a result of their actions.

1682. Outside these cases civil society is one jural person equal to others. The fiscal privilege which gives it first place amongst creditors by removing jural equality is simply injustice, although that does not mean that we have to agree with the saying: 'Under a good ruler, taxation is the cause of the worst evil.'

[1682]

1683. 6. We said that the third way in which civil society could injure others' rights of ownership was by impeding possessors in their attempt to defend their rights or seek compensation for them, or by rendering this more difficult than it would be if individual means were used for the same purpose. Civil society can neither suspend nor entirely abolish the natural law, but only assist it to prevail in all those cases where it is powerless to prevail. Hence, even under civil laws, many cases are found in which the parties do justice for themselves. In all these cases, the state of nature subsists (cf. 147-151). Self-defence, mutual and reciprocal defence amongst relatives and friends, compensation or repossession of goods wrongly taken from a person, and other acts of this kind cannot be altogether eliminated under civil laws.[494] In such cases, human beings really are in the state of nature. Public authority must indeed intervene if these acts disturb or threaten tranquillity, produce conflicts or disorder, or exceed their limits. Otherwise, it should even protect and authenticate them.

Civil laws must not determine everything and constrain people of good faith to undergo legal procedures without necessity. Such procedures are always accompanied by inconvenience, postponements, deception and expense.

1684. 7. Civil society can injure others' rights of ownership in its own defence and by inflicting harm greater than necessary upon transgressors. Criminal laws cannot have a single degree of severity greater than that which is necessary to repress criminal activity. The degree of punishment must vary according to times and circumstances. In modern days, for example, it has been greatly moderated.[495]

---

[494] For example, English laws permit the destruction of a wall erected in such a way that light is excluded from a house. According to the phrase of one celebrated author, civil society is instituted to change 'the ways of fact' into the 'ways of right' for humanity. Preventing conflict and private wars at their source is the first object that falls within the responsibility of civil society.

[495] Aristotle noted the progress from severe to milder laws in the development of Greek civilisation, as we notice it in Christian development. When he compared the Spartan legislation of Lycurgus with the more ancient legislation drawn up for Crete by Minos, he said 'by and large, ancient ways are cruder than modern ways' (*Polit.*, 2: 8).

It is highly probable, however, that in days past great injust-ice was committed by society through undue attachment to criminal laws which remained unchanged, despite alterations in mores. The rigour which had once been necessary became useless, although it was retained until *public resentment*, expressed orally, in writing and by facts, opened the eyes of governments and often inculcated fear of public unrest.

How extraordinary, though, that when the time had come for balancing the rigour of the law with less harsh ways of life, neither supporters of ancient severity nor upholders of modera-tion succeeded in reaching the heart of the matter! Both sides judge according to the pretended principles of absolute justice, although the whole question revolved around relative justice. The liberals condemn the conservatives as unjust, barbarous and cruel; conservatives condemn modern reformers as unjust and weak in their attitude to vice, which they seem to encourage. Both sides would be correct if the reformers, instead of main-taining that ancient severity was unjust, had considered it as inopportune for modern times, and if conservatives praised the justice once proper to law, but no longer appropriate. The only way in which society can avoid committing injustice in estab-lishing the correct degree of severity in punishment is to carry through what must be done in every other field, that is, it must embrace and cultivate knowledge, which it has to accept whatever its source.

1685. 8. Civil society injures others' rights of ownership in another way when, having suffered harm itself, it requires compensation greater than the harm it has undergone. An example of this is found in victorious nations which, having gone to war for what they believe are good reasons, remain dissatisfied with reparation for the offence received from the conquered nation. They think that victory alone provides them with the right to lord it over the vanquished, treat them cruelly and dispose of them as they please.

1686. 9. Society (the supreme authority) not only injures others' rights by its own action, but also through its magistrates, officials and others when it remains silent or even approves the evil they do in its name. One example of this is the flood of human blood that has been shed uselessly in the case of *crimen laesae*. These abuses depend in great part on the way in which society is constituted. Not all these abuses can be avoided but, granted this, society still has a duty to organise itself so that the least inconvenience results. — It can do nothing immediately! — Let it do immediately what it can and as it can, and what it knows it can. The moment for carrying out this sacred duty will depend by and large on the degree of knowledge that society has. Ignorance on its part, therefore, is injustice. I repeat: society has to learn and to omit nothing that will continually clarify the way in which it has to carry out such an important obligation.

1687. 10. The obstacles it places to the increase of such cognitions is another way in which society injures the totality of human rights. By impeding the development of the philosophical or merely jural knowledge necessary for illuminating its own rights and those of others, or the manner in which they are to be exercised and sanctioned, society sins mortally on a moral and a political level. This is particularly the case relative to ethical knowledge, when it can sin by placing obstacles to the truth and by opening the way to error. This explains why society has to undertake to solve the following difficult problem: 'How is moral truth to obtain the greatest development, and moral error the least?'

1688. 11. Finally, civil society injures others' rights when it places obstacles to the verification of rights and correct decisions in litigation. The principal duty of social government is that of judging cases of contention amongst its members. It is, therefore, obliged to institute laws, tribunals and legal procedure in such a way that justice may be done to all with the greatest speed, the least expense, the least inconvenience and the greatest uprightness. It is not obliged to obtain all this in an instant, although it is obliged not to neglect anything whatsoever that would bring such things about and to embrace loyally any light and any means offered for achieving such a purpose. No one should be able to say with any degree of probability: 'I see that some improvement is needed in the administration of justice. But society gags me; it does not want to understand' [*App.*, no. 13].

Article 2.
The enduring inviolability of rights

1689. The title to a right is always constituted by a fact.

However, besides the species of facts constituting titles to rights, there is an infinite number of other facts which do not constitute titles to rights. These facts, despite their multiplicity and durability, can never produce the slightest change in right. Moreover, whenever there is an attempt to change right by means of *facts extraneous to the nature of right* violation and injury are present.

1690. Force, for example, is a fact foreign to the constitution of right. Someone stronger than I does not acquire any jural ownership of what he takes from me however long the despoliation may last; he will never cancel, nor even weaken my title; I remain the owner of that thing for as long as I want wherever it may be. The moral force of my right is altogether independent of space, time or any kind of external, material power.

1691. As we said, prescription and usucaption have no jural efficacy from a merely temporal point of view, nor from the mere fact of possession. They receive it indirectly from the special conditions to which we are subject in the exercise of reciprocal rights (cf. 1049).

1692. Let us consider just one of these conditions. In its moral essence, right is constituted by a spiritual act of intelligence and will. But right, unless expressed in some exterior sign or productive of action, would undoubtedly lack respect and be powerless to take possession of anything. As we said, an external sign is an integral part of right (cf. 508-520).

But we also need some means of knowing the sign itself. This can only be another sign. Two species of signs of right are present, therefore: *constitutive* and *demonstrative*. This is how human beings, in their mutual conduct, are conditioned to external signs. But let us apply all this to prescription.

As we have seen, time does not alter rights in their essence, but it can obscure our knowledge of them. The conditions normally applied to prescription, that is, good faith, continued possession and the nature of the thing which can fall under prescription (cf. 1049), show that prescription is regarded only as a *critical* circumstance for the verification of rights.[496]

Prescription, therefore, as a simple means of judging the existence of laws, holds the place of a title in written as well as in natural law, but with this single difference: the person in a state of natural law is himself judge of the matter; in the state of civil law, tribunals are established to judge the matter. Note, however, that these two states always co-exist together. As we have said, civil society does not altogether destroy the natural state. Even under civil law, human beings are still to a great extent in a natural state. In civil society itself, therefore, we have to consider prescription as on a par with any other demonstrative sign of rights, that is, in two respects: relative to the person who judges in his own case, and relative to the person who judges the claims of others.

1693. The difference is immense. In fact, the person who judges his own case has nothing hidden from himself, and consequently possesses a favourable circumstance assisting him to arrive at a sound judgment. This is not so when a judge adjudicates in the cases of others and on the basis of dispositions which are not always sincere. Prescription will never be valid therefore for a thief, conscious that he has stolen, however long he remains in tranquil possession of what he has stolen, because he can never hide this circumstance from himself. But a judge will have to decide in the thief's favour if the alleged theft is not proved.

1694. The person who judges his own case is, therefore, in possession of immutable rules according to which he may direct his conduct in similar cases, simply because he has no fear that facts may be altered through falsity on the part of others. But the rules according to which a judge has to arrive at a decision necessarily vary:

1. According to the degree of human malice and deceitfulness.

The judge always finds himself in danger of injuring one or

---

[496] Another effect of time is to bring about forgetfulness of offences, which in turn leads to the cessation or diminution of moral resentment. It would seem, therefore, that according to the indication given by nature an old offence ought not to be punished in the same way as a recent offence.

other of the two parties. In the case of prescription, the arguments which form the basis of his judgment, that is, facts from the distant past, cannot be other than probable. The judge's uprightness consists in making his decision in accordance with the *greatest possible probability of not doing harm*, that is, according to *jural certainty*. This kind of decision does no injury to anyone because people have to be content with it when other certainty is impossible. If there is a false judgment, this will be the fault of whoever concealed circumstances which could have thrown light on the case. At the same time, not all proofs have the same value, which changes according to malice and deceitfulness in human beings. For instance, it is extremely probable that a truth told on oath in a certain period and in a religious nation would have little force in another period and in an irreligious nation. The judge's decision has to change, therefore, according to the highest probability of avoiding harm, precisely because he has to form his judgment on arguments that change their value with times and circumstances. For the same reason, civil laws that prescribe a rule for judgment have to undergo change, that is, they have to change their assessment of the force of legal proofs according to the understanding and moral quality of the people to whom these proofs are applied, and in relationship to other circumstances.

Nevertheless, civil laws, even when changing with the times, cannot equal the justice of natural uprightness. In the majority of cases they can do no more than establish a basis for *jural certainty*. Consequently, the law, although able to establish the basis for finding jural certainty in most cases, is subject to error in particular cases and leads to a decision contrary to natural equity. We must now ask if the right of individuals as such is harmed by the civil law in cases of this kind. We have to reflect that this seems a necessary evil dependent upon the generality of law. But if civil society has the right to make general laws, an evil necessarily connected with such a right cannot be imputed to civil society.

Positive legislation will not be able to claim immunity from every fault, however, unless two conditions are verified: 1. that it does not claim civil law as the sole obligatory means to which citizens have to resort when their rights are in conflict. They should be able to decide for themselves according to the natural

[1694]

state in which they are, provided this can be done without disturbing public order; 2. that in particular cases the irregularity or injustice consequent on the generality of the law should be the *least possible*. Government should do everything possible to improve or reform laws, and reduce necessary evil to the minimum. In this way, everyone will be generously compensated for the few inevitable evils by the greater good promised and produced by the law.

1695. 2. The rules according to which the judge gives his decision have to vary also according to the value of the goods which are put in danger by the decision.

As we said, the judge's decision has to be given with the intention of causing the least possible probability of harm. It follows that this danger will be the minimum possible if, in the case of error, the error itself produces the least possible harm. For instance, let us imagine that the probability of being right is the same for both parties to a dispute. The judge, in passing a wrong decision, may do a great deal of harm to one party by finding in favour of the other. By favouring the other, he may, in the case of error, do little harm to the first party. In these circumstances, he will have to decide for the least harm if he cannot in any way divide it or compensate for it. If, however, the harm can be divided or compensated, this should be done.

Article 3.
The inviolability of rights in any circumstance

1696. There are circumstances in which it is hard to respect the rights of others, and pleasant to violate them. Rights are of a moral nature, and therefore independent of circumstances. This is easy to understand if we simply recall what has been said. Human beings are twofold in themselves: subject and object, feeling and intelligence. As feeling, they act through sensation; as intelligence, through the idea. *Sensation* ends in itself, without making anything known; human nature is rooted in sensation, through which we are subjects. The *idea* refers us to something different from ourselves: it supposes an act of intuition, and something intuited; it constitutes human understanding and brings the subject to unconditioned truth.

Human beings as mere subjects would have neither rights nor duties; they would act instinctively. Rights and duties, if they are to exist, require two entities: one with a duty and one towards which this duty is directed. The subject presents itself as only a single, simple thing.

The relationship of the human being as subject with the human being as object constitutes rights and duties. The human being sees himself; as seen, the human being is humanity itself participated by an intelligent individual. Reason prescribes respect towards humanity wherever it is found, wherever reason sees it, whether in other individuals or in the individual whose reason it is; reason judges that others and self are to be respected equally. Each human being sees other human beings through his reason, but he feels neither their pleasures nor their pains; he sees himself, and at the same time he feels his own pleasures and pains. In so far as he sees himself, he is object to himself; in so far as he feels his pleasures and pains, he is subject. Duty, however, can be exercised only towards an object; in this case (where the object — humanity — is equal in himself and others), the subject has an equal duty towards others and towards himself. The fact that he feels his own pleasures and pains, but not those of others, does not mean that he has an extra duty towards himself, or an extra right, or that his rights are preferable to those of other human beings.

It follows from this teaching that human beings have to act morally, independently of the pleasure and pain they can derive for themselves from their actions. The moral law, coming as it does from the object, has no regard for the subject, and utters its commands in total independence of pleasure and pain.

1697. Hence, the difficulty of virtue. On the one hand, human beings have to act solely in accordance with the object; on the other, in our condition as subjects we are borne towards pleasure independently of consideration of the object. Strife looms before us. Intelligence stands above it, totally disregarding instinctive activity while prescribing reasonable activity. Such is the absolute dominion intelligence wishes to have over instinct; such is the necessary triumph of idea over sensation.

[1697]

Here full liberty, that is, moral strength, the condition of all virtues, finds its home.

The consequence is clear: rights have to be respected in all circumstances whatever pain or pleasure they may cause.

1698. But isn't extreme necessity an exception to this rule?

If it could be proved that another's right existed at this point, it would be better to perish rather than infringe it. The question, therefore, is not concerned with the moral possibility of infringing a right, but with knowledge of its existence. We have seen the limits to external ownership, and how ownership, in order to be right, has to be moderated by the laws of reason. But these laws do not allow us to be so attached to any superabundance in what we own that we can deny it to a dying person. This would be immoral, and destroy right.

1699. On the other hand, the right to life involves a right to provide the necessities of life for oneself when this can be done without risk to the life of another. Sometimes human beings suffer slavery and the sharpest pain without moral resentment. Mental insensitivity in savages and slaves in this regard is a phenomenon that provides obvious proof of their lack of moral resentment at what they suffer. But this is never the case when we are dealing with life itself. When existence is in the balance, human beings throw off their lethargy. Danger to existence excites in them intellectual forces which even appear to be stultified in the midst of intense corporal misery. This shows that we never abandon the jural possession of our own existence. Reason confirms this: we have necessarily to admit that human beings naturally take possession of their own existence with an act of the understanding (cf. 53-58, 537). They have, therefore, an essential, special right to life which no one can injure; and life is that intimate union which forms a single individual, a single person, of body and soul. If, therefore, personship is inviolable, the life of the human being, a complement of personship, is inviolable.[497] There is no case in which

---

[497] Personship, indicated in Scripture by the noble phrase 'made in the image of God', is offered as proof of the gravity of the crime of homicide, and of this crime only. It is one of the Noachian precepts, expressed as follows: 'Whoever sheds the blood of man, by man shall his blood be shed; for God made man in his own image' (Gen 9: [6]).

one human being could be the cause of another's death without offending the other's right. We must conclude that in cases of extreme necessity no one can, without injury to another, prevent that person from using food which the owner does not need, and that in these straits a person in need can take for himself the food denied him by others.

This argument cannot be applied to other kinds of corporal suffering, however great, but only to the case of danger to life.

Article 4.
The inviolability of rights, however they are offended

1700. Others' rights may not be offended either directly or indirectly, with a positive or a negative act, by use of what is our own or belongs to others, by our own activity or by the consequences of our activity.

1701. Nevertheless, rights of *freedom* are distinguished from rights of *ownership* because injury is not the same in both cases. Rights of freedom can be limited in others without injury by means of *pre-occupancy* (when others' freedom is forestalled by the use of our own) and by the *exercise of our right of ownership*. For example, the right of passage along the public highway for oneself and one's goods, the right to a necessary stop-over, the right of hospitality provided for exiles, the right to cultivate uncultivated lands, the right to contract marriage, and similar rights to actions and things enumerated by authors, cannot be attributed in an unlimited way to aliens. Civil society has the right to block, restrict and bind these rights to determined conditions, if this proves useful or has common consent, although it cannot be done out of caprice, from hardness of heart or as a result of unfounded suspicion. Moreover, because even here action must be directed in accordance with the just calculations of prudence, it is necessary that civil society change its conduct according to circumstances. When people live simple lives, society has perhaps no right to deny strangers passage along the public highway. But this will not be the case where there is ground for suspicion. The fact that the Hebrews fought their way forward with the sword through the lands of the Idumeans and the Amorites does not prove that every people has the right to pass through the lands of others. At most, it shows that such a right needed to be recognised at that time, and that the Idumeans and the Amorites had no reason to fear a people who gave proof of their uprightness in the balanced treaties they concluded. The same can be said about all other rights to actions and things: provided that a person has a just motive for judging that the limit he places to others' freedom is of assistance to himself, and provided he does this by using his own ownership, he can place such a limit. And this is the case whether the good he expects is direct or indirect, immediate or a remote consequence of the limitation he has posited.

1702. On the contrary, the exercise of ownership by others cannot be limited without fault. It cannot be limited:

1. Directly or indirectly. — If by speaking we willingly gave occasion for a theft, we would already be accomplices to the crime.

2. By our own activity or its consequences. — If in defending our land from flooding, we diverted a river to another's land, we would injure his right of ownership.

3. Positively or negatively. If we permit our flock to pasture in another's wood, we are the cause of the harm because we did not prevent it.

1703. Peace is maintained by this mutual respect for others' rights, proper to reasonable beings. It also opens the way to mutual agreements. The owners of land along the banks of a river liable to flood could not, according to the Right of nature, undertake separate repairs if this meant harming one another, but they could unite for the sake of common protection with proportionate expenditure. And because leaving the river without adequate provision would mean that each would suffer considerable harm, they all have an obligation to unite and agree about what is best in the common interest. Anyone refusing to form part of such an agreement would harm the rights of the others who could then carry on without him. This is a new case in which the right of others cannot be injured even negatively, that is, by not acting.[498]

---

[498] The Austrian civil code itself recognises in general the owner's *right not to make use of something he owns* and *to allow it to perish*, but limits this right

CHAPTER 4
The right to defence

Article 1.
The distinction between the right to defence
and the right to satisfaction

1704. We shall first deal with the right to *defence*, which we have to distinguish from that of *satisfaction*.

1705. It is clear that the right to defence is exercised either before the sphere of our rights is invaded or during the act of invasion. Our right to satisfaction on the other hand is present only after the sphere of rights has been invaded, and injury and harm inflicted. Defence aims at preserving our rights safe from threatened and feared offences; satisfaction, at ensuring amends for offences inflicted.

Article 2.
Analysis of the right to defence:
1. the right to simple defence, and 2. the right to harm others
when defence is necessary

1706. We have to begin our study of the right to defence by analysing this right. Analysis indicates two parts to the right: on the one hand, we have simple defence of rights under attack without harm to others; on the other, harm to others when defence of our rights is necessary. These are quite different things.

when dealing with particular matters if harm would result to others' ownership from such behaviour. §858 includes such limitation of the principle admitted by the code: 'Normally the exclusive owner is not obliged to repair his broken wall or fence. He has a duty to keep it in good repair only if his neighbour fears harm as a result of the breach.' Care should be taken, therefore, to interpret rightly the rule: 'No one causes harm by using his own right.'

We have, therefore, to answer two questions:
1. Can we defend our rights with force?
2. Can we defend our rights to the extent of inflicting harm on others when defence is otherwise impossible?

Article 3.
The ethical foundation of the right to defence

1707. The ethical foundation of the right to defence can only be the law of justice.

1708. *Fact* is not *right*. *Right* in its formal part[499] pertains to the order of *possibilities*, and consequently to the order of idealities, as law does; fact pertains to the order of *realities*. We have to find, therefore, the idea, the moral law, which justifies self-defence, and thus show how defence obtains the nature and dignity of right. Obviously, the source of this nature cannot be other than the law which justifies and protects it. This law, applied to self-defence, becomes the *form* of the right to defence. It is equally clear, therefore, that authors who deal with such right without showing how it receives its being from the moral law take as their object only the material part of defence and neglect the formal part.

1709. Ethical law has therefore to justify two things in the right of defence: *defence* itself, and any *harm* to our fellows resulting from necessary self-defence.

Defence of a right, carried out with the use of force, is inherent to the right that is being defended. As we saw, defence is nothing more than a function of right.[500] The law which justifies, protects and informs right, also authorises its defence.

This law, which recognises in the personship of the human being a lawful, inviolable subject of rights, permits a person to employ all his forces in the exercise of the rights he has. But because this person has physical as well as intellectual force,

---

[499] The law, in so far as it protects human *activity*, is the formal part of right. But the law is 'a *notion* of the mind with which we judge of the morality of actions.' Cf. the defence of this definition in *PE*, 1.

[500] Cf. *ER*, 246-251.

such permission is equivalent to permitting *coercion*, which is simply the use of these forces to maintain right.

1710. But what kind of ethical law enables us to justify and authorise the *harm* caused to others on the occasion of necessary defence of one's own right? Can this *harm* be caused even in the case of harmless persons? We shall answer these questions first by examining the harm that can be done to the unjust offender when it is necessary to repel the attack made on our rights; and then by deciding if, as a result of the same necessity, harm can be caused to others who do not act unjustly in our regard.

Article 4.
Continuation. — The right to harm an unjust intruder when harm is necessary in defence of our rights

1711. The harm inflicted upon an unjust intruder by the need to defend our rights is justified by the law of penal justice which states: 'Whoever willingly causes evil must bear the penalty'; in other words, 'Moral evil and eudaimonological evil have to be balanced', just as moral good and eudaimonological good have to be balanced in the same subject.

The person who attacks others' rights 1. is the willing cause of the moral evil that he commits; and, 2. if the attack succeeds, the willing cause of the physical evil undergone by the innocent person who has experienced the attack.

Consequently the innocent victim who defends his right by inflicting necessary harm on the aggressor (that is, the harm needed to safeguard his right) fulfils the general law of justice which declares that an individual who does evil deserves punishment. Self-defence makes the victim himself a minister of justice. When unjust aggression brings matters to such a term that some harm is inevitable, all that remains is to decide whether the guilty or the innocent should suffer. Justice requires that the guilty author of such a collision should suffer its effects. As a result, this person must impute to himself the harm that is inflicted upon him.

Article 5.
The distinction between the right to defence and penal right.
— does a penal right exist in the state of nature?

1712. If we wish to call *penal Right* the right to inflict merited punishment, we shall find that the right to defence, where it includes the right to cause necessary harm to a guilty attacker in one's own defence, is simply a branch of penal Right. This Right finds in self-defence an occasion or opportunity to be activated, in so far as the infliction of just punishment becomes a condition attached to the exercise of the right of defence.

1713. However, *penal Right*, considered simply as a complex of laws prohibiting certain injurious actions by the sanction of determined punishments, or as the power to inflict these punishments, clearly has no further place in the state of nature. According to this meaning, penal Right is simply a production of a society in which people unite and consent to the establishment by government of such laws and punishments.[501]

1714. Taken in this sense, Romagnosi is correct when he states: 'Penal Right is simply the right to defence,[502] modified by social circumstances'.[503]

1715. But it is not true that the right to defence is limited in the state of nature only to the act of intrusion or attack upon another's right. It is certain that in such a state the human being cannot make true *penal laws* because the power to establish morally obliging laws supposes the existence of subjects, and superiority on the part of the legislator. It is clear, however, that

---

[501] According to Romagnosi, 'the social union would have the right to punish misdeeds on the supposition that several hundred savages united to live in society but declared that they did not want to submit to penal laws' (*Genesi del D. P.*, pt. 2, c. 24). It would be more coherent to say that such a society would still need to be formed because the savages rejected one of the indispensable conditions for the existence of society. As soon as Romagnosi supposes a *willing* association of savages, it is clear that this willingness must either refer to all the conditions indispensable for a society, or remain an insufficient cause of the society. In the latter case, neither the society nor the social right to punish has come into existence.

[502] Nevertheless, the Right to *satisfaction* has a part in *penal right* as well as in the right to defence because coercion is used in both.

[503] *Genesi del D. P.*, pt. 2, c. 18, §332.

[1712–1715]

even in the state of nature there are cases where the human individual can

1. defend himself against aggression when it is already under way;

2. defend himself against attack and preparations for attack on the part of unjust enemies seeking to assail him;

3. take precautions against future, probable offences in the manner and under the conditions we shall describe;

4. inflict correctional punishment or chastisement upon the offender to deter him from repeating the same offences in the case of a habit or some habitual, evil disposition;

5. deter others and make himself respected, if the offence is serious, by inflicting upon persons attacking his rights a severe, just punishment as an example to others, provided the deterrent is necessary for holding others in check and making them desist from their desire to impose harm upon him;

6. issue decrees and establish norms when he knows that he possesses sufficient force to make them prevail, provided they conform to natural law, according to which he attaches certain punishments to actions or attacks injurious and harmful to him.

1716. These norms and punishments, when intimated and threatened by a just, powerful individual against individuals co-existing but not associating with him, correspond — if considered in their *positive* nature — to so-called *merely penal laws*. If considered as faithfully enunciated expressions or determinations of the Right of nature, they have a genuinely obligating value.[504]

1717. 7. Finally, the individual can also do for others what he does in the state of nature for his own defence, provided he never exceeds the law of justice.

---

[504] Dr. Girolamo Scari made several sound comments on Romagnosi's *Genesi del Diritto Penale* in his article for the Viennese *Giornale di Giurisprudenza*. Amongst them we find: 'It seems contradictory to deny to isolated individuals the right to use violence as a safeguard when this right is granted to one people against another' (Cf. *Genesi*, pt. 1, Appendix 2).

Article 6.
The *lex talionis*

1718. Before moving ahead with our study, I would like to reflect on the *lex talionis*, examining it as the means used by many ancient legislations to actuate in society the Right to defence, or civil, penal Right. Several modern authors have objected to this law. Realising that the harm inflicted on others in self-defence must not exceed what is absolutely necessary to defend one's own rights, they condemned the *lex talionis* as an excessive, disproportionate measure for effecting necessary self-defence.

1719. This judgment, however, depends on the false supposition that the *lex talionis* is simply the right of defence determined quantitatively by public law. In fact, the *lex talionis* is related to *penal right* in general; it is not a special actualisation of *penal right* called the *right of defence*, or better the *right to inflict punishment* in order to defend oneself.

1720. Taken in its simplest form, *penal Right* has as its base the eternal principle of justice which requires 'moral evil to be balanced by eudaimonological evil, and moral good by eudaimonological good.' It is clear that this principle is deeply impressed in the minds of all peoples. It is found at the base of all legislations and forms part of the conscience of mankind.

1721. The *lex talionis* determines and applies in an approximate, general way the principle of penal Right, which declares as just that a person perpetrating an evil against his fellow should experience the same evil. This rule is a consequence of the natural dictate: 'Do to others what you would want done to yourself; do not do to others what you would not want done to yourself.' Whoever breaks this precept exposes himself to receive as much as he has given; we can only expect that others, all of whom are equal to ourselves, should treat us as we have first treated them. According to the universal law of natural justice, we have no right beyond this.

[1718–1721]

Article 7.
Humanity excludes purely penal Right, and revenge

1722. Here two questions arise: 1. Can an individual in the state of nature make himself the executor of penal law beyond what is required for self-defence, and go so far as to inflict on others the *lex talionis*? 2. Can civil society do the same?

1723. It is clear from what has been said that the *lex talionis* can be considered under two different aspects: either simply as a norm according to which penal justice can be carried out; or as a means of defence for the individual and society (that is, as an exemplary punishment which cannot be more suitably replaced).

1724. If we consider this law simply as a norm directing the execution of penal justice, we are immediately faced with the question we have posed: 'Can human beings (an individual, or society) be the minister of penal justice relative to another human being?' Those who say 'No', reason that one human being can never judge another because all human beings are equal, and judgment, they say, is proper to a superior, just as being judged is proper to an inferior.

1725. Careful examination of this argument shows its weakness. It is not true that judgment is proper to a superior alone; rather, judgment is proper to a person with the understanding necessary to judge. If, in fact, a superior existed who were not intelligent enough to judge according to the truth, he should abstain from judging; if there were an inferior intelligent enough to judge according to the truth, he should have the right to judge. After all, judgment is simply an act of reason.

1726. But do human beings *know* how to judge others?

First, it is certain that human beings do not always know how to judge faults in others. In these cases an indispensable condition for the application of punishment is lacking, and neither the individual nor still less civil society can exercise the Right to punish.

1727. Second, very many degrees of blameworthiness (degrees dependent upon profound, internal dispositions of spirit) remain unknown to human beings. Consequently neither the individual nor civil society has sufficient knowledge to balance

[1722–1727]

punishment against fault. Such knowledge is proper to him who 'tries the minds and hearts'. Neither the individual nor society can ever *fully* exercise penal Right.

1728. Third, it is certain that human beings (individuals and society) can possess sufficient proof to generate *jural certainty* of the *existence* of some crime and fault. Such proof is taken from confessions or statements on the part of the guilty person, and from two or three eye-witnesses. Although we cannot uncover all the degrees of fault, which depend upon interior, hidden and uncommunicated or incommunicable dispositions of spirit in the guilty person, we can, once the existence of internal fault has been ascertained, uncover those degrees of fault revealed through the *quantity of criminal action*. And punishment can justly be applied in accordance with this quantity.

1729. This is in fact the foundation of the *lex talionis*. When the existence of a crime has been verified (without reference to the degrees of fault arising from hidden dispositions), the *lex talionis*, and indeed all penal laws we may say, comes into being to apply the punishment according to the degrees exhibited in the external *quantity* of harm.

1730. This is enough to show that relative to the condition of necessary knowledge, some penal Right can be exercised justly, although not completely, by human beings.

1731. It is not correct to object that crime could be punished disproportionately if internal, hidden dispositions, which cannot be calculated, are neglected, because some of these internal dispositions could considerably attenuate the fault. Granted that penal Right is concerned with mere justice, such an objection fails to consider that external, physical punishment never balances moral fault. Punishments, therefore, can only be less than deserved in relationship to justice, not more.

1732. Nevertheless, we must note carefully that nothing said so far proves that human beings have the right to punish fault. It only proves that in certain cases we have sufficient knowledge to apply to a fault a punishment which is not greater than justice requires and which, although imperfect in proportion to the fault, is proportioned to its external degrees. We must therefore ask once more if human beings have the right to exercise penal justice within certain limits. This is the question we still have to solve.

1733. We can be moved to inflict punishment on our guilty fellow-creatures by four principles which produce a fourfold division in the question we have posed. We can be moved to punish human crime:

1. By mere *love of objective justice*. As intellective, moral beings we naturally want and desire justice not to be injured or, if injured, to be restored and vindicated.

2. By *self-love*, when the offender's action is turned against us. This is the origin of the rights of defence and satisfaction.

3. By *love of our fellows*, when the offensive action is turned against our fellows. This is the origin of our right to come to the defence of others, and constrain the offender to render just satisfaction.

4. By zeal, that is, *by love of God*, in cases where injury is inflicted or an attempt is made to inflict injury on God. Love of God, which is a natural conclusion of our desire to see God acknowledged, loved and honoured by all intelligent creatures, enkindles a most just zeal against those who impede it through their own fault or act contrary to the honour owed to God.

1734. We have already spoken about the first and fourth cases when we dealt with innate rights (cf. 141-238). What we said can be summarised as follows:

1. It cannot be maintained that we act unjustly if, in cases where we are able to pronounce a *certain judgment* on the guilt of actions, we vindicate the fault through pure love of justice in itself and of the honour due to God.

2. An *inclination* to justice exists within human beings which brings them in fact to punish guilty actions (demonstration of *human instinct*), especially those actions which injure the honour owed to God. Because this inclination tends towards what is just, it would seem to take its place amongst the inclinations forming the *roots* of natural rights.

3. However, human beings can easily abuse this tendency. Every time we judge rashly and consequently inflict unjust punishments, or are moved by individual passions, we render ourselves guilty and unjust. In this case, our activity goes completely beyond the terms we have proposed.

The extraordinary ease with which we exceed these terms, granted humanity's present state after its original fall, forces us to conclude, even for this reason, that there are very few cases in which human beings in the state of nature can exercise this right of penal justice without fear of error.

1735. If, after the fall, people had acted simply according to their great sense of penal justice, they would probably have brought mankind to disaster, or even destroyed it altogether. Reasonable beings have a natural persuasion that corporal punishment of any kind is insufficient to castigate infractions of justice, especially if the injustice is directed against God. Such a state would have prompted mankind to have recourse to the death penalty for all crimes. In fact, this is the position taken by and easily observed in the oldest legislations, all of them written in blood.

1736. God, however, who unites mercy with justice, came to the aid of humanity, which would have succumbed before such an evil. At the very beginning of the world, he forbade capital punishment, even in the case of murder. Cain's words: 'Whoever finds me, will *slay* me',[505] were the voice of human nature which sensed keenly the instinct and necessity of penal justice. But God opposed that fearful penal right with his own positive law of piety and grace when he said: 'If anyone slays Cain, vengeance shall be taken on him sevenfold.'[506]

Scripture goes on to say that God put a mark on Cain so that he might not be killed by anyone who found him. Some mark was needed in order to save the fratricide's life; without it, no one in that first period of time would have hesitated to carry out the just, obligatory work of mortal retribution. By setting his positive law in opposition to the natural law, and his goodness and mercy against naked, human justice, God tempered and limited such a dangerous right of nature from the beginning. Lamech himself took refuge in the benign, divine decree after his angry slaughter of a young man. The feeling of justice inserted in his heart gave rise to a great fear for his own life, even at the hands of his wives for whom he composed the verses:

'If Cain is avenged sevenfold,
truly Lamech seventy-sevenfold.'[507]

1737. Finally, as mankind and society continued to develop,

505 Gen 4: 14.
506 Gen 4: 19.
507 Gen 4: 24.

divine revelation increased and reached its zenith with the incarnate Word of God. At this point, the practical execution of the right to punish, as such, was taken away from human beings completely and reserved to God alone. Indeed, perfect faith, such as that possessed by the Christian, persuades people that God unfailingly and fully punishes all injustices in the way best suited for the greater good of mankind (by bringing mercy and truth together in the kiss of peace), and at the right moment. It is impossible for anyone with this kind of faith to want to take upon himself the responsibility of vindicating offended justice. In fact, he could not do this lawfully without contradicting his faith if love of justice alone were directing him in this matter. The merely natural right of punishment cannot be exercised today by a Christian — to his good fortune — unless he is stimulated to do so by some extraordinary movement of the divine spirit itself.

1738. We still have to speak, however, of the second and third cases we have mentioned. The second case deals with what, according to natural Right, an individual can do against someone who offends him. Here three rights have to be examined: the *right to retaliation*, the *right to defence*, and the *right to satisfaction*.

1739. What is the right to retaliation? Does it exist in the state of nature? Can it be exercised by human beings under positive revelation?

Retaliation is the punishment decreed by the law of justice when one person has offended the personal dignity of another. It concerns *injury*. The person injured naturally feels and requires some satisfaction or restitution of honour from the offender. When he cannot obtain this, the injured person believes that he naturally possesses a right to inflict upon the offender a punishment or dishonour equivalent to that which he has unjustly received.

1740. Considered in itself, this is just. Justice requires balance, an eternal sanction. Injured personship must be compensated with equal honour and the offender must receive equal punishment and indignity. Considering, therefore, only the intimate nature of things and of human beings, the existence of the right to retaliation is undeniable if we take our reflection no further.

All the constitutive elements for such a right are present, and may be summed up under two headings:

1. a natural tendency (a branch of human instinct), obedience to which forms an eudaimonological good for human beings;

2. the justice of this tendency with which the injured person endeavours solely to re-establish the balance of justice now disturbed to the detriment of his dignity.

1741. But the third question, 'Can an individual exercise such a right under positive revelation?', must be answered negatively. God positively reserved the execution of such retaliation to himself when he said: 'Vengeance is mine, and recompense.'[508] God's law of perfection tempers crude right here also. The reason is clear. God has never abandoned mankind, his own work, to itself. On the contrary, he has always kept it under his own rule and, as supreme ruler, governed and continues to govern it in such a way that justice must be reconciled with mercy and goodness — a reconciliation possible only to God, who intends mankind to produce that *maximum* of moral good (and consequently of eudaimonological good) which is the end of creation.

We have to consider carefully that natural rights, which pertain only to the class of *lawful* things, occupy the lowest place in the order of moral matters. Human nature, however, according to the great designs of the Creator, must be borne up to meritorious, generous and *perfect* matters, which occupy the highest places in the moral order. What is *lawful*, therefore, such as rights, must whenever required give way to the cause of virtue and of the moral perfection of the world. This was the most holy intention of God in establishing his law: VENGEANCE IS MINE.

On the other hand, moral reason itself, when it reaches a certain degree of perfection, suggests that individuals 'should altogether renounce the exercise of the right to retaliation by leaving it entirely to God.' However, we cannot give ourselves such excellent advice without first firmly believing that God exists, that he is the remunerator of good and evil, and moreover

508 Deut 32: 24.

that he distributes this remuneration with infinite justice, totality, wisdom and goodness. With this belief implanted in their spirit, human beings who nevertheless claim to exercise the right of naked retaliation on their own behalf and in their own favour clearly posit an immoral act against such faith. They act uselessly and unreasonably. But those who perform useless, irrational actions show that they are overly dominated and led by some blind passion. Consequently, the Redeemer's disciples are forbidden to retaliate of themselves and commanded to be *meek*. At the same time they are promised that God himself, who without passion acts according to holiness and justice, will avenge every injury they receive.

1742. The answers would be the same in the case of retaliation on behalf of others. In effecting such retaliation, we are dealing either with the first question about the exercise of merely penal justice if the motive is pure love of justice in general, or with the second question of retaliation in one's own cause — or at least with a similar problem if the motive is some kind of affection for the person on whose behalf we are acting. In both cases, the exercise of retaliation is excluded by revelation and by the state of moral perfection in which the human race is placed by divine goodness after the coming of Christ.

1743. Defence and satisfaction, therefore, are the only cases in which the right to penal justice can be exercised by human beings. There is a problem here, however. In such cases, how is it possible to exercise the right to penal justice without conflicting with the law of the Gospel, if indeed mere penal justice or retaliation cannot be exercised unless there is call for defence or satisfaction? If God avenges, will he not also compensate the harm suffered by the offended person?

1744. In my opinion, *the order of mere penal justice*, when considered without relationship to real harm done to human beings, and *the order of mere retaliation*, are things pertaining to the internal, spiritual, invisible world. Consequently, although some disorder remains for a time in the metaphysical world, it is soon corrected, while the external, physical, visible human world is neither disturbed in its course as a result, nor less conserved. It would be different however if harm were not impeded or put right. In this case, real harm disturbs the course of the human, external world and harms its conservation. *Harm*, therefore, should be foreseen, repulsed or immediately put right by public authority or by anyone motivated by a spirit of humanity and charity who comes to the aid of another. It is not innocuous or indifferent for society to wait for the end of the world when the supreme Judge will restore all things to the full order of justice, although the meek, however, waiting like this on their own behalf, never lose, but gain, in accordance with the guarantee given them by God.

1745. *Injuries* themselves, therefore, can be prevented or willingly set right whenever they can be the cause of harm, but only to this extent and no further. In other words, in so far as they are *injuries* which *inflict harm*, not in so far as they are mere injuries. Consequently, the right to defence and satisfaction includes the jural power to self-defence against such injuries and to satisfaction for harm undergone. This power is not operative in relationship to injury in itself, but to injury in its consequences, neither more nor less. God has not reserved for himself, by means of his positive, perfect law, the exercise of the right to defence and compensation. He has left this free for human beings provided they use it in a holy way. He has however reserved entirely for himself the right to the exercise of merely penal justice, and to retaliation for injuries *qua* injuries.

1746. With all these things clarified, we can now go back and comment on the *lex talionis*, which is found in almost all ancient legislations and consecrated by the law of Moses. We can say that it was a penal law intended to *defend* ancient societies. There was perhaps no other law as effective as this in proposing exemplary, efficacious punishments suitable for holding back criminal impulses. The reasons for this are as follows:

1. Those primitive, undeveloped societies did not have sufficient elements for the exact calculation of criminal impulses and the quantity of repression needed to contain them. As a result such societies had to rely on experience and the good sense of the legislators, on the basis of which they guessed the measure needed. The legislators were rather like Roman architects who depended upon practical, and often imaginary data for calculating the stresses and strains on vaults, but always tended to make their structures stronger than actually necessary.

2. One well-known characteristic of effective penal law is that everyone, the guilty included, can easily come to recognise

its justice.[509] But the *lex talionis* was universally recognised as just in virtue of the very feeling of nature. For this reason, other punishments, measured according to more complicated calculations, could not be easily understood.[510]

Article 8.
Can harm be done to an innocent person when this is necessary to defend one's own right?

1747. Purely material offences are not injuries to rights; human beings are not in any way their authors. Such injuries are to be attributed to accidental factors, such as disasters, for which no one is to blame. By common consent, therefore, legislators do not prescribe any compensation for them: *si res perit, domino perit*. Formal offences, however, have as their cause the human beings who commit them, and compensation can be required. Material offences cannot produce either moral displeasure or reasonable resentment. It is unreasonable, for example, to be indignant with hail or with other inanimate things that harm us.

1748. But is it impossible to defend oneself when a human being acts mechanically? Must the intrusion on one's rights be

[509] Romagnosi's *Genesi del Diritto* opens with this fine reflection: 'It is important, and indeed a right of the people, that legislation should not go beyond the unchangeable limits of just *moderation* in establishing punishment; but it is also important, and should be the care of the whole of a society, that its individual members be *persuaded* of the justice of the punishment. For the sake of social order, harmony between the guilty person and the onlooker as the punishment is inflicted is extremely desirable. The guilty person should say to himself, "I have deserved this," and the spectator, "This is just." This affirmation, springing from the indelible feeling of approval for what is just and true, is proper to moral, intelligent beings and is an oracle of nature itself. It is a happy people in which this feeling co-operates with legislation! We can without doubt declare that legislation then profits by the assistance of all the forces of reason, public opinion, moral sense and often of people's religion to restrain or at least slow down the fatal pressures towards crime' (*Introduzione*). — Romagnosi, after criticising the *lex talionis* in §54 of his *Genesi del D. P.*, considers it more favourably in §1511 and its footnote.

[510] If the satisfaction imposed by laws is a multiple of the harm inflicted, its proportion is dependent upon the *lex talionis*, and its justice could therefore be understood with equal ease.

tolerated in this case, or is it possible in general to harm an innocent person when self-defence requires this?

It is clear that if harm could be done to an innocent human being (which is manifestly contrary to the law of justice) to avoid harm to oneself, we would also have to ask about the limitation of such permission. A general permission would allow me to inflict any evil on others for the sake of avoiding evil to myself. But this is obviously absurd.

We should, therefore, establish the contrary principle, that is, 'It is never lawful to cause real harm to an innocent party in order to defend oneself from any harm whatsoever.'

1749. With this principle as our basis (a principle which I think leaves no room for doubt — it was known in antiquity),[511] I maintain: 1. I can do some momentary harm to an innocent person in order to defend myself from harm threatened by individuals or things, provided that such harm is indispensable for my defence and that I can compensate, as I am strictly obliged to do, the harm I inflict. In this case, I do not in fact harm anyone, but simply re-order the modality of their rights. I can, therefore, make use of what belongs to others, unknown to them or, in certain cases, even when they are expressly opposed to what I am doing. The latter is true, however, only when the owner evidently refuses his approval as a result of malice or simple obstinacy without any legitimate advantage to himself. It is obviously reasonable that he should, if he is suitably recompensed, put up with some momentary harm or moderate limitation of his ownership. This forms part of the moderation with which all are obliged to make use of their right of ownership. We have already seen that ownership, as right, is limited by the laws of *humanity* even in the state of nature,[512] and that every owner must permit some alteration to be imposed on the modality of his right when the needs of his peers require this. The only qualification to this truth is that

---

[511] Note Cicero's enduringly beautiful and true affirmation: 'Society is held together supremely when people realise that harming another for the sake of one's own benefit is more UNNATURAL than submitting to any external inconvenience of body or even of spirit which arises from injustice' (*De Off.* bk. 3, c. 6).

[512] *ER*, 263-267.

the alteration must effect not the *value*, but solely the *mode* of the right. The *mode* has no intrinsic value, and is not therefore a suitable subject of right; in other words, it lacks the third constitutive element of right.[513]

1750. It cannot be said, therefore, that this way of acting produces any real harm. The harm done, and its duration, is fully compensated and cannot be considered to have caused genuine harm. It does not offend the principle we have laid down ('An innocent person cannot be harmed for our own sake'), but rather explains and illustrates it.

1751. This teaching is applicable to innocent people whether they are the unwitting cause of the harm or not.

1752. Finally, our phrasing would be more to the point if, instead of saying that we exercise our right in such a case to do harm to another for the sake of self-defence, we said that we exercise our right to make innocuous use of what belongs to another.

1753. 2. If the threatened harm to ourselves puts our life in danger, we can use other peoples' external ownership as a means to save ourselves. This seems wholly in keeping with the nature of human justice (and true justice must always be human), even though we are unable to see how compensation can later be made. However, I still have the obligation to make restitution when the opportunity occurs. In fact, if I can avoid the danger by using what is mine, I am certainly not permitted to use what belongs to another. Moreover, such temporary use of what belongs to others never makes me absolute owner of it, that is, of its value. The truth of this conclusion is obvious if we consider that external ownership, in so far as it is a right, is limited to the other's need to preserve his life.

1754. 3. The problem becomes more difficult, however, when I can only save myself from imminent harm by depriving some innocent person of life. Here, it is certain in the first place that I must put up with the harm if it is not on a par with losing my life.

1755. If my life is in danger, however, and there is no other way of saving it than through the death of an innocent person,

[513] Cf. *ER*.

can I save it? The answer in general is 'No'. The principle we have expounded, which forbids causing harm to an innocent person as a substitute for ourselves, is absolute and, when properly understood, allows no exceptions. However, some distinctions have to be made if the principle is to be understood correctly. For instance, the cause of my mortal danger may be violence on the part of the innocent party, from which I free myself by killing him. On the other hand, the innocent person may not be a threat in any way. The first instance would be verified in the case of an attack from an armed madman; the second in the case of women and children in a narrow street whom I would have to knock down in order to escape on horseback from pursuit by bandits.

1756. In the first case, I could, if there were no other means of salvation, kill the offender despite his innocence. As Grotius observed, I am not obliged to suffer what others wish me to suffer, and can therefore *repel force with force*.[514] By acting like this, I am not the true cause of another's death; the offender himself is the cause. I am simply preventing him from entering the sphere of my rights by keeping him out. If he dies as a result, I neither wish nor intend his death, which indeed I deplore, but merely want to save my own life. If two innocent people, one an attacker and the other a defender, come to blows, the former is the cause of the fight, and it is just that he should suffer if one of the two has inevitably to die. Even charity in general does not oblige me to see to the preservation of his life rather than my own.

1757. I can give only a negative answer to the second case. In fact, it follows from the answer to the first case (cf. 1756) that if there were no other way of salvation,[515] the women who saw

[514] 'Even though he is free from sin — he may, for instance, be fighting in good faith, or think that I am someone else, or be mad or sleep-walking (we have read accounts of this) — I do not lose my right to self-defence. It is sufficient that I am not held to suffer what he wishes to inflict any more than I would be if some wild beast attacked me (*De jure B. et P.*, bk 2, c. 1, §3).

[515] Those who maintain that people have an absolute right to save themselves do not distinguish between lawful and unlawful *means*. Their argument runs as follows: 'People have a right to an end (self-preservation), and therefore they have a right to all the means necessary for this end.' This is a paralogism. We have no right to self-preservation except by the use of

that they would inevitably die as the horse bore down on them would have the right to defend themselves and their children against the rider, whether he was culpable (if he knew what he was doing) or innocent (if in the desperation of flight he had no time to reflect and realise that he would be killing innocent, peaceful people). In clashes of this kind, the true cause of death is always the offender, that is, the first to use force to eliminate an innocent person. The use of such force has a eudaimonological end (one's own salvation), not a moral end, and is intent on moral evil (the killing of another) — something which cannot be done for a eudaimonological end: 'Evil is not to be done to obtain good.'

Article 9.
Conclusion on the ethical foundation of the right to cause harm to others in one's own defence

1758. We may now conclude: 1. That I can repel force with force, that is, counter one material force about to do me harm with another even though the blameless person who harms me perishes or himself remains harmed as an accidental consequence of what I do. The Right of nature gives me this protection against material force because it does not oblige me to suffer death in order to save the life of someone who puts me in danger of death. In such a case I do not defend myself against the human person, who is inoperative, but solely against material forces. I do not cause harm to the person, but accidentally harm him as a result of a combination of circumstances.[516]

lawful means. But killing (as a direct, primary cause) the innocent is *per se* an unlawful and unjust means. I do not have the right, therefore, to save myself with such means. Grotius himself falls into the trap when he writes: 'Note that this right to self-defence arises *per se* and primarily because of nature's prompting, not from danger as a result of the injustice or sin of another' (*De J. B. et P.*, bk 2, c. 1, §3). It is clear that he has not distinguished the right to defence from the right to do harm to others in order to defend oneself in case of necessity. The first right arises 'from nature's prompting'; the second can only arise from *punitive justice*, and therefore 'on the occasion of, and from the injustice of another'.

[516] There is no doubt that a person can without any fault on his part attempt

1759. 2. That I can repel force even with the death of an unjust, blameworthy aggressor, if this is necessary. In this case, my action has penal justice as its ethical foundation. Such justice declares that the object of my action, that is, to inflict punishment on the blameworthy person, is just.

1760. In fact, two conditions have to be proved in order that I may do harm to a person:

a) The first is relative to the *object of the action*. In our case, it has to be proved, by comparing the punishment with the law of penal justice, that inflicting the punishment is just.

b) The second is relative to the *subject who carries out the action*. In our case the existence of the right to self-defence must be proved in order that I may have the right to inflict the just punishment.

Granted these conditions, the right to inflict punishment upon anyone guilty of attacking my rights is proved without doubt.

Article 10.
This teaching is consistent with the authority of divine Scripture

1761. Certain modern philosophers affirmed a useful truth when declaring that 'civil society must moderate the punishments it inflicts upon criminals to what is necessary for repressing criminal activity.' In other words, we need only sufficient

to kill another, for example, when the attacker acts in his sleep or is out of his mind, or when his mind is ruled by some invincible error. We have to admit, however, that in all these cases there is some disorder in the violent person who acts against the norm which human nature should follow. According to Catholic teaching, such disorder is reduced to original sin; death, illness and other unhappy consequences are penalties assigned by the Creator to original sin. Amongst them we have to number the death suffered by a blameless aggressor as a result of the necessity of self-defence on the part of the person he attacks (Cf. *Dottrina del peccato originale* in *Filosofia della Morale*, vol. 4).

[1759–1761]

punishment to defend society from criminal aggression. This truth is a consequence of the teaching previously explained by us according to which the exercise of the naked right of punishment, together with retaliation, is altogether excluded. There remains (for individuals and society) no other human right to impose any punishment except that united to self-defence.

1762. But the same philosophers were in serious error when they endeavoured to eliminate totally the *right to punish* and thought that the *right to self-defence* could stand on its own, as the sole right, to which all punishments that society imposes on malefactors could be reduced.

1763. This serious error, with which they deluded themselves that they could escape from the so-called prejudices of preceding ages, depended upon a false form of argument only too familiar to them and constantly under fire from us. It runs as follows:

People (individuals and society) have the right to self-defence.

But in order to defend oneself it is sometimes necessary to cause harm or hurt to others.

Therefore people have the right in this case to cause harm to others because the person with the right to an end also has the right to the means.

The fallacy always lies in supposing that there is an unlimited right to the defence of our rights.

On the contrary, I cannot defend my rights by infraction of the rights of others if, for instance, I took the life of an innocent person, or defended myself by means of some unjust and unlawful action. In order to show that I have the moral faculty to harm a peer in self-defence, I have to show that this harm is just in itself, that is, does not contain any infraction of the rights of others — I cannot do this, however, except in the cases we have mentioned, and especially in the case of a person guilty and blameworthy of the danger to which I am exposed. In other words, I have to depend on the principles of penal justice if I want to justify the harm I do to others in self-defence.

The philosophers we have mentioned vainly persuade themselves that the principles of punitive justice can be excluded from public laws for the sake of substituting an isolated, gratuitous right of defence in favour of society. If this were the case, they could never justify the punishment that society imposes for misdeeds. They would have been right however if they had limited themselves to saying what we have said, that is, 'social power can exercise punitive justice only in order to defend society against evil tendencies.'

The teaching of these philosophers is not only contrary to opinions dominating in periods preceding our own — barbarous periods, as they complacently call them; it is also contrary to the feeling of all the more civilised ancient nations, and of the whole of mankind which recognises as *acts of justice* (a phrase used in all languages) the pain and other punishments imposed on delinquents. Worst of all, this teaching is opposed to the express declarations of divine Scripture and to the way in which the Christian religion, true and meek as it is, considers the pain inflicted on the guilty.

The first letter of St. Peter, in speaking of rulers, says that they are sent by God 'to punish those who do wrong'.[517] This shows that punishment properly speaking is inflicted for the sake of justice, as we may see more clearly from the next phrase: 'and to praise those who do right'.[518] The author is not speaking, therefore, about a right of defence, but solely about the just retribution that serves as a defence. Likewise, according to St. Paul, the ruler is a just judge. 'He is the servant of God to execute his wrath on the wrongdoer.'[519] The concept expressed by the Apostle leaves no room for doubt, especially if we consider the force of the words 'servant of God' which correspond to St. Peter's 'sent by God'.

As we know, judging according to justice and vindicating justice are God's prerogative. For this reason, the Scriptures consider judges, who punish the guilty as a social necessity for the defence of the innocent, as persons entrusted with a function proper to God, and consequently sharing in divine authority. This feeling for things is constant in the holy books, and explains why judges and rulers are sometimes called 'gods'.[520]

[517] 1 Pet 2: 14.

[518] *Ibid.*

[519] Rom 13: 4.

[520] There was a special reason for calling 'gods' the judges of the Hebrew nation. They possessed a *divine law*, according to which they judged, and thus could be called by Christ those 'to whom the word of God has been

Psalm 81 [Douai], which describes the severe judgment God will make on wicked judges, begins: 'God has stood in the congregation of gods; and being in the midst of them he judgeth gods.' According to Bossuet,

> these gods judged by God are the kings and judges gathered under his sceptre to exercise justice. He calls them 'gods' because sacred language uses 'god' as a name for 'judge'; again, authority to judge is a share in the supreme justice of God, with which he has invested the kings of the earth,[521]

that is, any form of government of civil society.

This does not mean that the aim and the occasion of the exercise of penal justice is other than defence against malefactors. Scripture expressly assigns the defence of civil society, and of innocent individuals too weak to defend themselves against the powerful, as the end to be attained by public punishment of guilty parties. It does not, of course, speak systematically, as philosophers do, but uses generic language which embraces equally civil association and individuals, and can be applied both to the state of society and to the state of nature. In the Psalm we have quoted, God says to the judges whom he judges: 'Judge for the needy and the fatherless: do justice to the humble and the poor. Rescue the poor: and deliver the needy out of the hand of the sinner.'[522] The Apostle constantly considers as exemplary and terrifying the punishments that heads of society inflict upon malefactors. He imposes on all the duty to fear such penalties: 'For rulers are not a TERROR to good conduct, but to bad ... But if you do wrong, BE AFRAID; for he does not bear the sword of God in vain.'[523]

Scripture, therefore, teaches that the government of civil society must on the one hand exercise *punitive justice*, and on the other exercise it for the end expressed by the necessary *defence of society and of the individual* against the guilty. And this is also the conclusion of the rational theory of penal Right unfolded.'

[521] *Politique tirée des propres paroles de l'Écriture sainte, etc.*, bk. 8, art. 1.
[522] Ps 81: 3-4 [Douai].
[523] Rom 13: 3, 7.

[1763]

as we have presented it. This theory justifies the good sense of those who have gone before us on this earth.

Article 11.
Necessity: the principle determining the exercise of the right to defence

1764. The punishment decreed by justice for fault is the ethical foundation and, therefore, the true, formal origin of the right to defence. The merely factual necessity of defending one's own right could not have originated or justified such a function (defence) apart from the law of penal justice. In fact, the real necessity of defending oneself and one's belongings against aggressors is, if we prescind from the moral law of justice, a mere circumstance bereft of the dignity of right.

1765. Those who took *real necessity* as the source of the right to self-defence (Romagnosi was one) have to accept that their error depends upon their assimilation of philosophical sensism. This system blinded them to the *ideal order* and made them conclude that everything could be found in *reality* alone.

1766. *Necessity*, therefore, does not give rise to any right; it is simply a factual circumstance contemplated by the law, and shows that the moment has come for the law's application and actuation. In other words, the function of defence comes into being.

1767. I have already distinguished *law* from the *titles* contained in law. Titles are those factual conditions in which the application of law takes place.[524] In the right to defence, the *moral law*, in so far as it authorises harm to others, is *penal law*; the *title* actuating this authorisation is the *necessity* of defending one's own right. The title to actuation has, therefore, been confused with the law, from which alone the title itself obtains its power.

1768. We note, however, that it is the *title* which gives the law its special or particular act, and which consequently *determines* the limits or measure of such actuation. Every effect, as we

---

[524] Cf. *Storia comparativa de' sistemi morali*, c. 7, a. 7.

[1764–1768]

know, receives its measure from its cause. Hence, I 'can harm the one who attacks my rights only when such harm is truly necessary for the defence of my rights. Moreover, the harm done cannot exceed this necessity.'[525]

Article 12.
Limits to the exercise of the right to defence

1769. From these principles we can deduce the limits within which the *exercise* of the right to defence has to be contained. They spring from five sources, that is, from considering
    1. the *nature of the wrong-doing* used to attempt intrusion into another's right;
    2. the *jural-penal responsibility* of the offender;
    3. the *nature of the action* used for defence;
    4. the *necessity* for defence; and
    5. the *amount of* attempted *harm*.
We must now consider the limits placed on the exercise of the right to defence by each of these five points.

§1. *The limit to the exercise of the right to defence arising from the nature of the wrong-doing perpetrated by the offender*

1770. It seems that the right to defence cannot begin to be exercised until the criminal attempt to invade our right has actually begun. The mere thought of offending, together with

[525] Because Romagnosi accepted 'an unlimited right to self-preservation' and consequently 'a so-called penal right to be exercised by society as an unlimited right to defence', he was unable to place just boundaries to 'penal right'. De Scari's criticism of Romagnosi is apposite: 'The author's (Romagnosi's) assertion leads him to the conclusion that the foundation of every valid right is whatever need happens to be more imperative and important. In face of this, every right dependent upon lesser needs has to give way. Romagnosi does, in fact, uphold jural necessity and, what is more to the point, society's right to sacrifice an innocent person for the sake of its own salvation.' (Cf. the article already quoted from the Viennese *Giornale di Giurisprudenza*, reproduced in *Annali di Statistica*, vol. 27.

any malicious feeling whatsoever, cannot give rise to the exercise of the right to defence.

1771. This principle seems universally admitted today, although it is not easy to offer clear proofs of its truth. If we say that the offensive thought remains hidden, and that punishment cannot, therefore, be applied to its author, we find that the proof is only valid for thoughts which truly remain hidden, and not for those which we come to know.

1772. Burlamacchi's appeal to the mercy which should be characteristic of penal laws[526] would simply prove that it is better to leave thoughts unpunished; it would not prove that there was no right to punish them.

1773. Romagnosi's view is also inconclusive. He opts for defence against external execution alone and maintains: 'Criminal plans reduced to idle speculation and innocuous desires on the part of the imagination have no effect on the *stability* of the social fabric.'[527]

1774. Perhaps we should say that simple thought does not enter the sphere of my rights? But here we should distinguish two classes of thoughts.

Some thoughts have wrong-doing as their object, but without relationship to the will. These are merely speculative thoughts completely devoid of guilt and not meriting punishment.

Other thoughts are blameworthy because they intend wrong-doing. If, however, the object of these volitive, practical thoughts is moral, not jural wrong-doing, they merit punishment, according to universal justice, which can be inflicted only by God, not human beings. Other volitive, practical thoughts, have as their object not only moral, but jural wrong-doing, that is, an infraction of others' rights, such as murder.

The only possible question before us, therefore, is whether individuals, and consequently society, can defend themselves against a known deliberation to carry out a crime such as murder.

1775. It is certain that there is no possibility of self-defence against John or reason to inflict punishment upon him if we are completely ignorant of his intention to murder William. It is

[526] *Principes de Droit Politique*, part 3, c. 4, §28.
[527] *Genesi del Diritto Penale*, §634.

also certain that defence would not be necessary if we come to know what John intended when he had already abandoned all idea of putting it into practice. Thirdly, it is certain that there is no point in inflicting *exemplary punishment* on John for a guilty thought which has already been eliminated or rendered inoperative, not only because society has no further need to defend itself against sterile thoughts, but also (and this is far more important, as we said at the beginning) because mere thought does not enter the sphere of others' rights except in their quality as injury. We have already seen, however, that simple injuries must not be punished by human beings. Such punishment would be retaliation, which has to be left to God.

1776. But if the murderous thought were still present, and known either with certainty or a high degree of probability (as a result, say, of John's manifesting the time, place and other circumstances of its execution), would this not give us the right to defend ourselves by inflicting some punishment on John, if there were no other way of self-defence?

There is no doubt that it would. Such punishment, if imposed by society, may be given various names. It may be called, for instance, *policing*. But whatever name is used, the penalty is always some kind of coercion or punishment by which society defends one of its members and itself against an efficacious thought or deliberation before the external wrong-doing has begun. But we cannot say that there has been some *attempt* at wrong-doing if by 'attempt' we mean some external commencement in the fact of wrong-doing. John's simple manifestation of his notion of a planned, organised murder is not in the proper sense attempted murder, unless we wish to change the meaning of words.

I know that the police, if told in time, will take account of his plans and catch him red-handed when he appears armed at the time and place indicated. But I also know that if circumstances do not permit a person's being apprehended in this way, and there is no other means of preventing the crime, the police would have and should have no scruple about arresting someone who is certainly or probably guilty, and thus preventing him from carrying out his wicked plan. For instance, let us imagine that he wants to murder his wife with whom he lives, and that her pregnancy makes it difficult for others to inform her of his

[1776]

intention. In this case, the government would certainly not act unjustly by arresting the would-be murderer (although he was still only thinking about the crime), allowing his wife to think the detention sprang from some other cause, and using whatever means were necessary to foresee and block the evil project.

1777. Nevertheless, social authority, although acting justly while subjecting the guilty person to arrest (or whatever else is needed to save another's life), would no longer act justly as soon as it intended to go further and inflict an *exemplary* punishment on this individual, even though he were convicted of his evil plan and had confessed it. There are two reasons for this: first, the simple thought of murder without any practical effect, is an injury, but does no harm; second, exemplary punishment is not properly speaking effective when applied to thoughts alone. No one is afraid of being convicted for wicked thoughts, which we rightly think are always immune from punishment. In fact, there is nothing easier than hiding a thought which has not produced any external effect. Exemplary punishment of thoughts would have a contrary effect to that intended; it would make people more careful about concealing their evil thoughts and thus enable them to think and plan their crimes more confidently.

This, I think, is a new reason for concluding that civil legislation cannot and must not punish thoughts with what we call 'exemplary' penalties.

1778. We can also deduce from what has been said that *jural-penal responsibility* originates with the first action that gives rise to the external commission of wrong-doing and increases until the act has been completed.

§2. *The limit to the exercise of the right to defence arising from the jural-penal responsibility of the offender*

1779. The limit arising from the jural-penal responsibility of the offender is relative to that part of the right to defence which is exercised, through *exemplary* punishment, by a powerful individual or by society against the criminal impulse of the masses.

1780. In this way of exercising the right to defence, we have to distinguish *jural-penal responsibility* from *moral imputation*, *moral responsibility* and *jural-restitutive responsibility*.

1781. *Moral imputation* means the attribution of a sin, any sin, to a person who is its free perpetrator. The degree of imputation depends upon the seriousness of the sin, and on the degree of freedom in the person committing it.

1782. *Moral responsibility* is the degree of punishment and satisfaction that a guilty person has to undergo to pay for his wrong-doing, according to the law of eternal justice.

1783. *Jural-restitutive responsibility* is the degree of harm caused for which a person is held to compensate, according to the laws of jural justice.[528]

1784. Finally, *jural-penal responsibility* is the degree of *exemplary punishment* that the perpetrator of a crime must expect from society, or from a person defending himself against criminal assault.

1785. It is true that no adequate comparison can be made between a moral evil, taken singularly, and a physical evil. Consequently, physical evil can, for reasons of justice, always be increased for the guilty person without going to excess. This principle can be applied, however, only to full, eternal justice, not to that part of justice which is poured out, as it were, in the *right of defence* proper to an individual or society.

1786. Exemplary punishment, which has to serve as a form of defence, was measured by Romagnosi in accordance with the calculated average of criminal impulse present in society.

1787. The factual criminal impulse which moves an individual delinquent to offend is simply one element in calculating average criminal impulse. This important teaching has to be developed in *Social Right*. Here, we shall have to be satisfied with the following brief comments.

1788. Criminal impulse results from two elements:

    1. natural instincts, which of themselves are not vicious;
    2. malice, which abuses these instincts.

---

[528] Some authors call this *civil responsibility*.

1789. *Jural-penal responsibility* varies properly speaking in proportion to the second element and its effects, not to the first. Consequently, different criminal legislations have rightly taken into consideration age, sex, and circumstances which attenuate or aggravate the malice of an act.

1790. But in badly ordered societies it is inevitable that punishments be brought into operation not only relative to the second, but also the first element. This, however, is opposed to what is required by reason of criminal justice, as we shall see better elsewhere.

1791. In fact, the wisdom and justice of governments has to prevent crime by satisfying, not irritating the demands of natural instincts. In addition, it ought not to impose punishment except on the degree of *wickedness* which, as we said, forms only a part of the criminal impulse.

§3. *The limit of the right to defence arising from the quality of the action used to defend oneself*

1792. This limit, arising from the kind of defence used, is reduced to the obligation of exercising the right to defence solely by means of actions which are not intrinsically unlawful and immoral.

§4. *The limit to the exercise of the right to defence arising from the necessity of defence*

1793. The right to defence cannot be extended further than is necessary to achieve one's defence; the end determines the means.

1794. But the right to self-defence does extend of itself to everything necessary for defence, provided that its exercise does not meet with any of the limits we have either already indicated or will indicate shortly.

1795. There are two immediate consequences of this:
   1. Our right to defence is moderated in such a way that it

cannot go beyond what is necessary in the defence of rights. In other words, we must defend ourselves with the minimum possible harm to the aggressor.

2. On the other hand the right of defence, considered in itself, is extended *ad infinitum*, as Grotius notes.[529] In other words, it extends to whatever is necessary for removing the evil threatening us.

1796. The *necessity* of the harm to be inflicted on others in our own defence has to be thought out and accurately determined. It often happens that the *spirit irritated* by an injury, the movement towards retaliation, and a hasty desire for immediate reparation make us believe in the necessity for some kind of defence which, considered calmly, would not be found acceptable.

1797. In the same way, *ignorance* and lack of reflection prevent our discovering a way to protect our rights without causing harm to others, or at least lesser harm. Instead, we defend ourselves by means of harm greater than necessary.

1798. If this ignorance and lack of reflection are not free, but arise from a low degree of development and intellective activity in the society to which the defender belongs, or in the individual himself, the harm done to others is *subjectively* just because it is necessary relative to the intellectual conditions of the subject.

1799. We could imagine, however, an assault taking place on a wise man able to defend his rights without finding it necessary to inflict any harm on his aggressor. In this case, the harm, if done, would be unjust relative to the wise man and considered in itself. Let us take an example.

Suppose that the sage saw no immediate way of defending his ownership without harm to an intruder, but contemporaneously realised that by letting himself be robbed he could receive full compensation either by recourse to public tribunals or through his own power and diligence. In this case, he could

---

[529] 'Although death and a blow are not on the same level, the person who prepares to inflict some injury on me gives me, by that very fact, a right, that is, a moral faculty of opposing him *ad infinitum* in so far I am otherwise unable to avoid this evil' (*De J. B. et P.*, bk. 2, c. 1, §10). The great jurist denies, however, that the exercise of such a right is unlimited if compared with the laws of humanity and the laws of the Gospel.

[1796–1799]

not inflict harm on the intruder because it would not be necessary. Our wise man simply has to accept a change in the *modality* of his right. We have already shown that according to rational Right human beings have to give way when *modality* alone is at stake. According to the definition we have given, modality has no worth and is not, therefore, an object of true right which here lacks its third constitutive element.

1800. The extension *ad infinitum* of the right to defence is proved from the ethical foundation of the right according to which, as we have seen, 'the *right* to defence is simply *penal right* exercised by the person offended or by others on his behalf against the guilty offender to the extent necessary for the defence of his rights.' The punishment, therefore, can be as extensive as defence demands without exceeding the bounds of justice: 'The quantity of *physical penalty* is never equal to moral *fault*.'

1801. This principle of justice from which we deduce the indefinite faculty for harming an offender, provided the harm inflicted is necessary for safeguarding rights, must however be moderated in its *exercise* by the laws of humanity, as we shall see.

1802. It has its full application when there is a question of defence by means of exemplary punishment which, however, does not aim at an actual offence but at an habitual offence on the part of the commonalty and, I would add, of the individual.

§5. *The limit of the exercise of the right to defence arising from the amount of the harm that may be inflicted*

1803. In fact, we have to distinguish defence that a person can make of his right during actual aggression from defence against continual, habitual evil-doing on the part of an individual or the commonalty.

1804. We shall speak first of the right of defence exercised during an attempt at aggression; then we shall say something in the same vein about the habitual evil-doing, or criminal impulse, that can be found in an individual or in a mass of individuals, whether associated or not.

1805. Consideration of simple, natural instinct and of the force of what we have called *ownership*, as distinct from the *right of ownership*, shows that during the act of aggression against even the smallest of our rights we could repel the aggressor by inflicting the greatest possible harm upon him, and even death, if that were inevitably necessary for effective defence.

1806. But in this case, the moral law of humanity greatly moderates the exercise of such a crude right to defence.

There seems no doubt that aggression against a person's life can be repelled at the cost of death to the aggressor.

1807. Nor does there seem any doubt that a father can kill anyone interfering with the purity, innocence or religious faith of his children, if no other means is available. I refer, of course, to the use by the offender of criminal or even violent acts, such as breaking into a house or at least entering against the owner's will, when the father acts either *vi vim repellere* or for the sake of punishing wrong-doing.

1808. The same can be done by anyone who, in the father's place, is moved by humanity and a sacred desire to safeguard the precious gifts enjoyed by his fellows.

1809. Finally, there can be no doubt that unjust assaults against our right can be defended, when other means are lacking, by inflicting harm upon the assailant equal to the worth of the right he threatens to assail. This is not contrary to the laws of natural justice nor to those of *humanity*. Renouncing such an exercise of our right would pertain in some cases only to evangelical perfection and generosity.

1810. It is not according to the law of humanity, nor rational right, to exercise the right to defence by taking the life of anyone assailing minor rights, or by killing a thief who has gorged himself on the fruit in our garden.

1811. First, as we have seen, we have to abstain from harming others in self-defence whenever we can prudently wait for full compensation for the harm inflicted upon us.

Second, humanity and rational right forbid us to defend minor rights with serious harm to fellow human beings who attempt to assail them, and even go so far as to demand that we sacrifice such rights or reserve a kind of credit enabling us to reassert them at some later date with less harm to the offender. *A fortiori*, therefore, we have less possibility of making our right to defence prevail when the good assailed is dependent upon some mistaken, prejudiced view we hold. And this is normally the case when we are dealing with so-called offences against our *honour*.

Honour consists entirely in moral virtue, that is, in the opinion of esteem which it merits and which is attributed to it. Every other sort of honour which cannot be referred to this kind of esteem is nothing more than a chimera arising from human ignorance and vanity. I leave it to the reader to judge how the notions of some moralists are totally at odds with reason and the Gospel when they permit a nobleman to run through with a sword a person attempting to slap his face.[530] This is not only an

---

[530] Let me quote the wise words of a Protestant who very rightly inveighs against these vain prejudices in favour of honour: 'It is very odd, when God's will is so clear in the Gospel, to find theologians — and Christian theologians at that —' (Here he quotes Navarr. c. 15: 4; Henr. *De irregul.*, c. 11, and *De jure belli*, n. 5) — 'who not only think that these things can be done to avoid a slap in the face, but to requite honour even if the assailant runs away after the slap. The reason would be to recover one's honour. This seems to me contrary to reason, and indeed impious. Honour is a view about excellence. But ANYONE PUTTING UP WITH SUCH AN INJURY SHOWS GREAT PATIENCE and INCREASES RATHER THAN DIMINISHES HIS HONOUR. It does not matter that people employ CORRUPT JUDGMENT in calling this virtue a fault; perverse judgments of this kind do not change either the thing itself or its worth. This was the view not only of ancient Christians, but even of philosophers who said that only the weak in spirit were unable to bear contumely, as we have said (cf. bk. 1, c. 2, §8).'

He goes on in a very Catholic way when he says: 'It is clear, therefore, that we cannot approve the opinion held by many that killing in self-defence is lawful, namely, approved by divine law — although I would not argue that this is the case if we consider only natural right' (This is the imperfect right of nature which ceases to be a right under the Gospel in so far as it is emended and perfected by the Gospel). 'And this is true even when the assailant can flee without danger. Flight itself is shameful in a nobleman. We conclude, therefore, that there is NO SHAME IN THE CASE WE ARE DISCUSSING, BUT ONLY A FALSE VIEW OF SHAME which is to be rejected by all who follow the path of virtue and wisdom. I am glad to find that Charles Molina is one of the jurisconsults who agree with me (*In add. ad Alex.*, cons. 119). Moreover, what I said about the slap and flight, I want to maintain about other things which do not harm TRUE ESTEEM. But what if someone says something about us which, when believed, weakens our esteem amongst good people? Some moralists teach that he can be killed, but this is false and against natural right because KILLING OF THIS KIND IS NOT A SUITABLE WAY FOR DEFENDING OUR ESTEEM' (*De jure B. et P.*, bk. 2, c. 1, §10).

example of excess in the *exercise* of right (for example, when we defend some small right of our own with grave harm to the aggressor); *right* itself is radically lacking because one of its constitutive elements (a good to be defended) is lacking. A false, prejudiced view which, for example, puts *honour* where it is not to be found, is not something good to be preserved, but an evil to be destroyed.

1812. These comments all show that the exercise of the right to do harm in self-defence is limited by the laws of *humanity* which forbids our inflicting supreme harm on another in order to avoid insignificant harm, or no harm at all, to ourselves.

1813. It is the moralists' difficult task to assign just boundaries to these relative quantities. The scholar who wishes to establish a true, non-deceptive Right will often need to turn to moralists in his work. Some brief remarks could perhaps be offered here about this thorny question.

1814. I think it would be reasonable, when setting the possible harm to be inflicted on an assailant in the exercise of self-defence according to the laws of humanity and equity,[531] to double the value of the threatened harm.

1815. The reason for this quantity is that it does not unbalance the equilibrium constituting what is just.

Let us imagine that one person wishes to inflict on another four degrees of unjust harm. By doing this he establishes for himself a law requiring that he receive the same amount of harm. But this harm, equal to that which he has inflicted, is his punishment or forfeit for wrong-doing; there is no doubt that just, strict justice is what he deserves. However, the account between assailant and assailed is not yet in order because their condition is still unequal. The attacker, who wished to inflict four degrees of *unjust* harm on his victim, himself receives four degrees of *just* harm. In other words, he has paid a debt, but he has not obtained any credit. For his condition to equal that of the

---

[531] Evangelical perfection is altogether more sublime. It says that the person who is struck on one cheek should prepare the other for a blow. Those who grasp such sublime teaching are happy indeed! We are simply explaining 'how the natural Right is moderated in its exercise by the laws of humanity', and how this exercise is thus made *lawful*. But *lawful* is very different from *perfect*.

victim, he has in his turn to be assailed — not because of a debt which is no longer his, but simply to enter a state equal to that of the one he has attacked. The person attacked, who owed nothing to anyone, was threatened with four degrees of harm. The assailant, therefore, after having paid his debt, can be threatened with equal harm by the other for the sake of what we have called the 'just balance'. Whether the attack has succeeded or not is accidental to the action; the assailant must in either case be considered as the blameworthy cause of harm.

It is true, of course, that such a balance of justice could not be actuated of itself by any human being, but it could come about in the case of just defence. I think, therefore, that the exercise of just defence is reasonably limited as follows: 'In order to defend his own assailed right, an individual can harm his assailant, provided there is no other form of defence, but not to more than double the value of the menaced, assailed right.'

1816. We have to note, however, that moderating humanely the exercise of one's own right can be understood and practised only when passions have been subdued and reflection elevated.

1817. Generally speaking, therefore, rights appear in all their force and simplicity in newly-founded nations where understanding has developed only to a low degree of reflection, human instinct is extremely powerful, and the necessity of moderating the exercise of rights through the moral laws of humanity has not been understood.

In fact, the human race, abandoned to itself, would never have understood this truth without the great light brought by the Gospel. The further we go back in history, the more we see legislations maintaining the crude exercise of rights without any human moderation. Radamantes' law, mentioned by Apollodoros, is a case in point. The legislator permitted anyone to defend himself by reacting to the violence of a first party without limit to possible harm.[532]

1818. Such moderation has no place, however, when the right

---

[532] Apollodorus writes: Linus 'having come to Thebes, where he became a citizen, died after being hit with a shield by Hercules, who had reacted angrily when Linus struck him. Hercules, on being accused of murder by some citizens, read to the tribunal the law of Radamantes which declared the innocence of anyone harming a person who had first attacked him' (bk. 2).

[1816–1818]

to self-defence is exercised not against a particular *act* of aggression, but against *habitual* wrong-doing and injustice which continually tends to invade the sphere of others' rights.

1819. This would be the case when, in the state of nature, one individual found himself under threat from another who showed constant signs of murderous hatred or other criminal passion. Continual injustice of this kind could be restrained and terrified by greater chastisements and punishments. The same is true in the case of defence against a plundering mob, or a group of pirates or a den of thieves.

Finally, such defence is perpetual in civil society, which has to defend its members and itself against criminal impulse by exemplary punishments.

In all these cases, because the harm threatened by habitual wrong-doing against which we exercise self-defence is of itself undetermined and almost infinite, the harm that can be used in self-defence is measured only by the quantity of *criminal impulse*.

However in order to avoid any misunderstanding of our concept in such delicate material we shall have to speak more at length about the right to self-defence against justly feared aggression.

Article 13.
The right to defence against probable and against certain offences

1820. The rules of conduct most frequently employed in human life are not those founded on certainty, but those whose basis is probability. Nothing is more difficult and nothing more distasteful to human beings than the attempt to establish rules of conduct in probable cases. Despite their difficulty, however, these cases forever demand solution, and in practice are more or less solved. But any attempt to deal with them in theory is universally resolved by classifying such research as useless subtlety or a search for undiscoverable truth. Cowardice, and the onslaught of difficulties hard to overcome, deceives us in an incredible way!

[1819–1820]

1821. We have a clear right to avoid probable harm.

1822. But in order that we may avoid it, can we do harm to the people from whom we fear it? And if so, to what extent? These are important questions which have to be constantly constantly.

1823. In order to reply to the first question, we have to distinguish, when threatened by probable harm from others, between the harm springing from blameworthy and non-blameworthy action.

1824. Probable harm threatening us can be attributed to another's fault in two ways:

1. Others have freely caused harm to us, or in some case have contributed to its being posited.

2. We have only indications on the basis of which we suppose that another person probably has an evil intention of doing us harm.

1825. Three cases exist, therefore, in which another person can cause us probable harm: he can be

1. an innocent cause;

2. guilty of some fact which makes it probable that we will suffer harm;

3. only a probably blameworthy cause of harm to us.

It is clear that here we are not dealing with an actual but a reasonably feared attack.

We must examine the right to defence in each of the cases mentioned.

§1. *The right to defence from some probable evil caused by another, but without his fault*

1826. In this first case, we can defend ourselves from probable harm, but we have no right to use means that could harm anything within the sphere of another's rights (except in the case of repelling brute force, as we have said above). The reason for this is clear: the person from whose action we fear danger is not the formal, but only the material cause of the harm. Our case supposes that he has done nothing except make lawful use of his own right.

1827. If he has inadvertently overstepped the sphere of his

[1821–1827]

own rights and entered that of ours, we should first show him where he has made the mistake. Only then, after he has refused to surrender to obvious truth, can we use force in our own defence and to his harm against the danger with which his action threatens us.

1828. If the matter is doubtful, force cannot be employed, but some friendly settlement would be needed. Only in the case of refusal to follow peaceful paths in the search for a balanced settlement would the other person render himself blameworthy and justly be subject to the coercion that the other could use against him. Jural reason prescribes this conclusion because true right cannot be deduced, as we have so often insisted, from mere *human instinct*, but from instinct regulated by reason (*rational*, not merely *natural* right).

1829. Something similar can be said if the action posited by another is an action pertaining of its nature to *innocuous freedom* rather than to the *right of ownership*, and if the person doing it is not aware of the harmful consequences to others. In this case, there would be no question of his using some right of his; he would simply be doing something *per se* lawful. It would cease being such, however, and no longer pertain to *innocuous freedom*, as soon as he realised that it could have harmful or dangerous consequences to others. Nothing could be done with such an individual except first let him know of the harm he is doing, but without threatening him with any harmful force. If he refused to surrender to obvious reason, self-defence against him would be in order, even if he were harmed. The good faith in which he is acting ceases as soon as he has been informed.

§2. The right to defence from danger caused by the fault of another

1830. A person can be blameworthy in our regard by doing anything which puts us in danger of harm. This can happen in at least five ways:

1. By departing from the sphere of his own rights and entering that of ours. This is a clear infliction of harm.

2. By departing from one of his rights of ownership, but in such a way that a *material force* acts accidentally on our ownership and to our harm. An example would be the case of an unrepaired wall of his falling on a wall of ours. Harm is done in this case also.

3. By departing from one of his rights without any benefit to himself and in such a way that our freedom is restricted. Once more, harm is done.

4. When an owner has two ways of making use of a right and maliciously choses that which will be prejudicial to our freedom. Again, harm results.

5. Or finally by carrying out actions pertaining to innocuous freedom but in such a way that their consequences place our ownership in danger. For example, someone may change the course of a stream on his land for the sake of setting up a manufactory, but in doing so puts my nearby field in danger of flooding.

When the blame has been verified in all these cases, we can defend ourselves, even by inflicting harm, against anyone who has unjustly placed us in danger.

1831. But there is no right to defence which causes harm to another if by his action he merely uses a right to his own advantage in the way least prejudicial to ourselves and without imposing force on the *object* of our ownership. In other words, the consequences of his use of force only limits our innocuous freedom.

§3. *The right to self-defence when we know in general that others' malice is the probable cause of our harm*

1832. We have to divide the third case in two: either 1. the arguments leading us to believe that the other individual intends to harm us are founded on his blameworthy actions; or 2. they are totally independent of him and in no way his fault.

1833. If the arguments making us suspect evil in a person are his fault, we have to decide whether they have any relationship with the threatened danger (if, for example, he threatened to kill or rob us, and so on) or have no relationship with it (if,

[1831–1833]

for example, his evil life provides only a general reason for suspicion).

1834. In the first case, by beginning to offend us the person has already provided us with a right to self-defence even at his own risk, if we have no other means of defence.

1835. This *species* of the right to defence is normally called the *right to prevention*.[533] According to Zeiller:

> My free activity is in fact impeded by anyone who, threatening me without lawful motive, causes me well-founded fear. In this case, I can repel him forcefully in the absence of milder means. This is even more true if, through carelessness or indulgence or tardiness on his part, more rigorous measures become necessary, and the defence of my rights is rendered more difficult or even totally impossible.[534]

1836. He adds a warning:

> A first attack is not justified by the simple possibility of harm, by threatening words (which are rather warnings that we should take care), by equivocal appearances or prejudiced opinions which lack objective reasons. These factors do serve, however, as an invitation to prepare a lawful defence.[535]

1837. In the second case, suspicion and fear arise from the evil life of an individual who is guilty not only of offending moral obligations, but tends to offend the rights of others. An evil life stained with crimes that offend against justice fully justifies:

1. The use of caution in dealing with an individual. A case in point is when we prohibit his entering the sphere of our rights as, for example, when we refuse to let him come into our house even if his entrance is of itself without prejudice to us, and others could, in the same circumstances, come in without our express permission.

---

[533] We consider the *right to defence* as the genus, and the *right to prevention* as the species, that is, as a special way of exercising the right to defence. Others consider the right of prevention as a right distinct from that of defence. This, however, seems to obscure the matter, or at least render its origin and foundation obscure.

[534] §176.

[535] *Ibid.*

[1834–1837]

2. A request for guarantees, even if this causes him some inconvenience.

3. Impeding acts pertaining to *innocuous freedom*, if by such acts he placed himself in a condition to harm us without our being any longer capable of withstanding his aggression. For example, we might have to make him keep his distance in some lonely place or, before allowing him near, ask him for guarantees sufficient to assure us against danger.

4. Watching him, and even forcefully obliging him not to evade our vigilance. This is the same as the previous number.[536]

1838. For the rest, however, we cannot cause this individual any direct harm on the basis of suspicion alone. On the contrary, we should if possible take suitable precautions by giving in ourselves and moving away, despite some light inconvenience, rather than causing him genuine harm.

1839. If the reasons for our suspicions of his malicious intention to harm us are independent of him and of any fault on his part, and spring at most from conjectures of an altogether different nature, we can take precautions and guard ourselves, or even demand guarantees that cost the person nothing and cause him no inconvenience. We could also encourage him to arrive at some agreement with us, provided it was harmless and without trouble to him. But we cannot defend ourselves by causing him harm.

1840. In fact, his evil intention cannot be fully proven. The suspicion depends neither on external things nor on him. It is not reasonable, therefore, for us to cause harm by defending ourselves against what we fear. 'Our fear,' as Grotius says, 'cannot diminish the rights of others;'[537] nor should we ever cause suffering to innocent people. Everyone must be presumed innocent until proved guilty.

1841. This was the opinion of the whole of antiquity, and it is natural that we should embrace even a single case in which we can think well of others. It would be injurious to think ill of someone as long as there remains even a single hypothesis for thinking well of him.

[536] These precautions justify the right of the police in civil society to carry out surveillance on suspects.

[537] *De jure B. et P.*, bk 2, c. 2.

[1838–1841]

1842. The reason for this lies in the supreme moral obligation, whose nature we have explained. It obliges us not to refuse to acknowledge things presented to our knowledge. In other words, we cannot deny the worth of what we know unless we see that it lacks this worth. In our case, to suppose that a person lacks some worth, without knowing if that is truly the case, is to offend that individual. The offence is more serious in so far as the worth is higher, and its possession a duty incumbent upon the person.

Because such worth is not necessary, it may be objected that we cannot know whether the person we are judging really has it. That, of course, is true, and it should induce us to suspend our judgment, which we can lawfully do. We may indeed have different degrees of inclination to judgment dependent upon various probabilities, although judgment itself remains suspended. In other words, there is no judgment. However, when our actions are directed to harming someone, we suppose that this person deserves harm; our behaviour is subsequent to a formed, completed judgment. Suspension of judgment, on the other hand, produces nothing — it simply suspends action.

We cannot, therefore, cause harm to anyone of whose guilt we are not certain. This is equivalent to saying that our rule of action must be favourable judgment until the contrary is proved. If a positive, favourable judgment cannot be formed, we have to *presume well* of the person, that is, we have to act *as if* a favourable judgment had been formed. Action supposes a formed judgment, which can only be favourable or unfavourable. It cannot be unfavourable without doing injustice. Our rule of action, therefore, must be a presumed, favourable judgment.

1843. Kant was wrong when he opposed this common-sense, moral attitude and substituted for it in Right this heart-breaking statement: 'Every individual is presumed evil until he has been proved good.'[538]

1844. He was also wrong about the consequences he wished to draw from his principle. One consequence affirms that ownership in the state of nature can only be *provisory*. Kant

[538] *Institutio in jus.*

reasons that the obligation of respecting others' ownership cannot be supposed unless others respect our ownership. This certainty is unobtainable, however, without some guarantee. Such a guarantee can only be verified in civil society, where alone therefore ownership can peremptorily exist.[539]

1845. He is wrong again when he deduces from his fearsome concept of human beings the necessity of an interchange of guarantees for all rights, and on this basis excogitates his *jural state* which, strictly speaking, is impossible and absurd. He actually calls for rights to be guaranteed by force without indicating how it is possible to have guarantees against the abuse of force itself.[540]

1846. Such a system, which can only be sustained on the basis of a necessarily wayward human nature, causes direct harm to humanity. Kant does, in fact, suppose a certain radical evil in humanity. We may grant this, but it is insufficient to make us consider other human beings as assailants against our rights unless, in addition to the radical evil in them, we also suppose that all mankind without exception is under some necessity to offend us. If, however, the human will is not necessitated in this way, it may easily be the case that people do not in fact offend us. Before we have some proof of their intention, therefore, we cannot know whether they do or do not wish to cause us harm. In this case, when we judge that they do, our judgment is false, rash and offensive to them. But we cannot harm them without judging them as assailants. We cannot, therefore, offend them, and have to conclude that favourable judgment is to be the guiding rule of our actions; we have to presume that others are good until they are proved evil.

1847. But what are we to say about the probability of a wayward intention in others, even when this probability is not founded in their own fault? Are we unable to take precautions against this probability? — Precautions can be taken, as we have seen, provided we cause no harm to the person concerned. We

[539] *Doctrina juris*, p. 1, c. 2, sect. 1.

[540] Grotius puts the matter excellently: 'Human life is such that complete security is impossible. We have to look for help against groundless fears not from force, but from providence and prudent caution' (*De jure B. et P.*, bk 2, c. 2, §17).

can, therefore, require declarations, guarantees and any kind of assurances from him, as we said, provided they are without harm and danger to him. Moreover, he is obliged to give them to us. If he does not, he begins to place himself amongst the guilty; it is reasonable that every individual should justify himself and render an account of himself when rational suspicion falls upon him.

1848. This enables us to deduce the obligation incumbent on all to form part of civil society which, while not fully assuring rights, greatly increases their security. The obligation does not begin, however, except when people ask it of one another and require it in words or in practice.

1849. Suspicion of another's evil intention can arise from two general arguments:

1. From analogy: for example, a person we know is suspect simply because he belongs to a society which is not unlawful in itself, but contains many evil people.

2. From a calculation made on the basis of comparison between average moral force and temptation.

We shall speak about both cases.

A.
The right to defence when another's malice
is known by analogy

1850. There can be some grade of reasonable suspicion about every human being because each one belongs to the society of mankind, which contains many wicked people. If we knew the comparative numbers of good and evil people in this society, we would be able to state the precise degree of probability of our suspicion.

1851. The same may be said about all particular societies, trades, and professions. Every one of them has its own number of good and bad people; the relationship between these two quantities indicates the degree of probable goodness or malice in each of the members otherwise unknown to us.

1852. The same reasoning applies to nations. We are more suspicious about unknown people if they belong to some corrupt or barbarian nation than if they belong to a fully-developed or civilised people.

1853. The probability of suspicion also varies, therefore, according to the times. The morality of human beings in general, of nations, and of more particular societies or classes of human beings is subject to variation, however they are composed. The actual degree of probability can only be discovered through experience: the things we have experienced, the interaction between evil people in given societies, cause us to be more or less diffident about all their members. But these experiences and known cases are not the same for all. This explains different judgments about the degree of trust we can place in unknown individuals who present themselves as belonging to a certain class of persons.

1854. Three questions arise therefore:

1. How can we defend ourselves against the suspicion clinging to a member of a moral body as a result of the evil people found at the core of the body to which he belongs?

2. How can we defend ourselves against the danger we fear from the moral body itself?

3. Can we do harm to an innocent person indirectly when we justly defend ourselves against a blameworthy moral body?

We shall say something about each of these cases.

I.

Self-defence when suspicion falls on a single member
of a moral body with many evil adherents

1855. As we said previously, this kind of doubt is insufficient to convict a person belonging to that body. We cannot do him harm, therefore, but can defend ourselves, and guarantee our defence with innocuous means. At most, we can require from him some reasonable, harmless agreement, guarantee or caution.

II.
Self-defence when we fear danger from the body itself

1856. We can defend ourselves against the threat of danger from a body provided that the body is an evil society according to its constitution, and its government has proved its wickedness by many acts of injustice, or the spirit of the society has in the same way shown itself evil by its unjust acts. The means of defence are those with which we can protect ourselves against individuals whose actions mark them as unjust. The only distinction we have to make, as we have already shown, is that between guilty actions which have threatened us in particular and those which have threatened and offended others.

1857. If, however, the fear we have about that body does not depend on the injustice of its constitution, nor from repeated acts of its government, nor from its spirit, we cannot cause it harm in order to avoid the danger we fear. Nevertheless, if our fears are well-founded, we can take precautions by making use of our rights and requiring agreements and guarantees. We can also require some change in the MODALITY of the body's rights provided that the VALUE of these rights is maintained. This kind of alteration must reasonably be granted us.

1858. We must note that the guarantees which we ask from the collective body we reasonably fear and in consequence of which we require some change in the MODALITIES, but not in the VALUE of its rights, can increase in accord with

    1. stronger reasons for fearing probable harm;

    2. fear of greater harm;

    3. higher possibilities of irreparable harm if precautions are not taken in time.

1859. At this point, the questions of balance of power between States and of the so-called *raison d'état* rises of its own accord. It may be expressed as follows: Can war be waged by one Power on another under the pretext of self-defence for the sole reason that the second Power is excessively strong? If the opportunity of defeating this Power is not grasped (so the argument runs), we would be threatened with ruin. Experience shows (the argument adds) that big fish eat small fish, and that in the long term a powerful people overcomes a weaker one.

[1856–1859]

1860. Alberico Gentile[541] answered the question in the affirmative; Grotius[542] very rightly answered it in the negative. History offers many examples of rulers who waged war moved by the secret motive of defeating rivals feared for their power.[543] Only rarely, however, do we see this motive openly and shamelessly affirmed.[544]

1861. It is true that we ourselves have heard the public offered *raison d'état* (the Napoleonic State) as the only motive for so many murderous wars. But we have to remember that the bully who spoke in such a bare-faced manner had set out on the road to conquest and military fortune. Conquerors have never held the compass of Right as their guide, nor has there ever been the slightest chance of their teaching and revealing what is just. We also have to remember that the philosophical theory of sensism and utilitarianism has firmly established in the world the theory of political balance of power, and allowed justice to be usurped by advantage. The very conscience itself of peoples seemed almost cloaked and obscured, and many strong, violent, armed people already struggled to replace the Right of eternal law with that of force which, they thought, was more to their advantage. Finally, we must remember that despite everything to the contrary, justice reacted with open disagreement in the secret depths of conscience, shone more brightly than ever, and finally

---

[541] Bk. 1, c. 14.

[542] *De Jure B. et P.*, bk. 2, c. 1, §17.

[543] Examples of wars caused only by fear of an excessively strong Power are: the war between Sparta and Athens (*Thucyd.*, 1, p. m. 48), between Lisymachus and Demetrius (Pausan., 1, 17; Plut., in Demetr.), between Rome and Antiochus (Appian, *De Bello Syria.*, c. 47) or Philip the Macedonian (Liv., 30, c. 42), between Turnus and Rutulus against the Aborigenes (Liv., 1, c. 2), between the Federates and Rome (Liv., 1, c. 14; Poly., 1, c. 10; Thuan., bk. 37). All these wars seem to have been execrated by public opinion and detested for their injustice.

[544] Machiavelli taught nations and tyrants to justify without shame their bloody contests. Indeed, the more subtle and less brazen doctrines of *raison d'état* and balance of power which began to flourish in the 17th century made statesmen declare more confidently and openly that rivalry between the great Powers was their reason for war. The fear of excessive power had already been used by the French to justify their war against the Emperor and Spain (Cf. Grammond, *Hist.*, bk. 4).

conquered mental aberrations as surely as it had overthrown terror inculcated by the legions.

1862. We would agree, however, that the feared greatness and power of others, although not justifying war, does justify alliances aimed at assisting victory on the part of those who wage just war on the feared Power (it is understood that the victory itself must not exceed Right). Helping someone who has justice on his side is not opposed by justice if counselled by prudence.[545]

1863. When fear is not inculcated by some just Power, but founded on the wickedness of human nature rather than on any fault on the part of those we fear, we have no authority to harm anyone in our own defence. This kind of fear simply authorises us

1. to strengthen ourselves by the use of things which lie within the sphere of our rights

2. by using our innocuous freedom and

3. by requiring from the party we reasonably fear agreements and guarantees that do not lessen the WORTH of their rights, but only change THEIR MODALITY, which has no jural worth.

1864. These things can be done or demanded to the extent that fear is soundly based. It is more soundly based in so far as:

1. the power to harm (forces, audacity) is greater in the other party;

2. the occasion for exercising the power is closer at hand and easier;

3. the good acquired by the other when he harms us is greater;

4. the hope of impunity is greater both in the case of material

---

[545] The constant norm of the Romans was to help their unjustly assailed allies, and thus overthrow the Power they justly feared. Caesar, speaking of his war with Ariosto, expressed this solemn maxim in the following way: 'The custom of the Roman people is not only to want their allies and friends never to be diminished, but to desire their increase in grace, dignity and honour' (*De B. G.*, 1, 25, 26). It is true that this principle was brought into play where it was least applicable, but the fact shows that it was held as just and equable by the nations to whose judgment it was submitted as a motive justifying war.

[1862–1864]

chastisement and in that of public opinion, which has either been falsified or which one hopes to falsify;

5. there is a general air of corruption about the feared collective body as a result of other cases of proven greed, total lack of moral restraint and complete shamelessness;

6. the probability of harm, calculated according to similar instances in history, is greater, and can in fact be very great;

7. finally the evil, if not attended to in time, is seen to be irreparable later.

1865. It often happens that all these reasons, especially the sixth and seventh, serve to exacerbate the relationships between nations. Constant experience shows that in the long term a small nation becomes the subject and prey of its great neighbour unless it takes advantage of favourable opportunities for waging war. Experience also reminds us that an evil is often irreparable if such an opportunity is neglected.

1866. Granted the immense danger present in such difficult circumstances, we should not be surprised that the right to request mutual guarantees in relationships between States has been fully developed. These guarantees change the MODALITY of each nation's rights without, however, diminishing their value.

1867. The obligation of nations to make treaties and draw up agreements for their own use is founded, therefore, on a strict RIGHT OF REASON. Any nation withdrawing from such pacts would be guilty before other nations, and could justly be forced to adhere to an agreement.

1868. This is international right, which is much better called RATIONAL than NATURAL. It was introduced, or certainly perfected on earth by Christianity which calmed passions, strengthened the understanding and established here below the principles of an eternal justice and, more importantly, of an eternal, supernatural power with infinite retribution. Our own eyes have witnessed marvellous progress in this Right in our own period which, more than any other, has seen protocols take the place of war. This all shows that such calmness of spirit and serenity of mind, which allows human beings to listen to *reason* rather than be impelled to act by *instinct*, will go on increasing. The motto, *cedant arma togae*, will become ever more attractive to Christian nations.

1869. The area to which international right extends can be

expressed in this way: 'The greater Power must give the guarantees requested by the lesser Power, not by decreasing the *value* of its own rights, but by changing their *modality* whenever the lesser nation's fear is reasonable.'

1870. This is a jural right founded in the principle of reason which states: 'An individual must not remain in a position dangerous to his neighbour when he can change that position without harm to himself, or when he can eliminate the danger.' Anyone not obeying this principle is guilty and responsible for the danger which he freely causes. Each individual 'must use his rights without harm or disturbance in that *way* which leaves others as unencumbered as possible.'

1871. It is clear that finding such a *mode*, which is the noble responsibility of *diplomacy*, is not always easy. In fact, the true scope of the science and art of diplomacy cannot be simply the advantage of the nation represented by a diplomat. Its aim rather is 'to find the *modality* of the rights of nations which will maintain and secure their mutual rights without any diminution of their worth — in other words, that modality which makes possible the fullest coexistence amongst nations. Diplomats, therefore, have to reconcile justice with an equal division of usefulness. They have to maintain rights, and obviate collisions by means of the form and attitude they give to rights.' Statesmen and diplomats have in hand a most noble ministry of justice and want to be considered today as judges and peacemakers between nations.

1872. It is obvious that the right of a State to demand *modalities* in the rights of other more powerful or equally powerful nations as mutual guarantee or security possesses enormous latitude which must always be moderated by need. Practically everything that forms part of a peace-treaty or trade-agreement is reduced to determining the *modality* of which we are speaking. This modality may be applicable to one or both parties, with or without compensation, as we see happening especially in questions of import tax.

1873. This part of Right has not yet been split up and specified as it deserves. Innumerable questions arise from it and come to our notice daily. Well-informed decisions about these questions are naturally of interest to the temporal advantage and peace of nations, but they are also necessary for public education. We

[1870–1873]

need to know thoroughly which treaty between nations is right and totally moral so that statesmen, instructed in these ideas, can work with greater surety.

Let me offer an example of this kind of question by referring to one of the most equivocal facts of modern history — the Copenhagen expedition undertaken by England to capture (as it did) the Danish fleet. At the time, Denmark was friendly with England and perfectly neutral.

1874. English intelligence had revealed that Napoleon had set his sights on capturing the fleet.[546] England thought it best to step in first, realising that Denmark would not be able to defend herself and her fleet against such a powerful aggressor. Did England have the right to do this?

In England itself there were disagreements about the uprightness and justice of such a step, which was government policy, and the proposal that those who had carried out the expedition should be thanked by Parliament met with considerable opposition in the House.

1875. In his *History of the Spanish Revolution*,[547] Mr. George Elliot tried to justify this undertaking with examples[548] and arguments. Examples, however, are of little use because they themselves need to be justified. Nevertheless, the judgment formed by the public on the facts used as an example is itself some kind of authority. Elliot writes:

> I do not think it difficult to prove that in the extremely extensive morality of the laws of nations every State has the *unalterable* right to look to its own security with every

---

[546] Only a short time before, the French fleet had been destroyed at the battle of Trafalgar at the very moment when Bonaparte was proclaiming at Ulm that he needed nothing except 'ships, colonies and commerce.'

[547] T. 2, p. 1.

[548] 'Pitt's proposition in 1761 that a rich Spanish flotilla should be intercepted for the sake of obtaining a secure pledge against the hostilities that nation was clearly planning against us was regarded as acceptable by all sensible people. If it had been actuated, it would with all probability have prevented the war declared by Spain shortly after the arrival of its treasure.' This example, however, is not on the same plane. It can be considered as an exercise of the *Right of prevention* against someone who has already begun to act against the rights of others.

[1874–1875]

means in its power, provided it can clearly prove that its
security is truly endangered.[549]

I could never approve of this. I must always maintain that
nations' right of defence is limited (as the individual's right is
limited) to the use of just, upright means alone. Equally harmful
and dangerous in our opinion are the author's other words :

> There would be little wisdom in the counsels of a nation
> which decided to perish through excessive delicacy of
> conscience.[550]

On the contrary, the business of nations must be governed
by the same delicacy of conscience that presides over private
business. Indeed, it must be even more delicate. We think that
this truth could and ought to be preached from the roof tops by
all writers on Right and morals and deeply impressed in the
spirits of peoples and their governments.

I grant that writers on ethics and rational Right are also called
to facilitate the practice of justice and holiness in public affairs.
Their responsibility is to identity special cases, and indicate the
ways in which they can be reconciled to the advantage of their
own nation, and with justice and morality towards all others.

1876. But let us return to the case we proposed and formulate
it as a general question: 'If a friend possesses a weapon that
could harm us and cannot defend himself against an enemy of
ours who would take it for use against us, can we first take that
weapon for ourselves.'

I have no doubt that rational Right leads us to an affirmative
answer on condition that we take possession of the weapon in
the right way and pay adequate compensation.

1877. The following are the conditions according to which we
can correctly exercise the *right of prevention*:

1. We must use all peaceful means to ensure that the weapon
is handed over by agreement, unless the use of peaceful means
are foreseen as totally useless or would compromise the outcome of the affair.

2. We cannot take possession of the weapon except as a
pledge to be restored after the danger has passed.

[549] Introduction.
[550] *Ibid.*

[1876–1877]

3. If in taking it by force we harm it, we must compensate the owner for the harm.

4. We must also compensate the owner for the harm accruing through his lack of the weapon, and for the income he has forfeited.

In this way the owner will lose nothing of the value of his rights; there is simply a change in their MODALITY for a just, necessary and urgent cause.

1878. Another question now arises: 'Can I prevent someone becoming much more powerful than myself, not because he threatens me, but in order to have some guarantee for my reasonable fear that human perversity finds it hard, as we know, to resist certain serious temptations for any length of time?' I would answer: 'Yes', if this individual were to employ disreputable ways of increasing his power, such as unjust conquests.

1879. If he declared war, and it were impossible to resolve doubts about its justice on either side, I could intervene as a mediator and peacemaker between the parties.

1880. I can ally myself with the opponent of the party I fear most if that side refuses either my mediation or some similarly fair way of resolving the differences peacefully. It is a duty of *rational justice* to reach an upright compromise and fair conclusion in a doubtful cause, and to avoid violence. Anyone refusing to do this offends against right.

1881. If, however, the person concerned makes due progress without giving cause for complaint, his development will entail the use of his rights within their own sphere (for example, by improving industry within his own State) or by acts of *innocuous freedom* intended to extend the sphere of his rights.

In the first case, it is certain that I cannot prevent his progress by causing harm; in the second, not only may I forestall his projected acquisition by occupying it myself and impeding his design, but I can even claim that he should either limit his innocuous freedom or offer sufficient guarantee against it. For example, one Power decides to occupy a great tract of abandoned territory which serves as a buffer between it and another Power. The second Power foresees that it would have no hope of resistance should the territory fall into the other's hands, but has no way of occupying the territory itself. In this case, it can require some explanation from the other, and even prevent occupation by war if no other means is available. As we said, *innocuous freedom* is not a right, but simply a means of acquiring rights. It can, therefore, be impeded and limited if it causes us some reasonable fear and thus ceases to be truly and completely *innocuous*. It can be impeded, however, only to the extent of the danger, and no further.

III.
Can we harm an innocent person indirectly as a result of our just defence against a guilty, collective body of which he is a member?

1882. Innocent people must undoubtedly be saved in a defensive war against a guilty collective body, if there is some way of saving them.

1883. But can I defend myself against a collective body intent on harming me if I have to involve innocent people in the harm I inflict? I think this can be done provided the defence is just, necessary and moderate, in the way we have previously described. In this case, the true cause of harm to the innocent is not myself, but the body which provoked the defence and wickedly imperilled the safety of its members, for which it is responsible.

1884. At this point, a most important, but little examined question could be raised about the solidarity formed at the heart of collective persons. This *solidarity* has two parts:

1. that by which each member considers himself associated with the action of the body;

2. that by which the whole body considers itself associated with the action of each member.

1885. It is clear that each member of a collective body with an evil end or wicked constitution shares in its wickedness by the fact of association, if the association is freely willed, not necessitated.

1886. If, however, a collective body has an upright end and constitution, it would not seem that all its members are invariably responsible for abuse of authority by the government. We have to conclude that guilty and innocent cannot be bracketed together if it is possible to separate them.

[1882–1886]

1887. Granted the impossibility of considering each member of the society as guilty of crimes perpetrated by the government, it is *a fortiori* impossible, generally speaking, to involve all the members in the faults of one of them.

1888. *Solidarity* taken in this sense has always been an immense source of injustices. One particularly inhuman example of this is reprisals, when prisoners of war, who are no longer capable of doing harm, are killed simply because the enemy has already done the same. I cannot see any way whatsoever for justifying such barbarity, by which one person is made to undergo the punishment merited by another. It should be outlawed from the Right of war amongst civilised people.

1889. I think the same has to be said about taking hostages for the sake of threatening their lives if their fellow citizens or relatives harm us or refuse to do what we want. In this case, we would be defending ourselves with innocent blood. It is impossible to justify this according to the principles of rational Right, which alone are worthy of a civilised people.

1890. In any case, we have to note that the *solidarity* attributed to all the members of a body in the case of crime by one of them is a right that has changed greatly in various times and periods of mankind's development, and has been given multiple *modes* by public opinion.

Natural, synergic unions were stronger at the beginning of human history. It would seem that the checks and balances applicable by underdeveloped reason and underactivated freedom exercised little influence on vehement feeling and instinct. In fact, freedom gains force only as reason develops, and through use. Unity in collective bodies, especially family unity, is tighter the further we reach back in antiquity. People were formed on the model of one another, through constant imitation and tradition. Children were the image of their fathers, whose feelings, passions, persuasions and customs they inherited. The whole family appeared a single person, marked with its own characteristics and distinct from all the others. This is, indeed, a special characteristic of Orientals. Hence, crime on the part of a single member was immediately imputed to the whole family, to all the clan; an entire city was punished for a single malefactor; an entire people were shamed by a few very

[1887–1890]

wicked members. No-one doubted the truth and justice of *crimine ab uno disce omnes*, a proverbial maxim accepted without hesitation by all.

1891. This reflection slightly diminishes, without removing altogether, the level of injustice found in the frequent judgments of ancient peoples which condemned the fathers for the children and the children for the fathers, or entire families and even cities for the wrong-doing of a single person. Another reflection makes it easy to explain this fact, without lessening its iniquity. In antiquity, the *faculty of abstraction* was little developed.[551] Consequently, it was difficult for the mind to separate one thing from another. Moses, for example, who evidently wished to educate the people and develop their understanding, ordered them to avoid as unjust some of these all-embracing judgments.[552] The immense development of the faculty of abstraction that has taken place in modern times is to a great extent the cause of the ever-growing exclusion, from our laws, of punishments founded on the principle of solidarity. Examples are confiscation, and so on.

1892. Moreover, it is too difficult to decide how much a body's uniformity in behaviour and nature, and unicity of spirit, could in remote times justify the harm that was done to an entire body for the sake of defence against the wrong-doing of a single member. We can say, however, that we would have to begin the calculation by carefully verifying the unity of the intent to harm, that is, of helping the guilty party in his wicked assault.

1893. It is lawful for everyone to take precautions against an entire body when he suspects that it harbours an individual malefactor. The means he uses, however, must not offend the rights of ownership of the body; they must be a mere use of his freedom. Pallas' family, for example, was able to avoid contracting marriage with the family of Agnusius because of

---

[551] Cf. *SP*, bk. 4, c. 35.

[552] Deuteronomy expressly states: 'The fathers shall not be put to death for the children, nor shall the children be put to death for the fathers; every man shall be put to death for his own sin' (24: 16). Scripture also notes that Amaziah, having put to death the murderers of king Joas, his father, spared their children, in accordance with the law of Deuteronomy that we have quoted (2 Kgs 14; 2 Chron 25). This moderation would have gone unnoticed if contemporary custom and natural feeling had not suggested the contrary.

the presence of a single traitor.[553] This kind of avoidance must not be the effect of hatred or of the spirit of retaliation, but of prudent fear and care not to take sides with the guilty or fall into the hands of the enemy.

B.
A comparison between average moral force and instant temptation gives rise to the right to defence against others' wrong-doing

1894. We have more reason to fear theft from people in a state of misery than from well-off people. Certainly the former are under greater pressure from temptation; necessity urges, and greater moral force is needed to resist it. Indigent people may indeed possess this force, but our ignorance of their state does not allows us to estimate their moral force as more than average. This in turn authorises us to be more suspicious of them than of comfortably-off or rich people. Moreover, average moral force, which is constant, leads us to increase our suspicion of the honesty of unknown people in proportion to the degree of temptation they experience.

1895. Consequently civil society has the right, relative to the poor, to require greater surety of their conduct than of others, to watch more carefully over the way of life of the poor, and so on. Society, however, has no right to lessen the rights of the poor or inflict the least harm upon them.

1896. Civil society may also assume a jural obligation to help the poor in cases of real indigence. This is the case in England, for example, where a poor-tax is imposed. It is clear that through this assistance and through the indigent who accept it, society gains a right to require work from the poor as a strictly jural obligation. Without such an obligation, it would be impossible to verify amongst the indigent those who had the *right* to assistance; the idle must be considered thieves under such a system.

1897. Generally speaking, it can be affirmed that all *methods of crime prevention* are defective and unjust whenever they are

---

553 Cf. Plutarch, *Theseus*.

employed by civil society in a manner disadvantageous to persons not convicted of the fault in question, or of any other fault producing some reasonable suspicion and fear in society.

§4. *An error easily committed in exercising the right to defence against feared, probable offences*

1898. We conclude this article with the observation that civil society sometimes does real harm to innocent people when it lays claim to the defence of its members, and at the same time wrongly imagines that its way of action is in accord with justice. The measures it takes seem necessary to its own safety or that of its members, but at the same time it believes that it can *abstract* from the harm inflicted upon innocent individuals.

1899. This abstraction, made by civil society and its government, does not diminish the real harm inflicted on the innocent, nor does 'another point of view' diminish the suffering experienced by the innocent.

1900. Torture, a genuine example of this kind of injustice, was justified in the past through a kind of legalistic abstraction, and used against the accused not as a punishment (so it was said) but as a means of knowing the truth.

Similarly, no pain or harm inflicted under the pretext that it is not imposed as punishment can be imposed on a person not yet proved guilty of a crime. A government, although sometimes obliged to take precautions against persons it suspects, must treat them with every consideration. Moreover it would seem, according to rational Right, that it must compensate them for disturbance caused, perhaps necessarily, for the public good. This compensation would ensure the preservation of the *value* of a person's rights; only the *modality* of the rights would be changed (cf. 1706). The English law of *habeas corpus* was dictated according to this principle of justice, which also suggested the fine instruction given by the Empress Catherine for the formation of the Russian code about preventative arrest.[554]

[554] Cf. Art. 10, q. 2.

[1898–1900]

Article 14.
How the right to defence is extended in accord with the development of the human race, and consequently takes different forms in the different ages of nations

1901. Right extends in so far as human understanding which possesses it knows how to draw more or less remote consequences from it.

1902. Right is offended in many ways: directly or indirectly, by positive or negative action, by the action itself, or by its consequences, and through the more or less remote consequences of our actions. Right is offended when its possessor suffers moral resentment, which varies in so far as he knows the consequences that another's action can have on his right.[555]

1903. Under this aspect, the sphere of innocuous freedom open to human beings is gradually restricted as intelligence increases and we come to know more about the remote consequences of our actions and their mutual relationships. As a result, an action which was thought innocuous at one time is considered offensive at another. The right of defence then appears to take on new laws, and be clothed in different *modes*.

1904. This observation enables us to explain in great part the new advances in our own days, the universally felt need for new theories of rights, the delicacy and mutual regard people have

---

[555] The most just way of measuring the value of an offence and its corresponding compensation would be on the basis of some possible calculation about the *value of the moral resentment* produced by the offence. The natural light of nations saw this truth, which in certain legislation was put into practice.

Amongst the Romans, 'according to the praetorian edict, the offended person took an oath that instead of submitting to a certain kind of injury, he would have preferred to lose a given sum of money. The judge added to this exposition of resentment or self-interest the modifications his caprice thought suitable' (the writer is accustomed to cutting short what he has to say, and unfortunately uses his poor stock of preconceived ideas too often), 'and that was that. . . When Roman laws came to light again after so many centuries of ignorance, this method was also reinstated, and is still accepted with respect by the majority of European nations' (Gioia, *Dell'ingiuria e de' danni*, etc., Preface).

The method adopted by the Romans drew on nature and justice, but its application requires a simple, religious people.

[1901–1904]

for one another, and the increase of mutual claims upon one another. In a word, understanding has taken possession of certain things that were formerly free: the individual who today possesses a right, possesses along with it all the useful, foreseen consequences of this right which, when he sees them, he appropriates. Formerly, the same things had not been seen, and hence not appropriated.

1905. This comment (which alone perhaps can pacify many angry disagreements amongst people and produce harmony between old and new opinions) will be better understood if we turn back to our division of rights and lawful acts pertaining to freedom, and to rights and lawful acts pertaining to ownership.

What is our ownership reduced to? As we have seen, it is inexact to speak, as civil laws do, about a right over the substance of things. The human being can only have a right over the *use* of things; he has no notion of what to do with their substance. It might just be possible to say, but even this would be inexact, that we have a right over the substance of which we are formed. The right over the substance of things, however, is entirely God's, who gives being to their substance, and maintains it. Ownership, therefore, is directly concerned only with the exclusive use of a thing, and consequently extends only as far as our knowledge of how to use it. But as ownership extends to more and more uses of a thing, so the possibility of harming others by our use of things is extended. It follows that the cases in which the right to defence can be brought into play are also extended.

1906. It may be objected that the exclusive use of some thing is exercised only through a series of actions in which we use the thing as a kind of matter or instrument. But an action is the proper object of our right only when we actually do it. Is there any difference, therefore, between freedom and ownership, between the right to actions and things, and the right over actions and things? Doesn't this kind of argument reduce ownership to freedom? Is the right I have over something, different from the right to certain actions?

I reply that the difference lies in this: the right over a thing brings me the right to all the actions which I can do with that thing in a way exclusive and proper to myself, that is, in such way that no one can limit me in my right. If, on the other hand,

[1905–1906]

I had the right to actions without this right being founded in something I already possessed, everybody could enforce limits on my actions in this regard. Possession of something is that which renders such actions possible for me; the thing itself can be regarded as a power to act, as an increase in my liberty.

The analogy between the two species of right already determined can be expressed as follows: in both we distinguish 1. the power to act; 2. the action itself. The power to act is either only our internal freedom or, in addition, is also the thing we have occupied. The first kind of freedom, which we have called *innocuous freedom*, is the source of our rights to acts and to things; the second is the source of the rights which consist in our use of a given thing. The *power* to act, whether it regards our internal freedom or the external thing, can never be touched or limited; the *acts* of such powers can, however, be limited by means of acts preceding our own.

As we were saying, therefore, we consider the external thing that we own as a power to act. I maintain that this power is extended and useful to us in so far as we know how to employ it and foresee its remote uses. Moreover, we do not possess this power except to the extent that we know how useful it will be. As our understanding increases, therefore, our rights acquire greater extension in accordance with the stricter moral bond between things and ourselves.

1907. Nations have become more jealous about their trade, navigation, rivers and so on, precisely because they have come to know better the consequences of these things.

To repeat: as right is further extended over things, so the right to defence is extended further at different times. In a word, because previously we were unable to calculate the remote consequences of an act in the way now possible to us, we can lawfully regard as harmful an action which at other times we considered as harmless, and defend ourselves against its consequences.

[1907]

CHAPTER 5
The right to satisfaction

1908. The *right of coercion* is exercised on two occasions: when an attempt is made to injure our rights, and when our rights have been injured. In the former, the right of coercion is called the *right to defence*; in the latter, the *right to satisfaction*.

1909. The right to defence and the right of satisfaction are therefore two actualisations of the right of coercion. The right of coercion can be considered as the genus, the other two as the species. We have spoken about the *right to defence*; we will now discuss the *right to satisfaction*.

Article 1.
The subject of this chapter

1910. But we must first distinguish between the right to satisfaction and the right to punish.

Because *satisfaction* presupposes *harm*, we need to see which actions inflict harm on others. Every immoral act implies a *debt* to moral being, but not every immoral act inflicts *harm* on others. The *debt* we incur to moral being contains in its concept our *duty of satisfying the debt* and the creditor's *right* to satisfaction. But in every immoral act the creditor is justice itself, that is, the supreme being where justice resides. Strictly speaking, this is called penal Right. *Penal Right* therefore deals with the violation of justice in its universal, objective nature.

1911. *Harm*, however, presupposes a created, intelligent being, capable of being harmed, and contains in its concept the *duty of rendering satisfaction* and, on the part of the person harmed, the *right to satisfaction*. Hence, the *right to satisfaction* is completely different from *penal right*, although it can be considered as connected with penal right. Strictly speaking, the right to satisfaction exists only in the case of unjust harm and debt to the harmed being, in addition to the debt to justice and the supreme being.

[1908–1911]

We have spoken about the *right to punish*. The reader must be careful not to confuse it with the *right to satisfaction*, which is the subject of our present discussion.

Article 2.
The nature of harm

1912. We must first determine the nature of injurious harm.

Some actions are *immoral* but do not injure others' rights. Other actions, such as failed aggression, are *immoral* and *injurious to rights* but in fact do no *harm*. Other actions do *harm* but are not immoral or injurious, for example, the use of innocuous freedom by which we restrict the sphere of another's freedom. Finally, some actions are *immoral, injurious* and *harmful*; only these are involved in the right to satisfaction.

1913. Injurious harm consists in a diminution of the good contained in a person's right, effected against his will.

1914. Every good, when reduced to its most general class, is both *moral* and *eudaimonological*.

Although an attack can be made against moral good, a human being cannot be robbed or despoiled of moral good against his will. If a person, by consenting to another's attack, is therefore deprived of moral good, the harm sustained cannot be classed among injurious harm because 'no harm is done to the person who knowingly consents'.[556]

1915. The only *jural offence* against moral good therefore is any *attack* against it. Consequently neither injurious harm nor right to satisfaction is involved. We spoke about this kind of injury and about possible defence against it when we dealt with innate right.[557]

---

[556] *Reg.* 27, in 6.

[557] In the case of a moral good under attack, it may appear contradictory to allow a *right to defence*, but not a *right to satisfaction* after a person has been seduced and robbed of virtue. Careful consideration however indicates that in the case of defence, where we wish to defend ourselves from seduction by forcefully repelling its occasions and means, we not only do not consent but we show ourselves opposed to the seduction. Here there is real injury and harm to the right we have of not being prevented from obtaining moral good.

[1912–1915]

We can require satisfaction therefore only for harm which involves the loss of any eudaimonological good. This perfects the proposed definition of injurious harm by determining the element of good, as follows:

1916. Injurious harm consists in the diminution, against our will, of some eudaimonological good which is ours by right.

1917. A question now arises which must be answered immediately.

According to what we have said, it would seem that no *right to retaliation*, distinct at least from penal right, exists between *penal right* which concerns punishment imposed on a sinner by the order of eternal justice, and the *right to satisfaction*. Human opinion and instinct is apparently the basis for the right of simple retaliation, but does this proposed right to retaliation in fact exist?

But when we have given in and been despoiled of moral good, the injury ceases precisely because we have given in. This is the only way moral good is lost, and because no injury is done to anyone who knowingly consents, no right to satisfaction is involved.

It is true that we can afterwards repent of our action and in doing so reject the seduction held out to us by declaring it contrary to our will. But this new state of will cannot restore to us our original right. Consequently, the seducer cannot in any way make restitution for the moral good whose loss he has merely occasioned rather than caused; its restitution, like its loss, depends on us. However, both we and the seducer deserve punishment. But this pertains to *penal right*, not to *right of satisfaction*.

It is also true that anyone who has given scandal to another has the obligation both to end the scandal if it is permanent and, if the scandal results in seduction, to give *edification* by compensating the person to whose loss the scandal has contributed. But the duty of *giving edification* is not an object of coercion, and does not therefore pertain to right. Hence, either the person is converted to good, in which case satisfaction is no longer necessary, or he remains in his evil, in which case he himself desires no satisfaction.

Everybody therefore has the right to defence against anyone who attacks their morality. Moreover, the assailant deserves *punishment* whether the desired fall is obtained or not. But there is no *right* to *satisfaction* unless some other harm has been done during the attack.

[1916–1917]

Article 3.
Is there in human beings a right to SIMPLE RETALIATION which protects the integrity of their rights and is distinct from penal right and from the right of coercion?

1918. As soon as human beings see justice offended they know, almost by intuition, that the order of justice requires the guilty to be punished in proportion to their guilt. Sensing a desire for order to be re-established by this means, they also rejoice in the punishment of the guilty. If punishment does not follow immediately, they call for it with zealous anger and feel incited to take some part in re-establishing the eternal order of being by inflicting on the guilty some suitable punishment. All these undeniable facts lie deep in human nature. At first sight they are easily explained, but later become mysterious, and finally, sublime consequences of human moral nature, rooted as they are in the intrinsic, immutable order of total, absolute, moral being.

But although all these facts do indeed witness to an essential *right to punish*, they do not witness to a right to *simple retaliation*.

The right to punish is objective, and consists in the clear need to re-establish the order of moral being by balancing fault with punishment. The feeling adherent to this right manifests itself in our spirit when we see any fault whatsoever, whether simply moral or even jural, and if jural, of a kind that infringes another's or our own right.

1919. But the right to simple retaliation is different. Properly speaking it is conceived as proper to an intelligent *subject* who has experienced injury and wants to vindicate himself against the perpetrator. This subject is motivated by the offence *against himself*, not by the mere requirements of the moral law considered objectively and universally. If the offence had been against someone else, it would not have motivated him in the same way. His intention is not only to re-establish the objective order but to have the perpetrator of the injury punished and thus obtain satisfaction for himself from the punishment and suffering. Does he, however, in the light of nature and human reason, have this right to simple retaliation?

[1918–1919]

1920. Note carefully: I do not deny the existence of the matter of a right whenever we are in the presence of an instinct truly proper to nature and therefore common to all human beings. It is also certain that human beings have an instinct for beholding the humiliation of one who has injured them and refuses to compensate the harm when confronted with it. But our case concerns the presence of a human instinct different both from the already mentioned instinct to punish, and from the instinct to gain satisfaction for harm done.

I say a *human instinct* because animality itself has its own inclination to react with angry feelings and warlike instinct against anything that upsets it. Relative to the animal, such a reaction is set in motion, as with all instinctive activities, by virtue of certain blind laws and in the absence of any ulterior intention. But relative to the governing providence of the animal, the purpose of the movement of anger is not retaliation at all but the defence of the animal against hostile forces.

All things considered, therefore, I maintain that no instinct for retaliation exists in the human being specifically different from the instinct to punish, defend oneself and obtain satisfaction for injurious harm. Consequently, a specific right to retaliation does not exist.

1921. Such a right is proper only to God, because only in God does a right to retaliation identify with *penal right*. Objective justice in God is also subjective, so that God can impose a punishment for fault considered as violation of justice (object) and offence against himself (subject).

1922. This solution is confirmed and clarified by the consideration that human beings deserve respect only in so far as they share in eternal law. Thus, *injury*, which comes within the orbit of this law, is not restricted to human beings. We do not have personship of ourselves; all injury against us is only relative, just as, in a similar but not equal way, an insult against an image is not confined to the image but wounds the subject presented in the image.[558]

1923. Nevertheless we can and must distinguish two functions of penal justice. Two *titles* draw into act the unique law of justice

[558] Cf. *PE*, 66-68.

when intelligent beings, as we are, suffer harm from another intelligent being. The first is the dignity of the *supreme Being*, where morality resides in all its essence; the second is the dignity of the *created, intelligent being* (human being). The dignity is essentially the same: it is always *being* that is not acknowledged. But the harm done to *being*, present in every person, is effected in human beings who share in being and therefore in its dignity. Because they feel *their dignity* is offended by the harm done to them, they seek *retaliation* and vindication in itself for the *being* that was harmed. This function of *punitive justice* can certainly be called '*right to retaliation*' but it is not specifically different from the right to punish, and is essentially different from the supreme Being's *right to retaliation*.

1924. Why then are human beings seen to be constantly moved by a greater impetus to retaliate for their own injuries rather than for the injuries of others?

Many explanations are given for this fact. First, human beings, as intellective, animal subjects, are subject to the passion of anger, a blind movement which (cf. 1920) affects the understanding and will, as do all the other animal passions. Viceversa, understanding and will move the passion of anger when they perceive an injury. It is not surprising therefore that such subjects show themselves more sensitive, active and energetic in obtaining retaliation for offences against themselves rather than against others.

1925. Second, the injuries are nearly always joined with harm either in itself or in its consequences.

1926. In the third place, human corruption must be borne in mind. Sadly, sinful humanity lost the knowledge of God. As a result, we necessarily became revengeful just as we had become proud and pleasure-seeking. We were necessarily pleasure-seeking because, having lost our greatest good, we could not find happiness except in creatures. Pride was necessary because, having rejected the first being and forgotten our proper Master, we showed ourselves as first being for ourselves, our own Master. Our reason necessarily became the God of the earth, since nothing superior to human reason was left. Consequently, we had also to be revengeful because on the one hand we were capable of knowing injustice but on the other no longer knew who was responsible for fully punishing and requiting injustice.

[1924–1926]

Moreover it was natural for us to claim the requital of injuries which had violated justice and been specifically perpetrated against us, although this right belonged to God alone (cf. 1921) whose position we usurped. Again, indignation, a passion arising from the knowledge of an offence, necessarily became more sensitive and inflamed in us; we had lost the vision of God and therefore felt the injury as if we were God ourselves. This explains why the passion of anger formed the heroes of paganism, whose archetype is Achilles, and why retaliation and cruelty are vices which contaminate all customs and laws of idolatrous peoples.

1927. To leave to God alone the exercise of the right to retaliation is a deliberation as difficult as our re-union with God.

The cities of sanctuary established by Moses for those who committed involuntary murder demonstrate how difficult it was to restrain blind indignation among the Hebrews, which took the form of a desire for retaliation. The least educated seek retaliation the most. To be able to reject the desire of retaliation we must be capable of controlling our anger and be convinced that God alone is the vindicator of every injustice, because he is the justice violated in us. These truths demand reflection, and to be effective, require a high degree of persuasion seen only in the people of the new Gospel. Certainly, human beings renewed by Christ, that is, newly joined to God, can fully understand the meaning of 'Vengeance is mine' because the law they follow also says: 'Love your enemies; bless those who hate you.'

1928. Let us conclude. The only *right to retaliation* within human competence is simply an actuality of the right to punish (cf. 1923). God however has reserved the exercise of this right to himself. We partake of personal dignity (the object of others' moral respect) by the light of truth, to which we adhere. We have a *moral exigency*[559] therefore as soon as we are known by other intelligent beings. If they do not give us the respect *required* by our dignity and will, we feel *injury* and the need to repair the *disorder*. Although this necessity originates from the objective exigency (of ourselves as objects), it affects the subject,

---

[559] Cf. *CS*, 115-140, for what I have said about the first form in which human beings feel the force of the moral law. I have shown that the *objects* themselves known by us act as law and exercise its obligating force.

because of the identity of object and subject. The subject now expects compensation and, if this is not willingly proffered by the offender, is moved to make the offender repent by punishing him. The punishment, considered relative to the exigency of the human being as object, is called 'chastisement'; considered relative to the offended *subject*, who naturally desires recompense, it is called *retaliation*. I repeat: there is no natural right to retaliation distinct from that of *chastisement*, but this right does exist in union with the right of chastisement.

According to human nature, human beings desire only a *retaliatory chastisement* for an offender, not simple retaliation. The reason is obvious: moral *exigency* (moral obligation) proceeds from real human beings in so far as they have a relationship with ideal human beings, that is, the exigency does not proceed from the subject as such but from the subject as object; it is the ideal human being, that is, the idea of human being, the objective human being, which enlightens the mind and says to it: 'This real human being requires respect.' Thus, ideal or object human being is the *law*; real or subject human being is the *title* to which the law is applied. Obligation in potency comes from the law, but potential obligation itself receives its actuality from the title. Ideal, object human being differs from real, subject human being: the former is eternal; the latter (a temporal thing) has indeed an essential but only a dependent relationship to the eternal. Thus, because obligation does not come from the real human being, he cannot have in himself the full right to retaliation, which he receives from the very same source as that of his own subsistence. Granted then the eternal law and the moral necessity of *chastisement* when the law is violated, we have the concept of what can be called the right to retaliation, that is, not simple retaliation but *retaliatory chastisement*. Hence, *retaliation* must be inseparable from *chastisement*, that is, from penal justice, and be fittingly returned to the control of Him who alone is just and the sufficient dispenser of all justice.

[1928]

Article 4.
Is penal right present in the right to satisfaction?

1929. Penal justice is present not only in the concept of just retaliation but in all the functions of right in which we cause pain to our fellows.

1930. I say 'In which we cause pain to our fellows', because, although the right to retaliation (as exercised by the supreme Being) and the right to punish are conceivable only together, the rights to *defence* and *satisfaction* can be conceived without necessarily having recourse to the right to punish. But inflicting pain on others, while not indispensable to these two rights, is inherently indispensable to retaliation.

1931. If the rights to defence and to satisfaction are therefore exercised without causing pain or loss to others, the right to punish, in such an exercise, is not present.

But it can happen that we need to use force and to inflict pain and loss in order to defend ourselves from others' injustice or to procure due indemnity from those harming us. In this case, the *right to punish* immediately becomes necessary to justify the pain or loss caused, because harming others is unjust if they are not guilty.

Article 5.
The existence of the right to satisfaction

1932. Granted these facts we can easily demonstrate the existence of the right to satisfaction both in itself and relative to its special function in which it resorts to force and causes pain to others so that satisfaction is obtained. The existence of the right is shown as follows.

The right of ownership is an activity, and also a force of a subject. By it the subject keeps united to himself some good object, which he uses as he pleases. This union, protected by the moral law, is moral order. On the other hand, removing the object is moral disorder, and anyone who attempts removal is culpable, that is, an author of moral disorder.

Thus, if I use my activity and force in an attempt to re-assert ownership, that is, to re-unite with myself the thing from which I was unjustly separated, I am simply re-establishing moral order. To re-establish moral order is to be author of something upright, and all of us are capable of this. Therefore my right of ownership extends to this action, because such action is conformable to the indication of human nature (simple ownership) and not contrary to the moral order (right of ownership).

1933. Hence, if the *right to satisfaction* extends to inflicting pain or loss on an assailant, the reason is found in his guilt. That a guilty person should suffer punishment conforms to penal justice. When I inflict punishment on a guilty person, therefore, I do nothing contrary to justice: my right extends even as far as this.

1934. But we must note that in this case also, penal Right is not exercised directly by me. I use only the amount necessary to maintain my right of ownership; it is always the right of ownership I exercise. Penal justice simply renders possible certain functions of this right.

1935. All these arguments clearly begin from the principle that 'the right of ownership can be exercised unlimitedly as long as nothing unjust or wrong in itself is perpetrated.'

Article 6.
The identity of the right to satisfaction exercised
by the individual and by society

1936. Such then is the nature of the right to satisfaction or indemnity. Its nature remains the same whether the right is exercised by a subject, by an *individual* in the state of nature or in the extra-societal state;[560] or even by *society* itself, the normal case when human beings are constituted in a civil state.

1937. We have already demonstrated the obligation to respect rights in whatever subject they are present. It would therefore be an error to seek the origin of the right of indemnity in the

---

[560] By *extra-societal* I mean that part of the state of nature which remains after civil society has been instituted.

[1933–1937]

social contract, as some have done, or, as others do, to think this right changes its nature for human beings united in society.

1938. Those who hold the second opinion believe that the right takes its origin from *public good*. According to them, public good is the end of civil society.

But I repeat, it is false to say that the end of civil society is the so-called *public good* (the good of the majority). The end of civil society is the good of every individual, and therefore the *common good* (the good of all).[561]

1939. The right to satisfaction exists before civil society. If society judges harm and determines compensation, it does so solely by taking the place of the offended person and protecting him, just as any person could take the place of every offended individual, defending each one in turn. In this way society produces the *common good* without diminishing the rights of each member. If a society is attacked or harmed (crimes against the State) and defends itself, it is still defending the *common good*, because its existence is of equal concern to all, and all desire it as a protector of their rights. We can only add that the public good, or good of the majority, becomes part of the purpose of society simply in the case of the indirect beneficence which society is called to exercise, but not in the case of justice.

Hence, political laws, while leaving intact the rights of all, permit or promote some useful institution and thus have as their end the good of the majority, that is, the public good, which is founded when particular goods merge to produce the common good.[562]

1940. Summarising, we can say that the government of civil society, as representative and agent of the individuals composing it, has the right to punish the guilty as a result of one of the following:

1. the right to defence against future and probable harm;

2. the right to restitution against harm already perpetrated.

1941. Thus society exercises these rights:

1. for its own defence, when its existence is attacked (universal or common good);

2. for the advantage of every collective or individual person

[561] Cf. *SP*, bk. 2.
[562] Cf. *SP*, bk. 4, c. 8.

[1938–1941]

within it, whenever these persons have recourse to it, or it spontaneously assumes the defence of the innocent (*particular* good, which merges with every other particular good to become *common* good).

Article 7.
The verification of harm

1942. For the right to satisfaction to be effective, the harm done must be verified.

1943. *Probability* of harm is not sufficient. Harm done to us must be *certain*, if we are to obtain satisfaction with force.

1944. To verify injurious harm, we need to know two things:
1. that which has to be proved;
2. how to prove it.

1945. These two things differ greatly from each other. What has to be proved can only be determined by the *Science of Right* in so far as it determines rights and corresponding obligations. The method of proof can only be determined by the *Art of Critique*, which makes known the value of the proofs.

1946. The *Art of Critique* applied to the verification of injurious harm differs greatly in the state of nature and in the civil state. In the state of nature people are generally judges in their own cause; in the civil state a third party is the deciding judge.

The kinds of proofs needed by a judge coming between accuser and accused are unnecessary for anyone judging his own cause. If a house-owner sees a thief escaping from his house with some of his possessions, he has sufficient proof of the crime. But without other witnesses or clues, the owner's assertion may possibly not be enough to convince the judge .

1947. In the state of nature the process of proofs of harm is much shorter than in the state of civil society where, besides a *treatise on judiciary proofs*, a *procedure* must first be established which regulates the way to find, organise and submit the proofs to judgment.

[1942–1947]

1948. Consequently the way of proving harm in civil society has both a necessary advantage and disadvantage compared with the way of proving harm in the state of nature. The disadvantage is that much of the real harm escapes legal proofs, which may not always be obtainable. The advantage is that passion is excluded from judgments about the harm done; a person judging in his own cause is usually under the influence of passion. Thus, the exclusion of passion prevents anyone either claiming satisfaction for imaginary, unreal harm or excessively estimating real harm. This is an invaluable advantage.

1949. Both the advantage and the disadvantage demonstrate that, although civil tribunals are very useful, they are not sufficient for accomplishing justice. They cannot, and therefore must not, render natural judgments (extra-societal) totally useless. To withhold private justice entirely from human beings would be to authorise injustice, and no civil legislation has ever pushed matters that far [*App.*, no. 14]. Any government claiming to carry the responsibility of civil legislation as far as this would be invading the territory of private life and assailing the family, the individual, everything; in a word, it would have attained extreme despotism.

1950. But even the majority of the defects noticeable when positive law determines judiciary proofs and their procedure are unnecessary. These defects can easily be removed by continual improvement in legislation. Indeed, the authority of a government of civil society is never sufficient to permit it to require for its courts proofs which offer no proof, or to omit those which do offer proof, or to accept an inept in place of an effective procedure. In such matters a government is always obliged to enlighten itself, and permit free discussion without rejecting any enlightenment coming to it from any source whatsoever.

Article 8.
The evaluation of harm

1951. We have discussed *how* harm must be proved, but it is no less important *to know* what must be proved.

[1948–1951]

In order to verify injurious harm, we need to prove three things:

1. the existence of a right in the person claiming to be harmed;

2. the fact by which the object of his right has been taken from him or harmed;[563]

3. that this fact is culpable, or rather it must not be proved that the harm happened by mere inculpable accident (on the supposition that human beings are generally considered to act reasonably).

1952. To prove the existence of right we must prove its constitutive elements, and this must be done for every right. Because a single action can offend many rights, each right must be proved; if the right is doubtful, injury to the right in question is also doubtful.

1953. The nature of certain rights (for example, the right of personship) is such that their mere enunciation is sufficient to prove them, as they pertain equally and inalienably to all human beings.

1954. Certain other rights are intimately connected with each other. For example, the right to the use of something is connected with the right of ownership, and the right to the pleasure obtained from the use of the thing is connected with the right to its use.

1955. Nevertheless, although a right may not always be proved, the rights naturally connected with, and rooted in it, are proved. Furthermore, certain results of a right escape our observation, affectivity and evaluation. In this case they are not yet rights posited in act.

It is very important to bear all this in mind because we find here the reason why certain actions, as we have already said, were at one time considered just and carried out peacefully but now are considered unjust. In earlier times, people had not taken possession of certain things with their understanding (intellectual bond) but have taken possession in modern times. A very clear example is found in slavery. In times of poor human

---

[563] This fact must be a *jural fault* because 'no one does harm unless he does what he has no right to do'. A jural fault can consist equally in a positive fact as in the non-execution of obligations.

development, many slaves did not want to come out of slavery when their masters offered them freedom. Among the Hebrews, a law and punishment did not suffice to make them all accept freedom.[564] By the very fact of preferring slavery to freedom such people certainly showed that they had not yet taken jural possession of their activity. Consequently slavery did not arouse any jural resentment in them. Today, on the contrary, civilised people resent even the slightest bond or restriction.

1956. Physical pain helps us to appreciate this better. Because it does not always activate our intelligence and will, physical pain does not always have the same value for everybody. It is of less importance to uneducated people, not because they feel less but because the pain they feel is judged less by their intelligence. The history of humanity demonstrates this. At various times and at different levels of active intelligence, physical pain was very differently evaluated by humanity; in certain periods we find people much more patient towards wrongful treatment and physical vexations than at other times.

1957. Finally, in order to evaluate the price, so to speak, of a right, we must note the following rules which derive from what we have said.

1. The increase in value given to things of sentimental importance is not calculated if the attachment is depraved, that is, if it depends on a vice or on a personal weakness, but the increase is calculated if the attachment depends on a virtuous or naturally human sentiment. We have no right to depraved pleasures; we have a right to natural and virtuous pleasures.

1958. In any discussion on injuries and harm, therefore, we must not calculate all those infinitely variable circumstances which are caused by disordinate attachments of the human heart. If the offended person should feel greater pain because of such attachments, his rights are not thereby increased; he must impute the increased pain to himself.[565]

---

[564] Ex 21.

[565] This is Gioia's principal error in *Dell'ingiuria, dei danni, del soddisfacimento, e relative basi di stima avanti i tribunali civili*. His so-called 'bases of evaluation' are very often mutually contradictory and without solidity

1959. On the other hand, we must calculate natural attachments, like those of father, son, spouse, etc. We must evaluate these relative to a just average of their actuation in a particular society according to the judgment of wise people.

1960. Virtuous attachments, at least those which are simultaneously natural and virtuous, and are in the highest degree legitimate and proper to the person who possesses them, ought generally to be calculated in the same way, as we said. Supernatural, perfect virtue however cannot be compensated on earth because it truly contains within itself all pleasure and restitution.

1961. 2. When harm involves a good which has a monetary equivalent and can therefore be restored by compensation, it is enough to estimate:

a) the value of the thing (in addition to the just attachment to it); and

b) the benefit deriving from this value during the time the possessor was deprived unjustly of the thing. In addition to this value, we need not determine the use of the thing, the pleasure derived from it, etc., because these are already contained in its *current value*.

1962. Hence we must observe in general that harmful consequences can no longer be evaluated separately if their value is also included in what is given as compensation for the harm. When however this value is not included, it must be satisfied separately, no matter how remote and indirect the harm may be.[566]

because taken from the accidents of human nature, not from its constant, universal laws. They are also based on the resentment revealed in human beings as a result of disordinate attachments and vices. This resentment can never indicate the true amount of harm, which is determined solely by what I have called JURAL, MORAL RESENTMENT.

[566] Civil laws sometimes limit restitution solely to immediate, direct harm. For example, the Albertine code prescribes: 'In cases where non-fulfilment of an agreement arises from the dishonesty of the debtor, the harm and interest relative to the lost suffered by the creditor, and the profit he was deprived of, must be extended only to the immediate, direct consequences of the non-fulfilment of the agreement' (art. 1242). It is difficult, in the light of rational, natural Right alone, to justify this limitation placed on restitution by positive law, at least in the case of real *harm*. Relative to *interest*, there is no *absolute* question of harm because interest produces interest only in those

We must therefore have recourse to the difficult and insufficiently known theory of the value or worth of things in order to make at least an approximately just evaluation of the harm that sometimes occurs in a very long series.

Article 9.
The different ways of satisfaction

1963. Not all harm can be satisfied in the same way. If it consists in stealing another's property without harm or destruction to the property, the harm is satisfied by returning the identical thing to its owner. This is the first way: *returning the thing*.

1964. But if something profitable was stolen, a cow, for example, then clearly the value of the calves which the cow would have borne, of the milk given and the manure during the time the owner was deprived of the beast, must be paid to him in addition to the value of the cow. The only payment excluded would be for the maintenance of the animal sustained by the thief during the time of its forced detention. This is the second way: *returning the thing together with compensation for its products*.

1965. If what was stolen, besides producing *benefits*, was also *useful*, and the owner, all things being considered, had suffered further harm because of the loss of its use, this harm caused by the non-use of the thing must be evaluated and restored. Let us suppose that the cow belonged to a poor farmer who had no means of acquiring another. He would not be able to work or

conditions of society in which the flow of money is rapid. It seems to me that Gioia was mistaken in condemning absolutely this limitation imposed by civil codes (*Dell'ingiuria*, etc., pt. 1, bk 3, sect. 3, c. 3). Moreover, rational right requires restitution of all certain, necessary harm (that is, arising necessarily from the evil action as from its cause), even though it is mediate, indirect, and remote from the evil action. This applies in so far as the harm could and should have been foreseen by the offender. It is perhaps this last clause that common sense and the sense of legislators see as a great limitation placed on restitution.

[1963–1965]

manure his field, with a consequent notable loss of produce and inevitable privation to his family. This serious, painful harm must be compensated by the thief — the farmer clearly has reason on his side. This is the third way: *return of the thing together with compensation for the harm arising from the loss of its use*, calculated according to the length of time of non-use, and within this time, the need and the opportunities for using it.

1966. If the thing has perished and cannot be returned as it was but its value can be established, indemnity is effected by *compensation*, that is, the equivalent is given in place of the thing — the fourth way.

1967. Sometimes however the harm does not consist in determined things but is multiple and general, maliciously caused by another. In this case the author of the harm compensates by removing the cause (of calumny, let us say) and, if that is not enough, makes up for the harm done by some further compensation. Some call this way of compensating the harm (by removing the cause) *restitution*, the fifth way.

1968. Finally, if spiritual things are involved, that is, dishonour or pain, without the removal of any material goods, the harm is restored by lending the victim something useful and enjoyable which in his opinion makes up for the harm, hurt and ignominy suffered. This way is called *satisfaction*, the sixth way.

1969. It is clear that returning the thing in its identical condition is the way prescribed by natural law; all other ways are simply a substitution for the non-restitution of the thing.

1970. It is also clear that the three kinds of satisfaction, *attestative*, *honorific*, and *pecuniary*, can and must be rendered, separately or together, according to the nature of the harm done. And if several are contemporaneously necessary for full reparation, it is an error to claim to be bound by only one of them, and nonsensical to ask which is the best of the three.

[1966–1970]

Article 10.
The different ways of doing harm

1971. Before we can apply the relevant just satisfaction to each way of doing harm, we need to classify all possible harm. As far as I know, this has not yet been fully done.

1972. One of the difficulties in compiling an accurate classification would be the effort to list specifically all important consequential harm. All harm is prolific and produces further harm. We must therefore start with the origin of harm, that is, its source, and follow it to its completion; we must faithfully record its development and ramifications. It is true that theoffender is not always responsible for all this series of impairments because, as we said, he neither could nor need foresee all of them. Nor does satisfaction have to be equivalent to the harmful consequences of the first harm, because what is given as satisfaction for harm produces its own consequences and ramifications of good, each of which should be counted in favour of the offender who satisfies the harm he has caused. Nevertheless, the following two questions are very different and must be considered individually:

1. What is the total harm from a natural series of impairments?

2. What is the total good from a natural series of benefits given in satisfaction?

If justice is to be satisfied, these two totals must be exactly equal.

1973. If I were asked how to classify all the harm done from its origin and thoughout its ramifications, I would say this is impossible without reducing the harm always and ultimately to the loss of some good (or to the imposition of the contrary evil, which for brevity's sake is understood), and without making the classification of harm match the exact classification of good. But all good is reduced to pleasure, if we take this word in its widest sense of 'good feeling'. Therefore the classification of good should be reduced to listing 1. *pleasures* and 2. the *means* which directly or indirectly produce these pleasures.

The means, it must be noted, are either different from us or are in us. Moreover, *occasions* for activating them are themselves means, the possession of which together with pleasures, leaves in us *good effects* (if, as we suppose, the pleasures are good), that is, they leave us more perfect and ennobled. Thus these effects are also classified among what is good. Finally, because the awareness of our own perfection, nobility and happiness is itself a good which completes our fulfilment, we must also take into account the *signs* of our *perfection* and *nobility*, consciousness of which is produced in us by the signs. These signs also produce a favourable opinion (our *honour*, our good name) about us in others. This is the division we could usefully make of various kinds of good as objects of a right, and therefore of impairments. It could be expressed by the schema shown overleaf.

[1973]

Notes for the Schema

(1) Person is the universal *subject* of all rights; we reserve the word 'subject' for it alone. But person can be considered in itself or in these faculties which depend on it. Because the faculties *depend* on it they are called *personal*; each of them is a *subject* of right. But here I consider person only in itself, not as governing and moving the lower faculties. Four personal *activities* can be distinguished in person considered in itself. Each of these also constitutes a *subject* of rights directly involving person. They are: 1. jural freedom; 2. the intellective faculty; 3. the moral faculty; 4. the eudaimonological faculty.

(2) *Jural freedom* in itself has no determined object; it is, as it were, its own object (cf. 588-591).

(3) Cf. *SP*, bk. 4, c. 6, where these effects are discussed.

(4) We might ask whether injury and harm is experienced when the esteem and good name we *falsely* enjoy is diminished. False esteem and false credit certainly has its value but it is not ours. Nevertheless, when *false* esteem is founded on a universal prejudice (for example, the esteem generally paid to tall people, etc.) the prejudice may be lawfully removed from people's minds. But while the prejudice lasts, the esteem we are given individually may not be lawfully denied us, if we truly have the quality on which it is based.

SCHEMA
OF THE VARIOUS KINDS OF GOOD CONSIDERED AS OBJECTS OF RIGHTS

FACULTIES, SUBJECTS OF RIGHTS		VARIOUS KINDS OF GOOD, OBJECTS OF RIGHT
PERSON,[1] essential, subsistent Right, has four faculties, subjects of rights:	1. Jural freedom	[2]
	2. Intellective faculty	truth
	3. Moral faculty	virtue
	4. Eudaimono-logical faculty	happiness
The subjects of rights whose object is the classified kinds of good are the faculties corresponding to each good and contained in Class 2 of the means, in so far as the subjects depend on the supreme-faculty, PERSON	Class 1	Means of enjoyment different from ourselves - ANY EXTERNAL GOOD A) removable by force (material things) B) removable only by seduction (persons, affections)
	Class 2	Means of enjoyment within us, FACULTIES A) natural activity: life, body, potencies, work in another's employ or other kind of work B) abilities, knowledge, good qualities
	Class 3	Means consisting in the certain or probable, proximate or remote OCCASIONS of our right TO USE A) means different from us (Class 1), or B) means within us (Class 2)
	Class 4	Means consisting in the certain or probable, proximate or remote OCCASIONS of our right TO ACQUIRE the means in classes 1, 2 and 3
	Class 5	Habitual and actual PLEASURES arising from A) the use of the means in Classes 1-4 B) the possession itself of these pleasures
	Class 6	Good EFFECTS left IN US[3] from A) the use of the means (Classes 1-4) B) the enjoyment of pleasures (Class 5)
	Class 7	SIGNS OF OUR OWN PERFECTION (favourable public opinion, glory, etc.) which produce A) a pleasant, confident feeling[4] B) our good name

1974. Granted an injurious, harmful action, therefore, we must calculate, relative to all the eight given classes of good, the amount of harm or loss *necessarily* caused by the action through the fault of its author. We also need to calculate the quantity and quality of evil that has resulted.

1975. We must note in fact how the medieval world — a time when society felt the direct influence of Christianity more strongly, despite a lack of culture in art and literature — included *spiritual* consequences in its calculation of harm. The modern world however limits itself strictly to immediate, *material* harm. This is certainly true when we compare today's legislation with medieval laws.

1976. Is it perhaps the fleeting effect of materialism and impiety that has so much influenced the world in the past three hundred years? Will laws acquire a more spiritual character when these accidental causes cease and liberated Christianity is able to exercise once more its natural, spiritual influence over civilised nations?[567]

Article 11.
The natural procedure for exacting
restitution of harm suffered

1977. Finally, something must be said about the *procedure* to be followed by the victim in the state of nature if he is to obtain the indemnity due to him.

Rational right prescribes the following rules:

1. If restitution is impossible, it cannot be claimed.

---

[567] 'The basis used by modern codes for determining satisfaction is solely the successive feelable changes in things. Barbarian codes however joined invisible changes in the spirit to visible changes of things. Thus, while the former codes are content if the value to be restored equals the value destroyed, the latter desire much more.

'To be convinced that our times are deficient compared with antiquity, let us take the total displeasure caused us by the destruction of something through harm, etc.' (Gioia, *Dell'ingiuria, dei danni*, etc., pt. 1, bk. 3, sect. 3, c. 2, §2).

[1974–1977]

1978. In murder, the victim cannot be restored to life. Restitution for murder therefore can only be made relative to its consequences. The living relatives and friends must be compensated for all the resulting harm.

1979. This explains why nearly all laws, particularly the Mosaic law, punish the killing of an adult with greater severity than that of a baby.[568]

1980. 2. Restitution for *harm culpably* inflicted must be distinguished from restitution for a *debt innocently incurred*.

Humanity requires a more lenient settlement for an innocent debtor than for a guilty debtor. If a guilty debtor persisted in his fault and in the evil disposition which caused the harm, he would make himself unworthy of the limitation which humanity applies to the force used against him by the creditor for the purpose of extracting due restitution, and which we have restricted to double the value of the harm. In this case, the restitution of culpable harm must, if possible, be made, no matter how harmful to the persistent offender. On the other hand, the creditor can never exact his money from the person to whom he lent or gave it as a deposit if this causes excessive harm to the debtor. If the person holding the money on deposit or on loan could not restore it without endangering his life or suffering very serious hardship, he would not, according to rational, human Right, be held to restitution.

1981. Hence some civil laws, in harmony with the law of reason, forbid the creditor to deny the debtor the means of subsistence, because, as the Mosaic law says, it would mean taking his life.[569]

---

[568] In Exodus 21 it is laid down that the death of a foetus resulting from blows to the pregnant mother is punished simply by compensating the father in accordance with the determination of the judges and the claim of the father (note here how *moral restitution* is taken into account). The child is granted no right of its own, but is considered as something belonging to the father. However, if the mother dies from the blows, the perpetrator is punished with death.

[569] Deut 24. — In the Middle Ages, when States began to write constitutions, one of the first rights to be recognised in agricultural workers was that of not depriving them of the tools with which they gained their living. In the English *Magna Carta*, which King John signed on 19th June 1215 in the field of Runnymede, many rights and privileges were granted and guaranteed to

1982. This then is the moderation with which alone we can use our rights if, by using them, we do not wish to harm others. If our ownership is strictly bound with others' ownership, we must prefer to forego ours rather than offend theirs. When duty and right conflict, the *observance of duty* must be preferred to the *exercise of right*.

1983. For the same reason the innocent author of harm is not bound to restitution except *in quantum factus est ditior* [in so far as he has profited from the harm], as in the case of a possessor in good faith.

1984. On the other hand, when harm has been unjustly inflicted, the offender can only blame himself if in making restitution he experiences grave distress and loss. Charity and human kindness can limit the distress but strict justice clearly prescribes unconditional restitution (provided restitution is possible) at whatever cost to the person responsible.

1985. Consequently two quantities are involved in the fulfilment of restitution:

    i) the amount of restitution required of the offender;

    ii) the amount of harm he himself suffers, which can also depend on the way he makes restitution.

1986. The first quantity equals the exact amount of harm done. Any errors in this amount will result from the wrongful evaluation of the harm I have already discussed. In the case of the second quantity, this must be the least possible.

1987. Provided the offended party is compensated without loss, he must not readily deprive the offender of reasonable comfort.

1988. Civil society, which accepts responsibility for determining the best way to make restitution, must not refuse any suggestion enabling it to determine more easily the best way of all, so that the least harm is done to the offender. If it rejects such a suggestion, it is guilty of injustice[570] as the willing cause of

the clergy, the barons, the lower nobility, to cities and the people, but only a single article was included in favour of the peasants. It said that 'they could not be deprived, by any penalty, of their ploughs, wagons and other agricultural implements.' We see how important this right, or at least the need to protect it, was considered.

570 Schmalz says that only a *jural*, not simply an *ethical duty* can be imposed

unnecessary harm. However such harm, when unavoidable, is excusable.

1989. 3. The offended party, who has the right to be compensated for the harm suffered, must not exact his retribution angrily or with the fury and blindness that result from anger. This is a consequence of the principle: 'Everyone must use his rights in the least burdensome way possible towards his fellows.'

1990. If mere instincts could constitute a right, the right to anger would certainly be possible. Such a right would in fact be the natural right, common to animals, which the authors of Justinian's *Institutes* mistakenly imagined. *Natural* right co-exists with *rational* right. Hence we said that 'the offended party must be satisfied when fully compensated in such a way that the offender suffers least harm in making restitution.'

Consequently, if 'the offender is ready to make full and just restitution, the offended party, who no longer has a right to use any force, nor to compensate himself by his own effort, must happily accept the restitution offered.'

1991. Such moderation in the exercise of the right of restitution was always known even to the Gentiles. When the Spartans were dissatisfied with the fair restitution offered them by the Thebans, Aristides rightly said that the just cause had passed from the Spartans, who were in the right, to the Thebans, who at first were in the wrong.[571]

on a people: 'The former can only be observed and violated externally; the latter consists solely in a disposition of the spirit. The former submits external actions to rules conforming to the dignity of right; the latter tends to give the spirit a power, that is, an internal sanction. A spirit of internal feelings, as attributed to an individual, cannot be attributed to a people; a people is a moral person whose existence rests solely on external actions.' This is clearly a paralogism. Certainly, a people considered abstractly exists only in external signs, but their government exists, as also does the person who acts on their behalf and represents them. These are the real persons who must exercise ethical duties conceived as joined to the collective person called 'nation' or 'people'. Schmalz himself, perhaps because he senses the difficulty of his observation, adds: 'Is there no moral duty incumbent on a people?' and replies that the body politic, which is helped by the duty, must perform it. But the body politic, if capable of performing the duty as something helpful, can surely perform it as something upright? (Cf. *Le Droit des gens européens*, bk. 1, c. 1).

[571] History shows many examples of princes who, under the pretext of

1992. This argument supplies an easy answer to the difficulty about self-defence on the part of an offending party against an offended party who uses force to claim restitution. If the offended party intends to use force, despite an offer of full, just compensation, the offending party can defend himself on the grounds that he also has been harmed and offended. Indeed, if the offended party obstinately continues his unnecessary recourse to violence, his action becomes subject to the suspicion that he is dissatisfied with the restitution due to him. Rather, he seems to claim more than the offender owes him.

1993. 4. Even when we are obliged to use force to exact due restitution, the same principles indicate that this must be done with the least harm to the offender; we must not claim from him more than the true value of the harm we have suffered through his fault.

1994. 5. Finally, if the harm is not certain, we cannot demand reparation. However, if the harm but not its amount were certain, the least certain harm must be accepted or an amicable settlement reached.

demanding restitution or satisfaction for harm and offences sustained by them, gave free rein to their ambition or to some other ignoble passion. Although Pontius the Samnite returned the booty taken from the Romans and handed over the author of the war, the Romans were not satisfied. According to Titus Livy, the Samnite said: 'The divine anger against us, caused by the broken treaty, has been expiated. I know well enough that the gods who wished to force us to surrender the booty did not intend that the Romans should so proudly spurn our expiation of the treaty.' We see from these words how the divinity was always considered as the supreme vindicator of justice, almost as subsistent justice itself. It was also thought that the war which the Romans wanted to fight, when just satisfaction had already been offered and given them, could not appear just to divine eyes. Among the best known cases of this kind of injustice is that related by Zonara of the emperor Argiropoulos against prince Calepius who offered peace and payment of the remaining tribute. Another, against the Crusade, is found in Cromero, bk. 17; another is Charles of Burgundy against the Swiss, who offered full compensation for a stolen wagonload of pelts (Comines, bk. 7).

[1992–1994]

CHAPTER 6

The origin of the right to predominance

1995. A consequence of the infraction of others' rights is subordination and jural predominance. Human beings are naturally equal but can, through their evil activity, subject themselves to others and give others the right to exercise a certain predominance over them.

1996. This truth is clear to anyone who considers the origin of human dignity. Human beings are ordered to truth and virtue; it is this relationship which constitutes their dignity. Truth and virtue are sublime objects to which they can aspire and which they can also renounce. If they renounce them, they renounce their dignity, and thus degrade themselves;[572] any respect which remains due to them on earth lies solely in the possibility they have of reforming and redirecting themselves to their sublime destination.

1997. We can see therefore that if someone, in offending truth and virtue, also offends his fellows, they acquire the right to *punish* him in their own defence and in retribution for the harm done. As we have seen, by punishing the offender, they cause pain and loss only in the name of, and as ministers of punitive justice. But anyone who punishes is in a predominant position relative to the person punished.

1998. When therefore we put into act not only the right to defence together with its four functions of *simple defence*, *prevention, exemplary repression* and *guarantee,* but also the right to restitution together with its functions of *revendication* and *compensation* (and the others we have listed), we attribute to ourselves a real predominance over anyone who has acted unjustly and harmfully. Our right endures as long as the title endures through which these rights are exercised. And the title

---

[572] St. Thomas Aquinas expresses this principle excellently: 'Through sin, human beings forsook the order of reason and lost their human dignity by which they are naturally free and EXIST FOR THEIR OWN SAKE. They fell in some way to the level of animal servitude and turned aside from themselves in so far as they became useful to others' (*S.T.,* II-II, q. 64, art. 2, ad 3).

[1995–1998]

can endure a long time, especially when it is a question of guarantee against the guilty.

1999. This is the only source of true SUBORDINATION and PREDOMINANCE among human beings.

Appendix

1. (544).

[Rosmini's philosophical and theological work had met with strong, but anonymous opposition. In particular, an author calling himself 'Eusebio Cristiano' had attacked Rosmini's ideas on original sin and on conscience. Rosmini's reply to this attack was in turn opposed by Fr. Dmowski S.J. Further exchanges led to this note to 544 which we reprint here as the first number of the Appendix]

The truth [that babies are moral beings] can be verified by philosophical observation and is confirmed by Christian theology. But our anonymous 'Eusebio Cristiano' protested strongly against it, as everybody knows. My reply to him is also known to everyone. Nevertheless Fr. Dmowski of the Society of Jesus has reiterated the opinion of the anonymous Eusebio in his so-called *Analisi* of my *Risposta* to the footnotes he inserted in his *Istituzioni filosofiche*, and I would like to use this opportunity to comment on this work (printed at Lucca in 1841).

First, he roundly expresses his surprise that I should be offended at his disagreement with me. But this is not true. What I said is in print and my sole complaint was that, instead of arguing philosophically, he preferred to spread doubts publicly about the soundness of my religious teaching.

Furthermore, he affirms that I have badly misunderstood what he proffers as a compliment when he says: 'I intended to be courteous to the intelligence of this author who in pursuing an idea is always trying to relate all knowledge and practice to it' (*Analisi*, p. 5) But this is not true — Father Dmowski did not compliment me on my intelligence but on what he sees as my attempt to make my system universal: *plurimum cl. autori gratulamur quod suum sistema universalissimum reddere satagat*. This in its turn is neither complimentary nor courteous nor sincere because 1. an author's attempt to make his system universal is not something to be complimented about; 2. the attempt is something Father Dmowski presumes (there was no attempt); 3. he could not be sincerely satisfied with an attempt to make universal a system of which he disapproves; 4. the words he then adds indicate that he cannot really see how the system will be widely accepted: *optaremus nihilominus illud eo usque minime promoveri, ut, etc.*; and finally, 5. according to the Father's judgment, such a system would change and exclude the common opinions of doctors of morals and would therefore be very pernicious: *optaremus nihilominus illud eo usque minime promoveri, ut communes praesertim moralium doctorum sententiae doctrinaeve nedum necessario immutandae, sed penitus quoque excludendae censeri debeant.* To say that I reduce all knowledge and practice to one single idea simply shows that Father Dmowski does not know my teaching. I teach that nothing real can be known with the idea of being alone (except for the necessary-real, God). Consequently neither knowledge nor practice can be drawn from it.

In the third place, Father Dmowski acknowledges the mistake he made by thinking that to the *definition* of law I applied the three conditions I had given only for the *application of the law* (*Analisi*, 19). But is this admission frank and honest, as he claims? — If so, why didn't he emend his mistake in the next edition of his *Istitutiones Philosophicae* (Turin, 1841) instead of reproducing and confirming it by adding to it? Surely it was his duty, after imputing error to me and admitting his mistake, not to communicate this error to the public? He did indeed apologise for his mistake (p. 19), trying to show that he had good reasons for making it. But even if this were true, he was still obliged to delete from later editions what, according to his own admission, was falsely imputed to me in the first edition against my express words.

Moreover, the very reasons with which he justifies attributing to me the opposite of what I expressly wrote are non-existent. Let us examine them:

1. He says: 'Defining law as a *notion used for making a judgment etc.*, (Rosmini) leads us to understand that, according to him, this notion, in order to be law, must be actually in the subject, that is, *received into the mind of the one making the judgment.*' — Not true; the notion, considered in itself, has the

aptitude to act as a norm for judging what is lawful and unlawful either in the mind of the Legislator or in any other mind whatsoever, and this aptitude is essential to the notion for it to be law. But any *particular subject* cannot really make use of the notion and apply it to judge actions if this subject has not received it into his mind. The condition applies to the *use* and *application* of the law, not to the law itself. Fr. Dmowski has confused the notion's *aptitude* for acting as a rule with the real use the obligated subject makes of it. He has confused potency with act.

2. 'Furthermore, I see the following words clearly and expressly stated in the second edition: "We can therefore say that the notion is promulgated in the subject and, properly speaking, begins to have the nature and force of law." From this he (Rosmini) argues that what *properly speaking* constitutes *the nature and force of law* necessarily pertains to the essential concept of law and therefore to the general definition which must express it' (pp. 19, 20). — This deduction extends further than my premises. I was speaking about the promulgation of the law in a *particular subject*, and said that once promulgated in a particular subject, it begins to have the nature and force of law. Because he has omitted the *particular subject* of which I was speaking, he concludes that, according to me, law can have the nature and force of law only when the second condition of promulgation in a particular subject is verified! With due respect, a law which is not promulgated in a particular subject has in no way the nature and force of law in that subject, although it certainly has the nature and force of law in itself, either in the mind of the legislator or of all those who know it but have not submitted to it. He wrongly claims therefore that, according to me, the second condition pertains to the definition itself of law.

Finally, Fr. Dmowski declares that it is *far from his intention* to spread doubt about the soundness of my religious teachings (*Analisi*, 4). Is this true? — The reader can judge from the footnotes and *Analisi*. I am content simply to quote a piece of his *Analisi* which clearly shows he agrees with the anonymous authors of the booklets published against me. He writes: 'To start by defining conscience totally differently from ancient and modern authors; to claim that all have erred concerning the very first element of moral science; to widen the sphere of *true morality* in such a way that there is true *morality* in willed but not *free* actions; to establish morality without conscience; to remove from moral science *duties towards oneself*, and reduce them to duties towards human nature in general — these teachings and many others of the same kind, if we examine them closely, tend to exclude the most accepted and solid ideas of teachers of morality. Rosmini's notions are indeed expressed in an entirely new moral language, but under cover of the words they significantly change basic concepts' (*Analisi*, 6). Are these assertions of Father Dmowski true or false? — I have given proofs of everything that I have said, proofs taken from the Fathers, from doctors and moralists, and I have shown how my teaching is the same as theirs. I have reconciled many different opinions by going to their roots and finding agreement with the majority of the greatest masters, precisely by reconciling their sometimes apparently different opinions. Are a few gratuitous words Fr. Dmowski enough to destroy an author's long, arduous studies?

And where did Fr. Dmowski find that I had ever claimed that all the ancient and recent doctors had made a great mistake in defining conscience? I would ask him to quote a single place in my works where according to him I have spoken with such little respect for the Doctors. On the contrary, I offered my definition of conscience as a more precise interpretation or expression of what *everybody*, even the uneducated, understand by conscience.

The fact that *morality* is sometimes present where there is no freedom or conscience is not something new but a DOGMA of the Catholic Church, which acknowledges a morally reprobate state, a state of sin, in a new-born baby, and a morally good state, a state of justice, grace and holiness in a baby reborn through baptism.

Finally, where did he find that I have done away with duties towards oneself? I certainly said that in my works on ethics I happily chose the more logical division of the Gospel instead of that of the philosophers, because JESUS CHRIST taught that there are two precepts of charity. I divided all duties into two classes, those towards God and those towards human beings, and I divided the latter into those towards oneself and those towards others. In doing this, I am surely not rejecting duties to self; I am surely not using 'an entirely new moral language', which 'under cover of words significantly changes basic concepts'?

I am only asking for the truth, therefore. Fr. Dmowski is free to think what he likes provided he speaks the truth.

2. (680).

Aristotle says that 'by nature some people are obviously free and others are bond-servants' (*Polit.*, 1, 3, 5). This celebrated passage shows that the truth I am expounding is accepted not only by Aristotle but by the common sense of the human race, which the philosopher, by saying 'it is obvious', claims to follow. Many modern thinkers have argued vigorously against this opinion of Aristotle because they have only partly understood it. He does not say, we must note, that 'some people are born bond-servants', as if he meant that the children of those made bond-servants by the civil law were justly made bond-servants. He says some 'are bond-servants by nature', that is, necessarily and justly subject to others, because relative to others their intellectual faculties are imperfect. This interpretation is so true that, after saying some people are bond-servants by nature, he adds that they are justly bond-servants because their servitude is useful to them. He is obviously speaking about a natural, limited subjection that by its nature does not harm but helps them.

Baroli defends Aristotle against the moderns who accuse Aristotle of favouring slavery in the ancient world (*Diritto Naturale*, §89), and cites another passage that removes all doubt by revealing Aristotle's true teaching on legal servitude. *By law*, the philosopher says, 'one person is certainly a bond-servant, another either free or a master, but the two are not different *by nature*. The difference (effected by positive law) therefore is unjust because it is does violence or involves harm' (*Polit.*, 1, 3). Aristotle's reason for rejecting the old legal slavery coincides with our principle of *jural resentment*. He places the harm in *violence*, that is, in acting against another's will and therefore with resentment on the part of the one suffering the action.

Finally, the place where he says 'all servitude is against nature' (*Polit.*, 1, 4) must be understood as against human nature, which is intelligent and therefore capable of understanding the consequences of actions and enjoying the freedom of action which flows from intelligence.

Furthermore, the natural superiority we are discussing is revealed not only in the feeling of individuals but in the feeling of peoples relative to other peoples. We can easily be convinced of this by reflecting on those places of Aristotle where he speaks about the natural superiority of Greece over the other nations. He is certainly not stating his own thought on the matter but the consciousness of all the Greeks expressed when Euripides makes Iphigenia say to Clytemnestra, 'The Greeks, Mother, must indeed command the barbarians, not the barbarians the Greeks. The barbarians are naturally bond-servants, the Greeks free' (*Iphigenia at Aulis*, act. 4).

A civilised people always feels like this towards a primitive people. Unfortunately human perversity and pride abuse the feeling. My intention however is to find (if possible) some traces of upright human nature under the devastation caused by passions.

3. (745).

We need to bear in mind that the purpose of civil laws was to sanction only a part, never the whole of rational Right. And this part did not, properly speaking, concern individuals but *families* and their preservation and development. This enables us to understand in their true spirit the many laws of different peoples which seem absurd and barbaric simply because we claim to find in them what the legislators did not intend, that is, the whole of rational Right rather than just that part of it which they intended for the purpose of their legislation. As I have said, legislators did not concern themselves so much with individuals as with the good of families or, more generally, with the human family. Consequently they valued individual rights not for what they are in themselves but for what they are relative to the good of entire generations. Clear proof of this will be given, I think, by an example taken from the laws with which some ancient peoples defended human life and animal life — the ox, for example, which was useful for family prosperity.

It would be a great injustice to think that the first legislators did not know that human life in itself was more valuable than the life of an ox; nevertheless, in their laws they sometimes showed that the latter had equal, if not more value than the former. They formed their laws, I repeat, to defend not the absolute value of rights but the relative value of the good of entire families, together with other social and humanitarian purposes. Varro writes as follows about the protection given by ancient laws to the ox, or rather to human society which was greatly helped by the ox: 'This (ox) is the friend of human beings, working in the fields and at the crops. Ancient people had such a desire to free themselves from this kind of work that anyone who killed an ox was punished by death. Attica and Pelopenesus testify to this' (*De re rustica*, 2, 5). Columella also says: 'Ancient peoples venerated the ox so much that capital punishment applied equally for killing an ox as for killing a citizen' (Bk. 6, *in proem.*). Hence the ox was respected as something sacred because of its great usefulness. Pausanias relates that on one occasion when the Athenians were sacrificing an ox to Jupiter, the priest had to flee to avoid being killed (*In Attic.*). Herodotus also narrates many things done by the Egyptians to honour a dead ox (*In Euterp.*). Cf. also Arist. *Polit.*, 1, 1; Plin., 8, 45; Val. Max., 8, 1; Aelian., *Historiae animalium*, 12, 34; Stobeus, *Serm.*, 42; Porphyr., *De non edendis animalibus*; Plut., *De esu animalium*. All these places indicate that laws, religion and philosophy concerned the utility of human *society* rather than simple right, that is, simple *individual justice*.

4. (fn. 222).

The word 'nature', taken as the opposite of 'reason', has a long history, and bears much the same meaning as that given by its etymology. In Latin, *natura* [nature] has the same root as *nascor* [I come to birth], while φύσις springs quite obviously from the verb φύο, 'I plant, produce, generate' and so on.

Reason, however, is not something that comes to birth or decays. Hence the famous distinction of Plato: all things are divided into those which generate and decay (γιγομενα), and those which, neither generating nor decaying, are eternal. Such a way of considering what is inherent to the use of words in very ancient languages shows how familiar to the human mind are the truths I have proclaimed about the nature of being. It shows that the system of philosophy which I have proposed has *per se* the consent of the human race; languages, our oldest and most trustworthy monuments, mirror this consent. I have shown that reason possesses an eternal element which is not the human being, although it is manifested in the human being; it is in no way subjective, although it is intimately united with the subject; finally, it is not a created, finite *nature* (*quod nascitur* [that which comes to birth]), but something superior to nature. The opposition between *nature* and *reason*, which is found in very ancient languages, is therefore the same opposition that I have endeavoured to establish between *subject* and *object*, that is, between created *human beings* and that *ideal being* which enlightens them, both without confusing itself with them, or coming to birth or perishing with them. It is the same opposition as that which we find between the intelligent *soul* and the *light* that renders the soul intelligent, and in the conjunction between the finite and the infinite, the human and the divine.

But we should also consider the other meanings of the word 'nature'. Here I shall quote from Aquinas, whose wonderful gifts included that of ascertaining the meaning of words with great acuteness and precision, a necessary condition for all good logic. He shows how other meanings of 'nature' derive from the most ancient use of the word. According to him, the following are the four meanings which the word 'nature' successively acquired: 'First, it was employed to signify the *generation* of living things, that is, their birth. Then it came to mean the *intrinsic principle* of all movement, metaphorically speaking — generation, as we know, springs from an intrinsic principle. It was then extended to mean both the *form* and the *matter* of things because the intrinsic principle is the cause of both. Then it was applied to the *essence* of things because essence receives its completion from form' (*S.T.*, I, q. 29, art. 1). — Now, when the Stoics said, 'It is the nature of the human being to be rational' and deduced a natural Right according to reason, and when Cicero, following their footsteps, wrote: 'Taking what is another's, and augmenting one's own well-being at another's expense, is more against NATURE than death, poverty, sorrow or anything else that can happen to the body or to external things' (*De Off.*, 3, 5), they used the word 'nature' in place of 'essence', that is, the essence of human beings. Cicero propounded his beautiful opinion — which contains the true principle of the Right of nature — because being rational, and consequently moral, is essential for human beings. And it is entirely in keeping with this essence that one should not harm others, even to help oneself.

5. (917).

According to Cicero, 'doing harm to another in order to help oneself is more contrary to human nature than death itself'. He proves this by showing that the opposite would destroy society, which of all things is the most in harmony with nature. His own words should be quoted here: 'First (such a maxim) destroys communal living and human society' (*tollit convictum hominum et societatem*: this is his distinction between *gregarious* living which, according to us, is present also in the state of nature, and *society*, which is more than 'gregarious living'). 'The society of mankind, which is more in harmony with nature than anything else, would be destroyed if we were formed in such a way that each individual could despoil and violate another for his own advantage' (*humani generis societatem*: he is not speaking of *domestic* or *civil* society, nor of any special form of society, but of universal society). 'For instance, if each member of the human body felt that it would be healthier by taking for itself the health of a neighbouring member, it would in fact be weakening and destroying the whole body. In the same way, if each of us took for himself the benefits and advantages of others, society and human community would be ruined.

'There is no opposition to nature if each one wants to acquire for himself, rather than for others, what assists his life; what is repugnant to nature is that we should increase our own faculties, ease and well-being at the expense of others. Not only nature, that is, the Right of the peoples, but the laws governing peoples and the State together, have established that it is not lawful to seek one's own advantage by damaging that of others' (here we find the *Right of nature* opposed to the *laws of civil society*; the latter lie therefore outside the former, although society in general proclaims itself as existing *maxime secundum naturam*). 'The aim and desire of laws is to maintain unbroken the connection between the citizens by punishing with death, exile, chains and fines those who attempt to break them. The very reason of nature (*ipsa naturae ratio*), which is the divine and human law, requires this. Those wishing to obey these laws (and all who live according to nature will obey them) never violate them by desiring and taking for themselves what belongs to others. This, and companionship, justice and freedom, are far more in harmony with dignity and greatness of spirit than greed, life and belongings. Despising these things and looking down upon them when we compare them to common utility is proper to great, noble spirits; withdrawing from others what is theirs for the sake of one's own benefit is more contrary to nature than death, pain and similar things' (*De Off.*, 3, 5).

Although Cicero shows here and in other places that society is *natural* to human beings, he acknowledges elsewhere the use we make of the word 'nature'. For instance, in speaking of exclusive ownership almost as though it were an essential element of civil society, he says that it is not constituted by nature, but by something *done* by human beings: 'Nothing is private by nature. Things are possessed either by lengthy occupation on the part of those who found them empty, or by victory in war, or by law, pact, agreement or lot.' A little later he says again that the individual who desires what is not his own 'will violate the law of human society', a phrase by which he distinguishes this social right from that of nature (*De Off.* 1, 7).

6. (958).

It may be objected that we sin by refraining from helping our neighbour when we are morally obliged to do so. But we have no right to sin. In this case, therefore, others will not be obliged by the moral law to respect our ownership. — Here the consequence is false; — the duty obliging me to beneficence comes from the eternal law and from the supreme Being before whom all my rights do indeed cease as a result of his full right to command me. The person in need does not, however, himself acquire any right. *Relative* to other human beings, my right does not decrease because of my duty to benefit others. In fact, although I have the *moral duty* to give others a part of my *ownership*, others nevertheless continue to have a moral duty not to touch but to respect my *ownership*, which remains as my relative right precisely because it is protected relative to other human beings by the moral law.

This obligation remains on others: 1. according to the nature of the moral law of benifecence whose effect is simply to *oblige* the owner to be beneficent without *disobliging* others from their duty not to harm the owner and without giving them any title of right over a substance owned by others; 2. because no one can establish the limits and determined modes of obligatory beneficence or the precise persons towards whom it must be exercised; 3. because the immorality of the person who could be beneficent, but is not, does not render ownership itself immoral. Its *title* remains lawful and just; there is nothing immoral about the title itself. This immorality, therefore, corrupts the spirit of the immoral person, not the nature of ownership; it is an accident which does not effect the substance of the right.

Take, for instance, the difference between this case and that in which a person neither draws nor wants nor is able to draw any advantage from his ownership. Here, others are not obliged to respect the so-called ownership because the *moral-physical bond* is lacking. Consequently, the pain of dispossession caused by others would not be *natural* for a reasonable being; it would originate from a capricious decision claiming to prevent others from profiting by what the owner has no desire to profit by. In the other case, on the contrary, the owner wants to profit from what he owns and is *naturally* upset at having to renounce the profit he could gain for himself. Any spontaneous renunciation of what he owns is therefore moved by the obligation of beneficence and becomes a willing sacrifice rewarded by merit.

If, however, others rob him of what is his own, the pain and disturbance he feels is natural and unjust.

Finally, see what I have said in *The Essence of Right*, 256-262, on the *lawfulness* of actions necessary to constitute Right.

7. (1290).

Was the right of *relative ownership*, which we have introduced here and shall use as we go along [1290 ss.], recognised by civil legislators? — We could bring forward innumerable examples of positive laws that could not have entered legislators' minds if they had been ignorant of the right of the relative ownership which we have shown to exist in nature. However, we shall limit ourselves to certain laws about dowries taken from Roman legislation.

Whatever the wife brought into a house, provided it did not come from her father, was called *dos adventitia* [fortuitous dowry] (*Leg. unic. § accedit Cod. De rei uxor. action.*) and formed part of the husband's succession if no other convention had been established (*L. dotis 7 § si res ff. De jur. dot.*). However, the dowry provided by the father, *dos profectitia* [the established dowry] (*L. profectitia 5 Cod. De jur. dot.*) was returned to the father if his daughter died without offspring (*L. dos a patre 4 Cod. solut. matrim. — L. jure 6 ff. De jure dot. — L. haeres 37 ff. de acquir. vel omit. haered. —* It was Martino and other jurisconsults who restricted Justinian law to the case of the wife who left no living children). It is clear that a law of this kind entails acknowledgement of some *relative ownership* in the father.

It is also true according to us that the person holding *relative ownership* cannot prevent another with *full ownership* of a thing from using it up (provided this is done within certain reasonable limits). To this extent, the action attributed to the father over the dowry of his deceased daughter by Roman laws differs from our *relative ownership*. Roman laws stated that the *established dowry* could not be alienated or used up by the spouses (Cf. Brisonio *ad legem juliam De Adulter.*, c. 20, *opp. minor.* p. 224, Louvain, 1749. — *Paulus recept. sentent.*, bk 2, tit. 21, n. 2, in

Schultingio *jurispr. et ret. ante-justinan.* t. 1, p. 309, Leipzig, 1737); our opinion, dependent upon our attempt to establish only that which seems in accord with the Right of natural reason without reference to any convention or civic view of things, states that the head of the house has the obligation simply to *indicate* what belongs to the spouse so that whatever remains (all of it, or any part) may be identified at the spouse's death. Moreover, the dowry of the deceased daughter should not be returned to the father, according to us, but should remain with the surviving husband, as we said.

In the same way, according to Roman laws, the established dowry was returned to the father at the death of the husband because it was thought that the daughter herself should return. But according to rational Right, the widow is free to return to her father's family, from which she was already divided, or to remain on her own. However, the father was forbidden to use up the daughter's dowry, which he had to restore to her if she wished to marry again (*L. dotium* 1 *ff. solut. matrim.* — Cf. Brisonio, c. 1, and Danello, *De jur. civil.*, 1, 9, c. 10, n. 23, and Hilliger's notes in the same place). This shows that the father was not considered as the *full owner* of the widowed daughter's dowry as long as she lived, but as its *defender* and tutor. Moreover, he was considered as the *owner relative to others*, but not relative to the daughter herself or to her family if she remarried. In his condition as *relative owner*, the father had the right, according to Roman right, to succeed the daughter who, in fact, was the principal and *full owner*.

We have a clear indication, therefore, in these laws about dowries, in laws about private property, and in innumerable other instances, of the obvious traces of that right of *relative and full* ownership that we have laid down in our treatise on rational Right. The Roman legislators, however, did not give this ownership a name.

8. (1298).

St. Augustine (*De C. D.*, 3, 21) condemns as completely unjust the Voconian law which excluded women from hereditary succession when a person died intestate, and allowed them no more than a quarter of the goods left in a will. Cardinal Mai, in his extremely erudite notes to Cicero's *Republic*, discovered by him (*De Rep.* 3, 10), surmises that St. Augustine's passage should read: *nisi unicam filiam* [with the exception of the only daughter] rather than *nec unicam filiam* [not even the only daughter].

This emendation has no support, however, in the Vatican codices nor in the oldest editions of the *City of God*. In fact, it seems that not even the only daughter enjoyed any privilege, and although Cicero defends Anius Asellus in the second Verrinum law for having made his only daughter his heir, the reason given in Anius' favour is his exclusion from any register (*census non erat*), (the Voconian law which applied only to those who had been civilly registered).

Dion provides more information when he tells us that females were able to inherit a maximum of 100,000 sestercii (*Cum lege Voconia mulieribus prohibetur ne quae majorem centum millibus nummum hereditatem posset adire*, bk. 6). Montesquieu's comments on the *census* referred to by the Voconian law can be read with profit (*Esprit des Lois*, bk. 27). But returning to St. Augustine, we note that his feeling in this respect coincides with French legislation. We agree with this in the case of daughters who are still at home when their father dies, but the matter would be different in the case of daughters who had ceased to form part of the paternal household and through marriage had already entered another domestic society. We shall consider this later, however.

If there is no reason in rational right for women to receive less than men in the case of intestate succession, we have to explain why the law of practically every State, especially ancient States, is so contrary to women and favourable to men. Listing all the causes which have served to produce such an effect would be a lengthy business, however, and we limit ourselves to a single observation.

Taken together, all the partial causes of which we have spoken result in a verification of the great law governing political societies (we deal with it at length in *Della naturale costruzione della società civile*). It runs: 'There is a continual tendency for *ownership* and *power* to arrive at a state of equilibrium.' Women were weak, men were strong. According to this law it was, therefore, necessary for female ownership to be less than male ownership if equilibrium was to result. Antiquity seemed to neglect women even more than modern times because they were weaker than they are now. In that period of human society, in which power was formed 'by the prevalence of bodily forces' (cf. *SC*, c. 16), it was inevitable that women would be subject to men and oppressed by them. Only moral qualities, as they begin to acquire weight in the balance of political power, can raise the condition of women. This has been and is being achieved by Christianity.

The truth of this (that is, that women's lack of influence in political power deprived them of many rights) may be seen by comparing various states in the same epoch. Such a comparison shows that women enjoyed greater advantages where their nature and education was stronger. In Sparta, where bodily strength was highly valued by the State, women were less oppressed in their rights precisely because they were more robust. Cesare Cantù says of the Spartans: 'Their married couples enjoyed mutual love, and greater spiritual harmony than other Greeks because in Sparta the women were less averse than elsewhere to male occupations and ways of behaviour. As a result, they were more highly esteemed by their husbands and shared not only their bed, but their way of life also' (*Legislazione*, no. 2, §16); cf. Plutarch for Spartan γυναικρατια (*Agis*, c. 7, and *Lycurgus* — *Numa*, c. 3), and Müller (*I Dorici*, p, 287).

It is odd to see how the law which unduly restricted women's right to inheritance was brought about by a tribune of the people, Quintus Voconius Saxa, who was in other respects completely favourable to the preservation of patrimonies. This shows the truth of the assertion that governmental action springs principally from an instinct arising from the general condition of the State. This condition gives rise to *prevalent opinion*, the mother of *governmental instinct*. Quintus Voconius acted against his responsibility as Tribune of the people when he established his law, although he thought he was doing the opposite. In effect, the *practical reason* of the masses influenced the speculative reason of the rulers of the people (Cf. *SC*, c. 10).

9. (1416).

Christianity has always shown an unceasing tendency to redirect positive laws, civil or political, to the simple Right of reason. With this in mind, it proceeded by bettering human beings so that we no longer need the multiple formalities and cautions with which human laws endeavour to make their point and bring us to conform to duty.

If we apply these considerations to wills, we note:

1. If we suppose civil society to be still imperfectly organised, as it always is when nations begin to exist, we can see why testaments and contracts of sale came into force only after receiving great publicity. Such public forms were the means by which all the people promise, as it were, to accept as valid the will of the testator and the contracting parties, and maintain it. The testator or the buyer enters into a kind of *pact* with all and sundry, and they with him by obliging themselves to respect his will as law.

2. It is no longer necessary to require this public promise from everyone when social government has been sufficiently organised and strengthened to maintain through its sole power the will of testators and contracting parties. It is sufficient that testators' wills be witnessed by a certain number of persons representing the people (who are still not completely submissive) and making their promise on behalf of the people. At the beginning, however, there has to be quite a large body of these persons in order to eliminate all doubt before the eyes of the people about the truth of the testament, and to provide a certain solemnity to the act of making a will — a solemnity which renders members of a society less likely to violate the will.

3. When government finally and completely prevails and the people are both more submissive and more enlightened, certain lesser formalities are required by the law for the sake of detecting more subtly the efficacy of proofs establishing the truth of testaments which are not so clear to the senses; eventually, only those formalities remain which 'are sufficient to make known this truth with certainty'. At this point, positive laws are already identified with rational laws.

We have to note — we have noted it at other times — that *formalities* not required by rational Right always result in harmful consequences, and must not therefore be introduced by legislators unless they are absolutely *necessary* to avoid greater evils. In fact, as more formalities are imposed upon jural acts to ensure their validity, a greater number of naturally valid acts are rendered invalid by positive law. This is the cause of grave inconvenience. Again, a great number of formalities increase rather than lessen litigation because they provide loopholes for those interested in endeavouring to render the act invalid.

In our case, the formalities imposed upon testaments by Roman law provided an excuse for declaring many wills worthless. The Church experienced this when she was called to succeed as heir or legatee. She was often disturbed by litigation that put in doubt the validity of wills through lack of some legal formality. This frequent disorder moved the Church, as far back as the 6th century, to declare that pious legacies had to be accepted as obligatory upon the *conscience of the faithful*, even when certain formalities of civil law were lacking, provided that the will of the testator could be proved with certainty.

The second Council of Lyons, for example, passed the following important decree (367 AD, c. 2): 'The Church has suffered greatly from the unfaithful who try to deprive her of gifts bestowed upon her. It is necessary, therefore, to observe inviolably the following: the testaments of bishops, priests or clerics in lower orders, or gifts or any acts of any kind by which anything is conferred upon the Church or anyone else, should consistently stand firm. In particular, we decree that the wills of any religious persons whatsoever, although either by necessity or through simplicity not altogether in keeping with the order of secular law, should as wills of the deceased remain firm and be preserved in all things with the help of God.' It was also declared that the will of the testator, although expressed only orally, had to prevail. Cf. the *Decretals* of Gregory IX (bk. 3, tit. 26, c. 4), which simply repeats a rescript of Gregory the Great (600 AD — *Ep.*, bk 12, ep. 30). Alexander III (1170 AD) ordered the judges at Velletri, who required seven or at least five suitable witnesses to validate pious legacies, to be satisfied with two or three witnesses: 'We command that when anyone is brought before you for examination in some case you should not treat the case according to the laws, but according to the STATUTES OF THE DECREES on the basis of three or two lawful witnesses. It is written: "Every word may be confirmed by two witnesses or three witnesses'" (bk. 3, tit. 26, c. 11). Innocent III declared to the bishop of Auxerre that a person confiding his last will to a third party did not die intestate (bk. 3, tit. 26, c. 13). These modifications of Right held sway in Christian nations.

The only controversy on the matter amongst jurists related to the quality of the formality requiring two or three witnesses. Was this formality absolutely necessary for validity or was it simply a sure proof? The second opinion is completely in harmony with the spirit of canonical Right which seeks unceasingly to draw people to rational Right.

The same *Decretals* of Gregory IX (bk. 3, tit. 26, c. 5) register another modification to civil laws which obliged the heir to satisfy even those legacies in which the testator had disposed of things not belonging to him. The question concerned a legacy left to a church and supported by civil laws. The Pope refuses the legacy and writes to the bishop of the legatee church: 'It is true that the laws of the world require an heir to carry out the obligation if a person has left as a legacy something not his own. But because WE LIVE BY THE LAW OF GOD, NOT BY THE LAW OF THIS WORLD, it appears very unjust to me that you, who are obliged to restore to others what belongs to them, should keep the things left to you which belong to any Church whatsoever.' This rescript of Gregory IX (1230) repeats that of Gregory the Great (AD 600). In a word, the spirit of the Church is the spirit of *jural reason*, never the spirit of *arbitrariness*.

10. (1426).

We have already said that Roman laws, especially the older laws, keep strictly to this principle (which we have noticed in nature): the family is a co-owning society whose head is by nature master and governor. As a result, Roman laws recognise rights of ownership amongst the members of the family, and between them and outsiders. These rights cease altogether only in relationship to the head of the house, and are therefore rights of *relative ownership*, as we have called them. Consequently Roman laws, although they subjected everything to the *patria potestas*, recognised the offspring as co-owners even during the father's lifetime, and certainly called them masters or owners relative to outsiders. Relative to the father, however, they were his, just as everything else was. All this is expressed in the following passage from Justinian: 'The heirs are called HIS because THOSE LIVING AT HOME' (those who form the domestic society) 'are heirs, and are considered, even during the father's lifetime, as MASTERS' (*Instit.*, bk. 2, tit. 19: 2). Normal ways of speaking, which give the title of 'lord' or 'master' to the children of a house although they are subject to their parents, are in accord with this. Again, the solid union between children and their father gives rise to the term *'necessary* heirs', as we have noted previously. Such is the co-ownership found in families, which ceases when a person leaves the family; it is ownership relative to outsiders, but not to all the members of the family itself.

Nevertheless, ownership relative to other members of a family can exist; for example, of a brother relative to another brother. This relative ownership amongst members of a family was admitted in Roman law under the name *'peculium'*, to which we give a more extended meaning here. The first *peculium* recognised by the Romans was called *peculium castrense* and was made up 'of that which was donated by the relatives or cognates to a soldier on active duty, or that which the son himself acquired during his military service and would not have acquired except for such service' (Pomponius, *Dig.*, bk. 49, tit. 17, leg. 11). We then have the *peculium quasi castrense* 'which was considered similar to the military *peculium*, and acquired by the son when in service with the palatine guard or employed civilly', according to Ulpian's definition (*Dig.*, bk. 37, tit. 6, leg. 1; and tit. 1, leg. 3). In fact, almost the only two ways of earning a wage open to Roman citizens were public offices in war and peace.

These *peculia* were disposed of by the children, and included in wills even during the father's lifetime. According to natural Right, therefore, they were owners in relationship to other members of the family, but according to an act of positive law, owners also relative to the father. Thus, in the Roman *peculium* there was an element founded in the law of nature, that is, the *peculium* belonged to whomsoever had earned it honestly for himself relative to everyone else; but this *peculium* also exceeded both the limit of natural law and the very spirit of Roman legislation in so far as it was made independent even of the *patria postestas*. This was one effect of the prevalence of the military condition which manifested itself in many guises, freed the testaments of soldiers (cf. *Dig.* bk. 29, tit. 1, leg. 1) and provided them with ample privileges. And in the end, it was this prevalence that destroyed the republic and the empire.

11. (1583).

Although public laws have declared that servitude is just, reason has sometimes protested, despite its speculative impotence, against the cruel decision of oppressive legislators. Aristotle mentions the criticisms brought against the laws:

> To some, it seems that seigniory is alien to nature, because human nature is the same for all. Only the law made some free and others bond-servants. Servitude therefore is evidently unjust because it does injury.

This argument of Aristotle against the servitude of his times shows that 1. *nature* and *violence* are seen as opposites; 2. nature is considered the source of justice and thus of natural law; violence, the source of injustice; 3. if injustice springs from violence which is the opposite of spontaneity, the symptom of injustice is natural resentment, as the ancient authors admitted. Aristotle adds that the critics of the laws are both right and wrong: right, because they speak of servitude established by the positive law, servitude that is very often contrary to nature; wrong, because they do not see that nature itself gives rise to a form of servitude. He says: 'It is easy to see that even those who oppose us' (those who affirm that *servitude* is opposed to *nature*) 'are in a way correct. A person can be said to be a bond-servant or to serve in two ways' (that is, by natural law or by positive law). 'According to the law, there are those who are slaves and serve. The law is a kind of consent in virtue of which booty in war belongs to those who take it. Many of those who practise law criticise this right, in the way that an orator who decrees evil is criticised.'

As usual Aristotle places himself between the philosophers who criticise the laws and the legislators who make them, and attempts to explain the origin of the diversity of opinions. According to him, legislators tended to believe that a conqueror's power was a sufficient title of right

> because that which overcomes and conquers always consists in a superior good. For this reason, force does not seem to lack some *virtue*.

But the difference between the two opinions lies in knowing whether *justice* is present in this virtue, or in something else:

> According to some, benevolence effects what is just, but in the opinion of others, it is just that the more powerful rule.

We must note that he also calls *just* whatever is established by positive law, although such justice is only relative. If we take 'just' to mean what is in conformity with both the positive law and the natural law, the servitude established by positive laws can be called both *just* and *unjust* at the same time:

> The cause of a war could be unjust, and no one will call bond-servants those who do not deserve to be bond-servants. Otherwise, even very noble people would become bond-servants.

Aristotle therefore, having accepted that servitude determined by state law can be contrary to nature, now applies himself to establish the opposite, namely, that a natural servitude exists. In order to be brief, we will present his thought partly in his own words and partly in ours. He says:

> It is impossible to stay alive and live comfortably without the necessities of life. If a work of some particular skill is to be completed, we have to use human industry; this applies to domestic possessions also. In order to produce them, we have to use tools, but before we can use them, we need someone capable of using them. Thus, if the instruments of a craft could do their work on the command and direction of their owner; if, like the tripods of Dedalus and Vulcan which, the poet tells us, 'enter spontaneously into the divine combat', shuttles could weave and plectra pluck

> zithers, then architects would not need builders, nor
> masters, bond-servants.

Human beings are necessary, therefore, if instruments are to produce what is needed for a domestic society. Thus, humans are bond-servants because they are clearly animate instruments moving inanimate instruments.

Having established the nature and necessity of servitude, we now need to see if servitude is founded in nature. First of all, if we consider all things in general, we discover seigniory and servitude everywhere, that is, that which commands and that which is subject; certain animals are subject to other animals, which in turn are subject to human beings. Even in human beings the body serves, and the spirit directs, provided their nature is rightly ordered. Moreover, it must be admitted that there are people who are naturally capable of mechanical and bodily skills but incapable of intellectual skills; they find it preferable and *helpful* to attend to their own skills and be directed by those with more intellectual ability.

> Hence, it is clear that some are by nature bond-servants, others, free. It is also clear that some have an innate aptitude of such a kind that they benefit from serving, in which case servitude is just, or have an aptitude such that they benefit from being free. According to different aptitudes, it is necessary for some to command, others to obey. Moreover, if to command is innate, it is also just. Anything done uselessly affects both parties; viceversa, what is helpful is helpful to the whole and the part, to the soul and the body. A bond-servant is in a way part of his master; he is as it were an animate part of his master's body but separate from him.

Aristotle concludes therefore that the difference between servitude established by law and servitude founded in nature is evident. Servitude founded in nature is of help to everybody, to the bond-servant and the master, provided these are disposed by nature to serve and to command respectively. But the contrary is true for bond-servants created by the law and with violence.

Such, it seems to me, are Aristotle's thoughts on the question of servitude. (Cf. *App.*, no. 2).

12. (1653).

Cicero, for example, glimpsed pure justice when he established as a general formula that *it was not lawful to harm another for the sake of one's own convenience* (*De Off.*, 3: 5). He offers this beautiful formula as one suitable for resolving every possible collision between justice and utility. Again, Cicero had a flash of light, and confessed: 'There are certain things so abominable that no sage would do them, even to preserve the fatherland' (*De Off.*, 1: 45). But is he consistent? Elsewhere he himself deduces the whole of morality or at least the whole of justice from the principle of *sociality*. Moreover, he calls such justice the mistress and queen of all other virtues (cf. *De Off.*, 3: 3). But when he endeavours to determine the superiority of one virtue to another, he finds himself in difficulty. On the one hand, his lack of clear knowledge of true spiritual good forces him to reduce everything to the external good of society, to which the individual is sacrificed; on the other hand, reason shows him the existence of goods different from and greater than social good. He comes to grief on this rock; his thought becomes obscure, confused, contradictory.

After distinguishing the four cardinal virtues, or the four parts of righteousness, he asks which of them has to be given precedence in the case of conflict. In his system justice, which he calls the *virtue of the community*, should be preferred to all the others. In fact, he immediately begins to show that it is preferable to prudence which he calls the *virtue of knowledge*. 'We willingly grant that duties springing from community are more in harmony with nature than those which spring from knowledge. This can be confirmed' (note this) 'if we think for a moment of the life of a wise man who abounds in every kind of affluence, has the leisure to consider and contemplate his possessions, which are worthy of thought, but is so cut off from others that he never sees anyone else. Such an individual would simply fade away and die' (1: 43). This wisest of Romans found nothing in the spirit of the lone person which could keep that person alive. To live, one had to immerse oneself in society. The individual is a spent force, without any life of his own; only the social human being is alive. But is there truly no virtue to be preferred to that which is relative to society? Is there no essential good for the human spirit more useful than that which can be drawn from society?

Here Cicero begins to flag. What he considered as the greatest virtue is no longer the greatest. Social justice, which he had placed above prudence, now falls below temperance. 'Perhaps we ought to ask whether this community, which is in harmony with nature TO THE HIGHEST DEGREE, is also to be preferred always to moderation and modesty. THIS WOULD NOT BE A HAPPY SOLUTION. There are some things which are so unseemly on the one hand, and so harmful on the other, that no sage would do them even for the sake of preserving the fatherland' (1: 45). His moral *feeling* irresistibly overthrows his error of *reasoning*. Nevertheless, he refuses to acknowledge the difficulty: 'But IT IS BEST TO SAY that there could be no moment in which it would be good for the republic if the sage had to do anything of this kind' (*ibid.*). Those who today wish to reduce everything to society and thus destroy the individual have led the human spirit into the same anguish of contradiction faced by paganism.

Even the phrase, 'The human being is born for the human being', offers no secure light relative to justice. Each individual could in fact ask why he should be born for others rather than for himself. *Humanity* renders his fellow human being worthy of respect, but humanity is found as much in him as in his fellow. Why, then, should he believe he was born for his fellow rather than for himself? The Stoics did not answer this question, and without an answer their maxim is worthless. Society, or humanity, which is found in other human beings, cannot be the unique, supreme source of justice. If humanity is to be revered in others, it is equally to be revered in ourselves. Society and I are therefore two persons, not one; and one cannot be sacrificed to the other.

13. (1688).

Those who take it upon themselves to criticise some public decision or propose some reform have to do so with the greatest consideration, while maintaining due reverence for authority. It would seem, therefore, that criticising laws is more fitting to older people, if they are learned and virtuous, than for the young, as Plato has said. At the same time government can indeed claim that suggestions made to it should be offered in a wise, seemly way. Nevertheless, it has the duty to accept every good proposal made, whatever its source, even if the proposer fails in his duty. The following quotation from Plato (*Laws*, bk. 1), where he mentions the proper mode of action for wishing to criticise anything in public laws, is I think a fine piece of writing. An Athenian guest, wishing to blame both Cretan and Spartan laws because they aim at making people strong in face of pain but not equally strong in face of pleasure, begins to speak about the matter with great delicacy to Clinia, a Cretan, and Megillo, a Spartan:

> *Athenian.* Indeed, if there is some careful investigator of truth and goodness amongst us who wishes to criticise something in the laws of our country, we would have to bear with him peacefully, and not let ourselves feel oppressed
> *Clinia.* That's right, my Athenian friend. And here I am, ready to obey you.
> *Athenian.* Yes, Clinia, it is fitting that people of your age and condition should act in this way.
> *Clinia.* Of course.
> *Athenian.* It would be different if it were a question of knowing who could justly criticise the Cretan and Spartan republics, but if we are simply referring to matters of common opinion, perhaps I am in a better position than either of you. Whether your laws have been well or poorly constituted, you certainly have one law that must be highly commended, that is, no young person should dare to question whether laws are rightly constituted or not. All together, with one mouth and one voice, should accept them as good and coming from the gods themselves; nothing said against the laws should be tolerated. But if one of the old men finds that after considering some point, he has something to say to the rulers and his own peers, he should take care that young people do not hear about this.
> *Clinia.* Well said! And even if your thoughts are far from those of the legislator, it seems obvious that you intuit such things with the wisdom of an oracle, and say things which

are altogether true.
Athenian. Look, there are no young people here. Alone, and granted our advanced age, we are licensed by the legislator to discuss such things without any fault.
Clinia. You're right! And it allows us to move on freely with our discussion about the laws. It is not in fact disrespectful to reveal whatever the laws contain outside the ambit of right. If the criticism is received benevolently, without animosity, the defect can be remedied.
Athenian. Yes, indeed! But I promise not to criticise anything without first having considered it as best I can.

This is an excellent way to review laws critically. Note, however, that imposing silence indiscriminately on all the young and obliging them to say something about which they are perhaps not persuaded, is out of keeping with freedom and Christian wisdom. Youth should be inspired by diffidence and modesty, but then allowed to speak.

14. (1949).

Whenever attempted harm must be promptly resisted, even civil laws allow the use of force and private justice. Thus, in the case of need, everyone can defend himself from an aggressor even by wounding or killing him. Furthermore, certain laws permit the physical harming of a nocturnal thief, etc. The reason is that a government's power is never so promptly available that it can usefully replace an individual's power, who in such cases has the natural right to defence or restitution. In civil society therefore individuals can always exercise a part of those rights of coercion which they have in the state of nature. This portion of exercise which they still retain pertains to that part of Right we have called the 'extrasocietal'.

It is certainly true that coercion by civil society cannot effect a full defence of all individual rights, nor the full restitution of all injuries resulting from harm. But this is not required by the perfection of civil laws; if civil laws attempted it, they would incur greater problems. M. Gioia correctly notes that

the means necessary for executing the law would simply cause a level of anxiety more harmful than the evil it wished to prevent (*Dell'inguria, de' danni*, etc, pt. 2, bk. 1, c. 6).

Moreover

> because many injuries 1. have no distinctive characteristic, granted their indefinite variety; 2. cannot easily be verified without a lot of movement and disturbance of witnesses; 3. are taking place nearly every moment, that is, there are too many malefactors; 4. are so difficult that no proportion can be determined between the supposed crimes and their punishment, it is clear that, even if all injuries constituted a crime in the eyes of the law, a great many would inevitably be left unpunished and courts would lose their credibility (*ibid.*).

Another reason why perfect legislation alone must not assume the punishment of all injuries and take responsibility for the restitution of all harm is that legislation must preserve the family without destroying paternal power. It must leave some authority to the parents and to those superiors who take the place of parents, like teachers, just as it must recognise ecclesiastical authority. Moreover, if the punishment of children, pupils and faithful were impossible, or if recourse to civil authority were always necessary, we would have a tyrannical situation destructive of nature and of the very law of God. Legislation would also be defective if those who are naturally subordinate were able to invoke civil authority every time they were dissatisfied with their natural superiors. Various medieval laws on this subject deserve our consideration; examples can be found in the collection of Canciani and in various municipal statutes (cf. the criminal statute of Brescia, c. 88, and of Tortona, bk. 4). One of these statutes excludes action against fathers and superiors for injuries to their children and dependents, against teachers for injuries to their pupils and against employers for injuries to their employees:

> In the case of disputes between husband and wife and between parents and children, even if blood has been drawn, provided death, disability or other lethal wound or blow do not follow, no action must or can be taken except in the foregoing cases or in danger of death. The same ruling applies to relatives and descendants to the fourth degree, also to those who without drawing blood strike a

member of their family for the sake of correction, and to teachers who correct or apply the rod to their pupils. Anything else is invalidated by the law itself (*Statuta criminalia Ripariae*, c. 96).

In this way the natural constitution of the family was up-held; and civil laws must certainly respect the sacred domestic hearth.

Civil laws can therefore abandon to individuals a part of the exercise of the rights to defence and restitution for two reasons: either 1. the responsibility does not pertain to civil laws so that a certain moderation on their part is praiseworthy and contributes to their perfection; or 2. responsibility does pertain to them, but they lack wisdom and energy, an indication of their imperfection which can be noted, amongst other differences, in those governments which make use of frequent fines against the condemned, or allow outlaws and the condemned to be punished [by citizens] for their crime, as did many municipal statutes in the Middle Ages.

Nevertheless it is extremely difficult to assign the precise *limit* of a civil government's rather than an individual's exer-cise of the rights to defence and restitution. Such a limit must certainly depend on the condition of peoples, the constitution of governments, the degree of civilisation, etc. There are consequently many cases which demand lengthy discussion and cannot be completely solved except by means of many delicate distinctions. For example:

1. Does it pertain to the perfection or weakness of civil laws whether a shepherd may be beaten, without any bone being broken, who fails to stop his animals wandering through crops (*Statute of Ferrara*, bk. 4, c. 50)?

2. Was that legislation perfect (as praised by M. Gioia) which allowed trees bordering public highways to be chopped for wood (this was previously prohibited by law) because it was feared they harboured robbers (*Statuta Casalis Majoris, De officio et jurisdict. officialis Stratorum, arzinorum et aquarum*)? And is there any wisdom in Gioia's suggestion that the same ruling be applied to rice fields established within limits of prescription by declaring that the rice belongs to the first occupier (Cf. *Discussione economica sul dipartimento d'Olona*)?

Index of Biblical References

Numbers in roman indicate paragraphs; numbers in italic indicate footnotes. Bible references are from RSV (Common Bible) unless marked †. In these cases, where the author's use of Scripture is dependent solely upon the Vulgate, the Douai version is used.

Index of Persons

Numbers in roman indicate paragraphs or, where stated, the appendix (app.); numbers in italic indicate footnotes.

General Index

Numbers in roman indicate paragraphs or, where stated, the appendix (app.);
numbers in italic indicate footnotes.

Movement
rights injured by, 278

Muslims
hopes in after-life, 170

Nations
conscience of, 1875
diplomacy and, 1871
intelligence in, *349*
law of, 932, 1412-1413, 1875; *233, 458, 460*
natural and ancient laws of, 1412 ss.
ownership and, 934-935, 937, 943
relationships between, 680
right of, 150, 165, 701, 935; *213, 233, 458, 460*
rights and progress of, 1011-1012, 1817; *406*
society and pagan, 133
trade and, 1676, 1907
treaties, 1867, 1873

Nature
meaning of, *app.* no. 4
reason and, *app.* no. 4
society and, *app.* no. 5

Natural Law,
civil, political and, 1413-1423
last wills and, 1414-1417
positive laws and, 1412, 1423
right relative to, 5, 6

Natural Right
connatural rights and, 283
meaning of, *255*
rational right and, 3-12, 1064
sacrifice of, 731-737

Nature
art and, 911
society and, *560*
state of, 504, 896 ss., 1052-1063; *406*

Obligation
beneficence and, 958; *app.* no. 6
feeling and, 813
fixed laws and, 762
inclination and, 7, 426-427
parents to children, 814
potential and actual, 1928
restoration as, 1624-1627; *244*
rights and, 1620-1621; *128, 234*

supreme moral, 1842
transmission of, 1465-1468

Observation
cause of errors, 403

Occupancy
conditions of, 452-453
errors about, 476-479
formal part of, 395
freedom modified by, 1561-1562
generation and, 816 ss.
persons and, 528 ss.
possession and, *238*
pre-occupancy, 1676, 1701
principles determining, 461-475
salvage and, *219*
self and, 529-530
see also **Ownership**

Original Sin
consequences of, *516*

Owner
direct, 993-994
use and, 993-994

Ownership
acquired, 312 ss.
actions and, 255; *81*
baby and, 45, 47, 264
benevolence and, 934
civil laws and, *137*
co-existence and, 879-894
common sense and, 432
common, 1396
communist system and, 446
concept of, 63
connatural rights and, 44, 47, 295
contracts and, 1051 ss., 1558-1559
co-ownership, 1003; *app.* no. 10
defence of, 239-244, 258
designation and, 508-520
dominion and, 535, 540-542; *346*
enjoyment of, 1454
error of, 455 ss.
exclusion of others, *223*
exercise of, 966-967, 973; *240*
fact and right of, 960, 968-969
feeling and, 1050, 1381; *347*
freedom and, 302-303, 479, 1631, 1701-1702
full, 1335-1339